CHILD AND ADOLESCENT
PSYCHOPATHOLOGY

CHILD AND ADOLESCENT PSYCHOPATHOLOGY

Irving B. Weiner
UNIVERSITY OF DENVER

JOHN WILEY & SONS

NEW YORK   CHICHESTER   BRISBANE   TORONTO   SINGAPORE

Library of Congress Cataloging in Publication Data:

Weiner, Irving B.
    Child and adolescent psychopathology.

    Includes bibliographical references and index.
    1. Child psychopathology. 2. Adolescent psycho-
pathology. I. Title. [DNLM: 1. Psychopathology—
In adolescence. 2. Psychopathology—In infancy
and childhood. WS 350 W423]
RJ499.W38   618.92 '89   81-21930
ISBN 0-471-04709-0   AACR2

Printed in the United States of America

10 9 8 7 6 5 4 3 2 1

PREFACE

This book provides a comprehensive description of the nature, prevalence, causes, course, outcome, and treatment of the major forms of psychological disorder and problem behavior occuring in children and adolescents. Along with this emphasis on description, attention is paid throughout the book to the influential concepts, controversial issues, and research findings that constitute current thinking and knowledge about developmental psychopathology, and the discussion embraces various theoretical approaches that have contributed to this knowledge.

The book begins with two introductory chapters that explain the distinction between normal and abnormal psychological development and discuss approaches to classify developmental psychopathology. Several chapters then present in detail what is currently known about seven major patterns of psychopathology in childhood and adolescence: mental retardation, minimal brain dysfunction/attention deficit disorder, childhood psychosis, adolescent schizophrenia, affective disorder, neurotic disorders, and school phobia. These are followed by four chapters concerned with problem behaviors that cut across diagnostic categories, including academic underachievement, delinquent behavior, suicidial behavior, and alcohol and drug abuse. A final chapter summarizes and integrates information on topics common to all of these disorders and problem behaviors, including their prevalence, causes, course, and treatment.

The discussion in each chapter focuses on describing the nature of developmental psychopathology, with case examples, and not on reviewing the literature, comparing alternative theories, or summarizing research. Nevertheless, contemporary clinical and research findings are cited extensively, both to document the description and to provide a reference source for advanced and professional readers. Hence the text should be easily readable by students with relatively little background while also satisfying the requirements of more experienced readers and providing a full bibliography on developmental psychopathology.

The discussion of individual topics stresses a data-based orientation that draws on facts irrespective of whatever theoretical framework has generated them. Most of the tables and figures used in the presentation have been prepared especially for this book from recent data. Each chapter concludes with a summary that can serve both as a study aid and as a handy guide to the topics that are amplified in the text. A glossary appears at the end of the book as an additional review and informative source.

Many people have helped me prepare this book. I am especially indebted to two good friends and former colleagues who shared their rich clinical experience with me. Dr. Donald Freedheim of Case Western Reserve University provided the case material on mental retardation that appears in Chapter 3, drawn from the files of the Mental Development Center operated by that university. Dr. James Michael of the University of

Rochester Medical Center furnished from his clinical practice the cases of childhood psychosis that are described in Chapter 5.

I am also grateful to Drs. Anthony Davids of Brown University, William Kessen of Yale University, and Herbert Quay of the University of Miami for their helpful comments and suggestions on preliminary drafts of the manuscript. Illustrative material has been reproduced with the permission of several publishers noted in the text and Drs. Stewart Agras of the Stanford University Medical School, K. Daniel O'Leary of the State University of New York at Stony Brook, Michael Rutter of the University of London Institute of Psychiatry, Norman Watt of the University of Dener, Edward Zigler of Yale University, and Joseph Zubin of the Pittsburgh Veterans Administration Hospital.

Finally, I want to acknowledge the skillful secretarial assistance I have had in completing this book. My special thanks are due to Mrs. Dorothy Rome, for her interest and help in all phases of preparing the manuscript, and to the staff of the Word Processing Center of the Denver Research Institue at the University of Denver, for their prompt execution of the final copy.

Irving B. Weiner

Denver, Colorado
October, 1981

CONTENTS

1

THE NATURE OF NORMAL AND ABNORMAL DEVELOPMENT

The study of child and adolescent psychopathology must begin with careful attention to the nature of normal development and abnormal development and how they differ. This task is complicated because psychological normality can be defined in several different ways. In addition, there are disagreements concerning whether normality and abnormality can be described in the same terms or whether they involve entirely different dimensions of personality.

The first two sections of this chapter will discuss alternative ways of defining normality and some issues related to whether it is considered continuous or discontinuous with abnormal behavior. Later sections will draw on available research to outline general guidelines for distinguishing normal from abnormal development.

DEFINITIONS OF NORMALITY

Normality is most often defined as *average, ideal,* or *adjustment.* Each approach has certain advantages and disadvantages, and each has different implications for how and where the line should be drawn between normal and abnormal behavior.

Normality as Average

Normality as average is a statistical concept that defines the typical behaviors among a group of people as being normal for that group and deviations from what is typical as being abnormal. Two common examples of this definition are parents who say to their child, "Why can't you be like the other kids?" and psychologists who label as "normal intelligence" the scores earned by the middle range of persons on an intelligence test. Normality as average has also been a popular concept among cultural anthropologists, as illustrated in the following remarks by Ralph Linton (1956): "Relative normality . . . is a matter of the individual's adjustment to the cultural milieu and of the degree to which his personality configuration approaches the basic personality of his society" (p. 63).

There are several advantages to defining normality in this way. First, deciding that a certain middle percent of persons is to be considered normal along some dimension provides a precise criterion for distinguishing between normality and abnormality in research studies. Second, adequate attention to typical patterns of behavior can help clinicians avoid seeing pathology where none exists. Leo Kanner, a distinguished pioneer in the field of child psychiatry, made a telling observation in this regard. He noted that various writers have referred to nail-biting in children as "a stigma of degeneration," "an exquisitely psychopathic symptom," and "a sign of an unresolved oedipus complex." But what are we to make of evidence that about 65 percent of school children are nail-biters at some time or other; "It is hardly realistic to assume that two-thirds of our youth are degenerate, exquisitely psychopathic or walking around with an unresolved Oedipus complex" (Kanner, 1960, p. 18).

As a third advantage, being aware of respects in which normality may be relative helps observers to evaluate behavior in light of important individual circumstances. For example, 8-month-old infants typically cling to their mothers when they are picked up,

Leo Kanner (1894–   ), who served for many years as director of the Child Psychiatry Clinic at Johns Hopkins Hospital, published the first English language textbook on child psychiatry in 1935.

whereas 3-year-olds are beginning to enjoy separating themselves from their mothers and are therefore much less likely to cling. Consequently, an infant who is indifferent to close contact with its mother and a 3-year-old who is reluctant to leave her lap are both showing signs of possible psychological disturbance (see Chapter 4). Similarly, delinquent acts committed in the company of peers who share asocial values are much less likely to reflect psychopathology than the same acts committed alone by a young person who has no friends or whose friends frown on such behavior (see Chapter 11).

There are also disadvantages to a statistical perspective on normality. If normal is defined as average, then the gifted as well as the retarded, the creative as well as the unproductive, and the extremely happy as well as the despondent person must be viewed as abnormal. Furthermore, in an extreme situation of mass panic or mob violence, people who act impulsively or irrationally would be considered normal, while those few who remain calm and clearheaded would be labeled abnormal.

As these examples should make clear, being *different* does not necessarily mean being *abnormal,* as the statistical approach implies. It is similarly unwarranted to assume that people in distress have no need of professional attention simply because everyone around them is experiencing the same distress. Influenza requires diagnosis and treatment whether it occurs as an isolated case or in epidemic proportions; the same can be said for distressing psychological conditions.

Normality as Ideal

Instead of being defined in statistical terms as average, normality can be defined in ideal terms as a state of perfection that people strive for but rarely achieve. This ap-

Sigmund Freud (1856–1939), the originator of psychoanalytic theory and therapy, wrote extensively on the relationship of childhood experience to the development of psychological disturbance.

proach, as reflected in the common expression "nobody's perfect," assumes that all people struggle with psychological limitations that prevent them from being as happy and successful as they would like to be. Sigmund Freud (1937, p. 235) worked from this perspective in formulating the classical psychoanalytic view of normality: "A normal ego . . . is, like normality in general, an ideal fiction." Barron (1963, p. 64) similarly concluded from a contemporary study of normal young adults that "psychopathology is always with us, and . . . soundness is a way of reacting to problems, not an absence of them."

Regarding normality as ideal avoids statistical decisions that label unusually intelligent, productive, or contented people as abnormal. At the same time, however, making normality a hypothetical ideal implies that everyone is more or less disturbed, which is a difficult concept to apply. It provides little help in separating normal from abnormal behavior for research purposes or in identifying circumstances that call for professional attention—unless one takes the debatable stance that everyone is more or less in need of psychotherapy.

Normality as Adjustment

Adjustment[1] consists of being able to cope effectively with life experience; more specifically, it refers to being able to enjoy rewarding interpersonal relationships and work productively toward self-fulfilling goals. When normality is defined in these terms, abnormality becomes a state of mind or a way of acting that impairs one's ability to deal

[1] Words in boldface are defined in the Glossary beginning on page 489.

successfully with the challenges and opportunities in his or her life.

The adjustment approach to normality is more useful than either the average or the ideal perspective in determining which conditions psychopathologists should study and clinicians should treat. This endorsement of an adjustment perspective on normality does not mean that it embodies the "true" definition, however. Definitions of normality, like definitions in general, cannot be judged right or wrong on the basis of argument or evidence. Instead, the merit of a definition lies in its clarity and its utility for some purpose. The adjustment approach is preferred here because it provides a clinically meaningful and useful concept of normality against which the presence and severity of psychological disturbance can be assessed. It is not to be taken as the "true" definition or even as necessarily the best definition for other purposes.

Furthermore, an adjustment approach should not be applied to the exclusion of certain features of other ways of looking at normality. The ideal approach, because it calls attention to what people can become, encourages active striving toward self-improvement and toward greater happiness and success. As stressed by writers concerned with "positive mental health" (Jahoda, 1958; Smith, 1959) and "self-actualization" (Maslow, 1968, 1971), such striving needs to be considered an integral part of dealing effectively with life experiences. Otherwise, the adjustment perspective can result in a stultifying focus on conformity at the expense of creativity, and on "not rocking the boat" at the expense of asserting one's individuality. Block and his colleagues, who have given much thought to the nature of good adjustment, make this point well: "The issues appear to reside in the way 'adjustment' is defined—as either optimal psychological functioning or a yielding to convention and properties, sometimes at great personal cost" (Siegelman, Block, Block, & von der Lippe, 1970, p. 283).

The average perspective holds that normality should be judged in terms of a person's reference group instead of according to any universal criteria. To illustrate this point with an age difference, being afraid of the dark is much less likely to indicate psychopathology among preschoolers, who very commonly have such fears, than among adolescents, in whom such fears are rare. Unless such normative data are accommodated within an adjustment approach to defining normality, many errors will be made in judging the severity and probable outcome of behavior problems.

At the same time, it can be argued that fear of the dark interferes with a child's sense of well-being, whatever his or her age, and is therefore worth trying to eliminate, no matter how common it is. This difference between the adjustment and average perspectives contains the essence of an ongoing controversy between advocates of *absolute* and *relative* criteria for assessing normality. Although this controversy cannot be resolved here, its implications merit a brief summary.

Speaking for a relative approach, social psychologists such as Miller (1970) argue that absolute criteria for normality should be avoided because they imply that what is best for one society or culture is best for all. For example, being aggressive may help a person adjust well in a competitive society, whereas being passive may foster good adjustment in an easygoing society that discourages competition. If both groups are judged by the standards of the competitive society, passive people in the easygoing society will be considered abnormal, even though they are getting along comfortably.

Such **ethnocentric judgments**—namely, that other people should do things our way—contain undesirable seeds of autocracy and intolerance.

Responding in favor of an absolute approach, personality theorists such as Block argue that people in a hostile, aggressive society who are devoting much of their energy to self-protection are not realizing their full human potential, and that the same can be said for complacent, unassertive people in a passive society; hence both are diminished persons compared to what they might achieve and enjoy, regardless of their "fit" within their society. As for the possible intolerance bred by judging normality according to absolute standards, Block et al. offer the following observations.

> If one rejects the possibility of an absolute basis for evaluating the psychological functioning of an individual, one rejects as well the possibility of evaluating the society or subsociety in which that individual lives. . . . Relativism provides a rationale for tolerance that is also a rationale for perpetuation of what is, rather than what might be (Block, Block, Siegelman, & von der Lippe, 1971, pp. 327–328).

However one feels about this issue, defining normality as adjustment is only a first step in distinguishing between normal and abnormal development. Deciding whether a person is coping effectively with life experience is largely a subjective matter. Except for instances in which people are obviously coping very well or extremely poorly, statements about abnormality and need for treatment are at best reasonable estimates. For this reason, experimental and applied psychopathology needs detailed guidelines for differentiating specific pathological conditions from each other and from normal variations. In addition to identifying differences among people, these guidelines must also take into account continuities that may exist between normal and abnormal behavior.

THE CONTINUITY OF NORMAL AND ABNORMAL BEHAVIOR

Normal behavior and abnormal behavior can be regarded as being either continuous or discontinuous phenomena. From the point of view of continuity, differences between disturbed and well-adjusted persons are *quantitative*. This means that normal and abnormal behaviors are presumed to derive from the same personality dimensions or traits, with maladjusted individuals simply having more or less than the optimum amount of certain traits.

For example, a moderate amount of self-control contributes to good adjustment, whereas too little self-control can lead to pathological impulsivity and too much self-control to pathological inhibition and rigidity. Similarly, a moderate capacity to reflect on one's experience tends to promote good adjustment, whereas insufficient reflection can lead to poor planning and excessive reflection to paralyzing indecision and self-consciousness. Thus from a continuity perspective every aspect of a disturbed person's behavior constitutes an exaggeration of a normal way of thinking, feeling, or acting, and every normal person can be expected occasionally to think, feel, or act the way disturbed people do. The key difference is one of degree—normal people behave in a less exaggerated fashion and do so less often than people who are psychologically disturbed.

By contrast, a discontinuity approach defines differences between normal and abnormal behavior as *qualitative*—that is, as differences in kind rather than degree. Discontinuity theory emphasizes the study of abnormal psychology in its own right, instead of as a part of normal psychology, in order to focus adequately on the unique circumstances that give rise to psychological disturbance and on the special kinds of care and treatment that disturbed persons require. For example, a 10-year-old boy with a delusion that he is a machine or that his stomach is missing would be considered to have a disordered way of thinking not found in normal youngsters and to need a form of intensive or residential care not used in helping normal children cope with developmental tasks.

Despite the apparent differences between quantitative and qualitative views of normality/abnormality, it is difficult to marshal conclusive evidence that one is more accurate than the other. In the first place, quantitative differences typically contribute to qualitative differences as they grow larger. Two youngsters with IQs of 110 and 115 may not differ very much in qualitative aspects of their intellectual functioning; however, if the quantitative difference in their measured intelligence were extended to IQs of 80 and 120, the children would probably deal with problem-solving and concept-formation tasks in qualitatively different ways that even an untrained observer could detect.

Second, even small quantitative differences can usually be looked at qualitatively as well. For example, in the case of two 10-year-old girls, one 54 inches tall and the other 58 inches, an observer could say that both are about average height for their age, but one is taller than the other. This would be a quantitative distinction emphasizing continuity between them. Another observer could simply describe the two girls as "the tall one" and "the short one." This would be a qualitative distinction emphasizing discontinuity. Both observers would technically be correct, and a preference for either point of view could be justified.

As in weighing definitions of normality, then, the important consideration is not whether continuity or discontinuity is the more accurate perspective, but what purposes each serves. The discontinuity approach, because of its stress on the uniqueness of psychopathology, can be extremely valuable in encouraging parents, teachers, and mental health professionals to recognize and respond to developmental disturbance. One risk of a continuity approach is that such disturbance will be minimized as being "only" an extension of normal behavior and hence of little concern.

On the other hand, the continuity approach helps avoid regarding disturbed persons as "different" from the rest of us. If we can think of these people as having more or less of something that we all have, not as being in an entirely different dimension, we are likely to do a better job of trying to understand and meet their psychological needs. The discontinuity approach risks regarding the psychologically disturbed as alien and unfathomable and relegating them to places where they will be out of sight and out of mind.

In order to maintain a focus on turning developmental disturbance into normal maturation, this book will work primarily from a quantitative perspective that identifies continuities between normal and abnormal behavior. At the same time, considerable emphasis will be placed on guidelines for differentiating between normal and abnormal development, in order to facilitate early recognition and prompt treatment of developmental disturbance.

To this end, it is necessary to begin with some general principles for differentiating normal from abnormal development, especially in instances of apparently minor maladjustments that represent early stages of more serious disturbance. The following two principles are proposed for this purpose.

1. *The Principle of Age-Appropriateness.* Children at all ages must deal with certain developmental tasks. Preschoolers must learn to separate themselves from their parents, 6-year-olds must learn to adjust to school, early adolescents must learn to accept rapid changes in their bodies, and so forth. These demands of growing up inevitably cause periods of stress and strain, even in young people who are developing normally. The principle of age-appropriateness holds that ways in which young people can be expected to behave as they cope with the particular developmental tasks of their age group constitute normal ways of thinking, feeling, and acting; conversely, ineffective behaviors that are not characteristic of a youngster's peers or that persist beyond the age at which they might be expected to occur are likely to reflect emerging psychopathology.

2. *The Principle of Future Implications.* One of the most important reasons for attempting to distinguish between normally and abnormally developing young people is to identify those who require professional help to improve their prospects for maturing into well-adjusted adults. The principle of future implications holds that problem behaviors that can be expected to lead to subsequent psychopathology are more likely to reflect abnormal development than problem behaviors that typically disappear of their own accord and do not result in later disturbance.

The remaining three sections of this chapter will expand on these principles in terms of research findings that help distinguish between normal and abnormal development. First, the principle of age-appropriateness will be elaborated with information on the nature of problem behaviors in normal and disturbed children. Next, data on the prediction of subsequent disturbance from childhood difficulties will be used to illustrate the clinical significance of the principle of future implications. Finally, both principles will be applied to the task of distinguishing between normal and disturbed adolescents.

PROBLEM BEHAVIORS IN NORMAL AND DISTURBED CHILDREN

As the heading for this section implies, problem behaviors in children do not necessarily indicate developmental disturbance. Both normally and abnormally developing children display problem behaviors. However, there are important age differences in the implications of such behaviors and useful data on the incidence of developmental disturbance, both of which help in making clinical judgments.

Age Differences in Childhood Behavior Problems

The fact that problem behaviors occur in normally as well as abnormally developing children was first documented in the Guidance Study, a long-term program of longitudinal research at the Institute of Human Development at the University of California at Berkeley (Eichorn, 1973). In this research the mothers of a representative sample of 248 children born in Berkeley between January 1, 1928, and June 30, 1929, were interviewed at regular intervals from the time their children were 18 months old until they reached age 14.

These interviews revealed that at one time or other, one-third or more of both the boys and the girls in the sample displayed such problem behaviors as bed-wetting, disturbing dreams, overactivity, lying, oversensitiveness, specific fears, mood swings, temper outbursts, jealousy, and excessive shyness (MacFarlane, Allen, & Honzik, 1954). On the other hand, most of these problems were *age-specific,* in that they tended to occur at one age but not at other ages. For example, bed-wetting and overactivity were common during the preschool years but not in elementary school, whereas disturbing dreams and specific fears were reported more often after these children reached school age than before.

A second landmark study of this kind was conducted by Lapouse and Monk (1958, 1959), who interviewed the mothers of 482 randomly selected 6- to 12-year-olds in Buffalo. Almost 50 percent of these apparently normal children were reported to have numerous specific fears and worries or frequent temper tantrums, and 27 to 30 percent of them were restless, had nightmares, or bit their nails. Of further interest, the younger children (ages 6 to 8) had many more behavior problems than the older children (ages 9 to 12) (Lapouse & Monk, 1964). Two conclusions suggested by the Berkeley and Buffalo studies have been confirmed in subsequent research: (a) most problem behavior in children is age-specific and tends to disappear with maturation; (b) problem behavior that differs substantially from what might be expected at a child's age—in terms of kind, severity, or duration—is what should be considered to constitute developmental psychopathology (Joint Commission, 1973; Kohlberg, LaCrosse, & Ricks, 1972; Robins, 1979; Thomas & Chess, 1976).

Age differences in the occurrence and implications of problem behavior are highlighted in a study by Schechtman (1970), who used a 91-item checklist to record deviant behaviors in 546 children at a mental health clinic. She found negative relationships between the ages of these children and the number of symptoms they displayed. The youngest children had the most symptoms, and the older the children were, the fewer symptoms they were likely to display. Similar results emerged from a study in which Cass and Thomas (1979) obtained parents' and teachers' reports on 38 problem behaviors shown by 200 patients in a child-guidance clinic. Taken together, these two studies found that behaviors significantly more likely to occur in children under 12 than among 12- to 17-year-olds included aggressiveness, attention-seeking, difficulty in concentration, restlessness, temper tantrums, sleep difficulty, bed-wetting, soiling, thumb-sucking, and excessive fearfulness. By contrast, only two behavior problems were consistently observed more frequently in older (age 12 to 17) patients of both sexes—truancy and running away.

Figure 1.1

Clinicians' ratings of degree of pathology reflected by problem behaviors at different age levels. (Based on data reported by Lessing et al. (1973).)

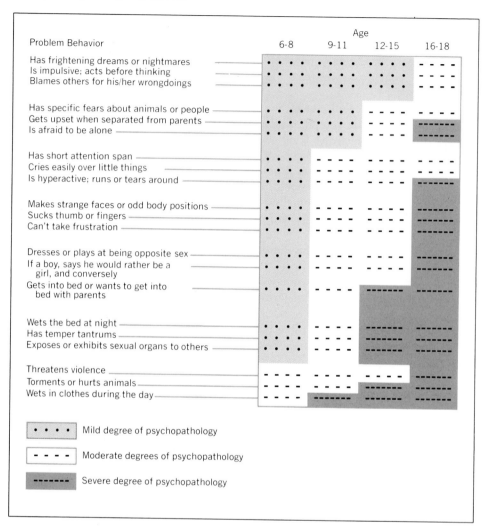

In another piece of research, Lessing, Beiser, Krause, Dolinko, and Zagorin (1973) asked 45 clinicians to rate the degree of psychopathology that various problem behaviors reflect when they occur at different age levels. Figure 1.1 indicates the changing significance they attached to 21 such behaviors as a function of a child's age. Apparent from these data is the extent to which a behavior problem that is viewed as reflecting little or no psychopathology at one age can take on implications for moderate or severe psychopathology if it persists or begins at a later age.

10   THE NATURE OF NORMAL AND ABNORMAL DEVELOPMENT

Findings of this kind leave little doubt that expected behavior at different stages of childhood provides the essential background for identifying abnormal development. The less age-appropriate a bit of problem behavior is, the more likely it is to consistitute a form of psychopathology and to call for professional attention.

The Prevalence of Developmental Disturbance in Childhood

The principle of age-appropriateness cannot be applied without also noting that some of the problem behaviors mentioned earlier did not occur any more frequently in the clinic children studied by Schechtman and Cass and Thomas than in the presumably normal children whose mothers were interviewed by MacFarlane et al. and by Lapouse and Monk. Similar observations are made by Shepherd, Oppenehim, and Mitchell (1966a, 1971) in the Buckinghamshire Child Survey, a countywide study of 5- to 15-year-old English children. Shepherd et al. report having no difficulty locating nonpatient children with the same behavior problems as 50 randomly selected patients from child-guidance clinics. The main difference between these two groups was in their patient's behavior. Compared to the parents of the nonpatients, the clinic children's parents were more anxious, more easily upset, less able to cope with their children, and more likely to seek other's help with their problems.

Shepherd et al. suggest on the basis of their data that whether children become patients may depend less on what their behavior is like than on how others react to it. Other research findings confirm that parents who are themselves maladjusted are more likely than normally functioning parents to perceive their children as being deviant and bring them to mental health clinics (Griest, Wells, & Forehand, 1979; Lobitz & Johnson, 1975). With this in mind, some writers have gone so far as to question whether certain child behaviors disturb other people because they are truly behavior problems, or whether these behaviors become defined as problems because people find them disturbing (Algozzine, 1977; Rhodes, 1967).

Any such conclusion may be ill-advised, however, especially if it involves believing that children called "normal" and "disturbed" may not really differ very much from each other. In the first place, the finding that some problem behaviors are as common in nonpatient as in patient children does not mean that all problem behaviors are equally frequent among them. Not listed in Figure 1.1, for example, are many behaviors that were identified by the clinicians in the Lessing et al. study as pointing to severe psychopathology no matter what the age of the child. These included such dramatic behaviors as talking nonsensically, claiming that peculiar things have happened to one's body, saying that one's mind or action is controlled by an outside force, and trying to kill someone. There is also evidence to indicate that even when many of the same behavior problems are found in patient and nonpatient children, the severity of these problems is likely to be significantly greater in the youngsters who have been referred for help (Therrien & Fischer, 1979). Thus even though some disturbed children who are receiving professional help may have certain problem in common with nonpatient and presumably normal children, other disturbed children will have different or more serious problems that can be clearly distinguished from common responses to developmental stress.

Second, similarities found between clinic and nonpatient children do not necessarily mean that the patients are normally developing youngsters whose parents or teachers cannot cope with them adequately. There is an alternative and more sobering possibility that clinic children are receiving help they need while many nonpatient youngsters with similar problems are developing abnormally in the absence of professional help that could benefit them. Regrettably, data from many sources point toward the latter conclusion—namely, that there is a substantial incidence of developmentally disturbed children whose needs for help are not being recognized or met.

Regarding the number of psychologically needy children, several large-scale surveys of representative samples indicate that 20 to 30 percent of children enter elementary school with behavior problems that are moderately or severely handicapping, and that of these youngsters about half have sufficiently severe emotional difficulties to warrant professional attention (Bower, 1969; Dohrenwend et al., 1980, Chapter 2; Rubin & Balow, 1978; Rutter & Graham, 1966; Zax, Cowen, Izzo, & Trost, 1964). With respect to the percent of needy children who receive attention, a study by Chamberlain (1974) is of particular interest. He collected information from the mothers of 190 four-year-olds who were patients in a private pediatric practice. Consistent with the above findings, 20 percent of these mothers believed that their children had a behavior or emotional problem. Yet, despite the presumed sophistication and resources of this advantaged private practice sample, 50 percent of these concerned mothers had never talked to anyone about their child's problem.

Similar results emerged from a detailed psychiatric study of 271 randomly selected 6- to 18-year-olds and their mothers by Langner, Gersten, Greene, Eisenberg, Herson, and McCarthy (1974). Marked or severe psychological impairment was found in 13.5 percent of these young people, but fewer than half (49.2 percent) of this needy group had ever been referred for psychological evaluation or treatment. All available research to date confirms that the majority of clinically maladjusted young people in the United States are not receiving treatment (Dohrenwend et al., 1980, Chapter 2).

Third, when comparisons are made between disturbed and nondisturbed children without regard for whether they happen to be receiving professional help, substantial differences appear in their frequency of behavior problems. In the most extensive study of this kind, Rutter and his colleagues examined the education, health, and behavior of all children and adolescents on the Isle of Wight, a small island of 100,000 people just off the southern coast of England and similar to England in social composition (Rutter, Tizard, Yule, Graham, & Whitmore, 1976). As one part of this study, 117 10- and 11-year-olds were identified as psychiatrically disturbed on the basis of interviews with them and their parents. These children were then compared with nondisturbed classmates on teacher ratings of 26 problem behaviors. The teachers, who had no information about the psychiatric evaluation, rated 17 of these 26 problem behaviors as occurring significantly more frequently in the disturbed than in the nondisturbed boys, and 23 of them significantly more frequently in the disturbed than in the nondisturbed girls (see Table 1.1).

On the basis of their findings, Rutter et al. agree with the majority of researchers that most problem behaviors can be found in at least some normal children at some point during their developmental years. This means that most problem behaviors, when oc-

TABLE 1.1 Teachers' Ratings of Problem Behaviors in Psychiatrically Disturbed Children and Their Nondisturbed Classmates (in percent)

Problem Behavior	Boys		Girls	
	Psychiatric Group	General Population	Psychiatric Group	General Population
Restless	55.4**	15.7	37.5**	6.5
Fidgety	60.8**	20.0	34.9**	9.8
Poor concentration	81.1**	35.3	69.8**	25.3
Irritable	39.2**	8.9	18.6**	5.3
Twitches	16.2**	4.9	23.3**	1.1
Not liked	45.9**	13.3	48.8**	9.5
Solitary	32.4**	17.0	27.9**	10.0
Truant	10.8**	1.8	7.0**	0.7
Destructive	23.0**	1.5	7.0**	0.4
Fights	50.0**	11.0	32.6**	3.7
Disobedient	62.2**	10.6	27.9**	3.6
Lies	47.3**	6.9	27.9**	2.0
Steals	35.1**	2.3	11.6**	1.4
Bullies	40.5**	4.2	14.0**	1.3
Worried	28.4	23.5	32.6	22.2
Miserable	20.3*	8.9	27.9**	6.8
Fearful	24.3	17.6	48.8**	6.0
Fussy	8.1	8.1	16.3	17.3
Tears on arrival at school	0.0	0.4	7.0*	0.8
Aches and pains	8.1	3.3	16.3**	3.4
Absent from school for trivial reasons	6.8	6.0	25.6**	5.2
Sucks thumb	8.1	4.8	23.3**	5.0
Bites nails	18.9	18.8	37.2*	18.8
Stutter	6.8	2.9	7.0**	0.3
Other speech disorder	16.2**	3.1	4.7	1.4
Wets or soils	4.1*	0.4	9.3**	0.6
Total number	74	1080	43	1079

*Statistically significant at 1 percent level of confidence.
**Statistically significant at 0.1 percent level of confidence.
Source. From Rutter et al. (1970). Reprinted by permission of Longman House.

curring by themselves, cannot be taken as presumptive evidence of abnormal development. Nevertheless, as Rutter et al. also stress, certain combinations of certain behavior problems are more likely than others to indicate psychopathology. To identify abnormal development, then, the principle of age-appropriateness must be supplemented by the principle of future implications. As noted earlier, this principle directs attention to specific patterns of childhood difficulty that, occurring at any age, constitute abnormal development by virtue of predicting subsequent psychological disturbance.

CHILDHOOD DIFFICULTIES PREDICTIVE OF SUBSEQUENT DISTURBANCE

Efforts to identify childhood difficulties that predict subsequent disturbance are an extremely important research focus in developmental psychopathology. Being able to predict psychological disturbances helps to determine what causes them. In addition, being able to recognize a disturbance in its early stages opens the door for interventions that can prevent it from ever becoming full-blown. The relationship of childhood difficulties to later disturbance has been studied primarily by **retrospective** and **life-history research methods.** This section will first describe these methods and then summarize what has been learned from them about estimating the future implications of problem behavior.

Retrospective and Life-History Research Methods

Retrospective research on the origins of psychopathology is based on the childhood recollections of disturbed adults and their families. This method was introduced by Freud in his early case studies (Breuer & Freud, 1893–1895), which influenced many other clinicians to construct developmental theories from the memories of their adult patients. The retrospective method lends itself well not only to individual case studies but also to systematic research. Investigators can fairly easily find an adequate sample of disturbed adults in the patient population of a clinic or hospital and an adequate comparison group of employees or nonpsychiatric patients at the same clinic or hospital. Since the data collection begins in the present, arrangements can be made to obtain the same kinds of information in the same way from all subjects.

Unfortunately, however, the retrospective method yields data of uncertain reliability. How accurately can adults recall the events of their childhood? To what extent does current emotional distress color memories of such events? How much are the recollections of a disturbed person's family influenced by what they know of his or her present condition? And, since patients and their families may feel a need to make certain kinds of impressions on clinic and hospital personnel, how many gaps are there between what they can recall and what they decide to report? Although there are no precise answers to these questions, the sources of unreliability they identify cast serious doubt on the utility of data from retrospective studies (Garmezy & Streitman, 1974; Jenkins, Hurst, & Rose, 1979; Yarrow, Campbell, & Burton, 1970).

To avoid such unreliability, researchers have become increasingly attracted to life-history methods, which use data recorded *during* the childhood of persons who became disturbed as adults. Information of this kind is much more likely to be reliable than what people can remember many years later, and it is also free from any distorting influence of knowing that the person has become disturbed. For this reason, life-history data are frequently referred to as *nonreactive;* that is, they exist independently of events (such as psychological disturbance) that have resulted in a person's being selected as a research subject (Roff & Ricks, 1970). Three somewhat different approaches are used in life-history research: *follow-back, follow-up,* and *follow-through.*

Follow-back Studies In follow-back studies the early lives of normal and disturbed adults are searched for clinic or school records that may identify differences in their childhood experiences and behavior. Like the other life-history methods, follow-back studies thus have the advantage of drawing on relatively reliable, nonreactive data. In addition, they share with retrospective studies fairly easy access to appropriate comparison groups of adult subjects (e.g., hospitalized psychiatric and nonpsychiatric patients).

The follow-back approach introduces some problems that retrospective researchers do not face. For one thing, early clinic records will be available only for those subjects who came to professional attention while they were children. Efforts to track adults through such records will therefore fail to yield data for many of them, and those for whom data can be found may be an unrepresentative sample—since they comprise only those members of the adult subject groups who were treated for childhood disturbances.

Follow-back researchers can avoid inadequate or nonrepresentative sampling by using school records, which can usually be found for most subjects. Unfortunately, however, school records often lack the historical detail and sensitive personality descriptions that appear in clinic records kept by mental health professionals. For example, a school record may indicate that a student had a discipline problem, but it will be less likely than a clinic record to suggest what kind of personality characteristics or psychopathology seemed to account for the problem.

A second difficulty is that clinic and school records dredged up from years past may be hard to use systematically. Having been written by many different people working in many different settings, these records tend to vary widely in focus and orientation. The same kind of behavior described by one observer as "overactivity" may have been described by another as "normal boyish enthusiasm." Likewise, one person's "oedipal conflicts" may be another's "typical family tensions." In addition, some key items of information may appear in some records but not in others, while some information that is crucial to an investigator's hypothesis may not appear at all.

Despite these problems, follow-back studies have provided important information on the childhood antecedents of adult psychopathology. As a leading example of this method, Watt and his colleagues used the complete list of 15- to 34-year-old first admissions to inpatient psychiatric facilities in Massachusetts from 1958 to 1964 to identify 145 patients who had attended the same Boston-area high school (Watt, 1972, 1978; Watt & Lubensky, 1976; Watt, Stolorow, Lubensky, & McClelland, 1970). Comparisons of these patients' school records with those of their classmates have yielded interesting findings that will be drawn on in later discussion.

Follow-up Studies   With the follow-up method children on whom data are collected when they are young are evaluated later to determine what aspects of their adult functioning might have been predicted from their childhood behavior. The follow-up approach allows investigators to begin with uniform and more or less complete childhood information on matters they consider important.

This approach also has some disadvantages. First, longitudinal work of this kind requires a long-term commitment, since the crucial results do not become available for many years. Second, subjects may be difficult to locate or unwilling to participate at follow-up time, and those from whom data can be obtained may not be an adequately representative sample of the original group. Third, the information gap between the initial and follow-up observations may limit what can be learned about how and when childhood difficulties begin to shade into adolescent psychopathology.

The length of time necessary to do follow-up research can be shortened by working from existing clinic or school records of children who are already grown. To avoid having to work from inconsistent or incomplete records, the study can be confined to a single setting in which all the children have been evaluated along similar lines. An excellent example of such research is the work of Robins and O'Neal, who began in the 1950s to collect 30-year follow-up data on 524 children who had been evaluated in the St. Louis Municipal Psychiatric Clinic between 1924 and 1929 (O'Neal & Robins, 1958; Robins, 1966; Robins & O'Neal, 1971). The previously mentioned research of Cass and Thomas (1979) is another important source of follow-up data on disturbed children. These investigators reevaluated their 200 patients 10 to 15 years after they were initially seen at the Washington University Child Guidance Clinic between 1961 and 1965. Information from both of these longitudinal studies will be presented at various points in this book.

Follow-through Studies   In follow-through research the data are collected at several regular intervals during the course of a longitudinal study, rather than at just the beginning and end as in follow-up studies. This improves the investigators' chances of keeping in touch with their subjects, and it also shortens their wait for useful findings to begin emerging. Moreover, because of the additional opportunities to observe change from one stage of childhood to the next, follow-through data are more likely than follow-up data to identify the circumstances in which psychopathology first appears.

Since most children do not grow up disturbed, however, only a fraction of youngsters randomly chosen for a follow-through study will ever furnish data about how and why psychopathology develops. For example, investigators studying schizophrenia must deal with the fact that only 1 of every 100 persons ever develop this condition (Babigian, 1975). This means that a follow-through study must start with a very large number of children in order to end up with an adequate sample of schizophrenic adults.

As one way of solving this problem some investigators recommend using a **high-risk method** in longitudinal studies (Garmezy, 1975, 1977; Mednick & McNeil, 1968). High-risk research begins with subjects who have an above-average likelihood of becoming psychologically disturbed. For example, children with a schizophrenic parent are about 15 times more likely than the average child to become schizophrenic as adolescents or adults (Zerbin-Rudin, 1972), and they are accordingly good subjects for follow-through studies concerned with the origin of schizophrenia. In addition to increasing the percentage of "vulnerable" subjects who will eventually become disturbed, the high-risk method provides valuable information on the development of "invulnerable" children—those who grow normally into adulthood despite being at risk by virtue of having disturbed parents.

Risk research was pioneered by Mednick and Schulsinger, who began in the early 1960s to follow 207 normally functioning Danish children with a schizophrenic parent (Mednick, 1966; Mednick & Schulsinger, 1965, 1968). The high-risk approach was subsequently extended to include children who are vulnerable to learning and behavior problems by virtue of complications during their mother's pregnancy and delivery. The life course of infants who have experienced such perinatal stress has been examined in two major projects: the Collaborative Perinatal Project, sponsored by the National Institute of Neurological and Communication Disorders and Stroke, in which 14 hospitals have been collecting data on the outcome of over 50,000 pregnancies (Niswander & Gordon, 1972), and the Kauai Longitudinal Study, which has evaluated the effects of perinatal stress in 660 young people at 1, 10, and 18 years of age (Werner, Bierman, & French, 1971; Werner & Smith, 1979).

Estimating the Implications of Problem Behaviors

Life-history research indicates that the implications of childhood behavior problems and the corresponding need for preventive intervention can be estimated most effectively by considering (a) the number of problems a child exhibits, (b) the kinds of problems these are, and (c) the age at which these problems become predictive of later difficulties.

Number of Problems   As noted earlier, research beginning with the Berkeley Guidance Study has demonstrated that most childhood behavior problems are age-specific, in that they appear in response to developmental stress and disappear with maturation and corrective experience. The fact that specific problems come and go does not necessarily mean that different children experience them. To the contrary, children who develop certain behavior problems at one age tend to be the ones who develop other problems at a later age. Furthermore, children who have many different problems at one point are likely to have many problems later, even though the nature of these problems changes (Robins, 1979; Robins & Wish, 1977).

This finding suggests the following guideline for distinguishing normal from abnormal development in children: the greater the number of behavioral difficulties a child has, even when each is seemingly age-appropriate, the greater the likelihood that the child will have multiple difficulties later and the firmer the basis for considering him or her to be developing abnormally and to require preventive intervention.

Kind of Problems   The work of Robins (1966), Cass and Thomas (1979), and others has demonstrated that certain kinds of childhood behavior problems are more likely than others to be followed by adult psychopathology. In particular, problems related to impaired cognitive functioning (school learning difficulties, confused thought processes, inadequate capacity for moral judgment) or antisocial tendencies (stealing, destructiveness, fire-setting, assaultiveness) are far more predictive of adult disturbance than emotional problems (anxiety, depression, nervousness, shyness, dependency). Accordingly, the more a childhood adjustment difficulty appears to have cognitive and antisocial behavioral components in addition to or instead of emotional components, the more likely it is that the child is developing abnormally rather than merely coping with normal developmental stress.

In using this guideline, however, care must be taken not to underestimate the implications of purely emotional problems. Children with such problems tend to be considered neurotic, whereas those with cognitive and antisocial behavior problems tend to be diagnosed as psychotic, brain damaged, or psychopathic. As will be elaborated in later chapters, it is the psychotic, brain-damaged, and psychopathic children in clinic populations who are found least likely to improve, even with treatment, whereas neurotic children are highly likely to improve, even without treatment (Glavin, 1972; Robins, 1979). Although these findings may at times discourage clinicians from working with more seriously disturbed children, they do not prevent them from recognizing the severity of their problems. For neurotic children, on the other hand, there is some risk that their relatively good prospects for improvement will result in minimization of their problems and inadequate attention to their needs.

For example, because Shepherd et al. (1966b, 1971) found in the Buckinghamshire survey that 61 percent of a group of mildly symptomatic children they followed for 2 years had improved without receiving treatment, they concluded that professional attention should be reserved for chronic disorders that are likely to persist into adulthood. But, we might ask, what about the 39 percent of untreated children in their study who failed to improve or became worse? How many of these children could have been helped by professional care? And for those who improved on their own in 2 years, how much could their improvement have been facilitated by appropriate mental health intervention?

These questions emphasize two important points about childhood neuroses: (a) the relatively favorable outlook for neurotic children does not mean that all of them will be so fortunate as to get better without help; and (b) even when professional help is not needed to prevent permanent psychopathology, it may speed recovery and thereby ease the burden that psychological disturbance places on children and their families.

Indeed, the fact that childhood neuroses are less likely to persist or predict adult disturbance than cognitive and antisocial behavior disorders does not constitute evidence that they have no such future implications. To the contrary, Waldron (1976) found in a follow-up study of neurotic children that 75 percent had some form of psychological disturbance as adults, compared to only 15 percent of a control group of their schoolmates. Rutter, Tizard, Yule, Graham, and Whitmore (1976) report that the 10- and 11-year-olds in the Isle of Wight study who showed emotional problems were more than twice as likely as the general population to have such problems at age 14 to 15. The neurotic children in the Cass and Thomas (1979) sample had a 44 percent rate of moderate or severe adjustment difficulties as young adults. These results challenge previously held beliefs that being neurotic as a child has no relationship to adult psychopathology (Kohlberg et al., 1972; Mellsop, 1972).

Age at Which Problems Become Predictive   It is important to know the age at which the number and kinds of behavior problems children have become predictive of later difficulties. If this age is overestimated, then abnormal developments may be overlooked beyond the point at which professional attention would have been most helpful. If the age is underestimated, then normally developing young children and their families may receive unwelcome and unnecessary attention from professionals who are seeing psychopathology in behavior patterns that do not yet have any predictive significance.

Available data suggest that behavior problems begin to show relationships to future psychological status at about the time children enter elementary school, at age 6 or 7. It is from this point on that having many problems increases the likelihood of having many problems later, and that cognitive and antisocial behavior problems are more predictive of subsequent disturbance than purely emotional problems (Robins, 1979).

Some particularly clear evidence for the need to take adjustment difficulties seriously beginning with the first grade has come from the Rochester Primary Mental Health Project, a long-term study of early detection and prevention of childhood psychopathology (Cowen, Pederson, Babigian, Izzo, & Trost, 1973; Zax, Cowen, Rappaport, Beach, & Laird, 1968). These investigators used interviews with mothers, direct observations, and psychological tests to rate first-grade children on their seeming potential for becoming disturbed. When these children were reevaluated in the third grade and again in the seventh grade, it was found that the first-grade ratings of their potential for later disturbance reliably predicted which of them would show the most signs of maladjustment, as measured by behavioral observations, school records, and achievement and personality tests. Other work confirms that teachers' behavior ratings, even in kindergarten, can predict academic achievement and classroom adjustment at the end of third grade (Spivack & Swift, 1977).

As a major exception to this age guideline, professional attention is indicated even before the school years in instances of serious developmental disturbances that are known to begin early in life and to cause persistent adjustment difficulties. These serious disturbances include mental retardation, minimal brain dysfunction, infantile autism, and childhood schizophrenia, which are discussed in Chapters 3 to 5.

With respect to mild adjustment difficulties, moreover, some researchers have found that prediction of later disturbance and appropriate intervention do not always have to wait until age 6 or 7. Westman, Rice, and Berman (1967) report that 3- and 4-year-old nursery school children whose teachers consider them to be immature or to get along poorly with other children are relatively likely to have poor interpersonal relationships later, to develop childhood neurotic disturbances, and to receive mental health services by the time they complete high school. Rickel, Smith, and Sharp (1979) describe an intervention program for 3- to 4-year-olds in a preschool program that helped withdrawn and aggressive children improve their behavior before they entered kindergarten. These findings may reflect that fact that nursery schools make many demands on children that they would not otherwise face until elementary school, such as having to participate in structured group activities. Hence this experience may reveal the beginnings of persistent adjustment difficulties earlier than in the case of children who do not begin such a school-type experience until age 6 or 7.

To summarize this discussion of distinguishing normal from abnormal development in children, it can be said that those children who demonstrate some diagnosable condition of the kinds to be discussed in subsequent chapters are developing abnormally. In addition, for children with behavior problems that do not justify any formal diagnosis, the likelihood that they are developing abnormally instead of merely coping normally with developmental stress is increased if (a) the problems they are displaying are not common or appropriate to their age group, (b) they are displaying many rather than just a few different problems, (c) they are displaying cognitive or antisocial behavior problems rather than only emotional distress, and (d) they have reached elementary school age.

PROBLEM BEHAVIORS IN NORMAL AND DISTURBED ADOLESCENTS

For adolescents as for younger children, the distinction between normal and abnormal development depends on the *age-appropriateness* and *future implications* of their behavior. Adolescents are developing abnormally when they are having adjustment difficulties that are not typical of their age group or that are known to predict later disturbance. Unfortunately, the picture of what constitutes age-appropriate and predictive behavior among teenagers has been blurred in many peoples' minds by the notion of

G. Stanley Hall (1844–1924), president of Clark University and the first president of the American Psychological Association, earned through his various writings the distinction of being referred to as the "Father of Child Psychology."

"normative adolescent turmoil." A brief review of this largely mythical notion will provide a context for presenting research findings that provide guidelines for differentiating the problem behaviors of normal and disturbed adolescents.

The Mythical Notion of Normative Adolescent Turmoil

There is an age-old conviction that adolescence disrupts the continuity of personality development and produces stormy, unpredictable behavior. Plato defined youth as "spiritual drunkenness," and G. Stanley Hall (1904), who was the first psychologist to write extensively about adolescent development, portrayed adolescence as an era of inevitable turmoil in which the major predictable feature of youthful behavior is its unpredictability. Adolescents, said Hall, is "suggestive of some ancient period of storm and stress when old moorings are broken. . . . The 'teens' are emotionally unstable and pathic. . . . We see here the instability of fluctuations now so characteristic" (Vol. I, p. xiii; Vol. II, pp. 74–75).

This view was subsequently expressed in clinical terms by Anna Freud (1936, 1958),

Anna Freud (1895–   ), the daughter of Sigmund Freud and a distinguished clinician in her own right, has contributed more extensively than any other psychoanalytic writer to the understanding of normal and abnormal child development.

who was among the first psychoanalysts to focus on adolescent behavior. In her words, which continue to exert a strong influence on psychoanalytic theory, "Adolescence constitutes by definition an interruption of peaceful growth which resembles in appearance a variety of other emotional upsets and structural upheavals" (1958, p. 267). Because "peaceful growth" is interrupted, she continues, adolescents normally display maladaptive thoughts, feelings, and actions that would suggest psychopathology if they occurred in adults. As a result, "The differential diagnosis between these adolescent upsets and true pathology becomes a difficult task."

A similar view of normative adolescent turmoil has emerged more recently from the work of Erik Erikson (1959, 1968) on **identity formation.** Identity formation is the process by which young people arrive at some fairly clear and enduring sense of what kind of person they are, what they believe in, and what they want to do with their lives. To succeed in this process, adolescents need to endure several years of uncertainty while they gradually expand their knowledge of themselves and their world and experiment with different ways of being.

Because this necessary uncertainty typically results in maladaptive reaction patterns and role diffusion, Erikson (1956) says, "Adolescence is . . . a *normative crisis*" (p. 72). The notion of a normative **identity crisis** has been elaborated to include many of the same behavioral features associated with the notion of adolescent turmoil, such as mood swings and unpredictable behavior. In Erikson's view, these and other features of an identity crisis indicate psychopathology when they occur in adults but are nor-

Erik H. Erikson (1902–   ) has become famous both for his views on personality development (including the concept of identity formation) and for his psychoanalytic interpretations of the lives of major figures in history (his *Ghandi's Truth* won both a Pulitzer Prize and a National Book Award).

mative and healthy in adolescents: "What under prejudiced scrutiny may appear to be the onset of a neurosis is often but an aggravated crisis which might prove to be self-liquidating and, in fact, contributive to the process of identity formation" (p. 72).

Beliefs in normative adolescent turmoil have also been reinforced by contemporary concerns about "adolescent alienation" and a "generation gap." Such well-known social scientists as James Coleman (1961), Kenneth Keniston (1965), and Margaret Mead (1970) have fostered the view that certain features of modern life and family living compel adolescents to form a youth culture that is cut off from and at odds with the adult world. Among the many reasons offered for this youthful alienation are (a) parental pampering and permissiveness, (b) a rapidly changing world that exposes adolescents to experiences their parents never had and cannot understand, (c) the long apprenticeship between childhood and adulthood that exists in a complex technological society, and (d) adolescents' disaffection for what they see as a materialistic and hypocritical adult generation that has done little to eliminate war, poverty, injustice, and human misery.

Both the professional literature and the popular media have waxed eloquent on how today's youth have responded to such alienating modern influences: with rebellion against their parents' wishes, rejection of traditional values, disrespect for authority, bad manners, laziness, insistence on immediate gratification, and involvement in delinquency, drug abuse, and sexual promiscuity. Deferring for the moment a look at whether these presumed manifestations of youthful alienation are in fact widespread, it is interesting to note that they are not as peculiarly modern as many writers suggest. Socrates, for example, is reputed to have aired the following complaint about the younger generation of his day: "Children now love luxury. They have bad manners, contempt for authority. They show disrespect for elders and love chatter in place of exercise. Children are now tyrants, not the servants of their households."

Things seemed little better in Shakespeare's time: "I would there were no age between ten and three-and-twenty, or that youth would sleep out the rest; for there is nothing in the between but getting wenches with child, wronging the ancientry, stealing, fighting" (*The Winter's Tale,* Act III, Scene iii).

Some further words from Hall's 1904 text are also to the point.

> *Modern life is hard, and in many respects, increasingly so, on youth. . . . Increasing urban life with its temptations, prematurities, sedentary occupations, and passive stimuli just when an active, objective life is most needed, early emancipations and a lessening sense for both duty and discipline, the haste to know and do all befitting man's estate before its time, the mad rush for sudden wealth and the reckless fashions set by its gilded youth (Vol. I, pp. xiv, vxi).*

Thus contemporary concerns about a gap between generations have not always been seen as adequately in their historical context as would be desirable. Nevertheless, the fact is that adolescent alienation is frequently regarded as contributing, along with identity crises, to normative adolescent turmoil. The notion of turmoil is central to the theme of this chapter because it has led many clinicians to form the following three opinions about problem behavior in adolescents.

1. *Most adolescents show signs of apparent psychological disturbance that do not really constitute psychopathology.*

   "One of the unique characteristics of adolescence . . . is the recurrent alternation of episodes of disturbed behavior with periods of quiescence" (Group for the Advancement of Psychiatry, 1968, p. 61).

   "Although puberty may take many courses, we think predominantly of stormy and unpredictable behavior marked by mood swings between elation and melancholy" (Eissler, 1958, p. 224).

   "The observed upheaval and turbulence is the inevitable by-product of the necessary transformation of the personality by which further growth and development to maturity can be achieved" (Shapiro, 1973, p. 117).

   "Adolescence, as is equally true of the neuroses and psychoses, is characterized by relative failure of the ego" (Josselyn, 1954, p. 225).

   "If there is anything that can be considered typical of the adolescent period, it is this quality of identity diffusion" (Giovacchini, 1978, p. 326).

2. *It is difficult if not impossible to distinguish normal from abnormal development during the adolescent years.*

   "The momentous biological and psychological changes are so great in this transition from childhood to young adulthood that the lines between normal and pathological are never more blurred or indistinct" (Redlich & Freedman, 1966, p. 693).

   "Despite the terrible turbulence of adolescence, which renders diagnosis a perilous affair" (Lief & Thompson, 1961, p. 38).

   "Frequently these young people give us a distorted picture, puzzling to the clinician. . . . At times, one can hardly differentiate between psychopathology and normal growth crises" (Ekstein, 1968, p. 347).

3. *Most instances of seemingly deviant behavior in adolescents are short-lived disturbances that will disappear of their own accord.*

   "My main therapeutic approach to the parents of adolescents. . . . the tried and true phrase of the men of the ancient church who, when beset by the unpredictable and seemingly uncontrollable, comforted themselves and one another with the words, 'It will pass. It will pass.' " (Gardner, 1947, p. 540).

   "The cure for adolescence belongs to the passage of time and the gradual maturation processes" (Winnicott, 1971, pp. 40–41).

What these opinions have in common is that they are based largely on impressions formed by clinicians in the course of their work with adolescent patients. There is no question that clinical observations can suggest rich hypotheses about human behavior. However, when generalizations about all people are made from the behavior of a small number of disturbed patients seen in individual clinical practice, numerous errors are likely to occur. This is precisely what has occurred with respect to adolescent turmoil. Findings from systematic research with representative groups of patient and nonpatient adolescents contradict all three of the above opinions by revealing (a) that relatively few adolescents become developmentally disturbed, (b) that normal and disturbed development can be clearly distinguished during adolescence, and (c) that both normal and disturbed behavior patterns tend to remain stable from adolescence to adulthood.

The Prevalence of Developmental Disturbance in Adolescence

In 1966 Douvan and Adelson reported an interview study with over 3000 adolescents representative of American youngsters in junior and senior high school. These young people showed little evidence of normative turbulence and instability. To the contrary, their relative freedom from conflict or turmoil led Douvan and Adelson to conclude that it is only the adolescent at the extremes "who responds to the instinctual and psychosocial upheaval of puberty by disorder" (p. 351).

Although Douvan and Adelson's interviewers were survey research staff members, and not mental health professionals, their results have been confirmed in many subsequent studies that have included extensive clinical evaluations of nonpatient adolescents. The best known of these studies is the Normal Adolescent Project conducted by Offer and his colleagues (Offer, 1969; Offer & Offer, 1973, 1974, 1975). In this 8-year project 73 typical middle-class midwestern boys were assessed by means of psychiatric interviews, psychological tests, and parents' reports on several occasions from their freshman to senior years of high school. Sixty-one of these young men were followed in the same way through 4 years of college.

The vast majority of the adolescents Offer studied gave few indications of personality upheaval from age 14 to 22. Many of them displayed "continuous growth," which is Offer's term for smooth and adaptive progress from adolescence into young adulthood. Many others displayed "surgent growth," which consists of adaptive but irregular progress toward maturity in which the young person sometimes stands still developmentally and at other times concentrates considerable energy on mastering developmental tasks, Just 21 percent of the group showed "tumultuous growth," which involves the kinds of inner unrest and overt behavior problems that are ascribed to all young people by the notion of normative adolescent turmoil. Other clinical studies of nonpatient adolescents have documented not only that turmoil and conflict are the exception rather than the rule, but also that developmental disturbance is most definitely *not* necessary for normal growth from adolescence to adulthood (Grinker, Grinker, & Timberlake, 1962; Hamburg, Coelho, & Adams, 1974; Oldham, 1978; Weiner, 1977).

Specific research on "identity crisis" and "adolescent alienation" leads to a similar conclusion. Longitudinal studies have found that identity crisis as defined by Erikson is a rare, not a common occurrence among adolescents (King, 1972; Offer, Marcus, & Offer, 1970). Adolescents *do* go through a several-year period of uncertainty and concern about their future during which they must work hard to sort out their values and preferences. For the most part, however, they do *not* experience any maladaptive states of crisis while they are working to achieve a stable sense of identity, nor do they display disturbing concerns about who or what they are in the present (Coleman, Herzberg, & Morris, 1977; Waterman, Geary, & Waterman, 1974; Waterman & Goldman, 1976). When instability of the self-image does occur among teenagers, it is much more likely to appear in early adolescence, when young people are coping with major changes in their body, than in later adolescence, when they are involved in integrating their sense of personal identity (Simmons, Rosenberg, & Rosenberg, 1973).

As for adolescent rebellion or a vast generation gap, Offer and Offer (1973) and Douvan and Adelson (1966) both report finding that most adolescents respect their parents, want to be like them, and maintain basically harmonious relationships with them and with other adults as well. The majority of the young people they studied were satisfied with their homes and tended to view their fathers as reliable and knowledgeable and their mothers as understanding and sympathetic. Meissner (1965) similarly found in a study of 1278 13- to 18-year-old boys that 89 percent were happy in their homes, 84 percent spent half or more of their leisure time at home, and 74 percent felt proud of their parents and enjoyed having them meet their friends.

Konopka (1976), in an interview study of 1000 12- to 18-year-old girls who were broadly representative of social-class, ethnic, and geographic groups in the United States, also found convincing evidence that differences between adolescents and adults do not constitute a generation gap. The majority of these girls felt close to their parents and very much wanted to have a warm, accepting family life based on mutual respect and good relationships with adults outside of their family. Lesser and Kandel (1969) similarly found that only 11 percent of 825 adolescents they surveyed felt removed from their mothers and only 23 percent felt removed from their fathers, whereas the rest felt at least moderately close to their parents.

Sorenson (1973) reports that 88 percent of a national sample of 13- to 19-year-olds stated in interviews that they held their parents in high regard, and 80 percent said they respected their parents' ideas and opinions. As a final note on this point, a large majority of college students asked about their relationships with their parents while they were in high school tend to describe their parents favorably and with enthusiasm and to report having had good relationships with them (Frankel & Dullaert, 1977; Sandell & Rossman, 1971; Stanton, 1974).

With respect to values, the evidence shows without doubt that typical high school and college students feel a keen sense of social and ethical responsibility, not a desire for immediate gratification, and that the majority support rather then reject the values of their parents. Beneath superficial appearances to the contrary, young people generally endorse the same standards of conduct and decency as their parents. Even among those adolescents who hold unconventional views, most are found to do so in agreement with their parents and not out of rebellion against them (Frederickson, 1972; Friesen, 1972; Lerner & Knapp, 1975; Thomas, 1974; Troll, Neugarten, & Kraines, 1969). In reviewing these and other similar findings, many social scientists in both the 1960s and 1970s came to the conclusion that "adolescent rebellion" and the "generatio gap" were largely myths, at least with respect to the overhelming majority of young people (Bandura, 1964; Bealer, Willits, & Maida, 1964; Conger, 1977; Tolor, 1976; Weiner, 1971, 1972, 1976).

Given that neither turmoil nor its origin in identity crises or alienation is widespread or necessary for normal maturation, what can be said about the incidence of developmental disturbance in adolescence? Two major research projects are helpful in answering this question. In the Symptomatic Adolescent Research Project, Masterson (1967a) evaluated 101 patients 12 to 18 years old consecutively seen for psychiatric consultation at the Payne Whitney Clinic and a comparison group of 101 nonpatient adolescents randomly selected from the schools attended by the patient group. He found that 20 percent of the nonpatient subjects had psychological symptoms that were moderately or severely impairing their ability to function in school or in social relationships; 63 percent had occasional symptoms, mainly anxiety and depression, that caused mild impairments of their ability to function; the remaining 17 percent were symptom-free.

Second, as part of the Isle of Wight study, Rutter and his colleagues examined the adjustment of 200 randomly selected 14- to 15-year olds (Rutter, Graham, Chadwick, & Yule, 1976). About 50 percent of these young people reported feelings of anxiety or depression, but only 16.3 percent were considered on the basis of a psychiatric interview to have significant psychological disorder.

Table 1.2 lists these and other findings on the incidence of psychological disorder among representative samples of nonpatient adolescents, as determined by clinical interviews. Taken together, the data in these studies indicate that about 20 percent of adolescents experience clinically significant developmental disturbances that interfere noticeably with their ability to function; another 60 percent have occasional episodes of anxiety or depression, but not to an extent that produces any major disruption in their daily lives; the remaining 20 percent show no signs at all of psychological disorder.

TABLE 1.2 Incidence of Psychological Disorder Among Representative Samples of Adolescents (based on clinical interviews)

Study	Subjects	Percent with Psychological Disorder
Hudgens, 1974	110 12–19-year-old nonpsychiatric hospital patients	23[a]
Kysar et al., 1969	77 randomly selected college freshmen	22.1[b]
Leslie, 1974	150 randomly selected 13–14-year-olds	17.2[c]
Masterson, 1967a	101 randomly selected 12–18-year-olds	20[d]
Offer & Offer, 1975	73 "typical" male high school students	21[e]
Rimmer et al., 1978	153 randomly selected college sophomores	15.3[a]
Rutter et al., 1976	200 randomly selected 14–15-year-olds	16.3[a]
Smith et al., 1963	86 randomly selected 18–20-year-old college students	12[a]

[a] Defined as diagnosable psychiatric disorder.
[b] Defined as clinically significant impairment of total psychological functioning.
[c] Defined as degree of disorder similar to psychiatric clinic patients.
[d] Defined as moderate or severe impairment of school and/or social functioning.
[e] Defined as tumultous growth.

Interestingly, these are about the same percentages that have been found in several large-scale normative studies of adult adjustment. This research indicates a range of 16 to 25 percent of American adults who suffer from moderate or severe psychological problems, with 51 to 58 percent having mild or fleeting problems and 18 to 19 percent having few or no problems (Dohrenwend et al., 1980; Leighton, Harding, Macklin, Macmillan, & Leighton, 1963; Regier, Goldberg, & Taube, 1978; Srole, Langner, Michael, Opler, & Rennie, 1962). Thus among adolescents and adults alike, close to 60 percent of persons demonstrate mild forms of symptom formation and the remaining 40 percent are about equally divided between symptom-free and moderately or severely impaired groups.

If anything, then, adolescents display slightly less tendency toward serious problems than adults and a correspondingly higher incidence of only mild disturbance. These minor variations aside, the normative data clearly demonstrate that developmental disturbance is far from being uniformly characteristic of adolescents, and furthermore that adolescents are no more likely than adults to display features of psychological maladjustment.

Distinguishing Normal from Abnormal Behavior in Adolescence

Normal adolescents, like normal children, often display problem behavior. Nevertheless, knowledgeable clinicians have little difficulty distinguishing between normal and disturbed adolescents. As in the case of younger children, the key to this distinction is careful attention to the number, kind, and persistence of any behavior problems that appear.

In the Symptomatic Adolescent Research Project, for example, Masterson (1967a) found that the patient group demonstrated far more frequent symptoms than the nonpatient comparison group. Despite the 63 percent incidence of mild difficulties among the nonpatients, the patients exceeded them by a 50 percent margin in the overall number of symptom patterns they displayed. Additionally, the symptomatic nonpatients showed mainly emotional problems, whereas the patients were more likely to display the kinds of cognitive and antisocial behavior problems noted earlier to have relatively serious future implications. Specifically, 54 percent of the nonpatients but only 33 percent of the patients had anxiety or depression as their principal symptom picture, whereas 57 percent of the patients but only 16 percent of the nonpatients displayed antisocial behavior, disturbed thinking, or other signs of serious personality disorder.

Masterson's work and other clinical studies identify the following three guidelines for distinguishing normal from abnormal development in symptomatic adolescents: (a) the more symptoms an adolescent displays, (b) the longer these symptoms persist, and (c) the more they involve cognitive and behavioral problems instead of or in addition to emotional upsets, the more likely the young person is to be psychologically disturbed. These guidelines allow clinicians to identify psychological disturbance as readily in adolescents as in any other age group (Gallemore & Wilson, 1972; Hudgens, 1974; Meeks, 1973; Weiner, 1970).

In fact, an adequate understanding of adolescent development allows the difference between normal and disturbed adolescents to be detected even from a self-report questionnaire. Offer and Howard (1972) developed such a questionnaire (the Offer Self-Image Questionnaire) and administered it to a broadly representative sample of over 3200 adolescents in the United States and Australia. They found dramatic differences between the ways in which normal and disturbed adolescents describe themselves with respect to their impulse control, emotional tone, self-image, social relationships, moral standards, family relationships, mastery of external problems, and educational and vocational goals. Similar results have been obtained in comparing the questionnaire responses of normal and disturbed adolescents in Ireland (Brennan & Loideain, 1980).

Clear distinctions between normal and abnormal adolescent development can also be made with respect to states of identity crisis and alienation. Studies comparing patient and nonpatient adolescents indicate that in those relatively few instances in which an identity crisis occurs, it is highly likely to reflect a sufficient degree of psychopathology to warrant professional help (Crist, 1972; Hauser & Shapiro, 1973). Among some of the indications of poor adjustment found among college students with identity crises are academic underachievement, social isolation, a disorganized life-style, and feelings of loneliness and inferiority (Donovan, 1975; Marcia, 1980; Orlofsky, Marcia, & Lesser, 1973; Waterman & Waterman, 1972). As for alienation, Figure 1.2, based on the Isle of Wight data, reveals a clear relationship between strained parent-child relationships at age 14 and the presence of psychopathology.

Figure 1.2
Parent-Child alienation and psychiatric disorder at age 14. (From Rutter, Graham, Chadwick, and Yule (1976). Reprinted with permission of Pergamon Press.

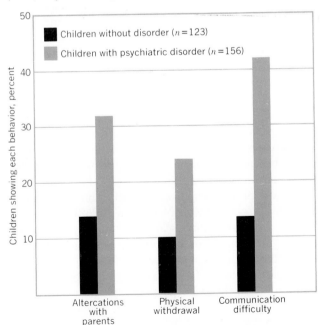

The Stability of Adolescent Behavior Patterns

Although adolescents have many years ahead of them in which to mature and change, research findings demonstrate that psychological and behavioral functioning are fairly stable from adolescence to adulthood. For better or worse, this means that adults tend to display many of the same general personality characteristics and the same relative level of adjustment they did as adolescents.

Two studies provide especially impressive evidence in this regard. Vaillant (1978) conducted a 35-year follow-through study of 268 college sophomores, 94 of whom were still available for interviews at age 54. The adequacy of the high school social adjustment of these men, as rated from the information they gave as college students, was significantly related to the adequacy of their adult psychological adjustment. Poor social adjustment in adolescence was clearly predictive of poor social adjustment at midlife in this sample.

Bachman, O'Malley, and Johnston (1979) report on an 8-year study of change and stability in the transition years from adolescence to adulthood. Their study involved a representative national sample of 1628 boys who were followed from entry into tenth grade to age 23. "Contrary to what might have been expected by those who view adolescence as a period of great turbulence and stress," the authors conclude, "we have found a good deal of consistency along dimensions of attitudes, aspirations, and self-concept" (p. 220). The dominant picture that emerged from their study of adolescent maturation, then, was of stability, not change.

These two studies and other longitudinal research confirming the stability of adolescent behavior patterns are listed in Table 1.3. These studies have not been selected to document stability while ignoring other studies with contrary results. As Offer and Offer (1975, p. 18) note, there are no studies that contradict this evidence for stability: "No published longitudinal or follow-up studies have isolated major changes in defenses utilized, strength of interpersonal relationships, nature of coping strategies, or even levels of adaptation of adolescents and young adults as outstanding features of these maturational periods."

The overall consistency of psychological and behavioral functioning from adolescence to adulthood applies to abnormal as well as normal development. Adolescents who manifest obvious symptoms of behavior disorder rarely outgrow them. Those who *appear* disturbed are likely to *be* disturbed and to *remain* disturbed unless they receive adequate treatment. In the Symptomatic Adolescent Research Project, for example, a 5-year follow-up revealed that 62 percent of the patients continued to have moderate or severe functioning impairments (Masterson, 1967b). Masterson (1968) concluded from these findings that clinicians should be very cautious about attributing adolescent symptoms to temporary turmoil, lest by so doing they delay treatment that is needed to prevent these symptoms from persisting or becoming worse.

Consistent with this conclusion, studies of college freshmen with behavior problems have found that only a small minority are likely to be passing through a temporary "adjustment reaction." In most cases they are either suffering from a continuation of high school problems that have not been treated adequately and are becoming worse, or they are experiencing new problems that will probably persist for several months or

TABLE 1.3 Longitudinal Studies Demonstrating Stability of Personality Characteristics and Level of Adjustment from Adolescence to Adulthood

Study	Sample	Length of Follow-up	Measures
Bachman et al., 1979	1628 male high school sophomores	8 years	Interviews and questionnaires
Bronson, 1967	31 male, 33 female 14–16-year-olds	To age 30	Interviews
Goldstein et al., 1978	23 male 15–16-year-olds	5 years	Interviews, personality tests
Grinker & Werble, 1974	37 male college freshmen	14 years	Questionnaires
Lief & Thompson, 1961	17 male and female high school students, average age 15	15 years	Interviews, personality tests
Offer & Offer, 1975	61 male high school freshmen, age 14	8 years	Interviews, Rorschach and Thematic Apperception Tests, self-ratings
Schimek, 1974	27 14-year-old boys	At age 24	Rorschach test
Symonds & Jensen, 1961	28 male and female high school students	13 years	Rorschach, Symonds Picture Story Test, interviews
Vaillant (1978)	94 male college sophomores, age 18–19	35 years	Interviews and questionnaires
Woodruff & Birren, 1967	35 male, 19 female college students, average age 19.5	25 years	California Test of Personality

even years to come (Deutsch & Ellenberg, 1973; Kysar et al., 1969; Selzer, 1960; Taube & Vreeland, 1972).

Additional data on this point are reported by Weiner and Del Gaudio (1976), who utilized a countrywide case register in Rochester, New York, to collect information on 1334 12- to 18-year-olds who had visited a psychiatric clinic, hospital, or office practitioner over a 2-year period. During a 10-year follow-up, 54.2 percent of these adolescents returned for further psychiatric care after their first course of treatment had been finished, which is far beyond what would be expected if their disturbances had simply been maturational phenomena that should pass in time.

The Weiner and Del Gaudio data also indicated that serious disturbances among adolescents are just about as stable and likely to persist as among adults. Table 1.4 shows the percentage of patients in four categories whose diagnosis remained approximately the same whenever they returned for help. Information from a similar study

TABLE 1.4   Diagnostic Stability over Time in Adolescent and Adult Psychiatric Patients

Diagnostic Category	Adolescents		Adults	
	n	Stability (in percent)	n	Stability (in percent)
Schizophrenia	90	72.2	179	82.1
Neurosis, personality disorder, and situational disorder	495	52.7	254[a]	71.3
Total	585	60.0	433[a]	75.8

[a] Includes some patients with diagnosis of acute brain syndrome and psychophysiological reaction.
Source.   Based on data reported by Weiner and Del Gaudio (1976) and Babigan, Gardner, Miles, & Romano, 1965.

with adult patients is included for comparison. It can be seen that adolescents show substantial overall diagnostic stability, although less so than adults (60.0 percent versus 75.8 percent), and that for the most serious of these conditions—schizophrenia—an adult degree of stability has pretty much been reached in adolescence (72.2 percent versus 82.1 percent).

Numerous reports from psychiatric hospitals confirm that adolescents who require inpatient treatment remain at high risk for psychopathology in adulthood. Follow-up evaluations up to 10 years after hospital discharge have indicated that although the majority of these disturbed youngsters improve, they are much more likely than the general adult population to have psychological difficulties and much less likely to be functioning completely adequately. Additionally, the severity of the psychopathology experienced in adolescence is consistently found in these studies to predict the level of adult adjustment in former patients (Gossett, Barnhart, Lewis, & Phillips, 1977; Shea, Hafner, Quast, & Hetler, 1978; Welner, Welner, & Fishman, 1979).

To summarize this discussion, the following three conclusions, each amply supported by research findings, can be offered to correct the mistaken opinions stated on page 24.

1. Psychological distress that results in symptoms other than fleeting episodes of anxiety or depression or that produces more than mild impairments of school and/or social functioning is not a normative feature of adolescent development.

2. Distinctions between normal and abnormal adolescent development can be readily made with adequate attention to the number, kind, and persistence of behavior problems an adolescent displays.

3. Apparent psychological disturbance in an adolescent is unlikely to disappear of its own accord; instead, in the absence of appropriate intervention, it tends to progress steadily into adult disturbance.

SUMMARY

Normality can be defined as *average,* which is the way most people are; as *ideal,* which is how most people would like to be; or as *adjustment,* which consists of being able to cope reasonably effectively with life experiences. Each way of looking at normality has certain advantages and disadvantages in studying and talking about human behavior. Because they are just definitions, however, none can be considered more or less correct; each is only more or less useful for some purpose. For the purpose of identifying psychopathological conditions that require professional attention, an adjustment perspective on normality seems to serve best. From this perspective abnormality involves a state of mind or way of acting that prevents a person from enjoying rewarding interpersonal relationships and working productively toward self-fulfilling goals.

Abnormal behavior can be regarded as either continuous or discontinuous with normal behavior. From the point of view of continuity, differences between disturbed and well-adjusted persons are *quantitative.* This means that normal and abnormal behavior are presumed to derive from the same personality dimensions or traits, with maladjusted individuals simply having more or less than the optimum amount of certain traits. By contrast, a discontinuity approach defines differences between normal and abnormal behavior as *qualitative*—that is, as differences in kind rather than degree. Like alternative definitions, these views represent only different ways of looking at the same phenomena, and neither can be proved more accurate than the other. However, because the continuity perspective emphasizes that disturbed behavior consists of exaggerations of normal ways of thinking, feeling, or acting, it has definite advantages in promoting both public and professional efforts to understand and meet the psychological needs of disturbed persons.

As the continuity perspective implies, problem behaviors occur in both normal and disturbed children and adolescents. Two principles are helpful in differentiating between problem behaviors associated with normal and abnormal development: (a) the *principle of age-appropriateness* holds that problem behavior that commonly occurs as young people cope with the developmental tasks of their age group is likely to reflect normal development, whereas ineffective behaviors that are not characteristic of a youngster's peers or that persist beyond the age at which they might be expected to occur are likely to reflect emerging psychopathology; (b) the *principle of future implications* holds that problem behaviors that can be expected to lead to subsequent psychopathology are more likely to reflect abnormal development than problem behaviors that typically disappear of their own accord and do not result in later disturbance.

Survey studies indicate that 20 to 30 percent of children enter elementary school with moderately or severely handicapping behavior problems, and that about 50 percent of these youngsters are sufficiently disturbed to warrant professional attention. Unfortunately, however, it appears that the majority of young people in the United States who need professional mental health care are not receiving it.

Research on the life history of children with behavior problems indicates that their need for professional help can be estimated fairly accurately from the number and kinds of problems they have. From the age of 6 or 7 on, children who have many different kinds of behavior problems are likely to continue to have multiple problems, even if the nature of these problems changes. Additionally, children who have problems related to impaired cognitive functioning or antisocial tendencies are more likely to experience persistent abnormal development than children with primarily emotional difficulties. Although these distinctions can help identify which children are most psychologically handicapped and most in need of help, it is important not to overlook or minimize the needs of less seriously disturbed children, who may be able to benefit considerably from only modest amounts of professional attention.

The principles of age-appropriateness and future implications apply in the evaluation of adolescent as well as child development. However, the picture of what constitutes appropriate and predictive behavior among teenagers has been blurred by widely held notions about "normative adolescent turmoil." These notions, which include the expectation that adolescents can be expected to pass through an "identity crisis" and become "alienated" from adult society, have contributed to clinical opinions that most adolescents show signs of psychological disturbance, that is is difficult if not impossible to distinguish normal from abnormal development during the adolescent years, and that most instances of seemingly deviant behavior in adolescents are short-lived disturbances that will disappear of their own accord.

Extensive research data indicate that this notion of normative adolescent turmoil is largely a myth and that the clinical opinions it has fostered are incorrect. Relatively few adolescents become developmentally disturbed. Most make steady progress toward identity formation without having a crisis, and most maintain mutually rewarding relationships with their families and with their society, without becoming alienated. Clinically significant developmental disturbances that interfere noticeably with their ability to function occur in approximately 20 percent of adolescents—which is just about the same percentage of moderate and severe psychological disturbance that is found in the adult population.

Adequately informed clinicians have little difficulty distinguishing normal from abnormal development in adolescence. As with younger children, the more behavior problems an adolescent displays, the longer these problems persist beyond an age when they might be expected; the more they involve cognitive and behavioral difficulties instead of or in addition to emotional upsets, the more likely the young person is to be psychologically disturbed.

Finally, both normal and disturbed behavior patterns tend to remain stable from adolescence to adulthood. Hence adolescents who manifest obvious symptoms of behavior disorder rarely outgrow them. Those who appear disturbed are likely to be disturbed and to remain disturbed unless they receive adequate treatment.

REFERENCES

ALGOZZINE, B. The emotionally disturbed child: Disturbed or disturbing. *Journal of Abnormal Child Psychology*, 1977, *5*, 205–211.

BABIGIAN, H. M. Schizophrenia: Epidemiology. In M. A. Freedman, H. I. Kaplan, & B. J. Sadock (Eds.), *Comprehensive textbook of psychiatry*. Baltimore: Williams & Wilkins, 1975.

BABIGAN, H. M., GARDNER, E. A., MILES, H. C., & ROMANO, J. Diagnostic consistency and change in a follow-up study of 1215 patients. *American Journal of Psychiatry*, 1965, *121*, 895–901.

BACHMAN, J. G., O'MALLEY, P. M., & JOHNSTON, J. *Adolescence to adulthood: Change and stability in the lives of young men.* Ann Arbor: Institute for Social Research, 1979.

BANDURA, A. The stormy decade: Fact or fiction? *Psychology in the School,* 1964, *1,* 224–231.

BARRON, F. *Creativity and psychological health.* Princeton, N.J.: Van Nostrand, 1963.

BEALER, R. C., WILLITS, F. C., & MAIDA, R. R. The rebellious youth subcultures—a myth. *Children,* 1964, *11,* 43–48.

BLOCK, J., BLOCK, J., SIEGELMAN, E., & VON DER LIPPE, A. Optimal psychological adjustment: Response to Miller's and Bronfenbrenner's discussions. *Journal of Consulting and Clinical Psychology,* 1971, *36,* 325–328.

BOWER, E. M. *Early identification of emotionally handicapped children in school.* (2nd ed.) Springfield, Ill.: Thomas, 1969.

BRENNAN, T. G., & LOIDEAIN, D. S. A comparison of normal and disturbed adolescent Offer Self-Image Questionnaire responses in an Irish cultural setting. *Journal of Youth and Adolescence,* 1980, *9,* 11–18.

BREUER, J., & FREUD, S. (1893–1895) Studies on hysteria. *Standard Edition,* Vol. II. London: Hogarth, 1955.

BRONSON, W. C. Adult derivatives of emotional expressiveness and reactivity-control: Developmental continuities from childhood to adulthood. *Child Development,* 1967, *38,* 801–817.

CASS, L. K., & THOMAS, C. B. *Childhood pathology and later adjustment.* New York: Wiley, 1979.

CHAMBERLAIN, R. W. Management of preschool behavior problems. *Pediatric Clinics of North America,* 1974, *21,* 33–47.

COLEMAN, J. S. *The adolescent society.* Glencoe, Ill.: Free Press, 1961.

COLEMAN, J., HERZBERG, J., & MORRIS, M. Identity in adolescence: Present and future self-concepts. *Journal of Youth and Adolescence,* 1977, *6,* 63–76.

CONGER, J. J. Parent-child relationships, social change and adolescent vulnerability. *Journal of Pediatric Psychology,* 1977, *2,* 93–97.

COWEN, E. L., PEDERSON, A., BABIGIAN, H., IZZO, L. D., & TROST, M. A. Long-term follow-up of early detected vulnerable children. *Journal of Consulting and Clinical Psychology,* 1973, *41,* 438–446.

CRIST, J. The adolescent crisis syndrome: Its clinical significance in the outpatient service. *The Psychiatric Forum,* 1972, *3,* 25–34.

DEUTSCH, A., & ELLENBERG, J. Transience vs. continuance of disturbance in college freshmen. *Archives of General Psychiatry,* 1973, *28,* 412–417.

DOHRENWEND, B. P., DOHRENWEND, B. S., GOULD, M. S., LINK, B., NEUGEBAUER, R., & WUNSCH-HITZIG, R. *Mental illness in the United States: Epidemiological estimates.* New York: Praeger, 1980.

DONOVAN, J. M. Identity status and interpersonal style. *Journal of Youth and Adolescence,* 1975, *4,* 37–55.

DOUVAN, E., & ADELSON, J. *The adolescent experience.* New York: Wiley, 1966.

EICHORN, D. H. The Berkeley longitudinal studies: Continuities and correlates of behaviour. *Canadian Journal of Behavioural Science,* 1973, *5,* 297–320.

EISSLER, K. R. Notes on problems of technique in the psychoanalytic treatment of adolescents. *Psychoanalytic Study of the Child,* 1958, *13,* 223–254.

EKSTEIN, R. Impulse—acting out—purpose: Psychotic adolescents and their quest for goals. *International Journal of Psycho-Analysis,* 1968, *49,* 347–352.

ERIKSON, E. H. The problems of ego identity. *Journal of the American Psychoanalytic Association,* 1956, *4,* 56–121.

ERIKSON, E. H. *Identity: Youth and crisis.* New York: Norton, 1968.

FRANKEL, J., & DULLAERT, F. Is adolescent rebellion universal? *Adolescence,* 1977, *12,* 227–236.

FREDERICKSON, L. C. Value structure of college students. *Journal of Youth and Adolescence,* 1972, *1,* 155–163.

FREUD, A. (1936) *The ego and the mechanisms of defense.* New York: International Universities Press, 1946.

FREUD, A. Adolescence. *Psychoanalytic Study of the Child,* 1958, *13,* 255–278.

FREUD, S. (1937) Analysis terminable and interminable. *Standard Edition,* Vol. XXIII. London: Hogarth, 1964.

FRIESEN, D. Value orientation of modern youth: A comparative study. *Adolescence,* 1972, *7,* 265–276.

GALLEMORE, J. L., & WILSON, W. P. Adolescent maladjustment or affective disorder? *American Journal of Psychiatry,* 1972, *129,* 608–612.

GARDNER, G. E. The mental health of normal adolescents. *Mental Hygiene,* 1947, *31,* 529–540.

GARMEZY, N. The experimental study of children vulnerable to psychopathology. In A. Davids (Ed.), *Child personality and psychopathology: Current topics.* Vol. 2. New York: Wiley, 1975.

GARMEZY, N. Observations on research with children at risk for child and adult psychopathology. In M. F. McMillan & S. Henao (Eds.), *Child psychiatry: Treatment and research.* New York: Brunner/Mazel, 1977.

GARMEZY, N., & STREITMAN, S. Children at risk: The search for the antecedents of schizophrenia. Part I. Conceptual models and research methods. *Schizophrenia Bulletin,* 1974, No. 8, 14–89.

GIOVACCHINI, P. L. The borderline aspects of adolescence and the borderline state. In S. C. Feinstein & P. L. Giovacchini (Eds.), *Adolescent psychiatry.* Vol. VI. Chicago: University of Chicago Press, 1978.

GLAVIN, J. Persistence of behavior disorders in children. *Exceptional Children,* 1972, *40,* 367–376.

GOLDSTEIN, M. J., RODNICK, E. H., JONES, J. E., MCPHERSON, S. R., & WEST, K. L. Familial precursors of schizophrenia spectrum disorders. In L. C. Wynne, R. L. Cromwell, & S. Matthyse (Eds.), *The nature of schizophrenia.* New York: Wiley, 1978.

GOSSETT, J. T., BARNHART, D., LEWIS, J. M., & PHILLIPS, V. A. Follow-up of adolescents treated in a psychiatric hospital. *Archives of General Psychiatry,* 1977, *34,* 1037–1042.

GRIEST, D., WELLS, K. C., & FOREHAND, R. An examination of maternal perceptions of maladjustment in clinic-referred children. *Journal of Abnormal Psychology,* 1979, *88,* 277–281.

GRINKER, R. R., SR., GRINKER, R. R., JR., & TIMBERLAKE, J. A study of mentally healthy young males (homoclites). *Archives of General Psychiatry,* 1962, *6,* 405–453.

GRINKER, R. R., & WERBLE, B. Mentally healthy young males (homoclites) fourteen years later. *Archives of General Psychiatry,* 1974, *30,* 701–704.

GROUP FOR THE ADVANCEMENT OF PSYCHIATRY. *Normal adolescence: Its dynamics and impact.* New York: Scribner's, 1968.

HALL, G. S. *Adolescence: Its psychology and its relation to physiology, anthropology, sociology, sex, crime, religion, and education.* Vols. I and II. New York: D. Appleton, 1904.

HAMBURG, D. A., COELHO, G. V., & ADAMS, J. E. Coping and adaptation: Steps toward a synthesis of biological and social adaptation. In G. V. Coelho, D. A. Hamburg, & J. E. Adams (Eds.), *Coping and adaptation.* New York: Basic Books, 1974.

HAUSER, S. T., & SHAPIRO, R. L. Differentiation of adolescent self-images. *Archives of General Psychiatry,* 1973, *29,* 63–68.

HUDGENS, R. W. *Psychiatric disorders in adolescents.* Baltimore: Williams & Wilkins, 1974.

JAHODA, M. *Current concepts of positive mental health.* New York: Basic Books, 1958.

JENKINS, C. D., HURST, M. W., & ROSE, R. M. Life changes: Do people really remember? *Archives of General Psychiatry,* 1979, *36,* 379–483.

JOINT COMMISSION ON MENTAL HEALTH OF CHILDREN. *Mental health: From infancy through adolescence.* New York: Harper & Row, 1973.

JOSSELYN, I. M. The ego in adolescence. *American Journal of Orthopsychiatry,* 1954, *24,* 223–227.

KANNER, L. Do behavior symptoms always indicate psychopathology? *Journal of Child Psychology and Psychiatry,* 1960, *1,* 17–25.

KENISTON, K. *The uncommitted: Alienated youth in American society.* New York: Harcourt, 1965.

KING, S. H. Coping and growth in adolescence. *Seminars in Psychiatry,* 1972, *4,* 355–366.

KOHLBERG, L., LaCROSSE, J., & RICKS, D. The predictability of adult mental health from childhood behavior. In B. B. Wolman (Ed.), *Manual of child psychopathology.* New York: McGraw-Hill, 1972.

KONOPKA, G. *Young girls: A portrait of adolescence.* Englewood Cliffs, N.J.: Prentice-Hall, 1976.

KYSAR, J. E., ZAKS, M. S., SCHUCHMAN, H. P., SCHON, G. L., & ROGERS, J. Range of psychological functioning in "normal" late adolescents. *Archives of General Psychiatry,* 1969, *21,* 515–528.

LANGNER, T. S., GERSTEN, J. C., GREENE, E. L., EISENBERG, J. G., HERSON, J. H., & McCARTHY, E. D. Treatment of psychological disorders among urban children. *Journal of Consulting and Clinical Psychology,* 1974, *42,* 170–179.

LAPOUSE, R., & MONK, M. An epidemiologic study of behavior characteristics in children. *American Journal of Public Health,* 1958, *48,* 1134–1144.

LAPOUSE, R., & MONK, M. Fears and worries in a representative sample of children. *American Journal of Orthopsychiatry,* 1959, *29,* 803–818.

LAPOUSE, R., & MONK, M. Behavior deviations in a representative sample of children. *American Journal of Orthopsychiatry,* 1964, *34,* 436–446.

LEIGHTON, D. C., HARDING, J. S., MACKLIN, D., MACMILLAN, A. M., & LEIGHTON, A. H. *The character of danger. Vol. III. The Stirling County study of psychiatric disorder and socio-cultural environment.* New York: Basic Books, 1963.

LERNER, R. M., & KNAPP, J. R. Actual and perceived intrafamilial attitudes of late adolescents and their parents. *Journal of Youth and Adolescence,* 1975, *4,* 17–36.

LESLIE, S. A. Psychiatric disorder in the young adolescents of an industrial town. *British Journal of Psychiatry,* 1974, *125,* 113–124.

LESSER, G. S., & KANDEL, D. Parent-adolescent relationships and adolescent independence in the United States and Denmark. *Journal of Marriage and the Family,* 1969, *31,* 348–358.

LESSING, E. E., BEISER, H., KRAUSE, M., DOLINKO, P., & ZAGORIN, S. W. Differentiating children's symptoms checklist items on the basis of judged severity of psychopathology. *Genetic Psychology Monographs,* 1973, *88,* 329–350.

LIEF, H. I., & THOMPSON, J. The prediction of behavior from adolescence to adulthood. *Psychiatry,* 1961, *24,* 32–38.

LINTON, R. *Culture and mental disorders.* Springfield, Ill.: Thomas, 1956.

LOBITZ, G. K., & JOHNSON, S. M. Normal versus deviant children: A multimethod comparison. *Journal of Abnormal Child Psychology,* 1975, *3,* 353–374.

MACFARLANE, J. W., ALLEN, L., & HONZIK, M. P. *A developmental study of the behavior problems of normal children.* Berkeley: University of California Press, 1954.

MARCIA, J. E. Identity in adolescence. In J. Adelson (Ed.), *Handbook of adolescent psychology.* New York: Wiley, 1980.

MASLOW, A. H. *Toward a psychology of being.* (2nd ed.) Princeton, N.J.: Van Nostrand, 1968.

MASLOW, A. H. *The farther reaches of human nature.* New York: Viking, 1971.

MASTERSON, J. F. *The psychiatric dilemma of adolescence.* Boston: Little, Brown, 1967a.

MASTERSON, J. F. The symptomatic adolescent five years later: He didn't grow out of it. *American Journal of Psychiatry,* 1967b, *123,* 1338–1345.

MASTERSON, J. F. The psychiatric significance of adolescent turmoil. *American Journal of Psychiatry,* 1968, *124,* 1549–1554.

MEAD, M. *Culture and commitment: A study of the generation gap.* New York: Doubleday, 1970.

MEDNICK, S. A. A longitudinal study of children with a high risk for schizophrenia. *Mental Hygiene,* 1966, *50,* 522–535.

MEDNICK, S. A., & McNEIL, T. F. Current methodology in research on the etiology of schizophrenia:

Serious difficulties which suggest the use of the high-risk group method. *Psychological Bulletin,* 1968, *70,* 681–693.

MEDNICK, S. A., & SCHULSINGER, F. A longitudinal study of children with a high risk for schizophrenia: A preliminary report. In S. Vandenberg (Ed.), *Methods and goals in human behavior genetics.* New York: Academic, 1965.

MEDNICK, S. A., & SCHULSINGER, F. Some premorbid characteristics related to breakdown in children with schizophrenic mothers. In D. Rosenthal & S. S. Kety (Eds.), *The transmission of schizophrenia.* New York: Pergamon, 1968.

MEEKS, J. E. Nosology in adolescent psychiatry: An enigma wrapped in a whirlwind. In J. C. Schoolar (Ed.), *Current issues in adolescent psychiatry.* New York: Brunner/Mazel, 1973.

MEISSNER, W. W. Parental interaction of the adolescent boy. *Journal of Genetic Psychology,* 1965, *107,* 225–233.

MELLSOP, G. W. Psychiatric patients seen as children and adults: The childhood predictors of adult illness. *Journal of Child Psychology and Psychiatry,* 1972, *13,* 91–101.

MILLER, D. R. Optimal psychological adjustment: A relativistic interpretation. *Journal of Consulting and Clinical Psychology,* 1970, *35,* 290–295.

NISWANDER, K. R., & GORDON, M. (Eds.) *The Collaborative Perinatal Study of the National Institute of Neurological Diseases and Stroke: The women and their pregnancies.* Philadelphia: Saunders, 1972.

OFFER, D. *The psychological world of the teen-ager.* New York: Basic Books, 1969.

OFFER, D., & HOWARD, K. I. An empirical analysis of the Offer Self-Image Questionnaire for adolescents. *Archives of General Psychiatry,* 1972, *27,* 529–533.

OFFER, D., MARCUS, D., & OFFER, J. L. A longitudinal study of normal adolescent boys. *American Journal of Psychiatry,* 1970, *126,* 917–924.

OFFER, D., & OFFER, J. Normal adolescence in perspective. In J. C. Schoolar (Ed.), *Current issues in adolescent psychiatry.* New York: Brunner/Mazel, 1973.

OFFER, D., & OFFER, J. Normal adolescent males: The high school and college years. *Journal of the American College Health Association,* 1974, *22,* 209–215.

OFFER, D., & OFFER, J. B. *From teenage to young manhood: A psychological study.* New York: Basic Books, 1975.

OLDHAM, D. G. Adolescent turmoil: A myth revisited. In S. C. Feinstein & P. L. Giovacchini (Eds.), *Adolescent psychiatry.* Vol. VI. Chicago: University of Chicago Press, 1978.

O'NEAL, P., & ROBINS, L. N. The relation of childhood behavior problems to adult psychiatric status: A 30-year follow-up study of 150 subjects. *American Journal of Psychiatry,* 1958, *114,* 961–969.

ORLOFSKY, J. L., MARCIA, J. E., & LESSER, I. M. Ego identity status and the intimacy vs. idolation crisis of young adulthood. *Journal of Personality and Social Psychology,* 1973, *27,* 211–219.

REDLICH, F. C., & FREEDMAN, D. X. *The Theory and practice of psychiatry.* New York: Basic Books, 1966.

REGIER, D. A., GOLDBERG, I. D., & TAUBE, C. A. The de facto US mental health services system. *Archives of General Psychiatry,* 1978, *35,* 685–693.

RHODES, W. The disturbing child: A problem of ecological management. *Exceptional Children,* 1967, *35,* 449–455.

RICKEL, A. U., SMITH, R. L., & SHARP, K. C. Description and evaluation of a preventive mental health program for preschoolers. *Journal of Abnormal Child Psychology,* 1979, *7,* 101–112.

RIMMER, J. D., HALIKAS, J. A., SCHUCKIT, M. A., & MCCLURE, J. N. A systematic study of psychiatric illness in freshman college students. *Comprehensive Psychiatry,* 1978, *19,* 249–251.

ROBINS, L. N. *Deviant children grown up.* Baltimore: Williams & Wilkins, 1966.

ROBINS, L. N. Follow-up studies. In H. C. Quay & J. S. Werry (Eds.), *Psychopathological disorders of childhood.* (2nd ed.) New York: Wiley, 1979.

ROBINS, L. N., & O'NEAL, P. L. The strategy of follow-up studies, with special reference to children. In J. G. Howells (Eds.), *Modern perspectives in international child psychiatry*. New York: Brunner/Mazel, 1971.

ROBINS, L. N., & WISH, E. Childhood deviance as a developmental process: A study of 223 urban black men from birth to 18. *Social Forces*, 1977, *56*, 448–473.

ROFF, M., & RICKS, D. F. (Ed.). *Life history research in psychopathology*. Vol. 1. Minneapolis: University of Minnesota Press, 1970.

RUBIN, R. A., & BALOW, B. Prevalence of teacher identified behavior problems: A longitudinal study. *Exceptional Children*, 1978, *45*, 102–111.

RUTTER, M., & GRAHAM, P. Psychiatric disorder in 10 and 11 year-old children. *Proceedings of the Royal Society of Medicine*, 1966, *59*, 382–387.

RUTTER, M., GRAHAM, P., CHADWICK, O. F. D., & YULE, W. Adolescent turmoil: Fact or fiction? *Journal of Child Psychology and Psychiatry*, 1976, *17*, 35–56.

RUTTER, M., TIZARD, J., & WHITMORE, K. *Education, health and behaviour*. New York: Wiley, 1970.

RUTTER, M., TIZARD, J., YULE, W., GRAHAM, P., & WHITMORE, K. Isle of Wight studies, 1964–1974. *Psychological Medicine*, 1976, *6*, 313–332.

SANDELL, S. D., & ROSSMANN, J. E. College freshmen view their parents. *Personnel and Guidance Journal*, 1971, *49*, 821–826.

SCHECHTMAN, A. Age patterns in children's psychiatric symptoms. *Child Development*, 1970, *41*, 683–693.

SCHIMEK, J. G. Some developmental aspects of primary process manifestations in the Rorschach. *Journal of Personality Assessment*, 1974, *38*, 226–230.

SELZER, M. L. The happy college student myth. *Archives of General Psychiatry*, 1960, *2*, 131–136.

SHAPIRO, S. H. Vicissitudes of adolescence. In S. L. Copel (Ed.), *Behavior pathology of childhood and adolescence*. New York: Basic Books, 1973.

SHEA, M. J., HAFNER, J., QUAST, W., & HETLER, J. H. Outcome of adolescent psychiatric disorders: A long-term follow-up study. In E. J. Anthony, C. Koupernik, & C. Chiland (Eds.), *The child in his family: Vulnerable children*. Vol. 4. New York: Wiley, 1978.

SHEPHERD, M., OPPENHEIM, A. N., & MITCHELL, S. Childhood behavior disorders and the child guidance clinic: An epidemiological study. *Journal of Child Psychology and Psychiatry*, 1966a, *7*, 39–52.

SHEPHERD, M., OPPENHEIM, A. N., & MITCHELL, S. The definition and outcome of deviant behaviour in childhood. *Proceedings of the Royal Society of Medicine*, 1966b, *59*, 379–382.

SHEPHERD, M., OPPENHEIM, B., & MITCHELL, S. *Childhood behaviour and mental health*. London: University of London Press, 1971.

SIEGELMAN, E., BLOCK, J., BLOCK, J., & VON DER LIPPE, A. Antecedents of optimal psychological adjustment. *Journal of Consulting and Clinical Psychology*, 1970, *35*, 283–289.

SIMMONS, R. G., ROSENBERG, F., & ROSENBERG, M. Disturbance in the self-image at adolescence. *American Sociological Review*, 1973, *38*, 553–568.

SMITH, M. B. Research strategies towards a conception of positive mental health. *American Psychologist*, 1959, *14*, 673–681.

SMITH, W. G., HANSELL, N., & ENGLISH, J. T. Psychiatric disorders in a college population. *Archives of General Psychiatry*, 1963, *9*, 351–361.

SORENSON, R. C. *Adolescent sexuality in contemporary America*. New York: Abrams, 1973.

SPIVACK, G., & SWIFT, M. "High risk" classroom behaviors in kindergarten and first grade. *American Journal of Community Psychology*, 1977, *5*, 385–397.

SROLE, L., LANGNER, T. S., MICHAEL, S. T., OPLER, M. K., & RENNIE, T. A. C. *Mental health in the metropolis: The Midtown Manhattan Study*. New York: McGraw-Hill, 1962.

STANTON, M. The concept of conflict at adolescence. *Adolescence*, 1974, *9*, 537–546.

SYMONDS, P. M., & JENSEN, A. R. *From adolescent to adult*. New York: Columbia University Press, 1961.

TAUBE, J., & VREELAND, R. The prediction of ego functioning in college. *Archives of General Psychiatry,* 1972, *27,* 224–229.

THERRIEN, R. W., & FISCHER, J. Differences in the severity of disturbance of behaviors in children receiving impatient and outpatient psychiatric treatment. *Journal of Personality Assessment,* 1979, *43,* 276–279.

THOMAS, A., & CHESS, S. Evolution of behavior disorders into adolescence. *American Journal of Psychiatry,* 1976, *133,* 539–542.

THOMAS, L. E. Generational discontinuity in belief: An exploration of the generation gap. *Journal of Social Issues,* 1974, *30,* 1–22.

TOLOR, A. The generation gap: Fact or fiction? *Genetic Psychology Monographs,* 1976, *94,* 35–130.

TROLL, L., NEUGARTEN, B., & KRAINES, R. Similarities in values and other personality characteristics in college students and their parents. *Merrill-Palmer Quarterly,* 1969, *15,* 323–336.

VAILLANT, G. E. Natural history of male psychological health: VI. Correlates of successful marriage and fatherhood. *American Journal of Psychiatry,* 1978, *135,* 653–659.

WALDRON, S. The significance of childhood neurosis for adult mental health. *American Journal of Psychiatry,* 1976, *133,* 532–538.

WATERMAN, A. S., GEARY, P. S., & WATERMAN, C. K. Longitudinal study of changes in ego identity status from the freshman to the senior year at college. *Developmental Psychology,* 1974, *10,* 387–392.

WATERMAN, A. S., & GOLDMAN, J. A. A longitudinal study of ego identity at a liberal arts college. *Journal of Youth and Adolescence,* 1976, *5,* 361–369.

WATERMAN, A. S., & WATERMAN, C. K. Relationship between freshman ego identity status and subsequent academic behavior. *Developmental Psychology,* 1972, *6,* 179.

WATT, N. F. Longitudinal changes in the social behavior of children hospitalized for schizophrenia as adults. *Journal of Nervous and Mental Disease,* 1972, *155,* 42–54.

WATT, N. F. Patterns of childhood social development in adult schizophrenics. *Archives of General Psychiatry,* 1978, *35,* 160–165.

WATT, N. F., & LUBENSKY, A. W. Childhood roots of schizophrenia. *Journal of Consulting and Clinical Psychology,* 1976, *44,* 363–375.

WATT, N. F., STOLOROW, R. D., LUBENSKY, A. W., & MCCLELLAND, D. C. School adjustment and behavior of children hospitalized for schizophrenia as adults. *American Journal of Orthopsychiatry,* 1970, *40,* 637–657.

WEINER, A. S. Cognitive and social-emotional development in adolescence. *Journal of Pediatric Psychology,* 1977, *2,* 87–92.

WEINER, I. B. *Psychological disturbance in adolescence.* New York: Wiley, 1970.

WEINER, I. B. The generation gap—fact and fancy. *Adolescence,* 1971, *6,* 155–166.

WEINER, I. B. Perspectives on the modern adolescent. *Psychiatry,* 1972, *35,* 20–31.

WEINER, I. B. The adolescent and his society. In J. R. Gallagher, F. P. Heald, & D. C. Garrell (Eds.), *Medical care of the adolescent.* (3d ed.) New York: Appleton-Century-Crofts, 1976.

WEINER, I. B., & DEL GAUDIO, A. C. Psychopathology in adolescence: An epidemiological study. *Archives of General Psychology,* 1976, *33,* 187–193.

WELNER, A., WELNER, Z., & FISHMAN, R. Psychiatric adolescent inpatients: Eight- to ten-year follow-up. *Archives of General Psychiatry,* 1979, *36,* 698–700.

WERNER, E. E., BIERMAN, J. M., & FRENCH, F. E. *The children of Kauai.* Honolulu: University of Hawaii Press, 1971.

WERNER, E. E., & SMITH, R. S. An epidemiological perspective on some antecedents and consequences of childhood mental health problems and learning disabilities. *Journal of the American Academy of Child Psychiatry,* 1979, *18,* 292–306.

WESTMAN, J. C., RICE, D. L., & BIERMANN, E. Nursery school behavior and later school adjustment. *American Journal of Orthopsychiatry,* 1967, *37,* 725–731.

WINNICOTT, D. W. Adolescence: Struggling through the doldrums. In S. C. Feinstein, P. L. Giovacchini, & A. A. Miller (Eds.), *Adolescent psychiatry.* Vol. 1. New York: Basic Books, 1971.

WOODRUFF, D. S., & BIRREN, J. E. Age changes and cohort differences in personality. *Developmental Psychology,* 1972, *6,* 252–259.

YARROW, M. R., CAMPBELL, J. D., & BURTON, R. V. Recollections of childhood: A study of the retrospective method. *Monographs of the Society for Research in Child Development,* 1970, *35,* No. 138.

ZAX, M., COWEN, E. L., IZZO, L. D., & TROST, M. A. Identifying emotional disturbance in the school setting. *American Journal of Orthopsychiatry,* 1964, *24,* 447–454.

ZAX, M., COWEN, E. L., RAPPAPORT, J., BEACH, D. R., & LAIRD, J. D. Follow-up study of children identified early as emotionally disturbed. *Journal of Consulting and Clinical Psychology,* 1968, *32,* 369–374.

ZERBIN-RUDIN, E. Genetic research and the theory of schizophrenia. *International Journal of Mental Health,* 1972, *1,* 42–62.

2

CLASSIFICATION IN DEVELOPMENTAL PSYCHOPATHOLOGY

POSSIBLE HARMFUL EFFECTS OF CLASSIFICATION

Psychological Dehumanization

Interpersonal Stigma

Prejudice and Rejection
Negative Expectations
Destructive Misinterpretations of Behavior

Social and Political Deprivation

BENEFITS OF CLASSIFYING BEHAVIOR DISORDER

Research Design

Treatment Planning

Communication

APPROACHES TO CLASSIFICATION

Descriptive-Behavioral Classification

Advantages
Disadvantages

Descriptive-Inferential Classification

Advantages
Problems of Reliability
Other Disadvantages

Advances in scientific knowledge require adequate classification of objects and events. To explore the differences between the liquid and solid states, for example, some substances must be designated as being liquids and others as solids; to examine the distinctive characteristics of dogs and cats, some animals must be considered as belonging to the class of "dogs" and others to the class of "cats"; to contrast the effects of inflation and recession, criteria must be established for determining when each is present. With such considerations in mind, the distinguished scientist James Conant (1951, p. 215) observed, "If factual information is considered important, then any classification, however arbitrary, is better than no system."

Classification in the physical, biological, and some social sciences—as in distinguishing between liquids and solids, dogs and cats, inflation and recession—provokes debates from time to time but tends to be relatively uncontroversial. When human behavior is involved, however, classification takes on consequences that are frequently viewed by some mental health professionals with enthusiasm and by others with alarm. The classification of behavior disorders in particular has provoked disagreement between people concerned about its possible harmful effects and people intent on realizing its benefits.

This chapter will first present the major arguments for and against classifying people who appear psychologically disturbed and summarize the primary benefits of doing so. Later sections of the chapter will review advantages and disadvantages of the most common approaches to developing a classification scheme and describe some alternative schemes that have been widely used in clinical and research work with young people.

POSSIBLE HARMFUL EFFECTS OF CLASSIFICATION

Mental health professionals who object to classifying behavior disorders argue that pinning labels of psychopathology on people is a psychologically dehumanizing act that results in interpersonal stigma and social and political deprivation. As elaborated in this section, however, each of these possible harmful effects can be avoided, at least in part, if classification is practiced by knowledgeable and ethically concerned clinicians. Moreover, adequate classification contributes to scientific communication, research design, and treatment planning for the psychologically needy in ways that far outweigh the consequences of its potential abuse.

Psychological Dehumanization

Carl Rogers, one of the most honored and influential psychologists of the twentieth century, has devoted much of his career to developing a *client-centered* orientation to personality theory and psychotherapy. Rogers concluded some 30 years ago that traditional relationships between patients and mental health professionals place patients in a dependent, subservient position that strips them of their dignity and self-esteem. The more responsibility the professional takes for telling patients what is wrong with them and what should be done about it, Rogers said, the less opportunity there is for them to retain a sense of worth and a feeling of being able to understand and do something about their problems on their own.

With this in mind, Rogers encouraged therapists to promote self-exploration and self-determination in their clients. To achieve this end, therapists were instructed to adopt a *nondirective* stance in which they avoid presuming to know any more than their clients about their problems and avoid passing any judgments on them. As one feature of his approach, Rogers (1951) argued against the classification of behavior disorders.

> *The very process of psychological diagnosis places the locus of evaluation so definitely in the expert that it may increase any dependent tendencies in the client, and cause him to feel that the responsibility for understanding and improving his situation lies in the hands of another. . . . There is a degree of loss of personhood as the individual acquires the belief that only the expert can accurately evaluate him, and that therefore the measure of his personal worth lies in the hands of another (pp. 223–224).*

Roger's concern about "personhood" subsequently became a central element of humanistic psychology, which was formulated by Maslow and others for the specific purpose of stressing human individuality: "I must approach a person as an individual unique and peculiar, the sole member of his class" (Maslow, 1966, p. 10). Humanistic psychologists object to personality classification because it labels people according to characteristics they supposedly share with others. Such labeling is regarded as a dehumanizing procedure that denies individual uniqueness and presumes the right of one person to pass judgment on another. Classification in clinical situations is seen by humanistic psychologists as nothing more than mechanistic pigeonholing that serves therapists' needs to label people but is of little value to the patient (Brown, 1972; Bugental, 1967, 1978; Buhler & Allen, 1971; Rogers, 1961).

In response to this concern, it certainly must be agreed that understanding and helping people in psychological distress requires respect for ways in which they are unique. However, the fact that classification *may* serve only to pigeonhole patients without helping them does not mean that it *must* be used in this way. Attention to individual uniqueness does not evaporate just because clinicians identify certain characteristics that people share in common. Learning about people as individuals and learning about them as members of a group are not mutually exclusive forms of clinical inquiry. Instead, how someone is like other people and how he or she is different from them are complementary bits of information that promote full understanding. To many clinicians, the main reason for classifying people is not to have labels for them, but to aid in selecting the form of treatment that will benefit them most (Appelbaum, 1976; Gough, 1971; Shevrin & Shectman, 1973; Sugarman, 1978).

Furthermore, there is much to be lost if individual differences are emphasized at the expense of adequate classification. Cumulative clinical wisdom depends on the identification of similarities among people. Unless similarities are identified, there is no way for previous learning about people who have certain characteristics to guide the evaluation and care of someone who currently has these characteristics. Classification helps prevent us from rediscovering the wheel, in other words; with it we can build on past experience without having to learn from scratch how best to deal with every new situation. Kendell (1975) expresses this point well in stressing that the value of classification lies in the aspects a person shares with some but not all other people.

> *If every patient is different from every other then we can learn nothing from our colleagues, our textbooks, or the accumulated experience of our predecessors. . . . Scientific communication would be impossible and our professional journals would be restricted to individual case reports, anecdotes, and statements of opinion (pp. 5–7).*

Interpersonal Stigma

In 1963 Erving Goffman, a sociologist, wrote an important book entitled *Stigma*. He defined *stigma* as an attribute of a person that makes him or her "different" in ways that other people consider undesirable. More specifically, a stigma is some "deeply discrediting" characteristic that causes others to view the afflicted person as bad, dangerous, or weak. "Because we believe the person with a stigma is not quite human," Goffman says, "we exercise varieties of discrimination, through which we effectively, if often unthinkingly, reduce his life chances" (p. 5). Many mental health professionals have been concerned that the classification of behavior disorders carries seeds of such stigma, which grow into prejudice and rejection, negative expectations that make psychological problems worse than they would otherwise be, and destructive misinterpretations of behavior based on the labels people carry rather than on how they actually conduct themselves.

Prejudice and Rejection It is widely believed that being labeled "mentally handicapped" or "emotionally disturbed" results in a person's being looked at unfavorably by others and excluded from close relationships with them. In support of this belief, some studies have found that people who are believed to have mental problems are viewed as less attractive than they would otherwise be as potential co-workers, neighbors, roommates, or lovers (Bord, 1971; Phillips, 1966, 1967; Yamamoto & Dizney, 1967). Through their everyday experience, most people have firsthand knowledge of someone who has been teased or shunned by peers, excluded from school activities, or been given low priority as a job applicant after having been labeled deviant or disturbed.

Like dehumanization, prejudice and rejection are difficult consequences to justify if they do in fact result from classification. Contrary to common belief, however, it is not at all clear that such is the case. In the first place, there is evidence to suggest that Americans have become increasingly knowledgeable about and tolerant of psychological disturbance to the point where the average person's attitude toward disturbed individuals can more accurately be described as accepting rather than rejecting (Aviram & Segal, 1973; Bentz & Edgerton, 1971; Lemkau & Crocetti, 1962, 1965).

Second, when prejudice and rejection are directed toward disturbed people, they appear to have much more to do with how these people are behaving than with how they are labeled. This conclusion is based on studies in which subjects have been asked to describe and express attitudes toward people whom they observed on videotape or whose "case report" they were given to read. The videotape performances and case reports used in these studies were designed to reflect varying degrees of behavior usually considered symptomatic of disturbance. In addition, both the relatively disturbed and the relatively nondisturbed behavior samples were presented for evaluation sometimes with and sometimes without a psychiatric label attached to them. What was found is that subjects doing these evaluations expressed prejudicial and rejecting attitudes primarily in relation to the extent of disturbed behavior they observed, and whether a label was attached to the behavior made little difference in their views (Kirk, 1976; Lehman, Joy, Kreisman, & Simmens, 1976).

Studies of schoolchildren similarly reveal that relatively little stigma is attached simply to being labeled "learning disabled," "mentally retarded," or "emotionally disturbed" and receiving special forms of instruction. Like adults, school-age children tend to judge each other according to how they perform rather than how they are labeled, and there is no firm basis for concern that attaching a classification to a youngster will by itself result in his or her being scorned or ridiculed. To the contrary, children appear to be fairly open to changing any negative attitudes they hold toward their handicapped peers, especially when they have opportunities for frequent contact with them (Cook & Wollersheim, 1976; Freeman & Algozzine, 1980; Hoffman, Marsden, & Kalter, 1977; Voeltz, 1980).

In an especially interesting study, Budoff and Siperstein (1978) found that sixth-graders, when asked about their attitudes toward children who were identified as academically incompetent, expressed more positive views toward those who were labeled "mentally retarded" than toward those who were not. Apparently the "retarded" label had the positive value of providing an explanation of the poor performance, and the children in this study could be more tolerant and accepting of incompetent behavior from a peer who could not be expected to perform well than one for whom there was no such excuse. In light of such findings, most writers who have reviewed the literature carefully agree that classification cannot by itself be held responsible for eliciting prejudice and rejection toward mentally handicapped or emotionally disturbed persons (Hobbs, 1975; Phillips, 1964; Sundberg, Snowden, & Reynolds, 1978).

Negative Expectations Concern is frequently expressed that classifying behavior disorders generates expectations that foster or at least reinforce the condition that is being labeled. This possibility is discussed in detail by Hobbs in *The Futures of Children* (1975), a very important book concerned with the effects of classification on handicapped, disadvantaged, and delinquent young people. Hobbs points out that calling a broken bone broken has never widened a fracture, but saying that a child is mentally retarded, emotionally disturbed, or antisocial can play a role in his or her being so. Parents who are told that their children are different in some way, for example, may treat them in a manner that encourages them to become different in that way. Thus children who are believed to be immature or incompetent may be "protected" from experiences that would help them mature or learn greater competence; adolescents believed to lack self-control or a sense of responsibility may be denied or "spared" opportunities to participate in social and school activities that require such personal skills but at the same time help young people to develop them.

Studies of teacher-student interaction in the schools have provided considerable evidence that youngsters who are labeled are likely to receive negative messages from their environment. Teachers expect more of students who are described to them as "intellectual bloomers" then they do of equally able students who are not so labeled, and they expect less of students assigned to special classes than they do of regular class students (Fine, 1967; Jones, 1977; Rosenthal & Jacobsen, 1968). As a result of such expectations, children who are believed to be relatively poor learners are called on less frequently in class, are given less time to answer questions, and receive less attention and encouragement than their classmates (Brophy & Good, 1974; Good & Brophy, 1972; Jones, 1972). These differences in how they are treated in turn lead children to behave in ways that agree with their teacher's expectations, so that those of whom less is expected make less academic progress, regardless of their intellectual capacity (Brophy & Good, 1970; Finn, 1972; Rosenthal & Jacobsen, 1968).

Because negative expectations can foster and perpetuate maladaptive behavior, Hobbs (1975) concludes that considerable caution must be exercised in classifying people in ways that lead to such expectations. However, just as children's attitudes toward each other are shaped more by how they act than by what they are called, teachers' expectations have been found to depend much more on their students' actual behavior than on any labels they carry. Research shows further that expectancy effects created by labels diminish rapidly over time, as teachers get to know their students better (Kedar-Voivodas & Tannenbaum, 1979; Reschly & Lamprecht, 1979).

Moreover, Hobbs's plea for caution can be seen as calling not for avoiding classification, but for doing a better job of it. Expectations threaten a child's well-being only when they are inaccurate—which is true of unjustified positive expectations as well as unjustified negative expectations. Children can suffer just as much when too much is expected of them as when their mental, physical, or social abilities are underestimated.

The way to prevent mistakes of both kinds is to have *accurate* expectations, and accurate expectations are promoted by careful and detailed classification. For example, having a child assigned to a special class may lead a teacher to expect less learning than the child is capable of; however, if the teacher knows in addition what the child's measured intelligence is, what the child's relative areas of strength and weakness are, and what kinds of learning typically occur in children with similar patterns of ability, then the teacher is likely to place appropriate demands on the child—neither too many nor too few.

For this reason, many clinicians advocate distinguishing between classification and diagnosis. Whereas classification may consist simply of pinning a label on a person, diagnosis involves explaining what that label means and how the person who wears it can be expected to behave. The more classification is approached with an eye to adequate diagnosis, the more likely it is to foster accurate rather than misleading expectations. Thus the potential to produce negative expectations is neither a necessary nor an inevitable consequence of classifying behavior disorders, but stands instead as an unfortunate and avoidable result of inadequate classification (Bachrach, 1974; Shectman, 1977; Spitzer, 1976; Weiner, 1972).

Destructive Misinterpretations of Behavior   A third aspect of interpersonal stigma that is sometimes felt to result from classifying behavior disorders is misinterpretation of behavior that leads directly to destructive consequences. The possibility of such a destructive outcome was dramatized by Rosenhan (1973) in a noteworthy paper entitled "On Being Sane in Insane Places." Rosenhan described the experience of eight normal people who, acting on his instructions, applied for admission to 12 different mental hospitals with the complaint of hearing voices. In each case the person was admitted to the hospital with a diagnosis of either schizophrenia (11 cases) or manic-depressive psychosis (1 case).

Once admitted, these "pseudopatients" stopped complaining of hearing voices and behaved in a presumably normal fashion. Nevertheless, they were kept in the hospital for an average stay of 19 days. Furthermore, according to Rosenhan, the experience of these nondisturbed people and their hospital records revealed a strong tendency for the staff to interpret their behavior in pathological terms when other alternatives were possible. For example, a patient observed pacing the floor was assumed to be anxious, not bored; patients observed writing frequently in a notebook (Rosenhan had instructed them to keep a detailed log on their experiences) were assumed to be doing something strange, not something creative or productive. In this way, Rosenhan (1973) concludes, psychiatric labels come to have a life and influence of their own: "Once a person is designated abnormal, all of his other behavior and characteristics are colored by that label. Indeed, the label is so powerful that many of the pseudopatients' normal behaviors were overlooked or profoundly misinterpreted" (p. 253).

Rosenhan's work has received a great deal of public attention and is frequently cited by opponents of classifying behavior disorder. Despite the importance of the concerns he addresses, however, his findings do not appear to support the conclusions he draws. First, there are very good reasons for presuming that a person who complains of hearing voices is seriously disturbed and most likely schizophrenic. When such a person voluntarily seeks admission to a mental hospital, there are very good reasons for admitting him or her. Following admission to a protective and supportive hospital environment, there is nothing unusual about even seriously disturbed persons displaying a rapid reduction in their symptoms, and it is good clinical practice to defer discharge until sufficient time has passed to ensure that such symptom relief is more than temporary. Accordingly, both admitting these pseudopatients to the hospital and keeping them there for average of 19 days represent appropriate responses to their behavior, rather than destructive misinterpretation of it (Davis, 1976; Millon, 1975; B. Weiner, 1975).

Second, Rosenhan's assertion that his pseudopatients behaved "normally" once they were admitted to the hospital is open to question. It seems reasonable to expect that normal people finding themselves in a mental hospital would tell the staff that they were sane and had always been sane, would say that they did not require whatever treatment they were receiving, and would ask to be discharged immediately. Instead, Rosenhan's pseudopatients said they were no longer "sick" but stuck to the ruse that they had been sick when they were admitted; they complied passively with all hospital and treatment procedures, and they made no requests to be released from the hospital. Added to the fact that they had voluntarily sought admission in the first place, these features of the pseudopatients' behavior would seem to have justified lingering concern about their adjustment, independently of any presumed effects of labeling.

Third, the information that Rosenhan provides falls short of demonstrating that the pseudopatients' behavior was misinterpreted in any way. Regarding the perception of pacing as a sign of nervousness instead of boredom, he himself states that the pseudopatients were in fact nervous about being in a mental hospital, especially under false pretenses. As for assumptions about the pseudopatients' writing behavior, the only relevant fact was that the nursing notes indicated, "Patient engages in writing behavior." It is Rosenhan's inference (and a questionable one) that this accurate record-keeping means that the activity was seen as pathological.

Furthermore, according to his report, the nurses' notes in the pseudopatients' records regularly contained the phrase "No abnormal indications." Rosenhan uses this fact to bolster his contention that these people were inappropriately kept in the hospital when they were no longer presenting symptoms of disturbance. The reason why people should be kept for observation even after their symptoms have diminished has already been mentioned. With respect to misinterpretations of behavior, the statement "No abnormal indications" suggests that the behavior of these pseudopatients was seen accurately, not colored or misinterpreted as a consequence of their having received a diagnostic label.

These shortcomings of Rosenhan's data do not eliminate the necessity for concern about possible destructive misinterpretations of behavior that can result from diagnostic labels. It is a well-documented finding in psychology that the "set" of observers and the context in which they are observing can influence what they perceive. However, it is important to be precise in deciding the extent to which a general tendency applies in certain specific circumstances. For Rosenhan's psuedopatients, the case for misinterpretations of behavior based on a diagnostic label is not made, despite the frequency with which his study is cited to this effect. Other research has more directly demonstrated that the accuracy with which people are observed may or may not be affected by labels attached to them, depending on various particular circumstances (Herson, 1974; Langer & Abelson, 1974; Romanoff, Lewittes, & Simmons, 1976). The compelling conclusion, then, is that such misinterpretations of behavior are a possible consequence of labeling and must be guarded against, but they are neither inevitable nor unavoidable.

Not only is the classification of behavior not to blame for much of the destructive misinterpretation that is laid on its doorstep, but it can help to prevent such misinterpretations from occurring. Crucial in this regard is the distinction made earlier between labeling and adequate diagnosis. If people are not merely classified by labels but are instead provided a diagnosis that accurately summarizes their assets and limitations, the likelihood of their behavior being misinterpreted is greatly reduced. Thus more rather than less information becomes an excellent way to nip destructive misinterpretation in the bud.

Social and Political Deprivation

Among psychiatrists concerned about the harmful effects of classifying behavior disorders, none has gained more attention than Thomas Szasz. In such books as *The Myth of Mental Illness* (1961), *Law, Liberty, and Society* (1963), *The Manufacture of Madness: A Comparative Study of Inquisition and the Mental Health Movement* (1970), and *The Myth of Psychotherapy: Mental Healing as Religion, Rhetoric, and Repression*

(1978), Szasz warns that psychiatric diagnosis has become a persecutory vehicle for dealing with "undesirable" people by locking them up in mental hospitals. Diagnosis is nothing more than "justificatory rhetoric," says Szasz; it has no substantive meaning, since mental illness does not exist in reality, and it furnishes a pretense for excluding people from society and depriving them of their civil rights whenever they disturb the social order or the sensitivity of those in authority. Similar concerns are raised by Halleck in *The Politics of Therapy* (1971), by Leifer in *In the Name of Mental Health* (1969), and by Magaro, Gripp, and McDowell in *The Mental Health Industry* (1978), all of which are thoughtful and scholarly books that deserve careful reading.

The specter of people being shipped off to mental hospitals because they are considered undesirable has been lent a very grim cast by vivid descriptions of brutalizing, dehumanizing, and nontherapeutic conditions that may exist in them. In *Asylums* Goffman (1961) provided a moving documentary of the dreary life he observed in mental hospitals during a year-long field study. Many semidocumentary and fictionalized accounts of dreadful conditions in such hospitals, from Ward's (1946) *The Snake Pit* to Kesey's (1962) *One Flew Over the Cuckoo's Nest,* have further dramatized the possible misery of being confined in them.

Depriving consequences of classification are not limited to the extreme situation of commitment to a mental hospital. Classification also contributes to such decisions as whether young people should be placed in a training school for the retarded or a correctional facility for delinquents. Are such placements justified and helpful, or do they reflect convenient use of a diagnostic label to send "undesirable" youngsters to undesirable places? A similar question can be asked about children who are assigned to a special class in school. Do they really belong there, or have they wound up there because teachers who disliked them or found them difficult to handle had labels available that could be used to limit their educational opportunities?

As in the case of possible dehumanization and stigma, such concerns must be recognized by all mental health professionals who take responsibility for classifying people on the basis of their behavior. These concerns must be approached with a balanced perspective, however, that preserves reason in the face of impassioned concern. With respect to classification serving as an agent of social and political deprivation, two questions from the previous discussions must be repeated once more: is this undesired outcome an inevitable consequence of classification, and, when deprivation does occur, is classification responsible for it?

Concerning what is inevitable, all of the fears of possible harmful effects of classification mentioned in this section relate to what is known as the *labeling theory of deviance.* According to this theory, people end up being labeled deviant not so much because of how disturbed they are as because they lack certain social or economic characteristics valued by their community. Furthermore, the theory holds, being labeled deviant is a primary cause of becoming deviant, so that classification causes more psychological maladjustment than it helps to prevent. Although this labeling theory has fostered numerous arguments for doing away with classification, there is considerable evidence to indicate that it is essentially invalid. As already noted, people are in fact much more likely to be treated according to how they act than according to how they are labeled (Gove, 1975; Gove & Fain, 1977; Scheff, 1974).

Turning to specific outcomes, the presumption that all of the places to which people may be sent following classification will do them harm ignores the existence of a very large number of mental hospitals, training schools, and special classes in which caring and dedicated staff provide beneficial services to people who sorely need them. For every *Snake Pit* and *One Flew Over the Cuckoo's Nest* that has appeared in the popular literature, there has also been an *I Never Promised You a Rosegarden* (an account of the determined, sensitive, and eventually successful effort of a hospital therapist to help a seriously disturbed adolescent girl regain contact with reality) and a *Victory over Myself* (the autobiological account by Floyd Patterson, former Olympic and professional boxing champion, of how he was turned away from a life of crime by a psychologist's intervention while he was in a reformatory) (Green, 1964; Patterson, 1963).

This is not to say that institutional deprivation in some cases should be considered acceptable so long as it is balanced by beneficial care in other cases. Injustice calls for corrective action whenever it occurs. The point is simply that while institutions or treatment programs are not always good for people, they are not always bad for them either. To the extent that classification results in people receiving needed help, it expands rather than limits their opportunities to find a fuller and more rewarding life. Hence a blanket statement that being classified inevitably works to a person's disadvantage finds no justification in the available facts.

But what about those circumstances in which being labeled disturbed, retarded, or delinquent does contribute to placement in a depriving or nonbeneficial environment? In part this question can be answered by efforts to improve these environments. Most people would agree that mental hospitals should not all be closed because some of them are "snake pits," nor should all special programs in the schools be terminated because some of them fail to teach children anything. A balanced perspective calls for avoiding sweeping conclusions that throw out the good with the bad.

As for instances in which depriving or nonbeneficial placements are imposed on people who are not psychologically needy, we are dealing not with the nature of classification, but with an *abuse* of classification. There is nothing inherently depriving about being classified; adequate classification merely provides accurate information about the amount and kind of professional help an individual may need. If people in authority pin an inaccurate label on someone to justify taking detrimental action against him or her, or if they take actions that ignore the implications of an accurate classification, they are abusing classification in ways that should not be tolerated. Rosenhan (1975), whose work is often cited by opponents of classification, comes to this same conclusion: "The thrust of any rational argument cannot be against classification, per se, but only against poor classification and misclassification as it occurs within certain systems and affects patients' welfare" (p. 473).

BENEFITS OF CLASSIFYING BEHAVIOR DISORDER

As the preceding discussion indicates, the classification of behavior disorder has widely acknowledged benefits for research design, treatment planning, and communication (Blashfield & Draguns, 1976; Kessler, 1971; Woodruff, Goodwin, & Guze, 1974). Some

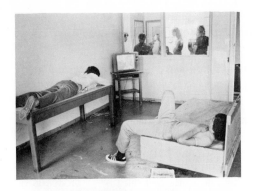

Some people are concerned that being classified as mentally or emotionally handicapped results in being relegated to depriving environments; others see classification as opening the doors to needed and beneficial services.

brief comments on these three areas of benefit will help to summarize the compelling reasons for continuing to use—and attempting to improve—classification.

Research Design

Research in psychopathology is intended to answer questions about the causes, manifestations, and outcomes of psychological disturbance. To this end, some people must be identified as psychologically disturbed in order to compare them meaningfully with nondisturbed people. Additionally, the systematic study of circumstances that contribute to or result from certain specific conditions (e.g., brain dysfunctions as opposed to schizophrenia or depression) requires subjects to be designated as displaying one or another of these conditions. By providing the necessary basis for identifying subject groups, then, classification plays a vital role in generating cumulative knowledge about psychopathology.

With the possible exception of those who object to scientific methods, there is little disagreement concerning this benefit of classification in efforts to expand knowledge. Observations to this effect by distinguished figures in clinical psychology and psychiatry include the following:

Attempts at categorization have resulted in advances in our knowledge and will . . . continue to provide valuable new insights in the field of psychopathology (Shakow, 1966, pp. 150–151).

Our ability to recognize and differentiate clinical syndromes . . . will be necessary for effective research on causes and for meaningful attempts to evaluate treatment (Eisenberg, 1967, pp. 179–180).

Without diagnosis or categories or typologies we have no science (Grinker, 1977, p. 73).

Even Rosenhan, who has raised so many concerns about the possible negative effects of personality classification, says that "scientific understanding . . . proceeds on the basis of classification," and that none of his remarks are intended to deprive researchers of their classificatory systems (Rosenhan, 1975, p. 473). However, he goes on to say that until a system of classification is fully validated, psychopathology researchers should keep their data in their files, where "they can do patients and treatment no harm." This provocative statement brings us to the role of classification in treatment planning.

Treatment Planning

The professional literature leaves little doubt that most clinicians regard an adequate personality evaluation and some type of diagnostic formulation as an essential first step in deciding the amount and kind of help a person may need (Chess & Hassibi, 1978, Chapter 6; Halleck, 1978, Chapter 2; Harrison, 1979; Pruyser & Menninger, 1977; I. Weiner, 1975, Chapter 5). The Joint Commission on the Mental Health of Children (1973, p. 110) is especially unequivocal on this point: "Individual psychodiagnosis is seen as the necessary condition for prescribing one of the many forms of psychotherapeutic interventions."

To know whether a problem exists and what to do about it, mental health professionals must be able to determine whether a person's behavior is similar to or different from the behavior of people who are considered to have certain kinds of problems that are alleviated by certain kinds of intervention. Classification of behavior disorder provides the basis for making such determinations.

On the other hand, Rosenhan is far from alone in his concern that available systems of classification are imperfect. Disagreements occur even among the most skillful clinicians, errors are frequently made by the less skillful, and the intervention believed to be indicated to relieve a particular condition may not in fact be the best one. These issues of reliability and validity will be considered in the next section. Granting that the reliability and validity of classification are imperfect, should clinicians follow Rosenhan's advice to keep diagnostic impressions locked in the files?

Ethical considerations argue strongly against any such paralysis of action. Clinicians are duty-bound to draw on whatever information and skills they have avilable to perform their function as helpfully as they can. Even in the face of imperfect knowledge, they must use their diagnostic impressions to formulate and carry out treatment plans. Failure to do all that seems possible because of what remains uncertain is an abdication of responsibility. The Joint Commission (1973) urges in similar words the best possible clinical utilization of diagnostic impressions.

> Yet, diagnoses must be made, and decisions regarding intervention cannot often be postponed. . . . It is incumbent upon the clinical investigator, therefore, to utilize the methodological tools and theoretical constructions available to him in such a manner that the task is accomplished as accurately as possible within the limitations imposed by existing conditions (pp. 77–78).

Communication

Classification helps mental health professionals talk both with each other and with the general public about psychopathology. Such communication is often the necessary first step in providing programs of service and support for psychologically handicapped people. Thus, although classification sometimes results in a child being excluded from a classroom or an adult being involuntarily committed to a mental hospital, it also can be the basis on which children are identified as being eligible for special instructional programs that will benefit them, or on which adults are identified as needing institutional care. From this perspective, it is failure to classify rather than classification that may have a depriving consequence. In one study confirming this effect, Cohen, Harbin, and Wright (1975) found that changes made in patients' diagnosis by psychiatrists who were concerned about "protecting" them from social stigma led to their receiving insufficient therapy.

As for programs of support, classification can facilitate calling public attention to the needs of people with psychological problems. In order to seek private and governmental funds, propose legislation, and promote community action on behalf of retarded, learning-disabled, or delinquent young people for example, it is necessary to be able to identify the groups whom these efforts are intended to help. Hobbs (1975) summarizes eloquently how these issues bear on the classification of children's problems.

> Classification can profoundly affect what happens to a child. It can open doors to services and experiences the child needs to grow in competence, to become a person sure of his worth and appreciative of the worth of others, to live with zest and to know joy. On the other hand, classification, or inappropriate classification, or failure to get needed classification—and the consequences that ensue—can blight the life of a child, reducing opportunity, diminishing his competence and self-esteem, and making him less a person than he could become. Nothing less than the future of children is at stake (p. 1).

APPROACHES TO CLASSIFICATION

To implement a conviction that developmental disturbances should be classified, clinicians and researchers should be able to call on a conceptually sound, internally consistent classification system that provides a highly valid basis for understanding disturbed youngsters and planning their treatment. Unfortunately no such system exists. Instead, there are several different approaches to classifying psychological disturbance, each of which has certain advantages and disadvantages and a sometimes bewildering variety of diagnostic schemes currently in use. The last section of the chapter will discuss specific classification schemes, and this section will describe the three most widely used approaches to classification—the *descriptive-behavioral* approach, the *descriptive-inferential* approach, and the *dynamic-etiological* approach.

Descriptive-Behavioral Classification

In the descriptive-behavioral approach disturbance is classified on the basis of observable behavior. People are labeled according to how they act in various situations, and no inferences are made about any underlying traits or personality characteristics that may account for their actions. For example, a youngster who shows excessive fear in the presence of a dog is simply classified as "phobic," one who is engaged in behavior that violates the law is classified as "delinquent," and one who has few friends and avoids other people is classified as "withdrawn." In each case the label is used solely as an adjective to describe the kind of behavior the young person is displaying; it is not intended to imply the existence of any general traits or characteristics that make him or her a phobic, delinquent, or withdrawn person.

The descriptive-behavioral approach is preferred by most behaviorally oriented psychologists because it is consistent with their view that what is real about people, aside from their physical attributes, is how they behave. People cannot experience personality problems or personality change, according to this view, but only behavior problems and behavior change; hence they should be differentiated from each other according to their behavior and not in terms of presumed personality characteristics that cannot be directly observed (Bem & Allen, 1974; Calhoun & Turner, 1981; Goldfried, 1976; Goldfried & Kent, 1972; Mischel, 1968, 1973).

Advantages   The descriptive-behavioral approach to classification has two pronounced advantages over other approaches. First, it provides a highly reliable means of labeling behavior disorders. Clinicians using this approach base their diagnoses on observable behavior only. So long as the clinicians are good observers with an adequate behavior sample to work from, there will usually be little room for them to disagree. Moreover, because the terminology used in descriptive-behavioral classification attempts only to say what a behavior is (as in *delinquent* behavior) and not what it may mean, this approach almost always results in an accurate description of a person being evaluated.

Second, descriptive-behavioral classification facilitates intervention planning and evaluation by identifying specific treatment "targets." When people are classified as "phobic," "delinquent," or "withdrawn," the diagnostic label indicates not only what the problem is but also what that treatment should aim to do—that is, help the person modify his or her phobic, delinquent, or withdrawn behavior. Such specific treatment goals guide therapists both in conducting treatment and in determining if and when the treatment has been successful.

Disadvantages   Because descriptive behavioral classification focuses on symptoms rather than on the person who has these symptoms, it may fail to distinguish among disorders that produce similar symptoms but have different causes, different appropriate treatments, and different outcomes. As elaborated in Chapter 11, for example, delinquent behavior appears to occur in at least five different kinds of youngsters: sociological delinquents, characterological delinquents, neurotic delinquents, psychotic delinquents, and organic delinquents. In each case the young person's delinquent acts result from different motives or personality impairments; in addition, the most helpful type of therapy and the likelihood of a favorable response to therapy vary widely across these five patterns of delinquency. Viewed from this perspective, a treatment approach targeted on specific symptoms may prove inadequate because it fails to address underlying personality problems or impairments that have caused the symptoms.

Behavioral psychologists respond to this criticism of descriptive-behavioral classification by reemphasizing that there is no such thing as an "underlying personality" and that the symptoms a person has *are* his or her disorder. If other kinds of behavior problems exist along with delinquency, such as poor reality testing or inadequate impulse control, then these problems should also be described and targeted for treatment. Once all the symptoms a person has are identified and modified by appropriate treatment, the person will no longer have any disorder.

Unfortunately this response does not fully solve the problem. Aside from the theoretical issue of whether people consist of more than the sum total of their observable behaviors, describing a complex disorder in behavioral terms alone is likely to result in a long list of symptoms, not a classification. Even though each of the symptoms in the list correctly describes the person and identifies a treatment target, the lack of any single diagnostic term that summarizes the person's major symptoms hinders scientific communication and research—two of the reasons for undertaking classification in the first place.

Furthermore, no matter how completely a list of behavioral terms describes a person's problems, it still says nothing about the origin of these problems or about the best way to treat them. For example, a list of what would generally be agreed to be psychotic behaviors contains few clues to whether the patient would benefit most from antipsychotic medication, a hospital-milieu program, intensive psychotherapy, behavior therapy, or some combination of these methods. By contrast, a diagnosis of "amphetamine psychosis" for this person would indicate that the observed psychotic behavior is the result of an overdose of amphetamines and that none of the above four methods is likely to be as important to successful treatment as simple withdrawal from the drug.

There has been considerable debate among clinicians who take a strong stand for or against a descriptive-behavioral approach to classification on the basis of these and other arguments. In the present discussion, it should be kept in mind that classification schemes share the characteristic of definitions noted in Chapter 1: they are never right or wrong, only more or less useful for some purpose. Accordingly the advantages and disadvantages of different approaches to classification should be weighed without getting caught up in any urgent need to "prove" that one approach captures the truth and the others should be discarded.

To summarize the merits of a descriptive-behavioral approach, it has the advantages of being highly reliable and identifying clearly the problems to be addressed in treatment. It has the disadvantage of providing little information about the nature of the person who has a certain problem, about the particular origin and meaning of the problem in the person's life, or about the treatment methods that are most likely to be helpful in eliminating the problem.

Descriptive-Inferential Classification

In descriptive-inferential classification certain combinations of observable symptoms or behaviors are presumed to indicate some form of underlying psychopathology that accounts for them. For example, a person who is displaying incoherent thinking, illogical reasoning, inaccurate perception of reality, inappropriate emotional responses, and withdrawal from people is likely to be classified as schizophrenic. These maladaptive behaviors are seen as resulting from the person's having a schizophrenic impairment of personality functioning, and the presence of schizophrenic disorder is *inferred* from the existence of these behaviors.

Most of the traditional diagnostic terms used in clinical settings involve the descriptive-inferential approach to classification. In addition to *schizophrenia,* these include such terms as *paranoia, obsessive-compulsive neurosis,* and *antisocial personality.* Some common behavioral terms may also be used in a descriptive-inferential manner. For example, *depression* can be taken as a strictly behavioral term that describes observable feelings of sadness or discouragement, or it can be used to describe an underlying disorder with multiple symptoms. In the latter case, depression is believed to consist of a sense of loss that results in apathy, slowed mental functioning, negative self-attitudes, and feelings of helplessness and hopelessness; the combination of these symptoms provides the basis for inferring a depressive disorder of personality functioning.

Advantages The chief advantage of descriptive-inferential classification is that it says something about a person who is manifesting behavior problems and about the origin of these problems in certain underlying personality impairments. In addition to allowing people to be seen as comprising more than merely the sum of their observable behaviors, this approach helps in selecting treatment methods focused on the basic problems that is causing the behavioral difficulty.

Problems of Reliability The advantage of an inferential approach over a purely behavioral approach to classification comes at a price, since terms based on inferences rather than direct observations alone open the door to unreliability. Two clinicians who see a man take off all of his clothes in the middle of the street will have little difficulty agreeing that he is displaying inadequate self-control (a descriptive-behavioral classification). However, if they are asked to make an inferential classification, it is easily possible for one to describe the man's behavior as resulting from a schizophrenic impairment of judgment and the other as resulting from a neurotic need to exhibit himself.

Because inferential classification allows even keen observers to disagree so widely, some critics have gone so far as to urge that traditional diagnostic categories should be discarded because of their unreliability (Adams, Doster, & Calhoun, 1977; Costello, 1970). Any blanket statement to this effect begs the question. Just because an inferential approach *may* result in unreliability does not mean that it *will* or *must.* To the contrary, clinicians working carefully from adequate data may be able to draw very similar inferences. Suppose, for example, that in the preceding illustration the man taking off his clothes was also shouting "I am Jesus Christ!" The clinician who had initially inferred a neurotic disorder would then be likely to change his or her mind, and both clinicians would probably agree that they were observing a person with a schizo-phrenic impairment of judgment and a schizophrenic delusional system.

The reliability of inferential descriptions can also be expected to vary from one condition to the next. If a particular disorder is widely believed to produce certain clear-cut symptoms that are unique to that disorder, clinicians are likely to agree fairly well on whether or not it is present. On the other hand, the more a disorder shares symptoms in common with other disorders and the less consensus there is about its having any unique features, the more frequently clinicians are likely to disagree on whether a disturbed person has that disorder.

For these reasons, an evaluation of descriptive-inferential classification cannot stop with merely saying that it is unreliable. It is necessary to look further into just how unreliable it is, what circumstances increase or decrease its unreliability, and which inferential diagnostic categories are more or less unreliable. To help answer these questions, Table 2.1 summarizes findings from 12 studies of diagnostic agreement among psychiatrists evaluating the same patients. The data are expressed as Kappa coefficients, a sophisticated index that contrasts an observed percent of agreements with the percent that could be expected by chance in the particular experimental situation; a Kappa of 0 indicates a chance agreement, and a Kappa of 1.00 indicates perfect agreement.

As interpreted by Spitzer and Wilson (1975), the average Kappas for the nine studies published from 1956 to 1973 suggest that clinicians can achieve satisfactory reliability in diagnosing organic brain damage and alcoholism, but only fair agreement for schiz-

TABLE 2.1 Reliability of Selected Diagnostic Categories in Several Major Studies (expressed as Kappa coefficients of agreement)

	Nine studies from 1956 to 1973[a]		Three More Recent Studies		
	Range	Average	Spitzer & Fleiss 1974	Robins et al. 1977	Helzer et al. 1977
Organic brain syndrome	0.59–0.90	0.77	—[b]	0.77	0.29
Alcoholism	0.65–0.77	0.71	0.66	0.88	0.74
Psychosis	0.43–0.73	0.54	—	—	—
Schizophrenia	0.30–0.77	0.54	0.84	0.84	0.58
Neurosis	0.22–0.52	0.36	—	—	—
Anxiety neurosis	0.45[c]	0.45	0.52	—	0.76
Neurotic depression	0.02–0.47	0.21	0.56	—	0.55
Personality disorder	0.11–0.56	0.29	—	—	—
Antisocial personality	0.53[c]	0.53	—	0.79	0.81

[a] As reported by Spitzer and Wilson (1975).
[b] Category not included.
[c] Category included in only one of these nine studies.

ophrenia and poor agreement for most other traditional diagnostic categories. Table 2.1 reveals not only a substantial variation among diagnostic categories in these nine studies, but also large differences for individual diagnostic categories from one study to the next. For example, the Kappa index ranges from 0.30 to 0.77 for schizophrenia and from 0.02 to 0.47 for neurotic depression.

Several careful analyses of these studies have indicated that their inconsistent results are due largely to differences in the methods they employ. Three factors have emerged as particularly important in this regard, because they directly influence the degree of reliability that can be expected to characterize diagnostic judgments: (a) the more experienced clinicians are and the more committed they are to the research, (b) the more they share the same clear and precise criteria for determining whether a particular condition is present, and (c) the more they obtain and use the same information in making their judgments, the more likely they are to agree (Kendell, 1975, Chapter 3; Robins, Gentry, Munoz, & Marten, 1977; Spitzer, Endicott, & Robins, 1978a; Ward, Beck, Mendelson, Mock, & Erbaugh, 1962; Zubin, 1967).

The first nine studies summarized in Table 2.1 fall short in one way or another of meeting these requirements for maximum potential reliability to occur. It is therefore likely that they underestimate the degree of agreement that is possible in using traditional diagnoses. The three more recent studies listed in Table 2.1 suggest in fact that improved research design can yield more encouraging results. These studies have employed structured diagnostic interviews and objective, precisely defined diagnostic criteria in order to maximize the likelihood that the clinicians would be working from the same frame of reference with the same data. The rates of agreement are almost uniformly higher than those observed in the earlier, less carefully designed research.

Spitzer and his colleagues have built further on this apparent reliability potential by developing the Research Diagnostic Criteria (RDC), a set of specific guidelines for diagnosing a selected group of disorders. They report that experienced and well-trained interviewers working with the RDC have achieved Kappa coefficients of agreement of 0.86 to 0.97 for alcoholism, 0.80 for schizophrenia, 0.88 to 0.90 for major depressive disorder, and 0.81 for minor depressive disorder (Spitzer, Endicott, & Robins, 1978b). These findings strongly suggest that the reliability problem of inferential diagnoses will give way in time to increasingly sophisticated specifications of the criteria for determining whether these conditions are present. Further information on reliability will be presented in the last section of this chapter, in specific relation to alternative schemes for classifying psychopathology in children and adolescents.

Before leaving the general topic of reliability, one more reference to the Rosenhan (1973) study of "pseudopatients" is in order. To recapitulate, eight normal people, complaining of hearing voices, sought admission to 12 different mental hospitals and were diagnosed as schizophrenic or manic-depressive. In addition to using his data to comment on the negative consequences of diagnostic labeling, Rosenhan also argued that traditional diagnostic categories are unreliable, since "It is clear that we cannot distinguish the sane from the insane in psychiatric hospitals" (p. 257).

This assertion loses sight of the fact that advances in knowledge about human behavior require data collection adequate to the task. Overgeneralization from inadequate or irrelevant data does more to undermine than to foster progress toward fuller understanding. The studies appearing in Table 2.1 accordingly involve several hundreds of subjects broadly representative of disturbed people receiving mental health care. Rosenhan's sweeping generalization that "we cannot distinguish the sane from the insane," on the other hand, is based on a sample of eight persons applying to 12 hospitals. Because his study has become widely cited as evidence of the unreliability of inferential diagnostic categories, it bears repeating that his data are inadequate to justify his conclusions.

Furthermore, no matter how large Rosenhan's sample had been, his findings would be irrelevant to the issue of diagnostic reliability. His method of study provides no information on whether psychiatrists can accurately detect "insanity" when it is present; all it reveals is that carefully coached imposters can mislead mental health professionals. As numerous critics of Rosenhan's work have noted, the unreliability or uselessness of a diagnostic method cannot be established by showing that pathological symptoms can be faked (Farber, 1975; Millon, 1975; Spitzer, 1976; Sundberg et al., 1978). Moreover, the previously mentioned frequency with which people applying for admission to mental hospitals with complaints of hearing voices turn out to be reliably diagnosable as schizophrenic gave the misled clinicians in the Rosenhan study good reason to act as they did (Davis, 1976).

To summarize the current status of knowledge in this area, then, inferential classification is less reliable than behavioral classification and may be especially unreliable for diagnostic categories that are not clearly understood or precisely defined. On the other hand, the reliability of inferential categories seems well on the way to being improved by increases in the uniformity of data collection and the clarity of diagnostic criteria used in clinical practice.

Other Disadvantages Unreliability is not the only potential disadvantage of a descriptive-inferential approach to classifying behavior disorders. In some cases it may result in treatment plans that focus too much on underlying personality disorder and too little on real-world behavior difficulties. Suppose, for example, that a child who is withdrawn from peer relationships is considered to have underlying neurotic concerns about being teased or rejected in social situations. Psychotherapy that helps this child overcome unrealistic fears will not automatically transform an isolated child into a social success. Maladaptive behavior patterns that have persisted for months or years tend to become habit-forming; that is, they develop an autonomy of their own, so they exist indepently of neurotic concerns that may have caused them and do not disappear just because these neurotic concerns have been resolved. Additionally, a once fearful, socially isolated child who is no longer fearful will still have some catching up to do in learning the social skills that contribute to good interpersonal relationships.

For this reason, a narrow focus on inferential classification may lead to a similarly narrow treatment focus on underlying pathology. Psychotherapists need to recognize that they have completed their task when the patient's adjustment has improved as much as seems possible, not when underlying adjustment has improved as much as seems possible, not when underlying personality problems appear to have been resolved. To the extent that inferential classification results in treatment aimed at under-lying disorder to the exclusion of concerns with adjustment, then, it carries a serious disadvantage into clinical practice.

Finally, although inferential categories provide more information about the nature of a person's problems than behavioral categories, they still fall short of explaining the problem. To say that a person has a schizophrenic, antisocial, or obsessive-compulsive disorder gives a description of disturbance, but it does not say anything specific about the origins of this disturbance, the circumstances in which it is manifest, or the kinds of ongoing events that sustain it. Bachrach (1974, p. 393) correctly notes in this regard that "Psychiatric categories most often refer to what is to be diagnosed (understood) rather than to what the diagnosis (understanding) is." As one important consequence of this limitation, the inferential-descriptive approach is not very helpful in suggesting how various kinds of disturbances might be anticipated and prevented.

Dynamic-Etiological Classification

The dynamic-etiological approach classifies maladaptive behavior in language that calls attention to the specific circumstances in which the problem behavior is manifest and to the kinds of biogenetic or psychosocial factors that have fostered and are sustaining the problem. *School phobia,* for example, refers to unrealistic fears of being in school that derive from excessive dependency of children on their parents; *homosexual panic reaction* refers to an anxiety state that emerges in situations of close contact with persons of the same sex and is caused by underlying conflicts over homosexual impulses.

Advantages Even more than descriptive-inferential classification, a dynamic-etiological approach to classification promotes understanding the disturbed person as an individual. Because the language of this approach summarizes the origins and the precipitating circumstances of a behavior problem, it conveys not only what the problem is, but also where it comes from, when it is likely to appear, what to do about it, and even how to prevent it. In the case of homosexual panic, for example, the diagnostic label tells us that the observed anxiety reactions (1) reflect underlying homosexual concerns, (2) tend to occur when the person is surrounded more closely than usual by members of his or her own sex (e.g., an 18-year-old male whose first experience in living away from home is Navy boot camp), (3) can be minimized by avoiding same-sexed groups and treated by working to resolve underlying homosexual concerns, and (4) can be prevented altogether by child-rearing experiences that help young people develop a clear and nonconflictual sense of their sex-role identity.

Disadvantages Unfortunately, the disadvantages of this approach mount in direct relation to the amount of additional information it provides. First, because dynamic-etiological classification strays even farther from the observable data than descriptive-inferential diagnosis and involves even more levels of inference, it is the least reliable of the three approaches being discussed. As a general rule, the more specifically behavior disorders are categorized according to their causes, the more opportunities there are for observers to disagree and the more difficult it becomes to formulate objective criteria that will minimize their disagreement.

Second, dynamic-etiological categories often imply more specificity between personality dynamics and problem behavior than is known to exist. With few exceptions, having a certain kind of underlying psychological concern does not mean that a particular behavior problem will *always* occur in certain circumstances; likewise, the appearance of a particular behavior problem in certain circumstances does not *always* mean that a certain kind of underlying psychological concern is present. Although a young man who becomes highly anxious in boot camp may have underlying concerns about homosexuality, he could just as easily be panicky about being away from home, submitting to authority, or meeting the physical demands of basic training. Conversely, many young men who are in fact troubled by underlying homosexual concerns may find ways of coping with boot camp without becoming especially anxious. As this example shows, dynamic-etiological classification runs the risk of concluding too quickly that one of several equally possible explanations of a behavior problem must be the correct one.

Third, many conditions are not sufficiently well understood to be classified in dynamic-etiological terms. For most of the disturbances discussed in subsequent chapters, alternative hypotheses outweigh established facts about their specific causes. In many cases there is particular uncertainty about the relative contribution of biogenetic and psychosocial factors in the origin of the condition. Because classification according to specific cause-effect relationships can therefore encompass only a small subset of behavior disorders, the dynamic-etiological approach cannot provide a basis for a comprehensive classification scheme.

ALTERNATIVE CLASSIFICATION SCHEMES

Mental health professionals have produced many different schemes for classifying behavior disorders. In doing so, clinicians have typically used observations of patients with various kinds of problems as a basis for deriving categories of disturbance. Researchers have more often worked from behavior ratings of disturbed people, on which they have used statistical analyses to identify dimensions of behavior that cluster together empirically. Neither the clinical nor the empirical method has yet resulted in a completely adequate or universally accepted classification scheme, especially with regard to the behavior problems of children and adolescents. Nevertheless, considerable progress has been made toward this end in recent years; it can be summarized by describing the major alternative schemes currently in use.

DSM-II

The most widely used classification scheme for behavior disorders was for many years the second edition of the *Diagnostic and Statistical Manual of Mental Disorders,* usually referred to as DSM-II, which was published by the American Psychiatric Association in 1968. DSM-II provides numerical codes for approximately 200 diagnostic categories and was the guidebook for official record-keeping in most mental health facilities from its inception until just recently. Most of the codes in this traditional psychiatric classification scheme refer to descriptive-inferential categories, such as *acute schizophrenic episode, obsessive-compulsive neurosis,* and *hysterical personality.* DSM-II also includes some categories that identify a specific etiology, such as *psychosis with intracranial neoplasm* and *involutional paranoid state;* other categories are expressed solely in descriptive-behavioral terms, such as *exhibitionism, habitual excessive drinking,* and *enuresis.*

In addition to lacking a consistent conceptual base, DSM-II has very little to say about developmental psychopathology. For the most part, children and adolescents must be assigned diagnostic categories intended for use with adults. The only exceptions are a category of "transient situational disturbances," which allows the diagnosis of *adjustment reaction* of infancy, childhood, or adolescence, and a category of "behavior disorders of childhood and adolescence," under which six specific diagnoses are possible: *hyperkinetic reaction, withdrawing reaction, overanxious reaction, runaway reaction, unsocialized aggressive reaction,* and *group delinquent reaction.*

In a study of 330 child and adolescent psychiatric patients diagnosed with DSM-II, Cerreto and Tuma (1977) found that 37.8 percent were labeled "transient situational disturbance" and 30.3 percent "behavior disorder," with most of the remaining youngsters receiving some adult diagnosis. In actual practice, then, DSM-II has had the shortcoming of resulting in fairly frequent use of adult diagnoses for young people, without their being specific criteria for identifying these conditions in children and adolescents. Of even greater concern is the fact that the narrow range of diagnostic categories available for young people leads to almost 40 percent being labeled in very general terms as having an adjustment reaction. Ceretto and Tuma (1977), along with many other authors, conclude that "transient situational disturbance" has been overused with young people, especially adolescents, at the expense of failing to call adequate attention to developing and potentially serious patterns of specific psychopathology (Fard, Hudgens, & Welner, 1978; Meeks, 1973; Weiner, 1980; Weiner & Del Gaudio, 1976).

The GAP Report

Dissatisfaction with the DSM-II approach has led to extensive efforts by concerned clinicians to improve on it. The major such effort with respect to children and adolescents was published by the Group for the Advancement of Psychiatry (GAP) in 1966 and revised in 1974. The aim of the GAP report was to provide a detailed classification of mental and emotional disorders in young people. As background for their work, the GAP committee reviewed 24 different schemes that various systematizers had previously proposed for classifying developmental psychopathology. They concluded that dynamic-etiological terms do not lend themselves well to classification, even though they may round out and deepen descriptive labels. Hence the GAP classification employs descriptive labels only, grouped into eight categories of disturbance: reactive disorders, developmental deviations, psychoneurotic disorders, personality disorders, psychotic disorders, psychophysiological disorders, brain syndromes, and mental retardation.

The GAP report constitutes a distinct improvement over DSM-II, primarily because it focuses specifically on developmental aspects of psychopathology and on criteria for identifying patterns of disorder in young people. However, it still mixes descriptive behavioral terms (e.g., *oppositional personality disorder, developmental sensory deviation*) with descriptive-inferential terms (e.g., *early infantile autism, hysterical personality disorder*). Moreover, it is a highly complex scheme involving more theoretical assumptions than are comfortable to many mental health professionals. As a result, the GAP classification scheme, although frequently referred to, has not shown much reliability in studies of how well people can agree in using it, and it has not enjoyed wide acceptance either for clinical or research purposes (Achenbach & Edelbrock, 1978; Beitchman, Dielman, Landis, Benson, & Kemp, 1978; Quay, 1979).

DSM-III

In 1980 the American Psychiatric Association published a substantially revised third edition of its *Diagnostic and Statistical Manual,* known as DSM-III (Spitzer, Williams, & Skodol, 1980). Several features of this revision are noteworthy.

First, mental disorders are presumed to be continuous to some extent with each other and with normal psychological functioning. This approach embodies the quantitative conception of psychopathology recommended in Chapter 1 (see p. 7) as a way of avoiding regarding disturbed people as qualitatively different from the rest of us. DSM-III in fact encourages a focus on classifying disorders rather than individuals; instead of referring to "schizophrenics" or "alcoholics," for example, DSM-III prefers such phrases as "individuals with schizophrenia" and "people who are dependent on alcohol."

Second, like the GAP report, DSM-III acknowledges that little is known about the etiology of most disorders and recommends a descriptive approach except for those rare instances in which the origin as well as the nature of a condition can be indicated by its label. Additionally, following the example set in developing the previously mentioned Research Diagnostic Criteria, DSM-III goes on to provide fairly specific behavioral criteria as guidelines for making each diagnosis it lists. Besides increasing the prospects for agreement among diagnosticians, these detailed objective criteria are likely to facilitate research on the validity of diagnostic categories by making it easier to examine how they correlate with other aspects of past, current, and future behavior. In fact, although DSM-III includes a number of inferential diagnostic categories, the behaviorally oriented guidelines provided for diagnosing them give the system many of the advantages of a strictly behavioral approach.

Third, DSM-III goes beyond a traditional labeling approach to diagnosis by employing a "multiaxial" scheme for a broad description of individual disorder. As summarized in Table 2.2, official diagnostic evaluation is covered by Axes I to III, which include all of the mental disorders and any physical condition that should also be taken into account. Axes IV and V then provide additional information about levels of stress and adaptive functioning that are helpful in planning treatment and predicting outcome.

Finally, DSM-III pays special attention to the classification of psychopathology in children and adolescents. Each feature of the system is illustrated for both younger and older persons; the manner in which primarily adult disturbances such as schizophrenic or affective disorders may become manifest in young people is described, and a separate section of the manual is devoted to disorders that first become evident in the

TABLE 2.2 Multiaxial Approach to Diagnosis Employed in DSM-III[a]

Axis	Information Provided	Sample Diagnosis and Code
I	Clinical syndromes	Depressive disorder, recurrent, mild (296.31)
II	Personality disorders (in adults) or specific developmental disorders (in children)	Dependent personality disorder (301.60)
III	Physical disorders and conditions considered pertinent to the cause or management of disorders on Axes I and II	None
IV	Severity of psychosocial stressors considered likely to have contributed to the current episode of disorder in Axis I (rated on 7-point scale)	Moderate stress (marital problems) (5)
V	Highest level of adaptive functioning during the past year (rated on 7-point scale)	Good adaptation (3)

[a] *Diagnostic and Statistical Manual.* Washington: American Psychiatric Association, 3d ed., 1980.

developmental years. These include approximately 45 diagnoses grouped under categories of mental retardation, attention deficit disorder, conduct disorders, anxiety disorders, eating disorders, stereotyped movement disorders, developmental disorders, and other disorders.

Turning to the important issue of reliability, research to date suggests that DSM-III is an improvement over DSM-II and can achieve good interjudge agreement in many categories. Table 2.3 shows overall Kappa coefficients of agreement for four axes of DSM-III as found in two phases of field trials involving several hundred adults. Within Axis I several of the diagnostic groups had reliability coefficients consistently above 0.70, which can be taken as indicating good agreement. These include organic mental disorders (0.76–0.79), substance use disorder (0.80–0.81), schizophrenic disorders (0.81), and affective disorders (0.69–0.83).

Although information concerning the interjudge reliability of DSM-III diagnoses of children and adolescents is still scanty, two research programs have provided some preliminary data that are encouraging. Cantwell and his colleagues compared DSM-II and DSM-III Axis I diagnoses given by a group of clinical raters working from case histories of child and adolescent psychiatric patients. These clinicians achieved reasonably good agreement with both systems for several major categories of disturbance (see Table 2.4). Some acceptable levels of agreement among these raters were also found for DSM-III Axis II (80 percent), Axis III (90 percent), Axis IV (63 percent), and Axis V

TABLE 2.3 Reliability Coefficients for Four Axes of DSM-III in Field Trials with Adults

	Phase One		Phase Two	
	Kappa	*n*	Kappa	*n*
Axis I Clinical syndromes	0.68	339	0.72	331
Axis II Personality disorders	0.56	339	0.64	331
Axis IV Severity of psycho-social stressors	0.60	308	0.66	293
Axis V Highest level of adaptive functioning past year	0.75	321	0.80	316

Source. Based on data reported in DSM-III (American Psychiatric Association, 1980, Appendix F).

(64 percent) (Cantwell Mattison, Russell, & Will, 1979; Cantwell, Russell, Mattison, and Will, 1979; Russell, Cantwell, Mattison, & Will, 1979).

Considering that the raters were using DSM-III for the first time, these results are promising with respect to the potential reliability level of this system. Although the DSM-III Axis I diagnoses just equaled rather than surpassed DSM-II in producing agreement about these young patients, this good start suggests that it will prove more reliable in the future as mental health professionals become increasingly familiar with its criteria.

In the other project Strober and his colleagues examined clinicians' agreements in evaluating 100 consecutively admitted adolescents at the UCLA Neuropsychiatric Institute. They found that 93 of these 100 youthful patients could be assigned an Axis I

TABLE 2.4 Interjudge Agreement on DSM-II and DSM-III Axis I Diagnoses with Child and Adolescent Patients (in percent)

	Psychotic Disorders	Depressive Disorders	Anxiety Disorders	Attention Deficit and Conduct Disorders	Mental Retardation and Organic Disorders
DSM-II	71	41	48	72	77
DSM-III	76	42	50	63	85

Source. Based on data reported by Mattison et al. (1979).

diagnosis, which speaks well for the clarity of the DSM-III criteria, and that 88 of the 93 could be given a more specific diagnosis than *adjustment reaction*. These findings support the point made in Chapter 1 that disturbed adolescents can and should have their conditions diagnosed and treated, rather than regarded as some murky manifestation of "adolescent turmoil" that will pass in time. As for reliability, these researchers found an overall Kappa coefficient of 0.74 for 14 DSM-III categories of disturbance, with coefficients over 0.70 for schizophrenic disorders, affective disorders, drug use disorders, eating disorders, conduct disorders, and attention deficit disorders (Strober & Green, in press; Strober, Green, & Carlson, 1981).

While DSM-III was being formulated, some psychologists expressed concern that it might bring an inappropriately broad range of human behavior and disability within the classification of psychiatric disorder, especially among young people (Garmezy, 1978; Schacht & Nathan, 1977). Yet from a psychological point of view DSM-III has the advantage of referring to "mental *disorder*," not "mental *illness*," and so far it appears to constitute more of an advance in classification than many behavioral scientists had anticipated. In 1980 the governing body of the American Psychological Association approved the following statement of support for the American Psychiatric Association's efforts in preparing DSM-III.

> Compared to its predecessors, and as a generic document, DSM-III represents progress in diagnostic procedure. . . . The inclusion of several new areas recognizing social and environmental influences on behavior and of a broader empirical data base with consequent increased objectivity and reliability make DSM-III more valuable than the DSM-I and DSM-II for treatment, training, and research (Moldawsky, 1981).

Empirically Based Classification

Although clinically derived classifications such as DSM-III can be evaluated experimentally, to determine how reliable and valid they are, they begin as *impressions*. Starting with impressions that some of the disturbed people they see have certain characteristics in common, clinicians decide that people who show these characteristics should be classified with a particular diagnostic label. Experimental methods can then be used to assess how well clinicians can agree on who should be assigned this label (interjudge reliability) and to what extent people who carry it share various past, present, and future behavior patterns (trait validity).

By contrast, empirically derived classification schemes originate from experimental methods. Behavioral descriptions of disturbed people (sad, angry, socially withdrawn), rather than inferences about what these characteristics might mean, constitute the raw data of such schemes. Multivariate statistical techniques are then used to determine which of these behavioral descriptions cluster together. When certain characteristics are regularly found to occur together, they are given a label that seems to fit them. For example, empirical evidence demonstrates that the characteristics of having bad companions, stealing in company with others, belonging to a gang, and being loyal to delinquent friends often co-occur, and this cluster of behaviors is often labeled *socialized-aggressive disorder*.

Like DSM-III, with its emphasis on behavioral descriptions, empirically based classification schemes classify types of disorders, not types of individuals. This helps sustain a quantitative approach to the nature of psychopathology, so that disturbed people are regulated as having more or less of some behavioral dimension than might be desirable, rather than as being qualitatively "different" kinds of people. In addition, because they are more closely related to actual behavior than clinical inferences, empirically derived categories of disturbance tend to be easier to agree on, validate, and communicate about.

A certain price must be paid for this advantage of empirically based classification, however. Most important, nothing more can emerge from a multivariate analysis of behavioral descriptions than is put into the descriptions in the first place. In clinical studies a dramatic but infrequent condition such as childhood psychosis will be clearly and readily identified. In most empirical studies, unless they are conducted in a treatment unit for seriously disturbed children, the behavioral dimensions that define childhood psychosis will occur too infrequently to emerge as a cluster of behaviors that should be labeled. Similarly, any sample of young people used in a multivariate analysis of behavior dimensions that happens not to include subjects with certain kinds of disorders will fail to generate adequate categories of diagnosis for these disorders.

Second, results of empirically based efforts at classification tend to fluctuate as a function of the data sources that are used. As reviewed in major contributions by Achenbach and Edelbrock (1978) and Quay (1979), research in this area has drawn on various combinations of parents', teachers', and mental health professionals' descriptions of children's past and current behavior. Many questionnaires, rating scales, and other measuring instruments have been used in this research. As a consequence, 37 multivariate studies summarized by Quay differ substantially in how they classify dimensions of disorder, and Achenbach and Edelbrock conclude that further advances in multivariate classification must await better standardization of the instruments and methods of analysis used in such studies.

Nevertheless, some common threads do run through empirically derived classification schemes. In reviewing 27 multivariate studies of behavior-disordered children and adolescents, Achenbach and Edelbrock (1978) found several regularly occurring clusters of characteristics. The syndrome labels most commonly given to these clusters by various researchers were *aggressive, hyperactive, delinquent, schizoid, anxious, depressed, social withdrawal,* and *somatic complaints.*

Edelbrock and Achenbach (1980) subsequently analyzed parents' descriptions on a behavior checklist of 2683 6- to 16-year-old boys and girls being seen at 30 mental health facilities. The behavioral clusters that emerged suggested seven types of disorder among the boys in their sample and eight types among the girls. As shown in Table 2.5, these dimensions of disturbance correspond closely to the syndromes identified in previous multivariate classification studies of youthful behavior disorder. In a reliability check of their typology, Edelbrock and Achenbach found a 74 percent agreement among raters and a Kappa coefficient of 0.64.

Quay (1979) integrates multivariate findings even further by suggesting that, except for psychotic disorder, the vast majority of deviant behaviors among young people can be subsumed within just four major patterns: *conduct disorder, anxiety-withdrawal, immaturity,* and *socialized aggressive disorder.* The characteristics most frequently associ-

TABLE 2.5   Types of Youthful Behavior Disorder Identified by Cluster Analysis of Parents' Descriptions

Boys		Girls	
Age 6–11	Age 12–16	Age 6–11	Age 12–16
Delinquent	Delinquent	Delinquent	Delinquent
Hyperactive	Hyperactive	Hyperactive	Hyperactive—immature
Schizoid	Schizoid	Schizoid—obsessive	Anxious—obsessive
Depressed—social withdrawal	Immature—aggressive	Depressed—social withdrawal	Anxious—obsessive aggressive
Schizoid—social withdrawal	Uncommunicative	Aggressive—cruel	Aggressive—cruel
Somatic complaints		Somatic complaints	Somatic complaints
	Uncommunicative—delinquent	Sex problems	Depressed—withdrawal delinquent

Source.   Based on data reported by Edelbrock and Achenbach (1980).

ated with these four patterns are listed in Table 2.6. There are two major differences between this summary of empirical efforts at classification and the work of Achenbach and Edelbrock: (a) Quay groups schizoid, anxious, depressed, and social withdrawal syndromes within the category of anxiety-withdrawal; (b) Quay believes that hyperactivity does not exist independently of other patterns of disorder and can be accounted for by characteristics of conduct disorder and immaturity.

Selecting Topics for this Book

Both the latest development in clinically based classification of developmental psychopathology—DSM-III—and recent advances in empirically based classification have much to recommend them. Each could be used as the outline for chapters to be included in a general text on child and adolescent psychopathology. Each has some limitations in this regard, however, at least from the perspective of the present author. Some DSM-III categories still exist too much in the eye of the clinical beholder to be presented and described in light of adequate research findings. Some empirically derived categories cut across more traditional and familiar diagnostic terms in ways that complicate communication among mental health professionals. Moreover, both kinds of schemes are focused on syndromes or disorders rather than on broad categories of problem behaviors that commonly result in young people being referred to mental health professionals.

The organization and content that have been chosen for this book are intended to maximize communication across these different possible approaches, as diverse as they may be, and to reflect our current state of knowledge, as imperfect as it may be. Accordingly, the next six chapters address specific kinds of disturbances: mental retardation (Chapter 3), minimal brain dysfunction or attention deficit disorder (Chapter 4),

TABLE 2.6 Characteristics Associated with Empirically Derived Dimensions of Behavior Disorder in Children and Adolescents

Dimensions of Disorder	Common Characteristics (in declining order of frequency)
Conduct Disorder	Fighting, hitting, assaultive
	Temper tantrums
	Disobedient, defiant
	Destructiveness of own or other's property
	Impertinent, "smart," impudent
	Uncooperative, resistive, inconsiderate
	Disruptive, interrupts, disturbs
	Negative, refuses direction; restless; boisterous, noisy; irritability, "blows up" easily
	Attention-seeking, "show-off"; dominates others, bullies, threatens
	Hyperactivity; untrustworthy, dishonest, lies
	Profanity, abusive language; jealousy; quarrelsome, argues
	Irresponsible, undependable
	Inattentive; steals
	Distractability; teases
Anxiety-Withdrawal	Anxious, fearful, tense
	Shy, timid, bashful; withdrawn, seclusive, friendless
	Depressed, sad, disturbed
	Hypersensitive, easily hurt
	Self-conscious, easily embarrassed
	Feels inferior, worthless
	Lacks self-confidence; easily flustered
	Aloof
	Cries frequently; reticent, secretive
Immaturity	Short attention span, poor concentration
	Daydreaming
	Clumsy, poor coordination
	Preoccupied, stares into space, absent-minded
	Passive, lacks initiative, easily led; sluggish
	Inattentive
	Drowsy
	Lack of interest; bored, lack of perseverence; fails to finish things
Socialized Aggressive Disorder	Has "bad" companions; steals in company with others
	Loyal to delinquent friends; belongs to a gang; stays out late at night; truant from school
	Truant from home

Source. Based on data provided by Quay (1979).

childhood psychosis (Chapter 5), schizophrenia (Chapter 6), affective disorders (Chapter 7), and neurotic disorders (Chapter 8). Chapter 9 concerns school phobia, which is sometimes considered a specific disturbance diagnosable in its own right and sometimes a general description of a problem behavior. The next four chapters deal with problem behaviors, each of which can involve various kinds of specific disturbance: academic underachievement (Chapter 10), delinquent behavior (Chapter 11), suicidal behavior (Chapter 12), and alcohol and drug abuse (Chapter 13). Finally, Chapter 14 reviews some unifying themes concerning the definition and prevalence, causes, course and outcome, and prevention and treatment of psychological disorders.

All of the categories of disturbance included in the major classification schemes are covered in one or more of the following chapters. Every effort is made to indicate similarities among the terms used in different schemes to refer to approximately the same condition, and special attention is paid to considerable differences of opinion that exist concerning which are the better terms and which should not even be used at all. Throughout, however, emphasis will remain on the fact that labels are only abstractions, more or less useful for clinical, research, and communication purposes. What is most important is what disturbed children and adolescents are like and how they can be helped to improve their prospects for a rewarding adult life.

SUMMARY

Although developmental psychopathology is widely acknowledged to exist, there is much disagreement on whether and how it should be classified. Opponents and advocates of classifying behavior disorders have engaged in spirited debate about the potential drawbacks and benefits of doing so.

Mental health professionals who object to classification argue first that labeling people according to characteristics they supposedly share with others is a psychologically dehumanizing procedure that denies individual uniqueness and presumes the right of one person to pass judgment on another. Advocates of classification respond that understanding and helping people in distress requires attention to ways in which they are both similar to and different from others. The identification of similarities among people does not necessarily preclude respect for their uniqueness, and it also provides the essential basis for cumulative clinical wisdom—that is, for previous learning about people who have certain characteristics to guide the evaluation and care of a person who now has those characteristics.

Second, opponents of classification express concern that labeling young people as mentally handicapped or emotionally disturbed is a stigmatizing procedure that results in (a) their being looked at unfavorably by others and excluded from close relationships with them, (b) their facing negative expectations that make their psychological problems worse than they would otherwise be, and (c) their suffering destructive misinterpretations of their behavior based on the label they carry rather than on how they actually conduct themselves. Advocates of classification respond by pointing to research evidence that interpersonal attitudes are determined much more by how people act than how they are labeled; that the antidote for negative expectations is not avoiding classification, but rather promoting accurate expectations by doing a more careful and detailed job of classifying individual children; and that the potential for misinterpretations of behavior can be minimized by replacing mere labels with adequate diagnoses that provide clear and extensive information about a person's assets and limitations.

Third, opponents of classification complain that diagnostic labels are too often used as a convenient justification for assigning people who are considered "undesirable" to such depriving environments as special classes, training schools, and mental hospitals. Advocates of classification respond that any unjustified deprivation as a consequence of an accurate psychological diagnosis represents an abuse of classification, for which its perpetrators should be held responsible, and is neither a necessary nor an inevitable result of classification; moreover, any sweeping indictment of institutions and programs for the emotionally disturbed or mentally retarded overlooks the large number that strive diligently to meet the needs of their patients.

Although the concerns expressed by opponents of classification merit careful and continuous attention, some compelling benefits of classifying behavior disorder derive from its role in promoting research design, treatment planning, and communication. Classification promotes systematic research by providing the necessary basis for selecting subject groups in studies of the causes, manifestations, and outcomes of various forms of psychopathology; it plays a vital role in diagnostic formulations that help identify the amount and kind of professional help a disturbed person may need; and it helps mental health professionals talk with each other and with the general public about the needs of psychologically handicapped people—often a necessary first step in making programs of service and support available to them.

Classification has most frequently been approached in one of three ways. In the *descriptive-behavioral* approach disturbance is classified on the basis of observable behavior. This approach has the advantages of providing a highly reliable means of labeling behavior disorders and identifying clearly the problems to be addressed in treatment. It has the disadvantages of providing little information about the nature of the person who has a certain problem, about the particular origin and meaning of the problem in the person's life, or about the treatment focus that is most likely to be helpful in eliminating the problem.

In *descriptive-inferential* classification certain combinations of observable symptoms or behaviors are presumed to indicate some form of underlying psychopathology that accounts for them. The chief advantage of this approach is that it says something about a person who is manifesting certain behavior problems, about the origin of these problems in personality impairments, and about selecting treatment methods focused on the basic problem that is causing the behavioral difficulty. The chief disadvantage of inferential classification is that it is less reliable than behavioral classification, although there is reason to believe that clinicians' agreement on inferential diagnostic categories can be improved by increasing the uniformity of the data they collect and the clarity of the diagnostic criteria they use. The inferential approach also has potential disadvantages of resulting in treatment plans that focus too much on underlying personality disorder at the expense of adequate attention to real-world behavior difficulties, and failing to provide information about means of preventing a problem from occurring or recurring.

Dynamic-etiological classification calls specific attention to the circumstances in which a particular problem behavior is manifest and the kinds of biogenetic factors or psychological conflicts that foster and sustain it. The language of this approach conveys not only what the problem is, but also where it comes from, when it is likely to appear, what to do about it, and even how to prevent it. Unfortunately, this advantage is offset by even greater unreliability than in inferential classification, by the risk of implying a greater degree of specificity between personality dynamics and problem behavior than actually exists, and by the fact that many conditions are not sufficiently well understood to be classified in dynamic-etiological terms.

Mental health professionals have produced many different schemes for classifying behavior disorders. In clinically derived schemes, impressions that some disturbed people have certain characteristics in common are used as a basis for deciding that people who show these characteristics should be classified with a particular diagnostic label. The currently most important of these clinical schemes is DSM-III, the third edition of the *Diagnostic and Statistical Manual* of the American Psychiatric Association. DSM-III pays special attention to the classification of psychopathology in children and adolescents and provides fairly specific behavioral criteria as guidelines for making each diagnosis it lists. Initial studies of DSM-III reliability with young people are encouraging with regard to its potential for interjudge agreement.

In empirically derived schemes, multivariate statistical techniques are applied to behavioral descriptions of disturbed people to identify characteristics that cluster together. Whatever characteristics are found to occur together regularly are then given a label that seems to fit them. Because they are more closely related to actual behavior than clinical inferences, empirically derived categories of disturbance tend to be easier to agree on, validate, and communicate about. On the other hand, multivariate analyses of behavior dimensions can overlook important but infrequent kinds of disturbance, and the results they yield tend to fluctuate widely as a function of the research methods used. Nevertheless, some common threads run through most empirically derived classification schemes, and these along with relevant DSM-III diagnostic categories are identified and defined within the context of the following chapters of this book.

REFERENCES

ACHENBACH, T. M., & EDELBROCK, C.S. The classification of child psychopathology: A review and analysis of empirical efforts. *Psychological Bulletin,* 1978, *85,* 1275–1301.

ADAMS, H. E., DOSTER, J. A., & CALHOUN, K. S. A psychologically based system of response classification. In A. R. Ciminero, K. S. Calhoun, & H. E. Adams (Eds.), *Handbook of behavioral assessment.* New York: Wiley, 1977.

AMERICAN PSYCHIATRIC ASSOCIATION. *Diagnostic and statistical manual of mental disorders.* (2nd ed.) Washington, D.C.: American Psychiatric Association, 1968.

AMERICAN PSYCHIATRIC ASSOCIATION. *Diagnostic and statistical manual of mental disorders.* (3d ed.) Washington, D.C.: American Psychiatric Association, 1980.

APPLEBAUM, S. A. Objections to diagnosis and diagnostic psychological testing diagnosed. *Bulletin of the Menninger Clinic,* 1976, *40,* 559–564.

AVIRAM, U., & SEGAL, S. P. Exclusion of the mentally ill. *Archives of General Psychiatry,* 1973, *29,* 126–131.

BACHRACH, H. Diagnosis as strategic understanding. *Bulletin of the Menninger Clinic,* 1974, *38,* 390–405.

BEITCHMAN, J. H., DIELMAN, T. E., LANDIS, R., BENSON, R. M., & KEMP, P. L. Reliability of the

Group for Advancement of Psychiatry diagnostic categories in child psychiatry. *Archives of General Psychiatry,* 1978, *35,* 1461–1466.

BEM, D. J., & ALLEN, A. On predicting some of the people some of the time: The search for cross-situational consistencies in behavior. *Psychological Review,* 1974, *81,* 506–520.

BENTZ, K., & EDGERTON, J. W. The consequences of labeling a person as mentally ill. *Social Psychiatry,* 1971, *6,* 29–33.

BLASHFIELD, R. K., & DRAGUNS, J. G. Toward a taxonomy of psychopathology: The purpose of psychiatric classification. *British Journal of Psychiatry,* 1976, *129,* 574–583.

BORD, R. J. Rejection of the mentally ill: Continuities and further developments. *Social Problems,* 1971, *18,* 496–509.

BROPHY, J. E., & GOOD, T. L. Teachers' communication of differential expectations for children's classroom performance: Some behavioral data. *Journal of Educational Psychology,* 1970, *61,* 365–374.

BROPHY, J. E., & GOOD, T. *Teacher-student relationships: Causes and consequences.* New York: Holt, Rinehart & Winston, 1974.

BROWN, E. C. Assessment from a humanistic perspective. *Psychotherapy: Theory, Research and Practice,* 1972, *9,* 103–106.

BUDOFF, M., & SIPERSTEIN, G. N. Low-income children's attitudes toward mentally retarded children: Effects of labeling and academic behavior. *American Journal of Mental Deficiency,* 1978, *82,* 474–479.

BUGENTAL, J. F. T. (Ed.) *Challenges of humanistic psychology.* New York: McGraw-Hill, 1967.

BUGENTAL, J. F. T. *Psychotherapy and process: The fundamentals of an existential-humanistic approach.* Reading, Mass.: Addison-Wesley, 1978.

BUHLER, C., & ALLEN, M. *Introduction into humanistic psychology.* Belmont, Calif.: Brooks/Cole, 1971.

CALHOUN, K. S., & TURNER, S. M. Historical perspectives and current issues in behavior therapy. In S. M. Turner, K. S. Calhoun, H. E. Adams (Eds.), *Handbook of clinical behavior therapy.* New York: Wiley, 1981.

CANTWELL, D. P., MATTISON, R., RUSSELL, A. T., & WILL, L. A comparison of DSM-II and DSM-III in the diagnosis of childhood psychiatric disorders. IV. Difficulties in use, global comparisons, and conclusions. *Archives of General Psychiatry,* 1979, *36,* 1227–1228.

CANTWELL, D. P., RUSSELL, A. T., MATTISON, R., & WILL, L. A comparison of DSM-II and DSM-III in the diagnosis of childhood psychiatric disorders. I. Agreement with expected diagnosis. *Archives of General Psychiatry,* 1979, *36,* 1208–1213.

CERRETO, M. C., & TUMA, J. M. Distribution of DSM-II diagnoses in a child psychiatry setting. *Journal of Abnormal Child Psychology,* 1977, *5,* 147–155.

CHESS, S., & HASSIBI, M. *Principles and practice of child psychiatry.* New York: Plenum, 1978.

COHEN, E. S., HARBIN, H. T. & WRIGHT, M. J. Some considerations in the formulation of psychiatric diagnosis. *Journal of Nervous and Mental Disease,* 1975, *160,* 422–427.

CONANT, J. B. *Science and common sense.* New Haven: Yale University Press, 1951.

COOK, J. W., & WOLLERSHEIM, J. P. The effects of labeling of special education students on the perceptions of contact versus noncontact peers. *Journal of Special Education,* 1976, *10,* 187–198.

COSTELLO, C. G. Classification and psychopathology. In C. G. Costello (Ed.), *Symptoms of psychopathology.* New York: Wiley, 1970.

DAVIS, D. A. On being *detectably* sane in insane places: Base rates and psychodiagnosis. *Journal of Abnormal Psychology,* 1976, *85,* 416–422.

EDELBROCK, C., & ACHENBACH, T. M. A typology of Child Behavior Profile patterns: Distribution and correlates for disturbed children ages 6–16. *Journal of Abnormal Child Psychology,* 1980, *8,* 441–470.

EISENBERG, L. The role of classification in child psychiatry. *International Journal of Psychiatry,* 1967, *3,* 179–181.

FARBER, I. E. Sane and insane: Constructions and misconstructions. *Journal of Abnormal Psychology,* 1975, *84,* 589–620.

FARD, K., HUDGENS, R. W., & WELNER, A. Undiagnosed psychiatric illness in adolescents. *Archives of General Psychiatry,* 1978, *35,* 279–282.

FINE, M. J. Attitudes of regular and special class teachers toward the educable mentally retarded child. *Exceptional Children,* 1967, *33,* 429–430.

FINN, J. D. Expectations and the educational environment. *Review of Educational Research,* 1972, *42,* 387–410.

FREEMAN, S., & ALGOZZINE, B. Social acceptability as a function of labels and assigned attributes. *American Journal of Mental Deficiency,* 1980, *84,* 589–595.

GARMEZY, N. DSM-III: Never mind the psychologists—is it good for the children? *Clinical Psychologist,* 1978, *31,* 1, 4–6.

GOFFMAN, E. *Asylums: Essays on the social situation of mental patients and other inmates.* Chicago: Aldine, 1961.

GOFFMAN, E. *Stigma: Notes on the management of spoiled identity.* Englewood Cliffs, N.J.: Prentice-Hall, 1963.

GOLDFRIED, M. R., & KENT, R. N. Traditional versus behavioral personality assessment: A comparison of methodological and theoretical assumptions. *Psychological Bulletin,* 1972, *77,* 409–420.

GOOD, T., & BROPHY, J. Behavioral expression of teacher attitudes. *Journal of Educational Psychology,* 1972, *63,* 617–624.

GOUGH, H. Some reflections on the meaning of psychodiagnosis. *American Psychologist,* 1971, *26,* 160–167.

GOVE, W. The labeling perspective: An overview. In W. Gove (Ed.), *Labeling deviant behavior:* Evaluating a perspective. New York: Halsted, 1975.

GOVE, W. R., & FAIN T. A comparison of voluntary and committed psychiatric patients. *Archives of General Psychiatry,* 1977, *34,* 669–676.

GREEN, H. *I never promised you a rosegarden.* New York: Holt, Rinehart & Winston, 1964.

GRINKER, R. R. The inadequacies of contemporary psychiatric diagnosis. In V. M. Rakoff, H. C. Stancer, & H. B. Kedward (Eds.), *Psychiatric diagnosis.* New York: Brunner/Mazel, 1977.

GROUP FOR THE ADVANCEMENT OF PSYCHIATRY. *Psychopathological disorders in childhood: Theoretical considerations and a proposed classification.* New York: Aronson, 1974.

HALLECK, S. L. *The politics of therapy.* New York: Science House, 1971.

HALLECK, S. L. *The treatment of emotional disorders.* New York: Aronson, 1978.

HARRISON, S. I. Child psychiatric treatment: Status and prospects. In J. D. Noshpitz (Ed.), *Basic handbook of child psychiatry.* Vol. III. New York: Basic Books, 1979.

HELZER, J. E., CLAYTON, P. J., PAMBAKIAN, R., REICH, T., WOODRUFF, R. A., & REVELEY, M. A. Reliability of psychiatric diagnosis. *Archives of General Psychiatry,* 1977, *34,* 136–141.

HERSON, P. F. Biasing effects of diagnostic labels and sex of pupil on teachers' views of pupils' mental health. *Journal of Educational Psychology,* 1974, *66,* 117–122.

HOBBS, N. *The futures of children: Categories, labels, and their consequences.* San Francisco, Jossey-Bass, 1975.

HOFFMAN, E., MARSDEN, G., & KALTER, N. Children's understanding of their emotionally disturbed peers: A replication. *Journal of Clinical Psychology,* 1977, *33,* 949–953.

JOINT COMMISSION ON MENTAL HEALTH OF CHILDREN. *Mental health: From infancy through adolescence.* New York: Harper & Row, 1973.

JONES, R. A. *Self-fulfilling prophecies: Social, psychological, and physiological effects of expectancies.* Hillside, N.J.: Erlbaum, 1977.

JONES, R. L. Labels and stigma in special education. *Exceptional Children,* 1972, *38,* 553–564.

KEDAR-VOIVODAS, G., & TANNENBAUM, A. J. Teachers' attitudes toward young deviant children. *Journal of Educational Psychology,* 1979, *71,* 800–808.

KENDELL, R. E. *The role of diagnosis in psychiatry.* Oxford: Blackwell, 1975.

KESEY, K. *One flew over the cuckoo's nest.* New York: Viking Press, 1962.

KESSLER, J. W. Nosology in child psychopathology. In H. E. Rie (Ed.), *Perspectives in child psychopathology.* Chicago: Aldine-Atherton, 1971.

KIRK, S. A. Labeling the mentally ill and the attribution of personal traits. *Journal of Consulting and Clinical Psychology,* 1976, *44,* 306.

LANGER, E. J., & ABELSON, R. P. A patient by any other name . . . . : Clinician group differences in labeling bias. *Journal of Consulting and Clinical Psychology,* 1974, *42,* 4–9.

LEHMAN, S., JOY, V., KREISMAN, D., & SIMMENS, S. Responses to viewing symptomatic behaviors and labeling of prior mental illness. *Journal of Community Psychology,* 1976, *4,* 327–334.

LEIFER, R. *In the name of mental health.* New York: Science House, 1969.

LEMKAU, P. V., & CROCETTI, G. M. An urban population's opinion and knowledge about mental illness. *American Journal of Psychiatry,* 1962, *118,* 692–700.

LEMKAU, P. V., & CROCETTI, G. M. On rejection of the mentally ill. *American Sociological Review,* 1965, *30,* 579–580.

MAGARO, P. A., GRIPP, R., & McDOWELL, D. J. *The mental health industry.* New York: Wiley, 1978.

MASLOW, A. H. *The psychology of science: A reconnaissance.* New York: Harper & Row, 1966.

MATTISON, R., CANTWELL, D. P., RUSSELL, A. T., & WILL, L. A comparison of DSM-II and DSM-III in the diagnosis of childhood psychiatric disorders. II. Interrater agreement. *Archives of General Psychiatry,* 1979, *36,* 1217–1222.

MEEKS, J. E. Nosology in adolescent psychiatry: An enigma wrapped in a whirlwind. In J. C. Schoolar (Ed.), *Current issues in adolescent psychiatry.* New York: Brunner/Mazel, 1973.

MILLON, T. Reflections on Rosenhan's "On being sane in insane places." *Journal of Abnormal Psychology,* 1975, *84,* 456–461.

MISCHEL, W. *Personality and assessment.* New York: Wiley, 1968.

MISCHEL, W. Toward a cognitive social learning reconceptualization of personality. *Psychological Review,* 1973, *80,* 252–283.

MOLDAWSKY, S. Report of APA council of representatives meeting. *Clinical Psychologist,* 1981, *34,* 2, 4.

PATTERSON, F. *Victory over myself.* New York: Bernard Geis Associates, 1963.

PHILLIPS, D. Rejection of the mentally ill: The influence of behavior and sex. *American Sociological Review,* 1964, *29,* 679–687.

PHILLIPS, D. Public identification and acceptance of the mentally ill. *American Journal of Public Health,* 1966, *56,* 755–763.

PHILLIPS, D. Identification of mental illness: Its consequences for rejection. *Community Mental Health Journal,* 1967, *3,* 262–266.

PRUYSER, P. W., & MENNINGER, K. Language pitfalls in diagnostic thought and work. In P. W. Pruyser (Ed.), *Diagnosis and the difference it makes.* New York: Aronson, 1977.

QUAY, H. C. Classification. In H. C. Quay & J. S. Werry (Eds.), *Psychopathological disorders of childhood.* (2nd ed.) New York: Wiley, 1979.

RESCHLY, D. J., & LAMPRECHT, M. J. Expectancy effects of labels: Fact or artifact? *Exceptional Children,* 1979, *46,* 55–58.

ROBINS, E., GENTRY, K. A., MUNOZ, R. A., & MARTEN, S. A contrast of the three more common illnesses with the ten less common in a study and 18-month follow-up of 314 psychiatric emergency room patients. *Archives of General Psychiatry,* 1977, *34,* 285–291.

ROGERS, C. R. *Client centered therapy.* Boston: Houghton Mifflin, 1951.

ROGERS, C. R. *On becoming a person.* Boston: Houghton Mifflin, 1961.

ROMANOFF, B. D., LEWITTES, D. J., & SIMMONS, W. L. Accuracy of "significant others" judgments of behavior changes. *Journal of Counseling Psychology,* 1976, *23,* 409–413.

ROSENHAN, D. L. On being sane in insane places. *Science,* 1973, *179,* 250–258.

ROSENHAN, D. L. The contextual nature of psychiatric diagnosis. *Journal of Abnormal Psychology,* 1975, *84,* 462–474.

ROSENTHAL, R., & JACOBSEN, L. *Pygmalion in the classroom.* New York: Holt, 1968.

RUSSELL, A. T., CANTWELL, D. P., MATTIONS, R., & WILL, L. A comparison of DSM-II and DSM-III in the diagnosis of childhood psychiatric disorders. III. Multiaxial features. *Archives of General Psychiatry,* 1979, *36,* 1223–1226.

SCHACHT, T., & NATHAN, P. E. But is it good for the psychologists? Appraisal and status of DSM-III. *American Psychologist,* 1977, *32,* 1017–1025.

SCHEFF, T. J. The labeling theory of mental illness. *American Sociological Review,* 1974, *39,* 444–452.

SHAKOW, D. The role of classification in the development of the science of psychopathology, with particular reference to research. *Bulletin of the Menninger Clinic,* 1966, *30,* 150–161.

SHECTMAN, F. Provocative issues in psychiatric diagnosis: A dialogue. In P. W. Pruyser (Ed.), *Diagnosis and the difference it makes.* New York: Aronson, 1977.

SHEVRIN, H., & SHECTMAN, F. The diagnostic process in psychiatric evaluations. *Bulletin of the Menninger Clinic,* 1973, *37,* 451–494.

SPITZER, R. L. More on pseudoscience in science and the case for psychiatric diagnosis. *Archives of General Psychiatry,* 1976, *33,* 459–470.

SPITZER, R. L., ENDICOTT, J. & ROBINS, E. The reliability of clinical criteria for psychiatric diagnosis. In H. S. Akiskal & W. L. Webb (Eds.), *Psychiatric diagnosis.* New York: Spectrum, 1978a.

SPITZER, R. L., ENDICOTT, J., & ROBINS, E. Research diagnostic criteria: Rationale and reliability. *Archives of General Psychiatry,* 1978b, *35,* 773/782.

SPITZER, R. L., & FLEISS, J. L. A reanalysis of the reliability of psychiatric diagnosis. *British Journal of Psychiatry,* 1974.

SPITZER, R. L., WILLIAMS, J. B. W., & SKODOL, A. E. DSM-III: The major achievements and an overview. *American Journal of Psychiatry,* 1980, *137,* 151–164.

SPITZER, R. L., & WILSON, P. T. Nosology and the official psychiatric nomenclature. In A. M. Freedman, H. I. Kaplan, & B. J. Sadock (Eds.), *Comprehensive textbook of psychiatry.* Baltimore: Williams & Wilkins, 1975.

STROBER, M., & GREEN, J. Diagnosis of adolescent psychopathology: A pilot study of the DSM-III nomenclature with adolescent patients. *American Journal of Orthopsychiatry,* in press.

STROBER, M., GREEN, J., & CARLSON, G. Reliability of psychiatric diagnosis in hospitalized adolescents: Inter-rater agreement using DSM-III. *Archives of General Psychiatry,* 1981, *38,* 141–145.

SUGARMAN, A. Is psychodiagnostic assessment humanistic? *Journal of Personality Assessment,* 1978, *42,* 11–21.

SUNDBERG, N. D., SNOWDEN, L. R., & REYNOLDS, W. M. Toward assessment of personal competence and incompetence in life situations. *Annual Review of Psychology,* 1978, *29,* 179–221.

SZASZ, T. S. *The myth of mental illness.* New York: Harper & Row, 1961.

SZASZ, T. S. *Law, liberty, and society.* New York: Macmillan, 1963.

SZASZ, T. S. *The manufacture of madness: A comparative study of the inquisition and the mental health movement.* New York: Harper & Row, 1970.

SZASZ, T. S. *The myth of psychotherapy: Mental healing as religion, rhetoric, and repression.* New York: Doubleday, 1978.

VOELTZ, L. M. Children's attitudes toward handicapped peers. *American Journal of Mental Deficiency,* 1980, *84,* 455–464.

WARD, C. H., BECK, A. T., MENDELSON, M., MOCK, J. E., & ERBAUGH, J. K. The psychiatric nomenclature: Reasons for diagnostic disagreement. *Archives of General Psychiatry,* 1962, *7,* 198–205.

WARD, M. J. *The snake pit.* New York: Random House, 1946.

WEINER, B. "On being sane in insane places": A process (attributional) analysis and critique. *Journal of Abnormal Psychology,* 1975, *84,* 433–441.

WEINER, I. B. Does psychodiagnosis have a future? *Journal of Personality Assessment,* 1972, *36,* 534–546.

WEINER, I. B. *Principles of psychotherapy.* New York: Wiley, 1975.

WEINER, I. B. Psychopathology in adolescence. In J. Adelson (Eds.), *Handbook of adolescent psychology.* New York: Wiley, 1980.

WEINER, I. B., & DEL GAUDIO, A. C. Psychopathology in adolescence: An epidemiological study. *Archives of General Psychiatry,* 1976, *33,* 187–193.

WOODRUFF, R. A., GOODWIN, D. W., & GUZE, S. B. *Psychiatric diagnosis.* London: Oxford University Press, 1974.

YAMAMOTO, K., & DIZNEY, H. Rejection of the mentally ill: A study of attitudes of student teachers. *Journal of Counseling Psychology,* 1967, *14,* 264–268.

ZUBIN, J. Classification of the behavior disorders. *Annual Review of Psychology,* 1967, *18,* 373–406.

3

MENTAL RETARDATION

Mental retardation is both an easy and a difficult topic with which to begin a discussion of developmental psychopathology. It is easy in three respects: (a) mental retardation has been clearly defined by a widely respected official organization, the American Association on Mental Deficiency (AAMD); (b) the psychological limitations of retarded persons are demonstrably related to the chief characteristic of their condition, low intelligence; (c) relatively little needs to be detailed about psychotherapeutic approaches to retardation, since it is treatable primarily by biological and educational methods.

For most of the conditions to be considered in subsequent chapters, by contrast, there are multiple definitions and a sometimes disheartening lack of consensus concerning the core characteristics of the disorders; there is more speculation than documentation concerning how the presumed characteristics of the disorders account for the behavior patterns associated with them; many thousands of pages in the professional literature are devoted to psychological methods of modifying the conditions.

Yet there are difficulties in leading off with mental retardation because efforts to define, understand, and treat it have raised some very thorny problems. First, the AAMD definition allows for some differences in emphasis that make considerable difference in who is considered retarded and what the prevalence of retardation is estimated to be. Second, the origin of mental retardation is both uncertain and controversial. In the majority of cases it has no identifiable cause, and hypotheses concerning the causative role of genetic inheritance and psychosocial experience in these cases touch on the age-old but still heated nature-nurture controversy in psychology. Moreover, the broader question of whether intelligence at all levels is determined primarily by genetic or experiential factors has implications for some hotly debated social and political issues, such as whether early enrichment programs for disadvantaged children have sufficient long-term benefits to justify their cost.

Third, even though mental retardation is not primarily treatable by psychotherapy, child psychopathologists must be familiar with numerous kinds of special educational programs, institutional placements, and other professional services that retarded youngsters may require. These aspects of intervention in mental retardation are unfortunately complicated by contradictory philosophies and uncertain data—concerning, for example, whether retarded youngsters should be educated separately from or together with normally intelligent children, and whether and when children with certain levels of retardation should be institutionalized.

With these difficulties in mind, this chapter will discuss current issues and our present state of knowledge in relation to the nature and prevalence of mental retardation, its categories and characteristics, its causes, and its prevention and treatment.

THE NATURE AND PREVALENCE OF MENTAL RETARDATION

As defined by AAMD, mental retardation refers to "significantly subaverage general intellectual functioning existing concurrently with deficits in adaptive behavior, and manifested during the developmental period" (Grossman, 1973, p. 11). Significantly subaverage intellectual functioning is defined as performance falling more than 2 standard deviations below the mean on a standard test of intelligence; for the two most frequently used intelligence tests, this means an IQ below 70 on the Wechsler and an

IQ below 68 on the Stanford-Binet. The "developmental period" signifies that the label of retardation is limited to conditions that appear during the first 18 years of life; previously normal adults whose measured IQ falls below 70 as the result of a brain injury or the aging process are not to be considered retarded. Finally, adaptive behavior consists of "the effectiveness or degree with which the individual meets the standards of independence and social responsibility expected of his age and cultural group" (Grossman, 1973, p. 11). This approach to defining mental retardation is very widely accepted and endorsed in DSM-III (American Psychiatric Association, 1980).

Unfortunately, however, differences between two parts of this seemingly precise definition make it possible to identify mental retardation in either *absolute* or *relative* terms. The part of the definition having to do with limited intelligence calls for an absolute approach, in the sense discussed in Chapter 1. The presence of mental retardation is determined by a low score on an IQ test that is considered applicable to all people, regardless of their circumstances. This low score is presumed to exist whether or not it is measured, and retardation is thus presumed to exist independently of whether or not it is recognized. From the absolute perspective mentally retarded people may be more or less well adjusted, but their level of adaptation has no direct bearing on their diagnoses.

By contrast, the AAMD reference to adaptive failure means that retardation should be assessed not only by intelligence tests but also through measures of how adequately a person is adapting in particular situations, relative to his or her particular age and sociocultural background. From this perspective retardation exists only when and where it is identified, and people may even be retarded in some situations but not others. In this vein, the President's Committee on Mental Retardation (1970) used the term *six-hour retarded child* to describe disadvantaged youngsters who may function at a retarded level in school while showing reasonably competent out-of-school behavior.

Because of these differences between absolute and relative perspective, the AAMD definition creates some uncertainty about who should be considered retarded. Taken literally, it means that only young people who display both limited intelligence and adaptive failure are retarded. In practice, however, retardation has commonly been diagnosed on the basis of a low IQ score alone. In a recent survey of state education agencies, for example, many of them were found to deemphasize or exclude adaptive behavior in their definition of mental retardation (Huberty, Koller, & Ten Brink, 1980). Traditional estimates of the prevalence of mental retardation run higher than those based strictly on the AAMD criteria. As indicated in a later section, factors related to degree of retardation, sociocultural background, and age reduce the observed prevalence of retardation when a relative instead of an absolute approach is used to make the diagnosis.

Traditional Prevalence Estimates

Traditional estimates based on intelligence test scores place the prevalence of mental retardation at 3 percent, which means that about 6.6 million people in the United States have IQs below 70 (Farber, 1968; Office of Mental Retardation Coordination, 1972). This figure is dramatic for the extent of mental retardation that it reveals, and also because 3 percent differs slightly from the prevalence that would be expected from statistical projections.

Most standardized intelligence tests are based on the assumption that intelligence is normally distributed in the population. Normal distribution tables therefore indicate exactly what percent of people should fall above or below a particular IQ score, depending on how many standard deviations above or below the mean that score is. A Wechsler IQ of 70 is 2 standard deviations below the mean, and the normal distribution curve tells us that 2.28 percent—not 3 percent—of the population should earn scores below this point.

The significance of this seemingly slight difference becomes apparent when it is explored further with respect to levels of IQ. Table 3.1, based on a model suggested by Dingman and Tarjan (1960), indicates that the additional prevalence of retarded persons beyond expectation occurs largely in the lower IQ ranges. For example, persons with IQs of 55 to 69 are only 1.24 times more numerous than would be expected (the "excess factor"), whereas the 25 to 49 IQ range includes almost 440 times more people than would be expected from the presumably normal distribution of IQ scores.

These findings have led many workers in the field to propose a "two-group" theory of mental retardation (Mercer, 1973a; Schoenbaum & Zinober, 1977; Zigler, 1967, 1969). According to this theory, most retardates are otherwise normal individuals who happen to have limited intelligence and who represent the lower end of the normal distribution of IQ scores. The actual estimated prevalence figures in Table 3.1 would match the predicted prevalence figures if only these "normally limited" people were included, the theory suggests, and close to 95 percent of them have IQs in the 55 to 69 range.

In addition to this group of "normal" or "familial" retardates, there is a group of "defective" retardates whose limited intellect is associated with demonstrable organic pathology. Although some of these individuals may have IQs of 55 to 69, most are

TABLE 3.1 Statistically Predicted versus Actual Estimated Prevalence of Mental Retardation

Level of IQ	Standard Deviations Below Mean[a]	Statistically Predicted Prevalence (%)[b]	Actual Estimated Prevalence (%)[c]	Excess Factor (actual %/ predicted %)
Below 70	More than 2	2.28	3.00	1.32
55–69	2–3	2.15	2.67	1.24
40–54	3–4	0.12966	0.18	1.39
25–49	4–5	0.000311	0.105	337.62
Below 25	More than 5	0.000029	0.045	1551.72

[a] Based on Wechsler IQ distribution with mean of 100, standard deviation of 15.
[b] Based on normal curve distribution.
[c] Based on AAMD estimates that 89 percent of retarded persons have IQs 55 to 69, 6 percent 40 to 54, 3.5 percent 25 to 49, and 1.5 percent below 25 (Grossman, 1973).

Figure 3.1

(a) Conventional representation of the distribution of intelligence. (b) Distribution of intelligence as represented in the two-group approach. (c) Actual distribution of intelligence. (From Zigler (1967). Reprinted with permission of the American Association for the Advancement of Science.)

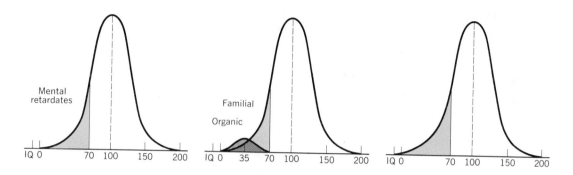

below this range. Hence organic abnormalities are responsible for an unexpectedly large number of retarded persons, especially at the lowest IQ levels. This "two-group" theoretical explanation of the data in Table 3.1, which is shown graphically in Figure 3.1, will figure prominently in the following discussions of the prevalence and the possible causes of mental retardation.

Factors Related to Degree of Retardation

Many people who earn low IQ scores show normal adaptive behavior with respect to such characteristics as self-help skills, social maturity, academic achievement, vocational attainment, and community participation. Mercer (1973a), for example, in a survey of 6998 people representative of the under-50 age population of Riverside, California, found that only 45 percent of those with IQs below 70 were unable to pass a measure of adaptive behavior. With the AAMD criteria in mind, she concluded from this result that the true prevalence of mental retardation should be estimated at 1.35 rather than 3 percent (Mercer, 1973b).

Of further significance, most of the low-IQ people in Mercer's study who did poorly on her measure of adaptive behavior had IQs below 50. With respect to degree of retardation, then, using the AAMD definition appears to reduce the estimated prevalence of mental retardation primarily in the 50 to 70 IQ range, where normal adaptive behavior often occurs. For persons with more severe intellectual limitations, on the other hand, prevalence estimates will be similar regardless of whether a one-dimensional (low IQ) or two-dimensional (low IQ plus adaptive failure) definition of mental retardation is used.

This distinction fits neatly with the two-group theory of mental retardation noted earlier. That is, many people with IQs only slightly below 70 happen to be at the low end of the distribution of intelligence scores but have otherwise normal adaptive capacities, whereas most people with IQs substantially below 70 have some sort of defect that interferes with their adaptive behavior as well as their intellectual functioning.

Factors Related to Sociocultural Background

Socioculturally disadvantaged groups in the United States, including the poor and many minorities, are known to have higher prevalence rates of low-IQ persons than the general population (Robinson & Robinson, 1976, Chapter 8). This difference exists almost exclusively within the 50 to 70 IQ range, however, and not at lower levels of intelligence. Whereas the majority of persons who earn scores of 50 to 70 on IQ tests come from disadvantaged backgrounds, those with IQs below 50 come proportionately from all segments of the population (Lemkau & Imre, 1969; Phillips & Williams, 1975; Reschly & Jipson, 1976; Sabagh, Dingman, Tarjan, & Wright, 1959; Tarjan, Wright, Eyman, & Keeran, 1973).

These findings, like those pertaining to degree of retardation, are consistent with the two-group theory: very low IQ can be conceived as the result of organic pathology that occurs independently of social class or ethnic differences, whereas IQs only slightly below 70 can be viewed as a developmental phenomenon that is influenced by such group differences. This does not mean that ethnic or racial variations in intelligence account for the overrepresentation of socioculturally disadvantaged persons among organically sound individuals with IQs of 50 to 70. Despite numerous efforts to prove otherwise, there is as yet no conclusive evidence for genetically determined ethnic or racial differences in intelligence (Gould, 1978; Loehlin, Lindzey, & Spuhler, 1975; Vernon, 1979, Chapter 21). On the other hand, there is good reason to believe that the intellectually impoverished circumstances in which many disadvantaged children grow up frequently contribute to their earning IQ test scores tht underestimate their functional ability.

For example, of the 55 percent of low-IQ people in Mercer's (1973a) study who performed normally on a measure of adaptation, all were black or Mexican-American and none were Anglo-American. In research having similar implications, Gerstein, Brodzinsky, and Reiskind (1976) compared black and white children at different IQ levels on a perceptual-cognitive measure of intellectual potential on the Rorschach test. For those with IQs in the 90 to 109 range, there was no difference between blacks and whites in intellectual potential as indicated by the perceptual-cognitive measure. Among those with IQs of 70 to 89, however, the black children earned significantly higher scores than the white children on the Rorschach index. Gerstein et al. conclude from their data that the intellectual capacities of some children may be underestimated by standard tests of intelligence, especially if they are low-IQ blacks.

These and numerous other studies suggest that standard tests of intelligence do not adequately measure the functioning ability of socioculturally disadvantaged youngsters, most probably because they require skills that receive relatively little emphasis in their home and school environments. Conversely, most advantaged children appear able to draw on past learning at home and in school to earn intelligence test scores above 70, unless they are handicapped by the kinds of organic pathology that reduce IQ below 50. Strict application of the two-dimensional AAMD definition thus tends to reduce prevalence estimates of mental retardation primarily among disadvantaged segments of the population, who can frequently give a better account of themselves on measures of adaptation than on IQ tests.

Factors Related to Age

Young children face relatively few intellectual demands and are not ordinarily subjected to intelligence testing. Hence retardation is rarely recognized before age 4, except in severely handicapped children who have obvious organic pathology or cannot cope even with the basic developmental tasks of the preschool years. By contrast, school-age children must deal with increasingly complex demands for intellectual attainment and social adaptation, and they are examined regularly on formal measures of intelligence and achievement. As a result, even those who are only mildly handicapped fall behind their peers, and their intellectual limitations are increasingly likely to be identified. Whereas just 1 child in 1000 is diagnosed as retarded before age 4, the detected prevalence grows during middle childhood to a peak of 30 per 1000 among 10- to 14-year-olds (Gruenberg, 1964; Lemkau & Imre, 1969; Office of Mental Retardation, 1972; Scheerenberger, 1964).

Following their school years, people are no longer likely to be examined, and those with intellectual limitations can often find occupations and living arrangements that do not overtax their abilities. Consequently, about 65 percent of people identified as retarded when they are young lose this label as adults; once they have finished school, they cease to be considered as retarded and merge into the general population. An initial diagnosis of mental retardation is rarely made in adulthood, and it is estimated that of all persons who are considered retarded, 75 percent are children and adolescents (Tarjan et al., 1973; Work, 1979).

Thus if adaptation as well as IQ is considered in assessing retardation, large numbers of preschool children and adults with IQs only slightly below 70 will not be identified as retarded—either because their IQ is not being measured or because they are adapting reasonably well. Only during the school years, when measurements are regularly taken and intellectual ability is especially important for adequate adaptation, will prevalence reach the traditional 3 percent figure. Tarjan et al. (1973), who argue that retardation exists only when it is identified in the two-dimensional AAMD sense, conclude that the actual prevalence of retardation is little more than 1 percent. Although 3 percent of all people born in the United States may be identified as retarded at some time in their lives, they say, just 1 percent of the population will be so identified at any one point in time.

One other item of information to note at this point concerns the frequency with which mental retardation is diagnosed among young people who come to the attention of mental health professionals. Such figures do not say much about the population prevalence of retardation, since they refer only to those children and adolescents who receive care in psychiatric clinics and mental hospitals. Moreover, they come from survey data that do not always indicate the definition of mental retardation that was used in assigning the diagnosis. Nevertheless, for purposes of comparison with frequency data cited in other chapters, it is of interest to report that mental retardation is the diagnosis carried by an estimated 17.9 percent of patients under age 18 in state and county mental hospitals in the United States and 1 to 1.5 percent of children and adolescents seen in outpatient mental health settings (Cass & Thomas, 1979, Chapter 4; Cerreto & Tuma, 1977; National Institute of Mental Health, 1978).

Choosing Between Absolute and Relative Definitions

The point was made in Chapter 1 that alternative definitions are never more or less valid, but only more or less clear and useful. Nevertheless, to proceed with this chapter, a choice must be made between the traditional absolute criterion for defining mental retardation (measure IQ below 70) and the relative criteria proposed by the AAMD (IQ below 70 plus adaptive failure relative to one's age and background). We have already seen that this choice determines whether 3 percent or somewhere between 1 and 1.5 percent of the population is considered retarded, and more specifically whether retardation is present in many slightly low-IQ, socioculturally disadvantaged, and nonschool-age persons. In order to consider systematically the characteristics, causes, and prevention of mental retardation, one or the other definition is necessary to determine for purposes of discussion who is to be considered retarded.

Prevailing practice and a clinical frame of reference suggest proceeding with an absolute definition of mental retardation. Regarding prevailing practice, numerous leaders in the field note that efforts to incorporate adaptive behavior within the definition of mental retardation have not been particularly successful. Not only is adaptive behavior a vague and difficult-to-measure concept, but generations of professionals and lay persons have become accustomed to thinking in IQ terms. Consequently, in most instances of classification for planning educational programs, conducting research, and writing legislation, mental retardation is implicitly equated with low IQ (Baroff, 1974, Chapter 1; Baumeister & Muma, 1975; Bialer, 1977).

From the clinical point of view, there are advantages to distinguishing between a handicap such as low IQ and a person's ability to adapt despite it. Emotionally disturbed children who are unmanageable at home and school may behave better in the structured setting of a residential treatment facility, but it cannot be assumed from their improved adaptation that they no longer have an emotional problem. Likewise, a youngster with an IQ of 68 who stands at the top of the class in learning and adjustment in a special program for retardates is still retarded.

Unless clinicians distinguish in this way between people's disabilities and their adaptation to more or less favorable circumstances, they may fail to anticipate their treatment needs as circumstances change. The apparently self-controlled child in an institution may lose control if returned home too soon, and the well-adjusted special-class student may become very upset if placed in a more demanding situation that exceeds his or her abilities. It is the responsibility of clinicians to guide their patients toward situations in which they can function well and away from situations in which they are vulnerable to breakdowns in adaptation. For these practical and clinical reasons, mental retardation is defined in IQ terms in the discussions that follow.

CATEGORIES AND CHARACTERISTICS OF MENTAL RETARDATION

Following guidelines recommended by AAMD, mental retardation is customarily categorized as *mild, moderate, severe,* or *profound.* The IQ ranges for these categories and their frequency among retarded persons appear in Table 3.2. Although there are individual exceptions, the category into which retardates fall has fairly clear implications for

TABLE 3.2 Categories of Retardation

| Category | Standard Deviations Below Mean of 100 | IQ Range | | Percent of Retarded Persons |
		Stanford-Binet[a]	Wechsler[b]	
Mild	2.00–2.99	52–68	55–69	89.0
Moderate	3.00–3.99	36–51	40–54	6.0
Severe	4.00–4.99	20–35	25–39	3.5
Profound	More than 5.00	0–19	0–24	1.5

[a] Standard deviation = 16.
[b] Standard deviation = 15.
Source. Based on Grossman (1973).

when their handicap is likely to be detected and for the developmental characteristics that are likely to accompany it.

Mild Retardation

Mildly retarded individuals, who have Wechsler IQs from 55 to 69 and constitute almost 90 percent of the retarded population, are frequently called **educable mental retardates** (EMR). As young children they may lag behind somewhat in developing social, motor, and communication skills, but they are typically not identified as retarded until they enter elementary school. Although they need special help to learn basic academic skills, these children can usually reach between a third- and sixth-grade level of education by the time they leave school.

Despite their intellectual limitations, most educable retardates are capable of a more or less normal social life. During the elementary school years they seek out friendships just as other children do, and as adolescents and young adults they become interested in dating, sex, love, and marriage. Hence they need and benefit from opportunities to learn interpersonal skills, and they profit from guidance in dealing with the postpubertal problems of heterosexuality faced by all young people (Hall, Morris, & Barker, 1973; Kohen-Raz, 1977).

As adults, the majority of educable retardates are able to hold unskilled or semi-skilled jobs, to become at least marginally self-supporting, and to achieve satisfactory adjustment in their community (Baller, Charles, & Miller, 1967; Cobb, 1972; Dinger, 1961; Ingalls, 1978, Chapter 17). Since minimum social competence in adulthood is not as noticeable as poor learning in school, many educable retardates may even "disappear." By holding jobs and meeting routine demands of social living, and in some cases marrying and having children, they take on what Edgerton (1967) has claled a "cloak of competence"; they may impress others as being "slow," but they are often not considered abnormal. These and other features of development and adaptation among mildly and more seriously retarded individuals are summarized in Table 3.3.

Only 1 percent of educable retardates are ever institutionalized for problems directly related to their limited intelligence (Robinson & Robinson, 1970). Nevertheless, they

TABLE 3.3 Developmental Characteristics of the Mentally Retarded

Degree of Mental Retardation	Age 0–5: Maturation and Development	Age 6–20: Training and Education	Age 21 and over: Social and Vocational Adequacy
Mild	Can develop social and communication skills, minimal retardation in sensorimotor areas; often not distinguished from normal until later age	Can learn academic skills up to approximately 6th-grade level by late teens; can be guided toward social conformity	Can usually achieve social and vocational skills adequate to minimum self-support but may need guidance and assistance when under unusual social or economic stress
Moderate	Can talk or learn to communicate; poor social awareness; fair motor development; profits from training in self-help; can be managed with moderate supervision	Can profit from training in social and occupation skills, unlikely to progress beyond 2nd-grade level in academic subjects; may learn to travel alone in familiar places	May achieve self-maintenance in unskilled or semiskilled work under sheltered conditions; needs supervision and guidance when under mild social or economic stress
Severe	Poor motor development; speech minimal; generally unable to profit from training in self-help; little or no communication skills	Can talk or learn to communicate; can be trained in elemental health habits; profits from systematic habit training	May contribute partially to self-maintenance under complete supervision; can develop self-protection skills to a minimal useful level in controlled environment
Profound	Gross retardation; minimal capacity for functioning in sensorimotor areas; needs nursing care	Some motor development present; may respond to minimal or limited training in self-help	Some motor and speech development; may achieve very limited self-care; needs nursing care

Source. Based on Grossman (1973).

suffer lifelong vulnerability to psychological and behavioral problems. As children and adolescents, retarded individuals are more likely to become emotionally disturbed than their normally intelligent peers, largely because of the greater stress they experience in attempting to master developmental tasks at home and in school (Chess, 1970; Jancar, 1977; LaVietes, 1978; Menaloscino, 1976; Philips & Williams, 1975).

As adults, their success in maintaining satisfactory social and vocational adjustment often depends on the availability of some other person, especially a spouse, who can help them deal with crisis situations as well as routine aspects of daily living. Without such a benefactor, mildly retarded adults usually have difficulty adjusting well enough to "pass" as nonretarded in the community (Edgerton, 1967). Moreover, even under the best of circumstances their adjustment is unstable. Although at any one time the majority may be getting along reasonably well, as individuals they frequently undergo periods of reversal in which vocational success, social relatedness, and an independent life-style give way to unemployment, isolation, loneliness, and an inability to provide for their own needs (Edgerton, 1975; Edgerton & Bercovici, 1976).

Case 1. *Mild Mental Retardation*

When Chris was 6 months old, his mother remembers thinking, "There was something about his eyes, they did not focus correctly; the way he held his spoon seemed different." Comparisons with an older brother emphasized these differences in development, and his mother suspected he had some problems. However, the family pediatrician reassured her that he was developing normally until at age 3½ it became apparent that he was not speaking clearly. The pediatrician then referred the family to an evaluation and treatment center for children with suspected mental retardation. At the center Chris was evaluated by a psychologist, a pediatrician, and a speech therapist. He was found to have an IQ of 64 on the Stanford-Binet Intelligence Scale, which placed him in the mildly or educably retarded classification. In addition to the mental retardation, Chris was found to have poor speech patterns that called for special attention to his speech development.

When Chris was 4 years, 3 months of age he entered a preschool program for mildly and moderately retarded children. He stayed in this preschool for 3 years until he was 7 years of age. During that time his speech improved considerably, and he developed a very friendly, outgoing personality. Chris then entered the special-education classes in his public school for educable retarded children. He remained in special classes until his graduation from the high school at 20 years of age. Although he was in segregated classes throughout his school years, he participated in school activities by being a manager for the football and wrestling teams. His outgoing personality and willingness to learn managerial tasks enabled him to become well liked in school and popular as a manager. During his school years, Chris had a number of IQ tests which ranged from mid-60 to mid-70 scores, thus confirming his intellectual functioning at the mildly retarded range.

Chris engaged in social activities with his brother and in his role as a manager of the football team, but he never dated or entered into a social grouping. He attended special programs at the local YMCA for handicapped children. He also attended a special camp for intellectually retarded children over the summers. During the latter years of high school, Chris began work-study programs to prepare him for some type of career. Immediately following his graduation, he was hired as an attendant in the men's department of a local department store, checking the men's fitting rooms. He continued to live at home, take public transportation to and from work, and maintain a regular, although somewhat isolated, career role. His social life was restricted to family and special programs available from time to time in local community centers for mildly handicapped individuals.

Future problems for him, yet to be encountered, include finding some kind of semiindependent living facility. Chris will need supervision in basic life skills, such as food preparation and shelter. However, his motivation to work, friendly personality, patience in taking directions, and ability to take responsibility have enabled him to sustain a job in the community, despite his mild mental retardation.

Moderate Retardation

Moderately retarded individuals have Wechsler IQs from 40 to 54 and are commonly referred to as **trainable mental retardates** (TMR). During their preschool years they are considerably slower than other children in developing social, motor, and communication skills, and their handicap is therefore usually recognized even before they confront school learning tasks. In school, trainable retardates typically cannot master functionally useful academic skills, and efforts to help them realize their limited potential must accordingly focus on their developing some capacity for self-care and social ad-

Sheltered workshops allow many retarded individuals to learn useful skills and help support themselves.

justment in a protected environment. With adequate training, moderately retarded persons may eventually be able to support themselves and enjoy social relationships within the context of sheltered workshops and carefully supervised residential living arrangements.

As they grow up and become increasingly unable to exercise the judgment and independence expected of people their age, many moderately retarded youngsters must be institutionalized. The final section of this chapter considers several factors that influence whether and when trainable retardates are likely to be placed in institutions and the impact such decisions can have on them and their family. It should be noted here that most trainable retardates do not require permanent custodial care. Institutionalization is necessary and should be used only for helping them develop and mature sufficiently to adjust to protected living and working environments that can be made available in the community. A case illustration of moderate retardation appears on page 94.

Severe and Profound Retardation

Severely and profoundly retarded individuals are known as **untrainable** or **custodial retardates.** Those who are severely retarded (Wechsler IQ 25 to 39) are largely incapable of taking care of themselves and require institutionalization, usually early in life. Under careful supervision they may eventually learn such basic self-care skills as feeding and dressing themselves, but they rarely outgrow their need for an institutional environment. Those who are profoundly retarded (Wechsler IQ below 25) need total nursing care throughout life. Because of their limited motor abilities, they may not even be able to master such basic skills as feeding themselves, controlling their bowels, or walking.

CAUSES OF MENTAL RETARDATION

About 25 percent of retarded individuals have biological defects that account for their intellectual limitations; the remaining 75 percent are usually described as having **familial retardation** (Jensen, 1970; Zigler, 1967). In familial retardation there are no obvious biological abnormalities, but there is a family history of one or both parents being retarded. Whether retardation has known biological causes or is familial, a variety of genetic and experiential factors may play a role in producing it, and experts in the field often disagree on which factors are most important.

Biological Causes of Retardation

Biological causes of retardation include inborn abnormalities that prevent normal mental growth from taking place and physical events that interfere with mental development early in life. Fortunately, most of the inborn abnormalities known to cause retardation occur only rarely (Cytryn & Lourie, 1980; Robinson & Robinson, 1976, Chapter 4). Two that merit special attention are **Down's syndrome,** which is the most common biological disorder resulting in retardation, and **phenylketonuria,** which is a genetically determined disorder that can be successfully treated. Among physical events that arrest mental development, the most important are maternal ill health during pregnancy, birth complications, and certain harmful postnatal experiences.

Down's Syndrome Down's syndrome, or *mongolism,* results from chromosomal abnormalities that almost always produce moderate or severe mental retardation. School-age children with mongolism living at home typically have IQs ranging from 40 to 54, whereas most of those living in institutions have IQs below 35. Whatever their IQ level, mongoloid children are typically most impaired in their language and concept-formation skills, while their ability to perform simple, routine tasks is relatively less limited (Cornwell, 1974; Lodge & Kleinfeld, 1973; Rohr & Burr, 1978). Down's syndrome has been found in various surveys to account for 10 to 30 percent of all cases of moderate or severe retardation and for 10 to 20 percent of all institutionalized retardates (Abramowicz & Richardson, 1975; Benda, 1969; Koch & de la Cruz, 1975; Stein & Susser, 1977).

In addition to retardation, Down's syndrome involves several distinctive physical characteristics that make the condition apparent at or soon after birth. These include small, egg-shaped eye sockets that give the impression of slanting; a wide, flat nose; a large, fissured tongue; and short, broad, square-shaped hands and feet. Children with Down's syndrome do not have any distinctive personality features. Sometimes they are described as placid, cheerful youngsters who are easy to manage at home and sometimes as being unable to adapt to family life and needing early and prolonged institutionalization. Contrary to either characterization, research findings indicate that Down's syndrome children show a wide range of personality styles and dispositions rather than any one typical pattern. Although many of them may eventually have to enter an institution, most can live comfortably at home during their developmental years and achieve better social adaptation than if they are separated from their families (Belmont, 1971; Carr, 1975; Gibson, 1978; Menolascino, 1974).

Case 2. *Moderate Mental Retardation in Down's Syndrome*

Tom and Sue Jones learned the day following the birth of their third child that she was a Down's syndrome baby. They had never heard the term *Down's syndrome,* which was then more commonly known as *mongolism* because of the slightly "oriental" look of the eyes of children with that condition. However, when they were told by the doctor that Jill would probably be severely retarded and unable to attend school, they had dread thoughts of the future.

While Sue Jones was still in the hospital, the doctor suggested that Jill be placed immediately in a nursing home where she would be taken care of and not be a burden to the Jones family. Although early placement was not unusual for severely retarded children at the time, Sue Jones wanted to have a second opinion. One of the nurses at the hospital who had known of a number of families with Down's syndrome children told the Joneses that many children with this condition were only moderately retarded, could benefit from special schooling with other handicapped children, and were very lovable. After much discussion with other children, relatives, and a few close friends, the Joneses decided to keep Jill at home and see how her adjustment developed.

During the first 2 years, Jill was treated and reacted like many other babies. Physi-

These youngsters show many of the distinctive physical features of Down's syndrome (mongolism), inborn chromosomal abnormality that typically results in moderate mental retardation.

cally, she could be distinguished as a Down's syndrome child because of her small eyes, round face, and sloppy posture. Also, she developed at about half the pace of the average child. She did not sit alone until about a year and did not walk until she was 2 years of age. She lagged in her speech development as well and spoke no understandable words at age 2.

With the help of a special center for retarded children, Sue Jones was alerted to developmental problems that Jill might encounter and was able to gear her expectations to the realities of Jill's development. The center had a preschool program for retarded youngsters, in which Jill was enrolled at 3 years of age.

After 3 years in the special program, Jill was taking on responsibility for dressing herself, she was almost completely toilet trained, and she could express her wishes verbally. She was a playful, happy child who was an object of delight to her brothers and sisters, as well as to her parents.

At age 6 Jill was able to enter a special class program for the retarded and begin a full day of school. During her middle childhood years, however, the discrepancy between Jill's actual age and her mentality became increasingly problematic. Her brothers and sisters had less time to play with her, and she became more isolated in her neighborhood. It was clear that there were not sufficient social and after-school activities to keep her occupied. In school she achieved about the predicted level for her IQ, which had been tested at between 50 and 55 over the years. However, other children in her classes seemed to take on greater responsibility and to have developed much clearer speech patterns.

As Jill entered her teen years, she became frustrated with the lack of attention and activities in her life. She began to have periods of anger and depression at home and was unable to entertain herself for any length of time. After several months of discussions with the staff at the center for the retarded where Jill had been seen earlier, Tom and Sue Jones decided to place her in a private residential facility for retarded children and adults. Just after Jill turned 14 the whole family went with her when she entered the facility. They arranged a regular schedule of visiting her every month and having her come home for brief summer and holiday visits. Jill adjusted well to the facility and continues to live there today. She works in the laundry, mainly sorting and stacking clothes. She has several friends with whom she enjoys talking and is a well-known, personable resident of the facility. She is likely to have a normal life expectancy and will continue to reside in the facility.

Recent advances in the early detection of inborn biological disorders have provided opportunities to reduce substantially the frequency of Down's syndrome, of which there are about 5000 new cases in the United States each year. In a fairly simple procedure known as **amniocentesis,** fluid extracted from the uterus of pregnant women 15 to 17 weeks following conception can be tested for chromosomal abnormalities, and the results indicate with almost perfect certainty whether the child will have Down's syndrome (Milunsky, 1976; Omenn, 1978). To the extent that parents elect this procedure and then choose to terminate a pregnancy rather than give birth to a child destined to be seriously handicapped, the number of new cases of Down's syndrome and eventually the prevalence of this condition will diminish.

Figure 3.2
As is true of many biological defects that develop between an infant's conception and delivery, the incidence of Down's syndrome increases with the mother's age at birth. (From Smith and Wilson (1973). Reprinted with permission of W. B. Saunders Co.)

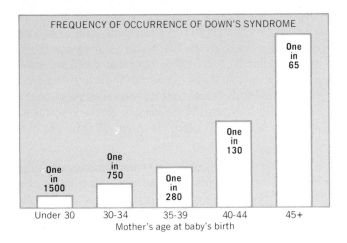

FREQUENCY OF OCCURRENCE OF DOWN'S SYNDROME

Mother's age at baby's birth

Amniocentesis can especially benefit older parents, since Down's syndrome is more common among children of older mothers. Approximately half of all mongoloid children are born to women over 35, and the risk of this condition increases from 1 in 1500 children of mothers under 30 to 1 in 65 children of mothers over 45 (see Figure 3.2)

Phenylketonuria (PKU)   PKU is a genetically transmitted metabolic disorder in which the body does not adequately absorb certain substances (phenylalanine) that are injurious to the brain. In children born with PKU, normal brain development is prevented by the ingestion of protein, which contains about 5 percent phenylalanine. These children show subtle developmental lags as early as 3 to 4 months of age, and the primary end result of untreated PKU is moderate or severe mental retardation. Without intervention, very few PKU youngsters will have IQs above 50, and many will be so seriously handicapped as to be bedridden and unable to talk. Those who escape serious physical handicap are still likely to have problems with motor coordination and to be hyperactive, unpredictable, unpleasant, and difficult to manage children (Berman, Waisman, & Graham, 1966; Berry, 1969; Knox, 1972).

PKU is fortunately a rare condition that appears just once in every 10,000 to 20,000 live births and accounts for only 1 percent of institutionalized retardates (Cytryn & Lourie, 1980). It merits attention because it differs from most other hereditary disorders in two important respects. First, soon after birth and before any of its observable manifestations appear, it can be detected by a blood test (the Guthrie test). Second, its effects can be almost entirely prevented by prompt treatment, which consists of a diet low in such high-protein foods as meat, fish, and eggs. When a properly controlled diet is begun in the first 3 months of life, most PKU children can grow normally, both physically and mentally, although their eventual IQs are still likely to be somewhat below the average in their family (Berman & Ford, 1970; Dobson, Kushida, Williamson, & Friedman, 1976; Hansen, 1977; Sutherland, Umbarger, & Berry, 1966).

Although adequate screening of newborns with the Guthrie procedure and subsequent diet control can thus eliminate PKU as a cause of mental retardation, it is uncertain how long an alanine-free diet must be continued. There are some data to suggest that after age 6, when most of the child's brain growth has occurred, a special diet is no longer necessary to avoid harmful effects of the PKU metabolic problem; other researchers caution that, depending on the specific levels of phenylalanine in their blood, PKU children older than 6 may suffer a decline in their rate of mental development if their special diet is discontinued (Brown & Warner, 1976; Dobson, Koch, Williamson, Spector, Frankenburg, O'Flynn, Warner, & Hudson, 1968; Holtzman, Welcher, & Mellits, 1975).

Maternal Ill Health   Various health problems in pregnant women increase the risk of their giving birth to a retarded child. During the first trimester the fetus is vulnerable to harmful effects of infectious disease, especially *rubella* (German measles). Half of the children whose mothers contract this illness early in pregnancy are likely to have some resulting mental or physical handicap. Many of these children will be deaf, and about 25 percent will be mentally retarded. In recent years, a vaccine developed to prevent rubella has made it possible to begin eliminating the childhood defects that once followed in the wake of epidemics of this disease (Chess, Fernandez, & Korn, 1978; Krugman, 1977; Sever, Nelson, & Gilkeson, 1965).

Later in pregnancy poor nutrition can prevent normal brain growth in the fetus and impair subsequent mental development. This is especially true during the last 50 prenatal days, when brain tissue is in a peak growth period and increasing at the rate of 5 to 6 percent of its adult weight every 2 weeks (Birch & Gussow, 1970, Perkins, 1977; Susser, Stein, & Ruch, 1977). Excessive smoking or drinking, heavy drug use, and exposure to radiation during pregnancy can also affect fetal development in ways that produce mental defect (Apgar, 1964; Dalby, 1978; Koch, 1976; Uchida, Holunga, & Lawler, 1968; Wood, Johnson, & Omori, 1967).

Special attention in this latter regard must be paid to a condition known as fetal alcohol syndrome (FAS). FAS is a pattern of facial deformities, growth deficiency, and mental retardation that occurs in one-quarter to one-third of children born to alcoholic mothers. Offspring of women who drink heavily during pregnancy are thus at high risk for physical and mental defects. Although not all FAS children are retarded, the average IQ reported for them is around 68 (Abel, 1980; Rosett & Sander, 1979; Streissguth, 1977; Streissguth, Landesman-Dwyer, Martin, & Smith, 1980; Thompson, 1979).

Birth Complications   Certain complications during the birth process increase the risk of subsequent mental and physical handicaps. Especially important is *prematurity,* which is defined as weighing less than 5.5 pounds (1500 grams) at birth. Infants who are born prematurely have a significantly lower intellectual level than full-term babies on the average and a higher incidence of achievement problems in school. The less the birth weight, the greater the risk of some handicap, and below 3.3 pounds (1500 grams) at birth there is a 15 percent likelihood of subaverage mental ability (Drillien, 1967, 1972; Dweck, Saxon, Benton, & Cassady, 1973; Kopp & Parmelee, 1979; Rubin, Rosenblatt, & Balow, 1973).

Birth complications, which are often referred to as *perinatal stress,* include two other noteworthy potential sources of retardation: **anoxia** (an inadequate supply of oxygen to the brain), which can occur when there are difficulties in getting a newborn to start breathing, and birth injuries caused either by instruments used in the delivery or by problems arising in the infant's passage through the birth canal (Goldstein, Caputo, & Taub, 1976; Drillien, 1970; Gottfried, 1973; Towbin, 1970). Delivery in the *breech* position (feet first rather than head first) is especially likely to result in subsequent development problems; in one study, 25 percent of a large sample of breech-delivered children were found to have repeated one or more grades in school by age 9 (Morgan & Kane, 1964; Muller, Campbell, Graham, Brittain, Fitzgerald, Hogan, Muller, & Ritterhouse, 1971).

A well-known condition that is due to birth injury is **cerebral palsy,** a neurological disorder in which damage to the brain produces motor difficulties and often a mental handicap as well. Children with cerebral palsy suffer from various kinds of muscle paralysis or weakness, involuntary movement, and impaired coordination, and 45 to 60 percent of them are mentally retarded (Hohman & Freedheim, 1958; Molnar & Taft, 1973; Moxley, 1978; Stephen & Hawks, 1974).

Although there is no question that mental retardation and neurological disorders can result from such birth complications, the relationship between perinatal stress and subsequent handicap is more complex than was once thought. Results from two major

Cerebral palsy often results in mental retardation as well as muscle weakness or paralysis in various parts of the body.

research undertakings mentioned in Chapter 1—the Collaborative Perinatal Project and the Kauai Longitudinal Study—and other related studies have suggested the following three conclusions:

1. When complications of the birth process contribute to biological defects, they are often adding to damage that has already been done prenatally, as a result of harmful influences during the pregnancy period. In particular, there are relatively few instances in which birth injuries alone are responsible for mental retardation or cerebral palsy in children whose prenatal development was entirely normal.

2. When birth complications play a role in producing handicaps, evidence of abnormality is usually apparent at birth or soon after. Children who have experienced perinatal stress are not especially likely to become abnormal in middle childhood or adolescence if they did not show developmental problems early in life.

3. Despite the risk of deviance that perinatal stress may pose, most infants in whom such complications occur develop normally. Moreover, differences between children who have been exposed to perinatal complications and those who have not are most pronounced during infancy and early childhood and tend to disappear with age. In this regard, the course of developmental difficulties associated with perinatal stress is strongly influenced by the socioeconomic status of the family. In advantaged families infants who have suffered perinatal complications tend to show few long-term ill effects, whereas infants from lower social classes with identical histories of complications are relatively likely to be handicapped in their later functioning. Thus the environment appears to have the potential for minimizing or maximizing early developmental difficulties, and an unfavorable outcome appears to result from an *interaction* between perinatal stress and poor social environmental conditions—including those mentioned in the next section (Sameroff, 1978; Sameroff & Chandler, 1975; Towbin, 1978; Werner & Smith, 1979).

Harmful Postnatal Experiences   In 9 of 10 cases in which physical events interfere with brain development, the damage has been done by the time the child is born (Yannet, 1957). Nevertheless, certain postnatal experiences can increase the risk of a child's growing up retarded. Infectious diseases accompanied by prolonged high fever—especially encephalitis and meningitis—may cause permanent damage to the brain if they occur early in life. Fifteen to 20 percent of children who suffer such illness as infants eventually show mental retardation (Cytryn & Lourie, 1980; Gibbs, 1966; Sells, Carpenter, & Ray, 1975; Yoeli, Scheinsesson, & Hargreaves, 1977).

Mental retardation can also result from head injuries and exposure to certain toxic substances early in life. Lead poisoning was at one time a special source of concern, since swallowing even a small amount of lead in paint that is flaking from walls or peeling off toys can cause severe mental retardation. However, legislation to limit the indoor use of lead-based paints has greatly reduced this particular risk (Needleman, 1977; Robinson & Robinson, 1976, Chapter 5; Routh, Mushak, & Boone, 1979).

Currently the most widely discussed postnatal cause of mental retardation is malnutrition, particularly among the poor parts of the world where food is in short supply. Dietary deficiencies early in life have been found to interfere with mental as well as physical development; the more severe and prolonged the malnutrition, especially if it extends from birth through the first year (a period of substantial brain growth), the greater the risk of retardation (Ashem & Janes, 1978; Hertzig, Birch, Richardson, & Tizard, 1972; Perkins, 1977; Richardson, 1977; Winick, 1976).

Unlike retardation caused by most other biological interruptions of brain development, the ill effects of malnutrition can often be reversed. Although it is still uncertain how much recovery of mental capacity can be expected, especially in relation to the severity of the problem, recent studies leave little doubt that an improved diet can accelerate both the mental and physical development of undernourished children who have fallen behind their peers (Brozek, 1978; Lloyd-Still, 1976; McKay, Sinisterra, McKay, Gomez, & Lloreda, 1978; Warren, 1973; Winick & Brasel, 1977).

Another reversible postnatal cause of retardation is **social isolation syndromes.** To develop normally, infants require a certain amount of social and sensory stimulation. When they are reared by emotionally depriving parents or grow up in an institutional setting where individual attention is limited, they may show retarded mental and physical growth (Buchanan & Oliver, 1977; Caldwell, 1970; Clancy & McBride, 1975; Garfunkel, 1977; Pollitt, Eichler, & Chan, 1975; Powell, Brasel, & Blizzard, 1967; Rosenheim & Ables, 1974). The developing human organism is more resilient than is often appreciated, however, so that a very extreme degree of isolation from human contact is necessary to interfere with normal mental development. Moreover, provided they have not been too severely deprived too early in life, young children have a remarkable capacity to recoup developmental lags associated with social isolation syndromes if their environment is enriched (Clarke & Clarke, 1977a; Koluchova, 1976; Langmeier & Matejcek, 1975; Rutter, 1974; Suedfeld, 1980, Chapter 4).

Familial Retardation

As noted earlier, in familial retardation the handicapped person has no apparent biological defect but does have a family history of mental retardation. Whereas biologically impaired retardates usually have IQs below 55, most familial retardates are in the 50 to 69 range. With this additional fact, the two-group concept of mental retardation mentioned earlier can now be summarized as follows: *biological* retardation involves moderate or severe intellectual handicap, is far more prevalent than would be expected from the normal distribution of IQ scores in the population, and occurs proportionately among different socioeconomic groups; *familial* retardation involves mild handicap, occurs in the frequency anticipated from the normal distribution of IQ, and has a much higher prevalence among socioculturally disadvantaged than among advantaged groups. The striking difference in the IQ distribution of biologically impaired and familial retardates was depicted in Figure 3.1. Aside from these descriptive findings, familial retardation is most frequently discussed in terms of genetic, environmental, and interaction views of its origins.

The Genetic View   Although its specific cause is not known, familial retardation is widely believed to be passed genetically from retarded parents to their children. This opinion is based largely on the important role that genetic factors appear to play in determining individual differences in intelligence. Careful reviews of available research

TABLE 3.4   Relatedness and IQ Scores

Category of Relatedness	Median Correlation Coefficient	Number of Groups Studied
Unrelated persons, reared apart	−0.01	4
Unrelated persons, reared together	0.23	5
Foster parent-child	0.20	3
Parent-child	0.50	12
Siblings reared apart	0.40	2
Siblings reared together	0.49	35
Two-egg twins	0.53	20
One-egg twins, reared apart	0.75	4
One-egg twins, reared together	0.87	14

Source.   Based on data compiled by Erlenmeyer-Kimling and Jarvik (1963).

indicate that the **heritability** of IQ—that is, the proportion of the variability among people in IQ test scores that can be ascribed to their genetic inheritance—ranges from 50 to 75 percent (Loehlin, Lindzey, & Spuhler, 1975; Scarr-Salapatek, 1975; Vernon, 1979, Chapter 2).

Especially important in this regard is evidence that the more closely two people are related, the more similar they are in measured IQ. As can be seen in Table 3.4, for example, one-egg (identical) twins are much more similar in intelligence than two-egg (nonidentical) twins, even when they have been reared apart. Likewise, the IQs of adopted children have been found in numerous studies to resemble those of their biological parents more closely than those of their adoptive parents (Holden, 1980; Munsinger, 1975; Vernon, 1979, Chapters 11 & 14).

There is also evidence that severely retarded children are less likely to have retarded parents and siblings than mildly retarded children (Johnson, Ahern, & Johnson, 1976). This finding is consistent with a two-group distinction between more seriously handicapped persons who are retarded as a result of some obvious biological abnormality and mildly handicapped persons whose retardation represents their genetic inheritance.

The Environmental View   Some writers argue that intelligence is determined more by children's experiences than by their inheritance and, accordingly, that retardation in the absence of any obvious biological disorder is due to psychosocial factors (Girardeau, 1971; Kamin, 1974). Data can be marshaled in support of this view as well as for the more widely held genetic position. For example, some extensive research has demonstrated a direct relationship between birth order and family size on the one hand and limited intelligence and school failure on the other hand; in other words, the more siblings children have and the lower their rank among them (second, third, etc.), the lower their measured IQ and the greater their risk of performing poorly in school. In two-child families this difference favoring the first-born holds independently of the age difference between the siblings (Belmont & Marolla, 1973; Belmont, Stein, & Wittes, 1976; Belmont, Stein, & Zybart, 1978; Zajonc & Marcus, 1975). Since family size and birth order are unrelated to any known genetic determinants, their relationship to intelligence would seem due to effects of experience. In particular, it is reasonable to suggest that early-born children in small families will receive more attention and intellectual stimulation from their parents than later-born children in large families.

Some researchers maintain that being reared by one or more retarded parents is cause enough for subnormal intelligence. From this point of view familial retardation is caused by the limited intellectual stimulation provided by retarded parents and the socioculturally impoverished environment in which they usually live. The higher prevalence of familial retardation among disadvantaged than advantaged children noted earlier is consistent with this position. Additionally, even though adopted children are more like their biological than their adoptive parents in IQ, children from low-income families who are adopted early in life into middle-class homes are found to show higher IQ scores and lower rates of school failure than would have been expected by virtue of their social class at birth. Supportive data in this regard suggest that one of the strongest predictors of children's intelligence is the amount of educational encouragement they receive in their homes (Bahr & Leigh, 1978; Scarr & Weinberg, 1977; Scarr-Salapatek & Weinberg, 1976; Schiff, Duyme, Dumaret, Stewart, Tomkiewicz, & Feingold, 1978).

In response to such an environmental view, some genetic theorists point out that being in a lower socioeconomic class can be regarded as an *effect* rather than a *cause* of retardation in families. According to this argument—known as the **cultural-drift hypothesis**—families whose retardation is inherited tend to drift toward a lower socioeconomic class because of their limited social and vocational capacities. Hence their poverty constitutes a result of their limited genetic endowment, not a reason for their retardation (Herrnstein, 1973).

The Interaction View Despite leaning toward either genetic or environmental views, most researchers doubt that subnormal intelligence can be fully explained by either. Instead, they regard the *interaction* between heredity and environment as determining whether and how much a particular child will be retarded (Clarke & Clarke, 1974; Rainer, 1976; Robinson & Robinson, 1976, Chapter 3).

In Table 3.4, for example, just as the environmental view cannot account for the similarity in IQ between one-egg twins reared apart, the genetic view cannot account for the greater similarity between unrelated persons when they are reared together than when they are reared apart. Moreover, for both subnormal and normally intelligent persons, motivational and emotional aspects of their lives and whether they have been reared in stimulating or impoverished environments are known to influence their intellectual functioning (Baroff, 1974, Chap. 4; Zigler & Balla, 1976). Figure 3.3 suggests how children at several intellectual levels might vary in their IQ test scores depending on how much their environment has encouraged or inhibited use of their intellectual capacity.

Figure 3.3
Possible relationships between environmental influences and range of intelligence test scores. (From Baroff (1974). Reprinted with permission of Hemisphere Publishing Corp.)

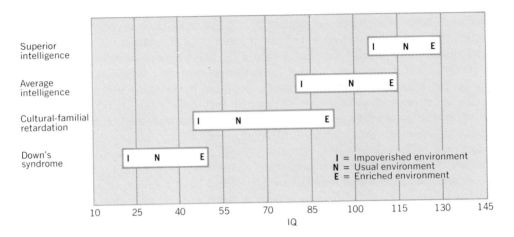

PREVENTION OF MENTAL RETARDATION

Clinicians concerned with treating psychopathology have traditionally concentrated on providing psychological services to people identified as experiencing some type of mental, emotional, or behavioral difficulty. Since the mid-1960s, however, increasing attention to community mental health needs has expanded traditional notions of *treatment* into the broader concept of *prevention*. This broader concept implies that clinicians should not only help people *overcome* psychological problems, but should help them *avoid* such problems in the first place (Albee & Joffe, 1977; Caplan, 1964; Cowen, Gardner, & Zax, 1967).

More specifically, it is becoming customary to speak of three kinds of preventive mental health action. *Primary prevention* involves steps taken to eliminate conditions before they occur, or at least to reduce the likelihood of their occurring. *Secondary prevention* consists of early detection and prompt action to limit or reverse an emerging condition before it becomes full-blown. *Tertiary prevention* refers to the treatment of already manifest conditions in an effort to correct them or to help people adapt as best they can to their effects. Attention to primary and secondary prevention has only a short history and has thus far yielded relatively little certain knowledge. Hence the treatment sections of Chapters 4 to 13 are concerned chiefly with tertiary measures— that is, attempting to do something about a problem that is already present. In the case of mental retardation, however, approaches to prevention have been sufficiently broad to provide concrete illustrations of all three kinds.

Primary Prevention

Good medical care is the best way currently known of preventing mental retardation from occurring, especially in instances where it would have been associated with biological abnormalities. Adequate nutrition during pregnancy, vaccination against such infectious diseases as rubella, and other types of prenatal attention that reduce the risk of fetal damage or birth complications all help to prevent women from giving birth to retarded children. Such postnatal measures as screening for PKU, good diet, and early treatment of infectious disease also prevent retardation by avoiding some of its identified causes.

As noted earlier, retardation involving Down's syndrome can be avoided when amniocentesis identifies chromosomal abnormalities and a decision is made to abort the pregnancy. However, such preventive action depends both on a family's access to this procedure and on the family's attitude toward abortion. For those who are normally opposed to terminating a pregnancy or are psychologically reluctant to do so, this route to primary prevention may not be taken.

These medical procedures are helpful mainly in preventing organic forms of mental retardation, and they have relatively little impact on the frequency of familial retardation. Nevertheless, it is estimated that full application of the knowledge and technology currently available in this area could reduce the number of biologically retarded persons in the United States by half, or over 1 million retardates (Sells & Bennett, 1977; Zigler, 1978).

Genetic counseling can also play a role in reducing the incidence of mental retardation, including the familial form. The facts that older women are more likely than younger women to give birth to retarded children and that retarded parents are more likely than normally intelligent parents to have retarded offspring have obvious implications for such counseling. Similarly, families with a genetic history of conditions associated with retardation might well be advised to think carefully about having children.

Whatever its potential effectiveness, genetic counseling poses some delicate moral, ethical, legal, and even political issues (Berg, 1977; Moraczewski, 1976; Switzky & Gaylord-Ross, 1977). Should science intrude on the natural laws of conception and childbirth? Do some people have the right to advise others against having children, and if so, who should these people be and under whose auspices should they give this advice? If a society is justified in seeking to reduce its number of defective children, who should decide what constitutes a "defect" and how can a line be safely drawn between genetic counseling and state control of who is allowed to reproduce? These and other complex questions raised by genetic counseling go beyond the scope of the present discussion. Nevertheless, it must be recognized that programs of primary prevention may have important implications for the rights of individuals to determine their own destiny.

Secondary Prevention

Many of the approaches to primary prevention of mental retardation are applicable to secondary prevention as well. For example, early detection of developmental delay caused by PKU followed by appropriate dietary control can prevent affected children from becoming as severely handicapped as they might otherwise be, even if the earlier opportunity for primary prevention has been missed. Similarly, as noted earlier, problems of mental and physical development related to poor nutrition can often be reversed if they are recognized and treated with an adequate diet.

Currently the best prospects for secondary prevention of intellectual handicap appear to be in programs of environmental enrichment. As noted already, growing up in an impoverished environment can contribute to mental underfunctioning and, when imposed on limited genetic endowment, increase the risk of mental retardation (see Figure 3.4). However, there is good reason to believe that the adverse effects of environmental impoverishment can often be reversed or at least minimized by adequate early intervention.

Although the findings were not fully appreciated until many years later, a pioneering observation of such secondary prevention was reported by Skeels and Dye in 1939. They wrote about 13 children with an average IQ of 64.3 who, because of overcrowding in an orphanage, were transferred to an institution for mental defectives when they were around 19 months of age. Whereas conditions in the orphanage had not provided these children very much stimulation or attention from adults, in the institution they were cared for individually by young women residents who "adopted" them and gave them a great deal of emotional and sensory stimulation.

When Skeels and Dye reassessed these supposedly retarded children 18 months after they had been transferred to the more stimulating setting, their average IQ had increased more than 27 points, to 91.8. Thus putting environmentally deprived children who appeared to be mentally defective into an enriched environment had enabled them to attain an average IQ level in less than 2 years. Skeels (1966) followed up on this group 30 years later and found that as adults they did not differ from the general population in their level of education, occupation, income, or intellectual level of their own children. Although the early Skeels and Dye research had some methodological weaknesses, their findings have largely been confirmed by subsequent investigators (Clarke & Clarke, 1977b).

Since the 1960s numerous programs of environmental enrichment for preschool children have been implemented (Caldwell, 1974; Horowitz & Paden, 1973). Of these the most ambitious effort at secondary prevention of mental retardation has been the Milwaukee Project carried out by Heber and his colleagues (Fallender & Heber, 1975; Garber, 1975; Heber, 1969). A group of children from a low-income background whose mothers had IQs below 75 were given daily sensorimotor and intellectual stimulation from the age of 6 months until they entered the first grade. For the first 3 years of this intensive program their mothers were trained in child-rearing and vocational skills. The IQs of these children and of a comparison group of children from the same background who did not receive the environmental enrichment were measured at periodic intervals by the Gesell Developmental Schedules (at 12 to 21 months), Cattell and Binet tests (at 24 to 66 months), Wechsler Preschool and Primary Scale of Intelligence (at 72 months), and Wechsler Intelligence Test for Children (at 84 months).

As indicated in Figure 3.4, the children receiving environmental enrichment (experimental group) earned substantially higher IQ scores than the nonstimulated (control) group throughout the program. At 60 months, the last measuring point prior to termination of the program, the mean IQ of the experimental group was 118, which was 26

Figure 3.4

IQ changes associated with environmental enrichment. (From Garber (1975). Reprinted with permission of University Park Press.)

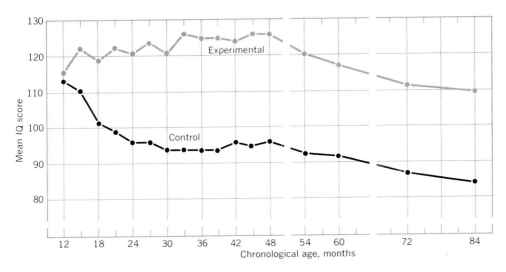

points higher than the control group's mean IQ of 92. During a 2-year follow-up period, both groups showed declines in measured IQ; however, those who had had the preschool enrichment continued to surpass the control group by more than 20 points in average IQ (106 versus 85 at 84 months of age).

The significance of these findings, notes Garber (1975), lies neither in the dramatic increase in IQ among the environmentally enriched children nor in the decline in their test performance once they were no longer receiving special attention. What is noteworthy is that (a) whereas the control group shows a declining trend in IQ and appears to be leveling off at close to their mother's intellectual level, as would normally be expected, (b) the experimental group, despite declining IQs following the termination of the enrichment program, appears to be leveling off in the average range of intelligence, considerably above what might be expected from their mother's IQ.

More longitudinal data are necessary to determine how long the beneficial effects of early enrichment programs persist once children from impoverished backgrounds are no longer receiving special attention. Nevertheless, the Milwaukee Project data indicate that, even though some of the gains realized during enrichment may only be temporary, there may be sufficient lasting effects to help children avoid subnormal levels of intelligence that would otherwise have been their lot.

Further research also needs to investigate the possibility that such intervention programs may produce benefits that cannot be measured in intellectual terms alone. Many researchers feel strongly that the intellectual capacity of young children is fairly fixed, especially if they are mentally retarded. However, the social competence of these children—and their ability to perform on IQ tests as well—may improve dramatically in response to early enrichment programs, particularly if they come from disadvantaged backgrounds (Goodman, 1977; Jason, De Amicis, & Carter, 1978; Zigler & Trickett, 1978).

Tertiary Prevention in the Schools

As indicated in Table 3.3, most retardates are mildly handicapped individuals whose limitations are first identified when they enter school and who can profit from special programs of academic, social, and vocational training. The public schools thus play an important role in determining whether the majority of retarded persons realize their potential to become at least moderately self-supporting and well-adjusted members of the adult community or whether they instead drift into the chronically unemployed and unhappy fringes of society.

Public schools in the United States began to respond to the needs of intellectually limited children in the 1920s. Slowly at first, but with gathering momentum following World War II, special classes for educable retardates were established as rapidly as money could be found for this purpose. By 1970 approximately 728,000 retarded children were receiving special instruction in the public schools (Metz, 1973), largely in small classes of similarly handicapped youngsters.

During the late 1960s, however, some educators became concerned that segregating retarded and other handicapped children in special classes might have the unintended effects of slowing their educational progress, hampering their social development, and subjecting them to stigma and rejection (Cushna, 1976; Dunn, 1968; Jones, 1972). Hobbs (1975) provides the following emphatic statement of these concerns.

> We see little to be gained by designing categorical programs that set these children apart from other children, accentuate their differences, and deny them access to individually designed learning opportunities that should be the right of all children. Furthermore, we see little to be gained from a system that deprives normal children of the opportunity to know exceptional children and to appreciate them as individuals, not as "retardates," "cripples," "psychos" (p. 10).

These views have given rise to the philosophy of **mainstreaming,** which holds that every possible effort should be made to keep children in their regular classes. Mainstreaming was legislated by Congress in the Education for All Handicapped Act of 1975, commonly referred to as Public Law 94-142. This law requires procedures "to assure that, to the maximum extent appropriate, handicapped children . . . are educated with children who are not handicapped." Schools are obliged under this law to prove that all of their handicapped students are being educated in the "least restrictive" alternative to special classes. The intent of the law is to reduce the number of children in segregated educational programs, which may deprive them of opportunities to learn, and some feel that it may also serve a valuable purpose in allowing nonhandicapped children to study with and perhaps be helpful to their less fortunate peers (Sarason & Doris, 1979).

Whatever the good intentions behind this legislation, McDaniels (1978) noted that it had at least one staggering and perhaps not fully appreciated implication: What happens when 750,000 retarded students receiving special instruction are returned to regular classrooms, where they will be the responsibility of teachers who may have had little preparation for meeting their special needs and may already be overburdened with a crowded classroom? In another important commentary on PL 94-142, Zigler and Muenchow (1979) observed that schools operating with limited budgets may interpret the "least restrictive" environment as being the least expensive alternative. In this circumstance the legal requirement to educate handicapped children as much as possible in regular classes could result in schools failing to provide sufficient special classes for children who really need them.

Time and experience will tell how successfully and with what variations this act of Congress is implemented. For the present, however, a brief review of the evidence will serve to indicate that neither an exclusive reliance on special classes nor a wholesale endorsement of mainstreaming is a perfect solution for meeting the needs of retarded children in school.

Educational Progress One of the strongest arguments in support of mainstreaming is the finding that special classes appear to hinder rather than promote learning; specifically, children with a low IQ generally do better academically in regular classes than in special classes (Fitzgibbon, 1967; Guskin & Spicker, 1968; Heintz & Blackman, 1977; Stanton & Cassady, 1964). These results hold even when steps are taken to make sure that special-class programs are not being undermined by poorly trained teachers who underestimate their pupils' capacity to learn (Carroll, 1967; Goldstein, 1967). Despite being academically ahead of special-class children, regular-class retarded youngsters are still usually found to be achieving less than could be expected from their measured abilities (Budoff & Gottlieb, 1976; Meyen & Hieronymus, 1970). It would therefore appear that neither regular- nor special-class placement as traditionally employed holds the key to maximum academic progress among retarded children.

Social Development Strong support for special-class programs comes from observations that educable retardates appear to adjust better and feel better about themselves in special classes, where they are competing and interacting with youngsters of their same ability, than in regular classes, where they are constantly overshadowed and outstripped by their brighter peers (Bruininks, Rynders, & Gross, 1974; Gottlieb, Gampel, & Budoff, 1975; Kehle & Guidubaldi, 1978). Hence the concerns of mainstreaming advocates that segregated classes hamper social development may be unwarranted; to the contrary, regular-class placement may run the greater risk of undermining retarded children's self-esteem and interpersonal skills.

Not all of the available data point in this direction, however. Some investigators have found that retarded children in regular classes are more likely to model themselves after their normally intelligent peers and to show more age-appropriate behavior than those in special classes (Barry & Overmann, 1977; Gampel, Gottlieb, & Harrison, 1974). These mixed results suggest that for social development as well as for academic progress, both special-class and mainstreaming approaches have something to offer retarded children but are not without flaws in meeting their needs.

Stigma and Rejection Advocates of mainstreaming generally subscribe to the **contact hypothesis,** which states that normally intelligent children will have more favorable attitudes toward retarded children they get to know in regular classes than toward those who are segregated in special classes. As suggested in Chapter 2, some research confirms that mainstreamed educable retardates who work closely with non-handicapped children in small groups do become more accepted by them over time (Ballard, Corman, Gottlieb, & Kaufman, 1977). However, despite the seeming logic of the contact hypothesis, other findings indicate the opposite. In the absence of special small-group activities, mildly retarded children in regular classrooms have been found to experience more rejection from their normal peers than those in segregated classes, and they are not considered any more socially acceptable (Gottlieb, 1975; Gottlieb, Semmel, & Veldman, 1978).

Concerns about social disadvantages of special-class students must also be tempered by the observation in Chapter 2 that interpersonal attitudes are more heavily influenced by how people behave than by how they are labeled. Gottlieb (1974) found in this regard that schoolchildren hold less favorable attitudes toward academically incompetent than competent peers independently of whether they are labeled mentally retarded or normal. Similarly, children tend to be accepting of peers whom they observe being treated positively by their teachers, independently of how they are labeled, and when they are asked to describe special-class retarded children they know, they rarely refer to their intellectual handicap or special-class placement; instead, they focus on their physical appearance and personal attributes other than academic ability (Clark, 1964; Foley, 1979; Renz & Simensen, 1969).

These and other findings have led numerous reviewers to the following two conclusions: (a) children's attitudes toward mentally retarded peers are determined by the quality and not the amount of contact they have with them; (b) there is as yet no conclusive evidence that being identified as "retarded" or placed in a special class has any long-lasting harmful effects (Bialer, 1977; Cook & Wollersheim, 1976; Guskin, Bartel, & MacMillan, 1975; MacMillan, Jones, & Aloia, 1974).

To summarize this important topic, research to date provides no clear weight of evidence favoring either special-class or regular-class placement of educable retardates in the schools. From a clinical perspective, moreover, the needs of individual children can rarely be served best by commitment to a single educational philosophy or treatment method. For these reasons, many child specialists caution against either unqualified embrace of mainstreaming or steadfast allegiance to special-class programs (Meyers, MacMillan, & Yoshida, in press; Zigler & Muenchow, 1979).

In light of current knowledge, it appears best for schools to maintain a range of educational approaches, to combine mainstreaming and special-class methods by keeping mildly retarded children with their regular class part of the time while also providing periods of small-group instruction with a special-education teacher who can offer extra help with learning and adjustment problems, and to arrange combinations from among available placement alternatives on an individual basis according to each child's particular academic and social needs (Anderson, 1976; Heintz & Blackman, 1977; Heron, 1978; MacMillan, Jones, & Meyers, 1976).

Figure 3.5
Intellectual level among residents of public institutions for the mentally retarded. (Based on data reported by Scheerenberger (1975).)

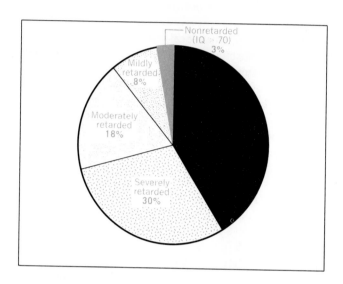

Tertiary Prevention in Institutions

Whereas education and training for mildly retarded children occurs primarily in the schools, the needs of moderately and severely retarded persons must often be met in residential settings. Just under 4 percent of retarded persons in the United States are institutionalized—about 181,000 in public institutions for the retarded, 28,000 in private institutions, and 29,000 with a primary diagnosis of mental retardation who are in state mental hospitals (Office of Mental Retardation Coordination, 1972). More than 70 percent of those in public institutions are severely or profoundly retarded, whereas only about 10 percent have IQs above 50 (Scheerenberger, 1975); see Figure 3.5.

Over the past 20 to 30 years the population of institutionalized retardates has gradually been growing younger and more severely handicapped. This trend reflects increased efforts to avoid permanent institutionalization wherever possible by returning less severely retarded individuals to their families and communities once they have derived what benefits they can from the institutional program. At one time decisions to send a child to an institution for the mentally retarded commonly constituted lifetime commitments. Now, however, it is widely agreed that moderately and especially mildly retarded youngsters should be institutionalized not for custodial care, but to help them develop and mature (Baumeister & Butterfield, 1970; Scheerenberger & Felsenthal, 1977).

Just as special classes in school are opposed by advocates of mainstreaming, even initial institutional care for retarded youngsters has been criticized by proponents of *normalization* or deinstitutionalization. These critics have voiced eloquent concern that public institutions for the retarded are overcrowded, understaffed "warehouses" that degrade and dehumanize their residents, cause deterioration in intellectual functioning, and promote permanent custodial care (Blatt, 1969; Braginsky & Braginsky, 1971; Thurman & Thiele, 1973; Wolfensberger, 1971). These facilities should be closed, the normalization position continues, and retardates should be kept at home or at least close to their families and communities through use of group homes, day-care centers, nursing homes, foster families, and, if necessary, small local institutions.

Despite considerable enthusiasm for it, deinstitutionalization has thus far not proved any more perfect a solution than mainstreaming to the tertiary prevention of mental retardation. First, community-based facilities are sometimes found to provide poorer care and fewer supportive services than large institutions. Second, the families of retarded persons may for numerous reasons be unable to care for them adequately at home or even provide good supplementary care in collaboration with a local facility. Third, for some retarded persons the relatively protected nondemanding setting of a large public institution may offer a more comfortable environment in which to live than full or partial residence with their families or in their communities. For these reasons, individual attention to retarded children's needs, the circumstances of their families, and the relative quality of available services should come before assertions that either institutional or community-based facilities are always the more desirable treatment alternative (Adams, 1971; Begab, 1975; Bronston, 1976; Sternlicht & Bialer, 1977).

Moreover, as noted in Chapter 2, all institutions should not be tarred with the same brush. The headlines captured by deplorable conditions in some institutions can easily obscure the constructive programs carried on by others. An important series of studies by Zigler (1973) and his colleagues confirms that the effects of institutionalization cannot be described in general terms, but that they vary with the history of the person and the particular institutional environment. In one of these studies 103 children from four different institutions showed no overall IQ change in the first 2½ years following admission (Balla, Butterfield, & Zigler, 1974). These and other data indicate that, contrary to the concerns of many who advocate normalization, institutional living under certain conditions and with certain retarded populations may improve or at least not detract from intellectual functioning (Sternlicht & Bialer, 1977).

In current practice, several factors influence whether and when retarded youngsters are institutionalized. As indicated earlier, mildly retarded children rarely enter a residential facility, whereas severely retarded children almost always do; in both cases this outcome is directly related to the extent of their handicap as educable and custodial retardates, respectively. For moderately retarded children, the likelihood of institutionalization is directly related to how low their IQ is, the number of physical disabilities and health problems they have, and the amount of supervision they require. In addition, the more uncomfortable their parents are about having them at home and the greater the availability of institutions that their parents can accept and afford, the sooner they are likely to be placed (Eyman & Call, 1977; Eyman, O'Conner, Tarjan, & Justice, 1972; Graliker, Koch, & Henderson, 1965; Hobbs, 1964).

On the other hand, parents who can tolerate and provide for a moderately retarded child at home and who dislike the idea of a residential placement may delay institutionalization indefinitely. Sometimes such a decision is best for all concerned. These parents may enjoy having their youngster at home and escape the feelings of guilt and loss that often come from sending a family member off to an institution. Moreover, some moderately retarded children may live more happily at home than they would in an institution, and they may be spared feelings of having been rejected.

At other times the decision to keep a moderately retarded child at home is made ill-advisedly and benefits no one. Parents who feel guilty for having given birth to a retarded child may feel duty-bound to provide for the child's total care, even if doing so disrupts their lives, fills them with resentment that causes them to be poor parents, and deprives their other children of a normal home life. Retarded youngsters who are kept at home under these circumstances may be less happy than they would be in an institution. They may also have less opportunity at home than in an institution to learn skills that could help them function as partially self-sufficient adults later.

Tertiary Prevention in Counseling and Psychotherapy

Because the primary characteristics of mental retardation are best treated by education and training, mental health specialists have often given short shrift to working with intellectually limited youngsters. One more barometer of change since the impact of federal attention to mental retardation in the early 1960s is that the psychological needs of retarded children and their families have gradually begun to attract the needed services of counselors and psychotherapists.

As noted earlier, retarded children display a broad range of emotional and behavior problems and are more susceptible to psychological disorders than their normally intelligent peers. Forced to grapple with social and achievement-related problems that most other people are better equipped to handle, they are especially vulnerable to feelings of loneliness and low self-esteem. Evidence that psychotherapy can help retarded persons deal with such emotional problems has fostered many different types of psychological treatment both in and outside of institutions (Bernstein, 1979; Gunzberg, 1974; LaVietes, 1978; Smith, McKinnon, & Kessler, 1976; Sternlicht, 1977; Watson, 1977; Wetherby & Baumeister, 1981).

As for the parents of retarded children, many are saddened and disappointed by having given birth to a defective child, to the point of becoming clinically depressed. Since one way of overcoming depression is to ignore or forget about events that led to it, these parents often tend to reject their retarded child. In other cases parents may feel guilty about having a handicapped child because, rightly or wrongly, they blame the handicap on their own heredity or behavior. These parents often tend to overindulge or overprotect a retarded child as a way of avoiding guilt, even though other children in their family may suffer as a result. Whichever way parents react, having a handicapped child often strains their marital relationship and may even increase the risk of separation and divorce (Carr, 1974; Ferholt & Solnit, 1978; Gath, 1977; Schild, 1976; Waisbren, 1980; Work, 1979).

Since parental rejection, overprotection, and disharmony increase the vulnerability of retarded children to adjustment problems, counseling aimed at minimizing these three reactions can be very helpful. In some cases depressed parents can be swayed from rejecting their retarded child by advice on the important role that a stimulating environment can play in enhancing intellectual functioning. In other cases guilty parents can be swayed from overprotection by information concerning biological causes of their child's retardation over which they had no control. Finally, general guidance concerning how best to manage all of the children in their family and their marital relationship can assist parents in providing the best possible home environment in which their retarded child can grow.

SUMMARY

Mental retardation is defined by the American Association on Mental Deficiency (AAMD) as significantly subaverage intelligence coexisting with poor adaptation to school, work, or social situations. In practice, however, retardation is commonly diagnosed simply on the basis of an IQ score below 70, which occurs in approximately 3 percent of the population—about 6.6 million people in the United States. Strict use of the AAMD definition of retardation as limited intelligence *plus* adaptive failure would reduce this prevalence figure considerably, especially among minimally handicapped, sociocultur-ally disadvantaged, and adult groups. Many low-IQ people who are in the 50 to 70 range and/or who have suffered sociocultural disadvantage perform adequately on measures of adaptation, and many who have difficulties during their school years man-age to adjust reasonably well as adults.

Mental retardation is customarily categorized as mild, moderate, severe, or profound. Mildly retarded persons are called *educable,* have Wechsler IQs from 55 to 69, and comprise 89 percent of all retardates. They are typically not identified as handicapped until they enter school, where with adequate instruction they can reach between a third- and sixth-grade education. They are generally capable of enjoying a reasonably normal social life, becoming at least marginally self-supporting adults, and adjusting satisfactorily in their community.

Moderately retarded individuals are commonly referred to as *trainable,* have IQs of 40 to 54, and include 6 percent of retardates. They show developmental lags as pre-schoolers and typically cannot master functionally useful academic skills. With adequate training in self-care and social skills they may become able to support themselves and enjoy social relationships in supervised settings. Although periods of institutional care may be necessary to achieve this end, most trainable retardates do not require perma-nent custodial care.

Severely retarded (IQ 25 to 39) and profoundly retarded (IQ below 25) persons constitute the remaining 5 percent of retardates and are referred to as *custodial.* They are largely incapable of taking care of themselves and require institutionalization, usu-ally from early in life.

About 25 percent of retarded individuals have biological defects that account for their intellectual limitations, whereas the remaining 75 percent are *familial* retardates who do not show any biological abnormalities but have a family history of retardation. Noteworthy among the known biological causes of retardation are Down's syndrome (mongolism), a chromosomal abnormality that produces distinctive physical character-istics and accounts for 10 to 30 percent of all cases of moderate or severe retardation; phenylketonuria (PKU), a genetically transmitted metabolic disorder that results in mod-erate or severe retardation unless children are placed on a low-protein diet early in life;

poor maternal health during pregnancy, especially malnutrition, infectious disease, and heavy alcohol or drug use; birth complications, particularly prematurity and injuries to the brain during the birth process; and various early-life events that interfere with mental development, including some infectious diseases, exposure to certain toxic substances, head injury, malnutrition, and social isolation.

Although the specific cause of familial retardation is unknown, it is widely believed to pass genetically from retarded parents to their children. In support of this belief, available research indicates that 50 to 75 percent of the variability among people in IQ test scores can be ascribed to their genetic inheritance. Nevertheless, some researchers argue that children's intelligence is determined more by what they experience than by what they inherit, and that being reared by one or more retarded parents is cause enough for subnormal intelligence. In acknowledging data consistent with this latter point of view, most child specialists consider subnormal intelligence as due neither to biological nor to psychosocial factors alone; instead, it is most likely the interaction between genetic and environmental influences that determines whether and how much a particular child will be retarded.

Preventive mental health action may be *primary* (steps taken to eliminate conditions before they occur), *secondary* (early detection and intervention to limit or reverse an emerging condition), or *tertiary* (treatment of an already manifest condition). The known biological abnormalities that account for about 25 percent of mental retardation provide many possibilities for achieving primary prevention, primarily through good medical care and genetic counseling. The best prospects for secondary prevention appear to lie in preschool programs of environmental enrichment, which have been demonstrated to improve the intellectual functioning of children from socioculturally impoverished backgrounds. However, it is not yet known how long the beneficial effects of early enrichment programs persist once children are no longer receiving special attention.

Tertiary prevention for mildly retarded children proceeds primarily through the schools. For about 50 years in the United States (1920–1970), public schools increasingly acted on the belief that retarded children could be taught best through special-class programs. More recently, advocates of *mainstreaming* have argued that mildly retarded children should be kept in their regular classroom, since segregating them in special classes slows their educational progress, hampers their social development, and subjects them to stigma and rejection. Research evidence appears to document the first of these concerns; on the other hand, there is reason to believe that the special-class environment can help retarded children maintain their self-esteem and learn interpersonal skills while not necessarily stigmatizing them in the eyes of their peers. For these reasons, schools currently tend to meet the needs of retarded children through individually tailored combinations of regular-class and special-class instruction.

Tertiary prevention for moderately and severely retarded children often requires residential care. Those who are severely retarded may need permanent institutionalization, but many moderately retarded youngsters can be helped to return to community-based facilities and should not be institutionalized for custodial care. There is much current interest in *normalization,* which calls for replacing large public institutions for the retarded entirely with smaller, community-based facilities or home care. Research findings to date indicate that good-quality care can be achieved through both large-scale and small-scale approaches, however, and is not ensured by either. As in the case of school problems, then, residential care needs to be planned on an individual basis that provides the best possible fit between an individual child's needs and an available treatment program.

Retarded children and their families are susceptible to numerous psychological problems for which counseling and psychotherapy may be indicated. Retarded children must often struggle with feelings of loneliness and low self-esteem, while their parents frequently tend either to reject or to overprotect them as a way of dealing with their feelings of sadness or guilt at having a handicapped child. Appropriate psychological intervention can help both retarded children and their parents feel better about themselves and find better ways of living together harmoniously.

REFERENCES

ABEL, E. L. Fetal alcohol syndrome: Behavioral teratology. *Psychological Bulletin,* 1980, *87,* 29–50.

ABRAMOWICZ, H. K., & RICHARDSON, S. A. Epidemiology of severe mental retardation in children. Community studies. *American Journal of Mental Deficiency,* 1975, *80,* 18–39.

ADAMS, M. *Mental retardation and its social dimensions.* New York: Columbia University Press, 1971.

ALBEE, G. W., & J. M. JOFFE (Eds.), *Primary prevention of psychopathology.* Vol. 1. *The issues.* Hanover, N.H.: University Press of New England, 1977.

AMERICAN PSYCHIATRIC ASSOCIATION. *Diagnostic and statistical manual of mental disorders.* (3d ed.) Washington, D.C.: American Psychiatric Association, 1980.

ANDERSON, E. M. Special schools or special schooling for the handicapped child? The debate in perspective. *Journal of Child Psychology and Psychiatry,* 1976, *17,* 151–155.

APGAR, V. Drugs in pregnancy. *Journal of the American Medical Association,* 1964, *190,* 840–841.

ASHEM, B., & JANES, M. D. Deleterious effects of chronic under-nutrition on cognitive abilities. *Journal of Child Psychology and Psychiatry,* 1978, *19,* 23–31.

BAHR, S. J., & LEIGH, G. K. Family size, intelligence, and expected education. *Journal of Marriage and the Family,* 1978, *40,* 331–335.

BALLA, D. A., BUTTERFIELD, E. C., & ZIGLER, E. Effects of institutionalization on retarded children: A longitudinal cross-institutional investigation. *American Journal of Mental Deficiency,* 1974, *78,* 530–549.

BALLARD, M., CORMAN, L., GOTTLIEB, J., & KAUFMAN, M. J. Improving the social status of mainstreamed retarded children. *Journal of Educational Psychology,* 1977, *69,* 605–611.

BALLER, W. R., CHARLES, D. C., & MILLER, E. L. Mid-life attainments of the mentally retarded. *Genetic Psychology Monographs,* 1967, *75,* 235–329.

BAROFF, G. S. *Mental retardation: Nature, cause, and management.* Washington, D.C.: Hemisphere, 1974.

BARRY, N. J., & OVERMANN, P. B. Comparison of the effectiveness of adult and peer models with EMR children. *American Journal of Mental Deficiency,* 1977, *82,* 33–36.

BAUMEISTER, A. A., & BUTTERFIELD, E. C. (Eds.) *Residential facilities for the mentally retarded.* Chicago: Aldine, 1970.

BAUMEISTER, A. A., & MUMA, J. R. On defining mental retardation. *Journal of Special Education,* 1975, *9,* 293–306.

BEGAB, M. J. The mentally retarded and society: Trends and issues. In M. J. Begab & S. A. Richardson (Eds.), *The mentally retarded and society.* Baltimore: University Park Press, 1975.

BELMONT, J. M. Medical-behavioral research in mental retardation. In N. R. Ellis (Ed.), *International review of research in mental retardation.* Vol. 5. New York: Academic, 1971.

BELMONT, L., & MAROLLA, F. A. Birth order, family size, and intelligence. *Science,* 1973, *182,* 1096–1101.

BELMONT, L., STEIN, Z. A., & WITTES, J. T. Birth order, family size and school failure. *Developmental Medicine and Child Neurology,* 1976, *18,* 421–430.

BELMONT, L., STEIN, Z., & ZYBERT, P. Child spacing and birth order: Effect on intellectual ability in two-child families. *Science,* 1978, *202,* 995–1006.

BENDA, C. E. *Down's syndrome: Mongolism and its management.* New York: Grune & Stratton, 1969.

BERG, J. M. Genetic counseling considerations in Down's syndrome. In P. Mittler (Ed.), *Research to practice in mental retardation.* Vol. 3. Baltimore, University Park Press, 1977.

BERMAN, J. L., & FORD, R. Intelligence quotients and intelligence loss in patients with phenylketonuria and some variant states. *Journal of Pediatrics,* 1970, *77,* 764–770.

BERMAN, P. W., WAISMAN, H. A., & GRAHAM, F. K. Intelligence in treated phenylketonuric children: A developmental study. *Child Development,* 1966, *37,* 731–747.

BERNSTEIN, N. R. Mental retardation. In J. D. Noshpitz (Ed.), *Basic handbook of child psychiatry.* Vol. III. New York: Basic Books, 1979.

BERRY, H. K. Phenylketonuria: Diagnosis, treatment, and long-term management. In G. Farrell (Ed.), *Congenital mental retardation.* Austin: University of Texas Press, 1969.

BIALER, I. Mental retardation as a diagnostic construct. In I. Bialer & M. Sternlicht (Eds.), *The psychology of mental retardation.* New York: Psychological Dimensions, 1977.

BIRCH, H. G., & GUSSOW, J. D. *Disadvantaged children: Health, nutrition and school failure.* New York: Harcourt, 1970.

BLATT, B. Purgatory. In R. B. Kugel & W. Wolfensberger (Eds.), *Changing patterns in residential services for the mentally retarded.* Washington, D.C.: President's Committee on Mental Retardation, 1969.

BRAGINSKY, D. D., & BRAGINSKY, B. M. *Hansels and Gretels: Studies of children in institutions for the mentally retarded.* New York: Holt, Rinehart & Winston, 1971.

BRONSTON, W. G. Concepts and theory of normalization. In R. Koch & J. C. Dobson (Eds.), *The mentally retarded child and his family.* (Rev. ed.). New York: Brunner/Mazel, 1976.

BROWN, E. S., & WARNER, R. Mental development of phenylketonuric children on or off diet after the age of six. *Psychological Medicine,* 1976, *6,* 287–296.

BROZEK, J. Nutrition, malnutrition, and behavior. *Annual Review of Psychology,* 1978, *29,* 157–177.

BRUININKS, R. H., RYNDERS, J. E., & GROSS, J. C. Social acceptance of mildly retarded pupils in resource rooms and regular classes. *American Journal of Mental Deficiency,* 1974, *78,* 377–383.

BUCHANAN, A., & OLIVER, J. E. Abuse and neglect as a cause of mental retardation: A study of 140 children admitted to subnormality hospitals in Wiltshire. *British Journal of Psychiatry,* 1977, *131,* 458–467.

BUDOFF, M., & GOTTLIEB, J. Special class students mainstreamed: A study of an aptitude (learning potential) x treatment interaction. *American Journal of Mental Deficiency,* 1976, *81,* 1–11.

CALDWELL, B. M. The effects of psychosocial deprivation on human development in infancy. Merrill-Palmer Quarterly, 1970, *16,* 260–277.

CALDWELL, B. M. A decade of early intervention programs: What we have learned. *American Journal of Orthopsychiatry,* 1974, *44,* 491–496.

CAPLAN, G. *Principles of preventive psychiatry.* New York: Basic Books, 1964.

CARR, J. The effect of the severely subnormal on their families. In A. M. Clarke & A. D. B. Clarke (Eds.), *Mental deficiency: The changing outlook.* (3d ed.) New York: Free Press, 1974.

CARR, J. *Young children with Down's syndrome: Their developmental upbringing and effect on their families.* London: Butterworth, 1975.

CARROLL, A. W. The effects of segregated and partially integrated school programs on self-concept and academic achievement of educable mental retardates. *Exceptional Children,* 1967, *34,* 93–99.

CASS, L. K., & THOMAS, C. B. *Childhood pathology and later adjustment.* New York: Wiley, 1979.

CERRETO, M. C., & TUMA, J. M. Distribution of DSM-III diagnosis in a child psychiatric setting. *Journal of Abnormal Child Psychology,* 1977, *5,* 147–155.

CHESS, S. Emotional problems in mentally retarded children. In F. J. Menolascino (Ed.), *Psychiatric approaches to mental retardation.* New York: Basic Books, 1970.

CHESS, S., FERNANDEZ, P., & KORN, S. Behavioral consequences of congenital rubella. *Journal of Pediatrics,* 1978, *93,* 699–703.

CLANCY, H., & MCBRIDE, G. The isolation syndrome in childhood. *Developmental Medicine and Child Neurology,* 1975, *17,* 198–219.

CLARK, E. T. Children's perceptions of educable mentally retarded children. *American Journal of Mental Deficiency,* 1964, *68,* 602–611.

CLARKE, A. D. B., & CLARKE, A. M. Formerly isolated children. In A. M. Clarke & A. D. B. Clarke (Eds.), *Early experience: Myth and evidence.* New York: Free Press, 1977a.

CLARKE, A. D. B., & CLARKE, A. M. Studies in natural settings. In A. M. Clarke & A. D. B. Clarke (Eds.), *Early experience: Myth and evidence.* New York: Free Press, 1977b.

CLARKE, A. M., & CLARKE, A. D. B. Genetic-environmental interactions in cognitive development. In A. M. Clarke & A. D. B. Clarke (Eds.), *Mental deficiency: The changing outlook.* (3d ed.) New York: Free Press, 1974.

COBB, H. *The forecast of fulfillment: A review of research on predictive assessment of the adult retarded for social and vocational adjustment.* New York, Teachers College Press, 1972.

COOK, J. W., & WOLLERSHEIM, J. P. The effects of labeling of special education students on the perception of contact versus noncontact peers. *Journal of Special Education,* 1976, *10,* 187–198.

CORNWELL, A. C. Development of language, abstraction and numerical concept formation in Down's syndrome children. *American Journal of Mental Deficiency,* 1974, *79,* 179–190.

COWEN, E. L., GARDNER, E. A., & ZAX, M. (Eds.) *Emergent approaches to mental health problems.* New York: Appleton-Century-Crofts, 1967.

CUSHNA, B. They'll be happier with their own kind. In G. P. Koocher (Ed.), *Children's rights and the mental health professions.* New York: Wiley, 1976.

CYTRYN, L., & LOURIE, R. S. Mental retardation. In M. A. Freedman, H. I. Kaplan, & B. J. Sadock (Eds.), *Comprehensive textbook of psychiatry.* (3d ed.) Baltimore: Williams & Wilkins, 1980.

DALBY, J. T. Environmental effects on prenatal development. *Journal of Pediatric Psychology,* 1978, *3,* 105–109.

DINGER, J. C. Former educable retarded pupils. *Exceptional Children,* 1961, *27,* 353–360.

DINGMAN, H. F., & TARJAN, G. Mental retardation and the normal distribution curve. *American Journal of Mental Deficiency,* 1960, *64,* 991–994.

DOBSON, J., KOCH, R., WILLIAMSON, M., SPECTOR, R., FRANKENBURG, W., O'FLYNN, M., WARNER, R., & HUDSON, F. Cognitive development and dietary therapy in phenylketonuric children. *New England Journal of Medicine,* 1968, *278,* 1142–1144.

DOBSON, J. C., KUSHIDA, E., WILLIAMSON, M., & FRIEDMAN, E. G. Intellectual performance of 36 phenylketonuria patients and their nonaffected siblings. *Pediatrics,* 1976, *58,* 53–58.

DRILLIEN, C. M. The incidence of mental and physical handicaps in school age children of very low birth weight. II. *Pediatrics,* 1967, *39,* 238–247.

DRILLIEN, C. M. Complications of pregnancy and delivery. In J. Wortis (Ed.), *Mental retardation: An annual review.* Vol. 1. New York: Grune & Stratton, 1970.

DRILLIEN, C. M. Aetiology and outcome in low-birth-weight infants. *Developmental Medicine and Child Neurology,* 1972, *14,* 563–574.

DUNN, L. M. Special education for the mildly retarded—is much of it justified? *Exceptional Children,* 1968, *35,* 5–24.

DWECK, H. S., SAXON, S. A., BENTON, J. W., & CASSADY, G. Early development of the tiny premature infant. *American Journal of Diseases of Childhood,* 1973, *126,* 28–34.

EDGERTON, R. B. *The cloak of competence: Stigma in the lives of the mentally retarded.* Berkeley: University of California Press, 1967.

EDGERTON, R. B. Issues relating to quality of life among mentally retarded persons. In M. J. Begab & S. A. Richardson (Eds.), *The mentally retarded and society.* Baltimore: University Park Press, 1975.

EDGERTON, R. B., & BERCOVICI, S. M. The cloak of competence: Years later. *American Journal of Mental Deficiency,* 1976, *80,* 485–497.

ERLENMEYER-KIMLING, L., & JARVIK, L. F. Genetics and intelligence: A review. *Science,* 1963, *142,* 1477–1479.

EYMAN, R. K., & CALL, T. Maladaptive behavior and community placement of mentally retarded persons. *American Journal of Mental Deficiency,* 1977, *82,* 137–144.

EYMAN, R. K., O'CONNER, G. O., TARJAN, G., & JUSTICE, R. S. Factors determining residential placement of mentally retarded children. *American Journal of Mental Deficiency,* 1972, *76,* 692–698.

FALLENDER, C. A., & HEBER, R. Mother-child interaction and participation in a longitudinal intervention program. *Developmental Psychology,* 1975, *11,* 830–836.

FARBER, B. *Mental retardation: Its social context and social consequences.* Boston: Houghton Mifflin, 1968.

FERHOLT, J. B., & SOLNIT, A. J. Counseling parents of mentally retarded and learning disorder children. In L. E. Arnold (Ed.), *Helping parents help their children.* New York: Brunner/Mazel, 1978.

FITZGIBBON, W. C. Public school programs for the mentally retarded. In A. A. Baumeister (Ed.), *Mental retardation: Appraisal, education, and rehabilitation.* Chicago: Aldine, 1967.

FOLEY, J. M. Effect of labeling and teacher behavior on children's attitudes. *American Journal of Mental Deficiency,* 1979, *83,* 380–384.

GAMPEL, D. H., GOTTLIEB, J., & HARRISON, R. H. Comparison of classroom behavior of special-class EMR, integrated EMR, low IQ, and nonretarded children. *American Journal of Mental Deficiency,* 1974, *79,* 16–21.

GARBER, H. L. Intervention in infancy: A developmental approach. In M. J. Begab & S. A. Richardson (Eds.), *The mentally retarded and society.* Baltimore: University Park Press, 1975.

GARBER, H., & HEBER, F. R. The Milwaukee Project: Indications of the effectiveness of early intervention in preventing mental retardation. In P. Mittler (Ed.), *Research to practice in mental retardation.* Vol. 1, Baltimore: University Park Press, 1977.

GATH, A. The impact of an abnormal child upon the parents. *British Journal of Psychiatry,* 1977, *130,* 405–410.

GERSTEIN, A. I., BRODZINSKY, D. M. & REISKIND, N. Perceptual intergration on the Rorschach as an indicator of cognitive capacity: A developmental study of racial differences in a clinic population. *Journal of Consulting and Clinical Psychology,* 1976, *44,* 760–765.

GIBBS, F. A. Mental retardation following common forms of encephalitis: Electroencephalographic aspects. In H. V. Eichenwald (Ed.), *The prevention of mental retardation through the control of infectious disease.* Washington, D.C.: USPHS Publication No. 1692, 1966.

GIBSON, D. *Down's syndrome: The psychology of mongolism.* London: Cambridge University Press, 1978.

GIRARDEAU, F. L. Cultural-familial retardation. In N. R. Ellis (Ed.), *International review of research in mental retardation.* Vol. 5. New York: Academic, 1971.

GOLDSTEIN, H. The efficacy of special classes and regular classes in the education of educable mentally retarded children. In J. Zubin & G. A. Jervis (Eds.), *Psychopathology of mental development.* New York: Grune & Stratton, 1967.

GOLDSTEIN, K. M., CAPUTO, D. V., & TAUB, H. B. The effects of prenatal and perinatal complications on development at one year of age. *Child Development,* 1976, *47,* 613–621.

GOODMAN, J. F. Medical diagnosis and intelligence levels in young mentally retarded children. *Journal of Mental Deficiency Research,* 1977, *21,* 205–212.

GOTTFRIED, A. W. Intellectual consequences of perinatal anoxia. *Psychological Bulletin,* 1973, *80,* 231–242.

GOTTLIEB, J. Attitudes toward retarded children: Effects of labeling and academic performance. *American Journal of Mental Deficiency,* 1974, *79,* 268–273.

GOTTLIEB, J. Public, peer, and professional attitudes toward mentally retarded persons. In M. J. Begab & S. A. Richardson (Eds.), *The mentally retarded and society.* Baltimore: University Park Press, 1975.

GOTTLIEB, J., GAMPEL, D. H., & BUDOFF, M. Classroom behavior of retarded children before and after integration into regular classes. *Journal of Special Education,* 1975, *9,* 307–315.

GOTTLIEB, J., SEMMEL, M. I., & VELDMAN, D. J. Correlates of social status among mainstreamed mentally retarded children. *Journal of Educational Psychology,* 1978, *70,* 396–405.

GOULD, S. J. Morton's ranking of races by cranial capacity: Unconsciuous manipulation of data may be a scientific norm. *Science,* 1978, *200,* 503–509.

GRALIKER, B. V., KOCH, R., & HENDERSON, R. A. A study of factors influencing placement of retarded children in a state residential institution. *American Journal of Mental Deficiency,* 1965, *69,* 553–559.

GROSSMAN, H. J. (Ed.) *Manual on terminology and classification in mental retardation.* (Rev. ed.) Washington, D.C.: American Association of Mental Deficiency, 1973.

GRUENBERG, E. M. Epidemiology. In H. A. Stevens & R. Heber (Eds.), *Mental retardation: A review of research.* Chicago: University of Chicago Press, 1964.

GUNZBERG, H. C. Psychotherapy. In A. M. Clarke & A. D. B. Clarke (Eds.), *Mental deficiency: The changing outlook.* (3d ed.) New York: Free Press, 1974.

GUSKIN, S. L., BARTEL, N. R., & MACMILLAN, D. L. Perspective on the labeled child. In N. Hobbs (Ed.), *Issues in the classification of children.* Vol. 2. San Francisco: Jossey-Bass, 1975.

GUSKIN, S. L., & SPICKER, H. H. Educational research in mental retardation. In N. R. Ellis (Ed.), *International review of research in mental retardation.* Vol. 3. New York: Academic, 1968.

HALL, J. E., MORRIS, H. L., & BARKER, H. R. Sexual knowledge and attitudes of mentally retarded adolescents. *American Journal of Mental Deficiency,* 1973, *77,* 706–709.

HANSEN, H. Specificity of phenylketonuria screening tests in newborns. In P. Mittler (Ed.), *Research to practice in mental retardation.* Vol. 3. Baltimore: University Park Press, 1977.

HEINTZ, P., & BLACKMAN, L. S. Psychoeducational considerations with the mentally retarded. In I. Bialer & M. Sternlicht (Eds.), *The psychology of mental retardation.* New York: Psychological Dimensions, 1977.

HERON, T. E. Maintaining the mainstreamed child in the regular classroom: The decision making process. *Journal of Learning Disabilities,* 1978, *11,* 210–216.

HERRNSTEIN, R. J. *IQ in the meritocracy.* Boston: Little, Brown, 1973.

HERTZIG, M. E., BIRCH, H. G., RICHARDSON, S. A., & TIZARD, J. Intellectual level of school children severely malnourished during the first two years of life. *Pediatrics,* 1972, *49,* 814–824.

HOBBS, M. T. A comparison of institutionalized and non-institutionalized mentally retarded. *American Journal of Mental Deficiency,* 1964, *69,* 206–210.

HOBBS, N. *The futures of children.* San Francisco: Jossey-Bass, 1975.

HOHMAN, L. B., & FREEDHEIM, D. K. Further studies on intelligence levels in cerebral palsy children. *American Journal of Physical Medicine,* 1958, *37,* 90–97.

HOLDEN, C. Identical twins reared apart. *Science,* 1980, *207,* 1323–1328.

HOLTZMAN, N. A., WELCHER, D. W., & MELLITS, E. D. Termination of restricted diet in children with phenylketonuria: A randomized controlled study. *New England Journal of Medicine,* 1975, *293,* 1121–1124.

HOROWTIZ, F. D., & PADEN, L. Y. The effectiveness of environmental intervention programs. In B. M. Caldwell & H. N. Ricciuti (Eds.), *Review of child development research.* Vol. 3. Chicago: University of Chicago Press, 1973.

HUBERTY, T. J., KOLLER, J. R., & TEN BRINK, T. D. Adaptive behavior in the definition of mental retardation. *Exceptional Children,* 1980, *46,* 256–261.

INGALLS, R. P. *Mental retardation: The changing outlook.* New York: Wiley, 1978.

JANCAR, J. Psychiatric aspects of mental retardation. In P. Mittler (Ed.), *Research to practice in mental retardation*. Vol. 1. Baltimore: University Park Press, 1977.

JASON, L. A., DEAMICUS, L., & CARTER, B. Preventive intervention programs for disadvantaged children. *Community Mental Health Journal*, 1978, *14*, 272–278.

JENSEN, A. R. A theory of primary and secondary familial mental retardation. In N. R. Ellis (Ed.), *International review of research in mental retardation*. Vol. 4. New York: Academic, 1970.

JOHNSON, C. A., AHERN, F. M., & JOHNSON, R. C. Level of functioning of siblings and parents of probands of varying degrees of retardation. *Behavior Genetics*, 1976, *6*, 473–477.

JONES, R. L. Labels and stigma in special education. *Exceptional Children*, 1972, *38*, 553–564.

KAMIN, L. J. *The science and politics of IQ*. New York: Erlbaum, 1974.

KEHLE, T. J., & GUIDUBALDI, J. Effect of EMR placement models on affective and social development. *Psychology in the Schools*, 1978, *15*, 275–282.

KNOX, W. E. Phenylketonuria. In J. B. Stanbury, J. B. Wyngaarden, & D. S. Frederickson (Eds.), *The metabolic basis of inherited disease*. New York: McGraw-Hill, 1972.

KOCH, R. Prenatal factors in causation (general). In R. Koch & J. C. Dobson (Eds.), *The mentally retarded child and his family*. (Rev. ed.) New York: Brunner/Mazel, 1976.

KOCH, R., & DE LA CRUZ, F. F. (Eds.) *Down's syndrome*. New York: Brunner/Mazel, 1975.

KOHEN-RAZ, R. Special education needs at adolescence. In S. C. Feinstein & P. Giovacchini (Eds.), *Adolescent psychiatry*. Vol. 5. New York: Aronson, 1977.

KOLUCHOVA, J. The further development of twins after severe and prolonged deprivation: A second part. *Journal of Child Psychology and Psychiatry*, 1976, *17*, 181–188.

KOPP, C. B., & PARMELEE, A. H. Prenatal and perinatal influences on infant behavior. In J. D. Osofsky (Eds.), *Handbook of infant development*. New York: Wiley, 1979.

KRUGMAN, S. Present status of measles and rubella immunization in the United States: A medical progress report. *Journal of Pediatrics*, 1977, *90*, 1–12.

LANGMEIER, J., & MATEJCEK, Z. *Psychological deprivation in childhood*. New York: Wiley, 1975.

LAVIETES, R. Mental retardation: Psychological treatment. In B. B. Wolman (Ed.), *Handbook of treatment of mental disorders in childhood and adolescence*. Englewood Cliffs, N.J.: Prentice-Hall, 1978.

LEMKAU, P. V., & IMRE, D. P. Results of a field epidemiologic study. *American Journal of Mental Deficiency*, 1969, *73*, 858–863.

LLOYD-STILL, J. D. (Ed.) *Malnutrition and infant development*. Littleton, Mass.: Publishing Sciences Group, 1976.

LODGE, A., & KLEINFELD, P. B. Early behavioral development in Down's syndrome. In M. Coleman (Ed.), *Serotonin in Down's syndrome*. London: North-Holland, 1973.

LOEHLIN, J. C., LINDZEY, G., & SPUHLER, J. N. *Race differences in intelligence*. San Francisco: Freeman, 1975.

MCDANIELS, G. Mainstreaming—not exactly new. *APA Monitor*, May 1978, 4.

MCKAY, H., SINISTERRA, L., MCKAY, A., GOMEZ, H., & LLOREDA, P. Improving cognitive ability in chronically deprived children. *Science*, 1978, *200*, 270–278.

MACMILLAN, D. L., JONES, R. L., & ALOIA, G. F. The mentally retarded label: A theoretical analysis and review of research. *American Journal of Mental Deficiency*, 1974, *79*, 241–261.

MACMILLAN, D. L., JONES, R. L., & MEYERS, C. E. Mainstreaming the mildly retarded: Some questions, cautions and guidelines. *Mental Retardation*, 1976, *14*, 3–10.

MENOLASCINO, F. J. Psychiatric aspects of retardation in young children. In R. Koch & J. C. Dobson (Eds.), *The mentally retarded child and his family*. (Rev. ed.) New York: Brunner/Mazel, 1976.

MENOLASCINO, F. J. Changing developmental perspectives in Down's syndrome. *Child Psychiatry and Human Development*, 1974, *4*, 205–215.

MERCER, J. R. *Labelling the mentally retarded*. Berkeley: University of California Press, 1973a.

MERCER, J. R. The myth of 3% prevalence. In G. Tarjan, R. K. Eyman, & C. E. Meyers (Eds.), *Sociobehavioral studies in mental retardation.* American Association on Mental Deficiency Monograph, 1973b (No. 1).

METZ, A. S. *Number of pupils with handicaps in local public schools, Spring, 1970.* DHEW Publication No. (OE) 73-11107. Washington, D.C.: National Center for Educational Statistics, 1973.

MEYEN, E. L., & HIERONYMUS, A. N. The age placement of academic skills in curriculum for the EMR. *Exceptional Children,* 1970, *36,* 333–339.

MEYERS, C. E., MACMILLAN, D. L., & YOSHIDA, R. K. Regular class placement of EMR students, from efficacy to mainstreaming: A review of issues and research. In J. Gottlieb (Ed.), *Educating mentally retarded persons in the mainstream.* Baltimore: University Park Press, in press.

MILUNSKY, A. Prenatal diagnosis of genetic disorders. *New England Journal of Medicine,* 1976, *295,* 377–380.

MOLNAR, G. E., & TAFT, L. T. Cerebral palsy. In J. Wortis (Ed.), *Mental retardation and developmental disabilities: An annual review.* Vol. V. New York: Brunner/Mazel, 1973.

MORACZEWSKI, A. S. Ethical aspects of genetic counseling. In M. A. Sperber & L. F. Jarvik (Eds.), *Psychiatry and genetics: Psychosocial, ethical, and legal considerations.* New York: Basic Books, 1976.

MORGAN, H. S., & KANE, S. H. An analysis of 16,327 breech births. *Journal of the American Medical Association,* 1964, *187,* 262–264.

MOXLEY, R. T. Cerebral palsy. In R. A. Hoekelman (Ed.), *Principles of pediatrics.* New York: McGraw-Hill, 1978.

MULLER, P. F., CAMPBELL, H. E., GRAHAM, W. E., BRITTAIN, H., FITZGERALD, J. A., HOGAN, N. A., MULLER, V. H., & RITTERHOUSE, A. H. Perinatal factors and their relationship to mental retardation and other parameters of development. *American Journal of Obstetrics and Gynecology,* 1971, *109,* 1205–1210.

MUNSINGER, H. The adopted child's I.Q.: A critical review. *Psychological Bulletin,* 1975, *82,* 623–659.

NATIONAL INSTITUTE OF MENTAL HEALTH. *Additions and resident patients at end of year, state and county mental hospitals, by age and diagnosis, by state, United States, 1976.* Rockville, Md.: NIMH Division of Biometry and Epidemiology, 1978.

NEEDLEMAN, H. L. Low level lead exposure and neuropsychologic function: Current status and future directions. In P. Mittler (Ed.) *Research to practice in mental retardation.* Vol. 3. Baltimore: University Park Press, 1977.

OFFICE OF MENTAL RETARDATION COORDINATION. *Mental retardation sourcebook.* Washington, D.C.: U.S. Department of Health, Education, and Welfare, 1972.

OMENN, B. S. Prenatal diagnosis of genetic disorders. *Science,* 1978, *200,* 952–958.

PERKINS, S. A. Malnutrition and mental development. *Exceptional Children,* 1977, *43,* 214–219.

PHILIPS, I., & WILLIAMS, N. Psychopathology and mental retardation: A study of 100 mentally retarded children. I. Psychopathology. *American Journal of Psychiatry,* 1975, *132,* 1265–1271.

POLLITT, E., EICHLER, A. W., & CHAN, C. Psychosocial development and behavior of mothers of failure-to-thrive children. *American Journal of Orthopsychiatry,* 1975, *45,* 525–537.

POWELL, G. F., BRASEL, J. A., & BLIZZARD, R. M. Emotional deprivation and growth retardation. *New England Journal of Medicine,* 1967, *276,* 1271–1283.

PRESIDENT'S COMMITTEE ON MENTAL RETARDATION. *Residential services for the mentally retarded.* Washington, D.C.: U.S. Government Printing Office, 1970.

RAINER, J. D. Genetics of intelligence: Current issues and unsolved questions. *Research Communications in Psychology, Psychiatry and Behavior,* 1976, *1,* 607–618.

RENZ, P., & SIMENSEN, R. J. The social perception of normals toward their EMR grade-mates. *American Journal of Mental Deficiency,* 1969, *74,* 405–408.

RESCHLY, D. J., & JIPSON, F. J. Ethnicity, geographic locale, age, sex, and urban-rural residence as variables in the prevalence of mild retardation. *American Journal of Mental Deficiency,* 1976, *81,* 154–161.

RICHARDSON, S. A. Malnutrition and mental development: An ecological perspective. In P. Mittler (Ed.), *Research to practice in mental retardation.* Vol. 3. Baltimore: University Park Press, 1977.

ROBINSON, H. B., & ROBINSON, N. Mental retardation. In P. H. Mussen (Ed.), *Carmichael's manual of child psychology.* (3d ed.) Vol. 2. New York: Wiley, 1970.

ROBINSON, N. M., & ROBINSON, H. B. *The mentally retarded child.* (2nd ed.) New York: McGraw-Hill, 1976.

ROHR, A., & BURR, D. B. Etiological differences in patterns of psycholinguistic development of children of IQ 30 to 60. *American Journal of Mental Deficiency,* 1978. *82,* 549–553.

ROSENHIEM, H. D., & ABLES, B. S. Social deprivation and "mental retardation." *Child Psychiatry and Human Development,* 1974, *4,* 216–226.

ROSETT, H. L., & SANDER, L. W. Effects of maternal drinking on neonatal morphology and state regulation. In J. D. Osofsky (Ed.), *Handbook of infant development.* New York: Wiley, 1979.

ROUTH, D. K., MUSHAK, P., & BOONE, L. A new syndrome of elevated blood lead and microcephaly. *Journal of Pediatric Psychology,* 1979, *4,* 67–76.

RUBIN, R. A., ROSENBLATT, C., & BALOW, B. Psychological and educational sequelae of prematurity. *Pediatrics,* 1973, *52,* 352–363.

RUTTER, M. *The qualities of mothering; Maternal deprivation reassessed.* New York: Aronson, 1974.

SABAGH, G., DINGMAN, H. F., TARJAN, G., & WRIGHT, S. W. Social class and ethnic status of patients admitted to a state hospital for the retarded. *Pacific Sociological Review,* 1959, *2,* 76–80.

SAMEROFF, A. J. Caretaking or reproductive causality? Determinants in developmental deviance. In F. D. Horowitz (Ed.), *Early developmental hazards: Predictors and precautions.* Boulder, Col.: Westview, 1978.

SAMEROFF, A. J., & CHANDLER, M. J. Reproductive risk and the continuum of caretaking causality. In F. D. Horowitz (Ed.), *Review of child development research.* Vol. 4. Chicago: University of Chicago Press, 1975.

SARASON, S. B., & DORIS, J. *Educational handicap, public policy, and social history: A broadened perspective on mental retardation.* New York: Free Press, 1979.

SCARR, S., & WEINBERG, R. A. Intellectual similarities within families of both adopted and biological children. *Intelligence,* 1977, *1,* 170–191.

SCARR-SALAPATEK, S. Genetics and the development of intelligence. In F. D. Horowitz (Ed.), *Review of child development research.* Vol. 4. Chicago: University of Chicago Press, 1975.

SCARR-SALAPATEK, S., & WEINBERG, R. A. I.Q. performance of black children adopted by white families. *American Psychologist,* 1976, *31,* 726–739.

SCHEERENBERGER, R. C. Mental retardation: Definition, classification, and prevalence. *Mental Retardation Abstracts,* 1964, *1,* 432–441.

SCHEERENBERGER, R. C. *Current trends and status of public residential services for the mentally retarded: 1974.* Madison, Wisc.: National Association of Superintendents of Public Residential Facilities, 1975.

SCHEERENBERGER, R. C., & FELSENTHAL, D. Community settings for MR persons: Satisfaction and activities. *Mental Retardation,* 1977, *15,* 3–7.

SCHIFF, M., DUYME, M., DUMARET, A., STEWART, J., TOMKIEWICZ, S., & FEINGOLD, J. Intellectual status of working-class children adopted early into upper-middle-class families. *Science,* 1978, *200,* 1503–1504.

SCHILD, S. The family of the retarded child. In R. Koch & J. C. Dobson (Eds.), *The mentally retarded child and his family.* (Rev. ed.) New York: Brunner/Mazel, 1976.

SCHONEBAUM, R. M., & ZINOBER, J. W. Learning and memory in mental retardation: The defect-developmental distinction re-evaluated. In I. Bialer & M. Sternlicht (Eds.), *The psychology of mental retardation.* New York: Psychological Dimensions, 1977.

SELLS, C. J., & BENNETT, F. C. Prevention of mental retardation: The role of medicine. *American Journal of Mental Deficiency,* 1977, *82,* 117–129.

SELLS, C. J., CARPENTER, R. L., & RAY, C. G. Sequelae of central nervous system enterovirus infections. *New England Journal of Medicine,* 1975, *293,* 1–4.

SEVER, J. L., NELSON, K. B., & GILKESON, M. R. Rubella epidemic, 1964: Effect on 6000 pregnancies. *American Journal of Diseases of Children,* 1965, *110,* 395–407.

SKELLS, H. M. Adult status of children with contrasting early life experiences. *Monographs of the Society for Research in Child Development,* 1966, *31,* No. 3.

SKEELS, H. M., & DYE, H. A study of the effects of differential stimulation on mentally retarded children. *Proceedings of the American Association on Mental Deficiency,* 1939, *44,* 114–136.

SMITH, O. W., & WILSON, A. A. *The child with Down's syndrome (mongolism).* Philadelphia: Saunders, 1973.

SMITH, E., MCKINNON, R., & KESSLER, J. W. Psychotherapy with mentally retarded children. *Psychoanalytic Study of the Child,* 1976, *31,* 493–514.

STANTON, J. E., & CASSADY, V. M. Effectiveness of special classes for educable mentally retarded. *Mental Retardation,* 1964, *2,* 8–13.

STEIN, Z. A., & SUSSER, M. Recent trends in Down's syndrome. In P. Mittler (Ed.), *Research to practice in mental retardation.* Vol. 3. Baltimore: University Park Press, 1977.

STEPHEN, E., & HAWKS, G. Cerebral palsy and mental subnormality. In A. M. Clarke & A. D. B. Clarke (Eds.), *Mental deficiency: The changing outlook.* (3d ed.) New York: Free Press, 1974.

STERNLICHT, M. Issues in counseling and psychotherapy with mentally retarded individuals. In I. Bialer & M. Sternlicht (Eds.), *Psychology of mental retardation.* New York: Psychological Dimensions, 1977.

STERNLICHT, M., & BIALER, I. Psychological aspects of institutionalization in mental retardation. In I. Bialer & M. Sternlicht (Eds.), *The psychology of mental retardation.* New York: Psychological Dimensions, 1977.

STREISSGUTH, A. P. Maternal drinking and the outcome of pregnancy: Implications for child mental health. *American Journal of Orthopsychiatry,* 1977, *47,* 422–431.

STREISSGUTH, A. P., LANDESMAN-DWYER, S., MARTIN, J. C., & SMITH, D. W. Teratogenic effects of alcohol in humans and laboratory animals. *Science,* 1980, *209,* 353–361.

SUEDFIELD, P. *Restricted environmental stimulation.* New York: Wiley, 1980.

SUSSER, M., STEIN, Z. Z., & RUCH, D. Prenatal nutrition and subsequent development. In P. Mittler (Ed.), *Research to practice in mental retardation.* Vol. 3. Baltimore: University Park Press, 1977.

SUTHERLAND, B. S., UMBARGER, B., & BERRY, H. K. The treatment of phenylketonuria. *American Journal of Diseases of Children,* 1966, *111,* 505–523.

SWITZKY, H. N., & GAYLORD-ROSS, R. J. Behavioral genetics and mental retardation. In I. Bialer & M. Sternlicht (Eds.), *The psychology of mental retardation.* New York: Psychological Dimensions, 1977.

TARJAN, G., WRIGHT, S. W., EYMAN, R. K., & KEERAN, C. V. Natural history of mental retardation: Some aspects of epidemiology. *American Journal of Mental Deficiency,* 1973, *77,* 369–379.

THOMPSON, R. J. Effects of maternal alcohol consumption on offspring: Review, critical assessment, and future directions. *Journal of Pediatric Psychology,* 1979, *4,* 265–276.

THURMAN, S. K., & THIELE, R. L. A viable role for retardation institutions: The road to self-destruction. *Mental Retardation,* 1973, *11,* 21–23.

TOWBIN, A. Central nervous system damage in the human fetus and newborn infant: Mechanical and hypoxic injury, incurred in the fetal-neonatal period. *American Journal of Diseases of Children,* 1970, *119,* 529–542.

TOWBIN, A. Cerebral dysfunctions related to perinatal organic damage. *Journal of Abnormal Psychology,* 1978, *87,* 617–635.

UCHIDA, I. A., HOLUNGA, R., & LAWLER, C. Maternal radiation and chromosomal aberrations. *Lancet,* 1968, *2,* 1045–1049.

VERNON, P. E. *Intelligence: Heredity and environment.* San Francisco: Freeman, 1979.

WAISBREN, S. E. Parents' reactions after the birth of a developmentally diabled child. *American Journal of Mental Deficiency,* 1980, *84,* 345–351.

WARREN, N. Malnutrition and mental development. *Psychological Bulletin,* 1973, *80,* 314–328.

WATSON, L. S. Issues in behavior modification of the mentally retarded individual. In I. Bialer & M. Sternlicht (Eds.), *Psychology of mental retardation.* New York: Psychological Dimensions, 1977.

WETHERBY, B., & BAUMEISTER, A. A. Mental retardation. In S. M. Turner, K. S. Calhoun, & H. E. Adams (Eds.), *Handbook of clinical behavior therapy.* New York: Wiley, 1981.

WERNER, E. E., & SMITH, R. S. An epidemiological perspective on some antecedents and consequences of childhood mental health problems and learning disabilities. *Journal of the American Academy of Child Psychiatry,* 1979, *18,* 292–306.

WINICK, M. *Malnutrition and brain development.* New York: Oxford University Press, 1976.

WINICK, M., & BRASEL, J. A. Early malnutrition and subsequent brain development. In N. H. Moss & J. Mayer (Eds.), *Food and nutrition in health and disease.* New York: New York Academy of Sciences, 1977.

WOLFENSBERGER, W. Will there always be an institution? II. The impact of new service models—residential alternatives to institutions. *Mental Retardation,* 1971, *9,* 31–37.

WOOD, J. W., JOHNSON, K. G., & OMORI, Y. In utero exposure to the Hiroshima atomic bomb: An evaluation of head size and mental retardation twenty years later. *Pediatrics,* 1967, *39,* 385–392.

WORK, H. H. Mental retardation. In J. D. Noshpitz (Ed.), *Basic handbook of child psychiatry.* Vol. II. New York: Basic Books, 1979.

YANNET, H. Classification and etiological factors in mental retardation. *Journal of Pediatrics,* 1957, *50,* 226–230.

YOELI, M., SCHEINSESSON, G. P., & HARGREAVES, B. J. Infectious diseases in etiology. In J. Wortis (Ed.), *Mental retardation and developmental disabilities: An annual review.* Vol. IX. New York: Brunner-Mazel, 1977.

ZAJONC, R. B., & MARKUS, G. B. Birth order and intellectual development. *Psychological Bulletin,* 1975, *82,* 74–88.

ZIGLER, E. Familial mental retardation: A continuing dilemma. *Science,* 1967, *155,* 292–298.

ZIGLER, E. Developmental versus difference theories of mental retardation and the problem of motivation. *American Journal of Mental Deficiency,* 1969, *73,* 536–556.

ZIGLER, E. The retarded child as a whole person. In D. K. Routh (Ed.), *The experimental psychology of mental retardation.* Chicago: Aldine, 1973.

ZIGLER, E. National crisis in mental retardation research. *American Journal of Mental Deficiency,* 1978, *83,* 1–8.

ZIGLER, E., & BALLA, D. Motivational aspects of mental retardation. In R. Koch & J. C. Dobson (Eds.), *The mentally retarded child and his family.* (Rev. ed.) New York: Brunner/Mazel, 1976.

ZIGLER, E., & MUENCHOW, S. Mainstreaming: The proof is in the implementation. *American Psychologist,* 1979, *34,* 993–996.

ZIGLER, E., & TRICKETT, P. K. IQ, social competence, and evaluation of early childhood intervention programs. *American Psychologist,* 1978, *33,* 789–798.

MINIMAL BRAIN DYSFUNCTION, ATTENTION DEFICIT DISORDER, AND LEARNING DISABILITY

TREATMENT OF MBD/ADD

Drugs

The Utility of Stimulant Medication
Concerns About Stimulant Medication

Psychological Intervention

Operant Conditioning
Verbal Mediation
Modeling

Educational Planning

Distraction-Free Versus Normally Stimulating Environments
Skill Training Versus Task Training
Regular Versus Special Classroom

Parent Counseling

SUMMARY

REFERENCES

On rating scales developed by Conners (1969, 1970), parents and teachers are asked to indicate how frequently children show the following 10 behaviors.

1. Restless or overactive, excitable, impulsive.
2. Disturbs other children.
3. Fails to finish things started.
4. Short attention span.
5. Constantly fidgeting.
6. Inattentive, easily distracted.
7. Demands must be met immediately, easily frustrated.
8. Cries often and easily.
9. Mood changes quickly and dramatically.
10. Temper outbursts, explosive and unpredictable behavior.

Children who exhibit most of these behaviors much of the time are widely agreed to have a discrete disorder with certain typical symptoms, a likely developmental course, some possible causes, and fairly predictable responses to various treatment approaches. Some writers have argued that there is no such disorder—that it is a myth created by parents and teachers to excuse their poor handling of difficult children or by drug companies to create a market for their products (Schrag & Divoky, 1975). Yet most people can identify relatives or acquaintances who probably suffered as children from some combination of the problem behaviors listed—in a very real and nonmythical way. Moreover, cases of children handicapped by this condition have been described in the literature for over 100 years, and extensive clinical and research data have been collected on it (Kessler, 1980; Klein & Young, 1979; Loney, 1980; Weiss & Hechtman, 1979).

It is consequently not difficult to maintain that the disorder measured by Conners's scales exists and to describe what is known about it. However, it is very difficult to decide what to call it. A continuing controversy over how to label this condition can be traced to the term **minimal brain dysfunction** (MBD), which was coined for it in 1966. MBD is usually defined as a disorder of behavioral and perceptual-cognitive functioning that is assumed to involve some impairment of the central nervous system. This term evolved over many years as a seemingly appropriate diagnostic label for children who have no detectable organic pathology but nevertheless display many of the functioning difficulties seen in people with known brain damage, including those covered by the Conners items (Clements, 1966; Gross & Wilson, 1974; Wender, 1971).

Numerous clinicians and researchers have objected to MBD as a diagnostic label, especially on the grounds that it implies brain damage when in fact no such damage can be demonstrated. Concern has also been raised that MBD is a difficult concept to explain to parents and conveys an inaccurate and unnecessarily frightening sense of their child's difficulties being irreversible (Kauffman & Hallahan, 1979; Satz & Fletcher,

1980; Saunders, 1979). A popular alternative is to label this condition not in terms of an inferential concept, such as MBD, but instead with behavioral terms that refer to some of its frequent characteristics.

For example, because the condition to be described in this chapter often involves a heightened level of activity, some writers prefer to call it **hyperactive child syndrome** (HACS) (Cantwell, 1975a; Weiss & Hechtman, 1979). As another example, because children with this condition are often found to be highly distractible, DSM-III refers to it as **attention deficit disorder** (ADD) (American Psychiatric Association, 1980). Significantly, however, those who write about HACS and ADD generally refer to the same deviant behavior patterns as those who speak of MBD, which means that these terms are essentially synonymous as descriptive diagnoses.

There are also child specialists who prefer to speak simply of hyperactive or distractible children and to avoid any diagnostic label that implies an underlying syndrome responsible for the heightened activity level or short attention span (Ross & Ross, 1976; Safer & Allen, 1976). In support of this position, some writers argue that whatever is measured by the Conners scales is either just a normal variation of being a highly active or temperamentally "difficult" child, or a reflection of immaturity or developmental lag (Carey, McDevitt, & Baker, 1979; Illingworth, 1980; Quay, 1979).

As already noted and will be elaborated further, however, there is considerable evidence that common abnormal threads run through the lives of children with this condition and can be distinguished from normal developmental variations or maturational lags. Furthermore, despite the fact that brain dysfunction cannot yet be proved to underlie this disorder, no purely psychological causes for it have been found. Accordingly, belief that it is constitutional in origin remains widespread, as does the use of the term *MBD* to refer to it. Indeed, some authors argue that MBD should continue to be preferred over HACS or ADD, since the latter two address only particular symptoms of the disorder that are not present in all cases (Conners, 1975a; Gardner, 1979; Silver, 1979).

At the same time, much of the best research on this condition is addressed to problems of activity level and attention span, and the inclusion of ADD in the official psychiatric classification scheme means that it will become widely used in clinical settings. Any definitive choice among these terms touches on the broader issue of behavioral and inferential approaches to classification discussed in Chapter 2 and cannot be resolved here. Instead, to promote communication across points of view, the discussion in this chapter will simply refer to the "MBD/ADD" condition.

The other subject of this chapter is **learning disability** (LD). As most commonly used, LD refers to some deficit in essential learning processes that causes children to achieve below expectation in school in the absence of any general intellectual deficit, emotional handicap, or inadequate opportunity to learn. Some writers use LD interchangeably with MBD, arguing that the two are synonymous (Cruickshank, 1977a, Chapter 1; Schroeder, Schroeder, & Davine, 1978). This practice should probably be avoided, however. LD can more usefully be viewed as one of the possible consequences of the cognitive and behavioral impairments associated with MBD/ADD and its most common consequence during the school-age years. Yet not all MBD/ADD children develop school learning difficulties, and MBD/ADD is thus a broader, more inclusive term than LD (Lahey, Stempniak, Robinson, & Tyroler, 1978; Lambert & Sandoval, 1980).

LD should likewise not be used to describe all children whose performance in school falls below their apparent capacity. Children underachieve for many different reasons. As discussed in Chapter 10, physical illness and psychological disorder of various kinds can contribute indirectly to school failure, and certain sociocultural attitudes and family interaction patterns often lead directly to underachievement. To distinguish these types of school difficulty from a learning disability, most authorities in the field urge limiting the LD label to children who have school learning problems attributable to the particular types of impairment that characterize MBD/ADD (Cruickshank, 1977b; Kinsbourne & Caplan, 1979; McCarthy & McCarthy, 1969; Ross, 1976).

The first two sections of this chapter are concerned with the prevalence of MBD/ADD and the nature of its primary manifestations. The third section describes the course and consequences of this disorder from infancy into adulthood, with particular attention to learning disability. The final two sections of the chapter discuss possible causes of MBD/ADD and alternative approaches to treating it.

PREVALENCE OF MBD/ADD

Surveys indicate that 5 to 6 percent of school-age children are considered by their parents, teachers, or family doctor to demonstrate MBD/ADD. When very strict criteria are used for the diagnosis, such as a consensus among parents, teachers, and physicians that its symptoms are present, the prevalence rates fall to 1 to 3 percent of kindergarten through ninth-graders in various studies (L. Belmont, 1980; Bosco & Robin, 1979; Lambert, Sandoval, & Sassone, 1978). Depending on how strictly MBD/ADD is defined, then, it affects possibly as many as 2.5 million 5- to 14-year-olds in the United States, and 1 child in every 20-child classroom.

For reasons that are not yet clear, MBD/ADD is three to seven times more common in boys than girls (L. Belmont, 1980; Campbell & Redfering, 1979; Miller, Palkes, & Stewart, 1973; Rutter, Tizard, & Whitmore, 1970). Further research is necessary to determine whether this sex difference results from some specific sex-linked determinant of MBD/ADD from a generally greater susceptibility among boys than girls to nervous system dysfunction, or from some other as yet unsuspected source.

MBD/ADD is usually present from birth or soon afterward. Like mental retardation, however, it is often not identified until middle childhood, when the academic and social demands of being in school bring an MBD/ADD child's limitations into sharper focus than before. Nevertheless, it is during the preschool years that the primary manifestations of the disorder first become apparent to the sensitive observer, and increasing research attention is accordingly being paid to the developmental course of MBD/ADD in early childhood as well as to its striking manifestations during the school years (Campbell, 1976; Cantwell, 1975a; Safer & Allen, 1976). In addition, books addressed to parents have expanded public awareness of indications of MBD/ADD among 2- to 5-year olds (Gardner, 1973a; Stewart & Olds, 1973; Walker, 1977).

PRIMARY MANIFESTATIONS OF MBD/ADD

MBD/ADD consists of several distinctive behavioral and perceptual-cognitive impairments (its *primary* manifestations) that lead to various academic, social, and emotional difficulties (its *secondary* manifestations). This section discusses the primary manifestations of MBD/ADD; its secondary manifestations will be considered in the following section on the course and consequences of this disorder.

Behavioral Impairments

The chief behavioral characteristics of MBD/ADD are *hyperactivity, distractibility, impulsivity,* and *excitability.* Each MBD/ADD child does not necessarily show all of these characteristics, nor do all MBD/ADD children show them to the same extent or in the same specific way. However, some combination of these behavior patterns usually indicates the presence of the disorder (Cantwell, 1975a; Denton & McIntyre, 1978; Douglas, 1972; Loney, Langhorne, & Paternite, 1978; Rosenthal & Allen, 1978; Wender, 1971, Chapter 1).

Most common are problems in controlling and coordinating motor activity. MBD/ADD children tend to be constantly on the go. There is a driven quality to their behavior that makes them restless, fidgety, and constantly at risk for bumping into people and objects as they dash from one place to the next. They almost always appear tense and keyed-up. Even when they sleep, which is less often than other children their age, they are fitful and unable to relax. In addition to being hyperactive in these ways, many MBD/ADD children are awkward and clumsy in their gross motor movements and slow in learning to sit up, stand, walk, skip, run, rollerskate, and ride a bicycle.

As a reflection of their distractibility, MBD/ADD children frequently have a short attention span and limited ability to concentrate. No person, project, game, television program, or other diversion can occupy them more than momentarily, and keeping them entertained or at work on a task tries the patience of even the most accepting and easygoing parents and teachers.

Because of their impulsivity and excitability, these youngsters have a low tolerance for frustration and little self-control. They overreact to stimulation, and they show rapid, unpredictable changes in mood. They are quick to anger, negativism, and aggressive outbursts. At the slightest provocation they may throw a violent temper tantrum or burst into tears, and they may alternate tantrums and tears with silly giggling or uproarious laughter, all in rapid succession and out of proportion to the circumstances.

Each of these primary behavioral manifestations of MBD/ADD is to some extent normal in young children. Especially among preschoolers, it is often difficult to determine just how much overactivity, distractibility, impulsivity, and excitability reflect abnormal rather than normal development—which is one of the reasons why MBD/ADD is often not identified until the school years. Many of these behaviors persist normally even into middle childhood, although they do become less frequent between ages 6 to 12 as children mature in their capacities for self-regulation and self-control (Abikoff, Gittelman, & Klein, 1980; Rosenthal & Allen, 1978; Stewart, 1976).

Special care must be taken to avoid either diagnosing MBD/ADD on the basis of

The overactivity and distractibility of many MBD/ADD children make them difficult for parents and teachers to handle.

behavior that is normal for a child of a particular age or failing to diagnose it because of a mistaken impression that observed behavior problems fall within the normal range. The best way to avoid either error is to pay close attention to normative data on expected behavior at different ages. Although fully adequate norms for this purpose are not yet available, researchers are currently working with various behavior rating scales to develop them (Gardner, 1979; Sandoval, 1977; Zukow, Zukow, & Bentler, 1978). Table 4.1 lists the items used in one of these scales and provides a useful summary of the behavioral manifestations of MBD/ADD.

Perceptual-Cognitive Impairments

MBD/ADD children are often impaired in their spatial perception, visual-motor coordination, memory, hearing, and speech. They have difficulty learning right from left and

TABLE 4.1 Items on the Hyperactivity Rating Scale

Restlessness
  Twists and turns in seat when should be sitting still
  Shifts position of hands and feet when should be still
  Squirms in seat, taps foot or fingers

Distractibility
  Has difficulty concentrating
  Doesn't finish work because other things capture attention
  Distracted by minimal stimulation

Work fluctuation
  Sometimes work is carefully done, other times carelessly
  Shows strong ups and downs in work performance
  Starts work with concentration, then becomes distracted

Impulsivity
  Shows little restraint when wishes to speak or act
  Talks first, thinks later
  Acts on the spur of the moment

Excitability
  Appears to be tense
  Startles easily
  Excited or agitated by changes in things around him

Low perseverance[a]
  Sticks to tasks until finished

If one effort to do a job is unsuccessful, will try again
  Tries hard at assignments, doesn't give up easily

Negativism
  Sulks if criticized
  Can't bear criticism, gets touchy or ill-tempered
  Gets angry when others disagree with his opinions

Poor coordination
  Has difficulty with delicate manual tasks
  Clumsy in handling small objects
  Handwriting difficult to read

Fatigue
  Looks sleepy or has blank expression
  Seems tired, not alert
  Functioning impaired by fatigue or sleepiness

Rapid tempo
  Talks rapidly
  Does things quickly
  Walks fast

Social withdrawal[a]
  Seeks out others to play or join in group
  Joins a group on his own during free time or games
  Spontaneously talks about what he likes or has been doing

[a] Low ratings on items in this category are associated with hyperactivity; for other categories, hyperactivity is indicated by high item ratings.
Source. From Spring, Blunden, Greenberg, and Yellin (1977). Reprinted by permission of Buttonwood Farms, Inc.

frequently confuse the two. They are inept at putting blocks or puzzles together and slow to master the intricacies of buttoning buttons, drawing circles, and catching a ball that is thrown to them. They are less able than other youngsters to remember past events and recent happenings. Because of mild hearing losses, they may be slow to develop language and may show mild articulation defects in their speech (I. Belmont, 1980; Chalfant & Scheffelin, 1969; Gardner, 1979; Lucas, 1980; Tsushima & Towne, 1977).

As one important illustration of the visual-motor handicaps that frequently aid in diagnosing their condition, about 75 percent of MBD/ADD children score 1 year or more below age level in copying the designs that constitute the Bender-Gestalt test of visual-motor functioning. They are particularly likely to rotate their drawings, "dog-ear" on their angles, and misplace points where lines are supposed to join or intersect (Klatskin, McNamara, Shaffer, & Pincus, 1972; Koppitz, 1963; see Figure 4.1).

Impaired motor coordination, visual-motor difficulties, and poorly articulated speech are among the "soft" signs used by neurologists to identify brain dysfunction in the absence of "hard" evidence of central nervous system damage, such as loss of sensation or paralysis in some part of the body (Gardner, 1979; Ingram, 1973; Rie & Rie, 1978; Schain, 1980). Neurological examinations of MBD/ADD children are likely to reveal imbalance, poor coordination, confused handedness, and uneven or unusually active reflexes. From 50 to 60 percent of MBD/ADD children show such soft signs,

Figure 4.1
Copy of the Bender-Gestalt designs made by a 9-year-old girl with MBD/ADD. (Test figures reproduced from the "Bender Visual Motor Gestalt Test" (adapted from Wertheimer) with permission of The American Orthopsychiatric Association.)

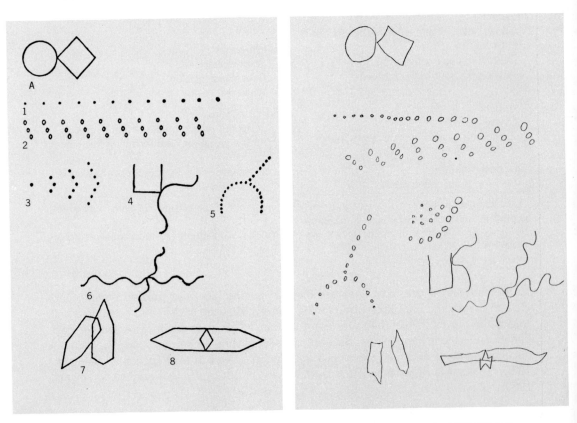

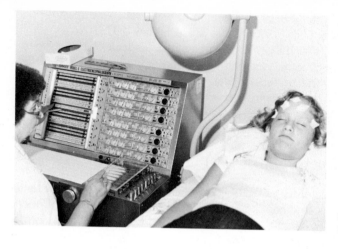

Brain-wave patterns, as measured by the electroencephalogram (EEG), are helpful in identifying central nervous system dysfunction.

which is significantly more often than appears in normal youngsters (Peters, Romine, & Dykman, 1975; Towbin, 1978; Werry, 1979; Wolff & Hurwitz, 1973). Similarly, about 50 percent of MBD/ADD children have abnormal brain waves on the **electroencephalogram** (EEG), compared to just 5 to 20 percent of normally behaving youngsters (Capute, Neidermeyer, & Richardson, 1968; Gross & Wilson, 1974; Satterfield, Cantwell, Saul, & Yusin, 1974).

COURSE AND CONSEQUENCES OF MBD/ADD

The prominent characteristics of MBD/ADD vary with age. During infancy the prelude to the disorder appears in the form of behavioral irregularities that make children difficult to manage. In early childhood the primary manifestations of the condition begin to become apparent. These primary symptoms persist into middle childhood but are then typically overshadowed by secondary difficulties they cause, especially in school learning and interpersonal relationships. These secondary consequences in turn persist into adolescence, where they are often accompanied or even eclipsed by adjustment difficulties involving low self-esteem and antisocial behavior. Among young adults the cumulative impact of these primary and secondary characteristics of MBD/ADD increases the risk of chronic impulse disorders and socioeconomic underachievement.

Infancy and Early Childhood: Prelude and Onset

Children later identified as MBD/ADD tend to be extremely active infants who eat and sleep poorly, cry frequently, and lag behind in acquiring motor and language skills. Their fitfulness makes them difficult to dress and bathe, their overresponsiveness to stimulation makes them difficult to soothe, and their unpredictable needs and moods undermine efforts to establish a comfortable routine in caring for them. Such temperamental irregularities put great strain on parents, who are usually also concerned or disappointed about their youngster's delay in learning to walk, talk, and master other skills (Denhoff, 1973; Stewart & Olds, 1973; Weiss & Hechtman, 1979).

This prelude to MBD/ADD, which closely resembles the "difficult child" temperament observed in extensive longitudinal research by Thomas, Chess, and Birch (1968, Chapter 7), is followed during the preschool years by the emergence of the primary manifestations of MBD/ADD—hyperactivity, distractibility, impulsivity, and excitability. Instead of appearing in any uniform fashion, however, these symptoms vary from one child to the next in both severity and primacy. Some MBD/ADD youngsters may be more hyperactive than others, for example, and some may be more characteristically excitable than hyperactive—that is, more prone to temper tantrums than to generally restless behavior.

Moreover, the degree to which MBD/ADD children manifest problem behavior tends to vary with their situation. In a study of situational variables, Schleifer, Weiss, Cohen, Elman, Cvejic, and Kruger (1975) compared 3- to 4-year-old hyperactive and normal preschoolers in a nursery school program. The hyperactive children were being seen by pediatricians to whom their mothers had complained about their being constantly overactive and difficult to manage. Despite this history, no behavioral differences were observed between the pediatric patients and the normal group during free-play activities. During structured play periods, however, when the children were supposed to stay in their seats and follow the teacher's instructions, the patient group was significantly more likely than the normal youngsters to show restless, out-of-seat, or aggressive behavior.

By following these same children for the next 3 years, into the second grade, Campbell and her colleagues were able to paint a graphic picture of the emergence of MBD/ADD and of its continuity from infancy into middle childhood. The more infant sleep difficulty these children were reported to have, the more hyperactivity and conduct problems they displayed at both 4½ and 6½ years of age. The more restless they were in the nursery school setting and the more frequently they left their seats, the more often they displayed out-of-seat and off-task behavior in the second grade, at age 7½. Finally, the more aggressive they were as preschoolers, the more frequently their second-grade teachers described them as engaging in disruptive behavior in the classroom (Campbell, Endman, & Bernfield, 1977; Campbell, Schleifer, & Weiss, 1978).

Middle Childhood: Learning Disabilities

As noted earlier, learning disabilities consist of underachievement in school that results from deficits in essential learning processes. Like mental retardation (see Chapter 3), LD is covered by Public Law 94-142—the Education for All Handicapped Act—and the following widely accepted definition has been developed in implementing this law.

"Specific learning disability" means a disorder in one or more of the basic psychological processes involved in understanding or in using language, spoken or written, which may manifest itself in an imperfect ability to listen, think, speak, read, write, spell, or do mathematical calculations. The term includes such conditions as perceptual handicaps, brain injury, minimal brain dysfunction, dyslexia, and developmental asphasia. The term does

not include children who have learning problems which are primarily the result of visual, hearing, or motor handicaps, of mental retardation, of emotional disturbance, or of environmental, cultural, or economic disadvantage (U.S. Office of Education, 1977).

As also mentioned in introducing this chapter, the impaired processes involved in LD are generally believed to result from some dysfunction in the central nervous system. Accordingly, the primary manifestations of MBD/ADD are usually agreed to put youngsters at risk for becoming learning disabled in middle childhood (Cruickshank, 1977a; Rie, 1980; Rourke, 1975). LD is in fact found to occur in 50 to 80 percent of MBD/ADD children, and 60 to 70 percent of MBD/ADD youngsters can be expected to fail one or more grades in school by the time they reach their teens (Lambert & Sandoval, 1980; Mendelson, Johnson, & Stewart, 1971; Safer & Allen, 1976, Chap. 2; Weiss, Minde, Werry, Douglas, & Nemeth, 1971).

Using the above definition, the U.S. Office of Education (1975) estimates a 3 percent prevalence of LD in schoolchildren. However, some writers report that as many as 10 percent of schoolchildren are referred each year for professional help with learning problems, and in various surveys of school populations from 5 to 40 percent of children are suggested to have LD. This broad range results from many different ways in which LD has been defined in these studies, and the larger prevalence figures reflect the unfortunate tendency noted earlier of some researchers to label all academic underachievers as learning disabled (Minskoff, 1973; Schroeder, Schroeder, & Davine, 1978). With LD more precisely defined as a deficit in learning processes secondary to MBD/ADD, the 3 percent LD prevalence of the Office of Education fits well with the evidence that MBD/ADD occurs in 5 to 6 percent of school-age children, of whom 50 to 80 percent have learning problems.

The behavioral and perceptual-cognitive impairments associated with MBD/ADD interfere with school learning in two ways. First, because MBD/ADD children are restless and distractible, they have difficulty paying attention to their teachers and assignments. They absorb less than other children from group discussions, they benefit less from individual study, they are slow to complete their homework and test papers, and they often fail to remember and follow directions (Bryan, 1974; Dykman, Walls, Suzuki, Ackerman, & Peters, 1970; Keogh, 1971; Lasky & Tobin, 1973).

In the classroom as in the nursery school, the extent of these behavior problems varies with how much structure is imposed. Jacob, O'Leary, and Rosenblad (1978) observed a group of 9- to 10-year olds referred by their teachers for treatment of hyperactivity in two classroom settings: an informal setting in which the children could choose tasks to work on and a formal setting in which the teacher specified what they were to do. Figure 4.2 depicts the amount of hyperactive behavior (such as changing position, being aggressive or negativistic, daydreaming, and making weird sounds) that these youngsters and a group of their normal classmates showed in the two settings. The data suggest that both hyperactive and normal children become better controlled in formal settings, but that hyperactive children show much less improvement in self-control than their normal classmates. In middle childhood as well as in the preschool years, then, the behavior problems of hyperactive youngsters are likely to be more apparent in structured than unstructured situations.

Figure 4.2
Mean levels of hyperactive behavior in hyperactive and normal 9- to 10-year-olds in formal and informal classroom settings. (From Jacob, O'Leary, and Rosenblad (1978). Reprinted with permission of Plenum Publishing Corp.)

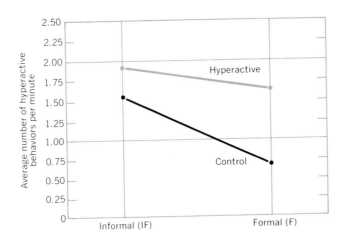

This first way in which MBD/ADD interferes with school learning is aptly referred to as *cognitive style disorder* in an important book by Kinsbourne and Caplan (1979). Consistent with the preceding description of learning problems, they define cognitive style disorders as inborn attentional and motor difficulties that make it hard for children to perform at grade level in school. By contrast, they also define a category of *cognitive power disorder,* which constitutes the second way in which MBD/ADD often impairs school learning. In cognitive power disorders, children are deficient in one or more specific intellectual functions that are necessary for mastering certain basic skills and subject matter.

Among the functions commonly affected in cognitive power disorders are the following: the ability to coordinate visual and motor functioning, which is required for putting puzzles together or doing other tasks in which the eyes must guide the hands; a sense of spatial relations, which is required to distinguish left from right or figure from ground; the integration of various sensory modalities, which is required to recognize that a spoken word is identical to the same word in print; the ability to understand the spoken word and to speak clearly; and adequate memory capacity (Ackerman, Peters, & Dykman, 1971; Adams, Koscis, & Estes, 1974; Black, 1976; Hallahan & Cruickshank, 1973; Kluever, 1971; Silver, 1976). Because MBD/ADD children are impaired in these functions, they often fall behind their classmates in learning such basic language skills as reading and writing. Later in elementary school and beyond, they are additionally likely to have difficulty with one or more specific subject areas.

Problems in Reading and Writing Specific patterns of reading retardation that result from MBD/ADD are commonly referred to as **dyslexia.** Dyslexia can be defined as reading attainment that falls significantly below the level that would be expected from a youngster's age, intelligence, and opportunities for reading instruction in his or her native language. Such specific reading disability is widely regarded as a variant or consequence of MBD/ADD and should be distinguished from general reading backwardness, which can result from limited intelligence or inadequate instruction. Like MBD/ADD, dyslexia is much more common in boys than girls and cuts across social class groups; by contrast, general reading backwardness shows an equal sex distribution and a predominance among socially disadvantaged youngsters (Dalby, 1979; Eisenberg, 1978; Pirozzolo, 1979; Rourke, 1975b, 1978; Rutter, 1978; Vellutino, 1978).

The relationship of MBD/ADD to reading problems is fairly easy to understand and demonstrate. First, the distractibility of many MBD/ADD children can interfere with their paying adequate attention to the printed page, which is one of the basic skills required in reading (Senf & Freundl, 1971; Willows, 1974). Second, their perceptual-cognitive impairments can handicap MBD/ADD children in looking at material with smooth left-to-right eye movements, in seeing letters accurately, and in combining letters to form words. As a result, they commonly make the kinds of reading errors listed in Table 4.2 (Heiman & Ross, 1974; Lefton, Lahey, & Stagg, 1978; Prawat & Kerasotes, 1978; Vande Voort & Senf, 1973; Vernon, 1979).

Some extensive longitudinal data on twins who were followed from 3 months of age into elementary school provides additional evidence of behavioral characteristics of MBD/ADD in the early lives of children who subsequently develop reading problems. Matheny, Dolan, and Wilson (1976) compared 46 twins having academic difficulties with normally achieving twins matched for age, sex, and social class. In reading level these LD twins averaged 1.9 grade-equivalents below their matched controls. Figure 4.3 indicates the difference between the two groups in several characteristics of MBD/ADD as reported by their mothers and observed by the research team during their infancy and early childhood.

Dyslexia is the most common and probably the most severe kind of learning disability. An estimated 15 percent of elementary school children fall 1 year or more behind grade level in their reading ability. Many of these poor readers are showing

TABLE 4.2   Common Reading Errors of Children with Dyslexia (Reading Disability)

Type of Error	Printed Word	What Child Reads
Reversal of word	"was"	"saw"
Transposition of letters within word	"sit"	"its"
Confusion of letters that are reversible	"dig"	"big"
Confusion of letters that look alike	"now"	"how"
Confusion of letters that sound alike	"town"	"down"

Figure 4.3

Preschool behaviors distinguishing between twins with and without subsequent reading disability. (Based on data reported by Matheny, Dolan, and Wilson (1978).)

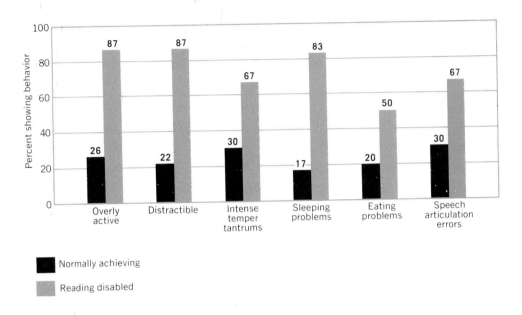

general reading backwardness rather than dyslexia; however, even when precise definitions are used, specific reading retardation is still found to occur in 4 percent of 9- to 11-year-olds and about two-thirds of schoolchildren with LD (Rutter, Tizard, & Whitmore, 1970; Satz, Taylor, Friel, & Fletcher, 1978; Schroeder, Schroeder, & Davine, 1978; Yule & Rutter, 1978).

With respect to its severity, dyslexia has a cumulative effect on almost all school learning. First, specific reading retardation tends to persist with age and to become increasingly pronounced relative to a child's age and grade. Second, most academic subjects require reading, and some measure achievement largely by how well a student can read and absorb large amounts of written material. Poor readers therefore have trouble in many of their courses, and without special remedial assistance they are likely to fall further and further behind their classmates each year. Not surprisingly, then, reading retardation becomes one of the major causes of both academic failure and school dropout in the adolescent years (Lenkowsky, 1977; Rutter, Tizard, Yule, Graham, & Whitmore, 1976; Satz et al., 1978; Trites & Fiedorowicz, 1976).

Many of the same kinds of confusion, reversal, and substitution of letters that hinder MBD/ADD children in reading also cause them problems in writing **(dysgraphia).** If these children have impaired fine motor coordination as well, as many MBD/ADD children do, their compositions and other written work (arithmetic problems, map drawing, spelling tests) may be so messy or illegible as to reduce further the grades they are able to achieve.

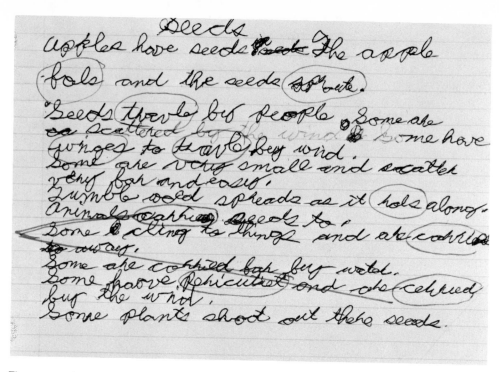

The perceptual-motor problems of MBD/ADD children often result in their producing poor written work in school.

Problems in Subject Areas   The particular kinds of learning difficulty MBD/ADD children experience vary with the relative strengths of their cognitive abilities (Ackerman, Dykman, & Peters, 1976). For example, LD children who are deficient in reading and spelling but relatively good at arithmetic show impairments primarily in basic verbal and auditory-perceptual abilities; in contrast, children whose reading and spelling are average or better but whose arithmetic performance is relatively poor tend to be weak primarily in visual-perceptual and visual-spatial abilities (Rourke & Finlayson, 1978).

Similarly, MBD/ADD children usually find that they are handicapped in certain subject areas required in the later years of elementary school and in high school. Those with serious and persistent reading problems are likely to receive relatively low grades in English and social studies, whereas those with impaired conceptual abilities may have special problems with science and mathematics.

Middle Childhood: Interpersonal Difficulties

MBD/ADD children typically develop social and interpersonal difficulties during the elementary school years. Their quick tempers and aggressive ways, their disruptive behavior in group situations, and their lack of self-control contribute to making them unpopular with peers, teachers, and other adults. Numerous studies confirm that MBD/ADD children are frequently disliked and rejected by their classmates (Bryan,

1978; Bruininks, 1978a, 1978b; Paulauskas & Campbell, 1979; Serafica & Harway, 1979). Their resulting isolation and their mounting academic and emotional frustrations often lead these youngsters into self-serving antisocial acts, especially fighting, stealing, lying, and cheating (Cantwell, 1975b; Schechter, 1974).

As an additional psychological stress in middle childhood, the perceptual-motor handicaps of MBD/ADD children limit their achieving the skills and sense of mastery that normally promote initiative and self-confidence. Some of these youngsters may already have emotional problems when they begin school, particularly if their parents have reacted negatively to their slow motor development and limited self-control. Others with understanding and supportive parents who have gotten along well as preschoolers become emotionally troubled in the classroom, as they find themselves unable to compete with their classmates or to realize their intellectual potential.

Growing awareness of their limitations often gives MBD/ADD children a low opinion of themselves. Frequently their classmates make matters worse by teasing them for errors they make, such as getting lost on the way to school (because of their poor sense of direction) or bumping into or dropping things (because of their poor coordination). Often their teachers single them out for criticism of their classroom performance or warnings about their behavior (Bryan & Pearl, 1979; Chapman, Larsen, & Parker, 1979; Helper, 1980). In an effort to salvage some feelings of worth and importance in the face of such attitudes, MBD/ADD children may behave in silly, wild ways that are intended to attract attention and admiration—but that usually make them even less popular than before.

The school learning and behavior problems of MBD/ADD children are also difficult for their parents to accept, especially if they were not anticipated. Like peers and teachers, parents may react in ways that make interpersonal problems worse. Some become angry and rejecting, as if their child were to blame for his or her handicap; some become overindulgent and overprotective, as if convinced that their child has no chance to become a responsible and self-reliant person; others deny the handicap and accuse either the child for being willful and lazy or the school for picking on their child and not doing a proper job of teaching.

The frequently strong negative reaction of parents to a learning disability can be attributed in part to what McCarthy and McCarthy (1969) call a "taste of honey." Unlike retarded or severely emotionally disturbed children, LD children display essentially normal intelligence and many normal abilities (the "taste of honey"), which makes it difficult for parents to understand or accept their subnormal areas of functioning. Because they may expect more from their child than is realistically possible, these parents are often more disappointed and frustrated than the parents of children with more devastating handicaps, from whom less is expected. Such negative attitudes make LD youngsters feel even less adequate and worthwhile than they would otherwise and discourage them from trying to overcome their handicap.

Case 3. *MBD/ADD in Middle Childhood*

The case of Charles illustrates how manifestations of MBD/ADD typically come to light during the school years, and it also anticipates some important treatment issues to be discussed later in the chapter. Charles was the oldest of three children reared in advantaged circumstances by well-educated and happily married parents. His mother's pregnancy was uncomplicated, his early developmental milestones were passed on schedule, and his parents' only early concern was that he seemed poorly coordinated—in his mother's words, "When he was little he ran like a cripple." Nevertheless, when he began school he was required to repeat kindergarten because of being "immature" and having an extremely short attention span.

When Charles was age 9 and in the third grade, the school psychologist recommended a thorough evaluation for possible brain dysfunction. At this time he was still poorly coordinated and barely able to ride a bicycle, and he was having a very difficult time learning to read and do arithmetic. He felt picked on by his classmates and often acted the role of a clown when they teased him. At home he was at odds with both of his parents. His highly intelligent father wanted to sympathize with his son's learning problems but found himself instead losing interest in "this apparently untalented child." His mother was frequently upset with him for what she described as his "negativistic" behavior, and she summarized her view of her son as follows: "He can't do anything in sports, he can't do anything in school, he has no friends, he can't do anything well."

Charles and his parents were seen at this time by their pediatrician, a child psychiatrist, and a child psychologist. All three agreed that although Charles might be lagging a bit in cerebral development, his problems were mainly the result of underlying anxieties. Psychotherapy was recommended, and he and his parents were seen over the next 2 years by a skillful, psychologically oriented clinician. During this therapy Charles's behavior improved dramatically. He became more involved in school and other activities, he got along much better with his peers, and he reestablished a comfortable relationship with his parents.

His school learning, however, which had not been a focus of the treatment plan, continued to deteriorate. At age 13 he was just completing the sixth grade and was not going to be allowed to continue further in the private school he had been attending. His parents again sought help, this time regarding Charles's intellectual abilities and academic potential. Psychological examination revealed clear evidence of perceptual and visual-motor handicaps consistent with MBD/ADD and a broad spread of abilities, ranging from above-average verbal skills to well-below-average ability in conceptual and numerical skills. In addition, although he was generally attentive and not distractible, Charles tended to give up easily and make careless guesses rather than persevere in trying to solve a difficult problem.

In addition to explaining these aspects of his intellectual functioning to Charles and his parents, the psychologist provided information about what could be expected of him in the future and made recommendations for a program of appropriate remedial education, course selection, and help with study habits. It may be that such attention to educational planning in the treatment program prescribed for him in the third grade would have averted the learning difficulties he still had in the sixth grade; it may even be that adequate attention to the immaturity and distractibility he was noted to have in kindergarten could have prevented a learning disability from developing in the first place.

Adolescence: Low Self-Esteem and Antisocial Behavior

The primary behavior manifestations of MBD/ADD tend to diminish during adolescence. Although MBD/ADD youngsters may remain more restless, distractible, impulsive, and excitable than other children, they gain increased self-control as they mature and become much less different from their classmates than before in these respects. However, in the absence of adequate treatment or spontaneous recovery, the secondary consequences of MBD/ADD that begin in middle childhood become worse in adolescence—especially learning difficulties, low self-esteem, and antisocial behavior (Campbell, 1976; Milich & Loney, 1979; Minde, Weiss, & Mendelson, 1972).

The cumulative nature of learning difficulties had already been noted. As subject matter becomes more difficult during high school and builds on previous learning, students with deficient skills and spotty prior learning find it increasingly difficult to keep up. Mildly learning-disabled children who have managed to struggle through junior high school science and mathematics, for example, may fall by the wayside in algebra and chemistry, and those who read well enough to handle seventh- and eighth-grade assignments may not be able to maintain the reading pace required in ninth- and tenth-grade English and history.

The generally unpromising academic future of LD children has been documented by Ackerman, Dykman, and Peters (1977a), who followed a group of 8- to 11-year-old boys who were performing 1 year or more below grade level despite average or better intelligence and no physical, emotional, or sociocultural handicaps. At age 14 all of these boys had made some progress in school, but only 15 percent had overcome their basic skill deficits. The rest held the same relatively low position among their classmates in reading, spelling, and arithmetic (15th to 20th percentile) as they had 3 to 6 years earlier.

Other research had demonstrated that, despite improvements, some of the basic cognitive deficits that contribute to school learning difficulties also continue into adolescence. As a group, formerly hyperactive children examined at age 15 perform significantly worse than their normal peers on tasks of sustained attention, visual-motor coordination, and motor development (Hoy, Weiss, Minde, & Cohen, 1978; Zambelli, Stamm, Maitinsky, & Loiselle, 1977).

With respect to self-esteem, the cumulative failure and rejection that MBD/ADD youngsters experience during middle childhood frequently contribute to their becoming withdrawn and self-depreciating as adolescents. Like people with depressive disorders (see Chapter 7), they frequently go through periods of feeling sad and incompentent, uninterested in doing anything, and pessimistic about the future. Socially they either have few friends or seek the company of younger children, who pose less threat to their fragile sense of adequacy than other adolescents (Brumback & Weinberg, 1977; Hoy et al., 1978; Helper, 1980; Stewart, Mendelson, & Johnson, 1973).

In a similar way, the mounting frustrations and needs for attention that cause some MBD/ADD children to engage in antisocial behavior often lead to increasingly serious conduct problems during adolescence. Sometimes delinquent behavior may obscure all of the other difficulties these youngsters have during the teenage years, and in some cases youngsters with previously overlooked learning problems are referred for help for the first time as adolescents because of aggressive behavior, major conflicts with authority, and other antisocial conduct. Various follow-up studies have found 25 to 60 percent of MBD/ADD children in such difficulty as adolescents, including frequent contact with the police (Ackerman, Dykman, & Peters, 1977b; Minde et al., 1972; Weiss & Hechtman, 1979).

Case 4. *MBD/ADD in Adolescence*

David was 13 years old and in the eighth grade when he first came to professional attention. The occasion was a call from the school about his having scratched a mirror in the lavatory. His parents sought psychological help, since they regarded this as the last straw in a series of events that had been worrying them recently, including (a) wide variations in David's academic performance, (b) his inability to sustain any friendships, (c) his frequently getting into fights, mainly because of being highly sensitive to personal slights and easily provoked to anger, and (d) persistent bed-wetting. For years they had tended to gloss over these problems, primarily because "he was never left back in school, so things couldn't have been that bad."

Now, however, having finally decided that David's problem behavior called for attention, they were able with the psychologist's assistance to recall some diagnostically significant features of his earlier life as well. He was anoxic at birth and required emergency measures to start him breathing after he already appeared blue and lifeless. As a preschooler, he "walked funny" and sometimes was difficult to understand because of "slurred speech." When he entered school he still seemed "clumsy," and in the third grade a school psychologist described him as very poorly coordinated.

David's own view of himself at age 13 was "I'm a big, stupid clod," and he felt that the only way he could avoid being mocked or taken advantage of by others was to "show them who's boss" and "make them sorry for fooling with me." In fact, he was neither stupid nor any longer clumsy. Testing indicated average intelligence, with an IQ of 105, and he showed only very slight difficulties in perceptual-motor coordination or in tasks requiring attention, concentration, and concept formation. Moreover, his above-average size and strength were making him respected more and teased less by his peers than before.

Nevertheless, after years of struggling to preserve his self-respect with lashing out at others as his only tool, David already bore numerous personality scars. In particular, he seemed on the verge of becoming a characterologically impulsive, self-centered, aggressive individual with little consideration for the rights and needs of others. Psychotherapy was recommended in the hope of helping David avoid any further movement toward an adult impulse disorder.

Adulthood: The Long-Term Consequences

The characteristic course of MBD/ADD described in the preceding pages is not inevitable. As indicated in Figure 4.4, most MBD/ADD children improve in response to treatment or their own maturation, and only one-third continue to suffer the same severity of disturbance during their adolescence.

Yet MBD/ADD is a chronic disorder, which means that failure to improve during

Figure 4.4
Long-term outcome in MBD/ADD children. (Based on data reported by Mendelson et al. (1971) and Minde et al. (1971).)

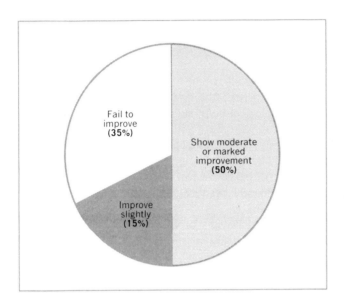

adolescence is often followed by an unrelenting downhill course in early adulthood. An undetermined but probably substantial number of adults who were diagnosed MBD/ADD in childhood will continue to have serious adjustment difficulties, and there is reason to believe that the problem behavior of many adults who are thought to have "impulse disorders" of purely psychological origin may derive in fact from the same causes as the antisocial conduct seen in MBD/ADD children and adolescents (Morrison, 1979; Weiss, Hechtman, Perlman, Hopkins, & Wener, 1979; Wood, Reimberr, Wender, & Johnson, 1976).

In an interesting study of such long-term consequences of MBD/ADD, Borland and Heckman (1976) interviewed 20 men who had been referred for MBD/ADD symptoms 20 to 25 years earlier, at an average age of 7½. These men reported a considerable decrease in their symptoms over the years. In comparison to their similarly aged brothers, however, who were also interviewed, they showed significantly more nervousness, restlessness, and irritability. These formerly MBD/ADD children also tended as adults to be more impulsive than their brothers, to become depressed more frequently, and to have fewer friends. Nine (45 percent) of them had a diagnosable emotional disorder, compared to none of the brothers, and as a group they had achieved less socioeconomic status than their brothers, despite comparable intelligence and levels of education.

CAUSES OF MBD/ADD

Like mental retardation, MBD/ADD is a condition of multiple etiology. It has many possible causes, and it is likely to appear for different reasons in different children. Most of the same harmful prenatal and early life events that can result in mental retardation also increase the risk of MBD/ADD (see page 98), and there is also evidence for both genetic and environmental factors in certain instances of the disorder (Dubey, 1976; Rourke, 1978; Stewart, 1980; Werner & Smith, 1979).

Prenatal and Early Life Events

Among prenatal events, heavy smoking or drinking by pregnant women has been identified in particular as contributing to the kinds of behavioral and perceptual-cognitive impairments associated with MBD/ADD (Denson, Nanson, & McWatters, 1975; Dunn & McBurney, 1977; Streissguth, 1977). In one study of such possible effects, the smoking patterns of pregnant women were compared with the reading performance of their children at age 7 in a large-scale longitudinal project involving approximately 14,000 British children. The data indicated that a decrease in smoking from 10 cigarettes per day to none during pregnancy accounted for a gain of 4 months in reading level among the 7-year-olds (Davie, Butler, & Goldstein, 1972).

Birth complications such as prematurity, anoxia, and injury by surgical instruments also occur in a greater proportion of children later identified as MBD/ADD than of normally functioning youngsters. Galante, Flye, and Stephens (1972), for example, found an unusual birth history in approximately 40 percent of a group of sixth-grade children whose reading achievement was one-half year or more below what could be expected from their general intellectual level, compared to only 14 percent among classmates who were reading at or above expectancy. Considerable other research strongly suggests a relationship between complications of pregnancy and birth and subsequent MBD/ADD and learning problems (Balow, Rubin, & Rosen, 1975–1976; Colletti, 1979; Rubin & Balow, 1977; Towbin, 1978). In addition, such early life events as head injuries, meningitis, malnutrition, and lead poisoning have been related to subsequent manifestations of MBD/ADD (National Institute of Child Health and Human Development, 1976; Levin & Eisenberg, 1979; Martin, 1980; Needleman, 1973).

It should be noted that some of the data relating prenatal and early-life events to subsequent manifestations of MBD/ADD come from retrospective ("follow-back") studies. As discussed in Chapter 1, efforts to reconstruct the earlier history of subjects in follow-back research may suffer from inadequate previous records and unreliable recollections of parents and other informants. Fortunately, however, follow-back researchers working on MBD/ADD have typically had access to key data that were reliably recorded when they occurred, especially data from medical records of pregnancy and the birth process.

Moreover, the apparent relationship between physically harmful early life events and increased risk of MBD/ADD has also emerged in longitudinal studies in which children have been followed carefully from birth into middle childhood. Two major projects of this kind are the British National Child Development Study, from which the Davie et al. (1972) data mentioned earlier were taken and which included 90 percent of all children born in Great Britain from March 3 to 9, 1958, totaling 13,958 youngsters, and the Collaborative Perinatal Project on early childhood origins of neurological disorders, mentioned in Chapter 1, in which researchers at 14 university medical centers followed 55,908 pregnant women between 1959 and 1965, before and after delivery, and subsequently examined their children at intervals from birth to age 7 (Niswander & Gordon, 1972; Runck, 1977).

Genetic Factors

MBD/ADD tends to run in families. Data from three studies summarized in Figure 4.5 indicate that the parents of MBD/ADD children are more likely to have been hyperactive themselves as youngsters, and their brothers are currently more likely to show symptoms of MBD/ADD, than the first-degree relatives of normal youngsters. As adults, moreover, the parents of the hyperactive children in these studies had a higher than usual prevalence of alcoholism and impulsive behavior disorders. It has also been found that both parents and siblings of learning-disabled children show more deficits than relatives of normally achieving children in reading ability, spelling, auditory memory, perceptual speed, and verbal reasoning (Foch, DeFries, McClearn, & Singer, 1977; Herschel, 1978; McClearn, 1978).

Although the familial incidence of MBD/ADD is well established by these and other studies, there are important limitations to what they reveal. First, even if as many as 16 percent of MBD/ADD children have MBD/ADD fathers, as Figure 4.5 shows, 84 percent do not. Hence any genetic factors suggested by this finding account for only a small proportion of cases. Second, what modest concordance there is for MBD/ADD among parents and siblings could easily result from environmental determinants. As was discussed in relation to mental retardation, relatives can share psychological difficulties either because they share certain common genes or because they share certain common experiences in living.

Research with twins has helped to pursue these alternative possibilities further. Willerman (1973), studying the activity level of 93 pairs of same-sexed twins, found a heritability index of 0.71 for hyperactivity.[1] The much greater concordance of MBD/ADD symptoms among twins than among children and their parents supports the existence of genetic factors, although it might be argued that the very closely shared developmental experiences of twins account for many striking environmentally determined similarities between them. This argument can be tested by comparing identical, monozygotic (MZ) and nonidentical, dizygotic (DZ) twins. If genetic factors contribute to MBD/ADD, MZ twins should be highly concordant for it, while DZ twins, who have different genes, are less concordant, at about the rate for siblings; if environmental factors are all-important, MZ and DZ twins, who share the same developmental experiences, should have similar concordance rates, both higher than in siblings.

The data in this regard are clear: MZ twins show greater concordance for manifestations of MBD/ADD than DZ twins, and DZ twins show the same concordance as siblings (Matheny, Dolan, & Wilson, 1976). Yet even these findings leave some room

---

[1] See page 102 for an explanation of heritability.

Figure 4.5
Prevalence of MBD/ADD symptoms among the parents and brothers of MBD/ADD and normal children. (Based on data reported by Cantwell (1972), Morrison and Stewart (1971), and Welner, Welner, Stewart, Palkes, and Wish (1977).)

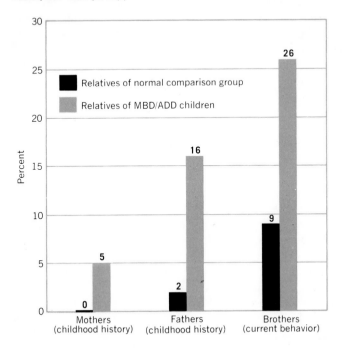

for an environmental explanation of familial incidence. It may be that MZ twins receive more similar treatment than DZ twins—for example, being dressed alike—and there is some evidence that MZ twins more frequently suffer potentially harmful prenatal and birth events than DZ twins (World Health Organization, 1966).

In addition to the family and twin studies, a third and even more conclusive line of evidence for genetic factors in MBD/ADD has come from adoption studies. Most significantly, it has been found that parental concordance is limited to biological fathers and mothers of MBD/ADD children, whereas parents with adopted MBD/ADD children are no more likely than the parents of normal children to show current or past indications of MBD/ADD (Cantwell, 1975c; Morrison & Stewart, 1973). Child-parent concordance thus appears to depend much more on who gives birth to MBD/ADD children than on who rears them. Similarly, in a study of siblings and half-siblings of MBD/ADD children reared apart in foster homes from an early age, Safer (1973) found a 53 percent concordance between the full siblings but only a 9 percent concordance among the half-siblings. Taken together, the available research has led most reviewers to conclude that genetic factors play a definite causative role in at least some instances of this disorder (Cantwell, 1976; Glow & Glow, 1979; Silver, 1979; Stewart, 1980).

Environmental Factors

The most important environmental factors that may contribute to features of MBD/ADD involve the impact on children of certain child-rearing styles and behavioral examples of their parents. Tense, impulsive, excitable parents tend to treat their children in ways that foster their becoming overly active, emotional, and intolerant of frustration. Consequently, MBD/ADD children grown into adulthood may be especially likely to have MBD/ADD children themselves, not for genetic reasons but because they transmit the disorder on a strictly experiential basis. It is also conceivable that children with difficult temperaments trigger anxious, demanding, and impatient parental behavior that can in turn contribute to their developing MBD/ADD characteristics (Campbell, 1979; Cameron, 1978; Field, 1979; Scholom & Schiff, 1980).

Moreover, all children learn certain behaviors as a result of copying them from available models. Research studies have demonstrated in particular that children exposed to active, aggressive models act more this way themselves (Bandura, Ross, & Ross, 1961; Elkind & Weiner, 1978, Chapter 8; Kaspar & Lowenstein, 1971). Hence it is possible for some excited, impatient, and temper-prone parents to foster behavioral manifestations of MBD/ADD in their children by virtue of the example they set. However, there is as yet little direct research evidence for either child-rearing or modeling effects in causing the broad range of behavioral and perceptual-cognitive impairments that define MBD/ADD. They must accordingly be viewed as potential contributing factors in some cases rather than as documented sufficient causes of the disorder.

Two other suggested environmental causes of MBD/ADD should be noted, although definitive data are not yet available on them. Feingold (1975a, 1975b) has asserted that chemical food additives lead some children to develop characteristics of MBD/ADD, including hyperactivity, impulsivity, aggressiveness, poor motor coordination, impaired perceptual-cognitive functioning, and learning disability. He reported a 75 percent improvement rate among children with such difficulties when they are placed on a special additive-free diet.

Subsequent research has raised more questions about this possible effect than it has answered, however. First, compared with Feingold's 75 percent improvement rate, other clinical investigators report successful dietary treatment of MBD/ADD children in a range from 50 percent of cases to none at all. Second, even when it occurs, successful treatment by an additive-free diet does not quite prove that the additives caused the problem in the first place. Third, efforts to prove such a cause-effect relationship in the laboratory have found that the dose of chemical food additives necessary to affect behavior is larger than children are likely to ingest through a usual diet (Conners, 1980; Mayron, 1979; Rapp, 1979; Spring & Sandoval, 1976; Swanson & Kinsbourne, 1980).

Mayron and his colleagues have concluded that radiation from fluorescent lighting contributes to hyperactivity and learning problems in school-age children (Mayron, 1978; Mayron, Mayron, Ott, & Nations, 1976; Mayron, Ott, Nations, & Mayron, 1974). In support of this hypothesis, some of their data suggest that hyperactive behavior in the classroom can be reduced by limiting the children's exposure to standard fluorescent lamps. As in the case of additive-free diets, however, the nature of a successful treatment method does not necessarily indicate the cause of a disorder. Moreover, other investigators have thus far failed to replicate Mayron's findings, and no conclusions about this possible environmental cause of MBD/ADD appear justified at the moment (O'Leary, Rosenbaum, & Hughes, 1978a, 1978b).

TREATMENT OF MBD/ADD

Most of the primary and secondary manifestations of MBD/ADD can be minimized by treatment programs involving some combination of drugs, psychological intervention, educational planning, and parent counseling. Each of these approaches addresses some aspects of MBD/ADD more than others, and adequate treatment planning for an individual child requires careful selection of those methods most likely to relieve his or her particular difficulties.

Drugs

For reasons that are not yet fully understood, stimulant drugs have proved helpful in curbing the hyperactivity, distractibility, and impulsivity of MBD/ADD children. Dextroamphetamine (Dexedrine) and methylphenidate (Ritalin) in particular have a calming effect on these youngsters; those who respond favorably show less restless and disruptive behavior, a longer attention span, and fewer aggressive outbursts (Barkley, 1979; Henker, Whalen, & Collins, 1979; Quinn & Rapoport, 1975; Thurston, Sobol, Swanson, & Kinsbourne, 1979).

Additionally, MBD/ADD children receiving these drugs frequently achieve improved performance on tests of memory and perceptual-motor coordination and show fewer handwriting difficulties (Gittelman-Klein & Klein, 1976; Humphries, Swanson, Kinsbourne, & Yiu, 1979; Lerer, Artner, & Lerer, 1979; Spring, Yellin, & Greenberg, 1976; Werry, 1975). No single drug or combination of drugs always gives these results, however, nor is there any known way of predicting in advance whether an individual child will benefit from drugs, or from which drug, or from what amount of the drug (Fish, 1971; Millichap, 1973; Satterfield, 1976).

The Utility of Stimulant Medication   Research reports indicate that 60 to 70 percent of MBD/ADD children improve substantially in response to stimulant medication; most of the remaining youngsters improve either slightly or not at all, and 5 to 10 percent may become even more behaviorally disturbed (Campbell & Small, 1978; Cantwell, 1977; Satterfield, 1976). Significantly, however, these generally good results are limited to the primary behavioral and perceptual-cognitive manifestations of the disorder. Stimulant drugs have not been found to improve the academic achievement of MBD/ADD children or to help them overcome interpersonal difficulties or low self-esteem (Aman, 1980; Barkley, 1979; Gittelman-Klein & Klein, 1975; Rie, Rie, & Stewart, 1976; Wolraich, Drummon, Salomon, O'Brian, & Sivage, 1978).

These youngsters do get along better with their parents and teachers when they are being medicated. They tend to become more responsive to their parents' wishes, and their parents in turn become less controlling and more positive in their attitudes toward their children than they were before the medication was started. In studies in the classroom, teachers who have no knowledge of which of their students are receiving stimulant medication are found to be less intense and controlling toward MBD/ADD youngsters who are on Ritalin than those who are not (Barkley & Cunningham, 1979; Whalen, Henker, & Dotemoto, 1981). Yet despite such improved circumstances, as well as behavioral and perceptual-motor improvements, follow-up studies reveal that a substantial proportion of MBD/ADD children whose improvements are related solely to stimulant medication fail to maintain their gains during adolescence and adulthood when they are no longer taking any drugs (Barkley, 1977; Campbell, 1976; Whalen & Henker, 1976).

Because stimulant medication typically calms MBD/ADD children, this drug effect was at one time called "paradoxical." Accumulating evidence now suggests that the *overactive* behavior in MBD/ADD results from *underactive* or *underaroused nervous-system functioning*, especially in parts of the nervous system that help to inhibit sensory input and motor outflow. This means that stimulant drugs reduce the hyperactivity of MBD/ADD children not because they have a sedative effect, which would be paradoxical, but probably because they bring the nervous system up to a more normal state of arousal; with more adequate activity in the inhibitory centers of their nervous system, MBD/ADD children are able to exercise greater control over their attention, emotions, and actions (Fish, 1975; Hastings & Barkley, 1978; Satterfield, 1975; Zahn, Abate, Little, & Wender, 1975; Zahn, Rapoport, & Thompson, 1980).

Concerns About Stimulant Medication Stimulant drugs frequently have such undesirable side effects as insomnia, loss of appetite, tearfulness, headaches, stomachache, nausea, and vomiting. Although these ractions may be mild and short-lived, the distress they cause children and their parents should be considered in decisions to include drugs in a treatment program (Barkley, 1977; Cantwell, 1977).

Additionally, stimulant medication produces marked suppression of growth while children are receiving it. Children on Dexedrine, for example, average only 62 percent of their annual expected weight gain and 75 percent of their expected increase in height. This growth suppression may result only from children having less appetite and eating less while taking this drug, and a normal growth rate does reappear when the medication is stopped. However, it is not yet known if this rebound is sufficient to make up for all of the growth that is lost during long-term medication (Lipman, 1978; Safer & Allen, 1975a; Safer, Allen, & Barr, 1975; Satterfield, Cantwell, Schell, & Blaschke, 1979).

As a further concern in using stimulant medication, the sometimes dramatic improvement in the primary manifestations of MBD/ADD when children begin drug treatment may obscure persistent secondary difficulties and prematurely convince parents and teachers that the problem is solved. Seeing that their child is calmer and more self-controlled, parents may not recognize his or her continuing needs for help and understanding in coping with social and emotional difficulties the condition has caused. With a more attentive and less disruptive pupil, teachers may lose sight of continuing learning deficits in children who have fallen a year or more behind their classmates in reading, writing, and other basic academic skills (Rie, Rie, Stewart, & Ambuel, 1976; Schaefer, Palkes, & Stewart, 1974; Sroufe, 1975; Weithorn & Ross, 1976).

Some other concerns about stimulant medication of MBD/ADD children have received considerable public attention but proved unjustified. Newspaper articles about supposedly widespread, inappropriate drugging of difficult-to-manage schoolchildren prompted a congressional inquiry in 1970 (Gallagher, 1970), and some professionals have voiced alarm that we are seeing an "epidemic" of unwarranted stimulant medication of the young that constitutes child abuse (Adelman & Compas, 1977; Brown & Bing, 1976; Freeman, 1976). Yet the best available research indicates in fact a range from 0.76 to 1.73 percent of schoolchildren who are receiving medication for hyperactivity. This figure does not seem out of line, given the estimated 5 to 6 percent prevalence of MBD/ADD and the reasonable expectation that about 65 percent will benefit from drugs. Urban children are somewhat more likely than rural children to receive medication for behavior problems. Yet in contrast to some claims in the public media that disadvantaged groups are singled out to be drugged rather than cared for in other ways, children are slightly more likely to be on medication in school districts with above-average family income than in districts with below-average family income (Bosco & Robin, 1979; Conway, 1977; Krager & Safer, 1974; Lambert, Sandoval, & Sassone, 1979).

Concern is also expressed at times that placing young children on a drug regimen, for whatever purpose, will make them susceptible to drug addiction later. Once again, in contrast to public alarm, no available research evidence points to subsequent addiction as a long-term consequence of stimulant medication in the treatment of MBD/ADD (Beck, Langford, MacKay, & Sum, 1975; Laufer, 1971; Safer & Allen, 1975b).

Nevertheless, enthusiasm for the utility of drugs in treating MBD/ADD children must be tempered by their likely side effects, their unpredictable impact in the individual case, and their minimal bearing on secondary consequences of the disorder. Children placed on stimulant medication should be carefully monitored for negative drug reactions, primary symptom change, and persisting social, emotional, and learning problems. Most clinicians concur further that drugs should constitute only one facet of a multimodal treatment approach in working with MBD/ADD children, and some physicians recommend using drugs only after psychological and educational approaches have been tried, unless the primary symptoms are severe (Barkley, 1977; Lambert et al., 1979; Loney, 1980; Satterfield, Cantwell, & Satterfield, 1979; Sprague, 1977).

Psychological Intervention

Various psychological intervention techniques are effective in reducing the primary manifestations of MBD/ADD and some of its secondary consequences as well. The most important of these are *operant conditioning, verbal mediation,* and *modeling.*

Operant Conditioning　The use of rewards to shape behavior has found useful applications in working with MBD/ADD children. Even such a simple procedure as giving children a piece of candy for performing well in a classroom situation helps them reduce their amount of hyperactive behavior and show a longer attention span. Similarly simple and effective is training teachers to increase the ratio of approving to disapproving comments in their interactions with students, known as "accentuating the positive" (Kazdin, 1978; Lahey, Delamater, & Kupfer, 1981; Loney, Weissenburger, Wollson, & Lichty, 1979; Rosenbaum, O'Leary, & Jacob, 1975).

O'Leary and his colleagues have developed an extensive program for hyperactive schoolchildren in which specific classroom goals are set for each child, efforts to achieve these goals are evaluated and praised on a daily basis, and regular reports are sent to parents, who are encouraged to reward progress with extra television time, spending money, family outings, and the like. When this program is integrated as a regular, ongoing feature of their school experience, 80 percent of the children participating achieve improved daily reports on their classroom behavior and learning (O'Leary & Drabman, 1971; O'Leary, Drabman, & Kass, 1973; O'Leary & O'Leary, 1976).

Verbal Mediation   This cognitive approach teaches learning-disabled children certain ways of thinking or talking to themselves about academic tasks that help them achieve better results. For example, hyperactive children who are encouraged to use self-directed verbal commands to "stop, look, and listen" become more capable of following directions, working deliberately, and avoiding careless errors. Numerous similar strategies that these youngsters can repeat to themselves have the same benefit, including "go slow," "check it over," and "work on one problem at a time" (Abikoff, 1979; Cameron & Robinson, 1980; Douglas, 1972; Meichenbaum & Burland, 1979).

Modeling   Impulsive schoolchildren become more reflective in their study habits when they work with teachers who model a reflective style. This same observational learning effect has been found after such youngsters view films of other children working on tasks in a careful, reflective manner (Allyon & Rosenbaum, 1977; Carter & Shostak, 1980; Ridberg, Parke, & Hetherington, 1971). Both teacher and peer modeling can accordingly contribute to helping children overcome learning disabilities.

Success to date in applying these behavioral methods in treating MBD/ADD children has been very encouraging, especially since they avoid the side effects of stimulant medication. Many psychologists urge continuing development of such nondrug approaches and thorough trials with them before drugs are considered necessary or appropriate in treating an individual child (Allyon, Layman, & Kandel, 1975; Prout, 1977; Weissenburger & Loney, 1977).

Traditional psychotherapy has little effect on the primary symptoms of MBD/ADD or on learning disabilities. However, this mode of treatment may be essential in combating the secondary emotional consequences of this disorder, which generally do not respond either to drugs or the behavioral interventions mentioned earlier. Particularly important in this regard is helping MBD/ADD children understand and deal with interpersonal difficulties, overcome negative self-attitudes, and avoid the feelings of failure and alienation that often contribute to antisocial behavior and other negative outcomes (Gardner, 1973b, 1975; Milich & Loney, 1979; Silver, 1979).

Educational Planning

Because young people spend so much of their time in school during middle childhood and adolescence, educational planning plays an important role in treating those who show signs of MBD/ADD. However, opinion is divided concerning three central aspects of working with MBD/ADD children in the schools: whether they should learn in distraction-free or normally stimulating environments; whether their instruction should focus on training in basic perceptual-motor skills or training in academic tasks; whether they should be taught in a regular or a special classroom.

Distraction-Free Versus Normally Stimulating Environments   Since learning and behavior problems of MBD/ADD children result partly from their distractibility, these problems might logically be expected to diminish when external stimulation is reduced. Cruickshank and his colleagues applied this logic in a well-known study involving specially engineered classrooms for hyperactive children (Cruickshank, Bentzen, Ratzeburg, & Tannhauser, 1961). Students' desks were placed far apart, to prevent them from distracting each other, and there were small, enclosed cubicles where they could be sent to work in semiisolation. The cubicles and the walls of the classroom were painted the same neutral color; no maps, pictures, or bulletin boards were hung; windows were fitted with translucent rather than transparent glass; wall-to-wall carpeting and acoustic ceilings were installed; the experimental room itself was located in a remote part of the school building. In short, everything possible was done to eliminate perceptual contrasts and reduce visual and auditory stimulation.

Some hyperactive children showed more academic progress in the Cruickshank setting than comparison groups in a regular classroom, and many special educators have subsequently recommended minimal stimulation programs in working with MBD children (Alabiso, 1972; Cruickshank, 1975; Kirk, 1972). Cruickshank (1977, p. 177) has remained clear on his view: "The first, and perhaps the most important, requirement of a setting for learning disabled children is that stimuli be reduced to a minimum." Nevertheless, there are several reasons for questioning the effectiveness of teaching children in distraction-free environments.

First, although some of the children in the original Cruickshank experiment benefited from the engineered classroom, most did not. Second, those who did benefit may well have been responding to general aspects of the special attention they were receiving

There is considerable disagreement concerning whether learning-disabled children should be taught in this kind of specially engineered, distraction-free classroom.

and not specifically to stimulus reduction. Third, whether effective in the classroom or not, such a contrived situation deprives children of necessary opportunities for learning to handle distracting stimulation in the real world (Forness, 1975; Ross & Ross, 1976, Chapter 6). Finally, there is increasing evidence to suggest that hyperactive and learning-disabled children are less restless and achieve better task performance in learning situations that include ordinary background sights and sounds than in situations where meaningful external stimulation has been reduced (Carter & Diaz, 1971; Rugel, Cheatam, & Mitchell, 1978; Zentall, 1980; Zentall & Zentall, 1976).

Although these latter findings run counter to the popular practice of teaching MBD/ADD children in distraction-free environments, they fit well with the recent advances in understanding the nature of this disorder. To the extent that MBD/ADD children suffer from nervous system underarousal, the logic behind the original Cruickshank experiment fails to hold. If MBD/ADD children are overactive and distractible because the inhibitory functions of their nervous system are underaroused, placing them in a stimulus-reduced environment may only aggravate their problems. On the other hand, if their limited self-control derives from underarousal, then providing adequate external stimulation can, like stimulant medication, have a calming effect that allows them to function better in school.

Skill Training Versus Task Training Some special educators believe that the best way to help MBD/ADD children overcome learning and behavior problems in school is to train them in specific perceptual-motor skills in which they are deficient (Arbitman-Smith & Haywood, 1980; Frostig & Maslow, 1979). In some research based on this belief, perceptually deficient first-graders given systematic perceptual-stimulation exercises showed significant improvement in their reading achievement; as second-graders, furthermore, they surpassed the achievement of a comparison group who had received only regular academic tutoring in reading (Arnold, Barnebey, McManus, Smeltzer, Conrad, Winer, & Desgranges, 1977; Silver, Hagin, & Hersh, 1972).

Other professionals argue that the effectiveness of any training for handicapped children depends on how closely it relates to actual tasks they are expected to master. There is considerable supporting evidence that direct training in an academic task produces better results than basic skill training. As one example, children who have difficulty reading because they cannot scan well from left to right benefit more from ordinary reading instruction than from contrived exercises to improve their eye movements. In other respects as well, numerous studies show a disappointing lack of success in remediating learning disabilities through perceptual training (Lyon, 1977; Mann, 1970; Schroeder, Schroeder, & Davine, 1978).

This disagreement can be partly resolved by considering a child's age. At the kindergarten level a significant relationship exists between perceptual-motor skills and school readiness, but this relationship and its implications for school learning decline sharply as children advance through the grades (Mann & Goodman, 1976). Hence it may be that skill training is helpful to learning-disabled children early but needs to be replaced increasingly with task training as children grow older. Regrettably, this means that skill training may already be too little and too late by the time a learning disability is identified. Especially among adolescents, there seems to be little basis for attempting to teach basic learning processes at the expense of remedial education in academic subject matter (Lerner, Evans, & Meyers, 1977).

Regular Versus Special Classrooms As in the case of educational planning for retarded children, opinions differ concerning the best place for working with MBD/ADD children in the schools. Some feel strongly that these youngsters should be kept in their regular classroom if at all possible (mainstreaming), some maintain that their special needs can be adequately met only by specially trained teachers working with them in special classes, and others favor combining regular class placement with a "resource" room in which children can spend part of their time each day receiving individualized special instruction (Bruininks, 1978b; Leviton, 1978; Ribner, 1978). The issues involved in preferences for one or the other of these alternative approaches are largely the same as discussed in Chapter 3 and will not be repeated here.

Mention should be made of a widespread trend toward what is called a **psychoeducational approach** in working with learning-disabled children. This approach avoids any assumptions about a single treatment plan that is best for all. Instead, it begins with a careful diagnostic assessment of why children are having learning difficulties and what will best serve their needs. These needs—for special skill training, tutoring in certain subject areas, programs to improve study habits or self-control, efforts to enhance self-esteem, or whatever—are met by whatever combination of behavior modification, psychotherapy, teaching methods, and classroom placement seems most likely to achieve the desired ends. Thus all available knowledge of what might be helpful to individual children is utilized without imposing any particular treatment philosophy on them (Brooks, 1979; Cruickshank & Hallahan, 1975; Gredler, 1978; Schere, Richardson, & Bialer, 1980).

Parent Counseling

Treatment of MBD/ADD children proceeds best when their parents are appropriately counseled about the nature of the condition and about what they can realistically expect of their youngsters. Parents often blame themselves when one of their children has a defect from early in life, and they may feel especially overwhelmed if the defect results in unpredictable, unmanageable behavior. Both self-blame and feelings of helplessness interfere with constructive parenting, and both can be relieved through parent counseling, whether individually, in groups, or in family sessions. Parents can also be trained to supplement and even take over certain functions of the professional therapist, particularly in caring for their child in ways that encourage positive growth rather than intensified disorder (Diament & Coletti, 1978; Feighner, 1975; Ferholt & Solnit, 1978; Kaslow & Cooper, 1978; Philage, Kuna, & Becerril, 1975).

Among the helpful responses parents can learn from counseling are to reward their youngsters for what they are able to accomplish and not to make excessive demands on them, to accept their children's handicap without subjecting them to countless evaluations in the hope of finding an expert who will refute the MBD/ADD diagnosis, and to allow them to do as many things as possible that other children do, rather than to overprotect them or accentuate their sense of being different. Such constructive parental management preserves the self-esteem of MBD/ADD children and also helps them benefit more from whatever other treatment they are receiving (Abrams & Kaslow, 1977; Kozloff, 1979; Loney, Comly, & Simon, 1975).

SUMMARY

Minimal brain dysfunction (MBD), also referred to as attention deficit disorder (ADD), is a disorder of behavioral and perceptual-cognitive functioning that is often assumed to involve some impairment of the central nervous system. Learning disability (LD) refers to some deficit in essential learning processes that causes children to achieve below expectation in school in the absence of any intellectual or emotional handicaps or lack of opportunity to learn. LD is one of the possible consequences of MBD/ADD and probably its most common consequence during the school-age years.

Surveys indicate that 5 to 6 percent of school-age children are considered by their parents, teachers, or family doctor to demonstrate MBD/ADD. For reasons that are not yet clear, MBD/ADD is three to seven times more common in boys than in girls. Although it is usually present from early in life, it is often not identified until middle childhood, when the demands of attending school bring an MBD/ADD child's limitations into sharper focus than before.

The primary behavioral characteristics of MBD/ADD are hyperactivity, distractibility, impulsivity, and excitability. Some combination of these behavior patterns usually indicates the presence of the disorder; however, care must be taken to distinguish the normal extent of such behavior in young children from abnormal patterns indicative of MBD/ADD. The primary perceptual-cognitive characteristics of MBD/ADD are impaired spatial perception, visual-motor coordination, memory, hearing, and speech. These impairments are among "soft" signs used by neurologists to identify brain dysfunction. From 50 to 60 percent of MBD children show neurological soft signs, and about 50 percent have abnormal brain waves.

The prominent characterists of MBD/ADD vary with age. As infants, children later identified as MBD/ADD tend to be extremely active, eat and sleep poorly, cry frequently, and lag behind in acquiring motor and language skills. These behavioral irregularities are followed during the preschool years by the emergence of the primary manifestations of MBD/ADD mentioned earlier. These primary symptoms persist into middle childhood but then typically become overshadowed by secondary difficulties they cause, especially in school learning and interpersonal relationships.

From 50 to 80 percent of MBD/ADD children develop school learning difficulties, and 60 to 70 percent fail one or more grades by the time they reach their teens. Their restlessness and distractibility interfere with attention to their teachers and assignments, and their perceptual-cognitive deficits interfere with their mastery of certain basic skills and subject matter. The most common and severe specific learning disability is inability to read at grade level, which has a cumulative negative impact on almost all subsequent learning. The aggressive, disruptive, and poorly self-controlled behavior of MBD/ADD children makes them unpopular with peers, teachers, and other adults. Their resulting social isolation, combined with mounting frustration in their efforts to master school learning and other skills, frequently contributes to these youngsters' forming a low opinion of themselves and engaging in various kinds of antisocial behavior.

The primary behavioral manifestations of MBD/ADD tend to diminish during adolescence. However, many perceptual-cognitive deficits persist, as do such secondary consequences of the disorder as learning difficulties, low self-esteem, and tendencies toward antisocial behavior. As adolescents MBD/ADD youngsters become increasingly prone to withdrawn and self-deprecating behavior, periods of depression, and delinquent acts, which together may obscure their perceptual-cognitive and learning difficulties. Fortunately, most MBD/ADD children improve in response to treatment or their own maturation, and only about 30 percent pass through this characteristic course of persisting disorder. For this group, continuing serious adjustment problems in adulthood are likely—especially chronic impulse disorders and socioeconomic underachievement.

Like mental retardation, MBD/ADD, has many possible causes and is likely to appear for different reasons in different children. Most of the harmful prenatal and early life events that can result in mental retardation also increase the risk of MBD/ADD, including excessive smoking and drinking by pregnant women, birth complications, and certain health problems in infancy. Evidence from family, twin, and adoption studies leaves little doubt that genetic factors contribute to some instances of MBD/ADD, although the majority of youngsters with this disorder do not show patterns of familial incidence. There is also reason to believe that parents who are themselves aggressive, excitable, and impatient can foster characteristic MBD/ADD behavior patterns in their children by the type of child-rearing they practice and the example they set with their own behavior.

Adequate treatment of MBD/ADD requires a careful combination of drugs, psychological intervention, educational planning, and parent counseling, tailored to meet an individual child's needs. Stimulant drugs have proved helpful in curbing the hyperactivity, distractibility, and impulsivity in 60 to 70 percent of MBD/ADD children, apparently because they bring an underaroused nervous system in these children up to a normal level of ability to control motor and sensory functions. However, these drugs have some undesirable side effects, and they have no directly beneficial impact on learning difficulties or other secondary consequences of MBD/ADD.

Various psychological intervention techniques are effective in reducing both the primary manifestations of MBD/ADD and related learning difficulties. These include using rewards to shape controlled achievement behavior (operant conditioning), teaching children certain ways of talking or thinking to themselves that help sustain task-oriented behavior (verbal mediation), and exposing children to teachers and peers who set good examples of careful, reflective work (modeling). In addition, traditional psychotherapy can often help MBD/ADD children understand and deal with interpersonal difficulties, overcome negative self-attitudes, and avoid feelings of failure and alienation.

Educational planning plays an important role in treating MBD/ADD children during the school years. Opinions differ concerning (a) whether children should learn in distraction-free or normally stimulating environments, (b) whether instruction should focus on skill or task training, and (c) whether learning-disabled children should be taught in regular or special classrooms.

Prevailing evidence indicates that although some highly distractible children may benefit from being isolated in special environments, most learn better in situations that include ordinary background sights and sounds. Training in specific perceptual-motor skills may help some MBD/ADD children overcome learning and behavior problems, especially in the preschool and early school years, but direct training in academic tasks generally produces better results than basic skill training and increasingly so as children grow older. Specific decisions for regular or special class placement or some combination of the two through use of a resource room must be made on the basis of individual psychoeducational assessments.

Finally, whatever combination of drugs, psychological intervention, and educational planning may be employed, treatment of MBD/ADD children proceeds best when their parents are appropriately counseled about the nature of the condition and what they can realistically expect of their youngsters. In addition, parents can often be trained effectively to care for their child in ways that will encourage positive growth rather than an intensified behavioral disorder.

REFERENCES

ABIKOFF, H. Cognitive training interventions in children: Review of a new approach. *Journal of Learning Disabilities,* 1979, *12,* 123−135.

ABIKOFF, H., GITTELMAN, R., & KLEIN, D. F. Classroom observation code for hyperactive children: A replication of validity. *Journal of Consulting and Clinical Psychology,* 1980, *48,* 555−565.

ABRAMS, J. C., & KASLOW, F. Family systems and the learning disabled child: Intervention and treatment. *Journal of Learning Disabilities,* 1977, *10,* 86−90.

ACKERMAN, P. T., DYKMAN, R. A., & PETERS, J. E. Hierarchical factor patterns on the WISC as related to areas of learning deficit. *Perceptual and Motor Skills,* 1976, *42,* 583−615.

ACKERMAN, P. T., DYKMAN, R. A., & PETERS, J. E. Learning-disabled boys as adolescents: Cognitive factors and achievement. *Journal of the American Academy of Child Psychiatry,* 1977a, *16,* 296−313.

ACKERMAN, P. T., DYKMAN, R. A., & PETERS, J. E. Teenage status of hyperactive and nonhyperactive learning disabled boys. *American Journal of Orthopsychiatry,* 1977b, *44,* 577−596.

ACKERMAN, P. T., PETERS, J. E., & DYKMAN, R. A. Children with specific learning disabilities: Bender Gestalt test and other signs. *Journal of Learning Disabilities,* 1971, *4,* 437−446.

ADAMS, R. M., KOSCIS, J. J., & ESTES, R. E. Soft neurological signs in learning-disabled children and controls. *American Journal of Diseases of Children,* 1974, *128,* 614−618.

ADELMAN, H. S., & COMPAS, B. E. Stimulant drugs and learning problems. *Journal of Special Education,* 1977, *11,* 377−416.

ALABISO, F. Inhibitory functions of attention in reducing hyperactive behavior. *American Journal of Mental Deficiency,* 1972, *77,* 259−282.

ALLYON, T., LAYMAN, D., & KANDEL, H. J. A behavioral-educational alternative to drug control of hyperactive children. *Journal of Applied Behavioral Analysis,* 1975, *8,* 137−146.

ALLYON, T., & ROSENBAUM, M. S. The behavioral treatment of disruption and hyperactivity in school settings. In B. B. Lahey & A. E. Kazdin (Eds.), *Advances in clinical child psychology.* Vol. 1. New York: Plenum, 1977.

AMAN, M. G. Psychotropic drugs and learning problems: A selective review. *Journal of Learning Disabilities,* 1980, *13,* 87−97.

AMERICAN PSYCHIATRIC ASSOCIATION. *Diagnostic and statistical manual of mental disorders.* (3d ed.) Washington, D.C.: American Psychiatric Association, 1980.

ARBITMAN-SMITH, R., & HAYWOOD, H. C. Cognitive education for learning-disabled adolescents. *Journal of Abnormal Child Psychology,* 1980, *8,* 51−64.

ARNOLD, L. E., BARNEBEY, N., MCMANUS, J., SMELTZER, D. J., CONRAD, A., WINER, G., & DES-GRANGES, L. Prevention by specific perceptual remediation for vulnerable first-graders. *Archives of General Psychiatry,* 1977, *34,* 1279–1294.

BALOW, B., RUBIN, R., & ROSEN, M. J. Perinatal events as precursors of reading disability. *Reading Research Quarterly,* 1975–1976, *11,* 36–71.

BANDURA, A., ROSS, D., & ROSS, S. A. Transmission of aggression through imitation of aggressive models. *Journal of Abnormal and Social Psychology,* 1961, *63,* 575–582.

BARKLEY, R. A. A review of stimulant drug research with hyperactive children. *Journal of Child Psychology and Psychiatry,* 1977, *18,* 137–165.

BARKLEY, R. A. Using stimulant drugs in the classroom. *School Psychology Digest,* 1979, *8,* 412–425.

BARKLEY, R. A., & CUNNINGHAM, C. E. The Effects of methylphenidate on the mother-child interactions of hyperactive children. *Archives of General Psychiatry,* 1979, *36,* 201–208.

BECK, L., LANGFORD, W. S., MACKAY, M., & SUM, G. Childhood chemotherapy and later drug abuse and growth curve: A follow-up study of 30 adolescents. *American Journal of Psychiatry,* 1975, *132,* 436–438.

BELMONT, I. Perceptual organization and minimal brain dysfunctions. In H. E. Rie & E. D. Rie (Eds.), *Handbook of minimal brain dysfunctions.* New York: Wiley, 1980.

BELMONT, L. Epidemiology. In H. E. Rie & E. D. Rie (Eds.), *Handbook of minimal brain dysfunctions.* New York: Wiley, 1980.

BLACK, F. W. Cognitive, academic, and behavioral findings in children with suspected and documented neurological dysfunction. *Journal of Learning Disabilities,* 1976, *9,* 182–187.

BORLAND, B. L., & HECKMAN, H. K. Hyperactive boys and their brothers: A 25-year follow-up study. *Archives of General Psychiatry,* 1976, *33,* 669–675.

BOSCO, J., & ROBIN, S. Hyperkinesis: How common it is and how is it treated: In C. Whalen & B. Henker (Eds.), *The social ecology of hyperactivity.* New York: Academic, 1979.

BROOKS, R. Psychoeducational assessment: A broader perspective. *Professional Psychology,* 1979, *10,* 708–722.

BROWN, J. L., & BING, S. R. Drugging children: Child abuse by professionals. In G. P. Koocher (Ed.), *Children's rights and the mental health professions.* New York: Wiley, 1976.

BRUININKS, V. L. Peer status and personality characteristics of learning disabled and nondisabled students. *Journal of Learning Disabilities,* 1978a, *11,* 484–489.

BRUININKS, V. L. Actual and perceived peer status of learning-disabled students in mainstream programs. *Journal of Special Education,* 1978b, *12,* 51–58.

BRUMBACK, R. A., & WEINBERG, W. A. Relationship of hyperactivity and depression in children. *Perceptual and Motor Skills,* 1977, *45,* 247–251.

BRYAN, T. H. Social relationships and verbal interactions of learning disabled children. *Journal of Learning Disabilities,* 1978, *11,* 107–115.

BRYAN, T. H., & PEARL, R. Self concepts and locus of control of learning disabled children. *Journal of Clinical Child Psychology,* 1979, *8,* 223–226.

BRYAN, T. S. An observational analysis of classroom behaviors of children with learning disabilities. *Journal of Learning Disabilities,* 1974, *7,* 35–43.

CAMERON, J. R. Parental treatment, children's temperament, and the risk of childhood behavioral problems. *American Journal of Orthopsychiatry,* 1978, *48,* 140–147.

CAMERON, M. I., & ROBINSON, V. M. Effects of cognitive training on academic and on-task behavior of hyperactive children. *Journal of Abnormal Child Psychology,* 1980, *8,* 405–419.

CAMPBELL, M., & SMALL, A. M. Chemotherapy. In B. B. Wolman (Ed.), *Handbook of treatment of mental disorders in childhood and adolescence.* Englewood Cliffs, N.J.: Prentice-Hall, 1978.

CAMPBELL, S. B. Hyperactivity: Course and treatment. In A. Davids (Ed.), *Child personality and psychopathology: Current topics.* Vol. 3. New York: Wiley, 1976.

CAMPBELL, S. B. Mother-infant interaction as a function of maternal ratings of temperament. *Child Psychiatry and Human Development*, 1979, *10*, 67–76.

CAMPBELL, S. B., ENDMAN, M. W., & BERNFELD, G. A three-year follow-up of hyperactive preschoolers into elementary school. *Journal of Child Psychology and Psychiatry*, 1977, *18*, 239–249.

CAMPBELL, S. B., SCHLEIFER, M., & WEISS, G. Continuities in maternal reports and child behaviors over time in hyperactive and comparison groups. *Journal of Abnormal Child Psychology*, 1978, *6*, 33–45.

CANTWELL, D. P. Psychiatric illness in the families of hyperactive children. *Archives of General Psychiatry*, 1972, *27*, 414–417.

CANTWELL, D. P. Clinical picture, epidemiology and classifications of the hyperactive child syndrome. In D. P. Cantwell (Ed.), *The hyperactive child*. New York: Spectrum, 1975a.

CANTWELL, D. P. Natural history and prognosis in the hyperactive child syndrome. In D. P. Cantwell (Ed.), *The hyperactive child*. New York: Spectrum, 1975b.

CANTWELL, D. P. Familial-genetic research with hyperactive children. In D. P. Cantwell (Ed.), *The hyperactive child*. New York: Spectrum, 1975c.

CANTWELL, D. P. Genetic factors in the hyperkinetic syndrome. *Journal of the American Academy of Child Psychiatry*, 1976, *15*, 214–223.

CANTWELL, D. P. Psychopharmacologic treatment of the minimal brain dysfunction syndrome. In J. M. Wiener (Ed.), *Psychopharmacology in childhood and adolescence*. New York: Basic Books, 1977.

CAPUTE, A., NEIDERMEYER, F., & RICHARDSON, F. The electroencephalogram in children with minimal cerebral dysfunction. *Periatrics*, 1968, *41*, 1104–1114.

CAREY, W. B., MCDEVITT, S. C., & BAKER, D. Differentiating minimal brain dysfunction and temperament. *Developmental Medicine and Child Neurology*, 1979, *21*, 765–777.

CARTER, E. N., & SHOSTEK, D. A. Imitation in the treatment of the hyperkinetic behavior syndrome. *Journal of Clinical Child Psychology*, 1980, *9*, 63–66.

CARTER, J. L., & DIAZ, A. Effects of visual and auditory background on reading test performance. *Exceptional Children*, 1971, *38*, 43–50.

CHALFANT, J. G., & SCHEFFELIN, M. A. *Central processing dysfunctions in children: A review of research*. Washington, D.C.: National Institute of Neurological Diseases and Stroke. Monograph No. 9. 1969.

CHAPMAN, R. B., LARSEN, S. C., & PARKER, R. M. Interactions of first-grade teachers with learning disordered children. *Journal of Learning Disabilities*, 1979, *12*, 225–230.

CLEMENTS, S. D. *Minimal brain dysfunction in children*. Washington, D.C.: National Institute of Neurological Diseases and Blindness. Monograph No. 3. 1966.

COLLETTI, L. F. Relationship between pregnancy and birth complications and the later development of learning disabilities. *Journal of Learning Disabilities*, 1979, *12*, 659–663.

CONNERS, C. K. A teacher rating scale for use in drug studies with children. *American Journal of Psychiatry*, 1969, *126*, 884–888.

CONNERS, C. K. Symptom patterns in hyperkinetic, neurotic, and normal children. *Child Development*, 1970, *41*, 667–682.

CONNERS, C. K. Minimal brain dysfunction and psychopathology in children. In A. Davids (Ed.), *Child personality and psychopathology: Current topics*. Vol. 2. New York: Wiley, 1975.

CONNERS, C. K. *Food additives and hyperactive children*. New York: Plenum, 1980.

CONWAY, A. Therapeutic drugs in the elementary schools: An urban phenomenon? *Education*, 1977, *97*, 299–301.

CRUICKSHANK, W. M. The education of children with specific learning disabilities. In W. M. Cruickshank & G. O. Johnson (Eds.), *Education of exceptional children and youth*. (3d ed.) Englewood Cliffs, N.J.: Prentice-Hall, 1975.

CRUICKSHANK, W. M. *Learning disabilities in home, school, and community*. Syracuse, N.Y.: University of Syracuse Press, 1977a.

CRUICKSHANK, W. M. Myths and realities in learning disabilities. *Journal of Learning Disabilities,* 1977b, *10,* 51–58.

CRUICKSHANK, W. M., BENTZEN, F. A., RATZEBURG, F. H., & TANNHAUSER, M. T. *A teaching method for brain injured and hyperactive children.* Syracuse, N.Y.: Syracuse University Press, 1961.

CRUICKSHANK, W. M., & HALLAHAN, D. P. (Eds.) *Perceptual and learning difficulties in children.* Vol. 1. *Psychoeducational practices.* Syracuse: Syracuse University Press, 1975.

DALBY, J. T. Deficit or delay: Neuro-psychological models of developmental dyslexia. *Journal of Special Education,* 1979, *13,* 239–264.

DAVIE, R., BUTLER, N., & GOLDSTEIN, H. *From birth to seven: A report of the National Child Development Study.* London: Longman, 1972.

DENHOFF, E. The natural life history of children with minimal brain dysfunction. *Annals of the New York Academy of Sciences,* 1973, *205,* 188–205.

DENSON, R., NANSON, J. L., & MCWATTERS, M. A. Hyperkinesis and maternal smoking. *Canadian Psychiatric Association Journal,* 1975, *20,* 183–187.

DENTON, C. L., & MCINTYRE, C. W. Span of apprehension in hyperactive boys. *Journal of Abnormal Child Psychology,* 1978, *6,* 19–24.

DIAMENT, C., & COLLETTI, G. Evaluation of behavioral group counseling for parents of learning-disabled children. *Journal of Abnormal Child Psychology,* 1978, *6,* 385–400.

DOUGLAS, V. I. Stop, look and listen: The problem of sustained attention and impulse control in hyperactive and normal children. *Canadian Journal of Behavioral Science,* 1972, *4,* 259–282.

DUBEY, D. R. Organic factors in hyperkinesis: A critical review. *American Journal of Orthopsychiatry,* 1976, *46,* 353–366.

DUNN, H. C., & MCBURNEY, A. K. Cigarette smoking and the fetus and the child. *Pediatrics,* 1977, *60,* 772.

DYKMAN, R., ACKERMAN, P. T., CLEMENTS, S. D., & PETERS, J. E. Specific learning disabilities: An attentional deficit syndrome. In H. Mykelbust (Ed.), *Progress in learning disabilities.* Vol. II. New York: Grune & Stratton, 1971.

DYKMAN, R. A., WALLS, R. C., SUZUKI, T., ACKERMAN, P. T., & PETERS, J. E. Children with learning disabilities: Conditioning, differentiation, and the effect of distraction. *American Journal of Orthopsychiatry,* 1970, *40,* 766–782.

EISENBERG, L. Definitions of dyslexia: Their consequences for research and policy. In A. L. Benton & D. Pearl (Eds.), *Dyslexia: An appraisal of current knowledge.* New York: Oxford University Press, 1978.

ELKIND, D., & WEINER, I. B. *Development of the child.* New York: Wiley, 1978.

FEIGHNER, A. Videotape training for parents as therapeutic agents with hyperactive children. In D. P. Cantwell (Ed.), *The hyperactive child.* New York: Spectrum, 1975.

FEINGOLD, B. F. *Why your child is hyperactive.* New York: Random House, 1975a.

FEINGOLD, B. F. Hyperkinesis and learning disabilities linked to artificial food flavors and colors. *American Journal of Nursing,* 1975b, *75,* 797–803.

FERHOLT, J. B., & SOLNIT, A. J. Counseling parents of mentally retarded and learning disordered children. In L. E. Arnold (Ed.), *Helping parents help their children.* New York: Brunner/Mazel, 1978.

FIELD, T. Games parents play with normal and high-risk infants. *Child Psychiatry and Human Development,* 1979, *10,* 41–48.

FISH, B. The "one child, one drug" myth of stimulants in hyperkinesis. *Archives of General Psychiatry,* 1971, *25,* 193–203.

FISH, B. Stimulant drug treatment of hyperactive children. In D. P. Cantwell (Ed.), *The hyperactive child.* New York: Spectrum, 1975.

FOCH, T. T., DEFRIES, J. C., MCCLEARN, G. E., & SINGER, S. M. Familial patterns of impairment in reading disability. *Journal of Educational Psychology,* 1977, *69,* 316–329.

FORNESS, S. Educational approaches with hyperactive children. In D. P. Cantwell (Ed.), *The hyperactive child.* New York: Spectrum, 1975.

FREEMAN, R. D. Minimal brain dysfunction, hyperactivity, and learning disorders: Epidemic or episode? *School Review,* 1976, *85,* 5–30.

FROSTIG, M., & MASLOW, P. Neuropsychological contributions to education. *Journal of Learning Disabilities,* 1979, *12,* 538–552.

GALANTE, M. B., FLYE, M. E., & STEPHENS, L. S. Cumulative minor deficits: A longitudinal study of the relation of physical factors to school achievement. *Journal of Learning Disabilities,* 1972, *5,* 19–24.

GALLAGHER, C. C. Federal involvement in the use of behavior modification drugs on grammar school children. Hearing before a subcommittee of the Committee of Government Operations, House of Representatives, September 29, 1970.

GARDNER, R. A. *The family book about minimal brain dysfunction.* New York: Aronson, 1973a.

GARDNER, R. A. Psychotherapy of the psychogenic problems secondary to minimal brain dysfunction. *International Journal of Child Psychotherapy,* 1973b, *2,* 224–256.

GARDNER, R. A. Techniques for involving the child with MBD in meaningful psychotherapy. *Journal of Learning Disabilities,* 1975, *8,* 272–282.

GARDNER, R. A. *The objective diagnosis of minimal brain dysfunction.* Cresskill, N.J.: Creative Therapeutics, 1979.

GITTELMAN-KLEIN, R., & KLEIN, D. F. Are behavioral and psychometric changes related in methylphenidate-treated, hyperactive children? In R. Gittelman-Klein (Ed.), *Recent advances in child psychopharmacology.* New York: Human Sciences Press, 1975.

GITTELMAN-KLEIN, R., & KLEIN, D. F. Methylphenidate effects in learning disabilities. *Archives of General Psychiatry,* 1976, *33,* 655–664.

GLOW, P. H., & GLOW, R. A. Hyperkinetic impulse disorder: A developmental defect of motivation. *Genetic Psychology Monographs,* 1979, *100,* 159–231.

GREDLER, G. R. Learning disabilities and reading disorders: A current assessment. *Psychology in the Schools,* 1978, *15,* 226–238.

GROSS, M. B., & WILSON, W. C. *Minimal brain dysfunction: A clinical study of incidence, diagnosis and treatment in over 1,000 children.* New York: Brunner/Mazel, 1974.

HALLAHAN, D. P., & CRUICKSHANK, W. M. *Psycho-educational foundations of learning disabilities.* Englewood Cliffs, N.J.: Prentice-Hall, 1973.

HASTINGS, J. E., & BARKLEY, R. A. A review of psychophysiological research with hyperactive children. *Journal of Abnormal Child Psychology,* 1978, *6,* 413–447.

HEIMAN, J. R., & ROSS, A. O. Saccadic eye movements and reading difficulties. *Journal of Abnormal Child Psychology,* 1974, *2,* 53–61.

HELPER, M. M. Follow-up of children with minimal brain dysfunctions: Outcomes and predictors. In H. E. Rie & E. D. Rie (Eds.), *Handbook of minimal brain dysfunctions.* New York: Wiley, 1980.

HENKER, B., WHALEN, C. K., & COLLINS, B. E. Double-blind and triple-blind assessments of medication and placebo responses in hyperactive children. *Journal of Abnormal Child Psychology,* 1979, *7,* 1–18.

HERSCHEL, M. Dyslexia revisited: A review. *Human Genetics,* 1978, *40,* 115–134.

HERTZIG, M. E., BORTNER, M., & BIRCH, H. G. Neurological findings in children educationally designated as "brain damaged." *American Journal of Orthopsychiatry,* 1969, *39,* 437–446.

HOY, E., WEISS, G., MINDE, K., & COHEN, N. The hyperactive child at adolescence: Cognitive, emotional, and social functioning. *Journal of Abnormal Child Psychology,* 1978, *6,* 311–324.

HUMPHRIES, T., SWANSON, J., KINSBOURNE, M., & YIU, L. Stimulant effects on persistence of motor performance of hyperactive children. *Journal of Pediatric Psychology,* 1979, *4,* 55–66.

ILLINGWORTH, R. S. Developmental variations in relation to minimal brain dysfunction. In H. E. Rie & E. D. Rie (Eds.), *Handbook of minimal brain dysfunctions.* New York: Wiley, 1980.

INGRAM, T. Soft signs. *Developmental Medicine and Child Neurology,* 1973, *15,* 527–530.

JACOB, R. G., O'LEARY, K. D., & ROSENBLAD, C. Formal and informal classroom settings: Effects on hyperactivity. *Journal of Abnormal Child Psychology,* 1978, *6,* 47–59.

KASLOW, F. W., & COOPER, B. Family therapy with the learning disabled child and his/her family. *Journal of Marriage and Family Counseling,* 1978, *4,* 41–49.

KASPAR, J. C., & LOWENSTEIN, R. The effect of social interaction on activity level in six- to eight-year-old boys. *Child Development,* 1971, *42,* 1294–1298.

KAUFFMAN, J. M., & HALLAHAN, D. P. Learning disability and hyperactivity (with comments on minimal brain dysfunction). In B. B. Lahey & A. E. Kazdin (Eds.), *Advances in child clinical psychology.* Vol. 2. New York: Plenum, 1979.

KAZDIN, A. E. The application of operant techniques in treatment, rehabilitation, and education. In S. L. Garfield & A. E. Bergin (Eds.), *Handbook of psychotherapy and behavior change.* (2nd ed.) New York: Wiley, 1978.

KEOGH, B. K. Hyperactivity and learning disorders: Review and speculation. *Exceptional Children,* 1971, *38,* 101–109.

KESSLER, J. W. History of minimal brain dysfunctions. In H. E. Rie & E. D. Rie (Eds.), *Handbook of minimal brain dysfunctions.* New York: Wiley, 1980.

KINSBOURNE, M., & CAPLAN, P. J. *Children's learning and attention problems.* Boston: Little, Brown, 1979.

KIRK, S. P. *Educating exceptional children.* Boston: Houghton Mifflin, 1972.

KLATSKIN, E., MCNAMARA, N., SHAFFER, D., & PINCUS, J. Minimal organicity in children of normal intelligence: Correspondence between psychological test results and neurologic findings. *Journal of Learning Disabilities,* 1972, *5,* 213–218.

KLEIN, A. R., & YOUNG, R. D. Hyperactive boys in their classroom: Assessment of teacher and peer perceptions, interactions, and classroom behaviors. *Journal of Abnormal Child Psychology,* 1979, *7,* 425–442.

KLUEVER, R. Mental abilities and disorders of learning. In H. R. Myklebust (Ed.), *Progress in learning disabilities.* Vol. 2. New York: Grune & Stratton, 1971.

KOPPITZ, E. *The Bender-Gestalt test for young children.* New York: Grune & Stratton, 1963.

KOZLOFF, M. A. *A program for families of children with learning and behavior problems.* New York: Wiley, 1979.

KRAGER, J. M., & SAFER, D. J. Type and prevalence of medication in treating hyperactive children. *New England Journal of Medicine,* 1974, *291,* 1118–1120.

LAHEY, B. B., DELAMATER, A., & KUPFER, D. Intervention strategies with hyperactive and learning-disabled children. In S. M. Turner, K. S. Calhoun, & H. E. Adams (Eds.), *Handbook of clinical behavior therapy.* New York: Wiley, 1981.

LAHEY, B. B., STEMPNIAK, M., ROBINSON, E. J., & TYROLER, M. J. Hyperactivity and learning disabilities as independent dimensions of child behavior problems. *Journal of Abnormal Psychology,* 1978, *87,* 333–340.

LAMBERT, N. M., & SANDOVAL, J. The prevalence of learning disabilities in a sample of children considered hyperactive. *Journal of Abnormal Child Psychology,* 1980, *8,* 33–50.

LAMBERT, N., SANDOVAL, J., & SASSONE, D. Prevalence of hyperactivity in elementary school children as a function of social system definers. *American Journal of Orthopsychiatry,* 1978, *48,* 446–463.

LAMBERT, N. M., SANDOVAL, J., & SASSONE, D. Prevalence of treatment regiments for children considered to be hyperactive. *American Journal of Orthopsychiatry,* 1979, *49,* 482–490.

LASKY, E. Z., & TOBIN, H. Linguistic and non-linguistic competing message effects. *Journal of Learning Disabilities,* 1973, *6,* 243–250.

LAUFER, M. W. Long-term management and some follow-up findings on the use of drugs with minimal cerebral syndromes. *Journal of Learning Disabilities,* 1971, *4,* 518–522.

LEFTON, L. A., LAHEY, B. B., & STAGG, D. I. Eye movements in reading disabled and normal children: A study of systems and strategies. *Journal of Learning Disabilities*, 1978, *11*, 549–558.

LENKOWSKY, R. S. Reading for the learning-disabled adolescent. *Academic Therapy*, 1977, *13*, 47–52.

LERER, R. J., ARTNER, J., & LERER, M. P. Handwriting deficits in children with minimal brain dysfunction: Effects of methylphenidate (Ritalin) and placebo. *Journal of Learning Disabilities*, 1979, *12*, 450–455.

LERNER, J. W., EVANS, M. A., & MEYERS, G. LD programs at the secondary level: A survey. *Academic Therapy*, 1977, *13*, 7–19.

LEVIN, H. S., & EISENBERG, H. M. Neuropsychological impairment after closed head injury in children and adolescents. *Journal of Pediatric Psychology*, 1979, *4*, 389–402.

LEVITON, H. The resource room: An alternative. *Academic Therapy*, 1978, *13*, 405–413.

LIPMAN, R. Stimulant medication and growth in hyperkinetic children. *Psychopharmacology Bulletin*, 1978, *14*, 61–62.

LONEY, J. Hyperkinesis comes of age: What do we know and where should we go? *American Journal of Orthopsychiatry*, 1980, *50*, 28–42.

LONEY, J., COMLY, H. H., & SIMON, B. Parental management, self-concept, and drug response in minimal brain dysfunction. *Journal of Learning Disabilities*, 1975, *8*, 187–190.

LONEY, J., LANGHORNE, J. E., & PATERNITE, C. E. An empirical basis for subgrouping the hyperkinetic-minimal brain dysfunction syndrome. *Journal of Abnormal Psychology*, 1978, *87*, 431–441.

LONEY, J., WEISSENBURGER, F. E., WOOLSON, R. F., & LICHTY, E. C. Comparing psychological and pharmacological treatments for hyperkinetic boys and their classmates. *Journal of Abnormal Child Psychology*, 1979, *7*, 133–143.

LUCAS, A. R. Muscular control and coordination in minimal brain dysfunctions. In H. E. Rie & E. D. Rie (Eds.), *Handbook of minimal brain dysfunctions*. New York: Wiley, 1980.

LYON, R. Auditory-perceptual training: The state of the art. *Journal of Learning Disabilities*, 1977, *10*, 564–572.

MCCARTHY, J. J., & MCCARTHY, J. F. *Learning disabilities*. Boston: Allyn & Bacon, 1969.

MCCLEARN, G. E. Review of "Dyslexia: Genetic aspects." In A. L. Benton & D. Pearl (Eds.), *Dyslexia: An appraisal of current knowledge*. New York: Oxford University Press, 1978.

MANN, L. Perceptual training: Misdirections and redirections. *American Journal of Orthopsychiatry*, 1970, *40*, 30–38.

MANN, L., & GOODMAN, L. Perceptual training: A critical retrospect. In E. Schopler & R. J. Reichler (Eds.), *Psychopathology and child development*. New York: Plenum, 1976.

MARTIN, H. P. Nutrition, injury, and illness. In H. E. Rie & E. D. Rie (Eds.), *Handbook of minimal brain dysfunctions*. New York: Wiley, 1980.

MATHENY, A. P., DOLAN, A. B., & WILSON, R. S. Twins with academic learning problems: Antecedent characteristics. *American Journal of Orthopsychiatry*, 1976, *46*, 464–469.

MAYRON, L. W. Hyperactivity from fluorescent lighting—fact or fancy: A commentary on the report by O'Leary, Rosenbaum, and Hughes. *Journal of Abnormal Child Psychology*, 1978, *6*, 291–294.

MAYRON, L. W. Allergy, learning, and behavior problems. *Journal of Learning Disabilities*, 1979, *12*, 32–42.

MAYRON, L. W., MAYRON, E. L., OTT, J. N., & NATIONS, R. Light, radiation, and academic achievement: Second year data. *Academic Therapy*, 1976, *11*, 397–407.

MAYRON, L. W., OTT, J. N., NATIONS, R., & MAYRON, E. L. Light, radiation and academic behavior: Initial studies on the effects of full-spectrum lighting and radiation shielding on behavior and academic performance of school children. *Academic Therapy*, 1974, *10*, 33–47.

MEICHENBAUM, D. H., & BURLAND, S. Cognitive behavior modification with children. *School Psychology Digest*, 1979, *8*, 426–433.

MENDELSON, W., JOHNSON, J., & STEWART, M. Hyperactive children as teenagers: A follow-up study. *Journal of Nervous and Mental Disease*, 1971, *153*, 273–279.

MILICH, R., & LONEY, J. The role of hyperactive and aggressive symptomatology in predicting adolescent outcome among hyperactive children. *Journal of Pediatric Psychology,* 1979, *4,* 93–112.

MILLER, R. G., PALKES, H. S., & STEWART, M. A. Hyperactive children in suburban elementary schools. *Child Psychiatry and Human Development,* 1973, 4, 121–127.

MILLICHAP, J. G. Drugs in management in minimal brain dysfunction. *Annals of the New York Academy of Sciences,* 1973, *205,* 321–334.

MINDE, K., WEISS, G., & MENDELSON, N. A 5-year follow-up study of 91 hyperactive school children. *Journal of the American Academy of Child Psychiatry,* 1972, *11,* 595–611.

MINSKOFF, J. G. Differential approaches to prevalence estimates of learning disabilities. *Annals of the New York Academy of Sciences,* 1973, *205,* 139–145.

MORRISON, J. R. Diagnosis of adult psychiatric patients with childhood hyperactivity. *American Journal of Psychiatry,* 1979, *136,* 955–958.

MORRISON, J. R., & STEWART, M. A. A family study of the hyperactive child syndrome. *Biological Psychiatry,* 1971, *3,* 189–195.

MORRISON, J. R., & STEWART, M. A. The psychiatric status of the legal families of adopted hyperactive children. *Archives of General Psychiatry,* 1973, *28,* 888–891.

NATIONAL INSTITUTE OF CHILD HEALTH AND HUMAN DEVELOPMENT. *Maturation, learning, and behavior.* Washington, D.C.: Department of Health, Education, and Welfare Publication No. (NIH) 76-1036, 1976.

NEEDLEMAN, H. L. Lead poisoning in children: Neurological implications of widespread subclinical intoxication. *Seminars in Psychiatry,* 1973, *5,* 47–53.

NISWANDER, K. R., & GORDON, M. (Eds.) *The Collaborative Perinatal Study of the National Institute of Neurological Diseases and Stroke: The women and their pregnancies.* Philadelphia: Saunders, 1972.

O'LEARY, K. D., & DRABMAN, R. Token reinforcement programs in the classroom. *Psychological Bulletin,* 1971, *75,* 379–398.

O'LEARY, K. D., DRABMAN, R., & KASS, R. E. Maintenance of appropriate behavior in a token program. *Journal of Abnormal Child Psychology,* 1973, *1,* 127–138.

O'LEARY, K. D. ROSENBAUM, A., & HUGHES, P. C. Fluorescent lighting: A purported source of hyperactive behavior. *Journal of Abnormal Child Psychology,* 1978a, *6,* 285–289.

O'LEARY, K. D., ROSENBAUM, A., & HUGHES, P. C. Direct and systematic replication: A rejoinder. *Journal of Abnormal Child Psychology,* 1978b, *6,* 295–297.

O'LEARY, S. G., & O'LEARY, K. D. Behavior modification in the school. In H. Leitenberg (Ed.), *Handbook of behavior modification and behavior therapy.* Englewood Cliffs, N.J.: Prentice-Hall, 1976.

PAULAUSKAS, S. L., & CAMPBELL, S. B. Social perspective-taking and teacher ratings of peer interaction in hyperactive boys. *Journal of Abnormal Child Psychology,* 1979, *7,* 483–493.

PETERS, J. E., ROMINE, J. S., & DYKMAN, R. A. A special neurological examination of children with learning disabilities, *Developmental Medicine and Child Neurology,* 1975, *16,* 63–78.

PHILAGE, M. L., KUNA, D. J., & BECERRIL, G. A new family approach to therapy for the learning disabled child. *Journal of Learning Disabilities,* 1975, *8,* 490–499.

PIROZZOLO, F. J. *The neuropsychology of developmental reading disorders.* New York: Praeger, 1979.

PRAWAT, R. S., & KERASOTES, D. Basic memory processes in reading. *Merrill-Palmer Quarterly,* 1978, *24,* 181–188.

PROUT, H. T. Behavioral intervention with hyperactive children: A review. *Journal of Learning Disabilities,* 1977, *10,* 141–146.

QUAY, H. C. Classification. In H. C. Quay & J. S. Werry (Eds.), *Psychopathological disorders of childhood.* (2nd ed.) New York: Wiley, 1979.

QUINN, P. O., & RAPOPORT, J. L. One-year follow-up of hyperactive boys treated with imipramine or methylphenidate. *American Journal of Psychiatry,* 1975, *132,* 241–245.

RAPP, D. J. Food allergy treatment for hyperkinesis. *Journal of Learning Disabilities,* 1979, *12,* 608–616.

RIBNER, S. The effects of special class placement on the self-concept of exceptional children. *Journal of Learning Disabilities,* 1978, *11,* 319–323.

RIDBERG, E. H., PARKE, R. D., & HETHERINGTON, E. M. Modification of impulsive and reflective style through observation of film-mediated models. *Developmental Psychology,* 1971, *5,* 369–377.

RIE, E. D. Effects of MBD on learning, intellective functions, and achievement. In H. E. Rie & E. D. Rie (Eds.), *Handbook of minimal brain dysfunctions.* New York: Wiley, 1980.

RIE, E. D., & RIE, H. E. An analysis of neurological soft signs in children with learning problems. *Brain and Language,* 1978, *6,* 32–46.

RIE, H. E., RIE, E. D., STEWART, S., & AMBUEL, J. P. Effects of Ritalin on underachieving children: A replication. *American Journal of Orthopsychiatry,* 1976, *46,* 313–322.

ROSENBAUM, A., O'LEARY, K. D., & JACOB, R. G. Behavioral intervention with hyperactive children: Group consequences as a supplement to individual contingencies. *Behavior Therapy,* 1975, *6,* 315–323.

ROSENTHAL, R. H., & ALLEN, T. W. An examination of attention, arousal, and learning dysfunctions of hyperactive children. *Psychological Bulletin,* 1978, *85,* 689–715.

ROSENTHAL, R. H., & ALLEN, T. W. Intratask distractibility in hyperkinetic and nonhyperkinetic children. *Journal of Abnormal Child Psychology,* 1980, *8,* 175–187.

ROSS, A. O. *Psychological aspects of learning disabilities and reading disorders.* New York: McGraw-Hill, 1976.

ROSS, D. M., & ROSS, S. A. *Hyperactivity: Research, theory, action.* New York: Wiley, 1976.

ROURKE, B. P. Brain-behavior relationships in children with learning disabilities: A research program. *American Psychologist,* 1975, *30,* 911–920.

ROURKE, B. P. Issues in the neuropsychological assessment of children with learning disabilities. *Canadian Psychological Review,* 1976a, *17,* 89–102.

ROURKE, B. P. Reading retardation in children: Developmental lag or deficit? In R. M. Knights & D. J. Bakker (Eds.), *Neuropsychology of learning disorders: Theoretical approaches.* Baltimore: University Park Press, 1976b.

ROURKE, B. P. Neuropsychological research in reading retardation: A review. In A. L. Benton & D. Pearl (Eds.), *Dyslexia: An appraisal of current knowledge.* New York: Oxford University Press, 1978.

ROURKE, B. P., & FINLAYSON, M. A. J. Neuropsychological significance of variations in patterns of academic performance: Verbal and visual-spatial abilities. *Journal of Abnormal Child Psychology,* 1978, *6,* 121–133.

RUBIN, E. Z. Cognitive dysfunction and emotional disorders. In H. R. Myklebust (Ed.), *Progress in learning disabilities.* Vol. II. New York: Grune & Stratton, 1971.

RUBIN, R. A., & BALOW, B. Perinatal influences on the behavior and learning problems of children. In B. B. Lahey & A. E. Kazdin (Eds.), *Advances in clinical child psychology.* Vol. 1. New York: Plenum, 1977.

RUGEL, R. P., CHEATAM, D., & MITCHELL, A. Body movement and inattention in learning-disabled and normal children. *Journal of Abnormal Child Psychology,* 1978, *6,* 325–337.

RUNCK, B. Conference on possible follow up NINCDS collaborative perinatal study. *Schizophrenia Bulletin,* 1977, *3,* 483–486.

RUTTER, M. Prevalence and types of dyslexia. In A. L. Benton & D. Pearl (Eds.), *Dyslexia: An appraisal of current knowledge.* New York: Oxford University Press, 1978.

RUTTER, M., TIZARD, J., & WHITMORE, K. *Education, health and behaviour: Psychological and medical study of childhood development.* New York: Wiley, 1970.

RUTTER, M., TIZARD, J., YULE, W., GRAHAM, P., & WHITMORE, K. Isle of Wight studies, 1964–1974. *Psychological Medicine,* 1976, *6,* 313–332.

SAFER, D. A familial factor in minimal brain dysfunction. *Behavioral Genetics,* 1973, *3,* 175–187.

SAFER, D. J. & ALLEN, R. P. Side effects from long-term use of stimulants in children. In R. Gittelman-Klein (Ed.), *Recent advances in child psychopharmacology.* New York: Human Sciences Press, 1975a.

SAFER, D. J. & ALLEN, R. P. Stimulant drug treatment of hyperactive adolescents. *Diseases of the Nervous System,* 1975b, *36,* 454–457.

SAFER, D. J., & ALLEN, R. P. *Hyperactive children: Diagnosis and management.* Baltimore: University Park Press, 1976.

SAFER, D., ALLEN, R., & BARR, E. Growth rebound after termination of stimulant drugs. *Journal of Pediatrics,* 1975, *86,* 113–116.

SANDOVAL, J. The measurement of the hyperactive syndrome in children. *Review of Educational Research,* 1977, *47,* 293–318.

SATTERFIELD, J. H. Neurophysiologic studies with hyperactive children. In D. P. Cantwell (Ed.), *The hyperactive child.* New York: Spectrum, 1975.

SATTERFIELD, J. H. Central and autonomic nervous system function in the hyperactive child syndrome: Treatment and research implications. In A. Davids (Ed.), *Child personality and psychopathology: Current topics.* Vol. 3. New York: Wiley, 1976.

SATTERFIELD, J. H., CANTWELL, D. P., & SATTERFIELD, B. T. Multimodality treatment: A one-year follow-up of 84 hyperactive boys. *Archives of General Psychiatry,* 1979, *36,* 965–974.

SATTERFIELD, J., CANTWELL, D., SAUL, R., & YUSIN, A. Intelligence, academic achievement and EEG abnormalities in hyperactive children. *American Journal of Psychiatry,* 1974, *131,* 391–395.

SATTERFIELD, J. H., CANTWELL, D. P., SCHILL, A., & BLASCHKE, T. Growth of hyperactive children treated with methylphenidate. *Archives of General Psychiatry,* 1979, *36,* 212–217.

SATZ, P., & FLETCHER, J. M. Minimal brain dysfunctions: An appraisal of research concepts and methods. In H. E. Rie & E. D. Rie (Eds.), *Handbook of minimal brain dysfunctions.* New York: Wiley, 1980.

SATZ, P., TAYLOR, H. G., FRIEL, J., & FLETCHER, J. M. Some developmental and predictive precursors of reading disabilities: A six year follow-up. In A. L. Benton & D. Pearl (Eds.), *Dyslexia: An appraisal of current knowledge.* New York: Oxford University Press, 1978.

SAUNDERS, T. R. A critical analysis of the minimal brain dysfunction syndrome. *Professional Psychology,* 1979, *10,* 293–306.

SCHAEFER, J. W., PALKES, H. S., & STEWART, M. A. Group counseling for parents of hyperactive children. *Child Psychiatry and Human Development,* 1974, *5,* 89–94.

SCHAIN, R. J. Medical and neurological differential diagnosis. In H. E. Rie & E. D. Rie (Eds.), *Handbook of minimal brain dysfunctions.* New York: Wiley, 1980.

SCHECHTER, M. D. Psychiatric aspects of learning disabilities. *Child Psychiatry and Human Development,* 1974, *5,* 67–77.

SCHLEIFER, M., WEISS, G., COHEN, N., ELMAN, M., CVEJIC, H., & KRUGER, R. Hyperactivity in preschoolers and the effect of methylphenidate. *American Journal of Orthopsychiatry,* 1975, *45,* 38–50.

SCHOLOM, A., & SCHIFF, G. Relating infant temperament to learning disabilities. *Journal of Abnormal Child Psychology,* 1980, *8,* 127–132.

SCHRAG, P., & DIVOKY, D. *The myth of the hyperactive child.* New York: Pantheon, 1975.

SCHROEDER, C. S., SCHROEDER, S. P., & DAVINE, M. A. Learning disabilities: Assessment and management of reading problems. In B. B. Wolman (Ed.), *Handbook of treatment of mental disorders in childhood and adolescence.* Englewood Cliffs, N.J.: Prentice-Hall, 1978.

SENF, G. M., & FREUNDL, P. C. Memory and attention factors in specific learning disabilities. *Journal of Learning Disabilities,* 1971, *4,* 94–106.

SERAFICA, F. C., & HARWAY, N. I. Social relations and self-esteem of children with learning disabilities. *Journal of Clinical Child Psychology,* 1979, *8,* 227–233.

SILVER, A. A., HAGIN, R. A., & HERSH, M. F. Reading disability: Teaching through stimulation of deficit perceptual areas. *American Journal of Orthopsychiatry,* 1972, *11,* 645–674.

SILVER, L. B. The playroom diagnostic evaluation of children with neurologically based learning disabilities. *Journal of the American Academy of Child Psychiatry,* 1976, *15,* 240–256.

SILVER, L. B. The minimal brain dysfunction syndrome. In J. D. Noshpitz (Ed.), *Basic handbook of child psychiatry.* Vol. 2. New York: Basic Books, 1979.

SPRAGUE, R. L. Psychopharmacotherapy in children. In M. F. Mc Millan & S. Henao (Eds.), *Child psychiatry: Treatment and research.* New York: Brunner/Mazel, 1977.

SPRING, C., BLUNDEN, D., GREENBERG, L. M., & YELLIN, A. M. Validity and norms of a hyperactivity rating scale. *Journal of Special Education,* 1977, *11,* 313–321.

SPRING, C., & SANDOVAL, J. Food additives and hyperkinesis: A critical evaluation of the evidence. *Journal of Learning Disabilities,* 1976, *9,* 560–569.

SPRING, C., YELLIN, A. M., & GREENBERG, L. Effects of imipramine and methylphenidate on perceptual-motor performance of hyperactive children. *Perceptual and Motor Skills,* 1976, *43,* 459–470.

SROUFE, L. A. Drug treatment of children with behavior problems. In F. D. Horowitz (Ed.), *Review of child development research.* Vol. 4. Chicago: University of Chicago Press, 1975.

STEWART, M. A. Is hyperactivity abnormal? and other unanswered questions. *School Review,* 1976, *85,* 31–42.

STEWART, M. A. Genetic, perinatal, and constitutional factors in minimal brain dysfunction. In E. E. Rie & E. D. Rie (Eds.), *Handbook of minimal brain dysfunctions.* New York: Wiley, 1980.

STEWART, M. A., MENDELSON, W. B., & JOHNSON, N. E. Hyperactive children as adolescents: How they describe themselves. *Child Psychiatry and Human Development,* 1973, *4,* 3–11.

STEWART, M. A., & OLDS, S. W. *Raising a hyperactive child.* New York: Harper & Row, 1973.

STREISSGUTH, A. P. Maternal drinking and the outcome of pregnancy: Implications for child mental health. *American Journal of Orthopsychiatry,* 1977, *47,* 422–431.

SWANSON, J. M., & KINSBOURNE, M. Food dyes impair performance of hyperactive children on a laboratory learning test. *Science,* 1980, *207,*1485–1486.

SYKES, D. H., DOUGLAS, V. I., & MORGENSTERN, G. Sustained attention in hyperactive children. *Journal of Child Psychology and Psychiatry,* 1973, *14,* 213–220.

THOMAS, A., CHESS, S., & BIRCH, H. G. *Temperament and behavior disorders in children.* New York: New York University Press, 1968.

THURSTON, C. M., SOBOL, M. P., SWANSON, J., & KINSBOURNE, M. Effects of methylphenidate (Ritalin) on selective attention in hyperactive children. *Journal of Abnormal Child Psychology,* 1979, *7,* 471–481.

TOWBIN, A. Cerebral dysfunctions related to perinatal organic damage: Clinical-neuropathological correlations. *Journal of Abnormal Psychology,* 1978, *87,* 617–635.

TRITES, R. L., & FIEDOROWICZ, C. Follow-up study of children with specific (or primary) reading disability. In R. M. Knights & D. J. Bakker (Eds.), *Neuropsychology of learning disorders: Theoretical approaches.* Baltimore: University Park Press, 1976.

TSUSHIMA, W. T., & TOWNE, W. S. Neuropsychological abilities of young children with questionable brain disorders. *Journal of Consulting and Clinical Psychology,* 1977, *45,* 757–762.

UNITED STATES OFFICE OF EDUCATION. *Estimated number of handicapped children in the United States, 1974–75.* Washington, D. C.: Bureau of Education for the Handicapped, 1975.

UNITED STATES OFFICE OF EDUCATION. *Federal Register,* 1977, *42,* August 23, Part II.

VANDE VOORT, L., & SENF, G. M. Audio visual integration in retarded readers. *Journal of Learning Disabilities,* 1973, *6,* 49–58.

VELLUTINO, F. R. Toward an understanding of dyslexia: Psychological factors in specific reading disability. In A. L. Benton & D. Pearl (Eds.), *Dyslexia: An appraisal of current knowledge.* New York: Oxford University Press, 1978.

VERNON, M. D. Variability in reading retardation. *British Journal of Psychology,* 1979, *70,* 7–16.

WALKER, S. *Help for the hyperactive child.* Boston: Houghton Mifflin, 1977.

WEISS, G., & HECHTMAN, L. The hyperactive child syndrome. *Science,* 1979, *205,* 1348–1354.

WEISS, G., HECHTMAN, L., PERLMAN, T., HOPKINS, J., & WENER, A. Hyperactives as young adults. *Archives of General Psychiatry,* 1979, *36,* 675–681.

WEISS, G., MINDE, K., WERRY, J., DOUGLAS, V., & NEMETH, E. Studies on the hyperactive child. VIII: Five year follow-up. *Archives of General Psychiatry,* 1971, *24,* 409–414.

WEISSENBURGER, F. E., & LONEY, J. Hyperkinesis in the classroom: If cerebral stimulants are the last resort, what would be a first resort? *Journal of Learning Disabilities,* 1977, *10,* 339–348.

WEITHORN, C. J., & ROSS, R. Stimulant drugs for hyperactivity: Some disturbing questions. *American Journal of Orthopsychiatry,* 1976, *46,* 168–173.

WELNER, Z., WELNER, A., STEWART, M., PALKES, H., & WISH, E. A controlled study of siblings of hyperactive children. *Journal of Nervous and Mental Disease,* 1977, *165,* 110–117.

WENDER, P. H. *Minimal brain dysfunction in children.* New York: Wiley, 1971.

WERNER, E. E., and SMITH, R. S. An epidemiological perspective on some antecedents and consequences of childhood mental health problems and learning disabilities. *Journal of the American Academy of Child Psychiatry,* 1979, *18,* 292–306.

WERRY, J. S. Methylphenidate and haloperidol in children: Effects on attention, memory, and activity. *Archives of General Psychiatry,* 1975, *32,* 790–795.

WERRY, J. S. Organic factors. In H. C. Quay & J. S. Werry (Eds.), *Psychopathological disorders of childhood.* (2nd ed.) New York: Wiley, 1979.

WHALEN, C. K., & HENKER, B. Psychostimulants and children: A review and analysis. *Psychological Bulletin,* 1976, *83,* 1113–1130.

WHALEN, C. K., HENCKER, B., & DOTEMOTO, S. Teacher response to the methylphenidate (Ritalin) versus placebo status of hyperactive boys in the classroom. *Child Development,* 1981, *52,* 1005–1014.

WILLERMAN, L. Activity level and hyperactivity in twins. *Child Development,* 1973, *44,* 288–293.

WILLOWS, D. M. Reading between the lines: Selective attention in good and poor readers. *Child Development,* 1974, *45,* 408–415.

WOLFF, P., & HURWITZ, I. Functional implications of the minimal brain damage syndrome. *Seminars in Psychiatry,* 1973, *5,* 105–115.

WOLRAICH, M., DRUMMOND, T., SALOMON, M. K., O'BRIEN, M. L., & SIVAGE, C. Effects of methylphenidate alone and in combination with behavior modification procedures on the behavior and academic performance of hyperactive children. *Journal of Abnormal Child Psychology,* 1978, *6,* 149–161.

WOOD, D. R., REIMBERR, F. W., WENDER, P. H., & JOHNSON, G. E. Diagnosis and treatment of minimal brain dysfunction in adults. *Archives of General Psychiatry,* 1976, *33,* 1453–1460.

WORLD HEALTH ORGANIZATION. The use of twins in epidemiological studies. *Acta Geneticae Medicae et Gemellologiae,* 1966, *15,* 109–128.

YULE, W., & RUTTER, M. Epidemiology and special significance of specific reading retardation. In R. M. Knights & D. J. Bakker (Eds.), *Neuropsychology of learning disorders: Theoretical approaches.* Baltimore: University Park Press, 1976.

ZAHN, T. P., ABATE, F., LITTLE, B. C., & WENDER, P. H. Minimal brain dysfunction, stimulant drugs, and autonomic nervous system activity. *Archives of General Psychiatry,* 1975, *32,* 381–387.

ZAHN, T. P., RAPOPORT, J. L., & THOMPSON, C. L. Autonomic and behavioral effects of dextroamphetamine and placebo in normal and hyperactive prepubertal boys. *Journal of Abnormal Child Psychology,* 1980, *8,* 145–160.

ZAMBELLI, A. J., STRAMM, S. S., MAITINSKY, S., & LOISELLE, D. L. Auditory evoked potentials and selective attention in formerly hyperactive adolescent boys. *American Journal of Psychiatry,* 1977, *134,* 742–747.

ZENTALL, S. S. Behavioral comparisons of hyperactive and normally active children in natural settings. *Journal of Abnormal Child Psychology,* 1980, *8,* 93–109.

ZENTALL, S. S., & ZENTALL, T. R. Activity and task performance of hyperactive children as a function of environmental stimulation. *Journal of Consulting and Clinical Psychology,* 1976, *44,* 693–697.

ZUKOW, P. G., ZUKOW, A. H., & BENTLER, P. M. Rating scales for the identification and treatment of hyperkinesis. *Journal of Consulting and Clinical Psychology,* 1978, *46,* 213–222.

5

CHILDHOOD PSYCHOSIS: INFANTILE AUTISM AND CHILDHOOD SCHIZOPHRENIA

People whose mental functioning is so impaired that they lose touch with reality and cannot meet the demands of ordinary living are generally considered to have a psychotic disorder. **Psychosis** thus corresponds to what is popularly called "insanity" or "madness." Technically, however, this term does not refer to any specific condition, but to a severe extent of disturbance that often accompanies certain conditions. These conditions include the following: (a) **organic psychosis,** in which the mental disturbance results from the brain-damaging effects of tumors or other disease processes, of deterioration associated with aging, or of alcohol or other toxic substances; (b) **affective psychosis,** which involves extreme states of elevated or depressed mood; (c) schizophrenia; (d) childhood psychosis. Organic psychosis occurs almost exclusively in adults and will not be considered further. Affective psychosis is discussed in Chapter 7, schizophrenia beginning in adolescence is the subject of Chapter 6, and the present chapter addresses childhood psychosis.

Childhood psychosis comprises two distinct patterns of disturbance: **infantile autism** and **childhood schizophrenia.** Infantile autism is a very serious disorder of mental and social development that begins early in life, almost always prior to 30 months of age. Although it is a rare condition, it has been widely studied and has many implications for identifying the limits of normal developmental variation in early childhood. Childhood schizophrenia is a serious breakdown in personality functioning beginning between 2½ and 12 years of age, but mainly after age 7. As a precursor of schizophrenia beginning in adolescence and adulthood, it offers a developmental glimpse into the most extensively researched of all mental health problems.

Although most child clinicians agree that childhood schizophrenia is an early form of adult schizophrenia, some question the statement that infantile autism is a distinct condition. Bender (1971), Bettelheim (1967), and Fish (1977), for example, all of whom are prominent contributors to the field, argue that infantile autism and childhood schizophrenia exist on a continuum with adult schizophrenia and differ only with respect to how the person's age colors his or her manifest symptoms. As will be elaborated, however, accumulating evidence indicates that psychosis beginning before age 3 differs substantially from psychosis beginning after age 7 not only in symptomatology, but also in its underlying pathology, its likely course, its probable origins, and its long-term outcome.

EPIDEMIOLOGY OF CHILDHOOD PSYCHOSIS

The **epidemiology** of a condition refers to how frequently it occurs in relation to age, sex, race, social class, place of residence, and other objective characteristics of people who develop it. Epidemiologic studies of mental disorders provide information on how these disorders are distributed in the population, and such information helps to identify how and when certain people become at risk for developing particular psychological disorders (Robins, 1978; Weissman & Klerman, 1978). Such research on childhood psychosis has yielded three consistent findings: (a) with few exceptions, it begins either before age 3 or after age 7; (b) it occurs very infrequently at all ages; (c) it is much more common in boys than in girls.

Figure 5.1
Age of onset in childhood psychosis. (Based on survey data summarized by Rutter (1974, 1978a).)

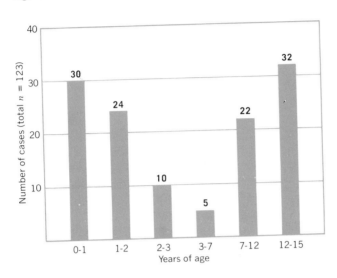

Age of Onset

All available data indicate that childhood psychosis occurs in two peaks of onset. As shown in Figure 5.1, one peak occurs in infancy and the second peak as youngsters move toward and into adolescence, with onset between ages 3 to 7 being relatively infrequent.

Some clinicians report a somewhat less infrequent onset of psychosis in 3- to 7-year-olds in their particular setting than is reflected in Figure 5.1 (Char & Lubetsky, 1979). As notable examples, Bender (1970) states that 28 percent of a group of psychotic children seen at Bellevue Hospital in New York first became disturbed at age 3½ to 6, following an apparently normal infancy; Bomberg, Szurek, and Etemad (1973) at the Langley Porter Children's Service in Los Angeles report a 10 percent frequency of initial onset from age 3 to 5. Yet even these reports reveal early and late peaks of onset with a relatively low frequency in between. In Bender's sample 59 percent showed onset of their psychosis before age 3, no cases of initial onset were recorded between 6 and 9, and there was a gradual increase in initial onset from 9 to 12. Among Bomberg et al.'s psychotic children, 62 percent became disturbed before age 3 and 28 percent at age 6 or older.

There is also reason to believe that many children who are first identified as psychotic between ages 3 and 7 are in fact autistic youngsters with psychological problems dating from infancy. Studying a group of clearly autistic children who averaged nearly 4 years of age when they were first accurately diagnosed, for example, Ornitz, Guthrie, and Farley (1977) found that half of their families had been concerned about their development by the time they reached their first birthday. Similarly, careful case histories taken from parents who report a deterioration in their child's behavior following 2 years of normal development often reveal subtle early signs of autism that have been overlooked, forgotten, or even denied (Ornitz & Ritvo, 1976a, 1976b).

Prevalence

Childhood psychosis occurs in 3 to 5 per 10,000 children, of whom 1 to 2 show the pattern of early onset indicative of infantile autism. More specifically, Lotter (1966) found 4.5 psychotic and 2.1 autistic children per 10,000 in a survey of the entire population of 78,000 8- to 10-year-olds in Middlesex, England. Treffert (1970), in the only other major prevalence study of this kind, reported 3.1 psychotic and 0.7 autistic children per 10,000 among all youngsters under 12 seen in mental health facilities in the state of Wisconsin over a 5-year period; 25 percent of these psychotic children (0.8 per 10,000) showed clear early onset and were considered autistic.

Because total population surveys tend to reveal a larger number of actual cases than surveys limited to children who have come to professional attention, the larger figures reported by Lotter are probably more reliable (Wing, Yeates, Brierly, & Gould, 1976). Slightly different prevalence rates are reported from time to time, depending on how precisely infantile autism is defined and differentiated from childhood schizophrenia. Especially misleading in this regard is the tendency of some writers to cite Lotter's 4.5 per 10,000 figure as if it referred to the prevalence of autism, rather than the broader category of childhood psychosis. Lotter's report clearly states that, of the psychotic children he identified, just 2.1 per 10,000 demonstrated the core features of infantile autism.

By contrast with how rare it is, childhood psychosis is diagnosed in about 9 percent of children age 12 and under seen in psychiatric clinics and hospitals (Bender, 1973; Cerreto & Tuma, 1977; Werry, 1979). This contrast reflects the fact that psychotic children, while constituting only a small proportion of young people in treatment, are especially likely to be referred for professional help. Indeed, psychotic disorder results in such referral more frequently than any of the other conditions discussed in this book, and some surveys suggest that virtually all psychotic children and adolescents in the United States are known to some treatment facility (Dohrenwend, 1980, Chapter 2).

Sex Differences

Childhood psychosis occurs far more frequently in boys than girls. Specifically, King (1975) reports a male:female ratio of 3.4 to 1 among 376 psychotic children in six major studies. As indicated in Table 5.1, this sex difference is consistent with a general tendency for boys to be more susceptible than girls to psychological disorders. These differences decrease with age, however. Among 5- to 9-year-olds the sex ratio for psychotic disorders is already below the overall 3.4:1 figure—which suggests a particular preponderance of males in early-onset psychosis—and by late adolescence sex differences no longer appear for either psychosis or all disorders combined. Consistent with this trend for psychotic disorders, schizophrenia in adulthood is equally common among men and women (Gottesman, 1978; Keith, Gunderson, Reifman, Buchsbaum, & Mosher, 1976).

The greater vulnerability of boys than girls to psychopathology of most kinds remains

TABLE 5.1 Ratio of Boys to Girls Receiving Treatment for Psychological Disorders in the United States

	Age		
	5–9	10–14	15–19
Psychotic disorders (excluding organic psychoses)	2.13	1.18	1.03
All psychological disorders	2.56	1.22	.91

Source. Based on data reported by Gove (1979).

a mystery. For conditions involving brain dysfunction or genetic determinants, the explanation may lie in sex-linked inheritance or differential susceptibility to nervous system impairment, as noted in Chapter 4. From a broader biosocial point of view, Gove (1979) offers the following line of reasoning: boys experience more psychological stress than girls because more is expected of them and because they mature less rapidly; with maturity, boys catch up in biological and social maturation while girls encounter increasing social pressures; hence girls are less susceptible to psychological disorders as children but become equally susceptible during adolescence. Further research is needed to determine the accuracy of this hypothesis or other possible explanations of youthful sex differences in psychopathology.

CHARACTERISTICS OF CHILDHOOD PSYCHOSIS

All psychotic children share the impaired sense of reality and the inability to cope with normal demands of living that identify severe psychological disturbance. Those who are psychotic from early in life show certain distinctive characteristics that are rarely seen in those who first become disturbed in middle childhood; conversely, late-onset psychosis in children involves certain characteristics that seldom appear in autistic children. It is helpful for this reason to consider the nature and course of infantile autism and childhood schizophrenia separately and then to summarize the differences between them.

The Nature and Course of Infantile Autism

Infantile autism was first identified as a special form of child psychosis by Leo Kanner (1943) and is sometimes referred to as "Kanner's syndrome." Kanner described the two chief characteristics of the condition as *interpersonal isolation* and an abnormal concern with the *preservation of sameness,* both beginning in infancy. He observed further that almost all autistic children display marked *language peculiarities* by the time they reach school age. Subsequent research has indicated that *cognitive and intellectual impairments* are also a prominent feature of the condition. As elaborated below, these manifest symptoms of autism change somewhat with age; once established, however, the basic condition runs a continuous and unrelenting course (American Psychiatric Association, 1980; Kernberg, 1979; Schopler, Reichler, DeVellis, & Daly, 1980).

Children who are later identified as autistic frequently show as infants a dislike or disinterest in being held or cuddled.

Interpersonal Isolation   Autistic children are strikingly unresponsive to other people. As infants they lag far behind in showing such signs of social interest as following people with their gaze, making direct eye contact, and smiling. When they do look directly at someone, their gaze often seems disinterested, impersonal, and without feeling. Autistic children also often fail to make the kinds of anticipatory movements normally seen in infants who are about to be picked up, and, when they are picked up, they tend to keep their bodies stiff instead of cuddling up against the person who is holding them.

Later these children tend not to form the kinds of attachment to their parents that typically occur in 1- to 3-year-olds. Whereas most toddlers follow their parents around the house, cry when they go out somewhere, and rush to greet them when they return, autistic children remain indifferent to whether their parents are around. They seem entirely content to be left alone, and typically they treat people as if they were inanimate objects—and not very important ones at that (Block, Freeman, & Montgomery, 1975; Massie, 1975; Richer & Coss, 1976; Rimland, 1974).

Preservation of Sameness   Autistic children cling tenaciously to sameness in their activities and their environment. In their actions they sometimes seem to lack any interest in what is going on around them and may sit motionless for hours, staring off into space. At other times they may become intensely absorbed in odd, repetitive behaviors, such as turning a vacuum cleaner switch on and off, passing a toy back and forth from one hand to the other, or touching each side of their crib or playpen over and over in succession. Whether they are doing nothing or performing some ritual, they cannot bear to be interrupted. If spoken to they show no sign of having heard; if objects are dangled in their line of vision, they pay no attention; if their self-preoccupation is forcibly intruded on, as by picking them up or taking an object away from them, they are likely to throw a violent temper tantrum. Similarly, these children have little tolerance for unpredictable events and may become frantic if their physical surroundings are changed—for example, moving their playpen or taking a piece of furni-

TABLE 5.2 Abnormal Early Life Behaviors Reported by Mothers of Autistic Children

Abnormal Behavior	Percent with Symptom
Seemed very hard "to reach" or be "in a shell"	90
Ignored people as if they did not exist	85
Avoided looking people directly in the eye	76
Acquired things by directing another's hand	74
Ignored or failed to respond to sounds	71
Excessively watched the motions of his/her hands or fingers	71
Looked through people as if they did not exist	65
Stared off into space as if seeing something that was not there	64
Ignored toys as if they did not exist	61
Preoccupied with things that spin	57
Preoccupied with minor visual details	57
Let objects fall out of hands as if they did not exist	53
Responded to affection by ignoring it	53
Responded to being held by clinging without interest	51
Preoccupied with scratching surfaces and listening to the sound	50
Became attached to an unusual object	48
Agitated at being taken to new places	48
Agitated by loud noises	42

Source. Based on data reported by Ornitz (1978a) on 74 autistic children with a mean age of 45.2 months.

ture out of their bedroom (DeMyer, Mann, Tilton, & Loew, 1967; Ferrara & Hill, 1980; Prior & Macmillan, 1973; Ritvo, Ornitz, & LaFranchi, 1968; Simons, 1974).

Table 5.2 lists some frequently observed abnormal behaviors of autistic children that paint a clear picture of these youngsters' interpersonal isolation and concern with preserving sameness.

Language Peculiarities About 50 percent of autistic children fail to achieve any useful speech by age 5, and over 75 percent of those who do learn to talk show specific speech peculiarities. These include **echolalia,** which consists of automatically repeating words that have been spoken to them; **pronomial reversal,** such as using "you" for "I"; referring to objects in terms of their location or function, as in "down" to mean "floor" or "sweep-the-floor" to mean "broom"; omitting or misusing parts of speech, as in "go walk shops" or "you sit for chair in table"; and referring to a whole concept with just one of its parts, as in asking for dinner by saying, "Do you want some ketchup?" (Baker, Cantwell, Rutter, & Bartak, 1976; Ricks & Wing, 1976; Rutter, 1978b; Simon, 1975).

In addition to these specific peculiarities, autistic youngsters display many more grammatical errors and a lower level of complexity in their speech than nonautistic children of comparable nonlinguistic mental ability (Bartolucci & Albers, 1974; Bartolucci, Pierce, & Streiner, 1980; Pierce & Bartolucci, 1977). They also respond peculiarly to the speech of others. Asked the color of a yellow stick held up in front of them, they are as likely to say "stick" as "yellow"; asked to place a small box *on top* of a block, they may place the box *over* the block or drop the block *into* it (Churchill, 1978a).

Those autistic children who learn to talk are usually slow in passing the various "milestones" of speech acquisition. On the average they lag a full year or more behind normal youngsters in when they first imitate sounds, use or repeat words spoken by others, and combine words into phrases. Finally, autistic children are limited in their ability to think of themselves in words, and they are less likely than other children to use gestures and other body movements for communication purposes (Cohen, Caparulo, & Shaywitz, 1976; Ornitz et al., 1977).

Because the language peculiarities of autistic children deviate so clearly from normal expectations, delays in speech development are frequently the first concern of parents seeking professional help (Ornitz & Ritvo, 1976b). Accordingly, knowledgeable clinicians always consider possible infantile autism in youngsters who are described as ignoring or not seeming to understand what is said to them, as if they were deaf or retarded, or as using language either infrequently or in strange ways. The pervasive language difficulties of children with an early-onset psychosis have also led many investigators to conclude that cognitive and perceptual handicaps lie at the core of the disorder. From this point of view, the unresponsive and self-preoccupied behavior of autistic children results from a faulty modulation of sensory input that interferes with their ability to understand sounds and produce language (Bartak, Rutter, & Cox, 1975, 1977; Churchill, 1978b; Gold & Gold, 1975; Ornitz, 1978a; Wing, 1978).

Cognitive and Intellectual Impairments   For many years following Kanner's original contributions, most child specialists regarded infantile autism primarily as a condition of social withdrawal; any apparent cognitive or intellectual impairment in autistic youngsters was considered only a secondary consequence of their emotional problems. More recently, research findings have produced a shift in the prevailing view: autism is now widely believed to be a developmental disorder consisting primarily of severe cognitive deficits that are probably due to some form of organic brain dysfunction and that account for the manifest symptoms of interpersonal isolation, preservation of sameness, and language peculiarities (Lovass, Koegel, & Schreibman, 1979; Ornitz, 1978b; Prior, 1979; Rutter, 1978b; Werry, 1979).

The strongest support for this change in view has come from studies of the intellectual functioning of autistic children. A substantial portion of these youngsters have always been found to perform poorly on intelligence tests. Earlier writers who attributed this poor performance to emotional factors described autistic children as normally intelligent youngsters whose IQ scores would increase if their social withdrawal could be overcome. To the contrary, however, research findings demonstrate that autistic children who score below 70 on IQ tests are as retarded as anyone else with an IQ below 70. Those with low scores in early childhood tend to have similarly low scores in late adolescence, whether or not their social functioning has improved. Regarding the extent of intellectual handicap among autistic children, approximately 75 percent will perform throughout their lives at a retarded level (DeMyer, Barton, DeMyer, Norton, Allen, & Steele, 1973; Kernberg, 1979; Rutter, 1970, 1978a).

As would be expected from their previously noted problems in communication, many autistic children also display specific cognitive defects on language-related tasks and on measures of auditory perception. They perform poorly in situations requiring speech, and they earn very low scores on nonverbal tasks that require some ability to think clearly in words, such as arranging a series of pictures to tell a sensible story (the Picture Arrangement subtest of the Wechsler Intelligence Scale for Children). By contrast, they succeed relatively well on nonverbal tasks that draw more on visual-spatial than lan-

guage skills, such as putting blocks together to form a design (the Block Design subtest of the Wechsler) (Lockyer & Rutter, 1970; Wolff & Barlow, 1979). The relatively good ability of some autistic children to handle complex visual stimuli may even obscure their cognitive deficits in other areas and make them appear more intelligent than they are (DeMyer, 1976).

Unlike MBD/ADD youngsters, who characteristically suffer visual-spatial perceptual defects, autistic youngsters are perceptually impaired primarily in the auditory sphere— as so clearly reflected in their difficulty in responding appropriately to the spoken word. This special cognitive deficit involving auditory and language processes also distinguishes low-IQ autistic youngsters from mentally retarded but nonautistic children,

Autistic children taking the Wechsler Intelligence Scale for Children often perform better on Block Design, which is a relatively abstract test of visualization and manipulation of objects, than on Picture Arrangement, which requires social judgment and some degree of thinking to oneself in words.

TABLE 5.3 Motor Development in Autistic and Normal Children

Motor Milestone	Age of Achievement (in months)	Percent of Children Capable of Behavior	
		Autistic	Normal
Child first held head erect while in upright position	Under 3	27.0	33.3
	3 or 4	45.9	45.8
	5 or 6	10.8	20.8
	Over 6 or never	16.2	0
Child first rolled onto back	Under 3	29.6	21.9
	3 or 4	42.6	75.0
	5 or 6	13.0	3.1
	Over 6 or never	14.8	0
Child first sat up without support	Under 7	36.2	65.7
	7 or 8	40.6	34.3
	Over 8 or never	23.1	0
Child first moved around on hands and knees	Under 7	24.2	48.5
	7 or 8	21.2	45.4
	9 or 10	24.2	6.1
	Over 10 or never	30.3	0
Child first pulled self to a standing position	Under 9	29.7	63.6
	9 to 11	31.2	36.4
	Over 11 or never	39.0	0
Child first walked without support	Under 11	12.5	31.6
	11 to 14	34.7	65.8
	15 to 18	26.4	2.6
	Over 18 or never	26.4	0

Source. Based on data reported by Ornitz, Guthrie, and Farley (1977). Autistic children ranged in age from 16 to 75 months, with a mean age of 45.2; normal comparison group ranged from 17 to 84 months of age, with a mean of 46.0.

who typically show no such special deficit (Prior, 1979; Rutter, 1978a, 1978b).

Three additional lines of evidence support the possibility that the cognitive impairments of autistic children are associated with some kind of brain dysfunction. First, these children show notable delays in their motor development, including lags in such early motor milestones as learning to sit up, stand, and walk (see Table 5.3). Second, autistic children frequently display peculiar motor movements, such as repetitively flapping their arms or hands with the wrist or elbow held in a fixed position, whirling around without any apparent reason, walking on their toes, rocking their body back and forth for long periods of time, and rolling or banging their heads. More than 75 percent of autistic children have been found to show this strange flapping behavior and more than 50 percent the whirling and rocking behaviors (Ornitz, 1978a; Ornitz & Ritvo, 1976b; Weber, 1978).

Third, many of the soft signs of neurological disorder discussed in Chapter 4 occur

This autistic boy is absorbed with his shadow while he flaps his arms at the elbow, which is one of the peculiar motor movements seen in a majority of youngsters with this condition.

in a large percentage of autistic children, especially brain-wave indices of cerebral dysfunction. Significantly, such evidence of cerebral dysfunction is more commonly found among psychotic children with early onset of disturbance than among those who first become psychotic in late childhood (Hier, LeMay, & Rosenberger, 1979; James & Barry, 1980; Kolvin, 1971; Ornitz, 1978a; Tanguay, 1976).

These findings provide good reason to regard infantile autism as a special kind or variant of MBD/ADD. Like MBD/ADD, it is a behaviorally defined syndrome that seems attributable to basic defects in central nervous system modulation of sensory input and motor output. However, the behavioral characteristics that define MBD/ADD—hyperactivity, impulsivity, excitability, and irritability—rarely appear in autistic children, who are deviant by virtue of their generally unresponsive rather than overresponsive behavior. Conversely, MBD/ADD children rarely show the unrelatedness, repetitive and self-preoccupied behavior, and language peculiarities that characterize infantile autism.

The Course of Infantile Autism   As mentioned earlier, close observation of autistic children during their first year of life will often reveal an unusual lack of responsiveness and some delays in motor development. However, it is from age 1 to 5 that the primary features of autism become most obvious, and this is the time when the diagnosis is most commonly made. Even then it is the amount and not the kind of unusual behavior that distinguishes these youngsters from other preschoolers. Normal children may show aloofness and emotional isolation, repetitive and self-preoccupied behavior, and speech peculiarities from time to time. In normal children these deviations come and go quickly, whereas in autistic youngsters they persist all day, every day, year after year.

Starting at age 5 or 6, many autistic children begin to outgrow their interpersonal indifference and to become more socially responsive than before. Nevertheless, they continue throughout their developmental years and into adulthood to have difficulty grasping the reality of social situations and judging the appropriateness of what they do and say to other people. They consequently make few friends and get along poorly in group situations, which they usually avoid. Many of the odd repetitive behaviors that reflect autistic youngsters' concern with sameness also disappear during middle childhood. In their place, however, these children often begin to organize their daily lives into compulsive routines or become preoccupied with bus routes, time schedules, and other impersonal sets of facts and figures (Rutter, 1978a; Wing, 1976b).

Among those autistic children who learn to talk, language problems also persist into adolescence and adulthood. In many cases echoing, grammatical disorders, and concrete use of words continue to mar their speech. Others who manage to achieve nearly normal language usage tend to talk in a flat monotone, with little variation in emphasis or inflection. They tend to speak in short, staccato phrases and to express themselves in a stiff, overly formal way. Especially in social situations, they often have difficulty keeping to the rules of conduct and alternating talker-listener roles that govern conversation (Baltaxe, 1977; Rutter, 1970, 1978b; Shapiro & Huebner, 1976).

As already noted, a majority of autistic children are also mentally retarded and function at a retarded level throughout their lives. For example, as schoolchildren 80 percent of autistic youngsters with IQs below 70 fail to learn to multiply and divide with double-figure numbers, and as adults scarcely any with low IQs achieve regular paid employment (Bartak & Rutter, 1976; Rutter, 1978b). In their adolescent and adult years autistic children also become increasingly likely to display definite indications of neurological abnormality. By late adolescence, for example, as many as one-third of autistic children, including some who have not previously shown "soft" neurological signs, display such hard evidence of brain dysfunction as epileptic seizures and definitely abnormal brain-wave patterns (Deykin & MacMahon, 1979; Lotter, 1974; Rutter, 1970).

Autistic children grown up therefore tend to resemble certain seriously impaired adults. Those who never achieve language appear similar to adults with **aphasia,** a brain disorder that interferes with the ability to understand or express thoughts in words. Those with prominent neurological disorder share many features in common with adults who suffer from epilepsy. Those with very low IQs appear much the same as other retarded adults. The remaining few who have normal or nearly normal language, intellectual, and neurological capabilities tend to live out their lives as socially withdrawn, marginally independent adults.

Case 5. *Infantile Autism*

Brad was the third child born to Peter and Alice Smith, both college graduates and in good health. Although they planned to have several children, Alice Smith would have preferred a longer interval between their second child and Brad's arrival. She nevertheless adjusted well to the pregnancy, and there were no complications before or at birth.

Brad developed slowly as an infant, not sitting up until 8 months of age and not walking until 20 to 22 months. Since the Smiths' oldest boy had not walked until 17 months, they were not overly concerned. Moreover, Brad showed good manual dexterity, especially in learning to feed himself at an early age. On the other hand, he had begun by age 2 to require many rituals at mealtime. His food had to be cut and placed in a certain way before he would begin to eat; his cereal had to be removed from the bowl and placed on the table; his toast had to be cut and handed to him in a prescribed manner. Any deviation from these rituals triggered whining and refusal to eat. In Alice Smith's words, Brad was "different from the beginning."

Brad's social behavior was also strikingly deviant. When called, he typically acted as if he were deaf, which his parents regarded as "wilful disobedience." He disliked being held or cuddled and was quite happy to be left alone in his crib. He had little interaction with his siblings and spent much of his time in isolation, often just sitting and rocking back and forth.

Also beginning during his second year of life, Brad was rarely observed without a pail. He had a large and extraordinary collection of pails that were his major fascination. These ranged from small sandbox pails, which he took to bed, to the large refuse variety. Brad also seemed to like music and would listen for hours to a recording of Ravel's *Bolero*, the tune of which he could hum perfectly.

When Brad was 2½, the Smiths' pediatrician referred them to a child psychiatry clinic at a university hospital, where he was evaluated by a psychiatrist, a psychologist, and a pediatric neurologist. Brad carried a pail to his first diagnostic session. As he passed by his parents in the waiting room without acknowledging their presence, his father said, "Have a good time, Brad; this is *only* your father talking."

When seen in a playroom, Brad did not play with any of the toys. Instead, he remained preoccupied with his pail and with the wastebasket in the room. He never looked directly at the examiner and spent most of the session walking in a circle, pail in hand, humming a tune, and seeming oblivious to his surroundings.

The Cattell Infant Intelligence Scale was administered at a later session, and the most notable features were Brad's preoccupation with a cup and some cubes used in this test and his lack of direct eye contact. When he wanted the examiner to get something for him, he would not look at his face but instead at his hand and push or pull it toward the desired object.

Brad's overall performance yielded an IQ of 46, in the range of moderate mental retardation. A subsequent neurological examination showed no gross abnormality and ruled out a hearing deficit. The observed symptoms—including disturbances of relating, of developmental rate, of speech and language, and of motility—supported the diagnosis of infantile autism.

For several years following this diagnostic study, numerous treatment approaches were used with Brad, including individual and group play therapy, a day treatment program with emphasis on developing communication skills, and, beginning at age 7, residential treatment. Various drugs were also employed in conjunction with these other treatments in an effort to control some of his bizarre behaviors. From age 3, for example, he showed increasingly severe self-abuse, such as punching himself and tearing skin from his face with his fingernails with no overt signs of pain. Brad remains institutionalized in his teenage years and continues to manifest the symptoms of autism.

The Nature and Course of Childhood Schizophrenia

Schizophrenia constitutes a serious breakdown in certain cognitive, interpersonal, and integrative capacities. Normally functioning individuals are generally able to think coherently, logically, and at appropriate levels of abstraction; they perceive themselves and their environment accurately; they can establish and maintain rewarding relationships with other people; they are able to exert adaptive control over their thoughts, feelings, and impulses. In contrast, schizophrenia is characterized by *disordered thinking, inaccurate perception* of reality, *interpersonal ineptness,* and *inadequate controls* over ideas, affects, and behavior (American Psychiatric Association, 1980; Arieti, 1974a; Bellak, Hurvich, & Gediman, 1973; Cancro, 1980; Carpenter & Strauss, 1979; Weiner, 1966). These impairments characterize schizophrenia among adolescents and adults as well as children; as is true for most patterns of psychopathology, however, the age of the disturbed person colors the specific nature of his or her manifest symptoms.

Disordered Thinking   The most prominent feature of schizophrenic disturbance is incoherent, illogical, or inappropriately abstract thinking. Incoherent thinking, which is often referred to as **dissociation,** involves a disruption in the sequence of thoughts so that one thought does not flow continuously from another. Dissociated people may lose track of what they are saying, right in the middle of a sentence, or they may express a series of loosely related ideas that are difficult to follow and do not seem to go together. Asked "How are you?" a dissociated child may reply, "I'm okay but my father never takes me fishing do you like to bait hooks?"

Dissociation may also occur between a question asked and the answer given, as if the person were responding to a completely different question. Thus the response to "How are you?" may be "I'm around ten" or "The same as my brother." Among mildly disturbed schizophrenic children and those just beginning to develop this disorder, this type of dissociation is often very subtle. The answer may be just slightly off the point, so that it is not immediately certain whether the child has responded peculiarly or has simply misheard or misunderstood the question (Harrow & Prosen, 1978; Rosenberg & Tucker, 1979).

Illogical thinking consists of reaching unreasonable conclusions on the basis of minimal or circumstantial evidence. Seeing a number of people standing in front of a police station, a boy concludes that they are all police officers; when it is pointed out that they are in civilian clothes, he decides that they are "secret agents"; when he is told that they are in fact just an assorted group of people waiting for a bus that stops nearby, he refuses to be "tricked" into changing his initial conclusion. What is faulty in such reasoning is not the boy's considering the possibility that the people might be police, but his unwillingness to consider other possibilities in light of additional evidence.

These examples of subtle dissociation and circumstantial reasoning may appear to reflect childishness rather than psychopathology. Such ways of thinking are normal only among yound children and seldom persist beyond age 7—except as initial evidence of an emerging late-onset childhood psychosis. Moreover, circumstantial reasoning provides the basis for two prominent symptoms of serious schizophrenic disturbance, **delusions** and **ideas of reference.**

Delusions are unrealistic but fixed beliefs that derive from faulty reasoning. For example, a schizophrenic man, having grown a beard, may decide that he is Jesus Christ; his faulty reasoning has been "Jesus has a beard, I have a beard, therefore I am Jesus Christ." Ideas of reference involve interpreting general and public events as having specific and unique reference to oneself. Thus a schizophrenic woman may believe that the content of a television program or newspaper article is meant directly and only for her ("The president confided in me last night"), or that two people she observes in earnest conversation are without doubt talking about her, or perhaps plotting against her.

School-age children who become schizophrenic may similarly become unrealistically fearful that other children are "out to get them," and they may tell bizarre stories about what these supposedly dangerous enemies are doing to them and about imaginary friends or powers they can rely on for protection. Some schizophrenic children develop delusions of being an animal or a machine; some become convinced that their bodies are either impervious to harm ("I'm Superman"), or are falling apart, or are lacking some vital organ (Despert, 1968; Kernberg, 1979; Miller, 1974).

As a result of thinking at inappropriate levels of abstraction, schizophrenics at all ages often use words in an overly concrete or literal manner, much in the fashion of autistic children. For this reason the meaning of puns or other comments that involve a play on words escapes them. Told to "stop pulling my leg," they may respond with puzzlement, "I'm not even touching your leg." At the overly abstract end of the scale, they may become preoccupied with numbers, shapes, or philosophical ideas at the expense of adequate attention to more basic or ordinary ways of dealing with their experiences. Asked in what way a cat and a mouse are alike, they may say, "They're both made by God" (Andreasen, 1979a).

Inaccurate Perception   The perceptual distortions that characterize schizophrenic disturbance are reflected primarily in poor judgment. People with impaired capacity to assess their experience realistically tend to act in odd or queer ways, to say things that are out of place, and to harbor farfetched ideas. A schizophrenic girl told that a psychologist would like to ask her a few questions says, "How many days will it take?"; asked what you should do if you see thick smoke coming from the windows of your neighbor's house, she answers, "Blow it away." A slightly built, poorly coordinated college student with no athletic background goes out for the football team, not as a joke, but with the expectation that he can make All-American; another student calls her professor in the middle of the night to ask about a routine assignment. The lives of schizophrenic persons regularly involve such instances of poor judgment in which their behavior reflects an unrealistic assessment of a situation, of themselves, or of the consequences of their actions.

In their most extreme form breakdowns in perceptual accuracy result in **hallucinations,** sensory impressions for which in reality there are no external stimuli. Schizophrenic children and adults who are hallucinating may hear voices accusing them of sinful behavior or instructing them to perform various actions, and they may carry on conversations with these voices or become so absorbed in them that they cannot pay attention to anything else. At other times they may report vague sensations of sound, smell, or taste that are not noticeable by anyone else—music playing, manure odor, excess salt in their food, and so forth. In some studies of schizophrenic children, 80 percent were found to have auditory hallucinations and 50 percent visual or bodily hallucinations (Kolvin, 1971).

Interpersonal Ineptness Good interpersonal relationships require certain social skills and also some interest in approaching and being close to others. Schizophrenic persons frequently display both poor social skills and withdrawal from interpersonal contact. Regarding social skills, schizophrenics' disordered thinking and inaccurate perception often cause them to overlook or misjudge the feelings, motives, and actions of others. They are consequently likely to behave in ways that other people find insensitive, self-centered, argumentative, presumptuous, suspicious, or in some other way objectionable. These manifestations of their poor social skills make it difficult for schizophrenic people to make or keep friends, even when they try.

The withdrawal of schizophrenics may be either physical or emotional. Those who withdraw physically become loners, preferring solitary activity in both their work and recreation and avoiding situations that might bring them into close contact with others. Those who withdraw emotionally may actually seek out and enjoy crowds of people, particularly when they are all sharing some interest, as at a concert or baseball game. Such public events sometimes help schizophrenics preserve the fiction that they are meaningfully involved with other people; in fact, however, they remain alone in the crowd, their isolation from others emotional rather than physical. Even when mingling with other people, they hold them at a psychological distance by keeping their thoughts and feelings to themselves and interacting only on a formal, impersonal level.

Inadequate Controls Schizophrenic individuals are frequently unable to prevent anxiety-provoking and socially unacceptable ideas from occupying their mind. Uncontrollable aggressive and sexual fantasies and constant concern about terrible things they might do or that might be done to them are particularly likely to make the schizophrenic's existence a waking nightmare. Schizophrenics at all ages are consequently subject to severe bouts of anxiety and self-disgust, and they sometimes have difficulty distinguishing between their dreams and waking reality.

Schizophrenics also commonly suffer from poor integration of feelings and thoughts. As a consequence, they often express affect inappropriate to the situation. They may giggle while relating a violently aggressive fantasy or cry while describing how good they feel. For this same reason they also display two other frequent features of schizophrenia: emotional blunting, in which a person shows little or no emotional response to any situation, and **anhedonia,** which is a pervasive inability to experience pleasure in any setting or activity (Harrow, Grinker, Holzman, & Kayton, 1977).

Finally, schizophrenic persons may at times be unable to prevent their aggressive and sexual ideas from being directly expressed in their behavior. They may then erupt into sudden outbursts of violence against themselves or others or into inappropriate or assaultive sexual advances.

Not all schizophrenics manifest each of these disturbed behaviors, nor is any of them unique to schizophrenia. Dissociation occurs in extremely anxious persons, for example, delusions and hallucinations in states of drug intoxication, poor judgment in mentally retarded individuals, social withdrawal in shy, introverted persons, and inappropriate emotional responses in affective psychoses. Each of these phenomena has even been observed to occur transiently in otherwise normal people at times of acute stress. However, when several of the kinds of functioning impairments described in this section occur together and persist over any length of time, the presence of schizophrenia is usually indicated (Andreasen, 1979b; Harrow & Quinlan, 1977; Johnston & Holzman, 1980; Spitzer, Andreasen, & Endicott, 1978).

The Course of Childhood Schizophrenia Childhood schizophrenia begins during the elementary school years with the onset of the cognitive, interpersonal, and integrative impairments that give rise to disordered thinking, inaccurate perception, interpersonal ineptness, and inadequate controls. Initially the manifest symptoms of this breakdown come and go quickly and are difficult to distinguish from nonschizophrenic behavior. As schizophrenic children approach adolescence, however, their symptoms become more persistent and more pronounced. In the absence of some effective treatment, their condition is likely to become stable by the age of 12 or 13 and merge into the schizophrenia of adolescence and adulthood (Despert, 1968; Fish, 1977).

For this reason, the course of childhood schizophrenia is easier to describe than that of infantile autism. Whereas autistic youngsters may either remain primarily autistic or grow into retarded, epileptic, aphasic, or otherwise neurologically impaired adults, childhood schizophrenics become schizophrenic adolescents and adults. Specifically, follow-up studies indicate that approximately 90 percent of schizophrenic children subsequently show evidence of adult schizophrenia (Bender, 1973; Goldfarb, 1974a).

Case 6. *Childhood Schizophrenia*

Scott was Sarah Brown's first child, born when she was age 23 after a difficult pregnancy and a painful, 50-hour labor. Scott's early developmental milestones were within normal limits, although as an infant he cried for long periods of time, disliked being left alone, and wanted to be cuddled constantly. Scott resisted toilet training, which his parents were successful in achieving when he was 3½ by "threatening to rub his nose in it." However, he continued to wet the bed at night until age 6.

During his preschool years Scott developed severe asthma, had frequent night terrors, and showed little interest in other children. He seemed to get some enjoyment from mutilating insects and sticking pins into his stuffed animals. Occasionally he would light a match, blow it out, and touch the hot end to his skin.

In his early school years Scott's teachers found him a highly intelligent child who related poorly with his classmates, whom he frequently antagonized. At age 6 he had no friends, his night terrors were increasing, and he had begun to steal inexpensive objects. Because of these problems, the school advised the Browns to seek professional help.

The psychologist who examined Scott at age 6½ described him as a markedly anxious, fearful youngster who did not trust others to provide him with support or protection. On psychological tests he displayed unusually variable emotions, poor impulse control, and unrealistic grandiose fantasies. He was not considered psychotic at this time, however.

Scott was seen in individual psychotherapy for the next year, by which time his emotions were calmer, his night terrors had stopped, and he was stealing much less than before. Yet he continued to have difficulty controlling violent and destructive urges to kill things, and although his school grades were superior, he remained a loner.

In the sixth grade Scott began to get poor grades for the first time, especially on oral and written presentations. The school reports included the following comments: "Writing and thoughts seem to wander. . . . Ideas presented to the class are sometimes unrelated to the topic. A slight, nervous boy with an excellent mind. . . . The class treats him as an eccentric." Further professional help was strongly recommended at this point. However, Scott's father, Bill Brown, who had always been opposed to psychotherapy, felt the problems were not emotional but "a personality clash between mother and child." The difficulties in school increased, and Scott concentrated more and more of his time on his main pleasures of reading, watching television, collecting knives, and killing small game with a newly acquired BB gun.

Through all of his middle childhood, Scott's parents disagreed on how to discipline him. His mother believed in "logical and rational, patient explanations," whereas his father believed in physical punishment. When Scott was about 11, Bill Brown used the technique of striking him in the back of the head with his open hand in order to compel obedience. Both parents became increasingly exasperated with Scott's mischievous behaviors, and at one point locks were placed on almost everything in the house. One day when Scott was late in getting up for school in the morning, Bill Brown locked him outside the house in his pajamas and he went to school so attired.

When Scott was 12½, following a heated family argument over a poorly prepared school assignment, his mother found him sitting in the basement next to his father's tool bench, sobbing and holding a loaded and cocked .22 caliber shotgun. She contacted the school psychologist, to whom she expressed concern about his "lonely, depressed, and isolated state," but said nothing initially about the suicide gesture.

The school psychologist met with Scott twice and was struck by his "bizarre ideation and affect, and his desire to kill his father." Scott was hospitalized in the psychiatric unit of a university hospital for further evaluation. In the hospital he spoke readily but disjointedly about his suicidal gesture: "Everything went wrong. I was willing to give up the rare good days for all the bad days—I would have degraded my father." He expressed his poor self-image and feelings of loneliness and isolation as follows: "I'm itching for freedom—all my surly attributes have set things off—I was born with these attributes. My parents and I just don't fit together. I don't fit in any world but my own. I'm unhappily different from other kids—different from anyone else I have ever met." The diagnostic impression at this time was of a childhood schizophrenic disorder that had probably been present since shortly after he began elementary school.

Differentiating Infantile Autism and Childhood Schizophrenia

A brief comparative summary of the nature and course of infantile autism and childhood schizophrenia will serve to highlight some important symptomatic differences between them.

1. Infantile autism is characterized primarily by interpersonal isolation, abnormal concern with the preservation of sameness, and certain specific language peculiarities. By contrast, schizophrenic children may be awkward or hesitant in relating to other people, but they are unlikely to display the extreme social aversion or indifference of autistic youngsters; they may show some of the same compulsive routines and self-preoccupied behavior as autistic children, but they rarely display any unusual intolerance for changes in their environment; their speech may be difficult to understand at times because of their dissociation and literal use of words, but they seldom fail to develop language, and they seldom exhibit such language peculiarities as echolalia or pronomial reversal.

2. Childhood schizophrenia, like schizophrenia at all ages, is characterized primarily by disordered thinking, inaccurate perception, interpersonal ineptness, and inadequate controls. By contrast, autistic children may fail to think clearly or perceive their world adequately, but they do not exhibit dissociation or develop delusions and hallucinations; they avoid people because of disinterest or dislike, not because of poor social skills. Although they also have limited self-control, their behavior is unusual much more for their unresponsiveness than their overresponsiveness to situations.

3. Whereas infantile autism begins early in life, childhood schizophrenia constitutes a breakdown or deterioration in functioning after several years of apparently normal development.

4. Once begun, the symptoms of autism run a continuous, unrelenting course, whereas schizophrenia is an episodic disorder in which severe symptomatology alternates with periods of reasonably adequate functioning.

5. Childhood schizophrenia is continuous with and usually leads to adult schizophrenia, whereas autistic children do not become schizophrenic adults.

These and other differences between early- and late-onset child psychosis are summarized in Table 5.4, which also identifies the resemblance between infantile autism and central nervous system disorder on the one hand and child and adult schizophrenia on the other.

TABLE 5.4 Comparative Characteristics of Organic Syndromes, Childhood Psychoses, and Adult Schizophrenia

| Characteristic | Psychotic or Severely Retarded Children with Known Neurological Damage | Childhood Psychosis | | Adult Schizophrenia |
		Early Onset	Late Onset	
Extreme aloneness	+	+	−	−
Mental retardation	+	+	−	−
Males more often affected	+	+	+	−
Stereotyped ritualistic behaviors	+	+	+/−	+/−
Pronomial reversal	−	+	−	−
Echolalia	+/−	+	−	−
"Odd" since birth or infancy	+/−	+	−	−
Delayed speech, extreme	+/−	+	−	−
Bizarre motor movements	+	+	−	−
Perceptual disturbances	+	+	−	−
Abnormal EEG, seizures	+	+	−	−
Unremitting problems	+	+	−	−
Disordered stream of thought	−	−	+	+
Hallucinations	−	−	+	+
Blunted or inappropriate affect	−	−	+	+

+ = symptom fairly common; − = symptom rare; +/− = intermediate frequency.
Source. Modified from Hanson and Gottesman (1976). Reproduced by permission of Plenum Publishing Corporations.

ORIGINS OF CHILDHOOD PSYCHOSIS

The origins of childhood psychosis are not yet fully understood. Biogenetic theorists believe that psychotic children suffer inherited or acquired neurophysiological defects. Psychosocial theorists maintain that psychosis in the absence of clearly demonstrable brain damage results from severe interpersonal and environmental stress. Regrettably, firmly held positions of both kinds have sometimes run ahead of, or even contrary to, the available facts. As Hanson and Gottesman (1976) observe, "Debates over . . . the development of infantile autism and childhood schizophrenia often sacrifice scientific credibility to ideology" (p. 209).

Nevertheless, research findings on the origins of childhood psychosis appear to be pointing in certain directions, although somewhat differently for patterns of early and late onset. Infantile autism appears to be a multiply determined but primarily biological disorder in which neither genetic nor psychosocial factors play a major causative role. Childhood schizophrenia appears to result from an interaction between largely genetically determined predisposing factors and environmental precipitating factors.

Causes of Infantile Autism

Child specialists who consider infantile autism a primarily emotional disorder tend to believe that it results from harmful psychosocial influences. According to Bettelheim (1967), for example, autism is caused by personality defects in mothers that prevent them from being warm and loving toward their infants (so-called refrigerator mothers). From this point of view the interpersonal isolation of autistic children is a radical psychological defense against the massive rejection of mothers who would prefer them not to exist. Clinicians expressing this view have commonly described the parents of autistic children as undemonstrative, overly intellectual people who foster their child's disturbance by their lack of warmth and affection (Eisenberg, 1957a; King, 1975; Szurek, 1973).

Paralleling the previously noted shift toward an emphasis on primary cognitive deficits in autism, most researchers currently favor biogenetic theories of its origin. This change in view is due in large measure to accumulating evidence that contradicts psychosocial explanations. First, systematic research studies indicate that parents of autistic children are on the average no more likely to be cold or rejecting than parents of children with other developmental disorders. Many autistic children become disturbed despite having loving and attentive parents, and parents who are indifferent or detached include many who have become that way as a result, not as a cause, of their child's unresponsiveness to them (Cox, Rutter, Newman, & Bartak, 1975; DeMyer, 1975; DeMyer, Pontius, Norton, Barton, Allen & Steele, 1972; Hingten & Bryson, 1975).

Second, parents of autistic children tend to show as broad a range of personality characteristics as parents of other youngsters being treated in child guidance clinics, without any "typical" patterns, and they are no more likely to be disturbed themselves. Neither in kind nor degree, then, do these parents display any consistent behavioral trends or deviations that are likely to have accounted for their children's profound early disturbance (McAdoo & DeMyer, 1978; Schopler, 1978a).

Third, systematic observation of families with autistic children has failed to reveal any patterns of parent-child communication or interaction that distinguish them from other families (Byassee & Murrell, 1975; Cantwell, Baker, & Rutter, 1977, 1979). Taken together, these findings provide no support for viewing certain kinds of psychosocial stress as necessary for infantile autism to occur (Cantwell, Baker, & Rutter, 1978).

The only differentiating characteristic of the parents of autistic children that has received some research support is a suggestion that they tend to be more intelligent, better educated, and more affluent than the general population (Kernberg, 1979; Lotter, 1967; McAdoo & DeMyer, 1977). Whatever the possible implications of such a circumstance, Schopler and his colleagues have argued convincingly that it does not exist; according to their extensive data, autistic children probably do not come primarily from higher-social-class families, and autism can occur in any socioeconomic setting (Schopler, Andrews, & Strupp, 1979). Of particular interest, they found that being economically advantaged appears to have increased the likelihood of families traveling long distances to bring their disturbed children to major treatment centers—the source of most of the reports on this aspect of autism.

By contrast with the contradictions of psychosocial explanations, several lines of research support attributing autism to biological causes. First, there is the increasing evidence already noted for the primacy of basic cognitive defects in this condition. Second, autistic children have been found to experience an unusually high frequency of the kinds of harmful prenatal and early life events associated with MBD/ADD (see Chapter 4). These include pregnancy and birth complications, metabolic disorders, and infectious conditions, especially rubella (Chess, 1971; Chess, Fernandez, & Korn, 1978; Finnegan & Quarrington, 1979; Piggott, 1979). Third, there is the previously noted frequency of neurological abnormalities among autistic children. Fourth, autistic children show a more than normal frequency of minor physical anomalies, such as a large-size head and a highly arched palate, which suggests that they have undergone some deviant intrauterine experience (Campbell, 1978; Steg & Rapoport, 1975; Walker, 1977).

These data are by no means conclusive in demonstrating biological origins of infantile autism. Even though indications of biological hazards or disorder appear in almost half of autistic children, the majority do not have any such accompanying problems that can be detected through present methods. Furthermore, the accompanying presence of biological problems in an autistic child does not prove that they are causally responsible for his or her condition. Yet the accumulation of at least suggestive biological data has led most current researchers to regard autism as a brain disorder of multiple origins that, like MBD/ADD, can result from any of a number of circumstances that impair normal growth and development of the central nervous system (DeLong, 1978; Ritvo, 1976; Rutter, 1974; Werry, 1979).

As an important difference from MBD/ADD, however, the biological insults that appear to cause infantile autism have not yet been demonstrated to involve any significant genetic components. There is some suggestion that identical twins are more likely to be concordant for the disorder than nonidentical twins. By and large, however, early-onset psychosis does not run in families. Virtually none of the relatives of children who become seriously disturbed early in life are found to be psychotic themselves. Moreover, fewer than 20 percent of the parents and fewer than 10 percent of the siblings of autistic children show any kind of psychopathology, and neither of these figures exceeds the prevalence of disturbance in the general population of adults and children (Folstein & Rutter, 1977; Goldfarb, Spitzer, & Endicott, 1976; Hanson & Gottesman, 1976; Lennox, Callias, & Rutter, 1977; Lotter, 1974).

Causes of Childhood Schizophrenia

Some clinicians and researchers believe firmly that schizophrenia is transmitted genetically from parents to their children. Others are equally convinced that schizophrenia is caused by faulty social learning occurring in disorganized families. Schizophrenia has been studied more extensively than any other psychological disorder, and proponents of both points of view can cite research findings in apparent support of their position.

Genetic Factors   Unlike early-onset psychosis, late-onset psychosis occurs in families. Moreover, the elevated frequency of psychosis observed in the relatives of youngsters who become psychotic during middle or late childhood matches a similarly ele-

Figure 5.2
Schizophrenia in relatives of schizophrenics. (Based on data summarized by Jarvik and Deckard (1977).)

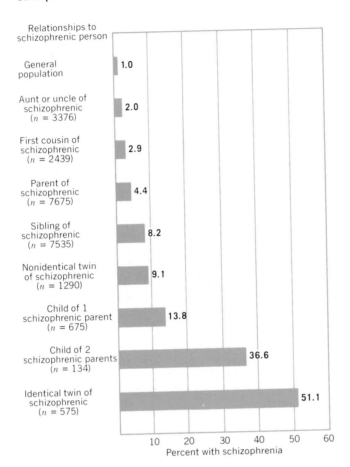

vated frequency found in the relatives of adolescent and adult schizophrenics (Hanson & Gottesman, 1976). These facts can be added to the reasons for distinguishing between infantile autism and childhood schizophrenia and regarding the latter as continuous with adolescent and adult schizophrenia.

Figure 5.2 indicates the average extent of famililial concordance for schizophrenia reported in over 70 studies. Compared to the 1 percent prevalence in the general population, any close relationship to a schizophrenic person can be seen to increase substantially the likelihood of also being schizophrenic—up to 51.1 percent for monozygotic (identical) twins. Additionally, the degree of concordance parallels the degree of relationship; that is, the more closely two people are related, the more likely it is that schizophrenia in one of them will be accompanied by schizophrenia in the other.

Two aspects of these data are especially suggestive of genetic factors in schizophrenia. First, schizophrenia is several times more likely to occur among children born to two schizophrenic parents (36.6 percent) than among children of just one schizophrenic parent (13.8 percent). Second, the concordance rate is considerably greater for monozygotic twins (51.1 percent) than for dizygotic (nonidentical) twins (9.1 percent), whose concordance approximates that of nontwin siblings (8.2 percent). As noted in Chapter 4, whether dizygotic twins are more like monozygotic twins, with whom they share similar experience, or more like siblings, with whom they share the same degree of genetic relationship, has compelling implications for whether a characteristic is inherited. In this case, the evidence appears to point to heredity instead of environment as the basis of the concordance.

Nevertheless, psychosocial theorists have favored other explanations of these findings. They suggest that schizophrenic individuals often have schizophrenic parents because such adults are likely to rear their children in a disorganized fashion, and two schizophrenic parents more so than one. Likewise, they see the high concordance of schizophrenia among siblings and twins as reflecting the fact that close relatives share the same social-learning environment, for better or worse, and monozygotic more so than dizygotic twins.

This shared-environment hypothesis cannot explain why nontwin siblings are just as concordant for schizophrenia as dizygotic twins. Furthermore, available evidence suggests that monozygotic twins are only slightly more likely than dizygotic twins to be treated the same way by their parents, which makes it difficult to account in environmental terms for the dramatic difference between them in concordance for schizophrenia (Allen, Greenspan, & Pollin, 1976; Cohen, Dibble, & Grawe, 1977; Lytton, 1977). Finally, monozygotic twins who have been reared apart, in completely different environments, are found to be just as highly concordant for schizophrenia as monozygotic twins reared in the same household (Cancro, 1979; Liston & Jarvik, 1976).

Studies of children reared apart from their biological families constitute an important advance in psychopathology research methods known as **cross-fostering.** The cross-fostering method compares children born to either normal or disturbed parents but, as a result of adoption or foster-home placement, reared by either normal or disturbed parents. This method distinguishes fairly clearly between hereditary and environmental influences. For example, if heredity is more important, then children born to schizophrenic parents should have an elevated frequency of schizophrenia regardless of who rears them; if the environment is more important, children born to schizophrenic parents but reared by normal parents should be no more likely than the general population to become schizophrenic.

The following findings from cross-fostering studies are extremely difficult to explain in psychosocial terms and point strongly toward genetic factors in the origin of schizophrenia.

1. Children born to schizophrenic mothers but placed for adoption early in life and reared by normal parents show about a 12 percent frequency of schizophrenia, which is almost identical to the risk of schizophrenia among children who are reared by as well as born to schizophrenic mothers (Haier, Rosenthal, & Wender, 1978; Heston, 1966; Wender, Rosenthal, Kety, Schulsinger, & Welner, 1974).

2. Children born to normal parents but reared by parents with a history of schizophrenia are no more likely to develop severe psychopathology than adopted children reared by nondisturbed parents (Wender et al., 1974).

3. Children born to and reared by schizophrenic mothers are no more likely to become psychologically disturbed than the offspring of schizophrenics who are reared by psychologically normal parents (Higgins, 1976).

In other words, there is no evidence to indicate that being reared by schizophrenic parents increases the risk of psychopathology beyond what would be expected on a genetic basis alone. This conclusion gains further support from extensive studies of the parents of young adult schizophrenics. Figure 5.3 indicates the frequency of psychopathology found in three groups: biological parents of schizophrenics, adoptive parents of schizophrenics, and biological parents of organically damaged (nonfamilial) retardates. This last group was included because they share with adoptive parents of schizophrenics the stress of having reared a severely handicapped youngster whose condition was not genetically related to any of their own characteristics. The data clearly show that the biological parents of schizophrenics are much more disturbed than parents who have reared either a schizophrenic youngster to whom they did not give birth or a mentally handicapped youngster whose condition was not inherited (Kety, Rosenthal, Wender, Schulsinger, & Jacobsen, 1978; Wender, Rosenthal, Rainer, Greenhill, & Sarlin, 1977).

Figure 5.3
Psychopathology in the parents of schizophrenic and organically retarded young adults. (Based on data reported by Wender et al. (1977).)

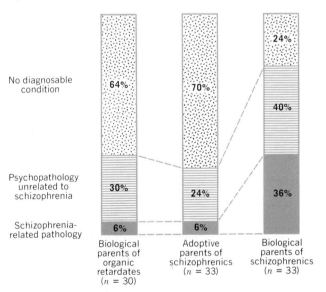

Other Biological Factors Psychotic children with an early onset of disorder are much more likely than those who become disturbed in middle or late childhood to show signs of neurological disorder or to have experienced complications during pregnancy or birth, as noted earlier. Nevertheless, such possible indications of brain dysfunction still occur with more than usual frequency in childhood schizophrenia. Kolvin (1971), for example, reports a 31 percent occurrence of evidence of cerebral dysfunction in late-onset childhood psychosis (compared to 54 percent in infantile autism), and Bender (1970) found pathological pregnancies or births in 11 to 18 percent of childhood schizophrenics she studied (compared to 36 to 54 percent of those with infantile autism).

Some studies report much higher frequencies of such difficulties in schizophrenic children: up to 65 percent (Gittelman & Birch, 1967; Walker & Birch, 1970; White, 1974). However, the psychotic children in these studies have typically not been carefully separated into early- and late-onset groups; this fact tends to obscure important differences between these two distinct conditions. Nevertheless, even when childhood schizophrenia is carefully defined for research purposes, ample evidence remains that brain dysfunction, whether inherited or acquired from early-life trauma, may play a causative role in at least some cases (Arieti, 1974a, Chapter 30; Mednick, 1970; Vaughan, 1978).

Several types of biochemical abnormality have also been proposed as contributing to schizophrenia, especially in the belief that any genetic determinants of the disorder would ultimately be expressed through biochemical processes. This area of research is still very new, however, and as yet no consistent evidence has appeared for a biochemical cause or correlation with childhood psychosis (Guthrie & Wyatt, 1975; Meltzer, 1979).

Social Learning Factors The findings in support of genetic factors in schizophrenia are impressive, and many reviewers have concluded that inherited characteristics are involved in the origin of this disorder (Hanson, Gottesman, & Meehl, 1977; Kessler, 1980; Kinney & Matthysse, 1978; Rieder & Gershon, 1978). However, as these reviewers acknowledge, genetics do not tell the whole story of the etiology of schizophrenia. In the first place, sophisticated research in this area has only a short history, and relatively small numbers of subjects have thus far been involved in definitive cross-fostering studies. Second, even if the data in Figure 5.2 are perfectly reliable, they still leave about 50 percent of children with a schizophrenic identical twin and more than 60 percent of children born to two schizophrenic parents who do *not* become schizophrenic. Whatever the genetic contribution to schizophrenia, then, there is considerable room for other than hereditary factors to determine who develops this condition.

Many clinicians and researchers propose social learning factors as such an additional source of schizophrenic disturbance, or even as the most crucial cause of the disorder. The strongest support for this position comes from reports of a high frequency of disturbed communication in the families of people who become schizophrenic. In particular, parents of schizophrenic offspring have been found to send many mixed messages. Often they say one thing when they mean another, and sometimes they are impossible to understand at all.

This "mystification" makes it difficult for their children to develop a firm sense of reality and to feel certain about what they should think or do. For example, a mother may overtly encourage her son to "stand on your own two feet," while at the same time she covertly conveys her pleasure in having him remain dependent on her. Such parental behavior puts children in a "double-bind" about how to act, and this kind of disturbed communication is believed by psychosocial theorists to result in children eventually learning schizophrenic ways of adapting to their world (Arieti, 1974b; Heilbrun, 1973; Laing & Esterson, 1970; Lidz, 1973; Schuham, 1968; Stierlin, 1978).

In a major research project that has made important contributions in this area, Wynne and Singer and their colleagues have examined styles of communication in approximately 600 families. They report a distinctive frequency of "communication deviance" among families, which consists of expressing oneself in ways that befuddle a listener. That is, people listening to deviant communication as defined by Wynne and Singer find themselves puzzled about the meaning of what they are hearing and about what they should think. These researchers maintain that their results and the outcome of similar studies demonstrate a predictive relationship between the type and severity of communication disorders in parents and the severity of psychological distrubances likely to appear in their late adolescent and young adult offspring (Singer, Wynne, & Toohey, 1978; Wynne, Singer, Bartko, & Toohey, 1977; Wynne, Toohey, & Doane, 1979).

In another noteworthy project Goldstein and Rodnick have collected 5-year follow-up data on adolescents and their parents first seen when the youngsters were referred at age 15 to 16 for help with disturbing but nonpsychotic emotional problem. Deviant parental communication styles as measured by psychological tests were used to assign these adolescents to high, intermediate, and low categories of risk for subsequent schizophrenia-related pathology. As indicated in Table 5.5, high risk determined in this way significantly increased the likelihood of schizophrenia at age 20 to 21 (Goldstein & Rodnick, 1975; Goldstein, Rodnick, Jones, McPherson, & West, 1978; Jones, Rodnick, Goldstein, McPherson, & West, 1977).

Neither the reliability nor the meaning of these findings is entirely clear. Although

TABLE 5.5 Parental Communication Deviance and Subsequent Psychopathology in Young Adult Offspring

Degree of Risk for Subsequent Schizophrenia at Age 15–16, as Inferred from Parental Communication Deviance	Type of Psychopathology at Age 20–21	
	Unrelated to Schizophrenia	Schizophrenia-Related
Low	1	0
Intermediate	6	1
High	2	6

Difference between high-risk and intermediate/low-risk groups is significant beyond the 0.05 level of confidence.
Source. Based on data reported by Goldstein et al. (1978).

research consistently confirms that the parents of schizophrenics are more likely to be disturbed and to have a disharmonious marital relationship than the parents of normal offspring, numerous investigators have failed to find evidence that they communicate with their children in any unusual or peculiar ways (Hirsch & Leff, 1975; Liem, 1974; Rutter, 1978c; Schopler, 1978a). Moreover, as noted earlier with respect to the parents of autistic children, there is no easy way to determine whether unusual attitudes or behaviors among the parents of schizophrenic offspring have caused the disorder or arisen in response to it (Liem, 1980).

There can be little doubt about the stress that psychotic children do place on their parents. The constant frustration of being ignored or spoken to strangely by their child; the daily uncertainty about the mood their child will be in and what might trigger a temper tantrum; the mounting dismay and dashed hopes over the years as their child continues to behave peculiarly, to fall behind in school, and to make few friends; the personal restrictions of having to schedule much of their lives around the needs of their disturbed child—these drains on their psychological resources are often observed to cause even well-adjusted parents to act inappropriately toward their youngsters and toward each other (Marcus, 1977).

Problems in separating cause from effect have likewise made it difficult to interpret some possibly important findings on the socioeconomic status of schizophrenic persons. Schizophrenia occurs at especially high rates among socially and economically disadvantaged urban populations, and psychosocial theorists suggest that the stressful life conditions such people experience contribute to their developing faulty conceptions of social reality (Dohrenwend & Dohrenwend, 1969; Kohn, 1973, 1976). Applying the cultural-drift hypothesis described in Chapter 3, it may be that families in which schizophrenia is transmitted from one generation to the next gravitate to the lower social classes as a result of their limited ability to cope with educational and occupational demands (Hammer, Makiesky-Barrow, & Gutwirth, 1978).

Risk Research In recent years many investigators have been turning to **risk research** as a means of distinguishing between cause and effect in studying factors associated with schizophrenia. As mentioned in Chapter 1, this method involves longitudinal studies of children who are considered at risk for becoming psychologically disturbed, usually because their parents have some identifiable psychological disorder. As time passes and some of these children become schizophrenic while others do not, the circumstances that have made some of them vulnerable to this disorder can be examined firsthand instead of after the fact. Consequently, because the data collected in risk research precede the onset of the disorder, circumstances that appear to lead to schizophrenia can be separated from those that appear to arise as a result of it (Garmezy, 1975, 1978; Mednick, 1978; Rieder, 1979).

Risk studies have fairly consistently found that children of schizophrenic parents who are not showing any obvious signs of psychological disturbance nevertheless perform less well than their peers on many measures of cognitive and interpersonal functioning, even after allowances are made for any differences in intelligence. For example, subtle difficulties in maintaining the continuity of their thoughts and in sorting concepts at appropriate levels of abstraction have been from age 3 to 15 among high-risk youngsters, and elementary school children with schizophrenic mothers have been found on the average to be less competent academically and socially and to show neurological soft signs more frequently than their classmates (Gamer, Gallant, Grunebaum, & Cohler, 1977; Oltmanns, Weintraub, Stone, & Neale, 1978; Orvaschel, Mednick, Schulsinger, & Rock, 1979; Rieder & Nichols, 1979; Rolf, 1972; Weintraub, Prinz, & Neale, 1978; Worland, Lander, & Hesselbrock, 1979).

Additional follow-up studies are required to determine what if any necessary relationship exists between such preexisting conditions and the eventual development of serious psychopathology. It is already known that early cognitive and social difficulties in high-risk children occur independently of their being reared by disturbed parents. Offspring of schizophrenic parents who are placed with nondisturbed foster parents early in life also show an elevated frequency of mild cognitive dysfunctions and social isolation prior to their beginning to display any clinically significant symptoms (Asarnow, Steffy, MacCrimmon, & Cleghorn, 1977; MacCrimmon, Cleghorn, Asarnow, & Steffy, 1980).

The Diasthesis-Stress Model The available evidence makes it unlikely that there is any single or specific cause of schizophrenia. Genetic factors are extremely difficult to rule out, especially in light of the cross-fostering data, yet most people with a family history of schizophrenia do not become schizophrenic. Biologically harmful prenatal and early-life events occur in some but not the majority of children who later become schizophrenic. Poor social learning environments have obvious potential to contribute to psychological disorder, yet many of the same kinds of stressful family and environmental circumstances that are associated with schizophrenia in some cases appear to produce no disorder or different disorders in other cases. Hence schizophrenia seems most likely to result from a combination of biogenetic predisposing factors and psychosocial precipitating factors.

This interaction view, called the **diasthesis-stress model** of schizophrenia, is currently the most widely endorsed view of schizophrenic causality. It presumes that certain biogenetic and psychosocial factors are both necessary for schizophrenia to become manifest, but that neither is sufficient by itself. The stronger the biogenetic predisposition (diasthesis) to the disturbance, the more likely it is to arise in response to minimal psychosocial stress. Conversely, persons with little or no predisposition to schizophrenia either cope adequately with severe family disorganization and environmental pressures or develop other forms of psychopathology (Fish, 1977; Kidd & Matthyse, 1978; Romano, 1978; Rosenthal, 1970; Schulsinger, 1980).

Zubin and Spring (1977) have formulated the diasthesis-stress model in terms of *vulnerability threshold*: the lower a person's vulnerability to becoming disturbed and the fewer challenging life events he or she faces, the higher the threshold against becoming psychologically disturbed; the higher the vulnerability and the more challenging events there are, the lower the disturbance threshold (see Figure 5.4). So long as the stress of life events stays below a person's vulnerability threshold, he or she will respond normally; when the stress exceeds the threshold, psychopathology is likely to develop.

Figure 5.4

Probable relationship between vulnerability and challenging events in determining an individual's threshold for psychopathology. (From Zubin and Spring (1977). Reprinted with permission of the American Psychological Association.)

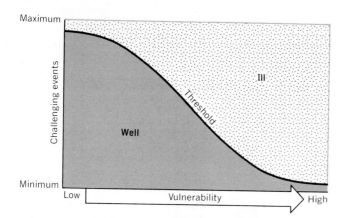

OUTCOME AND TREATMENT OF CHILDHOOD PSYCHOSIS

As a reflection of the severely disabling nature of childhood psychosis, its long-term prognosis is poor. Only about 25 percent of children with infantile autism make any substantial social or educational progress, and most of this group achieve no better than fair academic and interpersonal functioning. The remaining 75 percent do poorly throughout their lives, and about 50 percent of autistic children become permanently institutionalized by the time they reach adulthood (DeMyer, Barton, DeMyer, Norton, Allen, & Steele, 1973; Kanner, Rodriguez, & Ashenden, 1972; Lotter, 1974, 1978).

Schizophrenic children fare somewhat better on the average than those with autism. From one-third to one-half of childhood schizophrenics eventually show at least moderately good social adjustment, including about 20 percent who recover completely. The remaining half achieve only marginal or poor adjustment, however, and one-third or more face the prospect of progressive psychological decline and permanent residential care (Bender, 1973; Eggers, 1978; Eisenberg, 1957b).

This difference in outcome between infantile autism and childhood schizophrenia reflects the fact that age of onset predicts the outcome of these disorders. On the average, the older a child is before psychotic symptoms appear, the better his or her prospects for improvement or recovery (Harper & Williams, 1975; Rees & Taylor, 1975).

Three other factors that predict the outcome of childhood psychosis are intellectual level, language development, and severity of symptoms. As noted earlier with respect to intellectual level, scarcely any autistic children with IQs below 70 succeed in school or work situations. On the other hand, of the 25 to 30 percent of autistic youngsters who have nonverbal IQs above 70, about half are achieving adequately in the class-

Figure 5.5
Adult adjustment of psychotic children in relation to intelligence and age of onset. (Based on Bender's (1970) report on 50 early-onset and 50 late-onset psychotic children followed until age 22–46.)

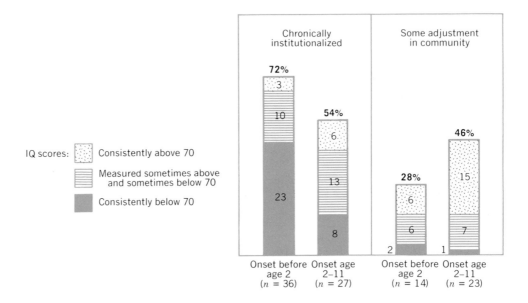

room or on the job by late adolescence or early adulthood (Rutter, 1978b). Figure 5.5 summarizes the combined impact of intelligence and age of onset on the subsequent adjustment of psychotic children in one long-term follow-up study; the high rate of eventual institutionalization among these children—63 percent—probably reflects the fact that they were initially seen between 1935 and 1952, prior to the development of many currently used treatment methods.

Regarding language, psychotic children who have not achieved communicative speech by the time they enter elementary school have especially poor prospects for improvement or recovery. Psychotic children who achieve good social skills as adolescents and young adults are almost always found to have been speaking clearly by age 5. Concerning severity, the more extreme the characteristics of infantile autism or childhood schizophrenia a child displays, the less likely he or she will be to overcome the disabling effects of the disorder. Accompanying evidence of neurological dysfunction and an inability to respond to initial treatment efforts are especially negative predictors in this regard (Bender, 1973, 1974; Goldfarb, Meyers, Florsheim, & Goldfarb, 1978; Lotter, 1974, 1978; Rutter, 1978b).

There is an important exception to the generally poor implications of symptom severity. Psychotic children who deal actively with their environment, even in disturbed ways, appear to fare better later than those who are less responsive and may therefore seem less deviant. Thus psychotic youngsters who actively reject physical contact with their parents have better prospects for recovery than those who passively tolerate it.

Similarly, those who engage in ritualistic play with toys or strike out aggressively against others are more likely to improve than those who are placid and apathetic, apparently because they are at least trying to master their circumstances (Rees & Taylor, 1975).

Aside from these features of their condition, psychotic children's prospects for improvement depend heavily on the availability of adequate treatment. Clinicians agree more on the importance of treating psychotic children than on what the nature of this treatment should be, however. Some favor a *psychodynamic* approach, some prefer a *behavioral* approach, and others have developed *combined* approaches using both psychodynamic and behavioral methods.

Psychodynamic Approaches

Psychodynamic approaches in therapy presume (a) that underlying sources of conflict and anxiety contribute to psychological distress and deviant behavior, whether or not they have caused it, and (b) that helping a disturbed person identify and understand these underlying concerns will facilitate his or her arriving at less-disturbed ways of feeling and acting. In this framework the main vehicle for promoting positive change in psychotic children is the personal relationship between child and therapist. Though emotional warmth, infinite patience, and sensitivity to the fears that often stand between psychotic children and their world, dynamically oriented therapists attempt to foster trust in the treatment relationship. Once established, this trust can generalize to the children's relationships with other people and free them to give up the psychotic symptoms that have been used to keep them and reality at a distance.

Bruno Bettleheim (1967, 1974) has been the most distinguished and influential proponent of psychodynamic therapy with psychotic children. Under his direction the Orthogenic School in Chicago, of which he became principal in 1944, became world-famous for its long-term residential treatment program for such youngsters. In addition to intensive individual psychotherapy and a primary focus on interpersonal relatedness, other hallmarks of Bettelheim's approach are almost total permissiveness—including approval of whatever a child chooses to do—and almost total separation of psychotic children from their parents—because of their presumed role in causing and sustaining the psychosis.

These latter features are not necessary for a psychodynamic approach, however. Other experienced clinicians have developed treatment programs in which individual psychotherapy is just one aspect of a therapeutic environment that includes (a) specific efforts to improve a psychotic youngster's self-control and reality contact, and (b) collaborative work with parents to help them understand and respond constructively to their psychotic child's behavior (Berlin, 1978; Ekstein, 1978; Goldfarb, 1971, 1974b; Ruttenberg, 1971; Szurek & Berlin, 1973).

Regrettably, there are no systematic data on the effectiveness of long-term, intensive, residential treatment of autistic and schizophrenic children. Case reports of successful outcomes abound, and many clinicians involved in these treatment programs feel strongly that they offer the best available opportunity for seriously disturbed youngsters to realize a rewarding adult life. Yet many child specialists have reservations about this approach, even if it works. Above all, questions are raised about its cost-effectiveness; that is, could the enormous amount of money and professional time invested in an individual child be better spent in providing shorter-term, less intensive treatment for many more children? There is as yet no satisfactory answer to this question.

Behavioral Approaches

Behavioral approaches in therapy involve the systematic use of rewards and punishments to modify maladaptive behavior. Therapists concentrate on *what* a disturbed person is doing, rather than *why,* and focus their efforts more on techniques for shaping behavior than on the patient-therapist relationship. Behavioral treatment of psychotic children aims specifically to eliminate such deviant responses as temper tantrums and rituals and to build a normal repertoire of cognitive, language, and social skills.

Early reports of successful behavioral treatment of psychotic children by DeMyer and Ferster (1962) and Lovaas, Schaeffer, and Simmons (1965) encouraged many clinicians to pursue this approach. Published reports soon documented that virtually any feature of child psychotic behavior could be altered by a carefully designed reinforcement schedule (Leff, 1968; 1971; Lovaas, 1976; Lovaas & Newsom, 1976; Lovaas, Schreibmen, & Koegel, 1976; Margolies, 1977).

For at least two reasons, however, the full potential of this approach was not realized for several years. First, simple rewards and punishments, such as giving or withholding food, were being used to shape very specific units of behavior, such as saying words. Often these rewards and punishments had only slight impact on seriously psychotic children, and at best they promoted only modest progress toward normal functioning. Second, the treatment programs were conducted for the most part by skilled professionals working very intensively with institutionalized children. Hence they involved the same high costs and other disadvantages of residential care as Bettelheim's approach. Moreover, follow-up studies revealed that virtually all of the gains achieved in these programs were lost shortly after the children returned home or were transferred to a residential setting that had no intensive behavioral program (Lovaas, Koegel, Simmons, & Long, 1973; Hemsley, Howlin, Berger, Hersov, Holbrook, Rutter, & Yule, 1978).

More recently, behavioral approaches to treating psychotic children have been modified in several promising ways. First, physical rewards and punishments have been replaced with more effective psychological reinforcers, such as giving or withholding affection, approval, or permission to engage in some desired activity. Expressions of affection might be anticipated to make matters worse rather than to reward psychotic children, because of their interpersonal isolation and ineptness, yet careful observation has indicated that whereas clumsy and demanding showers of attention do indeed cause psychotic children to withdraw even further, skillfully muted affection can lead these youngsters into pleasurable social involvements, even when it intrudes on self-preoccupied behavior (Hemsley et al., 1978).

Second, treatment aims have been expanded to go beyond specific units of behavior to more complex cognitive and social skills. Through a gradual shaping process psychotic children are encouraged to progress from using words to using language and then to engaging in social communication—and from looking at and listening to people to building an adaptive array of social skills. Third, parents are made part of a specific

Recent advances in treating psychotic children include training their parents to fill the therapist's role at home, thereby helping to reduce the amount of time they must spend in institutions. This mother is talking with a parent trainer while watching a therapist work with her son.

treatment contract in which they agree to participate in treatment sessions and to be trained themselves in the use of reinforcement techniques that will help their child achieve the treatment targets. Fourth, as soon as possible the treatment becomes home-based, so that the parents, perhaps helped by home visits from a professional therapist, take the major responsibility for regular training sessions with their child (Freeman & Ritvo, 1976; Hemsley et al., 1978; Lovaas, 1978; Rincover & Koegel, 1977; Schopler, 1978b; Schreibman & Koegel, 1981).

These advances have reduced sharply earlier disadvantages of long-term professional intervention in a residential setting. The participation of the parents in the treatment helps them overcome feelings of guilt or helplessness about their child's condition and also frees professional time to get other disturbed children and their parents started in treatment programs. The home-based treatment emphasis, in addition to minimizing the time these children spend in an institution, has been found to sustain and build on whatever gains they have made during a residential phase of treatment.

Combined Approaches

Although psychodynamic and behavioral approaches to treating psychotic children derive from very different theories, they share more common practices than is often recognized. Bettelheim, despite his emphasis on the treatment relationship rather than on any direct efforts to alter psychotic behavior, nevertheless includes limit-setting in his actual conduct of the therapy. About one disturbed boy he says, "Eventually his weird grin and trembling lips showed that this was another of his dangerous activities, and we declared it out of bounds" (1974, p. 257). Likewise, most behavior therapists comment that a positive therapist-child relationship allows adults to be more effective reinforcers than the mechanical administration of rewards and punishments (Helm, 1976).

Aside from these implicit common elements, some specialists have developed treatment approaches that explicitly combine psychodynamic, behavioral, and other features. Schopler and his colleagues encourage a highly structured and active teaching program that aims both to break down interpersonal isolation through a warm treatment relationship and to build up age-appropriate behaviors through behavior-shaping techniques. Known as "developmental therapy," this approach also includes intensive training of parents to take over the treatment of their child (Schopler, 1976; Schopler, Brehm, Kinsbourne, & Reichler, 1971; Schopler & Reichler, 1971).

Des Lauriers and Carlson (1969), in a method called "theraplay," similarly stress building a strong positive relationship with disturbed children and then using it as a basis for encouraging age-appropriate skills and behavior. Des Lauriers and Carlson believe that a high level of stimulation is a necessary feature of such treatment. Accordingly theraplay involves intensive and intrusive efforts by the therapist to establish physical contact with the disturbed child and constant effort to inject excitement, fun, and novelty into the treatment interaction.

In a third variation, Fenichel (1974) and others have recommended an *educational-milieu* approach in which the treatment setting is made as normal as possible. Instead of being institutionalized for even the initial stages of therapy, children attend a day school only and remain living at home. Instead of receiving "therapy," they are considered to be receiving special forms of "education." As in the other efforts at "normalization" in providing mental health services, this approach seeks to keep psychotic children and their parents as close as possible to ordinary patterns of family living.

Certain drugs may also be included in the treatment program for some psychotic children, although medication is neither as effective nor as widely used as in treating MBD/ADD. Stimulant medication, for example, which has a calming effect on hyperactive MBD/ADD children, usually makes psychotic children more upset than before, more out of touch with reality, and less in control of themselves. Psychotic symptoms in children can be controlled by several antipsychotic drugs developed in work with schizophrenic adolescents and adults. These drugs have sedative effects, however, and at doses sufficient to reduce disturbed behavior they tend to make children too sleepy and lethargic to benefit from relationship-building, behavior-shaping, or educational treatment efforts.

Since the aim in working with psychotic children is not to control their behavior but to help them correct delays and deficits in their development, drugs play at most an adjunctive role in their treatment. They may provide a temporary means of helping therapists make contact with these youngsters, but they do not have much direct impact on the cognitive and emotional impairments from which psychotic children suffer and should not be viewed as a long-term treatment modality (Campbell, 1975, 1976, 1978; Miller, 1974; Ornitz & Ritvo, 1976).

SUMMARY

Childhood psychosis comprises two distinct patterns of disturbance: infantile autism and childhood schizophrenia. Infantile autism begins early in life, almost always prior to 30 months of age, whereas childhood schizophrenia typically begins during middle or late childhood following several years of apparently normal development. Although some clinicians and researchers question whether these are distinct conditions, accumulating evidence indicates that psychosis beginning before age 3 differs substantially from psychosis beginning after age 7 in symptomatology, course, probable origins, and long-term outcome.

Childhood psychosis occurs in 3 to 5 per 10,000 children, of whom 1 to 2 show the pattern of early onset indicative of infantile autism. Boys are much more likely than girls to develop these and other psychological disorders. This sex difference gradually diminishes with age, however, so that by the end of adolescence young men and women, like older adults, are equally likely to become psychologically disturbed.

Autistic children with early-onset psychosis display (a) *interpersonal isolation,* which consists of striking unresponsiveness to other people and indifference or aversion to social contact; (b) an abnormal concern with the *preservation of sameness,* which results in ritualistic, self-preoccupied behavior that cannot easily be interrupted; (c) *language peculiarities* consisting either of the inability to acquire meaningful speech or numerous strange, overly literal, and ungrammatical forms of expression; (d) *cognitive and intellectual impairments,* often including auditory-perceptual defects, peculiar motor movements, other neurological indicators of brain dysfunction, and, in about 75 percent, persistent mental retardation.

Schizophrenic children with late-onset psychosis, in common with schizophrenic adolescents and adults, show (a) *disordered thinking,* which consists of the inability to think coherently, logically, and at an appropriate level of abstraction and results in such phenomena as dissociation, delusions, and overly abstract or concrete frames of reference; (b) *inaccurate perception* of reality and consequently poor judgment about the consequences of their behavior; (c) *interpersonal ineptness,* which involves poor social skills and either physical or emotional withdrawal from close contact with other people; (d) *inadequate control* over ideas, feelings, and impulses, resulting in disturbing preoccupations, inappropriate affect, and unpredictable behavior. In the absence of spontaneous recovery or adequate treatment, children with this pattern of disturbance become schizophrenic adolescents and adults; by contrast, autistic children become retarded or neurologically impaired adults who rarely show primary features of schizophrenic disturbance.

Biogenetic theorists believe that psychotic children suffer inherited or acquired neurophysiological defects, whereas psychosocial theorists maintain that childhood psychosis results from severe interpersonal and environmental stress. Although not yet definitive, available research suggests that early-onset childhood psychosis (infantile autism) is a multiply determined but primarily biological disorder in which neither genetic nor psychosocial factors play an important causative role; later-onset psychosis (childhood schizophrenia), on the other hand, appears due to an interaction between largely genetically determined predisposing factors and environmental precipitating factors.

Earlier efforts to attribute infantile autism to cold and rejecting parental rearing have been contradicted by evidence that many parents of autistic children do not behave in this way and that, as a group, these parents show as broad a range of personality characteristics as parents of youngsters with other psychological problems. At the same time, increasing evidence that autism involves primary cognitive defects and frequent neurological abnormalities, minor physical anomalies, and potentially harmful prenatal and early-life events supports biological origins of this condition similar to those in MBD/ADD. Specific patterns of family incidence pointing to genetic transmission of autism have not yet been demonstrated, however.

With respect to childhood schizophrenia, evidence from family studies indicates that the more closely two people are related, the more likely they are to be concordant for schizophrenia—if one has the disorder, the other will also. Such concordance holds whether or not close relatives are reared in the same family, and children of schizophrenic parents are much more likely than the general population to become schizophrenic even if they are reared from early in life by well-adjusted adoptive parents. On the other hand, many children with a strong family history of schizophrenia do not develop the disorder, which means that genetic factors, although often involved and perhaps even necessary for schizophrenia to occur, are not sufficient by themselves to cause it.

Although the sufficient conditions to precipitate schizophrenia in a predisposed person are uncertain, many clinicians and researchers assign this role to faulty social learning occurring in disorganized families. There is some evidence to suggest that parents of schizophrenics communicate in confused and confusing ways that make it difficult for their children to develop a firm sense of reality and feel certain about what they should think or do. It remains to be determined how much any unusual attitudes or behaviors among the parents of schizophrenic offspring have caused the disorder or arisen in response to it.

The long-term outcome of childhood psychosis is poor. Among autistic children, only about 25 percent make any substantial social or educational progress, and about half become permanently institutionalized by the end of adolescence. One-third to one-half of schizophrenic children eventually show at least moderately good social adjustment, but one-third or more also end up in permanent residential care. The prognosis is generally better for those children who have had a longer period of reasonably normal development before becoming psychotic, have acquired some language skills, show average or better intelligence, have relatively mild symptoms, are free from neurological dysfunction, and receive adequate treatment.

Some approaches to treating psychotic children focus on building a trusting relationship between child and therapist that will help the child come to relate better to other people and eventually give up his or her psychotic symptoms (psychodynamic approaches). Some approaches focus on the systematic use of rewards and punishments to eliminate psychotic behavior and shape a normal repertoire of cognitive, language, and social skills (behavioral approaches). Other combined approaches strive explicitly both to break down interpersonal isolation through a warm treatment relationship and to build up age-appropriate behaviors through behavior-shaping techniques. Recent advances involving all of these approaches have included training parents to serve as therapists with their own psychotic children and basing as much of the treatment program as possible at home or in a day school, not in a residential facility.

REFERENCES

ALLEN, M. G., GREENSPAN, S. I., & POLLIN, W. The effect of parental perceptions on early development in twins. *Psychiatry,* 1976, *39,* 65–71.

AMERICAN PSYCHIATRIC ASSOCIATION. *Diagnostic and statistical manual of mental disorders.* (3d ed.) Washington, D. C.: American Psychiatric Association, 1980.

ANDREASEN, N. C. Thought, language, and communication disorders. I. Clinical assessment, definition of terms, and evaluation of their reliability. *Archives of General Psychiatry,* 1979a, *36,* 1315–1321.

ANDREASEN, N. C. Thought, language, and communication disorders. II. Diagnostic significance. *Archives of General Psychiatry,* 1979b, *36,* 1325–1330.

ARIETI, S. *Interpretation of schizophrenia.* (2nd ed.) New York: Basic Books, 1974a.

ARIETI, S. An overview of schizophrenia from a predominantly psychological approach. *American Journal of Psychiatry,* 1974b, *131,* 241–249.

ASARNOW, R. F., STEFFY, R. A., MACCRIMMON, D. J., & CLEGHORN, J. M. An attentional assessment of foster children at risk for schizophrenia. *Journal of Abnormal Psychology,* 1977, *86,* 267–275.

BAKER, L., CANTWELL, D. P., RUTTER, M., & BARTAK, L. Language and autism. In E. R. Ritvo (Ed.), *Autism: Diagnosis, current research and management.* New York: Halsted, 1976.

BALTAXE, C. A. Pragmatic deficits in the language of autistic adolescents. *Journal of Pediatric Psychology,* 1977, *2,* 176–180.

BARTAK, L., & RUTTER, M. Differences between mentally retarded and normally intelligent autistic children. *Journal of Autism and Childhood Schizophrenia,* 1976, *6,* 109–120.

BARTAK, L., RUTTER, M., & COX, A. A comparative study of infantile autism and specific receptive language disorder. I. The children. *British Journal of Psychiatry,* 1975, *126,* 127–145.

BARTAK, L., RUTTER, M., & COX, A. A comparative study of infantile autism and specific developmental receptive language disorders. III. Discriminant function analysis. *Journal of Autism and Childhood Schizophrenia,* 1977, *7,* 383–396.

BARTOLUCCI, G., & ALBERS, R. J. Deictic categories in the language of autistic children. *Journal of Autism and Childhood Schizophrenia,* 1974, *6,* 131–144.

BARTOLUCCI, G., PIERCE, S. J., & STREINER, D. Cross-sectional studies of grammatical morphemes in autistic and mentally retarded children. *Journal of Autism and Developmental Disorders,* 1980, *10,* 39–50.

BELLAK, L., HURVICH, M., & GEDIMAN, H. K. *Ego functions in schizophrenics, neurotics, and normals.* New York: Wiley, 1973.

BENDER, L. The nature of childhood psychosis. In J. G. Howells (Ed.), *Modern perspectives in international child psychiatry.* New York: Brunner/Mazel, 1971.

BENDER, L. The life course of children with schizophrenia. *American Journal of Psychiatry,* 1973, *130,* 783–786.

BERLIN, I. N. Psychotherapeutic work with parents of psychotic children. In M. Rutter & E. Schopler (Eds.), *Autism: A reappraisal of concepts and treatment.* New York: Plenum, 1978.

BETTELHEIM, B. *The empty fortress: Infantile autism and the birth of the self.* New York: Free Press, 1967.

BETTELHEIM, B. *A home for the heart.* New York: Knopf, 1974.

BLOCK, M. B., FREEMAN, B. J., & MONTGOMERY, J. Systematic observation of play behavior in autistic children. *Journal of Autism and Childhood Schizophrenia,* 1975, *5,* 363–371.

BOMBERG, D., SZUREK, S., & ETEMAD, J. A statistical study of a group of psychotic children. In S. Szurek & I. Berlin (Eds.), *Clinical studies in childhood psychosis.* New York: Brunner/Mazel, 1973.

BYASSE, J., & MURRELL, S. Interaction patterns in families of autistic, disturbed, and normal children. *American Journal of Orthopsychiatry*, 1975, *45*, 473–478.

CAMPBELL, M. Psychopharamacology in childhood psychosis. In R. Gittelman-Klein (Ed.), *Recent advances in child psychopharmacology*. New York: Human Sciences Press, 1975.

CAMPBELL, M. Treatment of childhood and adolescent schizophrenia. In J. M. Wiener (Ed.), *Psychopharmacology in childhood and adolescence*. New York: Basic Books, 1977.

CAMPBELL, M. Pharmacology. In M. Rutter & E. Schopler (Eds.), *Autism: A reappraisal of concepts and treatment*. New York: Plenum, 1978.

CAMPBELL, M., et al. Minor physical anomalies in young psychotic children. *American Journal of Psychiatry*, 1978, *135*, 573–575.

CANCRO, R. The genetic studies of the schizophrenic syndrome: A review of their clinical implications. In L. Bellak (Ed.), *Disorders of the schizophrenic syndrome*. New York: Basic Books, 1979.

CANCRO, R. Schizophrenic disorders. In H. I. Kaplan, A. M. Freedman, & B. J. Sadock (Eds.), *Comprehensive textbook of psychiatry*. (3d ed.) Baltimore: Williams & Wilkins, 1980.

CANTWELL, D. P., BAKER, L., & RUTTER, M. Families of autistic and dysphasic children: II. Mothers' speech to the children. *Journal of Autism and Childhood Schizophrenia*, 1977, *7*, 313–327.

CANTWELL, D. P., BAKER, L., & RUTTER, M. Family factors. In M. Rutter & E. Schopler (Eds.), *Autism: A reappraisal of concepts and treatment*. New York: Plenum, 1978.

CANTWELL, D. P., BAKER, L., & RUTTER, M. Families of autistic and dysphasic children. I. Family life and interaction patterns. *Archives of General Psychiatry*, 1979, *36*, 682–687.

CARPENTER, W. T., & STRAUSS, J. S. Diagnostic issues in schizophrenia. In L. Bellak (Ed.), *Disorders of the schizophrenic syndrome*. New York: Basic Books, 1979.

CERRETO, M. C., & TUMA, J. M. Distribution of DSM-II diagnoses in a child psychiatric setting. *Journal of Abnormal Child Psychology*, 1977, *5*, 147–155.

CHAR, J., & LUBETSKY, S. Childhood psychosis in the preschool child. *Journal of Autism and Developmental Disorders*, 1979, *9*, 271–277.

CHESS, S. Autism in children with congenital rubella. *Journal of Autism and Childhood Schizophrenia*, 1971, *1*, 33–47.

CHESS, S., FERNANDEZ, P., & KORN, S. Behavioral consequences of congenital rubella. *Journal of Pediatrics*, 1978, *93*, 699–703.

CHURCHILL, D. W. LANGUAGE: The problem beyond conditioning. In M. Rutter & E. Schopler (Eds.), *Autism: A reappraisal of concepts and treatment*. New York: Plenum, 1978a.

CHURCHILL, D. W. *Language of autistic children*. Washington, D.C.: Winston, 1978b.

COHEN, D. J., CAPARULO, B., & SHAYWITZ, B. Primary childhood aphasia and childhood autism: Clinical, biological, and conceptual observations. *Journal of the American Academy of Child Psychiatry*, 1976, *15*, 604–645.

COHEN, D. J., DIBBLE, E E., & GRAWE, J. M. Parental style: Mothers' and fathers' perceptions of their relations with twin children. *Archives of General Psychiatry*, 1977, *34*, 445–451.

COX, A., RUTTER, M., NEWMAN, S., & BARTAK, L. A comparative study of infantile autism and specific developmental receptive language disorder: II. Parental characteristics. *British Journal of Psychiatry*, 1975, *126*, 146–159.

DELONG, G. R. A neuropsychological interpretation of infantile autism. In M. Rutter & E. Schopler (Eds.), *Autism: A reappraisal of concepts and treatment*. New York: Plenum, 1978.

DEMYER, M. K. Research in infantile autism: A strategy and its results. *Biological Psychiatry*, 1975, *10*, 433–452.

DEMYER, M. K. Motor, perceptual-motor and intellectual disabilities of autistic children. In L. Wing (Ed.), *Early childhood autism*. (2nd ed.) New York: Pergamon, 1976.

DEMYER, M. K., BARTON, S., DEMYER, W. E., NORTON, J. A., ALLEN, J., & STEELE, R. Prognosis in autism: A follow-up study. *Journal of Autism and Childhood Schizophrenia*, 1973, *3*, 199–246.

DEMYER, M. K., & FERSTER, C. B. Teaching new social behavior to schizoprhenic children. *Journal of the American Academy of Child Psychiatry*, 1962, *1*, 443–461.

DEMYER, M. K., MANN, N. A., TILTON, J. R., & LOEW, L. H. Toy-play behavior and use of body by autistic and normal children as reported by mothers. *Psychological Reports*, 1967, *21*, 973–981.

DEMYER, M. K., PONTIUS, W., NORTON, J. A., BARTON, S., ALLEN, J., & STEELE, R. Parental practices and innate activity in normal, autistic, and brain-damaged infants. *Journal of Autism and Childhood Schizophrenia*, 1972, *2*, 49–66.

DES LAURIERS, A. M., & CARLSON, C. F. *Your child is alseep: Early infantile autism.* Homewood, Ill.: Dorsey Press, 1969.

DESPERT, J. L. *Schizophrenia in children.* New York: Brunner/Mazel, 1968.

DEYKIN, E. Y., & MACMAHON, B. The incidence of seizures among children with autistic symptoms. *American Journal of Psychiatry*, 1979, *136*, 1310–1312.

DOHRENWEND, B. P. *Mental illness in the United States: Epidemiological estimates.* New York: Praeger, 1980.

DOHRENWEND, B. P., & DOHRENWEND, B. S. *Social status and psychological disorder: A causal inquiry.* New York: Wiley, 1969.

EGGERS, C. Course and prognosis of childhood schizophrenia. *Journal of Autism and Childhood Schizophrenia*, 1978, *8*, 21–36.

EISENBERG, L. The fathers of autistic children. *American Journal of Orthopsychiatry*, 1957a, *27*, 715–724.

EISENBERG, L. The course of childhood schizophrenia. *Archives of Neurology and Psychiatry*, 1957b, *78*, 69–83.

EKSTEIN, R. Psychoanalytically oriented psychotherapy of psychotic children. In J. Glenn (Ed.), *Child analysis and therapy.* New York: Aronson, 1978.

EME, R. F. Sex differences in childhood psychopathology: A review. *Psychological Bulletin*, 1979, *86*, 547–595.

FENICHEL, C. Special education as the basic therapeutic tool in treatment of severely disturbed children. *Journal of Autism and Childhood Schizophrenia*, 1974, *4*, 177–186.

FERRARA, C., & HILL, S. D. The responsiveness of autistic children to the predictability of social and nonsocial toys. *Journal of Autism and Developmental Disorder*, 1980, *10*, 51–57.

FINEGAN, J., & QUARRINGTON, B. Pre-, peri-, and neonatal factors in infantile autism. *Journal of Child Psychology and Psychiatry*. 1979, *20*, 119–128.

FISH, B. Neurobiologic antecedents of schizophrenia in children. *Archives of General Psychiatry*, 1977, *34*, 1297–1313.

FOLSTEIN, S., & RUTTER, M. Genetic influences and infantile autism. *Nature*, 1977, *265*, 726–728.

FREEMAN, B. J., & RITVO, E. R. Parents as paraprofessionals. In E. R. Ritvo (Ed.), *Autism: Diagnosis, current research and management.* New York: Halsted, 1976.

GAMAR, E., GALLANT, E., GRUNEBAUM, H. U., & COHLER, B. J. Children of psychotic mothers: Performance of 3-year-old children on tests of attention. *Archives of General Psychiatry*, 1977, *34*, 592–597.

GARMEZY, N. The experimental study of children vulnerable to psychopathology. In A. Davids (Ed.), *Child personality and psychopathology: Current topics.* Vol. 2. New York: Wiley, 1975.

GARMEZY, N. Observations on high-risk research and premorbid development in schizophrenia. In L. C. Wynne, R. L. Cromwell, & S. Matthyse (Eds.), *The nature of schiziphrenia.* New York: Wiley, 1978.

GITTELMAN, M., & BIRCH, H. G. Childhood schizophrenia: Intellect, neurologic status, perinatal risk. prognosis, and family pathology. *Archives of General Psychiatry*, 1967, *17*, 16–25.

GOLD, M. S., & GOLD, J. R. Autism and attention. *Child Psychiatry and Human Development*, 1975, *6*, 68–80.

GOLDFARB, W. Therapeutic management of schizophrenic children. In J. G. Howells (Ed.), *Modern perspectives in international child psychiatry.* New York: Brunner/Mazel, 1971.

GOLDFARB, W. Distinguishing and classifying the individual schizophrenic child. In S. Arieti (Ed.), *American handbook of psychiatry.* Vol. 2. New York: Basic Books, 1974a.

GOLDFARB, W. *Growth and change of schizophrenic children: A longitudinal study.* New York: Winston, 1974b.

GOLDFARB, W., MEYERS, D., FLORSHEIM, J., & GOLDFARB, N. *Psychotic children grown up.* New York: Human Sciences Press, 1978.

GOLDFARB, W., SPITZER, R. L., & ENDICOTT, J. A study of psychopathology of parents of psychotic children by structured interviews. *Journal of Austism and Childhood Schizophrenia,* 1976, *6,* 327–338.

GOLDSTEIN, M. J., & RODNICK, E. H. The family's contribution to the etiology of schizophrenia: Current status. *Schizophrenia Bulletin,* 1975, *14,* 48–63.

GOLDSTEIN, M. J., RODNICK, E. H., JONES, J. E., MCPHERSON, S. R., & WEST, J. L. Familial precursors of schizophrenia spectrum disorders. In L. C. Wynne, R. L. Cromwell, & S. Matthyse (Eds.), *The nature of schizophrenia.* New York: Wiley, 1978.

GOTTESMAN, I. I. Schizophrenia and genetics: Where are we? Are you sure? In L. C. Wynne, R. L. Cromwell, & S. Matthyse (Eds.), *The nature of schizophrenia.* New York: Wiley, 1978.

GOVE, W. R. Sex differences in the epidemiology of mental disorder: Evidence and explanations. In E. S. Gomberg & V. Franks (Eds.), *Gender and disordered behavior.* New York: Brunner/Mazel, 1979.

GUTHRIE, R. D., & WYATT, J. Biochemistry and schizophrenia: III. A review of childhood psychosis. *Schizophrenia Bulletin,* 1975, *12,* 19–32.

HAIER, E. J., ROSENTHAL, D., & WENDER, P. H. MMPI assessment of psychopathology in the adopted-away offspring of schizophrenics. *Archives of General Psychiatry,* 1978, *35,* 171–175.

HAMMER, M., MAKIESKY-BARROW, S., & GUTWIRTH, L. Social networks and schizophrenia. *Schizophrenia Bulletin,* 1978, *4,* 522–545.

HANSON, D. R., GOTTESMAN, I. I. The genetics, if any, of infantile autism and childhood schizophrenia. *Journal of Autism and Childhood Schizophrenia,* 976, *6,* 209–234.

HANSON, D. R., GOTTESMAN, I. I., MEEHL, P. E. Genetic theories and the validation of psychiatric diagnoses: Implications for the study of children of schizophrenics. *Journal of Abnormal Psychology,* 1977, *86,* 575–588.

HARPER, J., & WILLIAMS, S. Age and type of onset as critical variables in early infantile autism. *Journal of Autism and Childhood Schizophrenia,* 1975, *5,* 25–36.

HARROW, M., GRINKER, R. R., HOLZMAN, P. S., & KAYTON, L. Anhedonia and schizophrenia. *American Journal of Psychiatry,* 1977, *134,* 794–799.

HARROW, M., & PROSEN, M. Intermingling and disordered logic as influences on schizophrenic "thought disorder." *Archives of General Psychiatry,* 1978, *35,* 1213–1218.

HARROW, M., & QUINLAN, D. Is disordered thinking unique to schizophrenia? *Archives of General Psychiatry,* 1977, *34,* 15–21.

HEILBRUN, A. B. *Aversive maternal control: A theory of schizophrenic development.* New York: Wiley, 1973.

HELM, D. Psychodynamic and behavior modification approaches to the treatment of infantile autism. *Journal of Autism and Childhood Schizophrenia,* 1976, *6,* 27–41.

HEMSLEY, R., HOWLIN, P., BERGER, M., HERSOV, L., HOLBROOK, D., RUTTER, M., & YULE, W. Treating autistic children in a family context. In M. Rutter & E. Schopler (Eds.), *Autism: A reappraisal of concepts and treatment.* New York: Plenum, 1978.

HESTON, L. L. Psychiatric disorders in foster home reared children of schizophrenic mothers. *British Journal of Psychiatry,* 1966, *112,* 819–825.

HIER, D. B., LEMAY, M., & ROSENBERGER, P. B. Autism and unfavorable left-right asymmetries of the brain. *Journal of Autism and Developmental Disorders,* 1979, *9,* 153–159.

HIGGINS, J. Effects of child rearing by schizophrenic mothers: A follow-up. *Journal of Psychiatric Research,* 1976, *13,* 1–9.

HINGTEN, J. N., & BRYSON, C. Q. Recent developments in the study of early childhood psychoses: Infantile autism, childhood schizophrenia and related disorders. *Schizophrenia Bulletin,* 1975, *5,* 8–53.

HIRSCH, S. R., & LEFF, J. P. *Abnormalities in parents of schizophrenics.* London: Oxford University Press, 1975.

JAMES, A. L., & BARRY, R. J. A review of psychophysiology in early onset psychosis. *Schizophrenia Bulletin,* 1980, *6,* 506–525.

JARVIK, L. F., & DECKARD, B. S. The Odyssean personality: A survival advantage for carriers of genes predisposing to schizophrenia? *Neuropsychobiology,* 1977, *3,* 179–181.

JOHNSTON, M. H., & HOLZMAN, P. S. *Assessing schizophrenic thinking.* San Francisco: Jossey-Bass, 1979.

JONES, J. E., RODNICK, E. H., GOLDSTEIN, M. J., MCPHERSON, S. R., & WEST, K. L. Parental transactional style deviance as a possible indicator of risk for schizophrenia. *Archives of General Psychiatry,* 1977, *34,* 71–74.

KANNER, L. Autistic disturbances of affective contact. *Nervous Child,* 1943, *2,* 217–250.

KANNER, L., RODRIGUEZ, A., & ASHENDEN, B. How far can autistic children go in matters of social adaptation? *Journal of Autism and Childhood Schizophrenia,* 1972, *2,* 9–33.

KEITH, S. J., GUNDERSON, J. G., REIFMAN, A., BUCHSBAUM, S., & MOSHER, R. A. Special report: Schizophrenia, 1976. *Schizophrenia Bulletin,* 1976, *2,* 509–565.

KERNBERG, P. F. Childhood schizophrenia and autism: A selective review. In L. Bellak (Ed.), *Disorders of the schizophrenic syndrome.* New York: Basic Books, 1979.

KESSLER, S. The genetics of schizophrenia: A review. *Schizophrenia Bulletin,* 1980, *6,* 404–416.

KETY, S. S., ROSENTHAL, D., WENDER, P. H., SCHULSINGER, F., & JACOBSEN, B. The biological and adoptive families of adopted individuals who became schizophrenic: Prevalence of mental illness and other conditions. In L. C. Wynne, R. L. Cromwell, & S. Matthyse (Eds.), *The nature of schizophrenia.* New York: Wiley, 1978.

KIDD, K. K., & MATTHYSSE, S. Research designs for the study of gene-environment interactions in psychiatric disorders. *Archives of General Psychiatry,* 1978, *35,* 925–932.

KING, P. D. Early infantile autism: Relation to schizophrenia. *Journal of the American Academy of Child Psychiatry,* 1975, *14,* 666–682.

KINNEY, D. K., & MATTHYSSE, S. Genetic transmission of schizophrenia. *Annual Review of Medicine,* 1978, *29,* 459–473.

KOHN, M. L. Social class and schizophrenia: A critical review and a reformulation. *Schizophrenia Bulletin,* 1973, *7,* 60–79.

KOHN, M. L. The interaction of social class and other factors in the etiology of schizophrenia. *American Journal of Psychiatry,* 1976, *133,* 177–180.

KOLVIN, I. Studies in the childhood psychoses. *British Journal of Psychiatry,* 1971, *118,* 381–419.

LAING, R. D., & ESTERSON, A. *Sanity, madness, and the family.* (2nd ed.) New York: Basic Books, 1970.

LEFF, R. I. Behavior modification and the psychoses of childhood: A review. *Psychological Bulletin,* 1968, *69,* 396–409.

LEFF, R. I. Behavior modification and childhood psychoses. In A. Graziano (Ed.), *Behavior therapy with children.* Chicago: Aldine, 1971.

LENNOX, C., CALLIAS, M., & RUTTER, M. Cognitive characteristics of parents of autistic children. *Journal of Autism and Childhood Schizophrenia,* 1977, *7,* 243–261.

LIDZ, T. *The origin and treatment of schizophrenic disorders.* New York: Basic Books, 1973.

LIEM, J. H. Effects of verbal communications of parents and children: A comparison of normal and schizophrenic families. *Journal of Consulting and Clinical Psychology,* 1974, *42,* 438–450.

LIEM, J. H. Family studies of schizophrenia: An update and commentary. *Schizophrenia Bulletin,* 1980, *6,* 429–455.

LISTON, E. H., & JARVIK, L. F. Genetics of schizophrenia. In M. A. Sperber & L. F. Jarvik (Eds.), *Psychiatry and genetics.* New York: Basic Books, 1976.

LOCKYER, V., & RUTTER, M. A five-to-fifteen-year follow-up study of infantile psychosis. IV. Patterns of cognitive ability. *British Journal of Social and Clinical Psychology,* 1970, *9,* 152–163.

LOTTER, V. Epidemiology of autistic conditions in young children. I. Prevalence. *Social Psychiatry,* 1966, *1,* 124–137.

LOTTER, V. Epidemiology of autistic conditions in young children. II. Some characteristics of the parents and children. *Social Psychiatry,* 1967, *1,* 163–173.

LOTTER, V. Factors related to outcome in autistic children. *Journal of Autism and Childhood Schizophrenia,* 1974, *4,* 263–277.

LOTTER, V. Follow-up studies. In M. Rutter & E. Schopler (Eds.), *Autism: A reappraisal of concepts and treatment.* New York: Plenum, 1978.

LOVAAS, O. I. *The autistic child: Language development through behavior modification.* New York: Irvington, 1976.

LOVAAS, O. I. Parents as therapists. In M. Rutter & E. Schopler (Eds.), *Autism: A reappraisal of concepts and treatment.* New York: Plenum, 1978.

LOVAAS, O. I., KOEGEL, R. L., & SCHREIBMAN, L. Stimulus overselectivity in autism: A review of research. *Psychological Bulletin,* 1979, *86,* 1236–1254.

LOVAAS, O. I., KOEGEL, R. L., SIMMONS, J. W., & LONG, J. Some generalization and follow-up measures on autistic children in behavior therapy. *Journal of Applied Behavioral Analysis,* 1973, *6,* 131–166.

LOVAAS, O. I., & NEWSOM, C. D. Behavior modification with psychotic children. In H. Leitenberg (Ed.), *Handbook of behavior modification and behavior therapy.* Englewood Cliffs, N.J.: Prentice-Hall, 1976.

LOVAAS, O. I., SCHAEFFER, B., & SIMMONS, J. Q. Building social behavior in autistic children by use of electric shock. *Journal of Experimental Research in Personality,* 1965, *1,* 99–109.

LOVAAS, O. I., SCHREIBMAN, L., & KOEGEL, R. L. A behavior modification approach to the treatment of autistic children. In E. Schopler & R. J. Reichler (Eds.), *Psychopathology and child development.* New York: Plenum, 1976.

LYTTON, H. Do parents create, or respond to, differences in twins? *Developmental Psyctology,* 1977, *13,* 456–459.

MCADOO, W. G., & DEMYER, M. K. Research related to family factors in autism. *Journal of Pediatric Psychology,* 1977, *2,* 162–166.

MCADOO, W. G., & DEMYER, M. K. Personality characteristics of parents. In M. Rutter & E. Schopler (Eds.), *Autism: A reappraisal of concepts and treatment.* New York: Plenum, 1978.

MACCRIMMON, D. J., CLEGHORN, J. M., ASARNOW, R. F., & STEFFY, R. A. Children at risk for schizophrenia: Clinical and attentional characteristics. *Archives of General Psychiatry,* 1980, *37,* 671–674.

MARCUS, L. M. Patterns of coping in families of psychotic children. *American Journal of Orthopsychiatry,* 1977, *47,* 388–399.

MARGOLIES, P. J. Behavioral approaches to the treatment of early infantile autism: A review. *Psychological Bulletin,* 1977, *84,* 249–264.

MASSIE, H. N. The early natural history of childhood psychosis. *Journal of the American Academy of Child Psychiatry,* 1975, *14,* 683–707.

MEDNICK, S. A. Breakdown in individuals at high risk for schizophrenia: Possible predispositional perinatal factors. *Mental Hygiene,* 1970, *54,* 50–63.

MEDNICK, S. A. Berkson's fallacy and high-risk research. In L. C. Wynne, R. L. Cromwell, & S. Matthyse (Eds.), *The nature of schizophrenia.* New York: Wiley, 1978.

MELTZER, H. Y. Biochemical studies in schizophrenia. In L. Bellak (Ed.), *Disorders of the schizophrenic syndrome.* New York: Basic Books, 1979.

MILLER, R. T. Childhood schizophrenia: A review of selected literature. *International Journal of Mental Health,* 1974, *3,* 3–46.

OLTMANNS, T. F., WEINTRAUB, S., STONE, A. A., & NEALE, J. M. Cognitive slippage in children vulnerable to schizophrenia. *Journal of Abnormal Child Psychology,* 1978, *6,* 237–245.

ORNITZ, E. M. Neurophysiologic studies. In M. Rutter & E. Schopler (Eds.), *Autism: A reappraisal of concepts and treatment.* New York: Plenum, 1978a.

ORNITZ, E. M. Biological homogeneity or heterogeneity? In M. Rutter & E. Schopler (Eds.), *Autism: A reappraisal of concepts and treatment.* New York: Plenum, 1978b.

ORNITZ, E. M., GUTHRIE, D., & FARLEY, A. J. The early development of autistic children. *Journal of Autism and Childhood Schizophrenia,* 1977, *7,* 207–229.

ORNITZ, E. M., & RITVO, E. R. The syndrome of autism: A critical review. *American Journal of Psychiatry,* 1976a, *133,* 609–621.

ORNITZ, E. M., & RITVO, E. R. Medical assessment. In E. R. Ritvo (Ed.), *Autism: Diagnosis, current research and management.* New York: Halsted, 1976b.

ORVASCHEL, H., MEDNICK, S., SCHULSINGER, F., & ROCK, D. The children of psychiatrically disturbed parents. *Archives of General Psychiatry,* 1979, *36,* 691–695.

PIERCE, S., & BARTOLUCCI, G. A syntactic investigation of verbal autistic, mentally retarded, and normal children. *Journal of Autism and Childhood Schizophrenia,* 1977, *7,* 121–134.

PIGGOTT, L. R. Overview of selected basic research in autism. *Journal of Autism and Developmental Disorders,* 1979, *9,* 199–218.

PRIOR, M. R. Cognitive abilities and disabilities in infantile autism: A review. *Journal of Abnormal Child Psychology,* 1979, *7,* 357–380.

PRIOR, M., & MACMILLAN, M. B. Maintenance of sameness in children with Kanner's syndrome. *Journal of Autism and Childhood Schizophrenia,* 1973, *3,* 154–167.

REES, S. C., & TAYLOR, A. Prognostic antecedents and outcome in a follow-up study of children with a diagnosis of childhood psychosis. *Journal of Autism and Childhood Schizophrenia,* 1975, *5,* 309–322.

RICHER, J. M., & COSS, R. G. Gaze aversion in autistic and normal children. *Acta Psychiatrica Scandinavica,* 1976, *53,* 193–210.

RICKS, D. M., & WING, L. Language, communication and the use of symbols. In L. Wing (Ed.), *Early childhood autism.* (2nd ed.) New York: Pergamon, 1976.

RIEDER, R. O. Children at risk. In L. Bellak (Ed.), *Disorders of the schizophrenic syndrome.* New York: Basic Books, 1979.

RIEDER, R. O., & GERSHON, E. S. Genetic strategies in biological psychiatry. *Archives of General Psychiatry,* 1978, *35,* 866–873.

RIEDER, R. O., & NICHOLS, P. L. Offspring of schizophrenics. III. Hyperactivity and neurological soft signs. *Archives of General Psychiatry,* 1979, *36,* 665–674.

RIMLAND, B. Infantile autism: Status and research. In A. Davids (Ed.), *Child personality and psychopathology: Current topics.* Vol. 1. New York: Wiley, 1974.

RINCOVER, A., & KOEGEL, R. L. Research on the education of autistic children: Recent advances and future directions. In B. B. Lahey & A. E. Kazdin (Eds.), *Advances in child clinical psychology.* Vol. 1. New York: Plenum, 1977.

RITVO, E. R. Autism: From adjective to noun. In E. R. Ritvo (Ed.), *Autism: Diagnosis, current research and management.* New York: Halsted, 1976.

RITVO, E. R., ORNITZ, E. M., & LAFRANCHI, S. Frequency of repetitive behaviors in early infantile autism and its variants. *Archives of General Psychiatry,* 1968, *19,* 341–347.

ROBINS, L. N. Psychiatric epidemiology. *Archives of General Psychiatry,* 1978, *35,* 697–702.

ROLF, J. E. The social and academic competence of children vulnerable to schizophrenia and other behavior pathologies. *Journal of Abnormal Psychology,* 1972, *80,* 225–243.

ROMANO, J. On the nature of schizophrenia: Changes in the observer as well as the observed. *Schizophrenia Bulletin,* 1977, *3,* 532–559.

ROSENBERG, S. D., & TUCKER, G. J. Verbal behavior and schizophrenia. *Archives of General Psychiatry,* 1979, *36,* 1331–1337.

ROSENTHAL, D. *Genetic theory and abnormal behavior.* New York: McGraw-Hill, 1970.

RUTTENBERG, B. A psychoanalytic understanding of infantile autism and its treatment. In D. Churchill, G. Alpern, & M. DeMyer (Eds.), *Infantile autism.* Springfield, Ill.: Thomas, 1971.

RUTTER, M. Autistic children: Infancy to adulthood. *Seminars in Psychiatry,* 1970, *2,* 435–450.

RUTTER, M. Diagnosis and definition. In M. Rutter & E. Schopler (Eds.), *Autism: A reappraisal of concepts and treatment.* New York: Plenum, 1978a.

RUTTER, M. Language disorder and infantile autism. In M. Rutter & E. Schopler (Eds.), *Autism: A reappraisal of concepts and treatment.* New York: Plenum, 1978b.

RUTTER, M. Communication deviance and diagnostic differences. In L. C. Wynne, R. L. Cromwell, & S. Matthyse (Eds.), *The nature of schizophrenia.* New York: Wiley, 1978c.

SCHOPLER, E. Towards reducing behavior problems in autistic children. In L. Wing (Ed.), *Early childhood autism.* (2nd ed.) New York: Pergamon, 1976.

SCHOPLER, E. Limits of methodological differences in early family studies. In M. Rutter & E. Schopler (Eds.), *Autism: A reappraisal of concepts and treatment.* New York: Plenum, 1978a.

SCHOPLER, E. Changing parental involvement in behavioral treatment. In M. Rutter & E. Schopler (Eds.), *Autism: A reappraisal of concepts and treatment.* New York: Plenum, 1978b.

SCHOPLER, E., ANDREWS, C., & STRUPP, K. Do autistic children come from upper-middle-class parents? *Journal of Autism and Developmental Disorders,* 1979, *9,* 199–152.

SCHOPLER, E., BREHM, S. S., KINSBOURNE, M., & REICHLER, R. J. Effect of treatment structure on development in autistic children. *Archives of General Psychiatry,* 1971, *24,* 415–421.

SCHOPLER, E., & REICHLER, R. J. Parents as cotherapists in the treatment of psychotic children. *Journal of Autism and Childhood Schizophrenia,* 1971, *1,* 87–102.

SCHOPLER, E., REICHLER, R. J., DEVELLIS, R. F., & DALY, K. Toward objective classification of childhood autism: Childhood Autism Rating Scale (CARS). *Journal of Autism and Developmental Disorders,* 1980, *10,* 91–105.

SCHREIBMAN, L., & KOEGEL, R. L. A guideline for planning behavior modification programs for autistic children. In S. M. Turner, K. S. Calhoun, & H. E. Adams (Eds.), *Handbook of clinical behavior therapy.* New York: Wiley, 1981.

SCHUHAM, A. L. The double-bind hypothesis a decade later. *Psychological Bulletin,* 1968, *68,* 409–416.

SHAPIRO, T., & HUEBNER, H. F. Speech patterns of five psychotic children now in adolescence. *Journal of the American Academy of Child Psychiatry,* 1976, *15,* 278–293.

SCHULSINGER, F. Biological psychopathology. *Annual Review of Psychology,* 1980, *31,* 583–606.

SIMON, N. Echolalic speech in autistic children: Consideration of possible underlying loci of brain damage. *Archives of General Psychiatry,* 1975, *32,* 1439–1446.

SIMONS, J. M. Observations on compulsive behavior in autism. *Journal of Autism and Childhood Schizophrenia,* 1974, *4,* 1–10.

SINGER, M. T., WYNNE, L. C., & TOOHEY, M. L. Communication disorders and the families of schizophrenics. In L. C. Wynne, R. L. Cromwell, & S. Matthyse (Eds.), *The nature of schizophrenia.* New York: Wiley, 1978.

SPITZER, R. L., ANDREASEN, N. C., & ENDICOTT, J. Schizophrenia and other psychotic disorders in DSM-III. *Schizophrenia Bulletin,* 1978, *4,* 489–509.

STEG, J. P., & RAPOPORT, J. L. Minor physical anomalies in normal, neurotic, learning disabled, and severely disturbed children. *Journal of Autism and Childhood Schizophrenia,* 5, 299–307.

STIERLIN, H. The transmission of irrationality reconsidered. In L. C. Wynne, R. L. Cromwell, & S. Matthyse (Eds.), *The nature of schizophrenia.* New York: Wiley, 1978.

SZUREK, S. A. Attachment and psychotic development. In S. A. Szurek & I. N. Berlin (Eds.), *Clinical studies in childhood psychoses.* New York: Brunner/Mazel, 1973.

SZUREK, S. A., & BERLIN, I. (Eds.) *Clinical studies in childhood psychoses.* New York: Brunner/Mazel, 1973.

TANGUAY, P. E. Clinical and electrophysiological research. In E. R. Ritvo (Ed.), *Autism: Diagnosis, current research and management.* New York: Halsted, 1976.

TREFFERT, D. A. Epidemiology of infantile autism. *Archives of General Psychiatry,* 1970, *22,* 431–438.

VAUGHAN, H. G. Toward a neurophysiology of schizophrenia. In L. C. Wynne, R. L. Cromwell, & S. Matthyse (Eds.), *The nature of schizophrenia.* New York: Wiley, 1978.

WALKER, H. A. Incidence of minor physical anomaly in autism. *Journal of Infantile Autism and Childhood Schizophrenia,* 1977, *7,* 165–176.

WALKER, H. A., & BIRCH, H. G. Neurointegrative deficiency in schizophrenic children. *Journal of Nervous and Mental Disease,* 1970, *151,* 104–113.

WEBER, D. "Toe-walking" in children with early childhood autism. *Acta Paedopsychiatrica,* 1978, *43,* 73–83.

WEINER, I. B. *Psychodiagnosis in schizophrenia.* New York: Wiley, 1966.

WEINTRAUB, S., PRINZ, R. J., & NEALE, J. M. Peer evaluations of the competence of children vulnerable to psychopathology. *Journal of Abnormal Child Psychology,* 1978, *6,* 461–475.

WEISSMAN, M. M., & KLERMAN, G. L. Epidemiology of mental disorders: Emerging trends in the United States. *Archives of General Psychiatry,* 1978, *35,* 705–712.

WENDER, P. H., ROSENTHAL, D., KETY, S., SCHULSINGER, F., & WELNER, J. Cross-fostering: A research strategy for clarifying the role of genetic and experiential factors in the etiology of schizophrenia. *Archives of General Psychiatry,* 1974, *30,* 121–128.

WENDER, P. H., ROSENTHAL, D., RAINER, J. D., GREENHILL, L., & SARLIN, B. Schizophrenics' adopting parents: Psychiatric status. *Archives of General Psychiatry,* 1977, *34,* 777–784.

WERRY, J. S. The childhood psychoses. In H. C. Quay & J. S. Werry (Eds.), *Psychopathological disorders of childhood.* (2nd ed.) New York: Wiley, 1979.

WHITE, L. Organic factors and psychophysiology in childhood schizophrenia. *Psychological Bulletin,* 1974, *81,* 238–255.

WING, L. Epidemiology and theories of etiology. In L. Wing (Ed.), *Early childhood autism.* (2nd ed.) New York: Pergamon, 1976a.

WING, L. Diagnosis, clinical description and prognosis. In L. Wing (Ed.), *Early childhood autism.* (2nd ed.) New York: Pergamon, 1976b.

WING, L. Social, behavioral, and cognitive characteristics: An epidemiological approach. In M. Rutter & E. Schopler (Eds.), *Autism: A reappraisal of concepts and treatment.* New York: Plenum, 1978.

WING, L., YEATES, S. R., BRIERLY, L. M., & GOULD, J. The Prevalence of early childhood autism: Comparison of administrative and epidemiological studies. *Psychological Medicine,* 1976, *6,* 89–100.

WOLFF, S., & BARLOW, A. Schizoid personality in childhood: A comparative study of schizoid, autistic, and normal children. *Journal of Child Psychology and Psychiatry,* 1979, *20,* 29–46.

WORLAND, J., LANDER, H., & HESSELBROCK, V. Psychological evaluation of clinical disturbance in children at risk for psychopathology. *Journal of Abnormal Psychology,* 1979, *88,* 13–26.

WYNNE, L. C., SINGER, M. T., BARTKO, J. J., & TOOHEY, M. L. Schizophrenics and their families: Recent research on parental communication. In J. M. Tanner (Ed.), *Developments in psychiatric research.* London: Hodden & Stoughton, 1977.

WYNNE, L. C., TOOHEY, M. L., & DOANE, J. Family studies. In L. Bellak (Ed.), *Disorders of the schizophrenic syndrome.* New York: Basic Books, 1979.

ZUBIN, J., & SPRING, B. Vulnerability—A new view of schizophrenia. *Journal of Abnormal Psychology,* 1977, *86,* 103–126.

6

SCHIZOPHRENIA IN ADOLESCENCE

THE PRESENTING PICTURE IN ADOLESCENT SCHIZOPHRENIA

Mixed Symptomatology

Distinctive Profiles of Impairment

Thinking
Perception
Interpersonal Relatedness
Controls

Subtypes of Schizophrenic Disorder

Chronicity
Paranoid Status
Premorbid Adjustment
Borderline Disorder
Case 7. Schizophrenia with Acute Onset
Case 8. Schizophrenia with Chronic Onset

ADOLESCENT PREDICTORS OF SUBSEQUENT SCHIZOPHRENIA

The Schizoid Pattern

The Stormy Pattern

Sex Differences

PROGNOSIS IN ADOLESCENT SCHIZOPHRENIA

General Outcome

Specific Predictive Factors

The prevalence and severity of schizophrenic disturbance make it a major public health problem. At least 1 person in every 100 is likely to suffer an episode of schizophrenia during his or her life; some estimates of this lifetime prevalence run as high as 2 percent. Approximately 50 percent of the mental hospital beds in the United States and 25 percent of all hospital beds are occupied by schizophrenic patients. Schizophrenia is the second most frequently diagnosed condition among adults under age 45 seen in psychiatric clinics and hospitals, exceeded only by personality disorders in men and depressive disorders in women. About 180,000 persons in the United States are now hospitalized with a diagnosis of schizophrenia, and another 800,000 are being treated in outpatient clinics or showing active signs of the disorder. The treatment and rehabilitation of these people and their lack of productivity are estimated to cost nearly $20 billion each year (Babigian, 1975; Gunderson & Mosher, 1975; National Institute of Mental Health, 1972, 1978; Outpatient Psychiatric Services, 1973; Psychiatric Services in General Hospitals, 1972; Spitzer, Andreasen, Endicott, & Woodruff, 1978).

As for its severity, schizophrenia is a disabling disturbance that frequently runs a chronic or recurrent course. Among persons discharged from a hospital following a first admission for schizophrenia, 40 to 60 percent are likely to be readmitted for a subsequent episode within 2 years, and 15 to 25 percent will eventually receive continued care for a prolonged period of time. Only 20 to 25 percent achieve really good psychiatric status without relapses. Of those schizophrenics who remain living in the community, without ever being hospitalized, fewer than 40 percent are able to function successfully as a wage-earner or homemaker (Anthony, Cohen, & Vitalo, 1978; Harrow, Grinker, Silverstein, & Holzman, 1978; Mosher & Feinsilver, 1973; Tsuang, Woolson, & Fleming, 1979).

Improved methods of treating schizophrenia over the last 20 years have tended to obscure somewhat the persistence of this disorder. In particular, the development of effective antipsychotic medication in the late 1950s and the community mental health movement during the 1960s led to increasing numbers of schizophrenic patients being discharged from hospitals and returned to their family and community. Wide publicity for the resulting decrease in the mental hospital population fostered the belief in some quarters that schizophrenia was now being "cured" more frequently than in the past and, like polio and smallpox, was on the way to extinction.

In reality, however, the recently increasing number of discharges from mental hospitals has been accompanied by an equal increase in admissions. Figure 6.1 summarizes this trend in a typical public mental hospital, in which the admission-discharge activity grew as the average daily census shrank. This circumstance, common to most mental hospitals, has become known as the "revolving-door phenomenon." It reflects a trend toward short-term care in which schizophrenic and other seriously disturbed patients are more likely than before to move in and out of the hospital repeatedly rather than remain continuously hospitalized (Keith, Gunderson, Reifman, Buchsbaum, & Mosher, 1976).

Opinions differ concerning whether the revolving-door phenomenon is a change for the better or worse. Those who are enthused about it stress the benefits of reducing the costs of maintaining large mental hospitals and having disturbed people spend as

Figure 6.1

Changing admission trends in a typical public mental hospital. (Based on data reported for the Rochester Psychiatric Center (formerly Rochester State Hospital) by Romano (1977).)

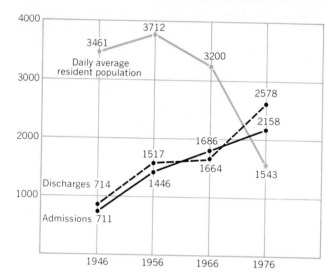

much time as possible in their community and with their family, instead of in long-term institutional care. Those who have reservations worry that short-term care may often be insufficient care, especially when readmission follows quickly on the heels of discharge; that sending disturbed people back into a world they are not yet equipped to handle may be cruel to them, burdensome for their family, and, in cases of potentially dangerous persons, a threat to their community; and that the overall cost to society of premature hospital discharge may exceed any savings from having smaller institutions (Drake & Wallach, 1979; Klerman, 1977; Stein & Test, 1980).

Whichever of these opinions is preferred, the readmission data leave little doubt that schizophrenia is not disappearing. To the contrary, the figure of approximately 980,000 persons in the United States who annually received treatment for schizophrenia in the mid-1970s is estimated to increase to 1.25 million by 1985—and to continue to increase along with population increases until research provides knowledge not currently available on how to prevent this disorder (Anthony, 1979; Kramer, 1978).

These basic facts about the schizophrenic population are pertinent to adolescent psychopathology because most forms of schizophrenic disturbance begin during or soon after the teenage years. Eugen Bleuler, a Swiss psychiatrist who coined the term *schizophrenia* from the Greek words *schizin* ("to split") and *phren* ("mind"), commented, "The adolescent age period seems to offer a particular predisposition to this disease" (1911, p. 340). Clinical observations and research findings over the 70 years since Bleuler's work have generally proved him correct in this regard (Arieti, 1974, Chapter 8; Holzman & Grinker, 1974; Spitzer, Andreasen, & Endicott, 1978).

Also noteworthy is the frequency of schizophrenia among adolescents who come to professional attention. This condition is diagnosed in 25 to 30 percent of all adolescents admitted to public mental hospitals, about 15 percent of those admitted to psychiatric units of general hospitals, and 6 to 8 percent of those seen in outpatient clinics. These frequencies make schizophrenia the most common diagnosis among adolescents in mental hospitals and the second or third most frequent condition in general hospital psychiatric units, after transient situational disorders in boys and transient situational and depressive disorders in girls (Rosen, Bahn, Shellow, & Bower, 1965; Strober & Green, in press; Strober, Green, & Carlson, 1981; Weiner & Del Gaudio, 1976).

Although schizophrenia in adolescence is continuous with adult schizophrenia, certain aspects of its presenting picture, predictive features, prognosis, and treatment relate specifically to this developmental stage. This chapter will elaborate these four topics.

THE PRESENTING PICTURE IN ADOLESCENT SCHIZOPHRENIA

As noted in Chapter 5, schizophrenia at all ages consists of disordered thinking, inaccurate perception, interpersonal ineptness, and inadequate controls. Among adolescents, however, especially in early phases of the disorder, signs of these impairments are often mixed with other kinds of symptoms and less apparent than in schizophrenic adults. Additionally, because adolescents have not yet achieved adult levels of cognitive and emotional maturation, they show somewhat distinctive profiles of impairment and subtypes of schizophrenic disorder.

Mixed Symptomatology

Clinical studies of schizophrenic adolescents indicate that no more than 30 to 40 percent initially show clear indications of a schizophrenic breakdown. The rest tend to present a mixed picture in which features of schizophrenia are secondary to or even obscured by other kinds of problems or complaints.

Two kinds of mixed-symptom picture are particularly likely to represent the early stages of schizophrenic breakdown. In one picture the young person shows some signs of schizophrenia but complains primarily of depression, with a loss of interest in people or activities, feelings of hopelessness, and thoughts about suicide. In the other picture indications of schizophrenia are overshadowed by an apparently antisocial personality disorder, with a history of family conflict, fighting, stealing, running away, truancy, and school failure (Feinstein & Miller, 1979; Hudgens, 1974, Chapter 7; Masterson, 1967, Chapter 5; Symonds & Herman, 1957).

Although prominent depressive or antisocial features in adolescents who are also showing signs of schizophrenia can alert clinicians to an early stage of schizophrenia, the initial onset of this disorder is still more difficult to detect in adolescents than in adults. Often the following three guidelines must provide the basis for an early diagnosis:

1. *Persistence of the Schizophrenic Features* The longer the schizophrenic features in a mixed clinical picture persist, the more likely a diagnosis of schizophrenia becomes. Emerging schizophrenia is especially clear when these features remain after other kinds of presenting complaints have become less noticeable, as in a

youngster who is no longer depressed but is still not thinking coherently. Unfortunately, the moment when persistent schizophrenic features become conclusive for the diagnosis varies considerably from one person to the next and is difficult to specify. Moreover, it may come too late to be of much help in planning an appropriate treatment program (Katz, 1967; Masterson, 1967; Spotnitz, 1961). In the short run, then, the next two guidelines often have more practical value.

2. *Extent of Usual Adolescent Concerns* Troubled but nonschizophrenic adolescents usually develop symptoms in the context of such developmental tasks as adapting to bodily changes in early adolescence, attaining independence from parents and gaining skill in heterosexual relationships during middle adolescence, and making commitments to life goals and values in late adolescence. Although involvement in such age-appropriate concerns cannot rule out the possibility of their becoming schizophrenic, this outcome is much less likely than when disturbed youngsters seem removed from being adolescents (Warren, 1949; Weiner, 1977).

More often than not, then, disturbed adolescents who are becoming schizophrenic show a marked inability or reluctance to grapple with usual adolescent concerns. Sometimes they remain strikingly immature in their attitudes, interests, and social relationships. A 15-year-old girl, for example, when asked what she enjoyed doing after school, replied, "I go out and play," which is what one would expect to hear from a 9- or 10-year-old. In other cases they may skirt the usual business of adolescence in favor of a deceptive pseudomaturity. Pseudomature adolescents present a calm, serious, mannerly facade that makes them seem "grown-up"; like immature adolescents, however, they suffer from not struggling with and learning to master the social and emotional challenges of adolescence.

Both immature and pseudomature adolescents may be viewed as reacting to an inadequate psychological preparation for the adolescent years by a maladaptive effort not to live them. Neither pattern by itself demonstrates schizophrenia in a disturbed adolescent. However, signs of schizophrenia in a mixed clinical picture are more likely to point to eventual schizophrenic breakdown in youngsters who show one of these patterns than in those with a well-developed pattern of age-appropriate interests and activities.

3. *Prominence of Formal Manifestations of Disturbance* *Formal* manifestations of disturbance refer to *how* a person is saying or doing something that is peculiar or inappropriate; they differ from *content* manifestations, which refer to *what* the person is saying or doing. To illustrate this difference, young people who report bizarre fantasies ("I think a lot about torturing people who haven't been nice to me") or unusual preoccupations ("I don't have time for my homework because I'm busy figuring out when the world will come to an end") are revealing content manifestations of disturbance. Yet, despite their disturbed content, these reports are expressed in a clear and comprehensible manner and are therefore not disturbed in a formal sense.

By contrast, formal manifestation of disturbance is illustrated by a boy who said, "I don't ever want to get married, because I don't have the physicalness for sexuality." In this case, even though some hunches may come to mind, the meaning is far from clear. *Physicalness* is a peculiar word that might refer to strength, stamina, potency, or even attractiveness, depending on what this boy is worried about; if he is worried specifically about having intercourse, sexuality is a rather odd and stilted way of referring to it; since sexuality can exist outside of marriage and some marriages involve relatively little sexuality, the exclusive relationship he appears to see between them involves some circumstantial reasoning.

Both formal and content manifestations of disturbance help identify schizophrenia. Among disturbed adolescents, however, the likelihood of an emerging schizophrenic disorder increases in direct relation to how prominent the formal manifestations are. In other words, it is not so much peculiar thought content but peculiar ways in which this content is arrived at and expressed that point to schizophrenia in the younger person (Machover, 1961; Piotrowski, 1962; Symonds, 1949, Chapter 16).

Distinctive Profiles of Impairment

Of the several types of impairment associated with schizophrenic disorder, some are as likely to indicate schizophrenia in adolescents as in older persons, whereas others occur more frequently in nonschizophrenic adolescents than nonschizophrenic adults. These similarities and differences contribute to some distinctive profiles of impairment among schizophrenic adolescents across the four areas of functioning described in Chapter 5.

Thinking　Adolescents can usually be expected to think as coherently as adults. Accordingly, incoherent or dissociated thinking that makes the person difficult to understand is equally suggestive of schizophrenia in adolescents and adults (Holzman & Grinker, 1974; Masterson, Tucker, & Berk, 1963; Rinsley, 1972; Spivack, Haimes, & Spotts, 1967). The following two interchanges with a 14-year-old schizophrenic boy involve subtle discontinuities in communication that pointed initially to the severity of his disturbance.

THERAPIST:　What kinds of things do you like to do?
PATIENT:　I like to play basketball; I'm a good aimer.
THERAPIST:　You're a good shot?
PATIENT:　Yes, last summer at camp we shot at targets with real bullets.

PATIENT:　The kids at school tease me and call me all kinds of names.
THERAPIST:　Like what?
PATIENT:　Oh, like "stupid" and "mental" and "retarded" and like that.
THERAPIST:　Do they call your brother those names (reference to patient's younger brother in same school)?
PATIENT:　No, no one calls me "brother."

The Rorschach inkblot test provides useful indices of a person's ability to think logically and perceive the environment accurately.

On the other hand, some aspects of cognitive development are still taking place during adolescence, and most teenagers have not yet attained adult levels of reasoning and concept formation. Most notably, adolescents often deal with the uncertainty they feel in trying to understand and integrate many new kinds of experiences by latching on to premature or abstract conclusions (Elkind, 1975; Inhelder & Piaget, 1958, Chapter 18; Neimark, 1975). Because they frequently strain to feel sure about things, even in the absence of concrete support for their convictions and in the face of inconsistent facts, adolescents are usually more likely than adults to show circumstantial reasoning and overinvolvement with abstract concerns.

The clearest evidence in this regard comes from research with the Rorschach test. Several large-scale studies indicate that nonpatient adolescents give a frequency of circumstantially reasoned and overly abstract Rorschach responses that in adults would suggest disordered thinking (Ames, Metraux, & Walker, 1971, pp. 290−293; Silverman, Lapkin, & Rosenbaum, 1962; Weiner & Exner, 1978). Significantly, however, disturbed adolescents in these studies, especially those known to be schizophrenic, produced an even greater frequency of such responses than the nonpatient youngsters. Circumstantial reasoning and preoccupation with abstractions therefore help to identify schizophrenic disturbance in adolescents, but they must occur more frequently than in adults to justify diagnosing the disorder. Figure 6.2 illustrates this important difference and highlights the need to make more allowances for instances of illogical thinking in the younger age group.

Perception Adolescents usually display the same level of perceptual accuracy as adults. Once more, the best evidence in this regard comes from studies with the Rorschach, which includes some highly reliable indices of a person's ability to perceive experience accurately and recognize conventional modes of response. Extensive normative data indicate that nonpatient adolescents receive the same scores on these indices as nonpatient adults. Table 6.1 shows that the average percent of perceptually accurate Rorschach responses and the average number of commonly given responses are as high among 13- to 16-year-olds as among 18- to 59-year-olds.

Figure 6.2

Percent of adolescents and adults showing illogical reasoning on the Rorschach test. (Based on data reported by Weiner and Exner (1978).)

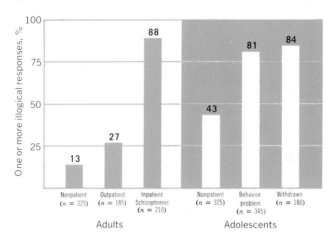

Distorted perception, especially as manifest in poor judgment and hallucinations, therefore has as serious implications for schizophrenia in adolescents as in adults. Whereas hallucinations are usually sufficiently dramatic to leave little doubt of a young person's disturbance, instances of poor judgment may involve only subtle misperceptions of the meaning of one's experience or the consequences of one's actions. For example, a 17-year-old boy beginning his senior year in high school said that he planned to enter college with a football scholarship the following fall. Asked about his high school football career thus far, he reported that he had never played football, because he wanted to avoid the risk of injury and "save myself for the big time." The unreality of expecting to play college football on a scholarship without having had any prior experience with the sport was among the first clues to a subsequently demonstrated schizophrenic disturbance in this boy, whose initial presentation was otherwise unremarkable.

TABLE 6.1 Rorschach Test Indices of Perceptual Accuracy in Nonpatient Adolescents and Adults

	Age				
	13	14	15	16	18–59
Rorschach Index	(n = 80)	(n = 100)	(n = 100)	(n = 100)	(n = 325)
Average percent of accurately perceived responses	82	84	80	84	81
Average number of commonly given responses	6.4	6.1	6.7	6.4	6.5

Source. Based on data reported by Exner (1978, Chapter 1).

Physical or emotional withdrawal from others may be an early sign of emerging schizophrenia in a disturbed adolescent.

Interpersonal Relatedness   Adolescents are still learning social skills and typically lack the interpersonal competence and self-assurance of mature adults. Nevertheless, there is nothing about adolescence itself that prevents young people from seeking out and establishing rewarding relationships, especially with their peers. Hence indications of physical or emotional withdrawal from others have the same implications for possible schizophrenia in adolescents as they do in adults. For some schizophrenic youngsters whose quiet, retiring, overcontrolled behavior conceals difficulties they are having in thinking clearly or perceiving reality accurately, an inability to engage in meaningful relationships with people their age may be the primary or sole manifest clue to their disturbance.

Any evaluation of adolescent social relationships must distinguish between *real* and *apparent* peer engagements, however. In real engagements young people take on group activities that they truly enjoy and in which they are involved participants. They are friendly with at least several different people whom they see regularly and with whom they share a variety of interests. These friendships are based on mutual respect, mutual decision-making, mutual exchange of favors, and mutual activity to maintain the relationship.

By contrast, some adolescents who appear engaged with their peers are only going through the motions of socially expected behaviors. Their group activities have been pressed on them by their parents or teachers, and they participate more as hangers-on and passive observers than as active enthusiasts. Their friendships are few, fleeting, and nonmutual. They have one friend at a time whom they see infrequently around a single shared interest, they float among various "friends" with whom they have little in common and to whom they never become close, or they get involved in relationships in which they are exploited or taken advantage of as the price of "friendship."

As was noted in Chapter 5, neither interpersonal ineptness nor any of the other impairments associated with schizophrenia is sufficient by itself to demonstrate presence of the disorder. However, when young people are clearly socially withdrawn or when their peer-group engagements turn out to be more apparent than real, the likelihood of an emerging schizophrenic disorder is increased considerably.

Controls Adolescents usually have the same capacity as adults to control their emotions and their actions. Adolescent immaturity sometimes produces fluctuating emotional states or impulsive decision-making that obscure these basic capacities, but there is no evidence to indicate that nondisturbed adolescents are inclined to lose control over aggressive and sexual impulses or to display clearly inappropriate emotional responses.

For this reason, loss of self-control and inappropriate emotions have serious implications for possible schizophrenia. Aggressive outbursts directed against a youngster's own person or property are especially serious in this regard—as in the case of a 17-year-old boy who took a hammer to his prized possession, a 10-speed bicycle, and smashed it to bits. Likewise, adolescents who show flat emotions or who giggle or weep for no apparent reason are displaying unusual behavior with pathological implications.

On the other hand, many young people do not yet show mature control of their thinking. More so than adults, adolescents are likely to become consciously aware of disturbing thoughts and images, especially involving aggressive and sexual content. The Rorschach responses in one study of several hundred nonpatient adolescents included almost 20 percent of such content themes as blood, guts, death, decay, destruction, and sex; in other research the average frequency of blatant sexual and aggressive content in Rorschach responses has been found not to differ among schizophrenic and nonschizophrenic adolescents (Ames et al., 1971; Rychlak & O'Leary, 1965; Silverman et al., 1962).

To summarize this section, schizophrenia in adolescence involves the same types of impairment as define adult schizophrenia. However, particularly in its mild or early stages, schizophrenia tends to produce some distinctive profiles of impairment in the younger age group. Perceptual distortions, social withdrawal, and inappropriate emotions are equally suggestive of schizophrenic disturbance in adolescents and adults, whereas circumstantial reasoning, preoccupation with abstractions, and limited control of thinking are less conclusive as signs of schizophrenia in adolescents than adults.

Subtypes of Schizophrenic Disorder

People diagnosed as schizophrenic differ considerably in the symptoms and course of their disorder and in how they cope with their experience. Indeed, one of the most consistent findings in clinical and research studies of schizophrenic patients is their variability from one person to the next (Carpenter, 1976; Chapman & Chapman, 1973; Lehman, 1975; Shakow, 1980; Strauss & Docherty, 1979).

Because schizophrenia is a heterogeneous disorder, numerous efforts have been made to divide it into cohesive subtypes. Unfortunately, little agreement has been reached about what these subtypes should be called. Some researchers have even concluded that none of the existing ways of subtyping schizophrenia provides categories that can be reliably distinguished from each other (Carpenter, Bartko, Carpenter, & Strauss, 1976; Carpenter & Strauss, 1979).

Nevertheless, accumulating evidence suggests that much of the interindividual variability among schizophrenics can be accounted for in terms of three dimensions—*chronicity, paranoid status,* and *premorbid adjustment* (Deckner & Cromwell, 1970; Houlihan, 1977; Lewine, 1978; Silverman, 1964). Along with describing these three dimensions of schizophrenia, attention must also be given to the category of *borderline disorder,* which overlaps in some ways with schizophrenia and has particular implications for adolescent disturbance.

Chronicity The more severely disabling a schizophrenic disturbance is and the longer it persists, the more likely it is to constitute a chronic disorder. Three other features associated with chronicity are (a) *insidious onset,* which means that the person's psychological functioning slowly deteriorates over a period of months or even years in the absence of any clearly precipitating events; (b) *symptom tolerance,* which means that the person displays little concern about the schizophrenic features of his or her behavior and lacks awareness that his or her problems derive from such impairments; (c) *prior maladjustment,* which means that the person was showing evidence of interpersonal and school or work difficulties even before the insidious onset began (Weiner, 1966, Chap. 13).

By contrast, *acute* schizophrenic disorder begins rapidly in response to clearly precipitating stressful experiences. Acutely schizophrenic individuals tend to recognize and worry about the unusual nature of their symptoms ("I don't know what's wrong with me; I just can't seem to think straight anymore"). Typically, their prior behavior has been unremarkable, at least in the eyes of untrained observers, so that their family and friends are surprised at their suddenly becoming disturbed. Finally, as these terms imply, episodes of acute schizophrenia respond more quickly to treatment than chronic schizophrenic disorder and are less likely to recur (Stephens, 1978; Vaillant, 1964, 1978).

Although the acute-chronic distinction is often used to separate schizophrenic people into two groups, especially for research purposes, it is better seen as a continuous dimension. Schizophrenia was originally described by E. Bleuler (1911, p. 256) as always being a more or less chronic condition: "I have never released a schizophrenic in whom I could not still see distinct signs of the disease." Many current writers share this view, and some research has identified persistent features of schizophrenic disorder, even in acutely disturbed persons, after they have apparently recovered (Astrachan, Brauer, Harrow, & Schwartz, 1975; Feighner, Robins, Guze, Woodruff, Winokur, & Munoz, 1972; Harrow & Silverstein, 1977). On the other hand, some researchers argue that what persists in schizophrenic persons is not their disorder, but their vulnerability to episodic psychotic breakdown (Zubin & Spring, 1977). Expressing still a different point of view, M. Bleuler (1978) presents data suggesting that at least 25 percent of all schizophrenics recover entirely and remain recovered for good.

In an effort to accommodate some of these differences in view, the new DSM-III classification scheme refers to schizophrenic-like reactions with rapid onset and short duration as **schizophreniform disorder** (lasting 2 weeks to 6 months) or **brief re-**

active psychosis (lasting less than 2 weeks). *Schizophrenia* in this scheme is reserved for disorders persisting at least 6 months. The course of schizophrenic disturbance would still be described with such terms as *chronic* (persisting more than 2 years), *subchronic* (persisting 6 months to 2 years), and *with acute exacerbation* (reemergence of prominent psychotic symptoms) (American Psychiatric Association, 1980).

Whatever terminology is preferred, the fact remains that schizophrenics vary in the chronicity of their disorder in ways that account for some important differences among them (Broen, 1968; Buss & Lang, 1965; Venables, 1964). With particular respect to schizophrenia beginning in adolescence, clinical observations indicate fairly distinct patterns of acute and chronic onset of disorder (Masterson, 1967, Chapter 5; Neubauer & Steinert, 1952; Symonds & Herman, 1957; Warren & Cameron, 1960).

In cases of *acute onset,* adolescents with no previous history of psychological difficulties break down in response to clearly precipitating stressful events. Typically there is a sharp demarcation in both time and behavior between their preschizophrenic and schizophrenic states, and the precipitating events usually consist of conflict or failure in working on the developmental tasks of adolescence.

In *chronic onset,* schizophrenia develops gradually and with little clear relationship to the biological and psychological events of adolescence. The young person's difficulties may appear to have begun at or following puberty, but a careful history reveals earlier behavior problems at home and in school. Whereas acute onset is often dramatic and unmistakable, the adolescent with chronic onset often lingers unrecognized on the fringes of teenage groups while a slow deterioration takes place—declining school performance, diminishing interest in peers and in personal appearance, retreat to solitary or meaningless activities, growing preoccupation with strange or pseudophilosophical ideas, and increasingly blunted emotions.

Paranoid Status   Paranoia consists of a distinctive cognitive style and set of attitudes toward the environment. Paranoid individuals tend to be alert and vigilant people who scan their surroundings carefully and miss little of what is going on around them; yet, because they are also rigid, inflexible, and narrow-minded, they fit new information into their previously held beliefs and rarely consider altering their views. Paranoid individuals see the world as a hostile, dangerous place, and they are accordingly cautious and suspicious in their dealings with it. They hesitate to trust other people, since they question their motives and fear being exploited or victimized by them. They relate to others with formal distance rather than easy intimacy; even with friends and relatives, they prefer to keep their own counsel rather than share their thoughts and feelings openly. Because they sense a constant need to protect themselves and their self-teem, they tend to be pompous and self-righteous individuals who criticize others freely and blame external circumstances for all of their own problems (Cameron, 1974; Meissner, 1978; Shapiro, 1965, Chapter 3; Walker & Brodie, 1980).

These characteristics can exist independently of schizophrenia, in which case they are usually referred to as a **paranoid disorder.** When they occur together with features of schizophrenia, they identify **paranoid schizophrenia.** The combination of paranoid styles and attitudes with schizophrenic impairments of thinking and perception produces such dramatic symptoms as delusions of persecution ("My food is being poi-

TABLE 6.2 Subtypes of Schizophrenia in Adolescent and Adult Patients (in percent)

Age and Sex	Subtype			
	Paranoid	Chronic Undifferentiated	All Other Subtypes	Total
Age 10–14				
Males (n = 355)	14.9	14.1	71.0	100.0
Females (n = 283)	9.2	26.1	65.7	100.0
Age 15–17				
Males (n = 1051)	26.5	20.7	52.8	100.0
Females (n = 1045)	16.1	26.4	57.5	100.0
Age 18–19				
Males (n = 1365)	28.8	27.3	43.9	100.0
Females (n = 1408)	20.0	28.3	51.7	100.0
Age 25–34				
Males (n = 6169)	45.6	26.2	28.2	100.0
Females (n = 9110)	33.4	27.5	39.1	100.0
Age 35–44				
Males (n = 4812)	48.9	26.1	25.0	100.0
Females (n = 9562)	39.9	25.6	34.5	100.0

Source. Based on General Hospital Inpatient Psychiatric Services (1969) data on 35,150 schizophrenic patients.

soned"; "Everybody is out to get me"), delusions of grandeur ("My mission on earth is to save humanity"; "I have superhuman eyesight and earsight"); and persecutory or grandiose hallucinations ("The voices keep saying terrible things will happen to me"; "I've been told I'll become a saint") (Arieti, 1974, Chapter 3; Weiner, 1966, Chapter 14).

Chronic and paranoid schizophrenia account for most of the schizophrenic subtypes diagnosed in clinical practice. Many statistical reports accordingly divide schizophrenia into these two subtypes and "all other schizophrenic reactions." Table 6.2 indicates how these three categories are distributed among adolescent and adult schizophrenics discharged from general hospital impatient psychiatric services. These data reveal little in the way of sex difference, except perhaps the trend at all ages for paranoid schizophrenia to be diagnosed more frequently in males than females. There are striking age differences, however, since approximately 70 percent of the adults but fewer than 40 percent of 10- to 19-year-olds are diagnosed chronic or paranoid, and these subtypes become increasingly frequent during adolescence.

Assuming that these diagnostic differences reflect actual differences in the patients' clinical status, they seem consistent with the frequently mixed picture of emerging schizophrenic disturbance during adolescence. That is, clear indications of chronicity or paranoid status are more likely to appear in older persons than in teenagers. Nevertheless, they occur sufficiently often among the younger patients to constitute an important facet of adolescent schizophrenia.

Premorbid Adjustment   The more adequately schizophrenic people have dealt with social, interpersonal, school, and work situations before becoming disturbed, the better their premorbid adjustment; conversely, personal incompetence, as reflected in emotional and behavioral problems that predate the onset of schizophrenic, identifies poor premorbid adjustment. This apparently simple distinction between "good premorbid" and "poor premorbid" schizophrenics has proved extremely valuable in accounting for differences within the schizophrenic population. In particular, poor premorbids tend to perform less well on measures of psychological functioning, to respond less favorably to treatment, and to suffer longer and more frequently recurring episodes of schizophrenia than good premorbids (Strauss, Kokes, Klorman, & Sacksteder, 1977).

These implications of premorbid adjustment identify some obvious overlap with the acute-chronic distinction. In addition, paranoid symptoms are found to be infrequent at the poorest levels of premorbidity and to increase progressively with better premorbid adjustment (Goldstein, 1978). Hence current thinking about these interrelationships holds that all three dimensions of schizophrenia share a developmental basis: namely, the higher the level of developmental maturity schizophrenic people have attained, the more likely they are to be acutely disturbed, to show paranoid features, and to have had a good premorbid adjustment (Lewine, Watt, & Fryer, 1978; Putterman & Pollack, 1976; Zigler, Levine, & Zigler, 1976).

Borderline Disorder   **Borderline disorder** is a form of psychopathology that combines certain features of psychotic, neurotic, and characterological disturbance. Some authorities consider it a type of schizophrenia, some regard it as a kind of personality disorder, and some classify it as a unique syndrome in its own right (Liebowitz, 1979; Stone, 1980). Much of the disagreement about the nature of borderline disorder derives from the fact that all three of the broad approaches to classifying psychopathology discussed in Chapter 2 have been used in defining it.

Work by Grinker has fostered a *descriptive-behavioral* approach in which the "borderline syndrome" is viewed as a set of characteristic ways that borderline people behave. The most notable of these characteristics are chronic fluctuations and instability in how they feel and act (Carpenter, Gunderson, & Strauss, 1977; Grinker, 1977, 1978, 1979; Grinker & Werble, 1977; Grinker, Werble, & Drye, 1968; Gunderson, 1977).

Knight and those he has influenced formulate the "borderline state" in *descriptive-inferential* terms as episodes in the lives of schizophrenic people during which neurotic symptoms obscure their underlying schizophrenic impairments. Although considered chronic, this state is seen as a variety of schizophrenia involving vulnerability to episodic breakdown, rather than as a personality style or distinct syndrome (Kety, Rosenthal, & Wender, 1968; Knight, 1953; Rieder, 1979; Weiner, 1966, Chapter 16).

Kernberg and others, working within a *dynamic-etiological* framework, regard "borderline personality organization" as the end result of early developmental arrest during the time when infants still tend toward **object splitting,** an immature interpersonal style in which other people are seen as either "all good" or "all bad." Whereas the

Grinker and Knight approaches are based on observations of patient behavior, Kernberg's formulations rest on theoretical speculations concerning early mental development (Kernberg, 1967, 1976, 1977; Masterson, 1975, 1976; Shapiro, 1978). Despite these conceptual differences, clinicians from all three points of view generally agree on the following five manifest features of borderline disorder (Gunderson & Singer, 1975; Gunderson & Kolb, 1978; Perry & Klerman, 1978):

1. *Intense Emotions*   Borderline individuals are subject to extreme episodes of anger, anxiety, and depression. Sometimes the intensity of their emotions makes people around them uncomfortable, because they seem so bristling with rage or wracked with worry.

2. *Poor Self-control*   The actions of borderline people are frequently poorly planned and poorly controlled. They are especially likely to engage in such self-destructive behavior as suicide attempts, drug abuse, and sexual promiscuity.

3. *Illusory Social Adaptation*   People with borderline disturbance usually appear to function adequately in situations that do not tax their abilities. Beneath these superifical appearances, however, they have little tolerance for stress or ambiguity. They cope poorly with challenge and uncertainty, and they typically have a history of failure or underachievement in meeting academic and vocational demands.

4. *Strained Interpersonal Relationships*   Although capable of managing superficial relationships with other people, borderline individuals cannot handle close or intimate relationships comfortably. They tend to vacillate between transient, distant acquaintanceships and intensely dependent and demanding attachments to other people.

5. *Vulnerability to Brief Psychotic Episodes*   Although borderline individuals are not overtly psychotic, they are highly vulnerable to psychotic breakdown, particularly in unstructured situations where they are unsure what is expected of them. These episodes tend to be short-lived, stress-related, and readily reversible.

As a reflection of these characteristics, people with a borderline disorder display a distinctive profile on psychological tests. In keeping with their illusory social adaptation, they often perform within normal limits on tests in which the questions and answers are unambiguous. On the Rorschach and other projective tests, however, which provide very little structure, their vulnerability to psychotic episodes surfaces in the form of dramatic evidence of disordered thinking, inadequate controls, and sometimes even distorted perception of reality (Weiner, 1966, Chapter 16).

There is also widespread agreement that borderline disorder is particularly likely to emerge during adolescence. For clinicians who consider borderline disorder a type of schizophrenia, it is simply one of the several forms of this disorder that first become apparent during the teenage years. For those who consider borderline disorder a distinct syndrome or a personality disorder, the developmental tasks of adolescence provide especially fertile ground for its characteristic instability, uncertainty, and problems with personal intimacy to blossom into a chronic pattern of maladjustment. From all points of view, moreover, the frequently mixed symptomatology of seriously disturbed young people may well reflect borderline disorder, with its characteristic mix of psychotic, neurotic, and characterological features (Giovacchini, 1978; Kernberg, 1978; Masterson, 1972; Schwartzberg, 1978).

Current trends in diagnostic practice, as formulated in DSM-III, are pointing toward the identification of two categories of borderline disorder. One category is labeled **schizotypal personality** (meaning "like schizophrenia"); this category includes those borderline individuals who are especially likely to show disturbances in thinking, perception, and self-control. The other category, which is labeled **borderline personality,** is intended for borderline persons in whom chronic instability in their moods and interpersonal relationships is the most prominent feature of their disorder. Although there is some overlap between these two diagnostic categories for borderline disorder, preliminary research suggests that they can be reliably differentiated from each other (American Psychiatric Association, 1980; Rosenthal, 1979; Spitzer & Endicott, 1979; Spitzer, Endicott, & Gibbon, 1979).

The following two cases illustrate many of the central features of emerging schizophrenia in adolescence. Both young people initially presented a mixed disturbance of uncertain diagnosis that eventually, on the basis of their past history, observed behavior, and psychological test performance, was identified as schizophrenia. In one case the disturbance involved a dramatic personality change with the sudden onset of aggressive, antisocial behavior; the other case featured a gradual, almost unnoticed breakdown involving mainly depression and withdrawal.

Case 7. *Schizophrenia with Acute Onset*

Until 6 months before being admitted to the hospital, 16-year-old Donald had been considered a bright and creative but quiet and retiring boy. He nevertheless had many friends, was well liked in school by all reports, and had never been a discipline problem. During the summer before his sophomore year in high school, he was struck by a car driven by another teenager who was trying to scare him but misjudged his braking distance. Donald suffered only a slight leg injury and did not have any lingering physical discomfort. Yet, in sharp contrast to his previous restraint and even temper, he began shortly after this frightening experience to display frequent angry outbursts. He would shout obcenities at his mother at the slightest provocation and would stamp around the house slamming doors whenever his parents disagreed with him.

When the school year began, Donald's previously above-average grades fell to Ds and Fs. He also got into disciplinary difficulty for the first time, and on one occasion he was among a group of boys caught breaking into the school building at night. In February of the school year, after 6 months of such problem behavior, he responded to his principal's asking him to get a haircut by storming out of school and refusing to return. At this point his parents sought professional help.

When first interviewed, Donald smirked most of the time and expressed little concern about his problem behavior and poor grades. Although he gave no clear sign of thought disorder, his apparently poor self-control and his strained relationship with his mother led to the decision to hospitalize him for further evaluation and treatment planning. However, the efforts of the hospital staff to help him control his aggressive, antisocial behavior were of little avail; if anything, he became worse. He regularly cursed at his therapist ("You're a shitty doctor"), broke furniture, and threw his shoes and other handy objects at fellow patients. Twice he ran away from the hospital. After 2 weeks his continued outbursts and some fleeting indications of dissociated thinking began to suggest schizophrenia. Subsequent psychological testing clearly identified schizophrenic impairments of his abilities to perceive reality accurately and exercise adequate social judgment.

Donald's stay at a university medical center ended abruptly after 30 days, when his parents' insurance coverage ran out. He was considered unimproved, and further care at a nearby state hospital was recommended. His parents decided to keep him at home, however, and to continue his treatment on an outpatient basis. In light of his stormy hospital course and apparent lack of improvement, Donald did surprisingly well at home. It was almost as if the hospital regimen had somehow perpetuated his misbehavior, so that only on returning to his natural environment could he display gains he had made in therapy. A follow-up evaluation 2 years later indicated that for the most part he had resumed the quiet, controlled personality style that had characterized him before the acute onset of his disorder. He continued to show some strange behavior, but he had returned to school without incident, was performing well in his studies, and had avoided any further behavioral difficulty.

Case 8. *Schizophrenia With Chronic Onset*

Karen was first seen at age 16 after she had expressed some thoughts of killing herself. She complained during the initial interview of having felt depressed for the past 2 to 3 years, following the death of two horses she had owned. Her apparently mistaken belief that she had in some way been responsible for these deaths had led her to give up riding, which had been her favorite pastime. Since then she had been troubled by poor appetite, difficulty in sleeping, preoccupation with the meaning of life, and a bleak view of her future. She described herself as a "loner" who cared little for being with people and had no interest in boys. Although her mood was clearly depressed, she talked freely and without obvious incoherence or circumstantiality. Nevertheless, because of the possible suicide risk, she was admitted to the hospital.

During the first week of her admission, Karen's behavior and some emerging details of her history began to suggest schizophrenic disturbance. She became markedly and strangely withdrawn. As if to shut out the world as much as possible, she would curl up in a corner of her room, with the blinds pulled and the lights out, wearing sunglasses. She frequently complained that "life is only pain and emptiness" and began to ask if she could remain in the hospital forever. She said that she felt close to no one, not even her parents—"I love them but I don't care about them." She also reported that there were times, mostly when she was alone, when she felt that eyes were watching her.

Elaborating her disinterest in boys, Karen stated that all boys expect heavy petting on the first date and that she did not want either to be touched or to have to "put men down." Hence she had never gone on a date. She reported further that she had always felt uncomfortable around youngsters of her own age and since age 7 or 8 had preferred associating with older people. The only two organized peer-group activities she had ever pursued were the 4-H Club and a horse club, both of which she had given up 2 years previously.

Karen's physical and emotional isolation from others, her unusual behavior, and her unrealistic ideas about dating and being watched suggested schizophrenic impairments, and her performance on psychological tests confirmed the presence of a schizophrenic disorder. After a month in the hospital, during which she remained depressed and withdrawn but no longer appeared to be suicidal, she was discharged to office treatment. Three months later she was back in the hospital, complaining, "I'm not myself, they changed me in the hospital; I started out thinking someone was going to kill me, and now I think everyone wants to kill me." She reported that she had done nothing but "sit around and lose all hope" since leaving the hospital, and she had developed the specific delusional idea that a tall man with a knife was after her to kill her.

Karen spent the next 8 months in the hospital, during which time her depression lifted somewhat and her paranoid thoughts diminished. Once again she was discharged to outpatient therapy, and several months later a second psychological evaluation was conducted to evaluate her progress. She showed much less fear of relationships with other people than she had previously, but her decreased interpersonal anxiety appeared to have been achieved at the cost of increased distance and withdrawal from other people. These developments, together with continued evidence of illogical thinking and inaccurate perceptions of reality, suggested that she was moving toward a basically chronic schizophrenic adjustment.

ADOLESCENT PREDICTORS OF SUBSEQUENT SCHIZOPHRENIA

The more that can be learned about features of behavior that signal emerging psychopathology in young people who are not yet overtly disturbed, the more opportunity there is to take steps to prevent the condition from occurring, or at least to minimize its eventual severity. For this reason many researchers have sought to identify youthful personality patterns that predict vulnerability to schizophrenia in late adolescence and early adulthood (Anthony, 1977; Spring & Zubin, 1977). By and large these studies have confirmed a classic view of Arieti (1974, pp. 103–107) that *schizoid* and *stormy* patterns are likely precursors of schizophrenia, and they have also revealed some interesting sex differences in this regard.

The Schizoid Pattern

A **schizoid personality pattern** is marked by shy, sensitive, seclusive behavior. Schizoid individuals have a "shut-in" personality, in the sense that their emotions and interests tend to be turned inward rather than directed toward other people (American Psychiatric Association, 1980; Chick, Waterhouse, & Wolff, 1979).

In a widely cited study some years ago, Bower, Shellhamer, and Daily (1960) reviewed the high school records and interviewed the teachers of 19- to 26-year-old hospitalized schizophrenic men and a comparison group of their classmates. Their find-

TABLE 6.3   Personality Descriptions of Preschizophrenic High School Students and a Comparison Group of their Classmates

Personality Description	Preschizophrenic Group (n = 44)	Comparison Group (n = 44)
1. Qualities of leadership in athletics or scholarship, "pride of school," eager for success	3	8
2. Apparently well adjusted and well integrated; moderately popular, sociable, no apparent school difficulty	9	31
3. No problem, seldom noticed, seclusive, and quiet; often hazily remembered by teachers; sensitive shy, passive, and colorless	4	0
4. Slight personality problems, different but not markedly so; shy, dreamy, lacked concentration, tempermental, and stubborn	19	3
5. Unusually striking personality, noted by others to be odd, peculiar, queer, or at times crazy	9	2

Note: Differences between groups statistically significant at 0.1% level of confidence.
Source.   Based on data reported by Bower, Shellhamer, and Daily (1960).

ings confirmed that withdrawn behavior in adolescence significantly increases the likelihood of subsequent schizophrenia. Although there are other routes to such an outcome, Table 6.3 indicates that more than half of the future schizophrenics showed little interest in social relations and group activities (descriptions 3 and 4), compared to less than 10 percent of their classmates. Moreover, in contrast to the 20 percent of the preschizophrenics who were seen as odd or peculiar, these withdrawn preschizophrenics would seem to have passed relatively unnoticed through their high school years.

This study has some of the limitations of retrospective research noted in Chapter 1, in that teachers' memories had to be relied on for certain data. To avoid this problem, Barthell and Holmes (1968) in a similar study used the recorded fact of how many times a graduating senior's picture appeared in the high school yearbook as an index of his or her participation in peer-group activities. Their sample of adult schizophrenics had significantly fewer such pictures than a comparison group of classmates. Other follow-back and follow-through studies as well have demonstrated a relatively high incidence of social isolation, weak friendship patterns, and underinvolvement in peer-group activities among preschizophrenic adolescents (Goldstein & Jones, 1977; Kreisman, 1970; Lewine, Watt, Prentky, & Fryer, 1980; Pitt, Kornfeld, & Kolb, 1963; Prentky, Watt, & Fryer, 1979).

The Stormy Pattern

Stormy personality refers to a conduct disorder in which young people complain of restlessness and difficulty concentrating and have a history of family conflict, stealing, fighting, running away, truancy, and school failure. In Robins's (1966) 30-year follow-up study of child guidance clinic patients, mentioned in Chapter 1, more than half of those who became schizophrenic as adults had shown this stormy pattern, whereas withdrawn and seclusive behavior in childhood was found generally not to be predictive of adult psychopathology. Nameche, Waring, and Ricks (1964), in a 7-year follow-up, also reported that a substantial portion of their youthful patients who later became schizophrenic had been referred because of antisocial behavior and rarely appeared quiet, withdrawn, or "shut-in."

Of further importance, both studies demonstrated that the predictive significance of antisocial behavior in stormy adolescents depends on the direction it takes. Antisocial youngsters who act selfishly and aggressively at home and toward their family and friends are especially likely to become schizophrenic later on. Those who direct their aggression primarily toward strangers, authority figures, and community establishments, on the other hand, tend to become antisocial rather than schizophrenic adults.

As for the apparently contradictory findings regarding schizoid and stormy precursors of schizophrenia, these data point up the significance of sampling differences in research studies. Children and adolescents are much more likely to be referred to mental health clinics for disturbing, antisocial behavior than for retiring, untroublesome behavior. Hence it is not surprising that the preschizophrenic clinic patients of Robins and Nameche et al. showed a high frequency of stormy behavior and not as much schizoid behavior as appeared in the nonpatient high school students whose records were examined by Bower et al. and Barthell and Holmes. Neither pattern should be discounted as a possible precursor or phase in the development of schizophrenia (Offord & Cross, 1969; Ricks & Barry, 1970; Woerner, Pollack, Rogalski, Pollack, & Klein, 1972).

Sex Differences

The follow-back studies of Watt and his colleagues, mentioned in Chapter 1, suggest that boys and girls who become schizophrenic as adults develop in different ways during childhood and adolescence. Preschizophrenic girls tend to be quieter, more passive, less mature, and more socially introverted than other girls in their early school years, from kindergarten through the sixth grade. Later, between seventh and twelfth grade, they become less passive but grow even more noticeably withdrawn. Preschizophrenic boys show few differences from other boys during elementary school, but during their high school years they became noticeably unpleasant, aggressive, self-centered, and defiant of authority. As shown in Figure 6.3, preschizophrenic girls are relatively likely to become wallflowers as adolescents and preschizophrenic boys to become behavior problems (Watt, 1974, 1978; Watt & Lubensky, 1976).

These findings are important because (a) they document that both schizoid and stormy personality patterns often precede schizophrenia, and (b) they relate these patterns to female and male personality development, respectively. Regarding such sex

Figure 6.3

Plot of developmental changes between grades K–6 and 7–12 in extraversion and agreeableness for preschizophrenic children and matched controls. Positive score indicates extraversion or agreeableness, whereas negative score indicates introversion or disagreeableness. (From Watt (1978). Reprinted with permission of the American Medical Association.)

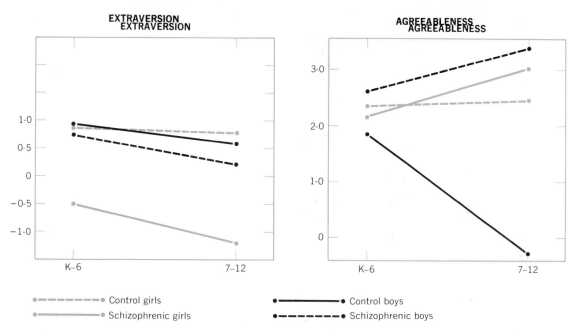

differences, Watt (1978) suggests that preschizophrenic girls who become dependent and socially insecure and preschizophrenic boys who become willful and aggressive may simply be following traditional sex-role stereotypes. Further research is necessary to explore this hypothesis. As a further caution, only a third to a half of the adult schizophrenics Watt studied showed these developmental changes during adolescence. This means that for a majority of schizophrenics, adolescent precursors that could identify the need for early intervention may not appear in either the schizoid or stormy form.

PROGNOSIS IN ADOLESCENT SCHIZOPHRENIA

The **prognosis** of a condition refers to its likely outcome in general and also to specific factors that help predict its course in the individual case. Generally speaking, the outcome of schizophrenia in adolescents is less favorable than in adults; as is true for most psychological disorders, the earlier in life the condition begins, the worse the person's prospects for full recovery. However, the individual factors that predict outcome in schizophrenia are pretty much the same for adolescents and adults.

Figure 6.4

Outcome in adolescents and adults hospitalized for schizophrenia. (Adolescent outcome data are pooled from studies by Annesley (1961), Carter (1942), Errara (1957), Masterson (1956), and Warren (1960); adult data are from reviews by Bleuler (1978), Stephens (1970), and Vaillant (1978).)

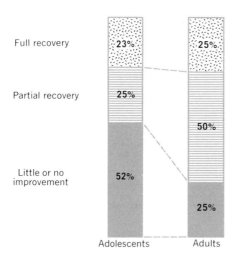

General Outcome

As indicated in Figure 6.4, about 25 percent of adolescents hospitalized for schizophrenia recover, 25 percent improve but suffer lingering symptoms or occasional relapses, and the remaining 50 percent make little or no progress and require continuing residential care. Schizophrenic adults are equally likely to recover, but more of them (about 50 percent) achieve periods of improvement and fewer (only 25 percent) remain permanently hospitalized or socially invalided.

Although these prognostic data document the seriousness of schizophrenic disorder, they also demonstrate that it is far from being a hopeless condition. There is little justification for old-fashioned but persistent inclinations in some quarters to write off hospiitalized schizophrenics as permanent psychological cripples—not when half of these adolescents and three-quarters of these adults escape such a grim course. Moreover, schizophrenic adolescents who can be treated entirely on an outpatient basis, without being hospitalized, probably have even less unfavorable long-term prospects than this. Unfortunately, there are no adequate data for determining the general outlook for non-hospitalized schizophrenic adolescents or for comparing them with a similar population of adults.

Outcome data must also be evaluated in light of the fact that being in residential care does not always signify serious or irreversible disturbance. Whether schizophrenics are hospitalized in the first place is influenced by the availability of appropriate facilities and by the attitudes of their families toward having them out of the home; whether and when they are discharged depends on the availability of continued outpatient care and their families' feelings about having them back (Cheek, 1965; Grob & Singer, 1974; Miller & Burt, 1977; Nealon, 1964).

Similarly, the likelihood of relapse following discharge from the hospital depends on how much life stress the person must face. Pressing demands for school or work performance, drastic changes in living arrangements, insufficient support from family and friends, excess encouragement from well-meaning but overbearing relatives—these and other stressful life events often precipitate relapse. Numerous studies confirm that such social circumstances influence the course of a schizophrenic disorder independently of how severe it is (Beck, 1978; Brown, Birley, & Wing, 1972; Clum, 1975; Wing, 1978). Hence the long-term implications of becoming schizophrenic need to be assessed not solely in terms of hospitalization and relapse rates, but also with respect to the schizophrenic person's capacity to cope with the particular environment in which he or she must live.

Specific Predictive Factors

The prospects for relatively favorable or unfavorable outcome in schizophrenia vary with certain aspects of (a) when and how the disturbance begins and (b) the schizophrenic person's initial symptom picture, premorbid adjustment, family history, and response to treatment. These specific predictive factors, as listed in Table 6.4, apply about equally to schizophrenic adolescents (Carter, 1942; King & Pittman, 1971; Masterson, 1956; Roff, 1976) and schizophrenic adults (Stephens, 1978; Stephens, Astrup, & Mangrum, 1967; Strauss & Carpenter, 1977; Vaillant, 1964).

With further regard to age of onset, schizophrenics who enter a hospital at age 15 to 19 are twice as likely to become chronically hospitalized as those who are initially hospitalized at age 20 to 29; in the same vein, both of these groups fare less well in later life than schizophrenics who are not initially hospitalized until after age 30 (Kris, Schiff, & McLaughlin, 1971; Pollack, Levenstein, & Klein, 1968). As for the next three factors in Table 6.4, the favorable implications of abrupt onset, initial distress, and previously good adjustment are consistent with the earlier discussion in this chapter of chronicity and premorbid development.

Special attention must be paid to aspects of social competence. Just as poor peer relationships in childhood and adolescence are a possible predictor of schizophrenia, they also contribute to a relatively poor prognosis should schizophrenia occur. Several follow-up studies have indicated that the more successful youthful schizophrenics have been in retaining social involvements and appropriate affects, despite their disturbance, the better their prospects for recovery. These emotional and interpersonal features of schizophrenics' past and current behavior are more predictive of the outcome of their disturbance than the extent to which their thinking is disordered (Janes, Hesselbrock, Myers, & Penniman, 1979; Knight, Roff, Barrnett, & Moss, 1979; Roff & Knight, 1978; Shea, Hafner, Quast, & Hetler, 1978).

Whether the unfavorable long-term implications of having schizophrenic relatives relate to their genetic or psychosocial impact on a schizophrenic adolescent is debatable, as has also been noted earlier. However, aside from whatever role genetic influences play in causing schizophrenia, schizophrenic relatives can certainly contribute to

TABLE 6.4 Factors Predicting Favorable and Unfavorable Outcome in Schizophrenia

Factor	Favorable Aspect	Unfavorable Aspect
1. Age of onset	Older when disturbance first appears	Younger when disturbance first appears
2. Nature of onset	Sudden onset in response to precipitating event	Gradual onset without apparent precipitating events
3. Initial symptom	Marked by confusion, distress, and moodiness	Marked by blunted or inappropriate affect
4. Premorbid	Previously good school, work, and social adjustment	Previously poor school, work, and social adjustment
5. Family history	No schizophrenic relatives; family pathology, if any, limited to nonschizophrenic disturbances	One or more schizophrenic relatives
6. Response to treatment	Meaningful engagement with therapist and early positive treatment response	Lack of involvement with therapist and failure to show early treatment response

perpetuating the disorder by being unable to provide an understanding and supportive environment. In one study, for example, half of a group of schizophrenic adolescents who failed to improve had at least one relative who was hospitalized with schizophrenia (Roff, 1974).

Finally, an early positive treatment response is an especially favorable indicator when the treatment program can be sustained. Youthful schizophrenics who are able to com-

Family attitudes have an important bearing on whether schizophrenic adolescents need residential care.

plete a planned course of residential care have better long-term prospects for recovery than those who leave the hospital prematurely. Likewise, the better the arrangements that can be made for continuing outpatient care, the better the outlook for maintaining and building on early improvement in hospitalized adolescents (Gossett, Barnhart, Lewis, & Phillips, 1977).

TREATMENT OF ADOLESCENT SCHIZOPHRENIA

The treatment of adolescent schizophrenia combines general procedures for treating this disorder with special attention to the developmental needs of young people. The major modalities used in working with schizophrenic adolescents are psychotherapy and drug therapy. Additionally, since schizophrenia is the most likely of all psychological disturbances in adolescence to require hospitalization, its treatment involves some important considerations in planning residential care.

Psychotherapy

As noted earlier, the key features that distinguish schizophrenic adolescents from youngsters with nonschizophrenic difficulties are their incapacity to form meaningful interpersonal relationships and their inaccurate perception of reality. Accordingly, *relationship building* and *reality testing* are the two Rs of effective therapy with these youngsters. Above all, the treatment must seek to help them (a) experience engaged, trusting, mutual relationships with other people and (b) correct their distorted impressions of themselves, their environment, and the consequences of their actions.

Relationship Building Successful psychotherapy with schizophrenic adolescents hinges on how well the therapist can impress them as a genuine, caring, empathic, and trustworthy person. It is because these adolescents have felt humiliated and rejected by other people that they have become physically or emotionally withdrawn. The therapist must be able to demonstrate that he or she is at least one person who wants to help, who can understand and be understood, and who can be relied on not to ridicule, scold, or reject. Such positive experiences of interpersonal relatedness, once established with their therapists, have the possibility of generalizing to the adolescents' dealings with other people in their lives.

This does not mean that therapists are always accepting and agreeable in working with schizophrenic adolescents. A tolerant approach can foster a helpful relationship when adolescents are frightened or depressed, but it has little impact when they are angry and rebellious, as in Donald's case (see pages 236–237). Antisocial adolescents tend to regard permissive adults as weaklings and fools or as people not to be trusted— why else would they remain pleasant in the face of abuse? Accordingly, building a good relationship with stormy adolescents requires actively challenging their views and setting strict limits on their behavior. Properly employed, this "hard line" conveys that the therapist cares enough and is strong enough to work through the adolescent's belligerence to help him or her achieve a more comfortable and rewarding life-style.

Great skill is required to treat schizophrenic adolescents with the balance between permissiveness and firmness that best meets their needs. For this reason, many years of training and experience are necessary for therapists to learn to work effectively with these youngsters. Moreover, because many schizophrenic adolescents have insulated themselves against emotional ties, therapists often cannot begin to build a treatment relationship until they have tuned in on their fears of intimacy. Thus to the youngster who says, "I'm a machine," a helpful response may be, "If you were a machine, you wouldn't have any feelings and you wouldn't have to worry about anyone hurting you." The role of such metaphorical communication and other procedures in establishing a therapeutic relationship with schizophrenic adolescents has been sensitively described in popular books by Beulah Parker *My Language is Me,* 1962) and Hannah Green (*I Never Promised you a Rosegarden,* 1964).

Reality Testing Psychotherapists working with schizophrenic adolescents need to provide them continual and direct corrections of their inaccurate perceptions. Severely disturbed young people who are having delusions or hallucinations must be helped to recognize that these impressions grow out of their fears and expectations and have no firm basis in reality. When reality testing is less severely impaired, as in subtle instances of poor social judgment, the therapy can focus on the learning of improved social skills. How could a particular situation have been seen more accurately? How could the impact of the actions taken have been anticipated more correctly? What alternative ways of responding were there that might have produced a more desirable outcome?

As in building a good treatment relationship with schizophrenic adolescents, helping them sharpen their reality testing demands great skill. It is not easy to challenge or correct how people view their world without seeming derogatory or hostile, and schizophrenic adolescents are especially quick to take criticism as meaning "You don't like me" or "You don't think much of me." Therapists cannot afford to be apostles of reality at the expense of undermining their positive relationship with a schizophrenic youngster. Hence they must learn to keep their efforts at improving reality testing within the limits of the youngster's ability to interpret these efforts as well-meaning help, rather than dislike or rejection (Gibson, 1974; Holmes, 1964, Chapter 10; Katz, 1970; Lulow, 1977).

Group and Family Approaches The goals of psychotherapy with schizophrenic adolescents can often be achieved as well in group or family sessions as in individual treatment. Typical group therapy involves one or two therapists meeting with a small number of youngsters, perhaps six to eight. For purposes of relationship building, this arrangement can be comforting to adolescents whose fears of intimacy make them highly anxious in a one-to-one conversation. The group setting helps them feel less "under the gun." With the therapist's attention spread among several people, they can be part of the group without always being the person who is expected to respond.

When two therapists are used, one is usually male and the other female. Different sexed cotherapists can facilitate the treatment for youngsters who would have difficulty reaching out to or confiding in a single therapist of one sex or the other. The group also provides an actual setting in which socially inept or withdrawn adolescents can be helped to learn rewarding ways of relating not only to a therapist but to other young people as well.

Group therapy is often useful in helping disturbed adolescents improve their interpersonal skills and perception of reality.

Group sessions likewise broaden the opportunities for schizophrenic adolescents to improve their perception of reality. The opinions and reactions of their peers help them identify their mistaken impressions, and they in turn can observe firsthand how the attitudes and actions of their copatients sometimes distort reality. To achieve these ends, however, whether as an alternative or a supplement to individual sessions, treatment groups must be carefully chosen to exclude youngsters who might exert a destructive influence on their peers or perhaps feel overwhelmed by them (Berkovitz, 1972; Berkovitz & Sugar, 1975; MacLennan & Felsenfeld, 1968; Weisberg, 1979).

In family therapy, the therapist meets jointly with the disturbed adolescent, his or her parents, and as many as possible of the siblings and other relatives who live in the home. Although the adolescent is usually referred to as the "identified patient" in this form of treatment, the approach focuses more on problems of family interaction than on the young person's abnormal behavior. Particular attention is paid to unusual or perplexing ways in which family members communicate with each other and to how their attitudes and actions affect each other. Understandably, this family approach is especially favored by clinicians who stress the role of deviant family communication in causing or sustaining schizophrenic disorder (Lidz, Fleck, & Cornelison, 1965; Shapiro, 1979; Wynne, 1974; Zuk & Rubinstein, 1965).

Like group therapy, family therapy provides a real-life situation in which the therapist can observe schizophrenic adolescents interacting with important people in their lives. It consequently offers many opportunities for seeing faulty reality testing and poor social skills and action and for working on ways to improve them.

Sometimes family therapy cannot be arranged or seems inadvisable, such as when the adolescent refuses to communicate in the presence of his or her family or when other family members are themselves seriously disturbed (Offer & VanderStoep, 1975). In these circumstances, active collateral work with schizophrenic adolescents' parents is important to effective therapy. Parents must be helped not to blame either themselves or their youngster for his or her difficulties, so they can avoid becoming either depressed and overprotective on the one hand or angry and rejecting on the other. In addition, most parents of schizophrenic adolescents need counseling to help them understand their child's conditions and avoid having expectations or making demands that will hamper his or her recovery.

Drug Therapy

A number of antipsychotic drugs, also referred to as major tranquilizers or neuroleptics, have proved effective in treating schizophrenia. These neuroleptic drugs act on the nervous system to decrease spontaneous motor activity, reduce reactivity to stimulation, and blunt emotional responses. The most widely used group of antipsychotic drugs are classified chemically as **phenothiazines,** and of these the best known is marketed under the trade name **Thorazine.**

For schizophrenics who are anxious, agitated, and out of control, neuroleptics exert a calming effect that curtails psychotic symptoms, promotes socially acceptable behavior, and increases accessibility to psychotherapy. For schizophrenics who are emotionally blunted or unresponsive to begin with, neuroleptics may be used in combination with energizing drugs to reduce underlying anxiety while at the same time fostering active participation in treatment (Lehman, 1975; May, 1975; Siris, Van Kammen, & Docherty, 1978).

Because adolescent schizophrenia is continuous with schizophrenia in adults, these general aspects of drug therapy apply to both age groups. However, decisions about medicating adolescents must take into account the still-formative stage of their cognitive and emotional maturation. As in work with psychotic children, the treatment goals are not merely to eliminate psychotic behavior and restore a previous level of functioning, but also to promote continued personality growth. Hence reliance on drugs should not preclude adequate attention to social and educational aspects of the treatment program.

As a second developmental consideration, adolescents are usually striving to achieve a sense of psychological independence from adults. They consequently take poorly to being controlled or manipulated by adults in ways they cannot understand. Before imposing tranquility on them through medication, then, therapists need to take special care to explain the nature of and need for the drugs and elicit their participation in planning this and other aspects of the treatment.

Third, the adolescent's psychological distress, no matter how painful, represents an active struggle to resolve adjustment difficulties, and it motivates the youngster to remain involved in a treatment program. If tranquilizing drugs are used to the extent of completely wiping out this distress, the therapist may sacrifice an important treatment ally: the patient's felt need to change. For these reasons, most clinicians who treat schizophrenic adolescents urge using drugs conservatively, to facilitate progress in a multifaceted treatment program rather than as the sole or primary agent for eliminating the disorder (Campbell, 1977; Campbell & Small, 1978; Conners & Werry, 1979; Goldstein, Rodnick, Evans, May, & Steinberg, 1978; McKnew, 1979; Matthews, Roper, Mosher, & Menn, 1979).

Planning Residential Care

Most clinicians prefer to treat disturbed adolescents outside of a hospital or residential facility, if possible. Hospitalization is a life-disrupting crisis that removes young people from their normal home and school surroundings, threatens their self-esteem, and may produce undesirable reactions toward them by their parents, teachers, and friends. Yet insufficient treatment of serious psychological disorders is much too high a price to pay for trying to avoid these problems, and there are at least three circumstances in which admitting adolescents to a hospital is necessary to meeting their needs.

1. *When a More Thorough Evaluation Seems Indicated than Can Be Accomplished on an Outpatient Basis*   Because of the frequently mixed symptomatology of adolescents who are becoming seriously disturbed, impending psychotic breakdown or even suicidal or homicidal tendencies may not be immediately apparent. When such possibilities are suspected, continued observation in the relative protection of an inpatient setting, until such risks can be ruled out, is far preferable to exposing adolescents and those around them to a calamitous loss of control.

2. *When the Adolescent Is Already Out of Control*   Young people who have a history of destructive acts against themselves and others and pose a present danger of such outbursts need the external controls imposed by a residential setting. In addition to protecting them and others from physical harm, these external controls can help to ease the painful psychological burden of feeling unable to control or predict their own behavior.

3. *When Environmental Stress Has Become Intolerable*   The pressures of a disturbed or rejecting family setting, an overly demanding school situation, or an inhospitable peer group may counteract even the most carefully planned outpatient treatment program. In such circumstances, even youngsters who are not seriously disturbed may need to be removed from their usual environment in order to benefit from therapy and learn more effective ways of coping with their real-life stress (Winsberg, Bialer, Kupietz, Botti, & Balka, 1980; Zinn, 1979).

Opinion has been divided for many years concerning whether hospitalized adolescents should be treated on an all-adolescent service or on mixed adolescent-adult units. Descriptions of all-adolescent services by Hendrickson and Holmes (1959) at the University of Michigan Neuropsychiatric Institute and by Nicklin and Toolan (1959) at Bellevue Hospital in New York influenced many experienced clinicians from leading hospitals around the country to endorse this approach (e.g., Barter & Langsley, 1968; Beckett, 1965; Coche & Thomas, 1975; Creson & Blakeney, 1970; Kris & Schiff, 1969). In their view, engagement with peers, rather than with adults from whom they feel alienated, is necessary for troubled teenagers to participate in the type of active open milieu in which psychological difficulties become readily accessible to psychotherapeutic intervention.

Yet other experienced clinicians from equally prominent treatment centers strongly oppose adolescent units for hospitalized teenagers (e.g., Besking, 1962; Garber, 1972; Miller, 1957; Norton, 1967). They argue that an all-adolescent service deprives youngsters of an opportunity to live in a normal interpersonal setting and makes them feel abandoned, deserted, and cut off from society. In a mixed adolescent-adult service, these writers continue, adolescents can maintain various levels of communication with people of different ages, just as the real world demands. Furthermore, they point out, the presence of adults helps prevent epidemics of misbehavior that frequently arise when groups of disturbed youngsters are isolated in a setting in which they can aid and abet each other in acting up.

The lines of this debate are sharply drawn. Regarding the greater ease of controlling behavior on a mixed than an all-adolescent service, Easson (1969, p. 16) says, "This adolescent patient dilution seems to be dictated more by the needs of the treating staff than by the requirements of the teenagers." In support of mixed services, Hartmann, Glasser, Greenblatt, Solomon, & Levinson (1968, p. 6) conclude that because of the small size and limited impact of all-adolescent units on serious disturbance, "The usefulness of all-adolescent units is limited."

These firmly held differences of opinion have not been put to any definitive test, and there is no evidence to suggest that either the all-adolescent or the mixed-patient treatment service works better for most disturbed youngsters. However, research has yielded two fairly conclusive findings that bear on residential care. First, the more severely adolescents are disturbed, the more rapidly they respond to treatment on a mixed rather than on an all-adolescent service. Specifically, youngsters with neurotic or characterological difficulties are relatively likely to benefit from a peer-group milieu, whereas schizophrenic adolescents appear to need the support and control provided by an adult environment in order to make maximum progress in therapy (Garber, 1972, Chapter 2; Hartmann et al., 1968, Chapter 1; Warren, 1965).

Second, regardless of whether it is administered on an all-adolescent or a mixed service, a program especially tailored for hospitalized adolescents improves their prospects for recovery (Beavers & Blumberg, 1968; Gossett, Lewis, Lewis & Phillips, 1973; Lordi, 1979). Such tailored programs consist of a core staff trained and committed to work with disturbed adolescents and a schedule of activities and procedures specially designed to meet the needs of this age group, from admission to discharge and beyond.

In light of these findings, schizophrenic adolescents who require residential care should usually be treated on a mixed adolescent-adult unit that has a special adolescent program. At their best, these programs combine individual and group psychotherapy, family therapy or collateral work with patients, drug therapy as necessary, and a supportive, protective, encouraging milieu. In addition, provision is made for adolescents to continue their education and to participate in social and recreational activities, in order to promote continuing development of skills that will aid their future adjustment (Adilman, 1973; Grob & Singer, 1974; Rinsley, 1968, 1974).

SUMMARY

Schizophrenia is a severely disabling disorder that occurs in approximately 1 percent of the population and frequently runs a chronic or recurrent course. It is a major public health problem that accounts for 25 percent of all hospital beds in the United States and costs nearly $20 billion each year in patient care and loss of productivity. These basic facts about schizophrenia are pertinent to adolescent psychopathology because most forms of schizophrenic disturbance begin during or soon after the teenage years. Schizophrenia is the most common diagnosis among adolescents admitted to public mental hospitals (25 to 30 percent of patients) and the second (in boys) or third (in girls) most frequent condition among those admitted to psychiatric units of general hospitals (about 15 percent).

Although schizophrenia in adolescence is continuous with adult schizophrenia, its signs are often less apparent in the younger age group. The majority of schizophrenic adolescents initially show a mixed picture in which features of schizophrenia are secondary to or obscured by other kinds of difficulty, most commonly depression or antisocial behavior. In these circumstances, an early stage of schizophrenia must be judged from how long the schizophrenic features in a mixed-symptom picture persist, how much they prevent the young person from coming to grips with usual adolescent concerns, and the extent to which they impair formal as well as content aspects of what the adolescent says and does.

Schizophrenic adolescents display the full range of impairments associated with this disorder. However, particularly in its mild or early stages, schizophrenia tends to produce some distinctive profiles of impairment in adolescents as compared to adults. Perceptual distortions, social withdrawal, and inappropriate emotional responses are equally suggestive of schizophrenic disturbance in adolescents and adults, whereas circumstantial reasoning, preoccupation with abstractions, and poorly controlled sexual and aggressive fantasies are less conclusive as signs of schizophrenia in the younger age group.

Schizophrenia is a very heterogeneous disorder, and one of the most consistent findings in studies of schizophrenic patients is their variability from one person to the next. Nevertheless, much of this interindividual variability can be accounted for in terms of three dimensions—*chronicity, paranoid status,* and *premorbid adjustment.* Chronicity refers to how severely disabling and persistent a schizophrenic disorder is. The more chronic the condition, the more likely it is to develop gradually in people who lack awareness of how disturbed they are and respond slowly to treatment. By contrast, *acute* schizophrenia begins rapidly, usually following precipitating stressful experiences, in people who recognize the unusual nature of their symptoms and are more likely than chronically schizophrenic people to show a quick and lasting treatment response.

Paranoid status defines a cognitive style and set of attitudes in which people are alert and vigilant but also rigid and inflexible. Paranoid individuals see the world as a hostile, dangerous place, and they are accordingly cautious and suspicious in their dealings with it. Chronic and paranoid forms of schizophrenia together account for most of the schizophrenic subtypes diagnosed in clinical practice. Although clear indications of chronicity or paranoid status are more likely to appear in older persons than in teenagers, they occur sufficiently often among younger patients to constitute an important facet of adolescent schizophrenia.

Premorbid adjustment refers to how adequately schizophrenic people have dealt with social, interpersonal, school, and work situations before becoming disturbed. Distinctions between "good premorbid" and "poor premorbid" schizophrenics overlap with the chronicity and paranoid dimensions, and all three seem related to the schizophrenic person's level of cognitive and social maturation.

Borderline disorder is a form of psychopathology that combines aspects of psychotic, neurotic, and characterological disturbance. Its chief manifest features are intense emotions, poor self-control, illusory social adaptation, strained interpersonal relationships, and vulnerability to brief psychotic episodes. There is currently disagreement concerning whether borderline disorder is a form of schizophrenia, a kind of personality disorder, or a unique syndrome in its own right. From each of these points of view, however, the condition is seen as particularly likely to emerge during adolescence.

Two youthful personality patterns are especially likely to predict vulnerability to schizophrenia in late adolescence and early adulthood: a *schizoid* pattern, which consists of shy, sensitive, seclusive behavior, and a *stormy* pattern, which is marked by family conflict and antisocial behavior. Preliminary evidence suggests that preschizophrenic girls are more likely to follow the passive, withdrawn route to schizophrenic disorder, whereas boys are more likely to follow the aggressive, defiant route.

Among adolescents who are hospitalized for schizophrenia, about 25 percent recover, 25 percent improve but suffer lingering symptoms or occasional relapses, and the remaining 50 percent make little or no progress and require continuing residential care. Although the long-term prospects are probably less grim for schizophrenic adolescents who can be treated entirely on an outpatient basis, adequate research to this effect is not yet available. The older adolescents are when a schizophrenic disturbance first appears, the better their prospects for recovery. Favorable outcome in the individual case is also relatively likely when (a) the disturbance begins suddenly in response to precipitating events; (b) confusion, distress, and moodiness are in the initial symptom picture; (c) previous school and social adjustment has been good; (d) there are no schizophrenic family members; (e) there is meaningful engagement in therapy and an early positive treatment response.

The major modalities used in treating schizophrenic adolescents are psychotherapy, drug therapy, and residential care. Psychotherapy with these youngsters focuses on *relationship building,* which seeks to help them experience engaged, trusting, mutual relationships with other people, and on *reality testing,* which aims at correcting their inaccurate perceptions of themselves, their environment, and the consequence of their actions. These goals can often be achieved in group or family sessions, both of which are frequently used as an alternative to or in combination with individual psychotherapy.

Certain antipsychotic drugs have proved effective in treating schizophrenia, especially with respect to calming anxious, agitated schizophrenics and increasing their accessibility to psychotherapy. In working with disturbed adolescents, care must be taken not to overrely on drugs to eliminate psychotic behavior at the expense of adequate attention to social and educational aspects of the treatment program that promote continued personality growth.

Hospitalization of disturbed adolescents becomes necessary when they need a more thorough evaluation than can be accomplished on an outpatient basis, when their behavior is out of control, or when they are facing intolerable stress in their environment. Some specialists favor caring for these youngsters on all-adolescent services in which peer engagement will promote progress in treatment. Others favor mixed adolescent-adult services in which interacting with people of varying ages will promote learning to deal with real-world demands. There is no evidence to suggest that either approach to residential treatment of adolescents is generally better than the other. However, the more severely disturbed adolescents are, especially if they are schizophrenic, the more likely they are to progress faster on a mixed than on an all-adolescent service. Whatever the treatment setting, the schizophrenic adolescent's prospects for improving are increased by the availability of a treatment program that is specifically designed to meet the psychological, social, and educational needs of young people.

REFERENCES

ADILMAN, P. H. Some concepts of adolescent residential treatment. *Adolescence,* 1973, *8,* 547–568.

AMERICAN PSYCHIATRIC ASSOCIATION. *Diagnostic and statistical manual of mental disorders.* (3d ed.) Washington, D.C.: American Psychiatric Association, 1980.

AMES, L. B., METRAUX, R. W., & WALKER, R. N. *Adolescent Rorschach responses.* (Rev. ed.) New York: Brunner/Mazel, 1971.

ANNESLEY, P. T. Psychiatric illness in adolescence: Presentation and prognosis. *Journal of Mental Science,* 1961, *106,* 268–278.

ANTHONY, E. J. Preventive measures for children and adolescents at high risk for psychosis. In G. W. Albee & J. M. Joffe (Eds.), *Primary prevention of psychopathology.* Vol. 1. *The issues.* Hanover, N.H.: University Press of New England, 1977.

ANTHONY, E. J. Prevention in schizophrenia. In L. Bellak (Ed.), *Disorders of the schizophrenic syndrome.* New York: Basic Books, 1979.

ANTHONY, W. A., COHEN, M. R., & VITALO, R. The measurement of rehabilitation outcome. *Schizophrenia Bulletin,* 1978, *4,* 365–383.

ARIETI, S. *Interpretation of schizophrenia.* (2nd ed.) New York: Basic Books, 1974.

ASTRACHAN, B. M., BRAUER, L., HARROW, M., & SCHWARTZ, C. Symptomatic outcome in schizophrenia. *Archives of General Psychiatry,* 1974, *31,* 155–160.

BABIGIAN, H. M. Schizophrenia: Epidemiology. In A. M. Freedman, H. I. Kaplan, & B. J. Sadock (Eds.), *Comprehensive textbook of psychiatry.* (2nd ed.) Baltimore: Williams & Wilkins, 1975.

BARTER, J. T., & LANGSLEY, D. G. The advantages of a separate unit for adolescents. *Hospital and Community Psychiatry,* 1968, *19,* 241–243.

BARTHELL, C. N., & HOLMES, D. S. High school yearbooks: A nonreactive measure of social isolation in graduates who later became schizophrenic. *Journal of Abnormal Psychology,* 1968, *73,* 313–316.

BEAVERS, W. R., & BLUMBERG, S. A follow-up study of adolescents treated in an in-patient setting. *Diseases of the Nervous System,* 1968. *29,* 606–612.

BECK, J. C. Social influences on the prognosis of schizophrenia. *Schizophrenia Bulletin,* 1978, *4,* 86–101.

BECKETT, P. G. S. *Adolescents out of step: Their treatment in a psychiatric hospital.* Detroit: Wayne State University Press, 1965.

BERKOVITZ, I. H. (Ed.) *Adolescents grow in groups: Experiences in adolescent group psychotherapy.* New York: Brunner/Mazel, 1972.

BERKOVITZ, I. H., & SUGAR, M. Indications and contraindications for adolescent group psychotherapy. In M. Sugar (Ed.), *The adolescent in group and family therapy.* New York: Brunner/Mazel, 1975.

BESKIND, H. Psychiatric inpatient treatment of adolescents: A review of clinical experience. *Comprehensive Psychiatry,* 1962, *3,* 354–369.

BLEULER, E. (1911) *Dementia praecox or the group of schizophrenias.* New York: International Universities Press, 1950.

BLEULER, M. E. The long-term course of schizophrenic psychoses. In L. C. Wynne, R. L. Cromwell, & S. Matthyse (Eds.), *The nature of schizophrenia.* New York: Wiley, 1978.

BOWER, E. M., SHELLHAMER, T. A., & DAILY, J. M. School characteristics of male adolescents who later became schizophrenic. *American Journal of Orthopsychiatry,* 1960, *30,* 712–729.

BROEN, W. E. *Schizophrenia: Research and theory.* New York: Academic, 1968.

BROWN, G. W., BIRLEY, J. L., & WING, J. K. Influences of family life on the course of schizophrenic disorders: A replication. *British Journal of Psychiatry,* 1972, *121,* 241–258.

BUSS, A., & LANG, P. Psychological deficit in schizophrenia: I. Affect, reinforcement, and conceptual attainment. *Journal of Abnormal Psychology,* 1965, *70,* 2–24.

CAMERON, N. Paranoid conditions and paranoia. In S. Arieti (Ed.), *American handbook of psychiatry.* (2nd ed.) Vol. III. New York: Basic Books, 1974.

CAMPBELL, M. Treatment of childhood and adolescent schizophrenia. In J. M. Wiener (Ed.), *Psychopharmacology in childhood and adolescence.* New York: Basic Books, 1977.

CAMPBELL, M., & SMALL, A. M. Chemotherapy. In B. B. Wolman (Ed), *Handbook of treatment of mental disorders in childhood and adolescence.* Englewood Cliffs, N.J.: Prentice-Hall, 1978.

CARPENTER, W. T. Current diagnostic concepts in schizophrenia. *American Journal of Psychiatry,* 1976, *133,* 172–177.

CARPENTER, W. T., BARTKO, J. J., CARPENTER, C. L., & STRAUSS, J. S. Another view of schizophrenic subtypes. *Archives of General Psychiatry,* 1976, *33,* 508–516.

CARPENTER, W. T., GUNDERSON, J. G., & STRAUSS, J. S. Considerations of the borderline syndrome: A longitudinal comparative study of borderline and schizophrenic patients. In P. Hartocollis (Ed.), *Borderline personality disorders.* New York: International Universities Press, 1977.

CARPENTER, W. T., & STRAUSS, J. S. Diagnostic issues in schizophrenia. In L. Bellak (Ed.), *Disorders of the schizophrenic syndrome.* New York: Basic Books, 1979.

CARTER, A. B. Prognostic factors of adolescent psychoses. *Journal of Mental Science,* 1942, *88,* 31–81.

CHAPMAN, L., & CHAPMAN, J. *Disordered thought in schizophrenia.* Englewood Cliffs, N.J.: Prentice-Hall, 1973.

CHEEK, F. E. Family interaction patterns and convalescent adjustment of the schizophrenic. *Archives of General Psychiatry,* 1965, *13,* 138–147.

CHICK, J., WATERHOUSE, L., & WOLFF, S. Psychological construing in schizoid children grown up. *British Journal of Psychiatry,* 1979, *135,* 425–430.

CLUM, G. A. Intrapsychic variables and the patient's environment as factors in prognosis. *Psychological Bulletin,* 1975, *82,* 413–431.

COCHE, E., & THOMAS, A. T. Evaluative research on a therapeutic community for adolescents. *Journal of Youth and Adolescence,* 1975, *4,* 321–330.

CONNERS, C. K., & WERRY, J. S. Pharmacotherapy. In H. C. Quay & J. S. Werry (Eds.), *Psychopathological disorders of childhood.* (2nd ed.) New York: Wiley, 1979.

CRESON, D. L., & BLAKENEY, P. M. Social structure in an adolescent milieu program: Implications for treatment. *Adolescence,* 1970, *5,* 407–246.

DECKNER, C. W., & CROMWELL, R. L. Commonality of word association response in schizophrenia as a function of premorbid adjustment, chronicity, and paranoid status. *Psychological Reports,* 1970, *26,* 503–509.

DRAKE, R. E., & WALLACH, M. A. Will mental patients stay in the community? A social psychological perspective. *Journal of Consulting and Clinical Psychology,* 1979, *47,* 285–294.

EASSON, W. M. *The severely disturbed adolescent: Inpatient, residential, and hospital treatment.* New York: International Universities Press, 1969.

ELKIND, D. Recent research on cognitive development in adolescence. In S. Dragastin (Ed.), *Adolescence in the life cycle.* Washington, D.C.: Hemisphere, 1975.

ERRERA, P. A sixteen-year follow-up of schizophrenic patients seen in an outpatient clinic. *Archives of Neurology and Psychiatry,* 1957, *78,* 84–87.

EXNER, J. E. *The Rorschach: A comprehensive system.* Vol. 2. *Current research and advanced interpretation.* New York: Wiley, 1978.

FEIGHNER, J. P., ROBINS, E., GUZE, S. G., WOODRUFF, R. A., WINOKUR, H., & MUNOZ, R. Diagnostic criteria for use in psychiatric research. *Archives of General Psychiatry, 1972, 26,* 57–63.

FEINSTEIN, S. C., & MILLER, D. Psychoses of adolescence. In J. D. Noshpitz (Ed.), *Basic handbook of child psychiatry.* Vol. 2. New York: Basic Books, 179.

GARBER, B. *Follow-up study of hospitalized adolescents.* New York: Brunner/Mazel, 1972.

GENERAL HOSPITAL INPATIENT PSYCHIATRIC SERVICES. Washington, D.C.: Department of Health, Education and Welfare, PHS Publication No. 1977, 1969.

GIBSON, R. W. The intensive psychotherapy of hospitalized adolescents. *Journal of the American Academy of Psychoanalysis, 1974, 2,* 187–200.

GIOVACCHINI, P. L. The borderline aspects of adolescence and the borderline state. In S. C. Feinstein & P. L. Giovacchini (Eds.), *Adolescent psychiatry.* Vol. VI, Chicago: University of Chicago Press, 1978.

GOLDSTEIN, M. J. Further data concerning the relation between premorbid adjustment and paranoid symptomatology. *Schizophrenia Bulletin, 1978, 4,* 236–241.

GOLDSTEIN, M. J., & JONES, J. E. Adolescent and familial precursors of borderline and schizophrenic conditions. In P. Hartocollis (Ed.), *Borderline personality disorders.* New York: International Universities Press, 1977.

GOLDSTEIN, M. J., RODNICK, E. H., EVANS, J. R., MAY, P. R., & STEINBERG, M. R. Drug and family therapy in the aftercare of acute schizophrenics. *Archives of General Psychiatry, 1978, 35,* 1169–1177.

GOSSETT, J. T., BARNHART, D., LEWIS, J. M., & PHILLIPS, V. A. Follow-up of adolescents treated in a psychiatric hospital: Precursors of outcome. *Archives of General Psychiatry, 1977, 34,* 1037–1042.

GOSSETT, J. T., LEWIS, S. B., LEWIS, J. M., & PHILLIPS, V. A. Follow-up of adolescents treated in a psychiatric hospital: I. A review of studies. *American Journal of Orthopsychiatry, 1973, 43,* 602–610.

GREEN, H. *I never promised you a rosegarden.* New York: Holt, Rinehart, & Winston, 1964.

GRINKER, R. R. The borderline syndrome: A phenomenological view. In P. Hartocollis (Ed.), *Borderline personality disorders.* New York: International Universities Press, 1977.

GRINKER, R. R. The borderline syndrome. In S. C. Feinstein & P. L. Giovacchini (Eds.), *Adolescent psychiatry.* Vol. VI. Chicago: University of Chicago Press, 1978.

GRINKER, R. R. Diagnosis of borderlines: A discussion. *Schizophrenia Bulletin, 1979, 5,* 47–52.

GRINKER, R. R., & WERBLE, B. *The borderline patient.* New York: Aronson, 1977.

GRINKER, R. R., WERBLE, B., & DRYE, R. C. *The borderline syndrome.* New York: Basic Books, 1968.

GROB, M. C., & SINGER, J. E. *Adolescent patients in transition: Impact and outcome of psychiatric hospitalization.* New York: Behavioral Publications, 1974.

GUNDERSON, J. G. Characteristics of borderlines. In P. Hartocollis (Ed.), *Borderline personality disorders.* New York: International Universities Press, 1977.

GUNDERSON, J. G. The relatedness of borderline and schizophrenic disorders. *Schizophrenia Bulletin, 1979, 5,* 17–22.

GUNDERSON, J. G., & KOLB, J. E. Discriminating features of borderline patients. *American Journal of Psychiatry, 1978, 135,* 792–796.

GUNDERSON, J. G., & MOSHER, L. R. The cost of schizophrenia. *American Journal of Psychiatry, 1975, 132,* 901–906.

GUNDERSON, J. G., & SINGER, M. T. Defining borderline patients: An overview. *American Journal of Psychiatry, 1975, 132,* 1–10.

HARROW, M., GRINKER, R. R., SILVERSTEIN, M. L., & HOLZMAN, P. Is modern-day schizophrenic outcome still negative? *American Journal of Psychiatry, 1978, 135,* 1156–1162.

HARROW, M., & SILVERSTEIN, M. L. Psychotic symptoms in schizophrenia after the acute phase. *Schizophrenia Bulletin, 1977, 3,* 608–616.

HARTMANN, E., GLASSER, B. A., GREENBLATT, M., SOLOMON, M. H., & LEVINSON, D. J. *Adolescents in a mental hospital.* New York: Grune & Stratton, 1968.

HENDRICKSON, W. J., & HOLMES, D. J. Control of behavior as a crucial factor in an all adolescent ward. *American Journal of Psychiatry,* 1959, *115,* 969–973.

HOLMES, D. J. *The adolescent in psychotherapy.* Boston: Little, Brown, 1964.

HOLZMAN, P. S., & GRINKER, R. R. Schizophrenia in adolescence. *Journal of Youth and Adolescence,* 1974, *3,* 267–279.

HOULIHAN, J. P. Heterogeneity among schizophrenic patients: Selective review of recent findings (1970–1975). *Schizophrenia Bulletin,* 1977, *3,* 246–258.

HUDGENS, R. W. *Psychiatric disorders in adolescents.* Baltimore: Williams & Wilkins, 1974.

INHELDER, B., & PIAGET, J. *The growth of logical thinking from childhood to adolescence.* New York: Basic Books, 1958.

JANES, C. L., HESSELBROCK, V. M., MYERS, D. G., & PENNIMAN, J. H. Problem boys in young adulthood: Teachers' ratings and twelve-year follow-up. *Journal of Youth and Adolescence,* 1979, *9,* 453–472.

KATZ, P. The diagnosis and treatment of borderline schizophrenia in adolescence. *Canadian Psychiatric Association Journal,* 1967, *12,* 247–251.

KATZ, P. The therapy of adolescent schizophrenia. *American Journal of Psychiatry,* 1970, *127,* 132–137.

KEITH, S. J., GUNDERSON, J. G., REIFMAN, A., BUCHSBAUM, S., & MOSHER, L. R. Special report: Schizophrenia, 1976. *Schizophrenia Bulletin,* 1976, *2,* 509–565.

KERNBERG, O. Borderline personality organization. *Journal of the American Psychoanalytic Association,* 1967, *15,* 641–685.

KERNBERG, O. Technical considerations in the treatment of borderline personality organization. *Journal of the American Psychoanalytic Association,* 1976, *24,* 795–829.

KERNBERG, O. The structural diagnosis of borderline personality organization. In P. Hartocollis (Ed.), *Borderline personality disorders.* New York: International Universities Press, 1977.

KERNBERG, O. The diagnosis of borderline conditions in adolescence. In S. C. Feinstein & P. L. Giovacchini (Eds.), *Adolescent psychiatry.* Vol. VI. Chicago: University of Chicago Press, 1978.

KETY, S. S., ROSENTHAL, D., & WENDER, P. H. The types and prevalence of mental illness in the biological and adoptive families of adopted schizophrenics. In D. Rosenthal & S. S. Kety (Eds.), *The transmission of schizophrenia.* New York: Pergamon, 1968.

KING, L. J., & PITTMAN, G. D. A follow-up of 65 adolescent schizophrenia patients. *Diseases of the Nervous System,* 1971, *32,* 328–334.

KLERMAN, G. L. Better but not well: Social and ethical issues in the deinstitutionalization of the mentally ill. *Schizophrenia Bulletin,* 1977, *3,* 617–631.

KNIGHT, R. A., ROFF, J. D., BARRNETT, J., & MOSS, J. L. Concurrent and predictive validity of thought disorder and affectivity: A 22-year follow-up of acute schizophrenics. *Journal of Abnormal Psychology,* 1979, *88,* 1–12.

KNIGHT, R. P. Borderline states. *Bulletin of the Menninger Clinic,* 1953, *17,* 1–12.

KRAMER, M. Population changes and schizophrenia, 1970–1985. In L. C. Wynne, R. L. Cromwell, & S. Matthyse (Eds.), *The nature of schizophrenia.* New York: Wiley, 1978.

KREISMAN, D. Social interaction and intimacy in preschizophrenic adolescents. In J. Zubin & A. M. Freedman (Eds.), *The psychopathology of adolescence.* New York: Grune & Stratton, 1970.

KRIS, A. O., & SCHIFF, L. F. An adolescent consultation service in a state mental hospital: Maintaining treatment motivation. *Seminars in Psychiatry,* 1969, *1,* 15–23.

KRIS, A., SCHIFF, L., & MCLAUGHLIN, R. Susceptibility to chronic hospitalization relative to age at first admission. *Archives of General Psychiatry,* 1971, *24,* 346–352.

LEHMANN, H. E. Psychopharmacological treatment of schizophrenia. *Schizophrenia Bulletin,* 1975, *13,* 27–45.

LEWINE, R. R. Response complexity and social interaction in the psychophysical testing of chronic and paranoid schizophrenics. *Psychological Bulletin,* 1978, *85,* 284–294.

LEWINE, R. R., WATT, N. F., & FRYER, J. H. A study of childhood social competence, adult premorbid competence, and psychiatric outcome in three schizophrenic subtypes. *Journal of Abnormal Psychology,* 1978, *87,* 294–302.

LEWINE, R. R., WATT, N. F., PRENTKY, R. A., & FRYER, J. H. Childhood social competence in functionally disordered psychiatric patients and in normals, *Journal of Abnormal Psychology,* 1980, *89,* 132–138.

LIDZ, T., FLECK, S., & CORNELISON, A. R. *Schizophrenia and the family.* New York: International Universities Press, 1965.

LIEBOWITZ, M. R. Is borderline a distinct entity? *Schizophrenia Bulletin,* 1979, *5,* 23–38.

LORDI, W. M. Hospital and residential treatment of adolescents. In J. R. Novello (Ed.), *The short course in adolescent psychiatry.* New York: Brunner/Mazel, 1979.

LULOW, W. V. Therapeutic technique: Treatment of a borderline adolescent girl. *American Journal of Psychotherapy,* 1977, *31,* 366–375.

MACHOVER, S. Diagnostic and prognostic considerations in psychological tests. In S. Lorand & H. I. Schneer (Eds.), *Adolescents: Psychoanalytic approach to problems and therapy.* New York: Hoeber, 1961.

MCKNEW, D. Use of psychotropic medication in adolescent psychiatry. In J. R. Novello (Ed.). *The short course in adolescent psychiatry.* New York: Brunner/Mazel, 1979.

MACLENNAN, B. W., & FELSENFELD, N. *Group counseling and psychotherapy with adolescents.* New York: Columbia University Press, 1968.

MASTERSON, J. F. Prognosis in adolescent disorders—schizophrenia. *Journal of Nervous and Mental Diseases,* 1956, *124,* 219–232.

MASTERSON, J. F. *The psychiatric dilemma of adolescence.* Boston: Little, Brown, 1967.

MASTERSON, J. F. *Treatment of the borderline adolescent.* New York: Wiley, 1972.

MASTERSON, J. F. The splitting defense mechanism of the borderline adolescent: Developmental and clinical aspects. In J. E. Mack (Ed.), *Borderline states in psychiatry.* New York: Grune & Stratton, 1975.

MASTERSON, J. F. *Psychotherapy of the borderline adult: A developmental approach.* New York: Brunner/Mazel, 1976.

MASTERSON, J. F., TUCKER, K., & BERK, G. Psychopathology in adolescence. IV. Clinical and dynamic characteristics. *American Journal of Psychiatry,* 1963, *120,* 357–366.

MATTHEWS, S. M., ROPER, M. T., MOSHER, L. R., & MENN, A. E. A nonneuroleptic treatment for schizophrenia: Analysis of the two-year post-discharge risk of relapse. *Schizophrenia Bulletin,* 1979, *5,* 522–533.

MAY, P. R. Schizophrenia: Overview of treatment methods. In A. M. Freedman, H. I. Kaplan, & B. J. Sadock (Eds.), *Comprehensive textbook of psychiatry.* (2nd ed.) Baltimore: Williams & Wilkins, 1975.

MEISSNER, W. W. *The paranoid process.* New York: Aronson, 1978.

MILLER, D. H. The treatment of adolescents in an adult hospital. *Bulletin of the Menninger Clinic,* 1957, *21,* 189–198.

MILLER, D., & BURT, R. A. On children's rights and therapeutic institutions. In S. C. Feinstein & P. L. Giovacchini (Eds.), *Adolescent psychiatry.* Vol. V. New York: Aronson, 1977.

MOSHER, L. R., & FEINSILVER, D. Current studies on schizophrenia. *International Journal of Psychoanalytic Psychotherapy,* 1973, *2,* 7–52.

NAMECHE, G. F., WARING, M., & RICKS, D. F. Early indicators of outcome in schizophrenia. *Journal of Nervous and Mental Disease,* 1964, *139,* 232–240.

NATIONAL INSTITUTE OF MENTAL HEALTH. *Schizophrenia: Is there an answer?* Washington, D.C.: Department of Health, Education & Welfare Publication No. HSM 63-9086, 1972.

NATIONAL INSTITUTE OF MENTAL HEALTH. *Additions and resident patients at end of year, state and county mental hospitals,* 1976. Rockville, Md.: National Institute of Mental Health, 1978.

NEALON, J. The adolescent's hospitalization as a family crisis. *Archives of General Psychiatry,* 1964, *11,* 302–311.

NEIMARK, E. D. Intellectual development during adolescence. In F. D. Horovitz (Ed.), *Review of child development research.* Vol. 4. Chicago: University of Chicago Press, 1975.

NEUBAUER, P. B., & STEINERT, J. Schizophrenia in adolescence. *Nervous Child,* 1952, *10,* 128–134.

NICKLIN, G., & TOOLAN, J. M. Twenty-year follow-up of an adolescent service in a psychiatric hospital. *Psychiatric Quarterly Supplement,* 1959, *33,* 301–316.

NORTON, A. H. Evaluation of a psychiatric service for children, adolescents, and adults. *American Journal of Psychiatry,* 1967, *123,* 1418–1424.

OFFER, D., & VANDERSTOEP, E. Indications and contraindications for family therapy. In M. Sugar (Ed.), *The adolescent in group and family therapy.* New York: Brunner/Mazel, 1975.

OFFORD, D. R., & CROSS, L. A. Behavioral antecedents or adult schizophrenia. *Archives of General Psychiatry,* 1969, *21,* 267–283.

OUTPATIENT PSYCHIATRIC SERVICES. Washington, D.C.: Department of Health, Education & Welfare Publication No. (ADM) 74-69, 1973.

PARKER, B. *My language is me: Psychotherapy with a disturbed adolescent.* New York: Basic Books, 1962.

PERRY, J. C., & KLERMAN, G. L. The borderline patient: A comparative analysis of four sets of diagnostic criteria. *Archives of General Psychiatry,* 1978, *35,* 141–150.

PIOTROWSKI, Z. A. Treatment of the adolescent. 1. The relative pessimism of psychologists. *American Journal of Orthopsychiatry,* 1962, *32,* 382–389.

PITT, R., KORNFELD, D. S., & KOLB, L. C. Adolescent friendship patterns as prognostic indicators for schizophrenic adults. *Psychiatric Quarterly,* 1963, *37,* 499–503.

POLLACK, M., LEVENSTEIN, S., & KLEIN, D. F. A three-year posthospital follow-up of adolescent and adult schizophrenia. *American Journal of Orthopsychiatry,* 1968, *38,* 94–109.

PRENTKY, R. A., WATT, N. F., & FRYER, J. H. Longitudinal social competence and adult psychiatric symptoms at first hospitalization. *Schizophrenia Bulletin,* 1979, *5,* 396–312.

PUTTERMAN, A. H., & POLLACK, H. B. The developmental approach and process-reactive schizophrenia: A review. *Schizophrenia Bulletin,* 1976, *2,* 198–208.

RICKS, D. F., & BARRY, J. C. Family and symptom patterns that precede schizophrenia. In M. Roff & D. F. Ricks (Eds.), *Life history research in psychopathology.* Minneapolis: University of Minnesota Press, 1970.

RIEDER, R. O. Borderline schizophrenia: Evidence of its validity. *Schizophrenia Bulletin,* 1979, *5,* 39–46.

RINSLEY, D. B. Theory and practice of intensive residential treatment of adolescents. *Psychiatric Quarterly,* 1968, *42,* 611–638.

RINSLEY, D. B. A contribution to the nosology and dynamics of adolescent schizophrenia. *Psychiatric Quarterly,* 1972, *46,* 159–186.

RINSLEY, D. B. Residential treatment of adolescents. In S. Arieti (Ed.), *American handbook of psychiatry.* (2nd ed.) Vol. 2. New York: Basic Books, 1974.

ROBINS, L. N. *Deviant children grown up.* Baltimore: Williams & Wilkins, 1966.

ROFF, J. D. Adolescent schizophrenia: Variables related to differences in long-term adult outcome. *Journal of Consulting and Clinical Psychology,* 1974, *42,* 180–183.

ROFF, J. D. Adolescent development and family characteristics associated with a diagnosis of schizophrenia. *Journal of Consulting and Clinical Psychology,* 1976, *44,* 933–939.

ROFF, J. D., & KNIGHT, R. Young adult schizophrenics: Prediction of outcome and antecedent childhood factors. *Journal of Consulting and Clinical Psychology,* 1978, *46,* 947–952.

ROMANO, J. On the nature of schizophrenia: Changes in the observer as well as the observed. *Schizophrenia Bulletin,* 1977, *3,* 532–559.

ROSEN, B. M., BAHN, A. K., SHELLOW, R., & BOWER, E. M. Adolescent patients served in outpatient psychiatric clinics. *American Journal of Public Health,* 1965, *555,* 1563–1577.

ROSENTHAL, D. Was Thomas Wolfe a borderline? *Schizophrenia Bulletin,* 1979, *5,* 87–94.

RYCHLAK, J. F., & O'LEARY, L. R. Unhealthy content in the Rorschach responses of children and adolescents. *Journal of Projective Techniques and Personality Assessment,* 1965, *29,* 354–368.

SCHWARTZBERG, A. K. Overview of the borderline syndrome in adolescence. In S. C. Feinstein & P. L. Giovacchini (Eds.), *Adolescent psychiatry.* Vol. VI. Chicago: University of Chicago Press, 1978.

SHAKOW, D. *Adaptation in schizophrenia.* New York: Wiley, 1979.

SHAPIRO, D. *Neurotic styles.* New York: Basic Books, 1965.

SHAPIRO, E. R. The psychodynamic and developmental psychology of the borderline patient: A review of the literature. *American Journal of Psychiatry,* 1978, *135,* 1305–1315.

SHAPIRO, R. L. Adolescents in family therapy. In J. R. Novello (Ed.), *The short course in adolescent psychiatry.* New York: Brunner/Mazel, 1979.

SHEA, M. J., HAFNER, J., QUAST, W., & HETLER, J. H. Outcome of adolescent psychiatric disorders: A long-term follow-up study. In E. J. Anthony, C. Koupernik, & C. Chiland (Eds.), *The child in his family: Vulnerable children.* Vol. 4. New York: Wiley, 1978.

SILVERMAN, J. The problem of attention in research and theory in schizophrenia. *Psychological Bulletin,* 1964, *71,* 357–379.

SILVERMAN, L. N., LAPKIN, B., & ROSENBAUM, I. S. Manifestations of primary process thinking in schizophrenia. *Journal of Projective Techniques,* 1962, *26,* 117–127.

SIRIS, S. G., VAN KAMMEN, D. P., & DOCHERTY, J. P. Use of antidepressant drugs in schizophrenia. *Archives of General Psychiatry,* 1978, *35,* 1368–1377.

SPITZER, R. L., ANDREASEN, N., & ENDICOTT, J. Schizophrenia and other psychotic disorders in DSM-III. *Schizophrenia Bulletin,* 1978, *4,* 489–509.

SPITZER, R. L., ANDREASEN, N., ENDICOTT, J., & WOODRUFF, R. A. Proposed classification of schizophrenia in DSM-III. In L. C. Wynne, R. L. Cromwell, & S. Matthyse (Eds.), *The nature of schizophrenia.* New York: Wiley, 1978.

SPITZER, R. L., & ENDICOTT, J. Justification for separating schizotypal and borderline personality disorders. *Schizophrenia Bulletin,* 1979, *5,* 95–104.

SPITZER, R. L., ENDICOTT, J., & GIBBON, M.. Crossing the border into borderline personality and borderline schizophrenia. *Archives of General Psychiatry,* 1979, *36,* 17–24.

SPIVACK, G., HAIMES, P. E., & SPOTTS, J. Adolescent symptomatology and its measurement. *American Journal of Mental Deficiency,* 1967, *72,* 74–95.

SPOTNITZ, H. Adolescence and schizophrenia: Problems in differentiation. In S. Lorand & H. I. Schneer (Eds.), *Adolescents: Psychoanalytic approaches to problems and therapy.* New York: Hoeber, 1961.

SPRING, B., & ZUBIN, J. Vulnerability to schizophrenic episodes and their prevention in adults. In G. W. Albee & J. W. Joffe (Eds.), *Primary prevention of psychopathology.* Vol. 1. *The issues.* Hanover, N.H.: University Press of New England, 1977.

STEIN, L. I., & TEST, M. A. Alternative to mental hospital treatment. *Archives of General Psychiatry,* 1980, *37,* 392—397.

STEPHENS, J. H. Long-term course and prognosis in schizophrenia. *Seminars in Psychiatry,* 1970, *2,* 464–485.

STEPHENS, J. H. Long-term prognosis and followup in schizophrenia. *Schizophrenia Bulletin,* 1978, *4,* 25–47.

STEPHENS, J. H., ASTRUP, C., & MANGRUM, J. C. Prognosis in schizophrenia: Prognostic scales cross validated in American and Norwegian patients. *Archives of General Psychiatry,* 1967, *16,* 693—698.

STONE, M. H. *The borderline syndromes.* New York: McGraw-Hill, 1980.

STRAUSS, J. S., & CARPENTER, W. T. Prediction of outcome in schizophrenia. III. Five-year outcome and its predictors. *Archives of General Psychiatry,* 1977, *34,* 159–163.

STRAUSS, J. S., & DOCHERTY, J. P. Subtypes of schizophrenia. *Schizophrenia Bulletin*, 1979, *5*, 447–452.

STRAUSS, J. S., KOKES, R. F., KLORMAN, R., & SACKSTEDER, J. Premorbid adjustment in schizophrenia: Concepts, measures, and implications. *Schizophrenia Bulletin*, 1977, *3*, 180–244.

STROBER, M., & GREEN, J. Diagnosis of adolescent psychopathology: A pilot study of the DSM-III nomenclature with adolescent impatients. *American Journal of Orthopsychiatry*, in press.

STROBER, M., GREEN, J., & CARLSON, G. Reliability of psychiatric diagnosis in hospitalized adolescents. *Archives of General Psychiatry*, 1981, *38*, 141–145.

SYMONDS, A., & HERMAN, M. The patterns of schizophrenia in adolescence. *Psychiatric Quarterly*, 1957, *31*, 521–530.

SYMONDS, P. M. *Adolescent fantasy*. New York: Columbia University Press, 1949.

TSUANG, M. T., WOOLSON, R. F., & FLEMING, J. A. Long-term outcome of major psychoses. *Archives of General Psychiatry*, 1979, *39*, 1295–1301.

VAILLANT, G. E. Positive prediction of schizophrenic remission. *Archives of General Psychiatry*, 1964, *11*, 509–518.

VAILLANT, G. E. A 10-year followup of remitting schizophrenics. *Schizophrenia Bulletin*, 1978, *4*, 78–85.

VAILLANT, G. E. The distinction between prognosis and diagnosis in schizophrenia. In L. C. Wynne, R. L. Cromwell, & S. Matthyse (Eds.), *The nature of schizophrenia*. New York: Wiley, 1978.

VENABLES, P. Input dysfunction in schizophrenia. In B. A. Maher (Ed.), *Progress in experimental personality research*. Vol. 1. New York: Academic, 1964.

WALKER, J. I., & BRODIE, H. K. Paranoid disorders. In H. I. Kaplan, A. M. Freedman, & B. J. Sadock (Eds.), *Comprehensive textbook of psychiatry*. (3d ed.) Baltimore: Williams & Wilkins, 1980.

WARREN, W. Abnormal behavior and mental breakdown in adolescence. *Journal of Mental Science*, 1949, *95*, 589–624.

WARREN, W. A study of adolescent psychiatric in-patients and the outcome six or more years later. II: The follow-up study. *Journal of Child Psychology and Psychiatry*, 1965, *6*, 141–160.

WARREN, W., & CAMERON, K. Reactive psychosis in adolescence. *Journal of Mental Science*, 1960, *96*, 141–160.

WATT, N. F. Childhood and adolescent routes to schizophrenia. In D. F. Ricks, M. Roff, & A. Thomas (Eds.), *Life history research in psychopathology*. Vol. 3. Minneapolis: University of Minnesota Press, 1974.

WATT, N. F. Patterns of childhood social development in adult schizophrenics. *Archives of General Psychiatry*, 1978, *35*, 160–165.

WATT, N. F., & LUBENSKY, A. W. Childhood roots of schizophrenia. *Journal of Consulting and Clinical Psychology*, 1976, *44*, 363–375.

WEINER, I. B. *Psychodiagnosis in schizophrenia*. New York: Wiley, 1966.

WEINER, I. B. Adjustment to adolescence. In B. B. Wolman (Ed.), *International encyclopedia of neurology, psychiatry, psychoanalysis, and psychology*. Princeton, N.J.: Van Nostrand Reinhold, 1977.

WEINER, I. B., & EXNER, J. E. Rorschach indices of disordered thinking in inpatient and nonpatient adolescents and adults. *Journal of Personality Assessment*, 1978, *42*, 339–343.

WEINER, I. B., & DEL GAUDIO, A. C. Psychopathology in adolescence: An epidemiological study. *Archives of General Psychiatry*, 1976, *33*, 187–193.

WEISBERG, P. S. Group therapy with adolescents. In J. R. Novello (Ed.), *The short course in adolescent psychiatry*. New York: Brunner/Mazel, 1979.

WING, J. K. Social influences on the course of schizophrenia. In L. C. Wynne, R. L. Cromwell, & S. Matthyse (Eds.), *The nature of schizophrenia*. New York: Wiley, 1978.

WINSBERG, B. G., BIALER, I., KUPEITZ, S., BOTTI, E., & BALKA, E. B. Home vs. hospital care of children with behavioral disorders. *Archives of General Psychiatry*, 1980, *37*, 413–418.

WOERNER, M. G., POLLACK, M., ROGALSKI, C., POLLACK, Y., & KLEIN, D. F. A comparison of the school records of personality disorders, schizophrenics, and their sibs. In M. Hoff, L. N. Robins, & M.

Pollack (Eds.), *Life history research in psychopathology.* Vol. 2. Minneapolis: University of Minnesota Press, 1972.

WYNNE, L. C. Family and group treatment of schizophrenia: An interim view. In R. Cancro, N. Fox, & L. Shapiro (Eds.), *Intervention in schizophrenia.* New York: Behavioral Publications, 1974.

ZIGLER, E., LEVINE, J., & ZIGLER, B. The relation between premorbid competence and paranoid-nonparanoid status in schizophrenia: A methodological and theoretical critique. *Psychological Bulletin,* 1976, *83,* 303–313.

ZINN, D. Hospital treatment of the adolescent. In J. D. Noshpitz (Ed.), *Basic handbook of child psychiatry.* Vol. III. New York: Basic Books, 1979.

ZUBIN, J., & SPRING, B. Vulnerability: A view of schizophrenia. *Journal of Abnormal Psychology,* 1977, *86,* 102–125.

ZUK, G. H., & RUBENSTEIN, D. A review of concepts in the study and treatment of families of schizophrenics. In I. Boszormenyi-Nagy & J. Frano (Eds.), *Intensive family therapy.* New York: Hoeber, 1965.

7

AFFECTIVE DISORDER:
DEPRESSION AND MANIA

Affective disorder consists of maladaptive changes in a person's mood, attitudes, energy level, and physical status. It occurs in two distinct types: **unipolar affective disorder,** which is manifest in espisodes of **depression,** and **biopolar affective disorder,** which involves episodes of **mania** or of both mania and depression (Winokur, 1973).

Depression is a common and familiar psychological state that most people have experienced in response to such disappointments and frustrations as misplacing a valued possession, failing to achieve a desired goal, facing the breakup of a close personal relationship, or becoming ill or incapacitated. Such events normally leave people feeling sad, discouraged, apathetic, or unwell. Especially distressing experiences, such as the death of a loved one, may cause a temporarily disabling depression, which is usually referred to as **grief.** Grief is also a normal reaction, so long as it does not persist for an unusually long time. When episodes of depression become more profound or last longer than events would seem to justify, they constitute a pathological depressive reaction, or unipolar affective disorder.

Mania falls at the opposite emotional pole from depression. Instead of sadness, discouragement, apathy, and malaise, its hallmarks are unflagging good spirits, unbounded optimism, enormous energy and enthusiasm, and pervasive sense of well-being. Feeling more or less happy, like feeling sad, is of course a normal reaction as one's life turns for better or worse; moreover, especially happy events may normally produce periods of **elation,** just as especially sad events cause moments of grief. When elation continues out of proportion to actual events, however, it constitutes a pathological manic reaction. Because mania usually occurs in people who also suffer depressive episodes, it has commonly been referred to as **manic-depressive disorder** as well as bipolar affective disorder.

Although unipolar and bipolar affective disorder involve the same dimensions of disturbance, they are not interchangeable conditions; that is, a person may have one or the other, but rarely both. Longitudinal studies indicate that only 4 to 5 percent of people diagnosed as having a unipolar disorder (depression alone) ever develop manic episodes that would change their diagnosis to bipolar disorder (manic-depression) (Dunner, Fleiss, & Fieve, 1976; Winokur & Morrison, 1973).

THE PREVALENCE OF AFFECTIVE DISORDER

The prevalence of affective disorder is somewhat difficult to determine, especially in young people, primarily because the frequency of depression and mania has been counted in three different ways: as *feeling states,* as *symptoms,* and as *syndromes.* In studies of feeling states, anyone who reports episodes of sadness or elation is counted, without distinction between normal and pathological degrees of these emotions. When depression and mania are studied as symptoms, attention is limited to affective states that are considered to reflect psychopathology. This approach casts a narrower net than the feeling-state definition and results in lower prevalence figures.

Symptom definitions count depression and mania whether they occur as a primary disturbance, or, as is sometimes the case, as a secondary reaction to other conditions (Akiskal, Rosenthal, Rosenthal, Kashgarian, Khani, & Puzantian, 1979; Andreasen &

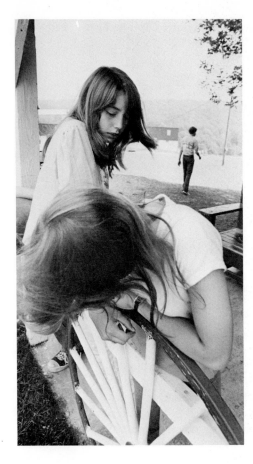

Disappointment causes most people to experience moments of depression from time to time.

Winokur, 1979; Krauthammer & Klerman, 1978a; Weissman, Pottenger, Kleber, Williams, & Thompson, 1977). Hence, symptom definitions produce larger prevalence estimates than syndrome definitions, which include only instances of primary affective disorder. Unfortunately, it is not always possible to determine from published reports whether the symptom approach or the more restrictive syndrome approach has been used in arriving at a particular prevalence figure.

To complicate matters further, attitudes toward the diagnosis of affective disorder have fluctuated over the years, particularly in the evaluation of younger people. Available prevalence estimates therefore vary with the vintage of the diagnostic data on which they are based. These various complications are illustrated in the following summary of recent studies of the prevalence of affective disorder.

Depression

The best current estimate of the prevalence of primary depressive disorder comes from work by Weissman and Myers (1978). Using carefully devised diagnostic criteria in a systematic population study, they found that approximately 25 percent of people born

TABLE 7.1 Patients in Age Groups with Diagnosed Depressive Disorder on Admission to Mental Health Facilities (in percent)

	Age		
Type of Facility	Under 18	18–24	25–44
State and county mental hospitals (n = 415,589)	4.3	8.6	10.1
Private mental hospitals (n = 129,832)	19.7	29.7	44.1
Outpatient psychiatric services (n = 1,405,065)	2.0	12.8	14.8

Source. From data in *Outpatient Psychiatric Services* (1978), *Private Mental Hospitals* (1978), and *State and County Mental Hospitals* (1978).

in the United States will suffer a diagnosable depressive reaction during their lifetime, and that at any one point in time close to 6 percent of American adults are definitely depressed.

Such firm estimates are not yet available for children and adolescents. In various surveys employing the *feeling state* and *symptom* approaches to counting, 20 percent of kindergarten through second-graders showed one or more symptoms of depressive disorder; 33 percent of seventh- and eighth-graders reported moderate to severe depressive feelings of sadness, worthlessness, and pessimism; and about 22 percent of 14- to 15-year-olds described having often felt "miserable or depressed" (Albert & Beck, 1975; Lefkowitz, 1977; Rutter, Graham, Chadwick, & Yule, 1976). Among young people referred to mental health facilities, over 70 percent are reported by their parents to show symptoms of depression, and one-third to one-half are found in fact to be significantly depressed (Brumback, Dietz-Schmidt, & Weinberg, 1977; Carlson & Cantwell, 1980a; Cass & Thomas, 1979; Hudgens, 1974; Masterson, 1967).

These reports leave little doubt that features of depression play a prominent role in the psychological disturbances of children and adolescents. However, they do not say much about the prevalence of primary depressive disorder among young people. Some relevant information on this point appears in Table 7.1, which shows the percentage of patients with diagnosed depressive reaction in three types of psychiatric service in the United States. These data indicate that depressive disorder is diagnosed in fewer than 5 percent of youthful patients seen in mental health facilities, compared to almost 20 percent of adults. Additional data reveal that these figures contain some interesting age and sex differences and may underestimate the actual frequency of child and adolescent depression.

Age Differences As shown in Figure 7.1, the prevalence of diagnosed depression among youthful patients varies considerably with their age. Very few children under 10 are diagnosed depressed (less than 1 percent), following which the frequency climbs dramatically. Taking the data for outpatient psychiatric services—which account for approximately 80 percent of youngsters under 18 seen in mental health facilities—we see

Figure 7.1
Percent of patients diagnosed with psychoneurotic depressive reaction in psychiatric clinics and hospitals. (From data in *Mental Health Statistical Note No. 148* (1978) and *Outpatient Psychiatric Services* (1969).)

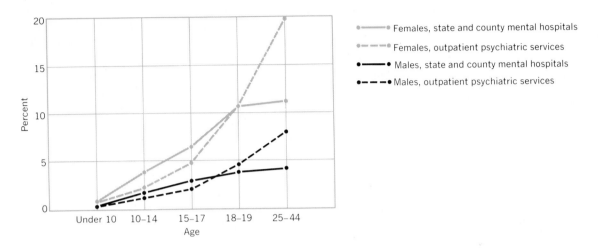

that the rate of depression for both sexes combined just about doubles between age 10 to 14 (1.7 percent) and age 15 to 17 (3.3 percent), and more than doubles again among 18- to 19-year-olds (7.6 percent). These 18- to 19-year-old patients are in turn only half as likely to be diagnosed depressed as 25- to 44-year-old clinic patients (14.8 percent). One possible conclusion from these age-related changes is that depression is more an adult than an adolescent disorder, with disturbed individuals becoming gradually more likely to show primary depression as they mature through the adolescent years toward adulthood.

A comparison of these diagnostic data with the clinical surveys just noted raises questions about how fully they capture the true prevalence of primary depression in young people. With respect to adolescents, for example, there is a large gap between the approximately 5 percent of young patients who are officially diagnosed as having a depressive disorder and the one-third to one-half who are found in research studies to be significantly depressed. Part of this gap could represent secondary depression, since only primary diagnoses appear in Table 7.1 and Figure 7.1. Yet the vast majority of depressive disorder—60 to 86 percent in various studies—has been found to be primary, not secondary (Robins, Gentry, Munoz, & Marten, 1977; Strober, Green, & Carlson, 1981; Weissman & Meyers, 1978). Thus at least some of the actual frequency of primary depressive disorder would seem to be missing from official diagnoses, and its true prevalence among adolescent patients probably exceeds the levels shown in Figure 7.1.

The negligible frequency of diagnosed depression in children under 10 differs even more strikingly from the survey findings for this age group. This difference almost certainly reflects the influence of a once widespread view that depressive disorder involves such complex psychological processes that young people are incapable of developing it until they have achieved almost an adult level of cognitive and emotional maturation (Rie, 1966). In addition, some current writers maintain that depressive symptoms are too common and fleeting in children to constitute a syndrome or call for any professional intervention (Lefkowitz & Burton, 1978).

The potential shortcomings of neglecting treatment of mild disturbances were noted in Chapter 1 (see page 18). More to the present point is the fact that contemporary theories of depression and careful studies of disturbed children, as elaborated in this chapter, clearly contradict the earlier notion that this condition is limited to late adolescents and adults. Many clinicians now regard depression as underdiagnosed in both children and adolescents, and future reports of recorded diagnoses may accordingly show a larger prevalence of youthful depressive disorder than appears in Table 7.1 (Cantwell & Carlson, 1980; Costello, 1980; Easson, 1977; Malmquist, 1975; Philips, 1979; Weiner, 1975).

Sex Differences Figure 7.1 reveals that, at least from age 10 on, female patients are more likely to be diagnosed depressed than male patients. This sex difference increases gradually during the adolescent years, and by adulthood depressive disorder is more than twice as frequent among female than male patients. A 2:1 ratio of females to males among adults treated for depression has been consistently observed in the United States for the last 40 years, and there is reason to believe that their greater vulnerability to depressive disorder derives from elements of the traditional female role in our society, especially low social status and discrimination in achievement-related situations (Brown & Harris, 1978; Chevron, Quinlan, & Blatt, 1978; Weissman & Klerman, 1977, 1979).

This last finding raises the interesting possibility that the female preponderance among depressed patients will diminish in the future, as progress is made in providing equal opportunities for women. For the present, however, the lack of such equality apparently continues to contribute to depression in women. In fact, the increasing female: male ratio as adolescents mature toward adulthood may reflect the increasingly depressing impact of perceived role limitations as girls grow into young women.

On the other hand, sex differences in depression cannot be attributed entirely to sociocultural factors. Radloff and Rae (1979) confirmed in a large-scale survey that women do encounter depressing life experiences more frequently than men. When men and women were matched for the frequency of such experiences, however, the women still showed more depression. Hence the greater susceptibility of females to becoming depressed seems to involve biological or learned sex differences as well as current experiences of sex-role limitation.

Mania

Pathologically elevated mood states occur much less frequently than depressive disorders. By contrast with the 25 percent lifetime prevalence of definite depressive episodes in the United States, bipolar affective disorder with some form of manic episode is estimated to occur in just 1.2 percent of the population. At any single point in time the prevalence of manic-depressive disorder is no more than 3 or 4 people per 1000 (Cohen,

1975; Krauthammer & Klerman, 1978; Weissman & Myers, 1978).

These data still mean that 1 of every 100 people born in this country will suffer a manic episode, a fact that has only recently been fully appreciated. For a long time clinicians in the United States regarded mania as a rare or at most a secondary condition and seldom recorded it as a primary diagnosis. In the late 1960s two developments began to change this situation: Research findings pointed increasingly to genetic factors in causing manic-depressive disorder, and clinical experience indicated that a drug called **lithium** could be used effectively in treating it. These new ideas about cause and treatment alerted clinicians more than before to the possibility of manic disorder in their patients, and the frequency with which it was diagnosed increased dramatically (Goodwin & Zis, 1979; Klerman & Barrett, 1973). Consequently the recorded prevalence of mania differs considerably in the pre- and postlithium eras, and some researchers believe that it is still much underdiagnosed (Pope & Lipinski, 1978).

With respect to young people, clinical surveys indicate that manic disorders rarely occur in children under the age of 10 to 12 (Anthony & Scott, 1960; Cytryn & McKnew, 1979). The data are less clear for adolescents. On the one hand, there is a widespread tendency to discount the occurrence of mania among teenagers, and categories of manic disorder typically do not even appear in prevalence reports on adolescent psychopathology. On the other hand, studies of manic-depressive adults reveal that 20 to 35 percent first showed overt signs of their disturbance when they were age 10 to 19 (Carlson, Davenport, & Jamison, 1977; Loranger & Levine, 1978; Winokur, Clayton, & Reich, 1969).

A report by Hudgens (1974) is interesting in this regard. He found that a clinical diagnosis of mania was assigned to just 4 percent of over 300 consecutively admitted 12- to 19-year-olds in a psychiatric unit of a general hospital. However, when a sample of 110 youngsters in this same unit were evaluated further against specific criteria for mania, 10 percent were judged to have this disorder. In the view of many current researchers in the field, these and other data indicate that manic-depressive disorder occurs in a substantial number of disturbed adolescents and is underdiagnosed in this age group (Carlson & Strober, 1978; Feinstein & Wolpert, 1973; Preodor & Wolpert, 1979; White & O'Shanick, 1977).

DIMENSIONS OF AFFECTIVE DISORDER

Affective disorder was defined at the beginning of the chapter as a maladaptive change in *mood, attitudes, energy level,* and *physical status.* Such events constitute the basic dimensions of both depression and mania (American Psychiatric Association, 1980; Beck 1970; Endicott & Spitzer, 1978; Kraepelin, 1921; Winokur, Clayton, & Reich, 1969).

Mood

As their label implies, affective disorders are predominantly disorders of mood, running to profound misery in the depths of depression and great ecstasy at the peaks of mania. Pathologically depressed moods typically involve feelings of sadness, spells of tearfulness and crying, loss of interest in people and previously enjoyed pursuits, and a diminished ability to experience pleasure.

Pathologically elevated moods, by contrast, are reflected in joyfulness, constant smiling and ready laughter, infectious good humor, enthusiasm spreading in all directions, and pleasure experienced at every turn. Depressed people withdraw into themselves emotionally, are difficult if not impossible to cheer up, and tend to have an unpleasant dampening effect on those around them. Manic individuals, on the other hand, actively reach out to other people and enliven social gatherings. However, because their bubbling gaiety persists even when the needs of others call for more serious behavior, they can make themselves socially distasteful.

Attitudes

Affective disorder frequently includes very negative or very positive attitudes toward oneself, the world, and the future. People who are depressed tend to have a poor opinion of themselves and a sense of helplessness. They view themselves as inadequate, unattractive, unlovable individuals who are incapable of doing anything to improve their situation in life, and they may also harbor a sense of guilt for having behaved improperly or sinfully. Their low self-esteem and self-depreciation lead to a degree of pessimism and hopelessness that often discourages depressed people from even trying to escape their unhappiness.

A youngster who sits listless in the classroom, unable to concentrate despite wanting to do well, may be suffering from depression.

Mania, on the other hand, is characterized by inflated self-esteem, unrealistically high expectations, and an uncritical sense of optimism. No task is too difficult to achieve, no obstacle too great to surmount, and no shortcoming too serious to be overcome. Manic people expect to be loved and admired by all and to succeed in everything they do. Should they recognize failure when it occurs, they attribute it to the inadequacy or interference of others rather than to any limitations of their own. Whereas depressive attitudes discourage activity, the grandiosity that accompanies mania and the rose-colored glasses through which manic individuals view the world fuel ambitious plans and an enormous investment in carrying them out.

Each of these attitude changes during an affective disorder distorts reality in some way. Hence both depression and mania can assume psychotic proportions, should the person's present and future expectations become extremely deviant from realistic considerations. Then, like schizophrenics, depressed and manic individuals may develop strange ideas about who they are and what they can or cannot do, and they may show poor judgment in conducting their daily lives. The more seriously depressed or manic people become, the more likely they are to suffer such a psychotic loss of touch with reality (Beck, 1971; Miller, 1975).

Energy Level

Depression robs people of their mental and physical energy and leaves them lethargic and unable to concentrate. Like a windup gadget that is running down, depressed individuals move slowly, talk slowly, and think slowly—a phenomenon sometimes referred to as **psychomotor retardation.** During episodes of depression people have difficulty accomplishing anything, because they cannot get their bodies to move or their minds to focus on a task.

In mania, the tide flows in the other direction. Vast stores of energy appear to be at the person's disposal, in even greater amounts than can be harnessed effectively. Speech pours out rapidly, and words may stumble over each other faster than they can be pronounced clearly (**pressure of speech**). Thoughts flow in quick succession, and the person may lose track of the point he or she was trying to make (**flight of ideas**). Actions proceed in many directions at once, so that manic people appear driven and disorganized and waste more effort than they use constructively.

Physical Status

The onset of affective disorder often brings changes in sleeping patterns, appetite, and physical well-being. People who are depressed tend to fall asleep slowly, sleep poorly, and wake up easily. When they are successful in avoiding insomnia, fitfulness, and early morning awakening, they are still likely to get up from long hours of sleep feeling fatigued and unrefreshed.

A person's appetite during episodes of depression often becomes either much smaller or much larger than usual. Depressed people, consequently, tend to lose or gain a great deal of weight, and some may alternate between periods of total disinterest in eating (**anorexia**) and excessive, insatiable needs to consume food (**bulimia**) (Bemis, 1980; Bruch, 1976; Daniel, 1970; Sours, 1980).

Depressed adolescents may turn to food as a source of gratification and become overweight.

Depression is also reflected in a general sense of feeling poorly physically and an exaggerated concern with health and bodily functions (**hypochondriasis**). Depressed people frequently regard themselves as being in poorer physical shape than they used to be, and they are in fact likely to experience an unusual number of aches, pains, and other somatic complaints that add to their worries about deteriorating health.

Manic individuals, by contrast, present a picture of robust good health. They sleep soundly and require less sleep than usual to feel rested. They eat heartily, describe themselves as being "in the pink of condition," and rarely complain of any physical symptoms. This description may make mania appear to be a desirable condition rather than a form of psychopathology. Unfortunately, however, in mania this sense of well-being persists despite actual physical problems that should in reality cause the person concern. Manic individuals are therefore likely to deny conditions that require medical treatment and to overlook symptoms that herald the onset of physical illness.

Contrary to the previously mentioned view that affective disorder does not occur in young people, each of these dimensions of depression and mania is in fact observed in children and adolescents as well as in adults. A growing number of studies reveal that the disturbances in mood, attitudes, and energy level traditionally associated with affective disorder in adults can be readily identified and reliably measured in 10- to 17-year-olds (Carlson & Cantwell, 1980b; Inamdar, Siomopoulos, Osborn, & Bianchi, 1979; Lefkowitz & Tesiny, 1980; Puig-Antich, Blau, Marx, Greenhill, & Chambers, 1978; Strober, Green, & Carlson, 1981; Weinberg & Brumback, 1976). Accordingly, clinicians and researchers are coming increasingly to agree that only minor modifications of the criteria used with adults are necessary to identify these conditions in young people (Cantwell & Carlson, 1979; Cytryn, McKnew, & Bunney, 1980; Kovacs & Beck, 1977).

Even the changes in physical status described above, which may seem largely problems of adulthood, frequently occur in affectively disordered children and adolescents. In one study, for example, disturbed patterns of sleep, appetite, and bodily functions were found in 85 percent of depressed children (Brumback, Dietz-Schmidt, & Weinberg, 1977). More broadly, Table 7.2 indicates the frequency of several typical symptoms of depression and mania observed in adolescents with affective disorder.

TABLE 7.2 Common Symptoms in Adolescents with Affective Disorder (in percent)

Dimension of Maladaptive Change	Depression		Mania	
Mood	Dejected	94	Elated	90
	Loss of interest	74		
Attitudes	Hopelessness	66	Grandiosity, sense of strength and importance	70
	Feelings of worthlessness	64*		
	Self-reproach	54*		
	Guilty thoughts	45		
	Excessive worry	45		
Energy level	Impaired concentration	86	Overactive	89*
	Loss of energy	60	Overtalkative	85
			Distractible	67*
			Flight of ideas	60
Physical status	Anorexia	70	Less need for sleep	65
	Insomnia	66		
	Weight gain or loss	57		
	Restless sleep	51		
	Somatic complaints	46		

*Asterisks indicate data from Carlson and Strober only.
Source.   Based on studies by Carlson and Strober (1979) and Hudgens (1974) of 47 depressed and 20 manic adolescents.

DEVELOPMENTAL VARIATIONS IN AFFECTIVE DISORDER

Although the same basic dimensions of disturbance characterize affective disorder at all ages, the most prominent symptoms of the disorder vary somewhat with age, in relation to maturational changes during childhood, early and middle adolescence, and late adolescence.

Childhood

Infants and young children sometimes show depressive behavior, especially in response to inadequate stimulation or separation from their parents. In these circumstances, they may become unhappy and apathetic, lose interest in their surroundings, and even fail to thrive physically despite being well cared for. Not until the age of 5 or 6 do children develop the cognitive maturity and language skills necessary to experience and communicate the kinds of attitudes that constitute an important dimension of affective disorder. For this reason, depressive-like states occurring in infants and preschoolers are usually referred to as "deprivation" or "social isolation" syndromes instead of affective disorder (Anthony, 1975; Arieti & Bemporad, 1978, Chapter 8; Elkind & Weiner, 1978, Chapter 6; Kovacs & Beck, 1977).

From 5 or 6 on, children and adolescents with affective disorder show essentially the same dimensions of disturbance as depressed or manic adults, as already noted. Nevertheless, because they still lack mature capacity to verbalize their moods and attitudes, elementary school children frequently manifest affective disorder through changes in their physical status. In addition to the previously mentioned problems with eating and sleeping, for example, depressed children from age 5 to 12 often show such symptoms as headache, abdominal pain, and enuresis (bed-wetting) as the initial or most apparent sign of their disorder (Arajarvi & Huttunen, 1972; Brumback et al., 1977; Leon, Kendall, & Garber, 1980; Ling, Oftedal, & Weinberg, 1970). Not surprisingly, then, depressed children may be seen and correctly diagnosed more frequently in pediatric and general medical settings than in mental health facilities, where clinicians are attuned more to mood and attitudinal changes than to physical signs of psychological disorder (Blumberg, 1978; Malmquist, 1977).

When disturbances of mood and attitude do occur at this age, the former tend to be more common up to 8 or so. Then, as a reflection of their maturing capacity to evaluate themselves and form sophisticated attitudes, children with affective disorder become increasingly likely to show a deflated or inflated sense of their worth and importance (McConville, Boag, & Purohit, 1973).

Early and Middle Adolescence

The developmental tasks that young people face from puberty until 15 or 16—including adjusting to rapid changes in their bodies, learning to become independent of their parents, and forming heterosexual friendships and dating relationships—pose serious challenges to their self-esteem. Youngsters of this age are consequently reluctant to admit any self-critical attitudes or concerns about being a competent person. Even thinking about being unable to cope can make them feel that they are being unacceptably childish or dependent. Hence they become relatively unlikely to experience or display the gloom, self-depreciation, and feelings of helplessness and hopelessness that appear in some depressed children and commonly characterize depression in adults.

For this reason, younger adolescents with an affective disorder are more likely to show easily recognizable signs of mania than of depression. When they become depressed, they often express their disorder in efforts to ward off depression through *restlessness, a flight to or from people,* and *problem behavior.*

Restlessness   Common lore tells people that keeping busy is a good way to "keep your mind off things" and avoid feeling depressed. Because younger adolescents are so intent on avoiding depressive feelings, they sometimes become more rather than less active in the face of depressing circumstances. However, this increased energy seldom results in any accomplishments. Instead, it makes these depressed youngsters restless and easily bored. Constantly in need of stimulation and excitement, they take up new pursuits with great enthusiasm, only to lose interest and drop them as soon as familiarity sets in. Routine of any kind becomes difficult for them to tolerate, quiet contemplation and low-key activities cannot be endured, and cravings for novelty and adventure become the order of the day (Inamdar, Siomopoulos, Osborn, & Bianchi, 1979; Weiner, 1975).

Flight to or from People   In their relationships with people, younger adolescents may exhibit an urgent need for companionship and a continuous search for new and "more interesting" friends. Like restlessness, such a flight toward people helps to keep the person stimulated and occupied, one step ahead of being overtaken by depressive thoughts or feelings.

Sometimes, however, when being around others exposes them to fears of being criticized or rejected, depressed youngsters may flee from, not toward, people. Since they may still feel a need to ward off depression through activity, these adolescents may then become intensely involved in solitary pursuits or with pets, with whom they can exchange affection with little risk of rejection (Weiner, 1975).

Problem Behavior   In some cases younger adolescents express depression primarily through temper tantrums, running away, stealing, truancy, and other defiant, rebellious, or antisocial acts. To the extent that such problem behavior is novel and exciting, it meets these youngsters' needs for stimulation and helps them avoid dwelling on what is troubling them. Public displays of resisting or outwitting authority may also bring them some notoriety that bolsters their self-esteem. Perhaps most importantly, problem behavior compels the attention of important people in a youngster's life and provides an indirect way of letting them know that he or she is struggling with depressing concerns that cannot be directly expressed (Anthony, 1968; Bonnard, 1961; Burks & Harrison, 1962; Spiegel, 1967).

Some writers refer to these and other efforts to ward off depression as "masked depression"; on occasion this concept is even applied to any manifestation of depression other than changes in mood and self-attitudes, including concentration difficulty, hypochondriasis, loss of appetite, and certain physical complaints (Glaser, 1967; Lesse, 1979; Malmquist, 1975; Toolan, 1974). There is little doubt that a diagnosis of "masked depression" often proved helpful in the past in identifying disturbed youngsters who could be treated most effectively by focusing on underlying depressive concerns that were not immediately apparent from their presenting symptoms.

Currently, however, a broadened understanding of the nature of depressive disorder in young people appears to have eliminated any need to speak of "masked" depression. When maladaptive changes in energy level and physical status are properly recognized as core dimensions of affective disorder, many of the features of "masked" depression become primary and readily apparent indices of depressive disorder. Likewise, efforts to ward off depression are now widely recognized as secondary consequences of the disorder that clearly reflect, rather than mask, the person's underlying concerns. An increasing number of clinicians therfore prefer to speak of "age-related changes" in the primary symptoms of depression and "secondary reactions" to depression, rather than of masked depression in children or adolescents (Arieti & Bemporad, 1978, Chapter 4; Carlson & Cantwell, 1980; Gittelman-Klein, 1977; Kovacs & Beck, 1977; Poznanski, 1979).

Case 9. *Depression in Early Adolescence*

Wilma was an academically average, plain-looking, eight-grade student, age 13, who lived in the shadows of her family and peer-group life. Her father owned a small business that monopolized his time, and her mother—a youthful, attractive, and fashionable woman whose appearance contrasted markedly with Wilma's characteristic drabness—was actively engaged in a business career of her own. During their limited moments at home, both parents concentrated their attention on Wilma's two younger brothers, to her considerable resentment. Although the parents recognized that Wilma felt less favored than her brothers, they believed she was being adequately cared for and had no grounds for her sullenness and constant complaining. From Wilma's perspective, however, she was the least able, least attractive, least loved, and least important member of her family.

Among her peers Wilma tagged along with many different groups, but more as a tolerated hanger-on than a valued member. "If I disappeared tomorrow," she said, "my friends wouldn't miss me or even notice I wasn't there." Wilma's parents disapproved of many of these friends and frequently criticized their sloppy dress and undisciplined behavior. Yet they never made any rules about Wilma's choice of companions or about how she should dress and act—in short, they gave little indication of caring what she did or what happened to her.

One day at school Wilma overheard some classmates describing some recent bomb scares at nearby schools as "neat" pranks. That same day she went to a telephone booth between classes and called the principal's office to report a bomb in the school. Within a few minutes an alarm was sounded, the building was evacuated, and the police arrived to search the premises.

Wilma confided to several classmates that she had made the call, swearing each to secrecy—which meant that her guilt quickly became common knowledge. Her parents were called in to meet with school officials and then with the police, who referred the family to juvenile court. Said Wilma, "It was the first time in months I was in a room with both of my parents at the same time." The court proceedings required many hours of her parents' time, they were ordered by the judge to keep a close watch on her behavior, and everybody in her school now knew precisely who she was and what she had done. For better or worse, the actions of this lonely, discouraged, ignored girl pulled her at least for the moment from the shadows into the spotlight.

Late Adolescence

As they mature, adolescents become more capable than before of thinking about themselves critically and sharing these thoughts with others. Accordingly they become more likely to resemble adults in both their manic and depressive symptoms should they develop an affective disorder. In some cases, however, older adolescents may still express depression indirectly, through maladaptive behavior. The most important behavioral indices of underlying depression that begin to emerge at age 15 or 16 are *drug abuse, sexual promiscuity, alienation,* and *suicidal behavior.* These problem behaviors do not necessarily indicate depression, since each has other possible causes. However, because they can and do arise as secondary reactions to depression, experienced clinicians evaluate and treat them with an eye to possible depressive concerns in their origin.

Drug Abuse The popular media often suggest that regular drug use has become a widespread and normal feature of contemporary teenage behavior. To the contrary, however, drug abuse characterizes only a small minority of adolescents and reflects serious maladjustment when it occurs. The more frequently high school students use drugs, for example, the more likely they are to do poorly in school, to be uninvolved in either academic or extracurricular school activities, and to lack any serious commitment to social, occupational, or recreational pursuits (McGlothlin, 1975; Stein, Soskin, & Korchin, 1975; Tec, 1972).

Although drug abuse has multiple causes, its association with the above signs of low interest and energy levels identifies the role that depression may play in it. In addition, persistent regular drug use may help a young person to ward off depressive feelings. The intoxicating effects of the drugs can offer escape from depressing concerns, the process of illegally obtaining and using drugs can satisfy needs for excitement and stimulation, and sharing a drug experience with other youngsters can establish at least a sense of companionship and provide a hedge against loneliness (Berlin, 1979; Hartmann, 1969; Levy, 1968; Paton, Kessler, & Kandel, 1977; Wieder & Kaplan, 1969). These and other aspects of adolescent drug abuse are elaborated in Chapter 13.

Sexual Promiscuity Sexual promiscuity, like abuse of drugs, is sometimes regarded as a common characteristic of today's teenagers. However, contrary to popular belief, abundant research findings demonstrate that there has been no "sexual revolution" in this country since the 1920s. Young people are more open and sophisticated about sexual matters than in the past and more inclined to become physically intimate in the context of a close, trusting, and relatively enduring relationship. However, they are no more likely than in previous years to approve of or engage in promiscuous sexuality, which consists of physical intimacy without personal intimacy and a rapid succession of multiple sex partners. Casual, indiscriminate sexuality is rare among young people, especially girls, and it is typically associated with psychological maladjustment when it occurs (Antonovsky, Shoham, Kavenaki, Lancet, & Modan, 1980; Binder & Krohn, 1974; Diepold & Young, 1979; Elkind & Weiner, 1978, Chapter 16; Sorenson, 1973).

Although adolescent girls are less active sexually than boys, they are more likely to use promiscuity to ward off depression. The reason for this sex difference is that sexual encounters ordinarily place more demands on the male than the female to be knowledgeable and to perform well. Since teenage boys are relatively inexperienced and uncertain of their ability to perform, sexual activity is a risky way for them to attempt to bolster their feelings of adequacy. The strong possibility of embarrassment or failure means that they could end up feeling worse instead of better about themselves.

For girls, on the other hand, being promiscuous requires only willingness, not performance. Hence they can more safely turn to sexuality to compensate for negative self-attitudes. In this regard, the promiscuity of a depressed adolescent girl is seldom sexual, in the sense of providing her erotic gratification. Instead, it serves primarily to bring her into intimate physical contact with other people. The attention she receives from boys and young men seeking her favors, the experience of feeling needed and wanted, and the sensations of being held and caressed all may help a depressed girl combat feelings of being unattractive, alone, and unloved.

Alienation   Reference to "alienated youth" has become fashionable in some quarters as a way of describing most young people in modern society. In fact, however, alienation is no more typical of adolescence than drug abuse or sexual promiscuity. Most adolescents are keenly interested in what is going on in their community and share with their parents and other adults the basic values of their society. Those who lack close ties with their families and broader community are maladjusted, not normally developing, young people (Weiner, 1971, 1976).

Among late adolescents who become depressed, then, some may develop a pattern of alienation in which they withdraw from efforts to make a place for themselves in the world. Concerned about their adequacy, they avoid any kind of effort that might end in failure and any kind of aspiration that might lead to disappointment. Typically this

Some young people join alienated groups to escape depressing feelings of being unable to make a place for themselves in conventional society. Here members of a religious commune in northern New Mexico are at prayer.

restricted personality pattern results in pronounced apathy that is justified by a cynical, "what's-the-use-of-it-all" view of the world.

Adolescents who are dealing with underlying depression in this way sometimes seek each other out to form groups of young people who become visible for their unconventional, antiestablishment ideas. Although some members of such groups may hold deep convictions, many are less concerned with the group's avowed purposes than with being able to use the group to escape from depressing feelings of being alone, unimportant, or ineffective (Cambor, 1973; Shainberg, 1966; Teicher, 1972; Unwin, 1970; Walters, 1971).

Suicidal Behavior Of all mental disorders, depression poses the greatest risk of actual or attempted suicide; the more depressed people become, especially with respect to negative attitudes toward themselves and their future, the more likely they are to contemplate taking their own lives (Minkoff, Bergman, Beck, & Beck, 1973; Silver, Bohnert, Beck & Marcus, 1971; Tsuang, 1978; Wetzel, 1976). As one prominent epidemiologist puts it, "Suicide is the mortality of depressive illness" (Silverman, 1968, p. 890).

This is not to say that suicidal individuals are always depressed. To the contrary, clinical depression is found in just 30 to 40 percent of adolescents who commit or attempt suicide, which means that the majority are not noticeably depressed (Schneer, Perlstein, & Brozovsky, 1975; Shaffer, 1974). Nevertheless, it is among young people who are depressed that clinicians must be most alert to possible suicidal behavior. Such behavior by depressed adolescents typically constitutes a desperate, last-ditch effort to get other people to recognize and help them with problems they can find no other way of solving (Jacobs, 1971). These and other aspects of youthful suicidal behavior are discussed more fully in Chapter 12.

Case 10. *Depression in Late Adolescence*

Donald was 16 when he made a suicide attempt with 20 aspirin tablets. The previous several years of his life had seen much family disruption. His mother had been hospitalized recurrently for a chronic schizophrenic condition, and when at home she had been too disorganized to function adequately as a parent. During his junior high school years, his father had sent him to live with his grandparents in another city to spare him the distress of their home life, and he had gotten along reasonably well. On returning home to begin high school, however, Donald discovered to his dismay that his father was having an affair with their neighbor, a divorced woman whose children were his schoolmates.

At this point Donald began increasingly to withdraw from activities and to isolate himself from his former friends, whom he felt embarrassed to face. He began to frequent bars, where he used false identification papers to be served, and he took to late hours, delinquent companions, and neglect of his studies. This period of withdrawal and problem behavior culminated in his running away to a distant city, where he spent 2 weeks hanging around bars, living in rooming houses, and developing an increasing sense of alienation.

He then returned home, only to learn that in his absence his father had gone to

Mexico for a divorce and had married their neighbor. Thus in 2 short weeks his home as he had known it had ceased to exist. He refused to move in with his father and stepmother and instead rented a room by himself. In this setting his efforts to ward off depression gave way to full-blown depressive changes in his mood, attitudes, and energy level. In his own words, his life at this point "seemed a big pointless nothing; nothing was good for me in the past, and I'll probably end up in a mental hospital or as a bum." After 4 days of progressive gloom, lethargy, and despair he swallowed the aspirins and then called his father to ask for help.

Donald's history of social withdrawal and his mother's known schizophrenic disturbance initially suggested that he might be developing schizophrenia himself. However, careful diagnostic study ruled out schizophrenic personality impairments, and he responded well to therapy aimed at his depressive concerns. He was discharged to outpatient care after a brief hospitalization and did not require rehospitalization during the subsequent 5 years in which follow-up was available.

CAUSES OF AFFECTIVE DISORDER

The causes of affective disorder have not yet been studied as extensively as the origins of schizophrenia, discussed in Chapter 5. So far, however, available evidence is pointing to a similar conclusion: that a certain level of genetic or constitutional disposition (*diasthesis*) and certain kinds of unpleasant experience (*stress*) interact to produce it. Specifically, there seems little doubt that affective disorder runs in families, that this familial incidence appears due at least in part to genetic factors, and that life events influence individual susceptibility to affective disorder and precipitate its expression in depressive and manic episodes (Dunner, Patrick, & Fieve, 1979).

Genetic Factors

For affective disorder, as for schizophrenia, the more closely two people are related, the more likely they are to share the condition. Most significantly with regard to genetic factors, identical (monozygotic) twins show a 69.2 percent average concordance for affective disorder in various studies, whereas nonidentical (dizygotic) twins show just a 13.3 percent concordance (Gershon, Bunney, Leckman, Van Eerdewegh, & De-Bauche, 1976).

The possibility that this difference results from identical twins sharing more common experiences, rather than from their being more genetically alike than nonidentical twins, is contradicted by two additional findings. First, identical twins who have been reared apart, and therefore have relatively little experience in common, still show close to a 70 percent concordance for affective disorder (Price, 1968). Second, when nonidentical twins are compared with other first-degree relatives (siblings, parents, offspring), who resemble them in genetic relatedness but usually have much less experience in common, they are found to show just about the same extent of concordance (Winokur, 1975).

The cross-fostering method described in Chapter 5 as so useful in identifying a genetic contribution to psychopathology has not yet been extensively applied in studies

TABLE 7.3 Frequency of Bipolar and Unipolar Affective Disorder in First-Degree Relatives (in percent)

Type of Affective Disorder in Index Person	Bipolar Disorder in Relatives		Unipolar Disorder in Relatives	
	Siblings	Parents and Offspring	Siblings	Parents and Offspring
Bipolar	8.6	5.1	6.8	8.4
Unipolar	0.6	0.3	7.1	4.8

Source. Based on research summarized by Gershon, Bunney, Leckman, Van Eerdewegh, & DeBauche (1976).

of affective disorder. However, one such study does lend support to the role of genetic factors. Cadoret (1978), studying people who had been placed for adoption after birth, found that three of eight biological children of mothers with affective disorder had become affectively disordered themselves (37.5 percent), compared to only eight of 118 (7 percent, the general population average) of adopted-away children of nondisturbed mothers.

Interestingly, the bipolar (manic-depressive) and unipolar (depression alone) types of affective disorder do not contribute equally to observed levels of familial concordance. Table 7.3 summarizes several studies in which elevated concordance appeared only in the bipolar type. Note that the first-degree relatives of persons with unipolar affective disorder showed no more than the general population frequency of manic-depressive disorder (less than 1 percent, as noted earlier) or depression (about 6 percent). The relatives of persons in these studies with bipolar affective disorder showed an elevated risk for being manic-depressive, but they too were only slightly more likely than people in general to have unipolar affective disorder.

Other more recent research is beginning to identify increased risk of depression in the family members of depressed people, however. Figure 7.2 shows concordance rates well above the 6 percent population average for twins, parents, and siblings. In another especially important large-scale study, Tsuang, Crowe, Winokur, and Clancy (1978) found depression in 9.4 percent of 413 first-degree relatives of depressed psychiatric patients but in just 5.5 percent of the first-degree relatives of 415 medically ill comparison subjects. Even in these studies the familial concordance falls below the figures for affective disorder in general, which indicates that manic-depressive disorder accounts for a greater share—and is therefore probably more dependent on genetic factors—than unipolar depression.

Yet, aside from how much of the familial concordance in affective disorder is eventually determined to reflect genetic factors, the fact remains that more than 30 percent and perhaps as many as 60 percent of the identical twins of persons with affective disorder avoid becoming affectively disturbed themselves. Hence there can be little doubt that life experience as well as heredity participates in causing this condition to

Figure 7.2
Familial concordance in depression. (Based on data summarized by Allen (1976) and Winokur (1975).)

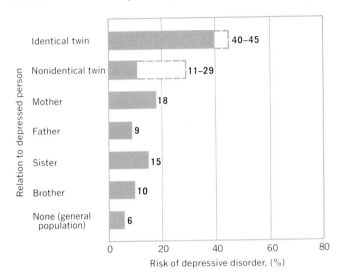

occur. Equally certain is the sex difference that appears in Figure 7.2, which has been confirmed by all investigators. The female relatives of persons with either bipolar or unipolar affective disorder are 1.5 to 2 times more likely than their male relatives to become affectively disturbed (Gerson et al., 1976; Johnson & Leeman, 1977; Winokur & Pitts, 1965). Although not fully understood, this sex difference in concordance is consistent with the generally greater frequency of affective disorder in females than males among both young people and adults.

Experiential Factors

Clinical and research findings indicate that depressive disorders emerge primarily in response to the experience of loss. Depression in response to loss is most apparent when a loved one dies, moves away, or rejects a person's affections, leaving him or her to mourn the lost relationship. Other experiences that often precipitate depression include damage to objects one holds dear, failure to achieve some desired goal, and loss of bodily integrity related to illness, physical handicap, disfigurement, or even normal biological changes (Bibring, 1953; Freud, 1917; Malmquist, 1976; Paykel, 1975; Toolan, 1978).

The sense of loss that causes a person to become depressed may be either *real* or *fantasied*. A real loss is an actual event that deprives people of something important to them. Among adolescents, for example, rejection by a boyfriend, finishing last in a race, or having to wear braces can deprive a youngster of a valued personal relationship, a highly desired success, or a gratifying sense of bodily integrity. A fantasied loss is an unrealistic concern that causes people to feel deprived in the absence of any apparent basis. Feelings of being rejected, having failed, or becoming unattractive, arising without solid basis in fact, are among the common fantasied losses that contribute to depression.

The distinction between real and fantasied loss in the origin of depression provides a basis for distinguishing between **reactive** and **endogenous depressions.** Real losses tend to precipitate reactive depressions, in which the depressing circumstances are readily identifiable. Like grief, reactive depression tends to be a self-limiting condition that heals with the passage of time and the replacement of lost objects and goals with new ones. The outcome of fantasied loss is likely to be an endogenous depression, in which the origins of the distress are often not apparent to the depressed person or to untrained observers. Endogenous depression is a chronic and lingering condition in which professional help is especially likely to be necessary to help the person unravel and take a more realistic view of the concerns that are depressing him or her (Easson, 1977; Endicott & Spitzer, 1979; Nelson & Charney, 1980; Strober et al., 1981).

Whatever the extent of a loss, whether real or fantasied, people differ in how they respond to it. What seem to be equivalent losses may cause one person to experience an overwhelming sense of deprivation and become deeply depressed, while another person takes the loss in stride without showing any adverse reaction. Aside from genetic factors that may affect a person's disposition to becoming depressed, such individual variation in sensitivity to loss appears due to certain kinds of developmental experiences. The nature of these experiences has been formulated somewhat differently by three influential theorists—Beck, Seligman, and Lewinsohn—whose views underlie most of the experimental work currently being done on depressive disorder.

Beck (1970, 1974) provides a *cognitive* model in which negative thoughts and attitudes are seen as the core feature of depression. Beck acknowledges that a sense of loss is the key event in people becoming depressed, but for him loss consists of coming to regard oneself as lacking some attribute that is considered essential to being happy. People become depression-prone, he concludes, when they have encountered unfavorable life situations that have disposed them to overreact to being deprived.

In this regard, numerous studies suggest that the disposition to becoming depressed in the face of loss is directly related to childhood experiences of parental deprivation that have sensitized a person to such losses (Blatt, Wein, Chevron, & Quinlan, 1979; Crook & Eliot, 1980; Jacobson, Fasman, & DiMascio, 1975; Seligman, Gleser, Rauh, & Harris, 1974). Parental deprivation does not necessarily follow from growing up in a broken home, however, even though such an assumption is often made. A child who is reared by one loving and devoted parent will experience much less deprivation than a child who lives with two parents, both of whom dislike or ignore the child. Actually depriving early experience, not just the absence of one parent from the home because of death, divorce, or separation, is the unfavorable developmental event that is likely to dispose youngsters to becoming depressed later.

Seligman (1974, 1975) formulates depression in terms of *learned helplessness.* Learned helplessness consists of the belief that one's actions have little impact on one's destiny. Children who learn helplessness as a way of viewing the world tend to attribute disappointment and failure to factors beyond their control, such as the behavior of others or their own lack of ability. Youngsters who grow into late childhood and adolescence believing that they have little control over their circumstances are inclined to respond to problem situations by feeling unable to cope and becoming depressed (Depue & Monroe, 1978; Dweck, 1979; Miller & Seligman, 1975).

Within this framework the experience of loss that precipitates depression is a loss of control. Accordingly, Seligman emphasizes that it is not merely unfavorable life experiences that dispose a person to become depressed, but experiences of lacking control over unhappy circumstances and not being able to do anything about them.

Lewinsohn (1974a, 1974b) presents a *behavioral* model in which depression represents the inability of a person to behave in ways that result in positive reinforcement. What the depressed person lacks from this point of view is an adequate repertoire of rewarding activities. Accordingly, people become disposed to depression when their developmental experiences provide them insufficient opportunity to learn gratifying ways of responding to people and events. As is always true of models attempting to account for the same phenomenon, these cognitive, learned-helplessness, and behavioral explanations of depression are not mutually exclusive. Each can be formulated in terms of the other, as in referring to a reduction in rewarding activity (behavioral) as reflecting an anticipation (cognitive) of failure (helplessness). Each, however, suggests useful directions for exploring the dimensions of a sense of loss.

Finally, the role of loss in causing depression helps to account for the rapid increase in the frequency of this disorder during adolescence. As reviewed earlier, the normal developmental process presents teenagers with many real losses and threats to their sense of adequacy. Dramatic bodily changes disrupt their sense of knowing themselves and cause doubts about their physical attractiveness. Societal expectations require them to loosen their ties to their parents and form new kinds of peer and heterosexual relationships. They must begin to take major responsibility for running their lives and planning their futures. Although adolescents typically welcome the prerogatives that such maturation brings, few can escape some qualms about giving up the protected position of their childhood and placing their self-esteem on the line in new social and achievement-related situations (Dwyer & Mayer, 1969; Weiner, 1977). Hence adolescence, like other transitional stages in the life cycle that involve major biological alterations and learning to live without previous sources of gratification, increases a person's susceptibility to becoming depressed (Benedek, 1975; Feinstein, 1975; Laufer, 1966).

Little clinical or research attention comparable to the work done on experiential factors in depression has yet been paid to manic episodes. Given the fact the primary mania occurs very frequently in people who also suffer episodes of depression, it may be that a stressful experience of loss precipitates both poles of bipolar affective disorder. If this is so, mania would arise in part as an effort to ward off depression subsequent to loss, and manic-depressive individuals would slide into depression at times when they were unable to muster or sustain manic behavior patterns. Confirmation of this or some other as yet unformulated hypothesis about experiential factors in mania will have to await systematic research.

TREATMENT OF AFFECTIVE DISORDER

Although affective disorder sometimes occurs as a lifetime susceptibility to recurring episodes of disturbance, the vast majority of cases show **spontaneous remission;**

that is, people tend to recover from even severe bouts of depression and mania within 6 to 18 months, without treatment (Brumback & Weinberg, 1977; Spitzer, Endicott, & Robins, 1978; Weissman & Myers, 1978). In this respect, affective disorder differs considerably from the conditions considered in the preceding chapters: mental retardation and minimal brain dysfunction/attention deficit disorder are chronic and persistent disorders, and childhood psychosis and schizophrenia carry a generally unfavorable long-term prognosis, especially in the absence of extensive treatment. In one long-term follow-up of several hundred adults who had been hospitalized with psychological disorders, 50 percent of the manic and 61 percent of the depressed patients subsequently achieved good psychiatric status, compared to only 20 percent of the schizophrenics; at the other end of the scale, subsequently poor overall adjustment was found in 54 percent of the schizophrenics but only 21 percent of the manics and 30 percent of the depressives (Tsuang, Woolson, & Fleming, 1979).

An apparent exception to this relatively good prognosis in affective disorder occurs when it begins in adolescence and is so incapacitating as to require hospital care. Preliminary findings with a small sample suggest that only about one-third of adolescents hospitalized with unipolar depression will recover completely, without further recurrences, and that those who are seriously incapacitated with bipolar disorder will almost always show a continuing course of disturbance (Welner, Welner, & Fishman, 1979).

Even when the outlook in affective disorder is favorable—as it is in that large majority of disturbed young people who do not have to be hospitalized—appropriate intervention can still help to shorten episodes of depression or mania and thereby limit the suffering experienced by young people and their families. Depending on the individual case, effective treatment includes various combinations of psychotherapy, environmental manipulation, and drug therapy. Because youthful mania has only recently begun to receive professional attention, very little is yet known or has even been suggested concerning its treatment other than by drugs. The first two sections that follow, on psychotherapy and environmental manipulation, accordingly speak only to treating depression.

Psychotherapy

As noted earlier, depressed youngsters are responding to experiences of loss that have caused a sense of being lacking or deprived. The origin of depression in experienced loss has two widely accepted implications for treating it psychologically. First, by entering depressed youngsters' lives as someone genuinely wanting to help, a therapist can reduce their feelings of being cut off from others and thereby begin to relieve their depression. Second, recovery from depression can be hastened by helping depressed youngsters come effectively to grips with the particular circumstances that are causing them to experience a sense of loss (Arieti & Bemporad, 1978, Chapter 15; Feinstein, 1975; Gilpin, 1976; Toolan, 1978; Weiner, 1975).

When loss has been experienced in relation to a real event, such as a broken friendship or failure in school, resulting depression often responds to relatively superficial discussions that help youngsters see the loss as less tragic, less permanent, and less irreparable than they have thought. If the sense of loss stems from fantasied or unrealistic concerns, however, especially when the young person is not fully aware of them, then more intensive exploration may be necessary to identify and get a less troubling perspective on the problem. Consistent with Beck's cognitive formulation of depression, he labels this effort to promote more realistic perspectives as "cognitive therapy" for depression (Beck, 1970, 1979; Zeiss, Lewinsohn, & Munoz, 1979).

Although tracing and resolving a sense of loss holds the key to psychological treatment of depression, a young person's presenting symptoms cannot be ignored in the process. Over time these symptoms can become so habitual that they persist even after the depressive concerns that prompted them have been dispelled. Hence these symptoms require direct treatment along with the therapist's efforts to provide depressed youngsters with a meaningful relationship and to help them work through their sense of loss.

For example, in combating lowered self-esteem and reduced energy levels, therapists need to find ways of getting depressed youngsters moving again. This involves learning where their talents lie, what situations they have enjoyed or done well in previously, and what remaining embers of aspiration might still be stirred into some blaze of enthusiasm. Any progress they can be encouraged to make in one or more of these directions creates an opportunity for pleasurable experience and drives a wedge into their symptomatic pattern of lethargy and self-depreciation. Each step a depressed youngster takes toward engagement in rewarding pursuits promises to replace apathy with activity and alienation with commitment.

Similarly, youngsters who have turned to problem behavior to escape feeling depressed need encouragement to give up these maladaptive efforts at avoiding psychological pain. Behavior change can rarely be legislated simply by a therapist or anyone else telling youngsters what they should or should not do, however. Instead, therapists require sufficient skill to demonstrate that symptomatic behavior is self-defeating, that it costs a personal price too great to justify any pleasure it gives, and that acting otherwise would be in these youngsters' own best interests. Such intrinsic motivation to change, once instilled, is far more powerful than pleas, promises, or threats in getting young people to give up problem behavior.

Environmental Manipulation

Psychotherapists can sometimes bring about changes in how a young person is being treated at home, in school, and in the community. To the extent that these changes diminish the frustration or disappointment depressed youngsters are experiencing, they can help relieve their distress; to the extent that they increase their opportunities for gratifying experiences, they can bolster their self-esteem and promote increased activity.

The best avenue for such constructive environmental manipulation is through discussions with the parents. Parents of depressed youngsters are often perplexed by what is going on. Often they alternate between being tense and anxious about why their child is feeling or acting as he or she is and being angry and resentful about it ("Why are you making things so difficult for us?"). Helping parents to understand how and why their child is depressed can reduce their tension, and convincing them of their child's needs for increased attention, affection, and reassurance can lead them to provide a more supportive home environment. Parents are not always able and willing to change their behavior in response to such counsel, but any step they can take in the right direction will help their youngster overcome his or her depression more quickly than might otherwise be possible.

Discussions with teachers and other adults in the community who figure prominently in a youngster's life may similarly help them recognize ways in which they can present fewer frustrations and provide more rewards. Environmental manipulation has its limits, of course. The world cannot be entirely reshaped to meet a disturbed youngster's needs, and therapists have neither the right nor the authority to determine how other people will conduct their lives. Nevertheless, new information and appropriate suggestions from a therapist, followed by some compromise and accommodation by key figures in the environment, have considerable potential for hastening a young person's recovery from depressive episodes.

Regrettably, few research findings can be added to this description of psychotherapy and environmental manipulation, which is based largely on clinical experience. Controlled studies of the effectiveness of psychological treatment of depressed children and adolescents are virtually nonexistent. As a reflection of this lamentable state of affairs, a recent handbook on the treatment of mental disorders in young people (Wolman, 1978) does not include a chapter or even part of a chapter on depression, and depression is not mentioned in a recent comprehensive review of research on psychotherapy with children (Barrett, Hampe, & Miller, 1978).

Drug Therapy

Some clinicians strongly advocate using antidepressant medication in treating depressed children (Frommer, 1967), whereas others state flatly that drugs are of little benefit (Krakowski, 1970; Lucas, 1977). Unfortunately, little research has yet been done that can help resolve this difference of opinion. Available studies deal for the most part either with individual cases or with mixed groups of youngsters with varied disturbances; the most that can be said is that no clear antidepressant drug effect in children with primary depression has yet been demonstrated (Campbell & Small, 1978; Conners & Werry, 1979; Rapoport, 1977).

When medication is used in treating depression in young people, the drugs most commonly prescribed are the **tricyclics,** which bear some chemical resemblance to the antipsychotic phenothiazines mentioned in Chapter 6 and have a demonstrable antidepressant effect in adults (Denber, 1979; Prange, 1975). Of the tricyclics, the most frequently chosen is **imipramine,** sold under the trade name of **Trofranil;** unlike many drugs powerful enough to relieve adult symptoms, imipramine has no serious side effects in children when cautiously used (Lucas, 1977). Studies with adults indicate that whereas both drugs and psychotherapy are effective in treating depression, a combination of the two produces even better results than either used alone (DiMascio, Weissman, Prusoff, Neu, Zwilling, & Klerman, 1979; Weissman, 1979). This finding also needs confirmation with respect to youthful patients.

For young people with mania, the most effective treatment currently known is lithium, the drug mentioned earlier in the chapter. Lithium has been consistently found to curb manic behavior in adults, and several studies indicate that it is equally effective in older children and adolescents, without untoward side effects (Carlson, 1978; Davis, 1979; Horowitz, 1977; Youngerman & Canino, 1978). This positive effect of lithium appears due to its acting as a mood stabilizer. Accordingly, it has also proved helpful in reducing excitable, explosive, or impulsive behavior in adolescents independently or whether they appear to have a primarily manic disorder (Lena, 1979; Lucas, 1977).

SUMMARY

Affective disorder consists of maladaptive changes in a person's *mood, attitudes, energy level,* and *physical status.* Unipolar affective disorder is manifest in episodes of depression that become more profound or last longer than events would seem to justify; bipolar affective disorder involves similarly persistent episodes of mania or of both mania and depression.

Approximately 25 percent of people born in the United States will suffer a diagnosable depressive reaction during their lifetime, and at any one point in time close to 6 percent of American adults are definitely depressed. Similarly precise figures are not available for children and adolescents. Although various surveys suggest that depression plays a prominent role in the psychological disturbances of young people, systematic prevalence studies of younger age groups using reliable diagnostic criteria for depression are just starting to be done.

In mental health facilities very few children, just under 5 percent of adolescents, and about 20 percent of adults are diagnosed as having a primary depressive disorder. This percentage increases sharply during the adolescent years, which might appear to suggest that disturbed individuals become gradually more likely to show primary depression as they mature through the adolescent years into adulthood. However, there is reason to believe that clinicians in the past have avoided diagnosing depression in young people because of preconceived notions that it is primarily an adult disturbance. Newer views of depression and recent studies of disturbed children contradict this earlier view, and future reports of recorded diagnoses are likely to show a greater percentage of depressed children and adolescents than appears in current data.

Female patients beginning at age 10 are more likely to be diagnosed depressed than male patients. This sex difference, which appears due to elements of the traditional female role in our society, becomes gradually more pronounced during the adolescent years and is most marked for adults, among whom females are more than twice as likely as males to be treated for depression.

Bipolar affective disorder with some form of manic episode is much less frequent than depression, occurring in just 1.2 percent of the population during their lifetime. Mania has typically been ignored in prevalence reports on younger people; even more so than depression, it has traditionally been viewed as an adult disorder. Recent studies show that 20 to 35 percent of manic-depressive adults first become disturbed when they are age 10 to 19, and other research is beginning to suggest that bipolar affective disorder has been substantially underdiagnosed in adolescents.

Certain dimensions of disturbance characterize depression and mania at all ages. First, affective disorders are predominantly disorders of mood. Pathologically depressed moods typically involve feelings of sadness, spells of tearfulness and crying, loss of interest in people and previously enjoyed pursuits, and a diminished ability to experience pleasure. Manic moods, by contrast, are reflected in joyfulness, constant smiling and ready laughter, infectious good humor, and abundant enthusiasm and pleasure in living.

Second, depressed people harbor negative attitudes toward themselves, the world, and the future, as a result of which they show low self-esteem, pervasive pessimism, and a sense of helplessness and hopelessness. Mania, on the other hand, is characterized by positive attitudes involving inflated self-esteem, unrealistically high expectations, and an uncritical sense of optimism.

Third, energy level becomes depleted in depression, leaving the person lethargic and apathetic and often producing psychomotor retardation. In mania, more energy is available than can be harnessed effectively, leading to disorganized activity and such phenomena as *pressure of speech* and *flight of ideas*.

Fourth, the onset of affective disorder often brings changes in physical status, especially in sleeping patterns, appetite, and sense of well-being. People who are depressed tend to sleep poorly, to undereat or overeat with marked loss or gain in weight, and to experience an unusual number of physical complaints that make them worry about being in poor health. Manic individuals, by contrast, sleep soundly, eat heartily but not too much, and consider themselves to be in the pink of condition.

Although each of these dimensions of depression and mania occurs in children and adolescents as well as in adults, the most prominent symptoms of affective disorder vary somewhat with age. Infants and young children sometimes show depressive behavior, especially when they lack adequate stimulation or are separated from their parents. However, these depressive-like states are usually referred to as "deprivation" or "social isolation" syndromes, because not until age 5 or 6 do children develop the cognitive maturity and language skills necessary to experience and communicate the kinds of attitudes that constitute an important dimension of affective disorder.

Elementary school children, who still lack mature capacity to verbalize their moods and attitudes, frequently manifest affective disorder through changes in their physical status. When disturbances of mood and attitude do occur, the former tend to be more common up to the age of 8 or so and the latter thereafter. From puberty to age 15 or 16 the developmental needs of young people make it difficult for them to admit self-critical attitudes. Younger adolescents with an affective disorder are therefore more likely to show easily recognizable signs of mania than of depression. When depressed they frequently express their disorder in efforts to ward it off through restlessness, a flight to or from people, or problem behavior.

As they mature, adolescents become increasingly capable of thinking about themselves critically and sharing these thoughts with others. They accordingly become more likely to resemble adults in both their depressive and manic symptoms should they develop an affective disorder. In some cases, however, older adolescents still express depression indirectly, through such maladaptive behavior as drug abuse, sexual promiscuity, alienation, and suicide.

Affective disorder is caused by the interaction of a certain level of genetic or constitutional disposition (diasthesis) and certain kinds of unpleasant experience (stress). The more closely two people are related, the more likely they are to be concordant for affective disorder; studies of twins reared apart and of children placed for adoption shortly after birth indicate that this familial incidence is due at least in part to genetic factors and cannot be accounted for solely by common experiences shared by family members. Genetic disposition contributes to both bipolar and unipolar affective disorder, although familial concordance is somewhat greater for manic-depressive conditions than for depression alone.

With respect to stress, depressive disorders emerge primarily in response to the experience of loss. Actual events that deprive people of something important to them (*real* losses) tend to produce *reactive* depressions, which are self-limiting conditions that heal with the passage of time and the replacement of lost objects and goals with new ones. Unrealistic concerns that cause people to feel deprived in the absence of any apparent basis (*fantasied* losses) result in *endogenous* depressions, which tend to be chronic and lingering conditions that are especially likely to require professional help.

Aside from genetic factors that may affect a person's disposition to becoming depressed, certain kinds of developmental experiences influence how sensitive people are to loss. As formulated in *cognitive, learned helplessness,* and *behavioral* models of depression, these early events that cause later susceptibility to depression involve experiences of viewing oneself as lacking or deprived, of being unable to control one's destiny, and of lacking a repertoire of rewarding activities. Little comparable clinical or research attention has yet been paid to experiential factors that precipitate manic episodes or dispose people to suffer them.

Affective disorders are by nature cyclical, and both depressive and manic episodes often show recovery without treatment. Appropriate intervention can shorten such episodes. Psychotherapy can hasten the recovery of depressed youngsters by providing a new, helpful relationship in the person of the therapist and by assisting them to come effectively to grips with the particular circumstances that have caused them to experience a sense of loss. Of further benefit is direct attention to such presenting symptoms as low self-esteem or problem behavior to prevent them from becoming habitual.

Environmental manipulation, to the extent that it can diminish frustration or disappointment that depressed youngsters are experiencing at home or in school, helps further to reduce the length and severity of their disorder.

Little information is available concerning psychological treatment of manic children and adolescents. Drug therapy, which has not yet been demonstrated as effective in treating depressed youngsters, has had wide acceptance in treating mania. *Lithium,* a mood stabilizer, has proved especially helpful in reducing excitable behavior in both adolescents and adults, without untoward side effects.

REFERENCES

ALBERT, N., & BECK, A. T. Incidence of depression in early adolescence: A preliminary study. *Journal of Youth and Adolescence,* 1975, *4,* 301–308.

ALLEN, M. Twin studies of affective illness. *Archives of General Psychiatry,* 1976, *33,* 1476–1478.

AKISKAL, H. S., ROSENTHAL, R. H., ROSENTHAL, T. L., KASHGARIAN, M., KHANI, M. K., & PUZ-

ANTIAN, V. R. Differentiation of primary affective illness from situational, symptomatic, and secondary depressions. *Archives of General Psychiatry,* 1979, *36,* 635–643.

AMERICAN PSYCHIATRIC ASSOCIATION. *Diagnostic and statistical manual of mental disorders.* (3d ed.) Washington, D.C.: American Psychiatric Association, 1980.

ANDREASEN, N. C., & WINOKUR, G. Secondary depression: Familial, clinical, and research perspectives. *American Journal of Psychiatry,* 1979, *136,* 62–66.

ANTHONY, E. J. Childhood depression. In E. J. Anthony & T. Benedek (Eds.), *Depression and human existence.* Boston: Little, Brown, 1975.

ANTHONY, E. J., & SCOTT, P. Manic-depressive psychosis in childhood. *Journal of Child Psychology and Psychiatry,* 1960, *1,* 53–72.

ANTHONY, H. S. The association of violence and depression in a sample of young offenders. *British Journal of Criminology,* 1968, *3,* 346–365.

ANTONOVSKY, H. F., SHOHAM, I., KAVENAKI, S., LANCET, M., & MODAN, M. Gender differences in patterns of adolescent sexual behavior. *Journal of Youth and Adolescence,* 1980, *9,* 127–141.

ARAJARVI, T., & HUTTUNEN, M. Encopresis and enuresis as symptoms of depression. In A. L. Annell (Ed.), *Depressive states in childhood and adolescence.* Stockholm: Almqvist & Wiksell, 1972.

ARIETI, S., & BEMPORAD, J. *Severe and mild depression.* New York: Basic Books, 1978.

BARRETT, C. L., HAMPE, E., & MILLER, L. Research on psychotherapy with children. In S. L. Garfield & A. E. Bergin (Eds.), *Handbook of psychotherapy and behavior change* (2nd ed.). New York: Wiley, 1978.

BECK, A. T. *Depression: Causes and treatment.* Philadelphia: University of Pennsylvania Press, 1970.

BECK, A. T. Cognition, affect, and psychopathology. *Archives of General Psychiatry,* 1971, *24,* 495–500.

BECK, A. T. The development of depression: a cognitive model. In R. J. Friedman & M. M. Katz (Eds.), *The psychology of depression.* Washington, D.C.: Winston, 1974.

BECK, A. T. *Cognitive therapy of depression.* New York: Guilford Press, 1979.

BEMIS, K. M. Current approaches to the etiology and treatment of anorexia nervosa. *Psychological Bulletin,* 1978, *85,* 593–617.

BENEDEK, T. Depression during the life cycle. In E. J. Anthony & T. Benedek (Eds.), *Depression and human existence.* Boston: Little, Brown, 1975.

BERLIN, I. N. Some implications of the development processes for treatment of depression in adolescence. In A. French & I. Berlin (Eds.), *Depression in children and adolescents.* New York: Human Sciences Press, 1979.

BIBRING, E. The mechanism of depression. In P. Greenacre (Ed.), *Affective disorders.* New York: International Universities Press, 1953.

BINDER, J., & KROHN, A. Sexual acting out as an abortive mourning process in female adolescent inpatients. *Psychiatric Quarterly,* 1974, *48,* 193–208.

BLATT, S. J., WEIN, S. J., CHEVRON, E., & QUINLAN, D. M. Parental representations and depression in normal young adults. *Journal of Abnormal Psychology,* 1979, *88,* 388–397.

BLUMBERG, M. L. Depression in children on a general pediatric service. *American Journal of Psychotherapy,* 1978, *32,* 20–32.

BONNARD, A. Truancy and pilfering associated with bereavement. In S. Lorand & H. I. Schneer (Eds.), *Adolescents: Psychoanalytic approaches* to problems and therapy. New York: Hoeber, 1961.

BROWN, G. W., & HARRIS, T. *Social origins of depression: A study of psychiatric disorder in women.* New York: Free Press, 1978.

BRUCH, H. Anorexia nervosa in adolescence. In J. R. Gallagher, F. P. Heald, & D. C. Garell (Eds.), *Medical care of the adolescent* (3d ed.). New York: Appleton-Century-Crofts, 1976.

BRUMBACK, R. A., DIETZ-SCHMIDT, S. G., & WEINBERG, W. A. Depression in children referred to an educational diagnostic center: Diagnosis and treatment. *Diseases of the Nervous System,* 1977, *38,* 529–535.

BRUMBACK, R. A., & WEINBERG, W. A. Childhood depression: An explanation of a behavior disorder of children. *Perceptual and Motor Skills,* 1977, *44,* 911–916.

BURKS, H. L., & HARRISON, S. I. Aggressive behavior as a means of avoiding depression. *American Journal of Orthopsychiatry,* 1962, *32,* 416–422.

CADORET, R. J. Evidence for genetic inheritance of primary affective disorder in adoptees. *American Journal of Psychiatry,* 1978, *135,* 463–466.

CAMBOR, C. G. Adolescent alienation syndrome. In J. C. Schoolar (Ed.), *Current issues in adolescent psychiatry.* New York: Brunner/Mazel, 1973.

CAMPBELL, M., & SMALL, A. M. Chemotherapy. In B. B. Wolman (Ed.), *Handbook of treatment of mental disorders in childhood and adolescence.* Englewood Cliffs, N.J.: Prentice-Hall, 1978.

CANTWELL, D. P., & CARLSON, G. Problems and prospects in the study of childhood depression. *Journal of Nervous and Mental Disease,* 1979, *167,* 522–529.

CARLSON, G. A. Lithium carbonate use in adolescents: Clinical indications and management. In S. C. Feinstein & P. L. Giovacchini (Eds.), *Adolescent psychiatry.* Vol. VII. Chicago: University of Chicago Press, 1979.

CARLSON, G. A., & CANTWELL, D. P. A survey of depressive symptoms in a child and adolescent psychiatric population—interview data. *Journal of the American Academy of Child Psychiatry,* 1979, *18,* 587–599.

CARLSON, G. A., & CANTWELL, D. P. A survey of depressive symptoms, syndrome and disorder in a child psychiatric population. *Journal of Child Psychology and Psychiatry,* 1980a, *21,* 19–25.

CARLSON, G. A., & CANTWELL, D. P. Unmasking masked depression in children and adolescents. *American Journal of Psychiatry,* 1980b, *137,* 445–449.

CARLSON, G. A., DAVENPORT, Y. B., & JAMISON, K. A comparison of outcome in adolescent and late onset bipolar manic-depression illness. *American Journal of Psychiatry,* 1977, *134,* 919–922.

CARLSON, G. A., & STROBER, M. Manic-depressive illness in early adolescence. *Journal of the American Academy of Child Psychiatry,* 1978, *17,* 138–154.

CARLSON, G., & STROBER, M. Affective disorders in adolescence. *Psychiatric Clinics of North America,* 1979, *2,* 511–526.

CASS, L. K., & THOMAS, C. B. *Childhood pathology and later adjustment.* New York: Wiley, 1979.

CHEVRON, E. S., QUINLAN, D. M., & BLATT, S. J. Sex roles and gender differences in the experience of depression. *Journal of Abnormal Psychology,* 1978, *87,* 680–683.

COHEN, R. A. Manic-depressive illness. In A. M. Freedman, H. I. Kaplan, & B. J. Sadock (Eds.), *Comprehensive textbook of psychiatry.* (2nd ed.) Baltimore: Williams & Wilkins, 1975.

CONNORS, C. K., & WERRY, J. S. Pharmacotherapy. In H. D. Quay & J. S. Werry (Eds.), *Psychopathological disorders of childhood.* (2nd ed.) New York: Wiley, 1979.

COSTELLO, C. G. Childhood depression: Three basic but questionable assumptions in the Lefkowitz and Burton critique. *Psychological Bulletin,* 1980, *87,* 195–190.

CROOK, T., & ELIOT, J. Parental death during childhood and adult depression: A critical review of the literature. *Psychological Bulletin,* 1980, 87, 252–259.

CYTRYN, L., & MCKNEW, D. H. Affective disorders. In J. D. Noshpitz (Ed.), *Basic handbook of child psychiatry.* Vol. 2. New York: Basic Books, 1979.

CYTRYN, L., MCKNEW, D. H., & BUNNEY, W. E. Diagnosis of depression in children: A reassessment. *American Journal of Psychiatry,* 1980, *137,* 22–25.

DANIEL, W. A. Obesity. In W. A. Daniel (Ed.) *The adolescent patient.* St. Louis: Mosby, 1970.

DAVIS, R. E. Manic-depressive variant syndrome of childhood: A preliminary report. *American Journal of Psychiatry,* 1979, *136,* 702–706.

DENBER, H. C. B. The pharmacologic treatment of depression. *American Journal of Psychotherapy,* 1979, *33,* 96–106.

DEPUE, R. A., & MONROE, S. M. Learned helplessness and the perspective of the depressive disorders: Conceptual and definitional issues. *Journal of Abnormal Psychology,* 1978, *87,* 3–20.

DIEPOLD, J., & YOUNG, R. D. Empirical studies of adolescent sexual behavior: A critical review. *Adolescence,* 1979, *14,* 45–64.

DIMASCIO, A., WEISSMAN, M. M., PRUSOFF, B. A., NEU, C., ZWILLING, M., & KLERMAN, G. L. Differential symptom reduction by drugs and psychotherapy in acute depression. *Archives of General Psychiatry,* 1979, *36,* 1450–1456.

DUNNER, D., FLEISS, J., & FIEVE, R. The course of development of mania in patients with recurrent depression. *American Journal of Psychiatry,* 1976, *133,* 905–908.

DUNNER, D. L., PATRICK, V., & FIEVE, R. R. Life events at the onset of bipolar affective illness. *American Journal of Psychiatry,* 1979, *136,* 508–511.

DWECK, C. S. Learned helplessness: A developmental approach. In J. G. Schulterbrandt & A. Raskin (Eds.), *Depression in childhood.* New York: Raven Press, 1977.

DWYER, J., & MAYER, J. Psychological effects of variations in physical appearance during adolescence. *Adolescence,* 1969, *3,* 353–380.

EASSON, W. H. Depression in adolescence. In S. C. Feinstein & P. Giovacchini (Eds.), *Adolescent psychiatry.* Vol. V. New York: Aronson, 1977.

ELKIND, D., & WEINER, I. B. *Development of the child.* New York: Wiley, 1978.

ENDICOTT, J., & SPITZER, R. L. A diagnostic interview: The schedule for affective disorders and schizophrenia. *Archives of General Psychiatry,* 1978, *35,* 837–844.

ENDICOTT, J., & SPITZER, R. L. Use of the Research Diagnostic Criteria and the Schedule for Affective Disorders and Schizophrenia to study affective disorders. *American Journal of Psychiatry,* 1979, *136,* 52–56.

FEINSTEIN, S. C. Adolescent depression. In E. J. Anthony & T. Benedek (Eds.), *Depression and human existence.* Boston: Little, Brown, 1975.

FEINSTEIN, S., & WOLPERT, E. A. Juvenile manic depressive illness. *Journal of the American Academy of Child Psychiatry,* 1973, *12,* 123–136.

FREUD, S. (1917) Mourning and melancholia. *Standard Edition,* Vol. XIV. London: Hogarth, 1957.

FROMMER, E. A. Treatment of childhood depression with antidepressant drugs. *British Medical Journal,* 1967, *1,* 729–732.

GERSHON, E. S., BUNNEY, W. E., LECKMAN, J. F., VANEERDEWEGH, M., DEBAUCHE, B. A. The inheritance of affective disorders: A review of data and of hypotheses. *Behavior Genetics,* 1976, *6,* 227–261.

GILPIN, D. C. Psychotherapy of the depressed child. In E. J. Anthony & D. C. Gilpin (Eds.), *Three clinical faces of childhood.* New York: Halsted, 1976.

GITTELMAN-KLEIN, R. Definitional and methodological issues concerning depressive illness in children. In J. G. Schulterbrandt & A. Raskin (Eds.), *Depression in childhood.* New York: Raven Press, 1977.

GLASER, K. Masked depression in children and adolescents. *American Journal of Psychotherapy,* 1967, *21,* 565–574.

GOODWIN, F. K., & ZIS, A. P. Lithium in the treatment of mania. *Archives of General Psychiatry,* 1979, *36,* 840–844.

HARTMANN, D. A study of drug-taking adolescents. *Psychoanalytic Study of the Child,* 1969, *24,* 384–398.

HOROWITZ, H. A. Lithium and the treatment of adolescent manic depressive illness. *Diseases of the Nervous System,* 1977, *38,* 480–483.

HUDGENS, R. W. *Psychiatric disorders in adolescents.* Baltimore: Williams & Wilkins, 1974.

INAMDAR, S. C., SIOMOPOULOS, G., OSBORN, M., & BIANCHI, E. C. Phenomenology associated with depressed moods in adolescents. *American Journal of Psychiatry,* 1979, *136,* 156–159.

JACOBS, J. *Adolescent suicide.* New York: Wiley, 1971.

JACOBSON, S., FASMAN, J., & DIMASCIO, A. Deprivation in the childhood of depressed women. *Journal of Nervous and Mental Disease,* 1975, *160,* 5–14.

JOHNSON, G. F. S., & LEEMAN, M. M. Analysis of familial factors in bipolar affective illness. *Archives of General Psychiatry,* 1977, *34,* 1074–1083.

KLERMAN, G. L., & BARRETT, J. E. Clinical and epidemiological aspects of affective disorders. In S. Gershon & B. Shopsin (Eds.), *Lithium: Its role in psychiatric research and treatment.* New York: Plenum, 1973.

KOVACKS, M., & BECK, A. T. An empirical-clinical approach toward a definition of childhood depression. In J. G. Schulterbrandt & A. Raskin (Eds.), *Depression in childhood.* New York: Raven Press, 1977.

KRAEPELIN, E. *Manic-depressive insanity and paranoia.* Edinburgh: E & S Livingston, 1921.

KRAKOWSKI, A. J. Depressive reactions of childhood and adolescence. *Psychosomatics,* 1970, *11,* 429–433.

KRAUTHAMMER, C., & KLERMAN, G. L. Secondary mania. *Archives of General Psychiatry,* 1978, *35,* 1333–1339.

LAUFER, M. Object loss and mourning during adolescence. *Psychoanalytic Study of the Child,* 1966, *21,* 269–293.

LEFKOWITZ, M. M. Discussion of Dr. Gittelman-Klein's chapter. In J. G. Schulterbrandt & A. Raskin (Eds.), *Depression in childhood: Diagnosis, treatment, and conceptual models.* New York: Raven Press, 1977.

LEFKOWITZ, M. M., & BURTON, N. Childhood depression: A critique of the concept. *Psychological Bulletin,* 1978, *85,* 716–726.

LEFKOWITZ, M. M., & TESINY, E. P. Assessment of childhood depression. *Journal of Consulting and Clinical Psychology,* 1980, *48,* 43–50.

LENA, B. Lithium in child and adolescent psychiatry. *Archives of General Psychiatry,* 1979, *36,* 854–855.

LEON, G. R., KENDALL, P. C., & GARBER, J. Depression in children: Parent, teacher, and child perspectives. *Journal of Abnormal Child Psychology,* 1980, *8,* 221–235.

LESSE, S. Behavioral problems masking severe depression—Cultural and clinical survey. *American Journal of Psychotherapy,* 1979, *33,* 41–53.

LEVY, N. J. The use of drugs by teenagers for sanctuary and illusion. *American Journal of Psychoanalysis,* 1968, *28,* 48–56.

LEWINSOHN, P. M. A behavioral approach to depression. In R. J. Friedman & M. M. Katz (Eds.), *The psychology of depression.* Washington, D.C.: Winston, 1974a.

LEWINSOHN, P. M. Clinical and theoretical aspects of depression. In K. S. Calhoun, H. E. Adams, & K. M. Mitchell (Eds.), *Innovative treatment methods in psychopathology.* New York: Wiley, 1974b.

LING, W., OFTEDAL, G., & WEINBERG, W. Depressive illness in childhood presenting as severe headache. *American Journal of Diseases of Children.* 1970, *120,* 122–124.

LORANGER, A. W., & LEVINE, P. M. Age at onset of bipolar affective illness. *Archives of General Psychiatry.* 1978, *11,* 1345–1348.

LUCAS, A. R. The treatment of depressive states. In J. M. Wiener (Ed.), *Psychopharmacology in childhood and adolescence.* New York: Basic Books, 1977.

MCCONVILLE, B. J., BOAG, L. C., & PURHOIT, A. P. Three types of childhood depression. *Canadian Psychiatric Association Journal,* 1973, *18,* 133–138.

MCGLOTHLIN, W. H. Drug use and abuse. *Annual Review of Psychology,* 1975, *26,* 45–64.

MALMQUIST, C. P. Depression in childhood. In F. F. Flach & S. C. Draghi (Eds.), *The nature and treatment of depression.* New York: Wiley, 1975.

MALMQUIST, C. P. The theoretical status of depressions in childhood. In E. J. Anthony & D. C. Gilpin (Eds.), *Three clinical faces of childhood.* New York: Halsted, 1976.

MALMQUIST, C. P. Childhood depression: A clinical and behavioral perspective. In J. G. Schulterbrandt & A. Raskin (Eds.), *Depression in childhood.* New York: Raven Press, 1977.

MASTERSON, J. F. *The psychiatric dilemma of adolescence.* Boston: Little, Brown, 1967.

MENTAL HEALTH STATISTICAL NOTE NO. 148. Changes in the age, sex, and diagnostic composition of additions to state and county mental hospitals, United States, 1969–1975. Washington, D.C.: U.S. Department of Health, Education, and Welfare, 1978.

MILLER, W. R. Psychological deficit in depression. *Psychological Bulletin,* 1975, *82,* 238–260.

MILLER, W., & SELIGMAN, M. E. P. Depression and learned helplessness in man. *Journal of Abnormal Psychology,* 1975, *84,* 228–238.

MINKOFF, K., BERGMAN, E., BECK, A. T., & BECK, R. Hopelessness, depression, and attempted suicide. *American Journal of Psychiatry,* 1973, *130,* 455–459.

NELSON, J. C., & CHARNEY, D. S. Primary affective disorder criteria and the endogenous-reactive distinction. *Archives of General Psychiatry,* 1980, *37,* 787–793.

OUTPATIENT PSYCHIATRIC SERVICES. Washington, D.C.: U.S. Department of Health, Education and Welfare, Public Health Service Publication No. 1982, 1979.

OUTPATIENT PSYCHIATRIC SERVICES. Distribution of admissions by primary diagnosis and age, 1975. Rockville, Md.: National Institute of Mental Health, 1978.

PATON, S., KESSLER, R., & KANDEL, D. Depressive mood and adolescent illicit drug use: A longitudinal analysis. *Journal of Genetic Psychology,* 1977, *131,* 267–289.

PAYKEL, E. S. Environmental variables in the etiology of depression. In F. F. Flach & S. C. Draghi (Eds.), *The nature and treatment of depression.* New York: Wiley, 1975.

PHILIPS, I. Childhood depression: The mirror of experience, interpersonal interactions, and expressive phenomena. In A. French & I. Berlin (Eds.), *Depression in children and adolescents.* New York: Human Sciences Press, 1979.

POPE, H. G., & LIPINSKI, J. F. Diagnosis in schizophrenia and manic-depressive illness. *Archives of General Psychiatry,* 1978, *35,* 811–828.

POZNANSKI, E. O. Childhood depression: A psychodynamic approach to the etiology of depression in children. In A. French & I. Berlin (Eds.), *Depression in children and adolescents.* New York: Human Sciences Press, 1979.

PRANGE, A. J. Pharmacotherpy of depression. In F. F. Flach & S. C. Draghi (Eds.), *The nature and treatment of depression.* New York: Wiley, 1975.

PREODOR, D., & WOLPERT, E. A. Manic-depressive illness in adolescence. *Journal of Youth and Adolescence,* 1979, *8,* 111–130.

PRICE, J. The genetics of depressive disorder. In A. Coppen & A. Walk (Eds.), Recent developments in affective disorders: A symposium. *British Journal of Psychiatry Special Publication No. 2.* Ashford: Headley, 1968.

PRIVATE MENTAL HOSPITAL INPATIENT UNITS. Distribution of admissions by primary diagnosis and age, 1975. Rockville, Md.: National Institute of Mental Health, 1978.

PUIG-ANTICH, J., BLAU, S., MARX, N., GREENHILL, L. L., & CHAMBERS, W. Prepubertal major depressive disorder: A pilot study. *Journal of the American Academy of Child Psychiatry,* 1978, *17,* 695–707.

RADLOFF, L. S., & RAE, D. S. Susceptibility and precipitating factors in depression: Sex differences and similarities. *Journal of Abnormal Psychology,* 1979, *88,* 174–181.

RAPOPORT, J. L. Pediatric psychopharmacology and childhood depression. In J. G. Schulterbrandt & A. Raskin (Eds.), *Depression in childhood.* New York: Raven Press, 1977.

RIE, H. E. Depression in childhood: A survey of some pertinent contributions. *Journal of the American Academy of Child Psychiatry,* 1966, *5,* 653–685.

ROBINS, E., GENTRY, K. A., MUNOZ, R. A., & MARTEN, S. A contrast of the three more common illnesses with the ten less common in a study and 18-month follow-up of 314 psychiatric emergency room patients. *Archives of General Psychiatry,* 1977, *34,* 269–281.

RUTTER, M., GRAHAM, P., CHADWICK, O. F. D., & YULE, W. Adolescent turmoil: Fact or fiction? *Journal of Child Psychology and Psychiatry,* 1976, *17,* 35–56.

SCHNEER, H. I., PERLSTEIN, A., & BROZOVSKY, M. Hospitalized suicidal adolescents. *Journal of the American Academy of Child Psychiatry,* 1975, *14,* 268–280.

SELIGMAN, M. E. P. Depression and learned helplessness. In R. J. Friedman & M. M. Katz (Eds.), *The psychology of depression.* Washington, D.C.: Winston, 1974.

SELIGMAN, M. E. P. *Helplessness: On depression, development, and death.* San Francisco: W. H. Freeman, 1975.

SELIGMAN, R., GLESER, G., RAUH, J., & HARRIS, L. The effect of earlier parental loss in adolescence. *Archives of General Psychiatry,* 1974, *31,* 475–479.

SHAFFER, D. Suicide in childhood and early adolescence. *Journal of Child Psychology and Psychiatry,* 1974, *15,* 275–291.

SHAINBERG, D. Personality restriction in adolescents. *Psychiatric Quarterly,* 1966, *40,* 258–270.

SILVER, M. A., BOHNERT, M., BECK, A. T., & MARCUS, D. Relation of depression to attempted suicide and seriousness of intent. *Archives of General Psychiatry,* 1971, *25,* 573–576.

SILVERMAN, C. The epidemiology of depression: A review. *American Journal of Psychiatry,* 1968, *124,* 883–891.

SORENSON, R. C. *Adolescent sexuality in contemporary America: Personal value and sexual behavior ages 13–19.* New York: World, 1973.

SOURS, J. *Starving to death in a sea of objects: The anorexia nervosa syndrome.* New York: Aronson, 1980.

SPIEGEL, E. Anger and acting out: Masks of depression. *American Journal of Psychotherapy,* 1967, *21,* 597–606.

SPITZER, R. I., ENDICOTT, J., & ROBINS, E. Research diagnostic criteria: Rationale and reliability. *Archives of General Psychiatry,* 1978, 35, 773–782.

STATE AND COUNTY MENTAL HOSPITALS. Admissions by age and diagnosis, 1978. Rockville, Md.: National Institute of Mental Health, 1978.

STEIN, K. B., SOSKIN, W. F., & KORCHIN, S. J. Drug use among disaffected high school youth. *Journal of Drug Education,* 1975, *5,* 193–203.

STROBER, M., GREEN, J., & CARLSON, G. Phenomenology and subtypes of major depressive disorder in adolescence. *Journal of Affective Disorders,* in press.

TEC, N. Some aspects of high school status and differential involvement with marihuana: A study of suburban teenagers. *Adolescence,* 1972, *7,* 1–28.

TEICHER, J. D. The alienated, older male adolescent. *American Journal of Psychotherapy,* 1972, *26,* 401–407.

TOOLAN, J. M. Masked depression in children and adolescents. In S. Lesse (Ed.), *Masked depression.* New York: Aronson, 1974.

TOOLAN, J. M. Therapy of depressed and suicidal children. *American Journal of Psychotherapy,* 1978, *32,* 243–251.

TSUANG, M. T. Suicide in schizophrenics, manics, depressives, and surgical controls. *Archives of General Psychiatry,* 1978, *35,* 153–155.

TSUANG, M. T., CROWE, R. R., WINOKUR, G., & CLANCY, J. Relatives of schizophrenics, manics, depressives, and controls: An interview study of 1331 first-degree relatives. In L. C. Wynne, R. L. Cromwell, & S. Matthysse (Eds.), *The nature of schizophrenia.* New York: Wiley, 1978.

TSUANG, M. T., WOOLSON, R. F., & FLEMING, J. A. Long-term outcome of major psychoses. *Archives of General Psychiatry,* 1979, *36,* 1295–1301.

UNWIN, J. R. Depression in alienated youth. *Canadian Psychiatric Association Journal,* 1970, *15,* 83–86.

WALTERS, P. A. Student apathy. In G. R. Blaine & C. C. McArthur (Eds.), *Emotional problems of the student* (2nd ed.). New York: Appleton-Century-Crofts, 1971.

WEINBERG, W. A., & BRUMBACK, R. A. Mania in childhood: Case studies and literature review. *American Journal of Diseases of Children,* 1976, *130,* 380–385.

WEINER, I. B. The generation gap—fact and fancy. *Adolescence,* 1971, *6,* 155–166.

WEINER, I. B. Depression in adolescence. In F. F. Flach & S. C. Draghi (Eds.), *The nature and treatment of depression.* New York: Wiley, 1975.

WEINER, I. B. The adolescent and his society. In J. R. Gallagher, F. P. Heald, & D. C. Garell (Eds.), *Medical care of the adolescent* (3d ed.). New York: Appleton-Century-Crofts, 1976.

WEINER, I. B. Adjustment to adolescence. In B. B. Wolman (Ed.), *International encyclopedia of neurology, psychiatry, psychoanalysis, and psychology:* Princeton, N.J.: Van Nostrand Reinhold, 1977.

WEISSMAN, M. M. The psychological treatment of depression. *Archives of General Psychiatry,* 1979, *36,* 1261–1269.

WEISSMAN, M. M., & KLERMAN, G. L. Sex differences and the epidemiology of depression. *Archives of General Psychiatry,* 1977, *34,* 98–111.

WEISSMAN, M. M., & KLERMAN, G. L. Sex differences and the epidemiology of depression. In E. S. Gomberg & V. Franks (Eds), *Gender and disordered behavior.* New York: Brunner/Mazel, 1979.

WEISSMAN, M. M., & MYERS, J. K. Affective disorders in a U.S. urban community: The use of research diagnostic criteria in an epidemiological survey. *Archives of General Psychiatry,* 1978, *35,* 1304–1311.

WEISSMAN, M. M., POTTENGER, M., KLEBER, H., RUBEN, H. L., WILLIAMS, D., & THOMPSON, W. D. Symptom patterns in primary and secondary depression. *Archives of General Psychiatry,* 1977, *34,* 854–862.

WELNER, A., WELNER, Z., & FISHMAN, R. Psychiatric adolescent inpatients: Eight- to ten-year follow-up. *Archives of General Psychiatry,* 1979, *36,* 698–700.

WETZEL, R. D. Hopelessness, depression, and suicide intent. *Archives of General Psychiatry,* 1976, *33,* 1069–1073.

WIEDER, H., & KAPLAN, E. H. Drug use in adolescents: Psychodynamic meaning and pharmacogenic effect. *Psychoanalytic Study of the Child,* 1969, *24,* 399–431.

WINOKUR, G. The types of affective disorders. *Journal of Nervous and Mental Disease,* 1973, *156,* 82–96.

WINOKUR, G. Heredity in the affective disorders. In E. J. Anthony & T. Benedek (Eds.), *Depression and human existence.* Boston: Little, Brown, 1975.

WINOKUR, G., CLAYTON, P. J., & REICH, T. *Manic depressive illness.* St. Louis: C. V. Mosby, 1969.

WINOKUR, G., & MORRISON, J. The Iowa 500: Followup of 225 depressives. *British Journal of Psychiatry,* 1973, *123,* 543–548.

WINOKUR, G., & PITTS, F. N. Affective disorder: VI. A family history study of prevalences, sex differences, and possible genetic factors. *Journal of Psychiatric Research,* 1965, *3,* 113–123.

WHITE, J., & O'SHANICK, G. Juvenile manic-depressive illness. *American Journal of Psychiatry,* 1977, *134,* 1035–1036.

WOLMAN, B. B. (Ed.) *Handbook of treatment of mental disorders in childhood and adolescence.* Englewood Cliffs, N.J.: Prentice-Hall, 1978.

YOUNGERMAN, J, & CANINO, I. A. Lithium carbonate use in children and adolescents. *Archives of General Psychiatry,* 1978, *35,* 216–224.

ZEISS, A. M., LEWINSOHN, P. M., & MUNOZ, R. F. Nonspecific improvement effects in depression using interpersonal skills training, pleasant activity schedules, or cognitive training. *Journal of Consulting and Clinical Psychology,* 1979, *47,* 427–439.

8

NEUROTIC DISORDERS

Neurotic behavior consists of repetitively immature, inappropriate, or maladaptive ways of responding to people and situations. It is typically less incapacitating than psychotic behavior, since it does not involve a marked loss of touch with reality or a marked inability to meet the demands of ordinary living. In comparison to psychotic disorders, neuroses typically run a shorter course, respond better to treatment, and more often show a full recovery. Yet a neurotic disorder can cause considerable psychological distress while it lasts, and it can seriously disrupt a person's academic, vocational, social, and interpersonal adjustment.

The study and treatment of neurotic behavior focuses on several discrete neurotic disorders, inclduding *phobic disorder, obsessive-compulsive disorder, conversion reaction,* and *habit disturbance.* As an introduction to discussing these disorders, it is important to review some general issues regarding the diagnosis and prevalence of neurosis.

THE DIAGNOSIS AND PREVALENCE OF NEUROSIS

The concept of "being neurotic" or "having a neurosis" has a long history, both in the mental health literature and in common parlance (Adams, 1979; Gray, 1978, Chapter 1). The term *neurosis* is currently in disrepute however—a victim of having been used too often with too little precision. In both professional and lay circles it has commonly been employed as a general synonym for maladaptive behavior, rather than as a label for discrete, clearly defined patterns of psychological disturbance. This sloppy practice has resulted in considerable unreliability in prevalence estimates and in the clinical diagnosis of neurotic disorders, especially among young people.

Problems of Unreliability

"Maladaptive behavior" can be defined in many ways, some of which are so broad as to include aspects of how most people conduct their lives. Overly broad definitions legitimize treatment efforts in some cases by providing diagnostic labels that could apply to most people. As noted in Chapter 1 in relation to ideal concepts of normality, however, the broader diagnoses are, the less precision they have and the less helpful they are in defining psychopathology. Because neurosis has traditionally been loosely defined, it has shown low reliability as a formal diagnosis, and estimates of its prevalence have varied widely. Surveys in the United States have reported prevalence rates for neuroses ranging from less than 1 percent to 40 percent of adults, with an average of about 15 percent. In light of other data presented in Chapter 1, there seems little doubt that many more people have been identified in some of these surveys than should really be considered psychologically disturbed (Dohrenwend, 1980, Chapter 3; Beck, Ward, Mendelson, Mock, & Erbaugh, 1962; Kendell, 1975, Chapter 3; Kreitman, Sainsbury, Morrisey, Towers, & Scrivener, 1961; Zubin, 1967).

For these reasons, very few psychopathologists currently refer in any general sense to people as "being neurotic." Instead, *neurosis* is used only as a convenient term for describing a specific group of discrete disorders, as in the present chapter (American Psychiatric Association, 1980; Spitzer, Sheehy, & Endicott, 1977). Time will tell whether *neurosis* is doomed to disappear entirely from professional usage and common parlance. Some writers question whether the term has any remaining utility, whereas others suggest that its long history and communication value will help it outlive those who prophesy its demise (Marks, 1981, Chapter 4).

Underdiagnosis of Youthful Neurotic Disorder

Scholars in clinical psychology and psychiatry are generally agreed that neurotic ways of dealing with experience can begin early in life and that neurotic symptom pictures can be identified after age 5 or 6 (Adams, 1979; Anthony, 1975). Yet practicing clinicians have traditionally shown a reluctance to diagnose neurotic disorders in young people. This reluctance is reflected in Table 8.1, which indicates the percent of youthful (under 18) and adult (age 25 to 44) patients receiving several diagnoses in three clinical settings.

Compared to adults, younger patients are relatively frequently diagnosed as having a situational, childhood, or "preadult" disorder and correspondingly infrequently as schizophrenic, depressed, or neurotic. For neurotic disorders the recorded diagnostic frequency differs substantially from estimates of their actual frequency among young people. Research-oriented surveys of child guidance clinics have yielded prevalence estimates for neurosis ranging from 5 to 50 percent of patients (Anthony, 1975; Cass & Thomas, 1979, Chapter 4; Chess & Hassibi, 1978, Chapter 11). This wide range reflects the previously noted lack of precision with which neurosis has traditionally been defined. Nevertheless, even the most conservative estimate in these surveys (5 percent) strongly suggests that the 1.7 percent rate of recorded neurotic diagnoses for clinic patients under 18 involves considerable reluctance to label them neurotic when they in fact are.

Some findings from the Isle of Wight studies noted in earlier chapters support such a conclusion. In this population survey definite neurotic disorder was identified in 2.5

TABLE 8.1 Youthful and Adult Patients Receiving Various Diagnoses (in percent)

	Clinical Setting					
	Outpatient Psychiatric Services		Private Mental Hospitals		State and County Mental Hospitals	
Diagnosis	Under 18	25–44	Under 18	25–44	Under 18	25–44
Schizophrenia	2.1	13.7	16.5	26.6	14.2	39.5
Depression	2.0	14.8	19.7	44.1	4.3	10.1
Neurosis	1.7	10.1	3.9	7.3	1.1	1.3
Transient situational disorder	21.2	14.2	31.8	6.0	0.8	0.4
Childhood or preadolescent disorder	39.1	0.3	9.7	0.0	40.6	0.0

Source. From data in *Outpatient Psychiatric Services* (1978), *Private Mental Hospitals* (1978), and *State and County Mental Hospitals* (1978).

percent of the 10- and 11-year-olds in a community and accounted for 37 percent of the diagnosable psychological disorder found among them (Rutter, Tizard, & Whitmore, 1970). Neurotic disorders thus appear to constitute a much larger proportion of youthful psychopathology than shows up in recorded diagnoses. They also occur much more frequently than schizophrenia, which does not have even a 1 percent prevalence in young people (see Chapter 5) but is more frequently diagnosed than neuroses in all of the settings noted in Table 8.1.

This discrepancy between the actual frequency of neurotic disorders in children and adolescents and the relative infrequency with which they are diagnosed in clinical settings appears due to three factors. First, as elaborated in Chapter 2, some clinicians dislike using diagnostic categories at all, particularly with young people. They regard diagnostic labeling as a dehumanizing, stigmatizing process that strips children of their individuality and causes more psychological problems for them than it helps to relieve. Clinicians holding such views may be compelled to make diagnostic judgments in the face of serious psychological handicaps that clearly reflect mental retardation, brain dysfunction, or schizophrenia. The milder neurotic disorders, however, provide them greater latitude for avoding a discrete diagnosis in favor of some nonspecific, presumably nonstigmatizing label such as "situational disorder" or "adjustment reaction."

Second, some clinicians who feel comfortable using traditional diagnostic categories with adult patients question whether they are applicable to childhood and adolescent difficulties. As noted in Chapter 1, this attitude presumes that youthful disorders are largely transient reactions to developmental circumstances. From this point of view, then, young people whose problems do not clearly identify chronic, severe psychopathology are likely to be described as having situational or adjustment disorders, rather than some discrete pattern of disturbance.

Third, because neurotic disorders on the average are less incapacitating and less persistent than the disorders discussed in previous chapters, they are less likely to come to the attention of mental health professionals. Parents and teachers do not perceive psychological problems as easily in a neurotic as in a psychotic youngster, for example. Should they become concerned about a neurotic young person's behavior, they are more likely to turn to their family doctor or clergy member than to a mental health professional; these people, when consulted, are less likely than in the case of a psychotic youngster to see a need for calling in a mental health specialist. Although parents are certainly well-advised to consult their family doctor or clergy when they are concerned about their youngster's behavior, these three factors taken together probably account for the underrepresentation of neurotic disorders among diagnoses recorded for children and adolescents in mental health settings.

PHOBIC DISORDER

Phobias are unrealistic, disruptive fears of relatively harmless objects or events. Unlike rational fears of dangerous situations, phobic dread serves no obvious protective purpose. It is typically out of proportion to any actual danger present, and it cannot be relieved by explanations or reassurances that there is nothing to fear.

To illustrate this disorder, a preschool boy with a phobia of dogs may panic at the sight of a small puppy and run trembling and weeping to his mother's arms. Her efforts to "cure" him by forcing him to confront the dog may only intensify his terror. His phobia may become so intense that it dominates his waking existence. He may hesitate to play outside, for fear a dog might be in the neighborhood; he may refuse to go shopping or visiting with his mother, lest they encounter a dog along the way; he may avoid looking at picture books or television programs that feature dogs. Phobias can also generalize, so that an irrational fear of dogs turns into an irrational fear of cats, squirrels, hamsters, and perhaps all four-legged animals.

Phobias do not always become this severe. In mild cases they may cause only moderate distress and become apparent only in specific situations. For example, a boy may feel threatened only by large dogs, or he may be able to remain calm near dogs so long as a parent is holding his hand. The milder phobic reactions are, the more difficult it becomes to distinguish them from normal childhood fears. Indeed, normal fears shade imperceptibly into phobias, and a thorough knowledge of common childhood fearfulness is required to identify phobic disorder (Anthony, 1975; Marks, 1969, 1977).

Childhood Fears and Phobias: Frequency and Course

From early in life certain kinds of fears commonly appear and disappear at various ages. At 6 to 8 months of age, as infants begin to form selective attachments to key people in their lives, they often become wary of unfamiliar people; this fear of strangers usually peaks at about 1 year of age and then gradually diminishes. Between 8 and 24 months most infants show fear reactions when they are separated from their parents or other people to whom they have become attached; such **separation anxiety** tends to diminish after age 2 and to be mastered by age 4 (Elkind & Weiner, 1978, Chapter 4).

During the preschool years (age 2 to 5), many children develop fears of spooks, robbers, imaginary creatures, being alone, and the dark. From 6 to 12 years these particular fears steadily decrease and are replaced by fears of physical injury, school-related events, and social situations. Some of these latter fears may persist into adolescence and adulthood. Fears of sexuality, suicide, abortion, and having defective children sometimes emerge in normal young people during adolescence, and these too may persist into adulthood. With these developmental patterns in mind, phobias must be defined to include not only exaggerated fears but also fears that continue beyond the age when they would be expected to diminish or disappear, such as an adolescent who is still afraid of the dark (Bauer, 1976; Deverensky, 1979; Miller, Barrett, & Hampe, 1974).

Various surveys indicate that preschoolers typically have an average of about three different fears. Although fearfulness in general tends to decrease from age 6 to 12, almost half of all elementary school children are likely to display some distinct fear at one time or another, and approximately 4 percent of 10- to 12-year-olds are described by their parents as still being very fearful of some situation (Lapouse & Monk, 1959; Miller, Barrett, Hampe, & Noble, 1972; Rutter et al., 1970). Girls tend to be somewhat more fearful than boys. This sex difference is indicated in Table 8.2, which shows the fears most commonly found in one large sample of 7- to 12-year-old youngsters.

In most cases youthful fears come and go quickly, cause relatively little anxiety, and

Young children are normally fearful of imaginary creatures in the dark. Such normal fears differ from phobias, which are unrealistic fears that are more pronounced or continue to a more advanced age than would ordinarily be expected.

do not interfere very much with a young person's life. Only about 5 percent of children are likely to develop an excessive, incapacitating fear of some object or event. Such phobic reactions can begin any time after age 2 and most commonly start between age 4 and 7 (Anthony, 1975; Miller et al., 1974; Sperling, 1952; Tyson, 1978; Wallick, 1979).

Minor or secondary phobic symptoms occur much more frequently than major or primary phobic disorder, however. Among adult psychiatric patients, fewer than 3 percent have a primary phobic disorder, but as many as 20 percent are estimated to show phobic symptoms (Marks, 1977). Agras, Sylvester, and Oliveau (1969) found similar differences for the general population in a survey of representative households in Burlington, Vermont. An estimated 77 people per 1000 (7.7 percent) had some kind of phobia, but in only 2.2 cases per 1000 (0.22 percent) was it severely disabling. As shown in Figure 8.1, Agras et al. also confirmed that phobias, although more prevalent in adults than children, have their highest peak of first onset (incidence) in the early elementary school years.

Like normal childhood fears, phobias in young people tend to be short-lived. More-

TABLE 8.2 Frequency of Unreasonable or Excessive Fears in 7- to 12-Year-Olds (in percent)

Girls		Boys	
Snakes	13	Criticism	7
Rats and mice	11	Shots	7
Dark	8	Snakes	6
War	8	Deep water	5
Being kidnapped	8	High places	4
Being seen naked	8	Tornados, floods, earthquakes	4
Being confined or locked up	7	Space creatures, monsters	4
Deep water	7	Seeing someone wounded	4
Family member dying	7	Family member dying	4

Source. Based on data reported by Miller, Barrett, & Hampe (1974) on 126 boys and 123 girls.

over, in phobic and other neurotic disorders, early onset is a favorable prognostic sign: the earlier the disorder appears, the more likely it is to disappear, whether of its own accord or in response to treatment. This is just the opposite from what occurs in psychotic disorders. Among schizophrenics, it may be recalled those who first become disturbed as adults have better prospects for recovery than those who break down as children or adolescents (see Chapters 5 and 6).

Figure 8.1
Incidence and prevalence rates for phobia within general population. (From Agras et al. (1969). Reprinted with permission of Grune & Stratton.)

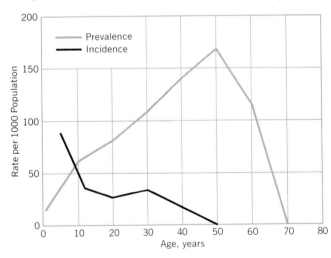

Figure 8.2

Changes over 5 years in intensity of untreated phobic disorder. (Based on longitudinal data reported by Agras et al. (1972).

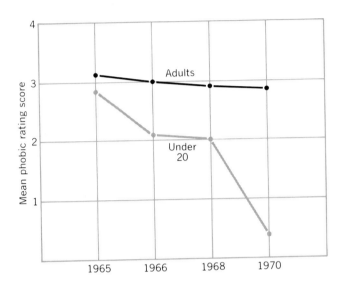

With specific respect to phobias, only 20 to 30 percent of adults who develop excessive fears overcome them completely, and just an additional 30 percent or so show some improvement. By contrast, at least 90 percent of phobic children are likely to get over their excessive fears (Agras, Chapin, & Oliveau, 1972; Glick, 1970; Hampe, Noble, Miller, & Barrett, 1973; Marks, 1971). This age difference seems to exist through adolescence, at least until age 20. As shown in Figure 8.2, a 5-year follow-up of untreated phobic persons identified in the Burlington, Vermont, study revealed a steady decline in fear level for those under 20 but a relatively unchanging picture for the adults.

Origins of Phobic Disorder

Because excessive fears are especially likely to occur during the preschool years and diminish thereafter, the disposition to phobic reactions can be understood partly in relation to the nature of early childhood experience. Preschoolers have matured enough cognitively to realize that they are small, weak, and helpless in relation to almost everything else in their environment but they have not yet matured sufficiently to comprehend which objects realistically threaten their safety or existence. This still-limited comprehension of the real world increases the susceptibility of young children to fears of external danger. The more frightened they are and the less they feel they can protect themselves, the more likely they are to develop phobic reaction patterns (Berecz, 1968; Poznanski, 1973). Anxious or physically timid children who actually become phobic have typically experienced certain real or imagined mishaps that have been modulated by the processes of *conditioning, modeling,* or *displacement.*

Conditioning   Under some circumstances phobias can be learned from frightening experiences. For example, being bitten by a dog may lead to a persistent, unreasonable fear of dogs that bears little relationship to the likelihood of being bitten again. Once acquired, any such excessive fear can generalize to other objects or events having some similar stimulus properties—as noted earlier, for example, from dogs to all four-legged animals.

John Watson, the founder of behavioristic psychology, demonstrated in a classic conditioning experiment that unreasonable fears can be learned from unpleasant experiences not only directly—as in becoming afraid of dogs after having been bitten by one—but also indirectly, by association with some fear-provoking event. Working with Albert, an 11-month-old boy, Watson made a loud banging noise (the unconditioned stimulus, of which Albert was afraid) every time the boy reached out toward a white rat (the conditioned stimulus, of which he was initially not afraid). Over a 7-day period Albert gradually came to show fear in the presence of the white rat, without any noise being made, and this fear subsequently generalized to include all furry objects (Watson & Rayner, 1920).

Although ample research confirms that phobias *can* result from conditioning, they rarely *do,* at least not outside of the laboratory or some other contrived situation. Only an occasional case of phobic disorder can be traced to a specific traumatic event, and phobic individuals who believe that such an event is the source of their problem are usually overlooking or unaware of its more complex origins (Anthony, 1975; Marks, 1977). Most phobias develop without the occurrence of obvious frightening experiences, through either modeling or displacement.

Modeling   Many of the fears of early childhood are acquired by observing and imitating parents who are themselves frightened by storms, the dark, visits to the doctor, or whatever. Children often develop the same fears as their parents, and frequently in unfamiliar situations they will look at their parents, to see how they are reacting, before showing their own reaction. In this way many phobic children come to have their excessive fears as a result of modeling themselves after parents who are extremely fearful themselves.

Excessive fears can be generated by verbal as well as behavioral messages, and copied from other children as well as parents. Phobia-prone preschoolers may become terrorized by the dire warnings of older children or adults that "garbage trucks gobble up little boys" or that "spiders like to scratch and bite little girls." Such teasing may cause fears of garbage trucks or spiders that assume phobic proportions, perhaps generalizing to all moving vehicles or all insects and making it difficult for a child to play outside. Likewise, exaggerated warnings about never accepting a ride from a stranger, embellished by gory recitals of the possible consequences, can cause basically fearful elementary school children to develop a phobic reluctance to leave the house or be among crowds of people—a condition known as **agoraphobia**—lest they be kidnapped or molested. Often, then, children fear what they are taught to fear (Deverensky, 1979).

Displacement   In other cases phobias may arise as a means of dealing with anxiety through displacement. **Displacement** is a process by which feelings and attitudes are

Children can acquire unreasonable fears and other neurotic behavior patterns by modeling themselves after parents who show such behavior.

transferred from their real source to a previously neutral object or situation. When phobias originate in displacement, the dreaded situation often has no particular significance other than as a convenient representation for something else that is feared.

The origin of phobias in displacement was first described by Freud (1909) in one of the best known cases in the psychoanalytic literature. Freud wrote about his lengthy conversations with the father of "Little Hans," a 5-year-old boy who was afraid of horses. Freud's analysis of the information he obtained suggested that Hans was really afraid that his father was angry at him and intended to harm him, and that he had displaced this fear onto horses. This allowed him to minimize his anxiety, since he could more easily avoid horses than he could his father; it also allowed him to maintain a reasonably comfortable relationship with his father, since he was not consciously aware of fearing him. Such displacement figures prominently in the formation of phobias about attending school, which are discussed in Chapter 9.

OBSESSIVE-COMPULSIVE DISORDER

Just as they have normal developmental fears, most preschool children go through a phase of insisting on certain kinds of routine and order in their lives. A particular doll or stuffed animal must be taken to bed every night, and no other toy will do; the shirt has to be put on before the pants because "that's the way it's supposed to be done"; a trip to the grocery store or to Grandma's house must be along the same route each time without variation.

Such attention to regularity among young children emerges as an effort to control their environment and their own behavior. The more regular and predictable they can make their lives, the more secure they can feel and the less they need to worry about some unexpected disaster taking place. Regularity also protects young children from letting their own impulses get out of hand; by sticking to definite routines they can avoid behaving in ways they might regret or be punished for (Kessler, 1972; Marks, 1977).

The more concerned children are about being the agent or the victim of physical violence, the more their routines are likely to become excessive or unusually persistent. In the same way that fears shade into phobias, then, routines can turn into maladaptive rituals and preoccupations. Elementary school children may become overly involved in collecting rocks, stamps, or batting averages, for example, at the expense of doing their homework; they may commit themselves to some very specialized interest or hobby, to the exclusion of all other activities; or they may develop a pervasive tendency to deal with their experience in a rigid, overcontrolled, excessively orderly, and perfection-istic manner (Adams, 1973, Chapter 1). This last development defines an **obsessive-compulsive personality style,** and the next step toward overt psychopathology is the emergence of specific obsessive-compulsive symptoms.

Obsessions consist of recurrent ideas, fears, or doubts that people cannot prevent from intruding on their conscious awareness despite finding them unpleasant and want-ing to avoid them. These ruminations, such as worrying about what happens to people who do bad things, rarely serve any constructive purpose and often paralyze the ob-sessional neurotic's capacity to come to any clear conclusion or take any definitive action.

Compulsions are repetitive, nonproductive acts that people feel required to carry out, even against their better judgment. Failure or inability to carry out certain self-prescribed rituals, such as washing one's hands every hour, fills the compulsive neurotic with a terrible sense of dread and impending catastrophe. Obsessions and compulsions often occur together, although not necessarily. The presence of either or both kinds of symptoms, occurring as a disturbed person's primary psychological difficulty, constitutes obsessive-compulsive disorder (Rachman & Hodgson, 1980).

The Frequency and Nature of Obsessive-Compulsive Disorder

Obsessive-compulsive behavior is fairly common in the general population but rarely crystallizes into discrete psychopathology. Most people can easily identify friends or relatives whom they regard as worriers and self-doubters or as being indecisive, perfec-tionistic, meticulous, or "uptight"—each involves some degree of an obsessive or com-pulsive personality style. In the Cass and Thomas (1979) study introduced in Chapter 1, 48 percent of the child-guidance clinic patients were described by their parents as showing some compulsive behavior. More specific obsessive-compulsive symptoms are found in only about 14 percent of the adult population, and primary obsessive-compulsive disorder is diagnosed in just 1.5 to 3 percent of the adults and about 1 percent of the children and adolescents seen in psychiatric clinics. At all ages males and females are equally likely to show the disorder (Adams, 1973, Chapter 1; Marks, 1981; Strober & Green, in press).

Although it is more prevalent among adults than among children and adolescents, obsessive-compulsive disorder often has a youthful onset. Among child-guidance patients, it occurs most frequently in the 6- to 10-year-olds, and obsessive-compulsive adolescents show an average age of onset of about 10. This identifies a somewhat later onset than in phobic disorders, which have their highest relative incidence among 4- to 7-year-old patients. Of all cases of obsessive-compulsive disorder, about 20 percent begin before age 15 and 50 to 60 percent before age 20 (Adams, 1973; Anthony, 1975; Hollingsworth, Tanguay, Grossman, & Pabst, 1980).

The essential nature of obsessive-compulsive disorder is the feeling of being driven by fate to take certain actions and/or think certain thoughts, regardless of how foolish they seem, regardless of how much trouble they cause, and regardless of how desperately the person wants to act or think otherwise. Obsessive-compulsive children will complain of constant worrying over which they have no control or of rituals they must carry out to prevent something terrible from happening to themselves or their family. Panic lingers constantly on the threshold of their experience, whether directly from their worries and self-doubts or indirectly in relation to what will happen if they fail to carry out their self-prescribed rituals. As Adams (1973, p. 92) aptly states, "The obsessive child, therefore, lives as if extermination were impending."

Pathological obsessions and compulsions are most likely to appear in people who have an obsessive-compulsive personality style. This personality style revolves around the "three Ps" of *parsimony, pedantry,* and *petulance.* Derived from original contributions by Freud (1908, 1913) on this style, the three Ps refer to the tendency of obsessive-compulsive people to be cautious and frugal, neat and orderly, and rigid and stubborn. More modern formulations have translated these characteristics into typical patterns of obsessive-compulsive ideation, affect, social relationships, and behavior (Adams, 1973, Chapter 3; Nemiah, 1980; Salzman, 1968; Shapiro, 1965, Chapter 2).

Ideation   Obsessive-compulsive people have strong needs to be absolutely sure of themselves and equally strong needs to ponder all aspects of a situation before coming to any conclusion about it. A thorough, cautious, conservative, reflective approach to forming judgments and making decisions thus reaches its ultimate in obsessive-compulsives, to the extent that chronic uncertainty and indecisiveness (**abulia**) becomes a hallmark of their personality style. For an obsessive-compulsive boy deciding whether to wear the blue shirt or the yellow shirt to school may go on for half an hour and still seem unsettled in his mind after a parent has made the decision for him.

Conversations with obsessive-compulsive children can also be trying affairs. These children are rarely satisfied with an explanation, since they cannot stop wondering whether all of the necessary facts and alternative possibilities have been considered. Because of their excessive need for certainty, moreover, they get hung up with the precise meaning of what other people are saying. They frequently ask for clarifications of how particular words are being used, and they may annoyingly use "I don't know what you mean" as their first response to any question or statement.

The cautious ideational style of obsessive-compulsive people colors their own speech as well. In their effort to touch all of the bases, they typically use many more words than are necessary to say something and clutter what they say with superfluous qualifications and elaborations. While trying to be precise and not misunderstood, then, they frequently end up being rambling, digressive, confusing, and very, very boring.

Affect   "Still waters run deep" captures the affective style of obsessive-compulsive individuals—strong undercurrents but nary a ripple on the surface. These people have very intense emotions that they keep largely to themselves. Underlying anger figures especially prominently in these emotions; it is not surprising to learn that children who live "as if extermination were impending" harbor hostile feelings either as a cause or result of seeing the word as such a dangerous place.

Despite feeling hate, love, and other emotions very deeply, obsessive-compulsive children typically show an unemotional face to the world. Their affective style is shaped by **isolation,** a process in which affective experience is minimized by separating emotions from thoughts they would ordinarily accompany. Stripped of their affect, the thoughts become somewhat colorless and seemingly unimportant. Whereas another kind of child might say, "I hate my mother," an obsessive-compulsive youngster would say, "Sometimes I think I don't like my mother very much."

In this fashion the verbal communications of obsessive-compulsives typically qualify ("sometimes"), intellectualize ("I think"), and minimize ("not very much") emotions. Their physical expressions of emotion are similarly constrained and unspontaneous. They rarely show joy and exuberance, nor do they laugh or cry easily. Occasionally obsessive-compulsive children will be commended by their parents or teachers for their "maturity." In these instances the adults are usually reacting to what they regard as grown-up emotional control; what they are in fact seeing is an abnormal degree of reserve in a drab, overcontrolled youngster who is falling behind his or her peers in learning to modulate affect adaptively and enjoy life.

Social Relationships   In keeping with their emotional restraint, obsessive-compulsive children do not mix well socially. They tend to be formal and reserved in how they relate to others, which often contributes to their getting along better with adults than with their peers. With all people, however, they have difficulty expressing their feelings and achieving any kind of easy intimacy. Hence they make friends slowly, if at all. The relatively few friendships they do form tend to become more intense and to last longer than is common for other children of their age; they have little capacity to be casual, whether in interpersonal relationships or in any other facet of their life.

Behavior   Caution, constraint, and rigidity color all of the observable behavior of obsessive-compulsive children. Activities, like interpersonal relationships, are never taken casually. Plans are made carefully in advance, leaving little to chance, and nothing is done on the spur of the moment. These children tolerate risk poorly, and they avoid situations that have an uncertain outcome. While thus making a production of everything they do, they pursue their interests doggedly, but rarely with enthusiasm, and they seem constantly to act out of a sense of what *should* or *ought to* be done, rather than what would be fun to do.

By virtue of their thrifty, conservative nature, obsessive-compulsive children often please their parents by taking very good care of their belongings. In this too, they pay a price: their excessive concern about making things last and stay in perfect working order prevents them from fully using or enjoying what they own. A boy's bicycle may still be like new after he has outgrown it, because he very carefully rode it only in clear weather, on smooth pavement, and at slow speeds. This same boy's closets and drawers may be overflowing because of his reluctance ever to throw anything away.

Above all else, obsessive-compulsive children impose orderliness on their lives. They are neat, clean, and well organized. Everything must be in its proper place, from the

Obsessive-compulsive young people often please their parents and other adults by being neat and well-behaved; however, such apparent "maturity" is achieved at the expense of being too reserved emotionally to get along well with their peers.

hairs on their head to the books on their desk. Being unable to get their hair combed just right, they may refuse to leave the house; a homework assignment will be painfully recopied rather than handed in with a minor mistake crossed out. Often their meticulousness, like certain other features of their affective and behavioral style, makes a favorable impression on adults. After all, points are awarded, not taken off, for neatness.

Obsessive-compulsive youngsters have gone beyond a reasonable degree of caution, however. Neatness is not an elective way of life for them, to be pursued when it brings pleasure or rewards and to be exchanged for sloppiness when they feel like it. Instead, it is a necessity, an obligation they must meet to avoid feeling uncomfortable, even when it results in punishment or ridicule. They submit a school assignment late, because they took time to recopy it, and get a lower grade than they would have by turning in the original messy copy on time. They dress meticulously for a casual occasion and have their peers snicker at rather than compliment them.

Finally, the rigidity of obsessive-compulsive youngsters may extend to their motor behavior. Often the way they hold themselves seems stiff and uncomfortable, as if they cannot relax their bodies any more than they can relax their thoughts and feelings. Their movements may look awkward and unnatural, even if they happen to be well-coordinated, athletic youngsters. When they use facial expressions or gestures, which is less often than most people, these too strike others as forced or restrained. One apt description of an especially constricted, obsessive-compulsive person included the statement, "When he smiles, it looks as if his face is going to crack."

Origins of Obsessive-Compulsive Disorder

The causes of obsessive-compulsive disorder are largely unknown. Partly because it is relatively infrequent and partly because it is one of the milder psychological disorders, it has not attracted as much attention from clinical investigators as disturbances that are either more common (e.g., depression) or more serious (e.g., autism). Nevertheless, there are some suggestive findings on the genetics of neurotic disorder and on possible experiential determinants of obsessive-compulsive neurosis.

The Genetics of Neurotic Disorder   A modest body of research indicates that neurotic disorders, like so many other features of behavior, run in families. Parents and siblings of a person with a neurotic disorder are more likely than people in general to show neurotic behavior themselves. Among twins, a small number of studies has found a significantly higher concordance for neurotic disorder in identical pairs (52 percent) than nonidentical pairs (23 percent). These studies also reveal a clear tendency for relatives to share the same kind of neurotic disorder, especially if they are identical twins (Cavenar & Caudill, 1979; Miner, 1973; Rainer, 1976; Shields & Slater, 1972).

The degree of familial incidence varies among neurotic disorders. First-degree relatives appear especially likely to share a high level of overt anxiety; conversion reactions, which are discussed in the next section, show a relatively small familial incidence; and phobic and obsessive-compulsive disorders occupy an intermediate position (Gottesman, 1963; Miner, 1973; Noyes, Clancy, Crowe, Hoenk, & Slymen, 1978). In studies of obsessive-compulsive disorder in twins, concordance has been found in 27 of 35 identical pairs but not in any of 7 nonidentical pairs. Approximately 10 percent of the parents of obsessive-compulsive children suffer from this disorder themselves, and from 40 to 70 percent in various studies show some obsessive-compulsive traits (Adams, 1973, Chapter 2; Anthony, 1975; Inouye, 1972).

Although these figures far exceed the general population frequencies for obsessive-compulsive disorder, they only suggest a possible genetic component. None of the neurotic disorders have yet been evaluated in the kinds of adoption (cross-fostering) studies described in earlier chapters as necessary to separate genetic from experiential factors in accounting for familial incidence. Although compelling genetic evidence may still be forthcoming, most clinicians and researchers currently believe that experiential factors, not genetic ones, account for the transmission of obsessive-compulsive personality features from parents to their offspring.

Experiential Factors in Obsessive-Compulsive Disorder   Many theories have been advanced concerning how obsessive-compulsive disorder evolves from experience. Common to most of these theories is the belief that obsessive-compulsive symptoms arise as a way of dealing with or defending against anxiety. Just as phobias keep people away from situations that frighten them, obsessions and compulsions help people avoid thinking or acting in ways that they consider unacceptable. In addition, most theorists believe that underlying anger plays an important role in obsessive-compulsive symptom formation. The focus on control that characterizes this disorder can easily be seen as reflecting a need to keep aggressive impulses from getting out of hand or even being expressed at all (Adams, 1973, Chapter 5).

However sensible these formulations may be, they do more to describe obsessive-compulsive disorder than to account for its origins. Even if obsessions and compulsions do in fact protect people from becoming upset, why do individuals choose these particular symptoms instead of phobias, conversion reactions, or some nonpathological behavior as a way of coping with anxiety? As for underlying anger, why do some aggressive youngsters develop obsessive-compulsive symptoms while many equally aggressive youngsters show other forms of psychopathology or none at all?

As a partial answer to these questions, theorists also agree that, among children whose circumstances precipitate neurotic symptom formation, a discrete obsessive-compulsive disorder is most likely to appear in those who have an obsessive-compulsive personality style. From this perspective, obsessive-compulsive symptoms are caused in part by developmental experiences that contribute to an obsessive-compulsive personality style. These experiences consist largely of having parents who treat their children in certain ways and provide them certain kinds of behavioral models.

Such child-rearing influences were first proposed by Freud (1908, 1913), who attributed an obsessive-compulsive personality style to difficult experiences with toilet training. Referring to this personality style as "anal character," he related its primary characteristics to excessive parental efforts to train bowel control: lavish rewards for the habit of retaining stools lead to frugality, he suggested; high praise for controlling excretion contributes to orderliness; and demandingness against which children rebel produces obstinacy.

Considerable research has confirmed that the traits Freud ascribed to the anal character do occur together consistently in certain people. There is also good evidence that the degree of "anality" people show is directly related to the intensity of "anal" attitudes present in their mothers. However, Freud's description of the anal character has stood the test of time better than his explanations of how it originates. The existence of an obsessive-compulsive personality style as he described it is an established fact, but numerous efforts have so far failed to demonstrate any relationship between how children are toilet trained and whether they will become frugal, orderly, and obstinate (Fisher & Greenberg, 1977, Chapter 3; Pollack, 1979).

It is possible, of course, to suggest that how children *experience* their toilet training, rather than how it looks to others, determines whether they develop an obsessive-compulsive personality style. However, such a hypothesis involves a type of circular reasoning that should be avoided: obsessive-compulsive people are presumed to have experienced their toilet training as harsh and traumatic; yet, because of the limited capacity of young children to conceptualize, verbalize, or recollect their experience, the only way to determine that they experienced stressful toilet training is from their showing obsessive-compulsive traits. Such circular reasoning results whenever there is no way to assess the quality of a person's experience independently of the outcome that this experience is presumed to cause. Hypotheses involving this type of reasoning cannot be disproved: if you don't get the outcome, you simply conclude that the experience didn't exist. Although sometimes useful as articles of faith, these hypotheses contribute little to the advancement of knowledge (Popper, 1959).

For this reason, most contemporary psychopathologists focus on observable features of how children are actually reared when they theorize about the origins of obsessive-compulsive traits and other normal and abnormal personality characteristics. Although toilet training cannot be singled out in this regard, parents do seem to promote obsessive-compulsive personality development by specifically encouraging and rewarding the ideational, affective, interpersonal, and behavioral features of this style while specifically discouraging other patterns. Adams (1973, p. 71) suggests the following specific actions as illustrative of how parents can foster an obsessive-compulsive orientation.

Encouraging a wakeful, frightened child to say his prayers again.

Telling a child with a nightmare to think good thoughts instead.

Showing fascination with a child's religiosity.

Talking away feelings instead of accepting them.

Advising half-heartedness, and feigning neutrality in matters of race, religion, politics, sexuality, economic inequality, etc.

Covering brutality with sweet, undoing talk.

In addition, some children acquire obsessive-compulsive ways of behaving from observing parents who conduct their lives in this fashion. As in other examples of the powerful impact of parental modeling, there is considerable truth in the old saying,

"The acorn falls close to the oak tree." Although children are not doomed to mirror their parents, for better or worse, all children take on at least some of their parents' characteristics, and some children take on many. The more clearly parents show obsessive-compulsive features, then, and the more extensively their children identify with them, the more likely the children are to develop an obsessive-compulsive style.

Case 11. *Obsessive-Compulsive Disorder*

Gerald was the only child of middle-class, emotionally stable parents. He showed no serious psychological problems as a child, but when he was 11 his parents sought professional help because he was doing poorly in school and had few friends. A thorough evaluation revealed that he was a shy, somewhat withdrawn boy with a compulsive personality style, but there were no indications of significant psychopathology. He and his parents were counseled briefly, and the next 4 years passed without psychological incident.

When Gerald was 15, his grandfather died suddenly after a brief illness. His grandfather had been a very important person in his life, and he had visited his bedside daily during his fatal illness. A few weeks following the funeral he began to develop compulsive rituals. His face had to be washed for 15 minutes in the morning; school assignments had to be read four times and written work recopied four times; his school locker had to be checked four times each time he locked it; and every object he handled had to be placed in a certain way. His waking life became governed by one or another of these rituals, and he was terrorized by thoughts that if he failed to carry them out to the letter "something terrible" would happen to his parents or "I'll be drafted into the army and sent to Vietnam and killed" (the year was 1965).

Gerald told his parents about this problem and asked for their help. They responded promptly, especially since they had remained concerned about his lack of friends, and arranged for him to enter therapy. He responded well to a behavioral focus on gaining control of his rituals and became essentially symptom-free over the next 2 months (see Weiner, 1967). He was also able to share with the therapist numerous fantasies that related his symptoms to underlying concern about aggression.

The number "4," which figured prominently in his rituals, reminded him of the 1940s, which in turn reminded him of World War II. He talked of being interested in reading war stories and having fantasies about being transported by a time machine back into that war, where he could fight, kill people, and take prisoners without having to risk being harmed himself. He also revealed that he was a physical culture enthusiast who kept to an arduous routine of daily calisthenics, was studying judo and karate, and liked to think about how he would "clean up on anyone who messed with me." In fact, however, he had never been in a real physical fight, and actually harming anyone, even in self-defense, would have been very upsetting to him.

When therapy was terminated, Gerald had become more relaxed and was beginning to mix a bit socially, in addition to having overcome his acute obsessive-compulsive symptoms. He retained his basically compulsive personality style, however, and probably remained relatively likely to develop neurotic rituals at times of great stress.

CONVERSION REACTION

Conversion reactions consist of sensory or motor impairments for which there is no organic cause. These reactions usually take the form of pain, numbness, or loss of muscle control in one or more parts of the body, and they derive their name from the belief that they involve anxiety being "converted" into somatic symptoms. Conversion reactions have been known to affect virtually every system of the body and even to produce blindness, fainting spells, or paralysis in people who are physically sound (Gross, 1979; Gross & Huerta, 1980; Loof, 1970; Nemiah, 1980; Templer & Lester, 1974).

Many psychopathologists endorse a very broad definition of conversion proposed by Engel (1970), who regards conversion reactions as a psychological process whereby ideas or wishes are expressed in bodily rather than verbal terms. This definition blurs somewhat the boundary between normal and abnormal behavior, since it seems to include common body language—such as using a thumbs-down gesture to express disagreement or disapproval. When Engel's approach is limited to maladaptive physical complaints for which no organic cause has been found, it helps avoid a serious mistake that clinicians sometimes make with regard to conversion, called *diagnosis by exclusion.*

Diagnosis by exclusion consists in the present context of deciding that a conversion reaction is present whenever organic origins of a somatic problem cannot be found. Although this circumstance is always a *necessary* basis for diagnosing conversion, it is never a *sufficient* basis. Undetectable organic causes can lie at the root of any physical complaint, and diagnosis simply on the basis of not finding them opens the door to many errors. Engel's definition helps minimize such errors by calling attention to certain other features of conversion that allow the condition to be diagnosed on positive grounds rather than merely by exclusion.

As one such feature, the psychological derivation of conversion symptoms means that they directly express some conflict or need or at least symbolize some unspoken thoughts or wishes. Second, these symptoms begin in some clear relationship to precipitating events that have had an easily understandable and painful psychological impact on the affected person. Third, because the symptoms constitute a conversion of anxiety that protects people against feeling upset, they are often viewed with a surprisingly casual attitude and lack of concern—a phenomenon sometimes referred to as *la belle indifference.* Unless symbolic meanings, precipitating events, and an indifferent attitude are in evidence, then, conversion is unlikely to be the reason for otherwise unexplainable somatic symptoms, and the search for organic causes should be continued (Friedman, 1973; Prazar & Friedman, 1980; Rock, 1971; Yates & Steward, 1976).

Frequency of Childhood Conversion Reactions

Opinions vary widely concerning the frequency of conversion reactions in young people. Some clinicians consider them as common, whereas others regard them as rare and most unusual (Anthony, 1975; Friedman, 1973). As is true for all neurotic disorders, this variation is due partly to unreliable diagnostic criteria. For conversion reactions, in addition, incidence reports differ considerably as a function of the clinical setting from which they come.

Because the presenting complaints in conversion reactions are physical symptoms, children who suffer them are more likely than other neurotic youngsters to be seen in medical rather than nonmedical settings, in hospitals rather than clinics, and by pediatric rather than mental health practitioners. Whereas reports from child-guidance and child-psychiatry clinics suggest a 4 to 5 percent prevalence of conversion among youthful patients, surveys in hospital pediatric units identify a 9 percent frequency (Proctor, 1958; Rae, 1977; Rock, 1971). Consistent in these studies, however, is an as yet unexplained sex difference: 60 to 70 percent of children with conversion are girls, and the remaining 30 to 40 percent are boys (Rae, 1977).

One relatively common conversion symptom is **tics,** which are repetitive, involuntary muscle movements, usually of the face, head, and neck. Typical ticking movements include blinking the eyes, clearing the throat, yawning, stretching the neck, and shaking the head. Such ticking movements are sometimes due to neurological disorders or to simple fidgeting and restlessness, and they do not always constitute conversion reactions. However, psychological factors usually play some role in this disorder, either as a cause or a complication, and most tiquers manifest other signs of being tense and anxious (Lucas, 1979; Werry, 1979; Yates, 1970).

Tics occur more commonly in children than adults. They tend to reach their peak frequency at about age 6 or 7 and to decline thereafter. Tics are observed in 5 to 10 percent of elementary school children, but in most cases they disappear of their own accord by the time youngsters reach adolescence. Follow-up studies of childhood tiqueurs show that almost half completely outgrow their tics, almost half improve substantially, and only 6 percent continue their ticking unchanged through adolescence and into adulthood (Bruun, Shapiro, Sweet, Wayne, & Solomon, 1976; Corbett, Mathews, Connell, & Shapiro, 1969; Lapouse & Monk, 1964; Torup, 1962).

A special form of tic disorder that has received considerable attention is **Gilles de la Tourette's syndrome.** This syndrome typically begins between age 4 and 10 with twitching movements of the face, arms, legs, neck, and eyelids. In addition, however, youngsters with Gilles de la Tourette begin around 10 or 11 to make repetitive, involuntary vocal noises, starting with throat clearing and leading to coughing, grunting, and loud barking sounds. Around puberty 50 to 60 percent of them develop **coprolalia,** which is an uncontrollable outburst of obscene speech and is perhaps the most distinctive feature of this syndrome. Like other tics, the symptoms of Gilles de la Tourette's syndrome often disappear over time. On the other hand, they are noteworthy for worsening at puberty, persisting into adolescence, and being associated with relatively poor social and personality adjustment during late adolescence and early adulthood (Goggin & Erickson, 1979; Shapiro, Shapiro, Bruun & Sweet, 1978; Shapiro & Wayne, 1973; Thompson, O'Quinn, & Logue, 1979; Woodrow, 1974).

Origins of Conversion Reactions

The origins of conversion reaction are not understood any better than the causes of phobic and obsessive-compulsive disorders. Just as phobias may be seen as an exaggeration of normal childhood fears and obsessive-compulsive symptoms as exaggerations of normal childhood rituals, conversion symptoms can be related to developmental concerns about how the body is growing and functioning. Also, in common with other neurotic disorders, conversion can be viewed as a means of avoiding or dealing with anxiety. Although these notions have prompted many theories about how conversion reactions begin, they constitute descriptions of the disorder, not explanations of why it originates.

To understand the origin of neurotic disorders, it is necessary to go beyond describing the processes they involve (such as conversion) and the purposes they may serve (such as defending against anxiety). Why do certain people but not others develop a neurotic disorder in the face of anxiety-producing stresses, and why do those who become neurotic develop one particular disorder rather than another? The best available answer to the first of these questions appears to lie in interactions between temperament and family environment that produce a disposition to neurotic disorder. The answer to the second question appears to lie in the development of a certain personality style—obsessive-compulsive style in the case of obsessive-compulsive disorder, as already discussed, and hysterical personality style in the case of conversion reactions.

Temperament and Family Environment   Although some suggestive evidence of genetic contributions to neurotic disorders was noted earlier, there is little reason to believe that any form of neurosis is directly inherited. What is inherited are certain kinds of temperament that dispose people to becoming neurotically disturbed in response to environmental stress (Adams, 1979; Cohen, 1974; Torgersen & Kringlen, 1978).

Temperament consists of inborn differences among people that affect how they respond to their experiences. Children differ from birth in many aspects of temperament. Some are more active than others, some are more sensitive to stimulation, some adapt more readily to new situations, and some have more regular patterns of eating and sleeping. In an extensive long-term research project, known as the New York Longitudinal Study, Thomas and his colleages demonstrated that youngsters who are temperamentally either extremely high or extremely low in activity level, sensitivity, adaptability, and regularity are more likely than their peers to develop psychological disorders during childhood (Thomas & Chess, 1977; Thomas, Chess, & Birch, 1968).

The family environment exerts considerable influence on the kind of disorder children develop if their temperament combines with stressful experience to make them neurotic. Mention has already been made of how parental models contribute to phobic and obsessive-compulsive symptom formation. Similarly, children who develop conversion symptoms usually come from families that are very much concerned about health, illness, and bodily functions. In such families physical complaints command much attention and sympathy, and often a child's conversion reaction bears a close resemblance to the symptoms of a real or imagined illness in a parent or relative with whom the child has a close relationship (Cavenar & Caudill, 1979; Laybourne & Churchill, 1972).

Hysterical Personality Style   Whether children in sickness-oriented families who become neurotic develop conversion symptoms seems substantially influenced by whether they are developing a **hysterical personality style.** Generally speaking, people with hysterical personality styles show just the opposite patterns of ideation affect, social relationships, and behavior from those of people with obsessive-compulsive styles (Adams, 1979; Chodoff, 1974; Horowitz, 1977; Krohn, 1978, Chapter 5; Shapiro, 1965, Chapter 4).

Unlike obsessive-compulsive people, hysterical people prefer to deal with their experience through affective rather than ideational channels. They are typically unreflective and prefer to do things rather than think about them. They take life at its face value instead of pondering its meanings. If anything, they err on the side of superficial judgments that take insufficient account of available facts and alternative possibilities. As a result, their attitudes and beliefs are not deeply held, and their readiness to change them makes them relatively unpredictable and easily swayed by outside influence.

The affects of people with a hysterical personality style are likewise superficial and changeable. Such people readily show emotions which allow them to be spontaneous and open in their dealing with others. However, their moods tend to be labile (rapidly and widely fluctuating) rather than stable, and they frequently impress others as being dramatic or overemotional. Lack of restraint, not the excessive reserve of the obsessive-compulsive, is thus one of the hallmarks of the hysterical style.

In their interpersonal relationships hysterical people tend to make friends more easily than the obsessive-compulsive person but more often move from one casual relationship to another. At any one point in time, they will have more acquaintances but fewer deep, long-term friendships than obsessive-compulsives. In their behavior hysterics tend to appear more relaxed than the obsessive-compulsive person but also to be relatively impulsive, careless, poorly organized, and self-centered.

Whereas an obsessive-compulsive personality style makes children seem more mature than they may actually be, the hysterical style produces a picture of immaturity. Emotional lability, superficiality, impulsivity, and self-centeredness are, after all, typical characteristics of young children. Whether such characteristics identify a developing hysterical personality style in children depends on the degree to which they exceed what would normally be expected and thereby make the youngster seem strikingly immature for his or her age. Conversion reactions are not limited to people who show this personality style. A hysterical style encourages the expression of ideas and wishes through bodily channels and thus contributes to the choice of conversion symptoms in the event of a neurotic disorder.

HABIT DISTURBANCES

Habit disturbances are undesirable traits that, in common with neurotic disorders, represent immature ways of behaving. At one time habit disturbances were referred to as "neurotic traits" and assigned considerable importance in discussions of developmental psychopathology. Unlike neurotic disorders, however, habit disturbances do not necessarily serve as ways of defending against anxiety. Instead, they occur simply as learned habits or as a result of delayed maturation, and they are not necessarily associated with other indices of maladjustment.

Current practice therefore tends not to consider habit disturbances as a form of neurosis or of any other specific category of disorder, and they could be omitted from this chapter without detracting very much from the presentation of neurotic disorders (Robinowitz, 1979). On the other hand, habit disturbances can and often do serve psychological needs, and their persistence over long periods of time may contribute to interpersonal problems between children and their parents and peers. Moreover, two habit disturbances—enuresis (bed-wetting) and thumb-sucking—occur with some frequency and give rise to parental concerns about whether a child is developing normally.

Enuresis

All children wet the bed at night from birth until 1 or 2 years after they have developed daytime bladder control. When nocturnal wetting persists beyond age 3, by which time most children have gained total control of their bladder, it is labeled **enuresis.** Approximately 15 percent of 4- and 5-year-olds are enuretic. This frequency drops sharply once children reach school age, but a sizable number continue to wet into middle childhood and even adolescence (see Figure 8.3). At most ages enuresis is about twice as frequent among boys than girls (Anders & Freeman, 1979; Largo & Stutzle, 1977; McKendry & Stewart, 1974; Sours 1978).

Enuresis occurs in two forms, primary and secondary. In *primary* enuresis the bed-wetting has persisted from birth and is caused by a delayed development of the neuromuscular control necessary to prevent urine from being discharged during sleep. This delay is usually the result of parents having provided inconsistent or inadequate toilet training—their enuretic children have simply not been helped to learn bladder control as rapidly as other youngsters. Primary enuresis typically disappears with age, as slower-maturing children gradually catch up with their peers in developing this control (Bin-

Figure 8.3
Frequency of nocturnal bed-wetting at selected ages. (Based on data reported by De Jonge (1973), Oppel, Harper, and Rider (1968), and Pierce (1975).)

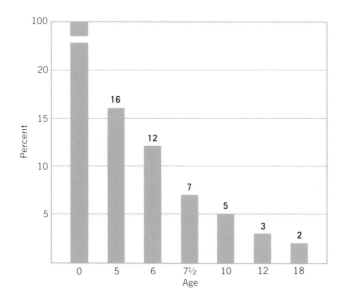

delglas, 1975; Cohen, 1975; Forsythe & Redmond, 1974; Greenberg & Stephans, 1977; Sours, 1978).

Primary enuresis accounts for about 75 to 80 percent of children with bed-wetting problems. The remaining 20 to 25 percent have *secondary* enuresis, which occurs as a regression after bladder control has been established. Secondary enuresis typically arises in reaction to some psychological stress, such as the birth of a sibling or moving to a new house, that causes a temporary return to less mature behavior patterns. Some clinicians have suggested that this particular regression may be a way for children who are angry at their mothers to express their feelings by symbolically urinating on her (the bedclothes), thereby giving her the extra work of changing and laundering their linen.

However it begins, enuresis can lead to adjustment difficulties if it becomes persistent. Parents whose grade-school children are still wetting the bed may worry that their child is sick or disturbed, and they may also resent the laundering problems the child is causing. In addition to having these disruptive effects on parent-child relationships, persistent enuresis can interfere with peer relationships if, for example, it prevents children from going to summer camp or staying overnight at a friend's house.

For these reasons, children with enuresis are more likely than their peers to develop emotional problems. Even though enuresis will probably disappear by itself in time—with the eventual maturation of bladder control or the passing of a stress situation—treatment should be undertaken to eliminate it when it persists into the elementary school years (McDonald, 1978; Werry & Corrsen, 1965).

Thumb-sucking

Thumb-sucking occurs normally in children up to about 3 or 4 years of age without any particular psychopathological causes or effects. Most infants do at least some sucking on their thumbs or fingers, and from 50 to 87 percent of healthy babies have been found in various studies to engage extensively in sucking behavior unrelated to getting food. Although the frequency of thumb-sucking declines rapidly as children approach school age, it continues as a learned habit in about 2 percent of 6- to 12-year-olds (Davidson, 1970; Lapouse & Monk, 1962).

Like enuresis, persistent thumb-sucking can lead to psychological problems. Grade-schoolers with this habit are likely to be criticized by their parents, scolded by their teachers, and teased by their peers, all with negative effects. In this case efforts to help older children get rid of their habit are well advised, and elementary school youngsters who overcome a thumb-sucking problem are usually found to show an improved psychological adjustment (Davidson, 1970; Safer 1978).

Because thumb-sucking shares with enuresis a likelihood of disappearing with age, treatment in early childhood should usually be avoided. Rather than fuss over preschool thumb-sucking or bed-wetting, and thereby stir parental concern and parent-child conflict, clinicians do better to counsel tolerance, patience, and perhaps some simple educative procedures, such as consistent toilet training. Only when these habits have persisted into the elementary school years, and thereby become a potential source of maladjustment, does a professional treatment program become indicated.

Various conditioning procedures have thus far proved to be the most effective means of eliminating habit disturbances. In the case of enuresis, for example, good results have been achieved with a specially designed mattress that is electrically sensitive to moisture. When a sleeping child begins to urinate, the mattress sets off an alarm that wakes him or her. In time the child becomes conditioned to wake up on feeling the need to urinate, but before actually doing so, which allows him or her to get up and go to the bathroom. This simple procedure can help approximately 75 to 85 percent of enuretic children learn bladder control in fairly short order (Anders & Freeman, 1979; Thorne, 1975; Werry, 1966). Other training procedures devised to reward bladder control, without using any conditioning apparatus, have also yielded good results (Azrin & Thienes, 1978).

TREATMENT

As noted in Chapter 1, neurotic disorders of childhood and adolescence tend to pass in time and to have relatively few implications for psychopathology later in life. Young people whose psychological problems do not involve antisocial conduct or the kinds of cognitive disorder seen in MBD/ADD or schizophrenia are often as well adjusted in adulthood as people in general (Cass & Thomas, 1979; Kohlberg, LaCrosse, & Ricks, 1972; Robins, 1979). This fact may appear to justify doing nothing about youthful neurotic disorders, other than waiting them out and counseling parental forebearance in the meantime.

On the other hand, as also previously observed, a *favorable* recovery rate is not a *perfect* recovery rate. Some neurotic young people, especially without treatment, will remain consistently and perhaps even progressively psychologically handicapped. Furthermore, those who will eventually overcome their neurotic symptoms on their own may be helped toward a speedier recovery by appropriate treatment, thus reducing the duration of the neurotic burden that they and their parents have to bear.

The treatment of choice for neurotic disorders in young people is psychotherapy. Koocher and Pedulla (1977) report some very interesting survey data on the effectiveness of psychotherapy with neurotic children, both in absolute terms and relative to other disorders. Using the membership of the American Academy of Child Psychiatry and the Child Section of the Clinical Division of the American Psychological Association, they chose a random sample of child psychotherapists from various parts of the United States. They received detailed information about their clinical practice from 85 of these child psychologists and 25 child psychiatrists, almost all of whom were actively seeing patients in outpatient clinic or private office settings. As shown in Figure 8.4, over 80 percent of these clinicians believed they were usually effective in treating neurotic children, whereas many fewer felt as good about their work with children suffering more serious disorders.

Dynamic and Behavioral Approaches in Psychotherapy

Psychotherapy with neurotic children and adolescents aims at removing or minimizing their neurotic symptoms and at promoting some understanding of what has caused or is perpetuating them. This second aim reflects primarily a *dynamic* approach in concep-

Figure 8.4

Frequency of therapists' rating their efforts as "usually effective" with various types of child patients. (Based on data collected by Koocher and Pedulla (1977) from 110 child psychotherapists.)

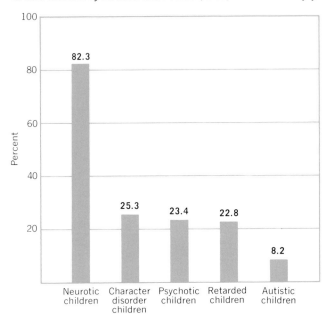

tualizing and treating neurotic disorder, and the first reflects primarily a *behavioral* approach.

In the dynamic approach, which derives from psychoanalytic theory, attention focuses primarily on how neurotic symptoms are being used to cope with underlying anxiety-provoking concerns. The treatment attempts to help people recognize and deal adaptively with these concerns, so that they will no longer have to resort to neurotic means of avoiding anxiety. In the case of Gerald (pp. 316), important parts of the therapy involved getting him to express his aggressive fantasies, to understand that he was unrealistically fearful of being the victim or perpetrator of violent acts, and to realize that in his compulsive rituals he was trying to avoid doing anything bad by exerting excessive control over his every action.

In the behavioral approach, which emerged from theories of learning, the focus is primarily on the manifest symptoms themselves, rather than on what is causing them. The treatment seeks to present people with experiences that will extinguish their maladaptive behavior patterns and/or foster learning of more adaptive ones. In Gerald's case a key element in his recovery was the therapist's prescribing certain routines that reduced the disruption in his life while allowing him to continue behaving in an orderly fashion. For example, he was instructed to wash his face by the clock and stop after exactly 3 minutes, a length of time he agreed would be sufficient to get his face clean. This simple procedure quickly eliminated his problem of being late for school in the morning.

At times, proponents of dynamic and behavioral approaches have criticized each other for having too narrow a perspective and failing to meet the needs of their patients fully. Dynamically oriented therapists have been accused of placing too much emphasis on gaining "insight" into problems, without adequate attention to whether this increased self-understanding leads to symptom reduction and improved adjustment. Child psychoanalysts in particular have been criticized for concentrating too much on what children say and do in the therapist's office and too little on how they relate to their parents, how they behave in school, and how they deal with various real-life events.

Behavior therapists have been accused of being mechanistic and impersonal in their use of conditioning procedures to shape behavior, at the expense of adequate attention to what people think and feel; of making authoritarian, unilateral decisions about how their patients' behavior should be changed; and of failing to involve their patients as understanding participants in the treatment process and thereby achieving only temporary symptom removal that is followed by relapse soon after the conditioning procedures are stopped.

None of these criticisms is fully justified. Within the dynamic framework, adequately trained spychotherapists are never satisfied with insight unless it leads to desirable behavior change or symptom relief. Self-understanding is only a means to an end, not the end itself, and contemporary child psychoanalysts state clearly that the goals of treatment are dissolution of symptoms and the patient's fullest possible ability to function effectively (Friend, 1972; Glenn, 1978; Scharfman, 1978). Also stressed among dynamically oriented child therapists are working closely with the family and promoting a therapeutic milieu in the young person's school and other real-life situations (Carek, 1979; Harley, 1974; Ornstein, 1976; Schimel, 1974).

In behavior therapy contemporary trends emphasize promoting self-control and self-determination. Instead of merely shaping behavior as they think necessary, modern behavior therapists try to help their patients manage their own lives and work toward their own self-determined objectives. Dealing with thoughts and feelings is regarded as an important way to help children recognize what is making them symptomatic and promoting long-term recovery (Goldfried & Merbaum, 1973; Graziano, 1978; McGee & Saidel, 1979; Mahoney, 1978; Meichenbaum, 1977; Ross, 1978).

In fact, despite their different origins and conceptions, dynamic and behavioral therapy as currently practiced have much in common. Both seek adaptive changes in thoughts, feelings, and behavior as their long-range goals. Although behavior therapists are somewhat more directive in their techniques than dynamic therapists, both encourage patients to express themselves freely, and both base their approach on establishing a warm personal relationship in which the therapist is seen as an emotionally neutral but friendly, interested, understanding, and nonjudgmental person (Bruinink & Schroeder, 1979; Murray & Jacobson, 1978).

Family Involvement

As the preceding discussion suggests, many child therapists combine dynamic and behavioral approaches in their work. For each individual child with a neurotic disorder, efforts to promote self-understanding and symptom relief are integrated into a treat-

Figure 8.5

Theoretical approaches rated by child psychotherapists as often or always useful. (Based on data reported by Koocher and Pedulla (1977).)

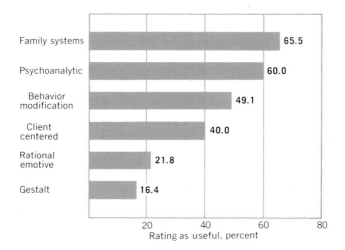

ment plan that best meets his or her needs. There is also almost universal agreement that family members must be involved in some way in the psychotherapy of children and adolescents. Among the therapists surveyed by Koocher and Pedulla (1977), 94 percent reported that most of the parents of their patients are seen concurrently as part of the child's treatment plan. Moreover, as shown in Figure 8.5, these therapists have a high regard for family systems theories, in which youthful disorders are conceived primarily in terms of how family members are interacting with each other.

Many different patterns of parental involvement are used in child and adolescent psychotherapy, depending on the particular situation. Sometimes parents are seen by the young person's therapist in "collateral" visits, which are used primarily to exchange information and review the progress of the treatment. Sometimes they are seen in "tandem" therapy, either by their child's therapist or by another professional, to explore their own personal concerns and to consider what role they may be playing in their child's disorder. Sometimes they are seen in "conjoint" treatment, in which child and parents, and perhaps the entire family, meet regularly with the therapist as a group.

The choice among these alternatives is determined by several factors, including how the family setting appears to be influencing the disorder, how willing the parents are to participate, and what the therapist's preferred style of working happens to be. Each pattern can be effective, so long as it is appropriately tailored to the family's situation and the therapist's talents. Although the discussion of treating neurotic disorders provides a good opportunity to describe these patterns, it is equally important to consider these alternatives in working with the parents of young people with other kinds of disturbance.

Despite differences in how parental involvement is arranged in actual practice, child therapists agree on the following basic principles of working with parents.

1. Both parents are important. Contrary to some traditional emphasis on working with just the mothers of disturbed youngsters, fathers should also be an integral part of the treatment plan.

2. Parents need to be helped to understand as fully as possible the nature of their child's problems and concerns.

3. Parents should not be blamed or made to feel responsible for causing their child's disorder. On the other hand, they should recognize how their behavior may be perpetuating the disorder, and they should accept responsibility for contributing to their child's improvement through the atmosphere they provide at home.

4. Within the limits of their ability to change, parents should be counseled or directed toward specific ways in which they can provide more effective, understanding parenting (Adams, 1978; Arnold, 1978; Reisinger, Ora & Frangia, 1976; Safer, 1978; Schomer, 1978; Sperling, 1979; Wells & Forehand, 1981; Whiteside, 1979).

Drug Therapy

Drugs play a minimal role in the treatment of children and adolescents with neurotic disorders. There is no documented evidence that any known drugs help young people overcome these disorders, with two exceptions among the symptoms mentioned in this

Psychotherapy sessions with an entire family are often useful in helping young people overcome neurotic difficulties.

chapter. *Haloperidol,* a tranquilizer, produces improvement in about 90 percent of children with Gilles de la Tourette syndrome, and *imipramine,* an antidepressant, reduces bed-wetting in about one-third of cases, although relapse usually follows withdrawal of the medication. In addition to their limited utility in milder disorders, drugs may have undesirable side effects, both physical and psychological, that should be avoided in young people if at all possible.

For these reasons, knowledgeable medical practitioners are very conservative in recommending psychoactive drug use with mildly disturbed youthful patients. By and large, tranquilizers and sedatives are included in the treatment plan only to reduce acute distress that cannot be relieved through psychological means and is preventing psychotherapy from getting under way. If used, these drugs are stopped as soon as it appears likely that the treatment can proceed without them (Black, 1979; Campbell & Small, 1978; Greenberg & Stephans, 1977; Patterson & Pruitt, 1977; Shapiro, Shapiro, Bruun, & Sweet, 1978).

SUMMARY

Neurotic behavior consists of repetitively immature, inappropriate, or maladaptive ways of responding to people and situations. The term *neurosis* has been defined in many different ways, sometimes so broadly as to include aspects of how most people behave. Consequently, estimates of the prevalence of neurosis vary widely, and many more people are included in some surveys than should really be considered psychologically disturbed. For these reasons, most psychopathologists avoid referring in any general sense to people "being neurotic," but use *neurosis* only as a convenient term for describing such discrete disorders as *phobic disorder, obsessive-compulsive disorder, conversion reaction,* and *habit disturbance.*

Neurotic ways of dealing with experience can begin early in life, and neurotic symptom pictures can be identified in young people after age 5 or 6. Nevertheless, for varying reasons clinicians have been somewhat reluctant to diagnose neurotic disorders in children and adolescents. Fewer than 2 percent of patients under 18 seen in psychiatric clinics are assigned a diagnosis of neurotic disorder, whereas research studies indicate that at least 5 percent of child-guidance clinic patients have such disorders.

Phobias are unrealistic, disruptive fears of relatively harmless objects or events. They are typically out of proportion to any actual danger and persist despite explanations or reassurances that there is nothing to fear. Most children have certain fears at different ages; when these fears become more pronounced or continue to a more advanced age than would ordinarily be expected, they shade into phobias. Only about 5 percent of children are likely to develop an excessive, incapacitating fear of some object or event, usually between age 4 and 7.

Unlike psychotic disorders, phobias and other neurotic disorders have a more favorable outcome the earlier in life they begin. Among adults who become phobic, approximately 20 to 30 percent recover completely, and an additional 30 percent show some improvement. By contrast, at least 90 percent of phobic children are likely to get over their excessive fears, and the younger they are, the more quickly they recover.

Preschool boys and girls who are anxious or physically timid are especially disposed to phobic disorders. Under some circumstances phobias can be learned from frightening experiences that produce an overgeneralized fear reaction to similar situations. Much more commonly, however, phobic children come to have their excessive fears as a result of modeling themselves after parents who are themselves extremely fearful of one thing or another. Phobias may also arise as the result of young people displacing fears from some real source to previously neutral objects or situations, which then become unrealistically feared.

Just as there are normal developmental fears, most preschool children go through a phase of insisting on certain kinds of routines and order in their lives. In the same way that fears can shade into phobias, routines can turn into maladaptive rituals and preoccupations that constitute obsessive-compulsive disorder. *Obsessions* are recurrent ideas, fears, or doubts that intrude on conscious awareness despite a person's wanting to avoid them. *Compulsions* are repetitive, nonproductive acts that people feel required to carry out, even against their better judgment.

Although obsessive-compulsive behavior is fairly common in the general population, it rarely crystallizes into discrete psychopathology. Primary obsessive-compulsive disorder is diagnosed in just 1.5 to 3 percent of the adults and 1 to 2 percent of the children and adolescents seen in psychiatric clinics and hospitals. Among child-guidance patients it occurs most frequently in the 6- to 10-year-olds, which points to a somewhat later onset than in phobic disorder.

Pathological obsessions and compulsions are most likely to appear in people who have an obsessive-compulsive personality style. These are people whose conduct is determined largely by traits of being cautious, frugal, neat, orderly, rigid, and stubborn. The causes of obsessive-compulsive disorder are largely unknown. Neurotic disorder, like many other features of behavior, runs in families, and some research suggests a possible genetic component in the familial incidence of obsessive-compulsive disorder. Definitive genetic studies have not yet been done in this area, however, and most clinicians and researchers currently believe that experiential factors account for the transmission of obsessive-compulsive personality features from parents to their offspring. In particular, there is good reason to believe that children develop an obsessive-compulsive style at least partly in response to parents who treat them in obsessive-compulsive ways or provide obsessive-compulsive models of coping with experience.

Conversion reactions consist of sensory or motor impairments that arise without any organic cause, usually in the form of pain, numbness, or loss of muscle control in one or more parts of the body. Absence of detectable causes of a somatic problem is never a sufficient condition for diagnosing conversion, however. There should also be evidence that these symptoms express some psychological conflict or need and began in relationship to some clearly precipitating psychological stress.

Opinions vary widely concerning the frequency of conversion reactions in young people, primarily among different clinical settings. Reports from child-guidance and child-psychiatry clinics suggest a 4 to 5 percent prevalence of conversion among youthful patients, whereas surveys in hospital pediatric units identify an approximately 9 percent frequency. One relatively common conversion symptom is tics, which are repetitive, involuntary muscle movements usually of the face, head, and neck. Ticking movements are sometimes due to neurological disorders or simple fidgeting and do not always constitute conversion reactions. Nevertheless, psychological factors usually play some role in tics, which are observed in 5 to 10 percent of elementary school children. Tics tend to reach their peak frequency of occurrence at about age 6 or 7, and over 90 percent of children with tics outgrow them by the time they reach adolescence.

The origins of conversion reactions are not understood any better than the causes of phobic and obsessive-compulsive disorders. To say that they arise as a way of avoiding anxiety by converting it into somatic symptoms describes the process they involve, but does not indicate why certain people develop conversion symptoms. There is evidence that some children are temperamentally disposed to becoming neurotically disturbed in response to psychological stress and that among these youngsters the family environment exerts considerable influence on the kind of disorder they develop. Just as parental models contribute to phobic and obsessive-compulsive symptom formation, children who develop conversion symptoms usually come from families in which considerable attention is paid to health, illness, and bodily functions.

In addition, conversion symptoms are especially likely to occur in children who are developing a hysterical personality style. People with this style generally show characteristics just the opposite from obsessive-compulsive people—they are superficial, changeable, impulsive, careless, and emotional. Conversion reactions are not limited to people who show this personality style, but a hysterical style encourages the expression of ideas and wishes through bodily channels and thus contributes to the choice of conversion symptoms in the event of a neurotic disorder.

Habit disturbances are undesirable traits that, in common with neurotic disorders, represent immature ways of behaving. Unlike neurotic disorders, they do not necessarily arise as ways of defending against anxiety. Nevertheless, habit disturbances can and often do serve psychological needs, and their persistence can contribute to adjustment difficulties. Enuresis, which is nocturnal bed-wetting that persists beyond age 3, occurs in about 15 percent of 4- and 5-year-olds and is still found in 5 percent of 10-year-olds and 2 percent of adolescents. At these ages the disturbance can cause numerous family problems and also interfere with normal peer relationships. Thumb-sucking, which occurs normally up to 3 or 4 years of age, continues as a learned habit in about 2 percent of elementary school children. Like enuresis, persistent thumb-sucking can lead to psychological problems by eliciting negative reactions from parents, peers, and teachers. Although both conditions disappear eventually, efforts to treat them with training or conditioning procedures are advisable once children reach school age, to help them avoid subsequent maladjustment.

Neurotic disorders of childhood and adolescence tend to pass in time and to have relatively few implications for subsequent psychopathology. Treatment of these disorders is nevertheless indicated to hasten recovery from them and to minimize the likelihood of persistent or progressively handicapping disorder. The treatment of choice for neurotic disorders in young people is psychotherapy, and over 80 percent of child psychotherapists believe they are usually effective in treating neurotic children.

Psychotherapy with neurotic children and adolescents aims at removing or reducing their neurotic symptoms and promoting some understanding of what has caused or perpetuated them. The treatment thus usually combines a *dynamic* focus on gaining self-understanding and a *behavioral* focus on symptom removal. These two approaches derive from different theoretical persuasions, and their advocates have at times been highly critical of each other. Yet dynamic therapy and behavioral therapy as currently practiced have much in common. Both seek to achieve adaptive changes in thoughts, feelings, and behavior, and therapists, of both persuasions have been found to conduct treatment sessions in surprisingly similar ways.

In addition to promoting both self-understanding and symptom relief, most child and adolescent therapists agree that the treatment must involve family members. Through either collateral, tandem, or conjoint participation in the therapy, parents and sometimes other family members as well need to be helped to understand as fully as possible the nature of the disturbed child's problems and concerns. Although not being held responsible for the disturbance, the family should accept responsibility for contributing to recovery from it through the atmosphere provided at home.

Drugs play little role in the treatment of children and adolescents with neurotic disorders. Because there is no documented evidence that drugs help young people overcome these disorders and because drugs may have undesirable side effects, knowledgeable medical practitioners include psychoactive drugs in the treatment plan only to reduce acute distress that cannot be relieved through psychological means and is preventing psychotherapy from getting under way.

REFERENCES

ADAMS, P. L. *Obsessive children*. New York: Brunner/Mazel, 1973.

ADAMS, P. L. Guiding parents of "neurotic" children in treatment. In L. E. Arnold (Ed.), *Helping parents help their children*. New York: Brunner/Mazel, 1978.

ADAMS, P. L. Psychoneuroses. In J. D. Noshpitz (Ed.), *Basic handbook of child psychiatry*. Vol. 2. New York: Basic Books, 1979.

AGRAS, W. S., CHAPIN, H. N., & OLIVEAU, D. C. The natural history of phobia. *Archives of General Psychiatry*, 1972, *26*, 315–317.

AGRAS, W. S., SYLVESTER, D., & OLIVEAU, D. C. The epidemiology of common fears and phobia. *Comprehensive Psychiatry*, 1969, *10*, 151–156.

AMERICAN PSYCHIATRIC ASSOCIATION. *Diagnostic and statistical manual of mental disorders*. (3d ed.) Washington, D.C.: American Psychiatric Association, 1980.

ANDERS, T. F., & FREEMAN, E. D. Enuresis. In J. D. Noshpitz (Ed.), *Basic handbook of child psychiatry*. Vol. 2. New York: Basic Books, 1979.

ANTHONY, E. J. Neurotic disorders. In A. M. Freedman, H. I. Kaplan, & B. J. Sadock (Eds.), *Comprehensive textbook of psychiatry* (2nd. ed.). Baltimore: Williams & Wilkins, 1975.

ARNOLD, L. E. Strategies and tactics of parent guidance. In L. E. Arnold (Ed.), *Helping parents help their children*. New York: Brunner/Mazel, 1978.

AZRIN, N. H., & Thienes, P. M. Rapid elimination of enuresis by intensive learning without a conditioning apparatus. *Behavior Therapy*, 1978, *9*, 342–354.

BAUER, D. H. An exploratory study of developmental changes in children's fears. *Journal of Child Psychology and Psychiatry*, 1976, *17*, 69–74.

BECK, A. T., WARD, C., MENDELSON, M., MOCK, J., & ERBAUGH, J. Reliability of psychiatric diagnoses: 2. A study of consistency of clinical judgments and ratings. *American Journal of Psychiatry*, 1962, *119*, 351–357.

BERECZ, J. M. Phobias of childhood: Etiology and treatment. *Psychological Bulletin*, 1968, *70*, 695–720.

BINDELGLAS, P. M. The enuretic child. *Journal of Family Practice*, 1975, *2*, 375–380.

BLACK, S. Minor tranquilizer use in adolescents. In S. C. Feinstein & P. L. Giovacchini (Eds.), *Adolescent psychiatry.* Vol. VII. Chicago: University of Chicago Press, 1979.

BRUININK, S. A., & SCHROEDER, H. E. Verbal therapeutic behavior of expert psychoanalytically oriented, gestalt, and behavior therapists. *Journal of Consulting and Clinical Psychology,* 1979, *47,* 567–574.

BRUUN, R. D., SHAPIRO, E., SWEET, R., WAYNE, H., & SOLOMON, G. A follow-up of 78 patients with Gilles de la Tourette's syndrome. *American Journal of Psychiatry,* 1976, *133,* 944–947.

CAMPBELL, M., & SMALL, A. M. Chemotherapy. In B. B. Wolman (Ed.), *Handbook of treatment of mental disorders in childhood and adolescence.* Englewood Cliffs, N.J.: Prentice-Hall, 1978.

CAREK, D. J. Individual psychodynamically oriented therapy. In J. D. Noshpitz (Ed.), *Basic handbook of child psychiatry.* Vol. 3. New York: Basic Books, 1979.

CASS, L. K., & THOMAS, C. B. *Childhood pathology and later adjustment.* New York: Wiley, 1979.

CAVENAR, J. O., & CAUDILL, L. H. Familial neurotic symptoms. *American Journal of Psychiatry,* 1979, *136,* 1474–1475.

CHESS, S., & HASSIBI, M. *Principles and practice of child psychiatry.* New York: Plenum, 1978.

CHODOFF, P. The diagnosis of hysteria: An overview. *American Journal of Psychiatry,* 1974, *131,* 1073–1078.

COHEN, D. B. On the etiology of neuroses. *Journal of Abnormal Psychology,* 1974, *83,* 473–479.

COHEN, M. W. ENURESIS. *Pediatric Clinics of North America,* 1975, *22,* 545–560.

CORBETT, J., MATHEWS, A., CONNELL, P., & SHAPIRO, D. Tics and Gilles de la Tourette's syndrome: A follow-up study and critical review. *British Journal of Psychiatry,* 1969, *115,* 1229–1241.

DAVIDSON, P. O. Thumbsucking. In C. G. Costello (Ed.), *Symptoms of psychopathology.* New York: Wiley, 1970.

DE JONGE, G. A. Epidemiology in enuresis: A survey of the literature. *Clinical and Developmental Medicine,* 1973, *48/49,* 39–46.

DEVERENSKY, J. L. Children's fears: A developmental comparison of normal and exceptional children. *Journal of Genetic Psychology,* 1979, *135,* 11–21.

DOHRENWEND, B. P. *Mental illness in the United States: Epidemiological estimates.* New York: Praeger, 1980.

ELKIND, D., & WEINER, I. B. *Development of the child.* New York: Wiley, 1978.

ENGEL, G. L. Conversion symptoms. In C. M. MacBride & R. S. Blacklow (Eds.), *Signs and symptoms: Applied physiology and clinical interpretation.* Philadelphia: Lippincott, 1970.

FISHER, S., & GREENBERG, R. P. *The scientific credibility of Freud's theories and therapy.* New York: Basic Books, 1977.

FORSYTHE, W. I., & REDMOND, A. Enuresis and spontaneous cure rate: Study of 1129 enuretics. *Archives of Diseases of Children,* 1974, *49,* 259–263.

FREUD, S. (1908) Character and anal eroticism. *Standard Edition,* Vol. IX. London, Hogarth, 1959.

FREUD, S. (1909) Analysis of a phobia in a five-year-old boy. *Standard Edition,* Vol. X. London: Hogarth, 1955.

FREUD, S. (1913) The disposition to obsessional neurosis. *Standard Edition,* Vol. XII. London: Hogarth, 1958.

FRIEDMAN, S. B. Conversion symptoms in adolescents. *Pediatric Clinics of North America,* 1973, *20,* 873–882.

FRIEND, M. R. Psychoanalysis of adolescents. In B. B. Wolman (Ed.), *Handbook of child psychoanalysis.* New York: Van Nostrand Reinhold, 1972.

GLENN, J. General principles of child analysis. In J. Glenn (Ed.), *Child analysis and therapy.* New York: Aronson, 1978.

GLICK, B. S. Conditioning therapy with phobic patients: Success and failure. *American Journal of Psychotherapy,* 1970, *24,* 92–101.

GOGGIN, J. E., & ERICKSON, H. M. Dilemmas in diagnosis and treatment of Gilles de la Tourette Syndrome. *Journal of Personality Assessment,* 1979, *43,* 339–348.

GOLDFRIED, M. R., & MERBAUM, M. A perspective on self-control. In M. R. Goldfried & M. Merbaum (Eds.), *Behavior change through self-control.* New York: Holt, Rinehart & Winston, 1973.

GOTTESMAN, I. I. Heritability of personality: A demonstration. *Psychological Monographs,* 1963, *77,* 1–21.

GRAY, M. *Neuroses: A comprehensive and critical view:* New York: Van Nostrand Reinhold, 1978.

GRAZIANO, A. M. Behavior therapy. In B. B. Wolman (Ed.), *Handbook of treatment of mental disorders in childhood and adolescence.* Englewood cliffs, N.J.: Prentice-Hall, 1978.

GREENBERG, L. M., & STEPHANS, J. H. Use of drugs in special syndromes: Enuresis, tics, school refusal, and anorexia nervosa. In J. M. Wiener (Ed.), *Psychopharmacoloy in childhood and adolescence.* New York: Basic Books, 1977.

GROSS, M. Pseudoepilepsy: A study in adolescent hysteria. *American Journal of Psychiatry,* 1979, *136,* 210–213.

GROSS, M., & HUERTA, E. Functional convulsions masked as epileptic disorders. *Journal of Pediatric Psychology,* 1980, *5,* 71–79.

HAMPE, E., NOBLE, H., MILLER, L. C., & BARRETT, C. L. Phobic children one and two years post-treatment. *Journal of Abnormal Psychology,* 1973, *82,* 446–453.

HARLEY, M. (Ed.) *The analyst and the adolescent at work.* New York: Quadrangle, 1974.

HOLLINGSWORTH, C. E., TANGUAY, P. E., GROSSMAN, L., & PABST, L. Long-term outcome of obsessive-compulsive disorder in childhood. *Journal of the American Academy of Child Psychiatry,* 1980, *19,* 134–144.

HOROWITZ, M. J. The core characteristics of hysterical personality. In M. J. Horowitz (Ed.), *Hysterical personality.* New York: Aronson, 1977.

INOUYE, E. Genetic aspects of neurosis: A review. *International Journal of Mental Health,* 1972, *1,* 176–189.

KENDELL, R. E. *The role of diagnosis in psychiatry.* Oxford: Blackwell, 1975.

KESSLER, J. W. Neurosis in childhood. In B. B. Wolman (Ed.), *Manual of child psychopathology.* New York: McGraw-Hill, 1972.

KOHLBERG, L., LACROSSE, J., & RICKS, D. The predictability of adult mental health from childhood behavior. In B. B. Wolman (Ed.), *Manual of child psychopathology.* New York: McGraw-Hill, 1972.

KOOCHER, G. P., & PEDULLA, B. M. Current practices in child psychotherapy. *Professional Psychology,* 1977, *8,* 275–287.

KREITMAN, N., SAINSBURY, P., MORRISEY, J., TOWERS, J., & SCRIVENER, J. The reliability of psychiatric assessment: An analysis. *Journal of Mental Science,* 1961, *107,* 887–908.

KROHN, A. *Hysteria: The elusive neurosis.* New York: International Universities Press, 1978.

LAPOUSE, R., & MONK, M. A. Fears and worries in a representative sample of children. *American Journal of Orthopsychiatry,* 1962, *29,* 803–818.

LAPOUSE, R., & MONK, M. Behavior deviations in a representative sample of children: Variation by sex, age, race, social class, and family size. *American Journal of Orthopsychiatry,* 1964, *34,* 436–446.

LARGO, R. H., & STUTZLE, W. Longitudinal study of bowel and bladder control by day and at night in the first six years of life. *Developmental Medicine and Child Neurology,* 1977, *19,* 598–606.

LAYBOURNE, P. C., & CHURCHILL, S. W. Symptom discouragement in treating hysterical reactions of childhood. *International Journal of Child Psychotherapy,* 1972, *1,* 111–123.

LOOF, D. H. Psychophysiologic and conversion reactions in children. *Journal of the American Academy of Child Psychiatry,* 1970, *9,* 318–331.

LUCAS, A. R. Tic: Gilles de la Tourette's syndrome. In J. D. Noshpitz (Ed.), *Basic handbook of child psychiatry.* Vol. 2. New York: Basic Books. 1979.

MCDONALD, J. E. Enuresis: A social problem. *Child Study Journal,* 1978, *8,* 235–241.

MCGEE, J. P., & SAIDEL, D. H. Individual behavior therapy. In J. D. Noshpitz (Ed.), *Basic handbook of child psychiatry.* Vol. 3. New York: Basic Books, 1979.

MCKENDRY, J. B. J., & STEWART, D. A. Enuresis. *Pediatric Clinics of North America, 1974, 24,* 1019–1027.

MAHONEY, M. J. Cognitive and self-control therapies. In S. L. Garfield and A. E. Bergin (Eds.), *Handbook of psychotherapy and behavior change* (2nd ed.). New York: Wiley, 1978.

MALMQUIST, C. P. Hysteria in childhood. *Postgraduate Medicine, 1971, 50,* 112–117.

MARKS, I. M. *Fears and phobias.* New York: American Press, 1969.

MARKS, I. M. Phobic disorders four years after treatment: A prospective follow-up. *British Journal of Psychiatry, 1971, 118,* 683–688.

MARKS, I. M. Phobias and obsessions: Clinical phenomena in search of laboratory models. In J. D. Maser & M. E. P. Seligman (Eds.), *Psychopathology: Experimental Models.* San Francisco: Freeman, 1977.

MARKS, I. M. *Cure and cause of neurosis.* New York: Wiley, 1981.

MEICHENBAUM, D. *Cognitive-behavior modification.* New York: Plenum, 1977.

MILLER, L. C., BARRETT, C. L., & HAMPE, E. Phobias of childhood in a prescientific era. In A. Davids (Ed.), *Child personality and psychopathology.* Vol. 1. New York: Wiley, 1974.

MINER, G. D. The evidence for genetic components in the neuroses. *Archives of General Psychiatry, 1973, 29,* 111–118.

MURRAY, E. J., & JACOBSON, L. I. Cognition and learning in traditional and behavioral psychotherapy. In S. L. Garfield & A. E. Bergin (Eds.), *Handbook of psychotherapy and behavior change* (2nd ed.). New York: Wiley, 1978.

NEMIAH, J. C. Neurotic disorders. In A. M. Freedman, H. I. Kaplan, & B. J. Sadock (Eds.), *Comprehensive textbook of psychiatry* (3d ed.). Baltimore: Williams & Wilkins, 1980.

NOYES, R., CLANCY, J., CROWE, R., HOENK, P. R., & SLYMEN, D.J. The familial prevalence of anxiety neurosis. *Archives of General Psychiatry, 1978, 35,* 1057–1059.

OPPEL, W. C., HARPER, P. A., & RIDER, R. V. The age of attaining bladder control. *Pediatrics, 1968, 42,* 614–626.

ORNSTEIN, A. Making contact with the inner world of the child: Toward a theory of psychoanalytic psychotherapy with children. *Comprehensive Psychiatry, 1976, 17,* 3–36.

OUTPATIENT PSYCHIATRIC SERVICES. Distribution of admissions by primary diagnosis and age, 1975. Rockville, Md.: National Institute of Mental Health, 1978.

PATTERSON, J. H., & PRUITT, A. W. Treatment of mild symptomatic anxiety states. In J. M. Wiener (Ed.), *Psychopharmacology in childhood and adolescence.* New York: Basic Books, 1977.

PIERCE, C.M. Enuresis and encopresis. In A. M. Freedman, H. I. Kaplan, & B. J. Sadock (Eds.), *Comprehensive textbook of psychiatry* (2nd ed.). Baltimore: Williams & Wilkins, 1975.

POLLACK, J. M. Obsessive-compulsive personality: A review. *Psychological Bulletin, 1979, 86,* 225–241.

POPPER, K. *The logic of scientific discovery.* New York: Basic Books, 1959.

POZNANSKI, E. O. Children with excessive fears. *American Journal of Orthopsychiatry, 1973, 43,* 428–438.

PRAZAR, G., & FRIEDMAN, S. B. Conversion reactions. In S. B. Friedman & R. A. Hoekelman (Eds.), *Behavioral pediatrics.* New York: McGraw-Hill, 1980.

PRIVATE MENTAL HOSPITAL INPATIENT UNITS. Distribution of admissions by primary diagnosis and age, 1975. Rockville, Md.: National Institute of Mental Health, 1978.

PROCTOR, J. Hysteria in childhood. *American Journal of Orthopsychiatry, 1958, 28,* 394–406.

RACHMAN, S. J., & HODGSON, R. J. *Obsessions and compulsions.* Englewood Cliffs, N.J.: Prentice-Hall, 1980.

RAE, W. A. Childhood conversion reactions: A review of incidence in pediatric settings. *Journal of Clinical Child Psychology, 1977, 6,* 69–72.

RAINER, J. D. Genetics of neurosis and personality disorder. In M. A. Sperber & L. F. Jarvik (Eds.), *Psychiatry and genetics.* New York: Basic Books, 1976.

REISINGER, J. J., ORA, J. P., & FRANGIA, G. W. Parents as change agents for their children. *Journal of Community Psychology, 1976, 4,* 103–123.

ROBINOWITZ, C. B. Habit disorders. In J. D. Noshpitz (Ed.), *Basic handbook of child psychiatry,* Vol. 2. New York: Basic Books, 1979.

ROBINS, L. N. Follow-up studies. In H. C. Quay & J. S. Werry (Eds.), *Psychopathological disorders of childhood* (2nd ed.). New York: Wiley, 1979.

ROCK, N. Conversion reactions in childhood: A clinical study on childhood neuroses. *Journal of the American Academy of Child Psychiatry, 1971, 10,* 65–93.

ROSS, A. O. Behavior therapy with children. In S. L. Garfield & A. E. Bergin (Eds.), *Handbook of psychotherapy and behavior change* (2nd ed.). New York: Wiley, 1978.

RUTTER, M., TIZARD, J., & WHITMORE, K. *Education, health, and behaviour.* New York: Wiley, 1970.

SAFER, D. J. Guiding parents of children with habit symptoms. In L. E. Arnold (Ed.), *Helping parents help their children.* New York: Brunner/Mazel, 1978.

SALZMAN, L. *The obsessive personality.* New York: Science House, 1968.

SCHARFMAN, M. A. Psychoanalytic treatment. In B. B. Wolman (Ed.), *Handbook of treatment of mental disorders in childhood and adolescence.* Englewood Cliffs, N.J.: Prentice-Hall, 1978.

SCHIMEL, J. L. Two alliances in the treatment of adolescents: Toward a working alliance with parents and a therapeutic alliance with the adolescent. *Journal of the American Academy of Psychoanalysis, 1974, 2,* 243–253.

SCHOMER, J. Family therapy. In B. B. Wolman (Ed.), *Handbook of treatment of mental disorders in childhood and adolescence.* Englewood Cliffs, N.J.: Prentice-Hall, 1978.

SHAPIRO, A., SHAPIRO, E., BRUUN, R., & SWEET, R. *Gilles de la Tourette Syndrome.* New York: Raven Press, 1978.

SHAPIRO, A. K., & WAYNE, H. L. The symptomatology and diagnosis of Gilles de la Tourette's syndrome. *Journal of the American Academy of Child Psychiatry, 1973, 12,* 702–723.

SHAPIRO, D. *Neurotic styles.* New York: Basic Books, 1965.

SHIELDS, J., & SLATER, E. Diagnostic similarity in twins with neurosis and personality disorders. In J. Shields & I. Gottesman (Eds.), *Man, mind and heredity.* Baltimore: Johns Hopkins University Press, 1972.

SOURS, J. A. Enuresis. In B. B. Wolman (Ed.), *Handbook of treatment of mental disorders in childhood and adolescence.* New York: Englewood Cliffs, N.J.: Prentice-Hall, 1978.

SPERLING, E. Parent counseling and therapy. In J. D. Noshpitz (Ed.), *Basic handbook of child psychiatry.* Vol. 3. New York: Basic Books, 1979.

SPERLING, M. Animal phobias in a two-year-old child. *Psychoanalytic Study of the Child, 1952, 7,* 115–125.

SPITZER, R. L., SHEEHY, M., & ENDICOTT, J. DSM-III: Guiding principles. In V. M. Rakoff, H. C. Stancer, & H. B. Kedward (Eds.), *Psychiatric diagnosis.* New York: Brunner/Mazel, 1977.

STATE AND COUNTY MENTAL HOSPITALS. Admissions by age and diagnosis, 1976. Rockville, Md.: National Institute of Mental Health, 1978.

STROBER, M., & GREEN, J. Diagnosis of adolescent psychopathology. *American Journal of Orthopsychiatry,* in press.

TEMPLER, D. I. The obsessive-compulsive neurosis: Review of research findings. *Comprehensive Psychiatry, 1972, 13,* 375–383.

TEMPLER, D. I., & LESTER, D. Conversion disorders: A review of research findings. *Comprehensive Psychiatry, 1974, 15,* 285–294.

THOMAS, A., & CHESS, S. *Temperament and development.* New York: Brunner/Mazel, 1977.

THOMAS, A., CHESS, C., & BIRCH, H. G. *Temperament and behavior disorders in children.* New York: New York University Press, 1968.

THOMPSON, R. J., O'QUINN, A. N., & LOGUE, P. E. Gilles de la Tourette's syndrome: A review and neuropsychobiological aspects of four cases. *Journal of Pediatric Psychology,* 1979, *4,* 371–387.

THORNE, D. E. Instrumented behavior modification of bedwetting. *Behavioral Engineering,* 1975, *2,* 47–51.

TORGERSEN, A. M., & KRINGLEN, E. Genetic aspects of temperamental differences in infants. *Journal of the American Academy of Child Psychiatry,* 1978, *17,* 435–444.

TORUP, E. A follow-up study of children with tics. *Acta Paediatrica,* 1962, *51,* 261–268.

TYSON, R. L. Notes on the analysis of a prelatency boy with a dog phobia. *Psychoanalytic Study of the Child,* 1978, *33,* 427–458.

WALLICK, M. M. Desensitization therapy with a fearful two-year-old. *American Journal of Psychiatry,* 1979, *136,* 1325–1326.

WATSON, J. B., & RAYNER, R. Conditioned emotional reactions. *Journal of Experimental Psychology,* 1920, *3,* 1–14.

WEINER, I. B. Behavior therapy in obsessive-compulsive neurosis. *Psychotherapy: Theory, Research and Practice,* 1967, *4,* 27–29.

WELLS, K. C., & FOREHAND, R. Childhood behavior problems in the home. In S. M. Turner, K. S. Calhoun, & H. E. Adams (Eds.), *Handbook of clinical behavior therapy.* New York: Wiley, 1981.

WERRY, J. S. The conditioning treatment of enuresis. *American Journal of Psychiatry,* 1966, *123,* 226–229.

WERRY, J. S. Psychosomatic disorders, psychogenic symptoms, and hospitalization. In H. C. Quay & J. S. Werry (Eds.), *Psychopathological disorders of childhood* (2nd ed.). New York: Wiley, 1979.

WERRY, J. S., & CORRSEN, J. Enuresis: An etiologic and therapeutic study. *Journal of Pediatrics,* 1965, *67,* 423–431.

WHITESIDE, M. F. Family therapy. In J. D. Noshpitz (Ed.), *Basic handbook of child psychiatry.* Vol. 3. New York: Basic Books, 1979.

WOODROW, K. Gilles de la Tourette's disease—a review. *American Journal of Psychiatry,* 1974, *131,* 1000–1003.

YATES, A. J. Tics. In C. G. Costello (Ed.), *Symptoms of psychopathology.* New York: Wiley, 1970.

YATES, A., & STEWARD, M. Conversion hysteria in childhood: A case report and a reminder. *Clinical Pediatrics,* 1976, *15,* 379–382.

ZUBIN, J. Classification of the behavior disorders. *Annual Review of Psychology,* 1967, *18,* 373–401.

9

SCHOOL PHOBIA

School phobia is a reluctance or refusal to go to school because of intense anxiety about being there. As a form of phobic disorder, it involves dread in the school setting that is out of proportion to any real danger and cannot be relieved by explanations or reassurances that there is nothing to fear.

Although school phobia shares the characteristics of phobic disorder discussed in the previous chapter, a separate chapter on it is indicated for two reasons. First, the nature and origins of school phobia and approaches to treating it have received much more attention in the literature than other youthful phobic disorders and most other broad categories of childhood neurosis. Second, school phobia more often goes undetected by parents and teachers than other neurotic disorders and hence merits special attention to promote its being recognized and responded to adequately.

This chapter on school phobia also provides a bridge between Chapters 3 to 8 on specific diagnostic categories—mental retardation, minimal brain dysfunction/attention deficit disorder, childhood psychosis, schizophrenia, affective disorder, and neurotic disorders—and Chapters 10 to 13, which deal with behavioral problems that cut across specific diagnostic categories. In fact, some writers prefer to call school phobia "school avoidance" or "school refusal" and to regard it as an adjustment difficulty that can derive from many types of neurotic or psychotic disorder, not just from phobic anxiety (Kahn & Nursten, 1962; Kahn, Nursten, & Carroll, 1980; Millar, 1961).

It is certainly useful to keep in mind that children may have difficulty attending school for many different reasons. However, nothing new is learned about this problem by recognizing that it can occur as a secondary consequence of being schizophrenic or depressed. Moreover, clinicians over the years have consistently identified cases of school refusal in which the anxiety has emerged just as in classic phobic symptom formation (Malmquist, 1965; Sperling, 1967; Waldfogel, Coolidge, & Hahn, 1957). Despite some objections to a narrow definition of it, then, *school phobia* has become a well-entrenched term that is favored in current usage over alternative labels (Coolidge, 1979; Shapiro & Jegede, 1973).

CHARACTERISTICS OF SCHOOL PHOBIA

School-phobic children typically express their reluctance to attend school through physical complaints that convince their parents to keep them home or the school nurse to excuse them from the classroom. The most common complaints are headache, abdominal pain, nausea, and sore throat. Although school-phobic children sometimes fabricate such complaints, they usually suffer real physical distress, including pain, diarrhea, vomiting, and even a mild fever. Occasionally they anticipate rather than suffer such problems, in which case they warn their parents that they are certain to become ill if they are sent to school. In other instances, either in addition to or instead of physical ailments, school-phobic children offer various criticisms of the school situation as their reason for not wanting to go: the teacher is mean and unfair, the work is boring or too difficult, the bus ride is too long, the other children are unfriendly, and so forth.

Whether expressed as physical complaints or criticisms of the school, the apprehensions of school-phobic children cannot be ignored or suppressed. If they are forced to go to school despite their complaints, these children often do become so ill or upset that they have to be sent home. Yet, consistent with their having a neurotic disorder, neither their physical discomfort nor their other complaints can be taken at face value.

The bodily symptoms of school-phobic children usually appear in the morning when they wake up and disappear shortly after a decision has been made that they do not have to attend school that day. If it is then suggested that they go to school in the afternoon, their symptoms reappear within the hour; if they are permitted to stay home for a day, their symptoms return the next morning; if the parents then decide to forget about school for the rest of the week, their child is likely to remain in good health and spirits until the following Monday, when the aches and pains return in full force. Weekends are an especially good time for school-phobic children, since they can be active and enjoy themselves without risking any pressures to go to school. The parents of these youngsters accordingly have a roller-coaster experience with them. A symptom-free afternoon or weekend lulls them into believing that the problem is over, while the dawn of the next day or the arrival of Monday morning puts them back with a sick child on their hands.

As for criticisms of the school raised by school-phobic children, these invariably turn out to be rationalizations rather than the real reasons for their not wanting to go. Attempts to respond constructively to the complaints—changing the teacher, putting the children into a less advanced class, driving them to school, or even sending them to a different school—bring only temporary results. At first the children are happy and appreciative and approach the changed school situation with enthusiasm. A few days or weeks later, however, they are back home again, complaining about some aspect of the new situation and refusing to return. As these observations indicate, the true origin of a school phobia lies not in any stated complaints, but in unstated and sometimes unconscious concerns these young people have about attending school (Coolidge, 1979; Eisenberg, 1958; Radin, 1967; Waldfogel et al., 1957).

These and other features of school phobia distinguish it from realistic fears about school and from truancy. As an example of realistic fears, a boy who has been threatened with a beating by the school bully or who faces an examination he expects to fail may be understandably apprehensive about going to school. If he learns that the bully has been expelled from school or that the examination has been canceled, his fears evaporate. Phobic anxiety, because it derives from exaggerated concerns that go beyond what is immediately apparent, rarely disappears following such obvious or superficial changes in the environment.

With respect to truancy, it is interesting that one of the first clinical descriptions of school phobia appears in a paper by Broadwin (1932) addressed to "the study of truancy." Broadwin reviewed his experience with youngsters who were consistently absent from school for extended periods of time during which they remained at home with their parents' knowledge. These youngsters could offer no comprehensible reason for their school refusal, other than that they were fearful and unable to function there. While at home, on the other hand, they remained happy, content, and symptom-free.

Subsequent clinical and research reports indicate that such a pattern of difficulty attending school has little in common with typical truancy. Truant youngsters usually dislike school and are doing poorly in their studies. They have little interest in academic pursuits and spend their truant time having fun away from home without their parents' knowledge or consent. By contrast, most school-phobic children linger at home with their parent's consent if not their approval. At school they are earning at least average grades, and they are concerned about falling behind in their studies. When asked, they say they enjoy school and would like to be able to return (Berg, Collins, McGuire, & O'Melia, 1975; Eisenberg, 1958; Hersov, 1960a; Szyrynski, 1976).

Acute and Chronic School Phobia

When school-phobic reactions first appear, they usually take the form of an *acute* disorder. The symptoms appear suddenly in a youngster who has not previously had school attendance or other behavioral problems, and their onset can be traced to precipitating events that have caused increased anxiety about being in school. Although episodes of acute school phobia may recur, they do not interfere with personality functioning or social development outside of school. Acute school-phobic children tend to be happy and industrious so long as they are allowed to remain at home. They continue to enjoy their friendships and peer-group activities, and they often keep up with their studies if their work is sent home.

Acute school phobia can occur at any age, from elementary school through high school and even among college students. Among adolescents and young adults, however, such an acute reaction becomes less likely to appear for the first time than as a recurrence of earlier childhood difficulties in attending school (Hodgman & Braiman, 1965; Levenson, 1961). Even more commonly as children grow older, school phobia no longer occurs as an acute or recurrent reaction to precipitating stresses, but instead constitutes a *chronic* and persistent disorder. Chronic school phobia develops gradually, in the absence of obvious precipitating circumstances, in youngsters who have a history of behavior problems, including acute school phobia. As an apt way of making this distinction, acute school phobia has been referred to as a "neurotic crisis" and chronic school phobia as a "way of life" (Coolidge, Hahn, & Peck, 1957; Kennedy, 1965; Miller, Barrett, & Hampe, 1974).

Unlike acute school phobia, chronic school phobia involves adjustment difficulties that go beyond the attendance problem. Chronic school-phobic children tend to withdraw not just from school but from other previously enjoyed activities as well. They mope around the house without accomplishing anything, neither studying nor pursuing hobbies. Additionally, their fears of school often become generalized to the environment. They consequently grow increasingly uncomfortable in interpersonal or unfamiliar situations and cling to their parents at the expense of maintaining social contact with their peers. The more repetitive and prolonged school-phobic reactions are, the more likely such widespread adjustment problems are to be present.

Prevalence of School Phobia

Despite the characteristic patterns of symptom formation that accompany school phobia, this disorder often goes unrecognized. The real physical distress of these children and their seemingly reasonable complaints about school frequently mask their actual pathologica anxiety about going to school. Parents and physicians often focus on the physical problems, without appreciating their psychological origin, while schools often fail to understand the emotional problems that underlie these particular problems of nonattendance. In one study, for example, it was found that fewer than one-third of a group of adults with a clear history of childhood school-phobic episodes had ever been referred for help (Tyrer & Tyrer, 1974).

Because of limitations in recognizing and reporting this condition, the frequency of school phobia is uncertain. Best estimates are that it occurs in 1 to 2 percent of the school population and in 5 to 8 percent of youngsters referred for professional care (Kahn & Nursten, 1962; Kennedy, 1965; Leton, 1962; Miller, Hampe, Barrett, & Noble, 1971; Tyrer & Tyrer, 1974). As a further clue to its frequency in clinical settings, Drotar (1977) reports that 35 percent of the children referred for psychological consultation in a pediatric hospital had unexplained physical complaints that were often accompanied by school avoidance.

Three other basic facts about school phobia have emerged from clinical surveys. First, it occurs about equally in males and females. Among several hundred cases of school phobia included in 17 different studies, 260 were boys and 267 were girls (Gordon & Young, 1976).

Second, school-phobic children do not differ from their classmates in intelligence or achievement level. Although numerous reports have suggested that school-phobic children tend to be brighter than average, systematic research indicates that both IQ scores and levels of attainment are distributed similarly in school-phobic youngsters and in the general school population (Hampe, Miller, Barrett, & Noble, 1973).

Third, the incidence of school phobia—that is, the number of new cases found within a particular period of time—shows two distinct peaks, one between age 5 and 8 and the other from age 11 to 14 (Rutter, Tizard, Yule, Graham, & Whitmore, 1976; Tyrer & Tyrer, 1974). School phobia is thus most likely to begin either in the early years of elementary school or when youngsters are entering junior and senior high school. These incidence peaks at times of major change or transition in a young person's life are consistent with what is known about common precipitating circumstances in the origins of school phobia, as discussed in the next section.

ORIGINS OF SCHOOL PHOBIA

Like other phobias, exaggerated fears of attending school are determined primarily by psychological experiences, rather than by any genetic or constitutional influences (see pp. 306–308). The probability that a phobic-prone child will become unreasonably afraid of going to school, instead of some other previously neutral object or event, stems from a particular set of disposing and precipitating factors that are typically found in association with this disorder.

Disposing Factors

The disposition to school phobia emerges from a pattern of family interaction that promotes excessive dependency. The mothers of school-phobic children tend to overprotect them early in life. These mothers strive continually to gratify their childrens' needs, to spare them from any deprivation or frustration, and to curry their love and affection.

They themselves appear to thrive on catering to their children's every wish. They are especially solicitous to any physical ills, and they tend to feel lonely and unfulfilled when their children are not at home requiring attention. In their needs to keep their children physically and psychologically close to them, such mothers commonly avoid sending them to a nursery school or taking them to someone else's house to play, and they may even give up their own social activities out of reluctance to leave them with a baby-sitter.

This type of mothering during the early years sets the stage for children to balk at going to school. Having had little or no experience away from their mother's protective presence, they may be extremely anxious at the prospect of separating from her and spending the day in a strange environment with unfamiliar people. Because of their own needs, moreover, these mothers are quick to accept their child's complaints as sufficient reason for them to stay home and be cared for. Some mothers may even directly encourage nonattendance by finding their own reasons for keeping their children at home, such as bad weather, a slight cough, or the advisability of resting up before a family trip (Berg, & McGuire, 1974; Clyne, 1966; Estes, Haylett, & Johnson, 1956; Waldron, Shrier, Stone, & Tobin, 1975).

The fathers of school-phobic children typically contribute to their overdependency in one of two ways. Most often they share with their wives a need to protect and cater to their children, as a way of keeping them close and winning their love. These fathers tend to be more concerned with maintaining peace in the family than with providing rules or administering discipline. Like their wives, they accordingly retreat from any hint of impending unpleasantness and yield to their children's demands at the first sign of tears or tantrums. They are also as quick as the mothers of school-phobic children to

In young children anxiety about separating from their parents may lead to phobic dread of going to school.

accept or even suggest themselves flimsy reasons why their youngsters should remain at home rather than go to school.

In some cases fathers foster the disposition to school phobia indirectly, not by being overprotective themselves but by encouraging their wives to be. These tend to be men who are detached from their family and too absorbed in their own activities to pay much attention to what goes on at home. This detachment encourages an overprotective mother and an overdependent child to draw even closer together. A close mother-child relationship suits the purposes of the disinterested father well, since he is spared from being bothered with parental responsibilities (Chotiner & Forrest, 1974; Coolidge, 1979; Malmquist, 1965; Weiss & Cain, 1964).

In response to such child-rearing attitudes, children who are disposed to school phobia usually develop three characteristic personality features. First, having been overprotected, they tend to grow up as dependent, clinging young people. Their poor preparation for independence exposes them to considerable anxiety in situations where they are expected or required to act on their own. Their inclination in such situations is understandably to withdraw to the safe dependency they have known at home under their parents' wing.

Second, because of the way in which their parents have catered to them and even encouraged them to impose their needs on the family, these children frequently become demanding and manipulative. They want what they want when they want it. They whine, plead, cry, yell, stamp their feet, hold their breath, make all sorts of promises and threats—whatever they think may be effective in bending a situation to their will. When they cannot get their own way, they take their marbles and go home—a metaphor that very much captures the nature of refusing to stay in school.

Third, as a result of their parents' reluctance to discipline or frustrate them, school-phobic children have usually developed an exaggerated sense of mastery. Often they have been able to govern not only their own affairs, but even such household matters as when meals will be served and when their parents will have company, with tantrums, threats, and physical complaints. While becoming expert at getting their parents to capitulate, however, school-phobic youngsters have usually had little opportunity for a realistic appraisal of how much mastery they can exert outside of their home. Typically, then, they approach the school situation with an unjustified belief in their own powers and little self-assurance to fall back on when they learn that the world does not fall at their feet the way their parents do (Jackson, 1964; Levenson, 1961; Leventhal & Sills, 1964).

These patterns of family interaction are neither unique to school phobia nor always predictive of it. Some school-phobic children and their parents may not fit the above description in every way; moreover, a family constellation of an overprotective mother, an equally overprotective or detached father, and a clinging, manipulative, overconfident youngster may be associated with a variety of pathological states or with no psychopathology at all. In addition, the onset of an overt school-phobic reaction requires the interaction of predisposing family patterns with precipitating events that intensify concerns about leaving home or attending school, discussed next. These qualifications notwithstanding, the family patterns outlined above will be found to characterize most instances of school phobia.

Precipitating Factors

Episodes of school phobia occur in response to experiences that increase children's anxiety about separating from their parents or being in school. These precipitating events are most obvious in acute school-phobic reactions and tend to be less apparent as school phobia becomes a more chronic way of life. Even gradually developing, long-standing inability to attend school begins somewhere, however, and careful study in these cases reveals distressing experiences that, although now remote, set the chronic school-phobic child's nonattendance in motion.

The most common precipitating factors in school phobia involve actual separations, changes, or embarrassments that children who are disposed to this condition cannot handle. With respect to *separation*, overdependent children often worry that something bad will happen to their parents when the family is not at home together. If a parent has become ill or if there has been a fire or burglary at home while they are at school, they may become very anxious about leaving the house. It is as if the child feels a responsibility to be at home to "make sure" that nothing happens (Nader, Bullock, & Caldwell, 1975). For these same reasons, such events as parents talking about a divorce or going away on a vacation or into the hospital for an operation can be involved in precipitating a school-phobic crisis.

Change is difficult for these children whenever it puts them in new situations in which they may have to act more independently than before. Moves to a new home, neighborhood, school, grade, or classroom are especially likely to be involved in the onset of a school phobia, because children must start fresh in establishing relationships with teachers and peers. This explains why school phobia is most likely to begin either during the early elementary school years or on entrance to junior or senior high school. Starting elementary school obviously makes many new demands on children for self-reliant behavior away from their parents' protection. Once they have settled into a familiar elementary school routine, however, even overdependent children may feel fairly secure. Hence the likelihood of becoming school phobic for the first time tails off in the fourth, fifth, and sixth grades.

With entrance to junior and particularly senior high school, young people must give up their single classroom and a primary relationship with one teacher. They change classes and teachers several times a day, under minimal supervision, and they are given increasing responsibility for budgeting their time, organizing their studying, and even choosing their subjects. Youngsters who are poorly prepared for such independence may experience a marked upsurge of anxiety when they move from a relatively structured elementary school program to such ambiguous junior and senior high school settings, and a reluctance to attend school may result.

As for *embarrassments*, school phobia especially in older children is often brought on by unpleasant school experiences that lead overdependent youngsters to prefer to remain safely at home. These experiences are seldom included among the reasons given by youngsters for not wanting to go to school, usually because they are too painful for them to talk or even think about. Particularly common among early adolescents who become school phobic are unpleasant experiences related to normal devel-

Adolescents who become school phobic are frequently reacting to unpleasant or embarrassing experiences in school.

opmental concerns at this age about the growth and adequacy of their bodies. Thus an athletically inept boy who is humiliated in his gym class may develop headaches or bouts of nausea that, significantly, appear only on the days when he has gym. Similarly, a physically precocious 10- or 11-year-old girl who is self-conscious about her breast development may become so upset about her classmates staring at her—whether or not they are in fact paying any special attention to her physical appearance—that she begins to find reasons for staying home.

In a more general sense, young people who are worried about how they look, whether for good or imagined reasons, may find school intolerable just because it puts them under constant scrutiny by teachers and peers. Whether because of feeling ugly or actually suffering some physical limitations or deformity resulting from handicap or illness, children disposed to school phobia may as early adolescents begin for the first time to prefer to remain at home (Lansky, Lowman, Vats, & Gyulay, 1975).

By high school the peak of normal bodily concern among adolescents has passed, and young people are increasingly caught up in developmental tasks related to success in dating and heterosexual relationships. School phobia then is likely to be precipitated by social rejections that make young people feel unable to participate as a member of their peer group. When going to school becomes a daily reminder of social inadequacy for adolescents who are already disposed to deal with stress by clinging to the bosom of their family, school-phobic reactions are highly likely to occur.

Case 12. *Acute School Phobia*

Beverly, a 12-year-old sixth-grade student, announced to her parents on a Monday morning that she would no longer attend school. When pressed for her reasons, she referred only to having been humiliated in class the previous Friday when several boys had laughed at her inability to answer a question. After failing for a week to get Beverly to change her mind, her parents sought professional help. They reported that although her school refusal had arisen suddenly, she had been increasingly irritable, short-tempered, and insistent on having her own way since she had begun to menstruate several months earlier.

Beverly was a large, well-developed girl who looked older than her 12 years. When interviewed she was pleasant and agreeable and expressed regret over the worry she was causing her parents. She denied having any problems or concerns and stated that she missed being with her friends and was ready to return to school. The therapist supported—and perhaps was manipulated by—these positive statements, and her return to school was planned for the next day.

The following evening the therapist received a telephone call from Beverly's father, during which she could be heard screaming in the background. She had talked her mother into allowing her to remain at home that morning ("Let me have just one more day to get myself ready"). When her father had come home from work in the evening and expressed displeasure at this turn of events, she had responded by breaking dishes until he stopped scolding her. He was able, however, to muster sufficient resolve to call the therapist, over her objections.

When the family was seen for their second interview the next day, their information left little doubt that Beverly kept her parents constantly on the defensive with insistent demands, rapidly changing decisions, and well-timed tantrums. She was an acutely sensitive girl who had become very skillful at exploiting what turned out to be very strong desires on her parents' part to placate her and equally strong fears lest they do the wrong thing as parents.

In interviews and telephone calls over the subsequent week, the therapist concentrated on encouraging Beverly's parents to deal with her firmly and to insist that she make good on her promise to return to school. Gradually, with constant reassurance that they were behaving properly, they became better able to ignore Beverly's tantrums, avoid getting into arguments with her, and stand fast in requiring her to attend school. They later reported having felt guilty while they were treating her so "cruelly." However, not only did Beverly return to school without further complaint once her parents stopped backing down, but to their pleasant surprise she also became much better tempered and less demanding as they resisted being pushed around.

The onset of Beverly's school refusal following an identified precipitating event—the humiliation in class—pointed to an acute school-phobic reaction. Consistent with this impression were the absence of other adjustment difficulties or peer-group withdrawal and her rapid recovery in response to brief intervention. Because of her prompt return to school the basic sources of her anxiety were not explored further. Certainly, however, her embarrassment seemed due to more than just being unable to answer a question. As a physically well-developed sixth-grader who had to stand to recite in her classroom, she may well have become upset about her physical attributes being on display—especially when according to her report it was some boys who had laughed at her. Also noteworthy in this case was the ability and willingness of the parents to modify their behavior, since the school-phobic reaction stopped as soon as they stopped accepting it as a way of dealing with whatever problems their daughter was having in school.

Case 13. *Chronic School Phobia*

Mary, age 16, became nervous and upset on the first day of classes as she began her junior year in high school. She attributed her nervousness to "just being around" her classmates and to a lack of confidence that she could perform adequately in her subjects—which was striking since she had been a consistent A and B student. She came home at midday, and her parents did not insist that she return. During the next two weeks she did not leave the house or make any attempt to contact her friends, some of whom had called to find out where she was. She seemed sad and lethargic at home, spoke very little, and expressed no interest in doing anything but reading a little and watching some television.

Her withdrawal and apparent depression, more than her refusal to go to school, eventually led Mary's parents to seek professional help. When Mary was interviewed, she was so anxious about being in a classroom that even talking about school caused her to become tearful and wring her hands in dismay. She was able to say that she had no idea why school had become unpleasant to her, and no specific events that had precipitated her phobic reaction could be identified. From her mother, however, it was learned that when Mary was in the fourth grade her convalescence from a mild midwinter illness had extended to the end of the school year. The parents had not encouraged her to return to school ("You can't rush these things") and had arranged instead for a medical exemption and home tutoring. Mary's mother went on to say that she was a former nurse and had always enjoyed having Mary at home under her care.

A very close mother-daughter relationship existed in this family in which the father played little part. He was a self-employed man who spent long hours at his business. He failed to join his wife and daughter for the initial consultation, which he had agreed to do, and during the subsequent therapy he neither expressed interest in his daughter's progress nor was mentioned by Mary unless the therapist specifically asked about him. The parents in this case, then, were an uninterested, uninvolved father and a nurturant mother who consistently communicated to her daughter that her presence at home was welcome. Mary in turn had apparently grown up disposed to withdraw to her home whenever she felt threatened. The past history in this case, together with the absence of precipitating events and accompanying problems of withdrawal and depression, identified a chronic school-phobic pattern.

This evaluation indicated that Mary had little prospect of being able to function in school in the immediate future and would require ongoing psychotherapy both for her school aversion and her depressive reaction. Regular therapy sessions and home tutoring were therefore arranged. During the first 6 months of treatment she kept up with her studies and began discussing with the therapist many concerns she had about her social adequacy and her ability to handle the dating relationships in which her friends were getting involved. In midwinter, as the first outward sign of progress in the treatment, she started getting out of the house and renewing her interest in peer-group activities—first going on shopping trips with her mother, then beginning to see her girlfriends again, and finally even going to school parties and out on dates. In the spring she decided she was ready to return to school: "I'm around people all the time and doing everything else with them, so I might as well be in class with them." She returned to finish out the last 2 months of the school year, without further complaint, and the therapy was terminated at the end of June.

In this case the school-attendance problem involved long-standing concerns that had been waiting in the wings for many years—Mary's feelings of social inadequacy—and accompanying depressive disorder. Hence getting her back into school was accomplished first by helping her to come to grips with these concerns, and then by the initiative she took with respect to her return.

OUTCOME AND TREATMENT OF SCHOOL PHOBIA

As noted in previous chapters, there is for the most part little relationship between childhood and adult neuroses. Children with neurotic difficulties are somewhat more likely than their normal peers to have psychological problems as adults, but most of them do not, and neurotic difficulties in childhood are generally not predictive of serious maladjustment later (Cass & Thomas, 1979; Kohlberg, LaCrosse, & Ricks, 1972; Robins, 1979). However, persistent school phobia that goes unrecognized and untreated constitutes an important exception. It takes young people out of the school and social arenas in which many significant learning experiences normally occur. As a result, it can seriously interfere with both academic progress and social development, and it often leads to poor adjustment in all work-related situations that demand a measure of independence and self-reliance.

School phobia, then, especially when it becomes chronic, is more predictive of psychological problems in adulthood than are other youthful neurotic disturbances. As in the general case of phobias, however, early onset offers a more favorable prognosis: school phobia beginning during the first peak period of onset for this condition (age 5 to 8) has fewer long-term implications for subsequent psychopathology than onset during the second incidence peak (age 11 to 14) (Gordon & Young, 1976; Pittman, Langsley, & DeYoung, 1968; Tyrer & Tyrer, 1974).

Because of the far-reaching consequences of prolonged school absence, treatment usually aims at getting these children back to school as soon as possible (Lassers, Nordan, & Bladholm, 1973). However, clinicians disagree as to what they mean by "soon." Some recommend that children undergo psychotherapy to help them understand and resolve their anxiety about being in school before they try to return. In this approach returning to school 6 to 12 months after beginning treatment is felt to be a successful outcome (Greenbaum, 1964; Hersov, 1960b; Talbot, 1957; Waldfogel, et al., 1957). Other clinicians believe that keeping a child out of school for psychotherapy reinforces the symptom of nonattendance and delays recovery. They argue that school phobia requires a "crisis" or "first-aid" approach in which reestablishing attendance is the first treatment priority, and working to understand the problem should come later (Kelly, 1973; Leventhal, Weinberger, Stander, & Stearns, 1967; Millar, 1961; Sperling, 1961).

These differences of opinion can be resolved by selecting the treatment approach that best meets the needs of the individual child or adolescent. If the school phobia has become chronic—that is, a way of life—some psychotherapy is usually necessary before a return to school is attempted, as in the case of Mary. Otherwise, a forced early return runs the risk of causing youngsters to become increasingly upset in school and to continue to lose ground both socially and academically. If the school phobia is acute, on the other hand, children may benefit most from vigorous efforts to get them back to school before they become too accustomed to staying at home (McDonald & Shepherd, 1976; Shapiro & Jegede, 1973; Sperling, 1967; Veltkamp, 1975).

Helping children with acute school phobia to stay in school and master their anxiety frequently taxes the ingenuity of therapists. Substantial progress has been made in developing a variety of effective behavioral and family-oriented methods. These include specific training exercises to help children feel less anxious in the classroom; reintroducing children to school gradually, as in having them attend for just an hour a day at first, then half a day, and finally a full day; asking children's mothers to go to school with them, perhaps even sitting for a while in their classroom and then gradually leaving as the children begin to feel more comfortable; and educating parents to avoid the kinds of overprotective behavior that encourage nonattendance at school (Allyon, Smith

Sometimes the best way to get school-phobic children back into the classroom is to have their mothers go with them.

& Rogers, 1970; Chapel, 1967; Garvey & Hegrenes, 1966; Hersen, 1971; Jones & Kazdin, 1981; LeUnes & Siemglusz, 1977).

When psychotherapy is undertaken together with or prior to returning school-phobic youngsters to the classroom, the focus—as in the treatment of other neurotic disorders—is on helping them express and evaluate the underlying concerns that have led to their symptoms. The more they are able to talk about their fears of being away from home or their unpleasant experiences in school, the more opportunity there is for them to assess the reality of their concerns and to consider alternative, more adaptive ways of feeling or acting. Family discussions can also be useful by promoting changes in the pattern of family interaction so as to reduce the youngster's dependence and demandingness and his or her parents' overprotection and willingness to be manipulated—as in the case of Beverly. In some cases even residential care is used to implement a comprehensive treatment program for school-phobic youngsters (Barker, 1968; Berg & Fielding, 1978; Malmquist, 1965; Pittman et al., 1968; Weiss & Cain, 1964).

Treatment programs that combine helping children understand why they are anxious about school with keeping them in the classroom generally yield good results. Such programs can help more than 70 percent of school-phobic children[b] return to school comfortably in anywhere from a few days to a few months. Consistent with the differences between acute and chronic school phobia, younger children generally have better prospects for improvedment than older ones. More than 90 percent of children 10 years of age or younger have been found to recover from school phobia in various treatment studies, whereas the recovery rate for those 11 years of age or older is no greater than 50 percent (Kennedy, 1965; Miller et al., 1974; Rodriguez, Rodriguez, & Eisenberg, 1959; Smith, 1979; Weiss & Burke, 1979).

SUMMARY

School phobia is a reluctance or refusal to go to school because of intense anxiety about being there. Like other phobias, school-phobic disorder involves dreads that are out of proportion to any real danger and cannot be relieved by explanations or reassurances that there is nothing to fear. School-phobic children typically express their reluctance to attend school through physical complaints that convince their parents to keep them home, especially headache, abdominal pain, nausea, and sore throat. In some cases, either in addition to or instead of physical ailments, they offer various criticisms of the school situation as their reason for not wanting to go.

Although school-phobic children are in reality disabled by their anxiety, neither their physical discomfort nor their other complaints can be taken at face value. Their bodily symptoms usually come and go quickly, depending on whether they are being pressed to go to school or allowed to stay home. Likewise, changes in the school situation made in response to their criticisms are quickly followed by a new set of complaints.

When school-phobic reactions first appear, they usually take the form of an acute disorder. The symptoms appear suddenly, independently of any other behavior problems, and they follow some precipitating events that have caused increased anxiety about being in school. As children grow older, such acute reactions are less likely to appear for the first time than as a recurrence of earlier episodes. Even more commonly among adolescents, school phobia occurs as a persistent, chronic disorder. Chronic school phobia is more a "way of life" than a crisis reaction, and it typically occurs in the absence of obvious precipitating circumstances in youngsters with past and current adjustment difficulties of other kinds as well.

School phobia is estimated to occur in 1 to 2 percent of the school population and in 5 to 8 percent of youngsters referred for professional care. Girls and boys are equally likely to become school phobic, and episodes of the disorder most frequently begin either in the early elementary school years (age 5 to 8) or at the time of entry into junior or senior high school (age 11 to 14).

Like other phobias, exaggerated fears of attending school are determined primarily by psychological experience, not by any genetic or constitutional influences. A disposition to school phobia emerges from a pattern of family interaction that promotes excessive dependency. Overprotective mothers and equally overprotective or detached fathers tend to cater excessively to their children, sparing them from any frustration or discipline and encouraging them to remain physically and psychologically close. Children reared in this way tend to become clinging, demanding young people who have an inflated sense of their mastery. They are poorly prepared to deal with situations that require self-reliance and give-and-take outside of their home, and they are prone to retreat to the safety of their parents' protection whenever they encounter threats to their security.

Children with this kind of disposition are likely to become school phobic in response to precipitating experiences that increase their anxiety about separating from their parents or being in school, although these precipitating events will be less apparent in chronic than in acute school-phobic reactions. Especially common are actual separations from parents or illness or other problems at home that make overdependent children worry about leaving the house; changes that put these children in new situations in which they may have to act more independently than before, such as moving to a new neighborhood or making the transition from elementary to junior high school; and specific unpleasant experiences at school that may be too embarrassing or painful for them to talk or even think about but that lead them to find reasons for staying home.

School phobia is more predictive of psychological problems in adulthood than are other youthful neurotic disturbances. Especially when it has been recurrent or persistent and is present after age 11, school phobia can interfere seriously with both academic progress and social development and lead to adjustment problems later. Because of the far-reaching consequences of prolonged school absence, treatment usually aims at getting these youngsters back to school as soon as possible. If the school phobia has become chronic, some psychotherapy may be necessary before a return to school can be implemented successfully. Children with acute episodes of school phobia, on the other hand, benefit most from vigorous efforts to get them back into the classroom before they become too accustomed to staying at home.

Treatment programs that combine helping children understand why they are anxious about school with keeping them in the classroom generally yield good results. More than 70 percent of school-phobic children can be helped to return to school comfortably in anywhere from a few days to a few months, with adequate treatment; consistent with the difference between acute and chronic school phobia, however, younger children generally have better prospects for rapid improvement than older ones.

REFERENCES

ALLYON T., SMITH, D., & ROGERS, M. Behavioral management of school phobia. *Journal of Behavioral Therapy and Experimental Psychiatry,* 1970, *1,* 125–138.

BARKER, P. B. The in-patient treatment of school refusal. *British Journal of Medical Psychology,* 1968, *41,* 381–387.

BERG, I., COLLINS, T., MCGUIRE, R., & O'MELIA, J. Educational attainment in adolescent school phobia. *British Journal of Psychiatry,* 1975, *126,* 435–438.

BERG, I., & FIELDING, D. An evaluation of hospital in-patient trteatment in adolescent school phobia. *British Journal of Psychiatry,* 1978, *132,* 500–505.

BERG, I., & MCGUIRE, R. Are mothers of school-phobic adolescents overprotective? *British Journal of Psychiatry,* 1974, *124,* 10–13.

BROADWIN, I. T. A contribution to the study of truancy. *American Journal of Orthopsychiatry,* 1932, *2,* 253–259.

CASS, L. K., & THOMAS, C. B. *Childhood pathology and later adjustment.* New York: Wiley, 1979.

CHAPEL, J. L. Treatment of a case of school phobia by reciprocal inhibition. *Canadian Psychiatric Association Journal,* 1967, *12,* 25–28.

CHOTINER, M. M., & FORREST, D. U. Adolescent school phobia: Six controlled cases studies retrospectively. *Adolescence,* 1974, *9,* 467–480.

CLYNE, M. B. *Absent: School refusal as an expression of disturbed family relationships.* London: Tavistock, 1966.

COOLIDGE, J. C. School phobia. In J. D. Noshpitz (Ed.), *Basic handbook of child psychiatry.* Vol. II. New York: Basic Books, 1979.

COOLIDGE, J. C., HAHN, P. B., & PECK, A. L. School phobia: Neurotic crisis or way of life? *American Journal of Orthopsychiatry,* 1957, *27,* 296–306.

DROTAR, D. Clinical psychological practice in a pediatric hospital. *Professional Psychology,* 1977, *8,* 72–80.

EISENBERG, L. School phobia: A study in the communication of anxiety. *American Journal of Psychiatry,* 1958, *114,* 712–718.

ESTES, H. R., HAYLETT, C. H., & JOHNSON, A. M. Separation anxiety. *American Journal of Psychotherapy,* 1956, *10,* 682–695.

GARVEY, W. P., & HEGRENES, J. R. Desensitization techniques in the treatment of school phobia. *American Journal of Orthopsychiatry,* 1966, *36,* 147–152.

GORDON, D. A., & YOUNG, R. D. School phobia: A discussion of etiology, treatment, and evaluation. *Psychological Reports,* 1976, *39,* 783–804.

GREENBAUM, R. S. Treatment of school phobia—theory and practice. *American Journal of Psychotherapy,* 1964, *18,* 616–634.

HAMPE, E., MILLER, L., BARRETT, C., & NOBLE, H. Intelligence and school phobia. *Journal of School Psychology,* 1973, *11,* 66–70.

HERSEN, M. The behavioral treatment of school phobia. *Journal of Nervous and Mental Disease,* 1971, *153,* 99–107.

HERSOV, L. A. Persistent non-attendance at school. *Journal of Child Psychology and Psychiatry,* 1960a, *1,* 130–136.

HERSOV, L. A. Refusal to go to school. *Journal of Child Psychology and Psychiatry,* 1960b, 1, 137–145.

HODGMAN, C. H., & BRAIMAN, A. "College phobia": School refusal in university students. *American Journal of Psychiatry*, 1965, 121, 801–805.

JACKSON, L. Anxiety in adolescents in relation to school refusal. *Journal of Child Psychology and Psychiatry*, 1964, 5, 59–73.

JONES, R. T., & KAZDIN, A. E. Childhood behavior problems in the school. In S. M. Turner, K. S. Calhoun, & H. E. Adams (Eds.), *Handbook of clinical behavior therapy*. New York: Wiley, 1981.

KAHN, J. H., & NURSTEN, J. P. School refusal: A comprehensive view of school phobia and other failures of school attendance. *American Journal of Orthopsychiatry*, 1962, 22, 707–718.

KAHN, J. H., NURSTEN, J. P., & CAROLL, C. M. *Unwillingly to school: School phobia or school refusal?* (3d ed.) New York: Pergamon, 1980.

KELLY, E. W. School phobia: A review of theory and treatment. *Psychology in the Schools*, 1973, 10, 33–42.

KENNEDY, W. A. School phobia: Rapid treatment of fifty cases. *Journal of Abnormal Psychology*, 1965, 70, 285–289.

KOHLBERG, L., LACROSSE, J., & RICKS, D. The predictability of adult mental health from childhood behavior. In B. B. Wolman (Ed.), *Manual of child psychopathology*. New York: McGraw-Hill, 1972.

LANSKY, S., LOWMAN, J. T., VATS, T., & GYULAY, J. E. School phobia in children with malignant neoplasms. *American Journal of Diseases of Children*, 1975, 129, 42–46.

LASSERS, E., NORDAN, R., & BLADHOLM, S. Steps in the return to school of children with school phobia. *American Journal of Psychiatry*, 1973, 130, 265–268.

LETON, D. A. Assessment of school phobia. *Mental Hygiene*, 1962, 46, 256–264.

LEUNES, A., & SIEMGLUSZ, S. Paraprofessional treatment of school phobia in a young adolescent girl. *Adolescence*, 1977, 12, 115–121.

LEVENSON, E. A. The treatment of school phobia in the young adult. *American Journal of Psychotherapy*, 1961, 15, 539–552.

LEVENTHAL, T., & SILLS, M. Self-image in school phobia. *American Journal of Orthopsychiatry*, 1964, 34, 685–695.

LEVENTHAL, T., WEINBERGER, G., STANDER, R. J., & STEARNS, R. P. Therapeutic strategies with school phobia. *American Journal of Orthopsychiatry*, 1967, 37, 64–70.

MCDONALD, J. D., & SHEPHARD, G. School phobia: An overview. *Journal of School Psychology*, 1976, 14, 291–308.

MALMQUIST, C. P. School phobia: A problem in family neurosis. *Journal of the American Adacemy of Child Psychiatry*, 1965, 4, 293–319.

MILLAR, T. P. The child who refuses to attend school. *American Journal of Psychiatry*, 1961, 118, 398–404.

MILLER, L. C., BARRETT, C. L., & HAMPE, E. Phobias of childhood in a prescientific era. In A. Davids (Eds.), *Child personality and psychopathology: Current topics*. New York: Wiley, 1974.

MILLER, L. C., HAMPE, E., BARRETT, C. L., & NOBLE, H. Children's deviant behavior within the general population. *Journal of Consulting and Clinical Psychology*, 1971, 37, 16–22.

NADER, P. R., BULLOCK, D., & CALDWELL, B. School phobia. *Pediatriatic Clinics of North America*, 1975, 22, 605–617.

PITTMAN, F. S., LANGSLEY, D. G., & DEYOUNG, C. D. Work and school phobias: A family approach to treatment. *American Journal of Psychiatry*, 1968, 124, 1535–1541.

RADIN, S. Psychodynamic aspects of school phobia. *Comprehensive Psychiatry*, 1967, 8, 119–128.

ROBINS, L. N. Follow-up studies. In H. C. Quay and J. S. Werry (Eds.), *Psychopathological disorders of childhood.* (2nd ed.) New York: Wiley, 1979.

RODRIGUEZ, A., RODRIGUEZ, M., EISENBERG, L. the outcome of school phobia: A follow-up based on 41 cases. *American Journal of Psychiatry*, 1959, 116, 540–544.

RUTTER, M., TIZARD, J., YULE, W., GRAHAM, P., & WHITMORE, K. Isle of Wight studies, 1964–1974. *Psychological Medicine*, 1976, 6, 313–332.

SHAPIRO, T., & JEGEDE, R. O. School phobia: A babel of tongues. *Journal of Autism and Childhood Schizophrenia,* 1973, *3,* 168–186.

SMITH, S. L. School refusal with anxiety: A review of sixty-three cases. *Canadian Psychiatric Association Journal,* 1970, *15,* 257–264.

SPERLING, M. School phobias: Classification, dynamics, and treatment. *Psychoanalytic Study of the Child,* 1967, *22,* 375–401.

SZYRYNSKI, V. School phobia, its treatment and prevention. *Psychiatric Journal of the University of Ottawa,* 1976, *1,* 165–170.

TALBOT, M. Panic in school phobia. *American Journal of Orthopsychiatry,* 1957, *26,* 286–295.

TYRER, P., & TYRER, S. School refusal, truancy, and adult neurotic illness. *Psychological Medicine,* 1974, *4,* 416–421.

VELTKAMP, L. J. School phobia. *Journal of Family Counseling,* 1975, *3,* 47–51.

WALDFOGEL, S., COOLIDGE, J. C., & HAHN, P. B. The development, meaning, and management of school phobia. *American Journal of Orthopsychiatry,* 1957, *27,* 754–780.

WALDRON, S., SHRIER, D., STONE, B., & TOBIN, F. School phobia and other childhood neuroses: A systematic study of the children and their families. *American Journal of Psychiatry,* 1975, *132,* 802–808.

WEISS, M., & BURKE, A. A five-to-ten-year follow-up of hospitalized school phobic children and adolescents. *American Journal of Orthopsychiatry,* 1970, *40,* 672–676.

WEISS, M., & CAIN, B. The residential treatment of children and adolescents with school phobia. *American Journal of Orthopsychiatry,* 1964, *34,* 103–114.

ACADEMIC UNDERACHIEVEMENT

Academic underachievement is a disparity between capacity and performance in which students receive lower grades than they are intellectually capable of earning. This definition does not include low grades that reflect limited intelligence. Instead, underachievers are students of average or better intelligence who show unexpectedly poor performance in their schoolwork. Such failure to realize their academic potential is estimated to occur in 25 percent of schoolchildren, and from 30 to 50 percent of young people seen in various psychiatric clinics are referred primarily because of school-learning problems (Cass & Thomas, 1979, Chapter 4; Gardner & Sperry, 1974; Schechter, 1974; Weisberg, 1978).

Two large-scale studies are of special interest in documenting the extent of school-learning difficulties in young people. Nader (1975), as part of an extensive assessment of child health in Rochester, New York, collected information from a random sample of 2043 5- to 17-year-olds and their families. He found that 28.9 percent of these young people were having trouble with their schoolwork, and the parents reported problems involving school as the most frequent behavioral difficulty their children were having. In the other study Schechtman (1970) examined the files of 548 5- to 17-year-olds who had been seen in a mental health clinic. At each year level and for both boys and girls, problems with schoolwork were consistently present in more than 25 percent of these youthful patients.

Young people who are unable or unwilling to utilize their intellectual potential typically squander educational and occupational attainments that would otherwise be within their grasp. Longitudinal studies show a high positive correlation between intellectual involvement and academic achievement during the teenage years, on the one hand, and achievement behavior and occupational level in adulthood, on the other. As an important case in point, young people who drop out of high school are twice as likely to be unemployed in their mid-20s than high school graduates. When dropouts are employed, furthermore, they are only one-third as likely as graduates to hold white-collar jobs. Even highly intelligent dropouts are relatively likely to show up in the ranks of the unskilled and unemployed later (Bachman, O'Malley, & Johnston, 1979; Hathaway & Monachesi, 1969; Howard & Anderson, 1978).

Because dropping out of school constitutes such a waste of youthful potential, it is a serious social problem. Contemporary America generally places a high value on graduating from high school. Yet approximately 20 percent of our adolescents fail to complete the twelfth grade, and more than half of these dropouts appear bright enough to get through high school (Johnston & Bachman, 1976; Howard & Anderson, 1978; Joint Commission, 1970, Chapter 2; Lichter, Rapien, Siebert, & Sklansky, 1962).

However important it may be to address academic underachievement among high school students, such concern may come too late. Underachieving patterns often emerge early in the school years and are already firmly entrenched by the time young people reach adolescence. In a study of equally bright achieving and underachieving high school students who had been classmates from the first grade on, Shaw and McCuen (1960) found that the underachieving boys had tended to receive lower grades than the achieving boys beginning in the first grade. These underachievers had dropped to a significantly lower performance level by third grade and had shown increasingly poorer achievement in each consecutive year up to tenth grade. A similar but later developing pattern was found for the underachieving girls, who began to receive lower grades than the achieving girls in sixth grade and declined to a significantly lower performance by ninth grade.

Other research with students doing poorly in high school indicates that 50 percent are likely to have experienced their first failure as early as second grade, 75 percent by the fourth grade, and 90 percent by the seventh grade (Fitzsimmons, Cheever, Leonard, & Macunovich, 1969). Once underway, moreover, underachievement has a snowballing effect. The poor background of underachieving students in subject matter they have previously failed, the lowered confidence they have in themselves as students, and their loss of motivation and pleasure in learning contribute to progressively larger gaps between capacity and performance as underachievement persists from one year to the next (Howard & Anderson, 1978; Marcus, 1966).

Academic underachievement results from many different causes. Among elementary school children, learning disabilities as described in Chapter 4 are probably the most common reason for poor school performance despite adequate general intelligence. Beginning in late childhood and continuing into adolescence, underachievement becomes increasingly due to sociocultural and psychological factors that include low motivation, limited opportunity, certain developmental and psychopathological states, specific aversions to the learning process, and maladaptive patterns of family interaction.

SOCIOCULTURAL FACTORS IN ACADEMIC UNDERACHIEVEMENT

For many underachieving young people the discrepancy between their academic performance and their intellectual capacity reflects social and cultural influences, rather than any form of psychopathology. These influences lead to unexpectedly poor grades primarily through producing *low motivation* for academic success or *limited opportunity* to attain it.

Low Motivation

For students to realize their academic potential, they must be motivated to work hard on their studies. Young people who do well in school tend to be interested in learning. They feel good about receiving high marks, and they see a clear relationship between achieving in school and realizing such long-range goals as getting into college or qualifying for a particular kind of job. In studies comparing equally bright high-achieving and low-achieving high school students, the achievers are consistently found to show stronger educational motivation and to place a higher value on school and work (Morrow, 1970; Pierce and Bowman, 1970).

By contrast, young people who are not oriented toward intellectual values or academic goals lack motivation to apply themselves in school. They may take pains to avoid the inconvenience and embarrassment of outright failure, but they see little reason to do any more than what is necessary to get by. Typically they dislike school and do not expect any inner satisfaction or external rewards to come from doing well. Academically unmotivated underachievers are especially unlikely to perceive their

Figure 10.1

Reasons given for dropping out of high school (in percent). (Based on data reported by Hathaway and Monachesi (1963) on 824 boys and 677 girls.)

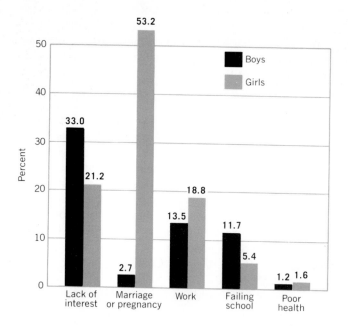

schoolwork as related to what they will be doing later or as helping them attain any long-range objectives (Hummel & Sprinthall, 1965; Schaefer, 1977).

Such lack of motivation also figures prominently in decisions to leave school. Contrary to what might be expected, fewer than 10 percent of high school dropouts quit school because of failing grades or lack of money. Instead, as shown in Figure 10.1, the most common reason boys leave school is "lack of interest"; for girls the most common reason is marriage or pregnancy. Research on the sociocultural origins of low academic motivation has not been abundant. Nevertheless, there is reason to believe that noneducational values and goals are fostered by certain family, school, peer-group, and sex-role influences.

Family Influences   Young people readily identify with their parents' feelings about school and education. Parents who value the educational process and respect the efforts of their children's teachers encourage positive attitudes, whereas parents who belittle teachers or brag about having accomplished a lot without much schooling often foster negative attitudes. Similarly, parents who *say* that education is important but do not *show* any personal interest in reading, learning, or intellectual discussions may discourage their children from caring about school Moreover, parents who doubt the usefulness of formal education as a way of getting ahead in life often pay little attention to how their children are doing in school. The rewards and punishments they employ in child-rearing seldom have anything to do with whether their youngsters are doing their homework or receiving good grades. As a consequence, their children are unlikely to develop much motivation to achieve academically.

Data from extensive longitudinal studies of child development conducted by the Fels Institute have confirmed clear relationships between how parents feel about school learning and how they react to the educational experiences of their elementary school children. The greater the value parents place on their own intellectual attainments, the more they value the intellectual attainments of their children and the more they participate in intellectual activities with them (Crandall, 1972; Katkovsky, Preston, & Crandall, 1964a, 1964b).

At the high school level, comparisons of achieving and underachieving high school students of equal intelligence demonstrate the following: (a) the parents of achievers are generally more encouraging with respect to achievement; (b) the families of achievers more actively promote intellectual interests in their children and foster a positive attitude toward teachers and toward the school; and (c) achievers are less inclined than underachievers to express negative attitudes about school or to view their teachers as unreasonable or unsupportive. Thus for both children and adolescents, lack of educational stimulation in the home and lack of parental interest in academic achievement have been found to be directly related to young people having school-learning problems and receiving relatively low grades (Boike, Gesten, Cowen, Felner, & Francis, 1977; Christopher, 1967; Gesten, Scher, & Cowen, 1978; Kelleghan, 1977).

Clinicians who work with young people frequently see parents who complain, "He just doesn't take any interest in his studies; how do we get him motivated?" In some cases this failure to become interested in schoolwork reflects one of the psychological difficulties discussed in the next section. With respect to value systems, however, this particular complaint often reveals that the parents, despite lip service to the contrary, harbor some underlying scorn for education that they have conveyed to their youngster.

A typical example is the self-made man who, having succeeded in the business world despite limited schooling or a poor academic record, scolds his underachieving son for his low grades and "poor attitude" but nevertheless considers him "a chip off the old block." In this vein, there is clear evidence that the less schooling parents have had themselves, the more likely their children are to receive low grades and quit school; even among fairly homogeneous groups of advantaged adolescents in academically oriented schools, grades correlate with parental years of education. Similarly, youngsters who feel negatively about school often lack examples in their family or neighborhood of adults who have benefitted from school (Berman & Eisenberg, 1971; Nielsen & Gerber, 1979).

As these findings suggest, parents' social class may be a factor in how their children feel about school. Middle- and upper-class parents tend to be well educated and to regard schooling as a way of preparing for life, socially and psychologically as well as vocationally. Hence they typically speak well of what school has to offer, and they follow their children's school activities closely. They also appreciate and discuss with their children the significance of what they are learning in school, and they reward their children's academic accomplishments. Lower-class parents, in comparison, are more

An intellectually oriented home environment can foster motivation to do well in school.

likely to be minimally educated, to regard the school as an alien and hostile institution, and to view their children's attendance just as a legal requirement or perhaps a way of getting a better paying job. They are less likely than white-collar parents to discuss school activities with their children, to understand and help them with their studies, or to praise their classroom achievements (Hess & Shipman, 1967; Katz, 1967).

Children from lower-class families may feel less positive toward school than middle- or upper-class children. For example, there is evidence that children form long-term occupational attitudes at an early age and by the eighth grade show clear social-class differences in their aspirations. Those from higher social-class groups tend to have relatively high educational goals and to be aiming at prestige occupations, whereas those from lower social classes tend already to have resigned themselves to less education and lower job status (Harvey & Kerin, 1978).

This general trend cannot be assumed to apply in all disadvantaged families, however. In the first place, parents within any subcultural group may hold widely differing attitudes. Comparing lower-class black fifth-graders who were doing well in school with a similar group of children who were doing poorly, for example, Greenberg and David-son (1972) found that the parents of the achieving children were more interested in their child's education, more knowledgeable about the school system, more likely to regard high school as preparation for college, and more likely to have books and adequate study space in the home. Buys, Field, and Schmidt (1976), studying lower-class Mexican-American high school students, similarly found that some perceived their home environment as more conducive to education than others, and that these students were more likely to regard school as worthwhile and a college education as necessary for a successful life.

Second, lower-class parents who do not encourage or support school activities may still foster positive attitudes toward verbal communication. This is important because verbal communication skills have been found to show a significant correlation with achievement among disadvantaged elementary school children (Slaughter, 1970). Furthermore, the influence of older siblings, aunts and uncles, and neighborhood adults who value education can lead lower-class children to feel positively about school even if their parents do not.

School Influences   For children in some lower-class or disadvantaged neighborhoods, the school may in fact be a hostile environment that contributes to low motivation to achieve. Despite much concern in the United States about addressing the heterogeneous needs of our diverse population, our schools remain largely middle-class, mainstream institutions. This means that middle-class, mainstream children experience considerable overlap between their school and home environments, particularly with respect to what is valued and rewarded and how language is used. For disadvantaged or minority youngsters, on the other hand, discontinuities between their school and home experiences frequently alienate them from the learning process. The more the patterns of thinking and acting they have acquired at home differ from what the school values and rewards, and the more their language differs from standard spoken English, the more likely they are to become unmotivated to achieve.

The sociocultural discontinuities between disadvantaged families and the schools their children attend affect parents and teachers as well as students. The parents may have difficulty understanding the goals and methods of the school or seeing how its curriculum will prepare their children for the future. If they cannot get good answers to these questions from the school or, as often happens, they find the school's response to their concerns patronizing or demeaning, they may deliberately direct their children's energies elsewhere. Teachers, who are well educated and mostly middle-class, frequently lack understanding of their disadvantaged students' home circumstances and subcultural environment (Elkind, 1971; Katz, 1967; Watts, 1978).

Regrettably, there is a tendency for teachers to expect less of children they regard as "culturally disadvantaged" and to give them less attention, encouragement, and support in the classroom than they give middle-class children (Richer, 1974; Schultz & Aurbach, 1971). Such negative expectations do little to build academic achievement motivation in minority youngsters. Research studies indicate that the more teachers praise and reward children for their academic work, the more the children will expect to succeed and the harder they will try. Conversely, fewer rewards lead to lower expectations, fewer achievement attempts, and poorer grades (Brookover, 1978; Buck &

Figure 10.2
The cycle of socioculturally determined academic underachievement experienced by some minority-group children.

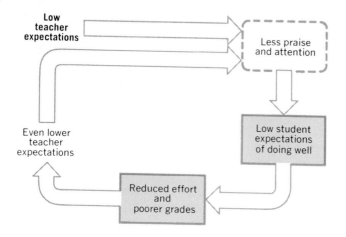

Austrin, 1971; Guttentag & Klein, 1976; Sattler & Van Wagener, 1975; Weinstein & Middlestadt, 1979) (see Figure 10.2).

Peer-Group Influences   Participation in a peer group that endorses nonintellectual values can also contribute to low motivation to achieve in school. Needs for acceptance within a peer group that belittles academic achievement can override any academic motivation that youngsters may otherwise have had. In some important early research on such peer-group influence, Coleman (1960, 1961) found that in schools where the student body generally valued academic performance, the most intelligent youngsters were getting the highest grades, as would be expected. In schools where the group devalued scholarship, on the other hand, the most able students were not the highest achievers, apparently because many of them were avoiding good grades to avoid being unpopular.

Cervantes (1965) reported another interesting confirmation of this peer-group influence, found among adolescents in an inner-city neighborhood. Those who were attending school expressed the belief that the majority of high school students in their neighborhood were planning to continue in school; those who had dropped out of school, on the other hand, said that most of their neighborhood group still in school were planning to leave. In other words, these young people from the same neighborhood perceived the neighborhood differently, according to their own particular situation.

Sex-Role Influences   Another important sociocultural determinant of academic motivation is the prevailing definition of sex roles in a youngster's subculture. In some groups academic effort and attainment are viewed as essentially feminine, and boys who are conscientious and successful in their studies risk being labeled not only as "brain" or "grind" but also as "square," "fag," "teacher's pet," or something else incompatible with being a "cool dude." As in the case of peer-group influences, then, such negative attitudes toward boys doing well in school lower their motivation to achieve.

In other groups scholastic excellence and career-mindedness are considered masculine characteristics, especially in late adolescence. Then girls who value their studies above their social life—especially if they are preparing to enter such predominantly masculine fields as engineering, law, and medicine—may find their femininity called into question by family and friends. Parents who doubt the compatibility of femininity and academic striving often reserve special pride for the intellectual achievements of their sons and take little interest or pleasure in their daughters' educational plans and accomplishments. The punishment that is experienced by able girls in such circumstances frequently dulls their academic enthusiasm and results in underachievement.

An interesting mixture of both sets of attitudes was found among academically motivated families in the Fels study reported by Crandall (1972). The parents in these families were more likely to communicate the importance of learning to their daughters than to their sons, but they set higher standards for their sons' than for their daughters' achievements. Crandall attributed these sex differences to commonly held sex-role stereotypes: boys should not get too wrapped up in their studies at the expense of more "masculine" activities, whereas for girls schoolwork is a natural and appropriate activity that is all right for them to enjoy; at the same time, doing well in school is more important for boys than for girls in the long run, since it is primarily the boys who will have to qualify for jobs and earn a living. From these stereotypes comes the apparently inconsistent result that parents provide more support for their daughters' viewing school as important but express more concern with the actual school performance of their sons.

Modern movements away from these traditional sex-role definitions appear to be reducing their influence on academic motivation. Certainly the premium that is placed in contemporary society on maximum educational advancement for all talented people has done much to eliminate the "gentleman's C" and the restriction of career-minded girls to teaching, nursing, and social work. At the college level in particular, the 1970s saw a substantial increase in masculine serious-mindedness and a marked reduction in feminine conflict between intellectual and personal needs. Frittering away opportunities to learn and prepare for a future career is no longer regarded as being "one of the guys," and students of both sexes are much less inclined than before to devalue competence, resourcefulness, and intelligence among their female friends (Wesley & Wesley, 1977, Chapter 9).

Such stereotypes die hard, however, and research indicates that they persisted at least through the 1970s as potential causes of low academic motivation. When elementary school children are asked what they want to be when they grow up, for example, the boys were still saying football player, policeman, doctor, dentist, priest, scientist, pilot, and astronaut, and the girls were saying teacher, nurse, housewife, mother, stewardess, and salesgirl (Hewitt, 1975; Looft, 1971; Scheresky, 1976; Williams, Bennett, & Best, 1975). Traditional sex-role notions thus continue to limit the level and range of occupation that grade-schoolers see as appropriate for females.

A study by Brown, Jennings, and Vanik (1974) suggests further that high school students of both sexes consider it more appropriate for men than women to achieve success in traditional male professions. The students in this reasearch, who ranged in age from 15 to 18, were asked to write stories in response to each of the following two cues: "After first-term finals, John finds himself at the top of his medical-school class"; "After first-term finals, Anne finds herself at the top of her medical-school class." The stories were scored for the presence of any negative imagery, such as doubting that such a thing could happen or suggesting that peer rejection or some other negative consequences would result from it.

Both the males and the females expressed more negative imagery about success when the medical student was "Anne" than when it was "John." In addition to demonstrating persisting sex-role stereotypes, the negative stories written by many of these high school students hinted at certain fears of being successful. Fear of success can be a major psychological determinant of academic underachievement, independently of sociocultural influences, as will be discussed in the next section. The point for now is that sociocultural attitudes toward sex roles continue to be largely traditional. The increasing value placed on intellectual competence among women has not yet been translated into consistent societal attitudes that encourage girls to be both competent and feminine (Sherman, 1976; Wesley & Wesley, 1977, Chapter 9). Weitz (1977, p. 250) provides the following assessment of how matters stand in this regard: "At the present time, it would be safe to say that most Americans, female and male, are living their lives within the structure of the traditional sex role system. . . . This role system is solidly entrenched, and the pace of change will probably be slower than any of us can imagine."

Limited Opportunity

Able youngsters who are adequately motivated to achieve in school may be prevented from realizing their goals by sociocultural factors that limit their opportunities to learn and study. Among the most widely publicized of these factors is the failure of elementary education to prepare young people adequately for high school and college work

Crowded, poorly equipped classrooms can limit opportunities for young people to develop academic skills.

(Silberman, 1970). This problem is most acute in inner-city and depressed rural areas, where educational resources are in shortest supply. Children who attend under-equipped and understaffed schools and who sit in crowded classrooms listening to bored or inept teachers may fail to acquire the basic academic skills and study habits they will need to handle high school work.

Young people who have had the benefit of attending good schools may still become inadequately prepared to achieve academically if illness or changes of school disrupt the continuity of their learning. For example, transferring in midyear from one school where the class is about to begin studying fractions in arithmetic to another school where the class has just finished fractions and is starting on decimals can leave a student temporarily behind or perhaps chronically deficient in his or her understanding of fractions.

Academic underachievement can also result from extracurricular circumstances that detract from youngsters' attention to their schoolwork. Adolescents who must work long hours at a job or take on burdensome responsibilities in the home may simply not have enough time and energy to do justice to their studies, even though they have the ability and the will to do well. Even the lack of a private or reasonably quiet place to study can contribute to students' failing to maintain grades commensurate with their abilities.

PSYCHOLOGICAL FACTORS IN ACADEMIC UNDERACHIEVEMENT

Psychological factors that contribute to young people failing to realize their academic potential include (a) developmental and psychopathological states that have no specific relationship to learning but handicap academic efforts; (b) specific aversions to the learning process that are also not directly related to academic achievement but secondarily interfere with it; and (c) maladaptive patterns of family interaction that produce a specific and primary nonachievement syndrome sometimes referred to as *passive-aggressive underachievement*. The first two of these factors will be discussed in this section, and the third will be considered separately in the next section.

Developmental and Psychopathological States

Several aspects of cognitive, physical, and emotional immaturity can impair scholastic performance. These developmental delays occur primarily in adolescence and are thus more likely to interfere with academic achievement at the junior and senior high school levels than during elementary school.

Cognitive Immaturity As first described by Piaget, young people begin during adolescence to advance from the primarily concrete operations that characterize the thinking of children toward the formal operational thinking that typifies mature cognition. They become better able than before to manipulate ideas verbally, in the absence of tangible referents; to formulate and grasp notions of how things might be as well as how they are, and thus to deal with possibilities, hypotheses, and even contrary-to-fact ideas as well as with facts; and to pass judgment on the logicality of their own ideas as well as the ideas of others (Elkind, 1974; Muuss, 1967; Neimark, 1975).

Because adolescents grow more capable of thinking in the abstract, their schoolwork becomes increasingly geared to their assuming abstract attitudes. With each advancing grade, teachers are more likely to present material and prepare examinations in ways that call for their students to exercise formal operational thinking. This means that otherwise normal adolescents who are lagging behind their peers in cognitive maturation may be handicapped in their studies by a temporary inability to abstract at grade level.

For example, an eighth-grader whose science teacher begins by saying, "Imagine that the earth is flat," cannot follow the discussion if all he or she can think about is having been taught previously that the earth is unquestionably round. Similarly, whereas 10-year-olds are likely to define "time" specifically in terms of the clock—that is, in hours, minutes, and seconds—15-year-olds can usually conceive of time as an interval between two points of measurement. This means that 15-year-olds whose class comments and test answers reflect such relatively concrete orientations as "time is what the clock tells" are almost certain to receive lower grades than equally intelligent peers whose more typical rate of cognitive development allows them to think abstractly of time as an interval of measurement.

In a recent review of adolescent thinking, Keating (1980) cautions that we may not yet know enough about formal operations to attribute underachievement to delays in their development. For example, it may be that formal operational thinking, like intelligence, is an ability that some people simply have more of than others. Young people may therefore differ in how capable they are of operational thought, aside from developmental factors, and some may never develop this capacity, even as adults (Dulit, 1972; Keating & Schaefer, 1975). From this perspective poor school performance in people who cannot think operationally would simply reflect limited ability and would not constitute underachievement.

On the other hand, we do know for sure that most young people show developmental changes in abstract thinking from childhood to adolescence. Accordingly, there are likely to be instances in which school performance falls off temporarily in youngsters who are slow in developing the thinking capacities of which they will eventually become capable (Gallagher & Noppe, 1976).

Physical Immaturity   Physical immaturity frequently impairs academic performance by virtue of the anxiety that usually accompanies delayed or arrested growth. Delayed development of puberty generates enough dismay among adolescents to disrupt their ability to function in many respects, including concentration on their studies. Not infrequently, then, physiologically immature adolescents who appear young and small for their age are found to have problems with academic achievement.

The generally negative psychological impact of delayed puberty has been confirmed in extensive research going back many years. Late-maturing boys are more likely than their normally developing peers to suffer serious doubts about their adequacy, and they are more likely to be personally and socially maladjusted during adolescence and to have difficulty making the transition to adulthood (Mussen & Jones, 1957, 1958; Petersen & Taylor, 1980).

Late-maturing girls are similarly found to have a depreciated view of themselves and corresponding adjustment problems. For girls, in addition, early as well as late maturation may be anxiety-provoking. Rapidly developing early adolescent girls who outstrip their peers in height and secondary sexual characteristics often experience at least temporarily a distressing sense of self-consciousness and isolation (Jones & Mussen, 1958; Livson & Peskin, 1980; Peskin, 1973). For some girls, then, physical precocity as well as immaturity may be a contributing factor in academic underachievement.

Emotional Immaturity   The role of emotional immaturity in poor school performance has been demonstrated primarily in relation to vocational attitudes, which constitute a meaningful index of maturity level. Specifically, adolescents who are undecided about their future plans have less vocational maturity than those who are pointing toward certain educational or career directions (Holland & Holland, 1977). Available evidence suggests that the lack of appropriate long-range occupational goals minimizes motivation to work to capacity and thereby contributes to academic underachievement. Among both high school and college students, achievers are more likely than underachievers to have decided on a specific vocational goal, and vocationally undecided students show less work involvement, earn lower grades, and more frequently drop out of school than those who have a goal in mind (Elton & Rose, 1971; Kelso, 1975; Lunneborg, 1975).

Psychopathological States   By disorganizing, distracting, or preoccupying young people, any form of anxiety state can interfere with academic achievement. Some specific patterns of psychological disturbance, including schizophrenia and depression, are especially likely to result in underachievement. Young people who cannot think clearly or maintain a normal energy level will understandably have difficulty earning grades in school that are commensurate with their intelligence. Moreover, such a secondary consequence often intensifies the primary disorder, which in turn leads to even poorer academic performance. For example, a depressed girl whose grades decline as she becomes unable to apply herself to her studies may become even more depressed by the fact that she is now a poor student, have even less energy for schoolwork, and then become an even poorer student.

Underachievement arising as a secondary consequence of psychopathology can often be predicted far in advance. In a 5-year follow-up study of a random sample of preschool children attending 90 public day-care centers in New York City, Kohn (1977) found that those who showed psychological problems prior to entering elementary school were relatively likely to be underachieving before the end of the fourth grade. Young children whose problems involved a notable degree of apathy or withdrawal were particularly likely to have academic difficulties when they entered elementary school. Kohn suggests that shy and inhibited children may do poorly in school simply because they do not make sufficient contact with the world to acquire knowledge about it. Among ninth-graders, also, those who display feelings of apathy or tendencies toward withdrawal are found to be more likely than their classmates to drop out of school later (Hathaway, Reynolds, & Monachesi, 1969a).

Specific Aversions to the Learning Process

In one of his best known books, *The Psychopathology of Everyday Life,* Freud (1901) suggested that certain types of forgetting, erroneous acts, and mistakes in speaking, reading, and writing are due to unconscious psychological influences. Such "Freudian slips" reveal needs or motives of which a person is not fully aware. If you suddenly "forget" the name of a friend you are about to introduce to another person, for example, you may be harboring some ill will toward that friend; if you leave your umbrella in his or her house or car, on the other hand, you may be signaling an underlying wish to return and spend more time with that person. Similarly, a child who says to his or her teacher, "Mother, I mean Mrs. Brown, can I go to the bathroom?" is probably saying something about underlying attitudes toward the teacher as a maternal figure.

Psychoanalytic theorists after Freud attempted to trace learning difficulties in normally intelligent, otherwise well-adjusted youngsters to such effects of unconscious needs or motives. In particular, certain aggressive or sexual aspects of the learning process were seen as causing "emotional blocks" in underachievers. For example, the taking in of information—as in looking at a page in a book—can be interpreted both as an active encounter with the environment and as an expression of curiosity. Aversions to the learning process can develop if this kind of activity makes children feel that they are being too aggressive or if being curious is linked with sexual curiosity that is taboo at home (for example, asking too many embarrassing questions or seeing things they are not supposed to see) (Harris, 1965; Hellman, 1954; Jarvis, 1958).

The specific content of course material can also produce aversions in youngsters with sexual or aggressive concerns. Adolescents who are struggling with inhibited or unsatisfied childhood curiosity about bodily and sexual functions may have difficulty concentrating on such subjects as biology. Similarly, youngsters troubled by their own aggressive fantasies may be uncomfortable with violence-filled novels assigned for English, dissections required in biology, or the study of wars and other catastrophes in history (Liss, 1955; Pearson, 1952; Sperry, Staver, & Mann, 1952).

Although such specific unconscious influences may be involved in learning difficulties that are primarily psychological in origin, they do not provide a particularly powerful explanation of such problems. In the first place, no matter how plausible or compelling these explanations may be to psychoanalytic clinicians, evidence for their validity is limited to case illustrations and has not yet emerged from any systematic empirical research. Second, clinical experience as well as research findings suggest that the vast majority of achievement problems in young people who are not intellectually or socioculturally handicapped can be adequately understood in terms of maladaptive patterns of family interaction, as discussed in the next section, without hypothesizing specific unconscious implications of the learning process itself (Weiner, 1971).

Nevertheless, one additional inhibiting effect of unresolved sexual concerns on school learning needs to be recognized. Some adolescents tend to become preoccupied with sexual fantasies or masturbatory urges when they are alone with nothing to do but think. For these youngsters the very process of studying, whatever the subject matter, may become so inefficient and fraught with anxiety as to bring their academic progress to a standstill (Lorand, 1961). The role of masturbatory problems in underachievement

Psychological reactions to the content of some courses may prevent students from doing well in them.

is vividly expressed in the following words of a bright 18-year-old boy who was in danger of flunking out of school:

> Whenever I sit down to study in my room, whether day or night, I get this tremendous urge to masturbate. If I fight it, I just don't get anything done; I find myself drumming my fingers, or looking out the window, or just staring at the page without seeing it. Sometimes I get up and walk around the room or even take a cold shower, but nothing relieves the pressure. Then, when I do finally masturbate, instead of feeling relieved I feel guilty and weak for not having any self-control, and I'm so preoccupied with being digusted with myself that I still find it hard to concentrate.

MALADAPTIVE PATTERNS OF FAMILY INTERACTION IN ACADEMIC UNDERACHIEVEMENT

When psychological factors cause primary problems in school learning, they typically involve maladaptive patterns of family interaction. These maladaptive patterns include (a) considerable anger that young people feel toward their parents but cannot express directly; (b) concerns about rivalry that generate marked fears of failure or of success; and (c) a preference for passive-aggressive modes of coping with stressful situations.

None of these patterns is unique to underachieving children or adolescents. However, they so frequently contribute to a reluctance or refusal to achieve, especially in families that value education, that underachievement can often be predicted for youngsters in whom they occur together. Learning difficulties determined by unresolved hostile impulses toward family members, fears of competing with parents and siblings, and a passive-aggressive behavior style constitute a fairly specific pattern of psychological disturbance that can be labeled **passive-aggressive underachievement** (Weiner, 1971).

Anger toward Parents

As measured by psychological tests, interviews, ratings by their teachers, and reports from their parents, underachieving adolescents seem basically angrier than equally intelligent students who are doing better in school. At the same time, they tend to display this anger not in overtly hostile behavior, but through such covert channels as snide remarks, hypercritical attitudes, and smoldering resentment (Dudek & Lester, 1968; Roth & Puri, 1967; Shaw & Grubb, 1958).

Other studies of underachieving youngsters have traced their anger specifically to resentment of parental authority that they perceive as restrictive and unjust. Low-achieving high school students are more likely than their equally intelligent but academically successful peers to describe their parents as too strict and overcontrolling (Davids & Hainsworth, 1967; Morrow & Wilson, 1961). These perceptions may or may not reflect their parents' actual behavior toward them, however. Some researchers have found parents of underachievers to be harshly critical of their youngsters and to endorse hostile control techniques in rearing them (Buck & Austrin, 1971; Nuttall & Nuttall, 1976), but in other studies it is the parents of *achieving* students who have been especially likely to endorse controlling attitudes and to be authoritarian and restrictive in their child-rearing practices (Davids & Hainsworth, 1967; Teahan, 1963).

These findings indicate that resentment of parental control among passive-aggressive underachievers does not necessarily represent a high level of parental authoritarianism. Instead, it comes from a disparity between what these youngsters perceive their parents' attitudes to be and what they would like them to be. Given these circumstances—underlying anger, difficulty in expressing this anger directly, and the source of the anger in how they perceive their parents' attitudes—passive-aggressive underachievers are drawn to poor academic performance as an indirect way of venting their anger and retaliating against their parents.

For such retaliation to succeed—that is, for unexpectedly low grades to serve as an aggressive act—the parents must care enough about their youngster's school performance to become visibly upset when it declines. Typically, then, in instances of passive-aggressive underachievement the parents will be highly concerned about their youngster's academic success and very distressed by his or her learning difficulties.

In addition, parental concerns and expectations will frequently have contributed to an underachiever's resentment in the first place. Common in this regard is the parents' imposition of academic goals that their children do not share. For example, the child of a lawyer or physician may be encouraged and expected to follow in his or her parent's footsteps, despite being uncertain of what he or she would like to do or perhaps preferring to become a history teacher or an architect. Or a youngster who is the only, the oldest, or the brightest child in the family may be selected to become its standard-bearer as a successful professional person, even though he or she would rather pursue a nonprofessional career or perhaps not even attend college. When such young people feel unable to question or reject their parents' demands openly, they may utilize underachievement to frustrate the parents' aspirations and take themselves out of the running for some goal in which they are not interested.

The following two case excerpts illustrate how young people may use underachievement as an indirect way of expressing anger toward their parents and how much anger can emerge in response to parental pressures.

Paul was a 14-year-old boy from a socially prominent family who was about to be dismissed from boarding school because of his poor academic record. His father had attended the same school and gone on from there to an elite preparatory school and distinguished university; he had planned for his son to do likewise. Discussion with Paul and his father revealed that the father was an emotionally cold, authoritarian person who demanded outstanding accomplishment and absolute obedience from his son. Paul rankled under his father's constant prodding and criticism and lack of overt affection. However, the prospect of ever disagreeing with his father or showing any anger was out of the question—"I'd just get clobbered," he said. In exploring with Paul his school failure, the interviewer suggested that this seemed to be one area in which he could exert some control over his father. Paul smiled broadly at this and responded, "You said it; there's not a darn thing he can do about it; when he got the call from the headmaster he hit the ceiling, but he can't do a thing about it!"

Karen was a 15-year-old sophomore whose grades had dropped from a B average in junior high school to just a shade above failing. Her clearly stated ambition was to attend vocational school after graduation from high school and be trained as a legal secretary, a career her mother had happily pursued for many years. Her father, however, had other plans for her. He was determined that she be a top student and attend a "first-rate" liberal arts college. Karen was enrolled in a college preparatory program at her father's insistence, despite her different wishes and the school's recommendation that she transfer to a less demanding curriculum consistent with her interests. Intelligence test scores indicated that Karen was bright enough to earn good grades in the precollege program if she wished to. However, deep resentment of her father's imposition of his values on her clearly seemed to be causing her declining performance, which represented an indirect aggressive action against him.

Concerns about Rivalry

Concerns about rivalry frequently lead people to avoid the competitive pursuit of excellence. Through inaction or by a variety of self-defeating maneuvers, they refrain from their best possible effort and never accomplish as much as they could. With specific regard to the classroom, passive-aggressive underachievers typically suffer from fears of failing or fears of succeeding that inhibit their academic efforts.

Fear of Failure Youngsters who fear failure doubt their own abilities and constantly seek to buffer themselves against the experience of having failed. Most notably, they are inclined to set high goals for themselves and then work only half-heartedly to attain these goals. This maneuver allows underachieving students to deny any limitations they may have and to dismiss any suggestions that they have actually been a failure. On the one hand, they do not have to feel embarrassed at not reaching their goals, since they were so ambitious to begin with. On the other hand, their admittedly lackadaisical effort lets them say to themselves and others, "I didn't really put much time in my schoolwork, you know, and if I had really cared or worked hard, I could have done a lot better." Were such youngsters to set goals realistically within their grasp and work diligently toward them, they would then risk failure without having such excuses to cushion the resulting blow to their self-esteem (Baker, 1979; Covington & Omelich, 1979).

Students who fear failure rarely take such risks; instead, they carefully hedge their bets. They seldom take a chance on being wrong, they consistently deny having worked hard even when they have, and they bolster themselves with false pride in how much they have been able to accomplish without extending themselves—"I think I did pretty well to pass, since I hardly cracked a book the whole term." As the insightful father of one underachieving boy put it, "I think he's afraid to work hard, because if he tried hard and still wasn't doing well, he would really have to feel terrible."

This underachieving pattern is particularly likely to emerge at certain transition points that confront students with more difficult subject matter or more demanding academic standards than they have had to face before. For example, youngsters who doubt their ability may find the promotions from elementary school to junior high school and then to senior high school sources of increased concern about failing. Likewise, fear-of-failure youngsters who transfer from one school to another and perceive their new classmates as brighter, more industrious, or better prepared than their former peers may retreat from competitive effort and begin to underachieve at this point in their schooling.

The challenge of making the transition from high school to college has also received special attention from clinicians and researchers. In one revealing study, Berger (1961) found that a group of superior high school students who began to underachieve when they reached college had consciously anticipated and become concerned about no longer being able to maintain superior grades. In comparison with these underachievers, a sample of achieving students seemed more able to accept their limitations: they denied extremely high standards, they were willing to exert and admit to maximum effort even in the face of possible failure, and they took pleasure in hard work.

Another feature of the discouraging impact of the transition from high school to college is elaborated by McArthur (1971), who describes the dilemma of college students whose family and friends expect them to maintain the same relative excellence they displayed in high school, despite the fact that they are now competing only with students who also did well in high school. Such youngsters often suffer what McArthur calls "big-league shock" when they realize the nature of their competition. Their despair of ever being able to compete successfully in the college environment may then lead them to retreat from the competitive effort and thus to underachieve.

Competitive concerns within the family are also common among underachieving youngsters whose self-defeating approach to their studies reflects fear of failure. Whatever their potential, students who fear failure have often suffered from unfavorable comparisons with a successful parent or sibling whose abilities they cannot match. Directly stated or implied disappointment that a youngster does not live up to family standards may then contribute to his or her giving up on doing the work that would earn grades commensurate with his or her ability—"What's the use of trying? I could never do as well as my brother did anyway."

Case 14. *Academic Underachievement Involving Fear of Failure*

After 2 years in the sixth grade 13-year-old John was about to fail the seventh grade when his parents first sought psychological help for him. His low achievement had begun in the third grade and had been attributed by his teachers primarily to his being inattentive in class and neglecting his daily assignments. He had never presented any behavior problems in school, and current psychological testing indicated high average intelligence, with an approximate IQ of 110 and no suggestion of cognitive deficits associated with brain dysfunction.

John's father spontaneously described himself as an authoritarian, bossy person who yelled a lot and was unpleasant to work with, and he added that perhaps he was too intolerant and punitive when his son did not behave exactly as he wanted him to. Although John did not overtly complain about his father's treatment of him, he did appear to resent many of his parents' actions. Yet he could never bring himself to any direct expression of anger or resentment. To the contrary, he consistently retreated from any situation that involved verbal or physical aggression and had a reputation among his peers for being unwilling to defend himself. His teachers' reports rounded out the picture of a shy, quiet, unassertive boy with little self-confidence.

John's parents reported that he characteristically set perfectionistic standards for himself, became extremely upset over minor setbacks, and avoided any situation in which he had once been a loser. Recently, during a game of catch with his father and some other boys and their fathers he had become so humiliated at dropping the ball, even though it had been badly thrown to him, that he left the game and would not return. John himself described clearly how his limited self-confidence and fear of failure interfered with his performance in school. His teachers were wrong in considering him inattentive in class, he said; in truth, he was just reluctant to volunteer or answer questions for fear he would say something wrong and give his classmates excuse for laughing at him.

John also faced major problems in competing with his 1-year-younger brother who, because of John's previous failure, was in the same grade. The brother was an outgoing, academically successful boy who at times joined in the teasing John received at school. The scholastic attainments of his brother and his professionally employed father intensified John's fears that he could never meet his family's standards and discouraged him even further from utilizing what academic ability he possessed.

Fear of Success Young people who fear success are concerned that doing well will bring them more unhappiness than failing to achieve. This seemingly paradoxical outcome of success was first noted clinically by Freud (1916), who described some patients in psychoanalysis who had apparently been "wrecked by success." These people had become psychologically disturbed just at the point when they had attained some highly valued goal for which they had worked long and hard. As subsequently elaborated in other psychoanalytic contributions, such fear of success derives from the expectation that one's achievements will be envied or resented by one's parents, siblings, or peers. In any competitive situation, then, the fruits of victory leave a bad aftertaste that prevents people from enjoying what they have achieved and encourages them to abandon their aspirations or undo their accomplishments (Ovesey, 1962; Schuster, 1955).

To avoid the disapproval or rejection they anticipate in the wake of achievement, success-fearing people approach achievement-related situations much differently from people who are concerned with failure. As noted above, fear-of-failure youngsters tend to set very high goals and not work very hard to reach them; in this way they escape the anxiety of a near-miss and can say that their attainments only partly reflect their true ability. By contrast, young people who fear success make light of their own abilities, even when they are considerable ("I'm not very good in math"); they set limited, unrealistically low goals that are easily within their grasp ("I'll be happy to get a C average, that's all I'm working for"); and they put in just enough effort to reach these minimal goals, after which they disavow any further aspirations ("I was lucky to do as well as I did"). By such attitudes toward their schoolwork, fear-of-success youngsters avoid any appearances or accomplishments that might threaten other people or give them cause to dislike or disapprove of them.

This underachieving pattern has been demonstrated in research studies as well as through clinical observations. When success-fearing people perform well on a task or are led to believe that they have performed well, they tend to become anxious and to experience difficulties in concentrating; on subsequent trials their performance level goes down. When they are doing poorly on a series of laboratory tasks, their performance gradually improves—until they are doing fairly well, at which point they become uncomfortable and slack off. In this same vein, when fear-of-success people happen to be successful, they attribute their accomplishments to external factors, such as luck; when

Public posting of grades can be very stressful for young people who are concerned about doing either better or worse than most of their classmates.

they fail, they attribute the outcome to internal factors, such as their own limited ability (Canavan-Gumpert, Garner, & Gumpert, 1978, Chapter 4; Zuckerman & Allison, 1976).

A further interesting difference between fear-of-failure and fear-of-success underachievers involves the accomplishments of their family and friends. Those who fear failure suffer from rivalry with *successful* people; the more their parents or siblings have achieved, the more afraid of failing they become and the more seriously they underachieve. By contrast, the school-learning problems of those who fear success are intensified by having *unsuccessful* family members. The more they regard their parents or siblings as less able than they are, the more they anticipate negative reactions to what they themselves accomplish. Family studies confirm that many fathers of underachieving sons regard themselves as less successful than they had hoped to be. These men tend to regard their sons as competitors, and they often find ways to discourage their sons from achieving in an apparent effort to protect themselves from even greater feelings of having failed (Grunebaum, Hurwitz, Prentice, & Sperry, 1962; Sperry, Staver, Reiner, & Ulrich, 1958).

Passive-aggressive underachievement that is due to a fear of success usually arises at a time when young people are in fact on the verge of surpassing their parents. This maladaptive reaction pattern is probably responsible in part for the relatively high frequency of high school dropout among children whose parents did not complete high school. It also accounts for many cases in which children of high-school-educated parents begin to do poorly in the final years of high school and thereby reduce their chances of getting into college—which has been referred to as **senior neurosis**—or do unexpectedly poorly in college after a strong high school performance (Hogenson, 1974).

This situation is particularly likely to develop if parents are overtly enthusiastic about college but communicate a different covert message. Parents may say to the college-bound youngster, "Now you'll be able to do all the things we never could." Such a message may imply pride and encouragement. Yet it can also convey underlying feelings of disappointment, envy, rejection, and even anger: "We've had a good life without a college education; now you're going to go away, and it will cost us a lot of money, and you'll get all kinds of new ideas, and it will never be the same between us again."

A growing body of research has considered possible age and sex difference in various fear-of-success attitudes. This work was stimulated by Horner (1968), who developed the projective measure of fear of success imagery mentioned earlier, in which subjects write a story to such cues as "John finds himself at the top of his medical-school class." Horner and others have suggested that females are more likely than males to report negative outcomes in their stories, thereby identifying more prevalent fear of success, and that these concerns increase dramatically for girls during the high school and early college years. If reliable, these differences might relate to persistent sex-role stereotypes about achievement. According to several literature reviews, however, no reliable age or sex differences in frequency of fear-of-success attitudes has yet been demonstrated (Canavan-Gumpert, Garner, & Gumpert, 1978; Condry & Dyer, 1976; Zuckerman & Wheeler, 1975).

On the other hand, high school boys and girls who show fear-of-success imagery do differ in the kinds of negative consequences they associate with doing well. Boys seem more able than girls to compete on a friendly basis, so that rivalry does not preclude friendship. Accordingly, they are more likely to stress envy and resentment as the outcome of success (Romer, 1975). For girls, the loss of affiliation is more often feared as the price of success. In a study by Dalsimer (1975), for example, a tenth-grade girl gave the following story to the clue, "Susan, a senior in a large high school, has just learned that she has gotten the best grades in the graduating class": "Susan is very worried about her friends being jealous and she is sorry that she got the best grades in her graduating class. She began to worry about maybe being a success in the career of her choice."

Passive-Aggressive Behavior Style

Passive-aggressive behavior consists of purposeful inactivity intended to vent underlying feelings of anger and resentment that cannot be expressed directly without causing considerable anxiety. Passive-aggressive youngsters feel put upon, but they fight back by inaction instead of outward behavior. They exert control not by committing disobedient acts, but by failing to do what is expected of them or what might please others. They frustrate and provoke the important people in their lives by just sitting there. Most underachieving youngsters whose school problems are primarily psychological in origin demonstrate such behavior patterns. To their parents and teachers they seem lazy, uninterested, and unmotivated—a stubborn lump under whom they would like to build a fire.

Consistent with this pattern, passive-aggressive underachievers study less than their achieving peers, delay completing their assignments, and reserve their enthusiasm for extracurricular activities (Morrow, 1970). Frequently they show a degree of concentrated effort and achievement in sports, hobbies, or part-time jobs that stands in sharp contrast to their do-nothing academic attitude. Often they will read widely and keep themselves well informed, while reading everything but material assigned in their courses and becoming informed about everything except matters they will be asked about in

Some students undermine their chances for good grades by managing to find time for almost anything except keeping up with their assignments.

class discussions or on examinations (Mondani & Tutko, 1969; Newman, Dember, & Krug, 1973).

Passive-aggressive underachievers also work hard to make sure that nothing happens to bring their grades up to their potential. They "forget" to write down assignments; they study the wrong material in preparation for examinations; they turn in test papers in which they have "overlooked" a section or an entire page; they sit silently through class discussions when they have something to contribute (Lacher, 1973). In these and numerous similar ways, young people use "mistakes" and inactivity to undermine their chances of receiving grades commensurate with their abilities.

Case 15. *Passive-Aggressive Style in Academic Underachievement*

Bob, an 18-year-old high school junior, had managed to get by in school with C grades through the ninth grade. At that point his parents, concerned that continuing mediocre performance would prevent him from getting into a prestigious college, had sent him against his wishes to a private boarding school. They hoped he would improve his academic credentials at this school; what happened instead was that he managed to fail every one of his courses and be asked not to return. Back home the next year he had repeated the tenth grade, with barely passing grades, and was now on the verge of failing grade 11.

Psychological examination revealed that Bob had superior intellectual abilities, with a measured IQ above 125. In commenting on this finding, Bob stated flatly that he received low grades because he disliked studying and consistently avoided doing his schoolwork. Contrary to his parents' educational aspirations for him, he was undecided about attending college, especially any prestigious school where he would have to study hard. As for his study habits, he reported that during the evening periods legislated by his parents as "study time," he typically read widely—books, newspapers, magazines—but seldom studied his school assignments or absorbed any information related to his courses.

Clearly, Bob was not lazy, nor was he untalented or generally averse to success. He pursued several nonintellectual activities with industry and enthusiasm. He liked to hunt, fish, and camp and was an accomplished outdoorsman; he was a skilled carpenter and had completed several ambitious woodworking projects around his home; he enjoyed painting, drawing, and ceramics, and during the previous summer had done very well in a special art course. Where it counted for his parents, however—getting good grades in a demanding school—he was successfully resisting their wishes by not doing what he was capable of, and punishing them in the process.

TREATMENT OF ACADEMIC UNDERACHIEVEMENT

As would be anticipated from the previous discussion, the treatment of academic underachievers varies with the nature of the particular sociocultural or psychological factors that are contributing to their school-learning problems.

Socioculturally Determined Underachievement

Young people who are minimally invested in school as a result of sociocultural factors that have lowered their motivation or limited their opportunities to learn are very difficult to treat. Underachievers whose parents or peers devalue academic achievement typically do not regard themselves as having a problem. Unlike MBD/ADD children (see Chapter 4) or psychologically troubled youngsters who are doing poorly in school, sociocultural underachievers see little to gain by improving their grades. They rarely come to professional attention unless forced to, and when they are seen by a therapist, they seldom show much interest in considering new ways of thinking or acting in relation to school.

In most cases therapists can modify the behavior of socioculturally unmotivated underachievers only by finding ways to convince them of potential advantages in doing as well as they can in school. Therapists who are skillful at fostering mutual confidence, trust, and respect in their work with young people, even those who are being seen unwillingly, may be able to help unmotivated underachievers identify and aspire toward goals that are not shared by their parents and peers.

This treatment prescription may appear contrary to customary cautions against therapists' imposing their own values on the people with whom they work. Nevertheless, helping youngsters to realize their potential by modifying their value systems seems consistent with ethical standards of practice. Although the clinical literature in this regard is sparse, contemporary biography records many cases of bright young people who were influenced by certain experiences or a special relationship with some adult to discard the antiintellectual values of their immediate sociocultural group and to achieve significant educational goals. In *Manchild in the Promised Land,* for example, Claude Brown (1965) tells vividly of how his reform school relationship with psychologist Ernst Papanek (1958) helped direct him away from his delinquent, dropout subculture toward college and law school.

When limited opportunity prevents otherwise able and motivated youngsters from utilizing their full academic potential, there may be little that mental health professionals can do, except in their role as public citizens. Problems of crowded schools, inferior instruction, and the necessity of long hours of after-school work are essentially social problems that extend beyond the capacities of psychotherapists to resolve.

Psychologically Determined Underachievement

When underachievement reflects normal variations in cognitive, physical, or emotional maturity, patience rather than professional intervention is usually the proper prescription. So long as slowly developing young people do not develop excessive concerns about being less mature than their peers, and so long as their parents and teachers do not jump to premature conclusions that they are academically inept, they will in time outgrow the concrete thinking, worries about growth, and lack of future orientation that can temporarily hamper their work in school.

When excessive concerns arise or patience wears thin, counseling may be indicated for these young people and for their parents and teachers as well. Such counseling focuses first on explaining how the academic difficulty stems from development lags rather than from more serious or lasting handicaps. Second, efforts are made to forestall any overreactions to this temporary problem that might cause it to persist beyond the time when these late-maturing underachievers catch up with their peers.

When young people are underachieving as a secondary consequence of schizophrenia, depression, or other forms of psychopathology not directly related to learning, improved schoolwork usually follows successful treatment of the primary disturbance. In cases of passive-aggressive underachievement, in which school difficulties constitute the primary manifestations of psychological disturbance, the therapy typically addresses the origin of the problem in unexpressed anger and resentment toward parents, against whom the youngster's inactive, self-defeating scholastic style is serving as an aggressive weapon.

When passive-aggressive underachievement is of recent onset and derives mainly from negative reactions to the imposition of parental goals, brief counseling with just the parents often helps to resolve the problem. Parents are given accurate information about their underachieving youngster's intellectual potential, they are reassured that his or her declining grades do not mean that future failure is inevitable, and they are encouraged to relax whatever pressures they are placing on him or her for academic excellence or attainmsnt in some specific area. Relaxation of parental pressure frequently undercuts the motivation to passive-aggressive school failure; when parents cease to fret about their youngster's performance, he or she ceases to perceive poor grades as an effective way of acting aggressively toward them.

In older adolescents whose reservations about imposed goals have recently contributed to the onset of underachievement, brief counseling can be effectively directed toward them rather than toward their parents. Such counseling seeks to help them recognize their abilities and interests, clarify their own value systems and preferred goals, and pursue their studies to serve their own purposes rather than to meet or frustrate the needs of others. This approach aims at speedy improvement by focusing specifically on conscious attitudes toward academic goals and efforts and avoiding any extended exploration of underlying feelings or personality style. Group as well as individual counseling along such lines has proved successful with underachieving students at both the high school and college levels (Broedel, Ohlsen, Proff, & Southard, 1960; Gilbreath, 1968; Goldburgh & Penney, 1962).

For young people whose academic underachievement has persisted for some time and is entrenched in problems with anger and rivalry, ongoing psychotherapy rather than brief counseling may be necessary to reverse their academic decline. Definitive psychotherapy in such instances is not necessarily long term, however. For many underachieving youngsters just enough therapeutic help to recognize and express underlying resentments toward their parents is sufficient to break the underachievement pattern. When passive-aggressive youngsters' parental resentments can be elicited and related to their academic efforts, they may with a few months of psychotherapy achieve a markedly improved school performance (Blaine & McArthur, 1971; Parens & Weech, 1966).

Despite this generally favorable outlook in treating passive-aggressive underachievement, certain other considerations temper the success that can be expected. First, the less accessible an underachieving youngster's underlying feelings toward his or her parents are and the more his or her learning difficulties are complicated by concerns about competition and success, the more likely it is that extended psychotherapy will be necessary to produce significant improvement (McIntyre, 1964; Mandel, Roth, & Berenbaum, 1968). Second, passive-aggressive underachievers, especially those who require extended treatment, are seldom motivated to participate actively in it. The likelihood of a good treatment outcome is much better for those who come willingly rather than reluctantly to therapy, and any success at all for those who come unwillingly depends on how effectively the therapist gets them to recognize that they have difficulties that need attention (Altmann, Conklin, & Hughes, 1972; Lacher, 1973).

Additionally, recent advances in behavioral treatment methods indicate that school failure can be avoided or reversed in many cases through school-based programs involving both underachieving students and their parents and teachers. In addition to counseling along the lines discussed earlier, these programs focus on increasing parental and teacher rewards for academic attainment and on providing certain forms of programmed instruction (Bry & George, 1980; Jones & Kazdin, 1981).

SUMMARY

Academic underachievers are young people who receive lower grades in school than would be expected from their average or better intelligence. Such failure to realize their academic potential occurs in approximately 25 percent of schoolchildren; from 30 to 50 percent of young people seen in psychiatric clinics have been referred primarily because of school-learning problems. About 20 percent of adolescents in the United States fail to complete twelfth grade, and more than 50 percent of these dropouts have enough ability to get through high school. Underachievement during the school years is highly predictive of occupational underachievement later and constitutes a serious waste of youthful potential.

Among elementary schoolchildren, learning disabilities related to minimal brain dysfunction/attention deficit disorder are probably the most common reasons for poor school performance despite adequate general intelligence (see Chapter 4). Beginning in late childhood and continuing into adolescence, underachievement becomes increasingly due to sociocultural and psychological factors that include low motivation, limited opportunity, certain developmental and psychopathological states, specific aversions to the learning process, and maladaptive patterns of family interaction.

With respect to *low motivation*, young people who do well in school tend to be interested in learning and to see a clear relationship between achieving in school and realizing some long-range goals, Students who are not oriented toward intellectual values or academic goals, on the other hand, lack motivation to apply themselves in school and are at high risk to underachieve or drop out. Such noneducational values and goals typically come from certain kinds of family, school, peer-group, and sex-role influences.

Parents who value the educational process encourage positive attitudes toward school in their children, whereas parents who ignore or belittle the importance of what their youngsters are doing in school foster negative attitudes. Lower-class parents, who tend to have had fewer positive educational experiences in their own lives than middle- and upper-class parents, are especially likely to promote low academic motivation in their youngsters. There is considerable variability within social-class groups in this regard, however, and the trend for children from lower-class families to feel less positive toward school than middle- or upper-class children cannot be presumed to apply in all disadvantaged families.

Nevertheless, schools are basically middle-class institutions run by well-educated teachers and administrators. Many disadvantaged or minority youngsters consequently experience discontinuities between their school and home experiences that alienate them from the learning process. The more the patterns of thinking and acting they have acquired at home differ from what their school values and rewards, and the more their language differs from standard spoken English, the more likely they are to become unmotivated to achieve. In addition, teachers tend to expect less of children they regard as "culturally disadvantaged," which often reduces their academic motivation even further.

Peer-group and sex-role influences can lower academic motivation when they surround young people with views that working hard to earn good grades is not quite the "right" thing to do. If their friends or parents suggest that high achievement is inconsistent with being popular, or that it is a feminine characteristic in boys and a masculine characteristic in girls, young people can easily lose interest in doing their best in school. Modern movements tend to be replacing such reservations about being a good student with a premium on maximum educational attainment for all talented people. Nevertheless, old stereotypes die hard, and concerns about social opinion still persist as a potential cause of low academic motivation.

Limited opportunity contributes to underachievement primarily when inferior elementary schools fail to prepare young people adequately for high school and college work. In addition, adolescents who are overburdened with responsibilities outside of school may underachieve because they lack the time and energy to do justice to their studies.

The *developmental states* that can impair scholastic performance include several aspects of cognitive, physical, and emotional immaturity. Some young people fall behind their peers during adolescence in advancing from the primarily concrete thinking of children toward the formal operational thinking that characterizes mature cognition; some show a relatively late growth spurt that disrupts their sense of well-being; and some are slower than others to develop the vocational maturity that points young people in certain educational or career directions. Each of these developmental lags can interfere temporarily with young people working to capacity in school, and each has been found in association with academic underachievement.

Similarly, any form of *psychopathology* that disorganizes, distracts, or preoccupies young people can handicap their academic efforts. Underachievement as a secondary consequence of psychopathology is in fact predictable for children who show various kinds of psychological problems prior to entering school. In some cases these problems may include *specific aversions* to the learning process that are based on early childhood experiences that have inhibited a youngster's curiosity.

Maladaptive patterns of family interaction that contribute to academic underachievement typically involve (a) considerable anger toward parents that cannot be directly expressed; (b) concerns about rivalry that generate marked fears of failure or of success; and (c) a passive-aggressive style of coping with stress. None of these patterns is unique to underachieving children or adolescents. When they occur together, however, especially in families that value education, they pose a strong likelihood that passive-aggressive underachievement will arise.

The anger of passive-aggressive underachievers toward their parents typically derives from resentment of parental authority that they perceive as restrictive and unjust. Especially common in this regard is the parental imposition of academic standards or career goals that their children do not share. Underachievement serves to frustrate such parental aspirations when young people feel unable to resist them directly.

Concerns about rivalry lead passive-aggressive underachievers to refrain from making their best possible effort. Some, who fear failure, doubt their own abilities and seek to buffer themselves against the experience of having failed; most notably, they set high goals for themselves and then work only halfheartedly to attain these goals. Others, who fear success, worry that doing well will cause others to resent or reject them; accordingly they make light of their own ability, set limited goals for themselves, and work only hard enough to reach these minimal goals.

The passive-aggressive style found in this pattern of underachievement consists of purposeful inactivity used to vent the underlying feelings of anger and resentment that cannot be expressed directly. Passive-aggressive underachievers study less than their achieving peers, delay completing their assignments, and reserve their enthusiasm for extracurricular activities. Through various "mistakes," such as copying the wrong assignment or "forgetting" that a test has been scheduled, they prevent what they have learned from being translated into grades as high as they are capable of earning.

Treatment of socioculturally determined underachievement is difficult, since these young people typically do not see themselves as having a problem. Often change can be fostered only by finding ways to convince them of potential advantages in doing as well as they can in school. Psychologically determined underachievement requires patience and parental counseling in cases of developmental lag; direct treatment of the primary problem when it is secondary to some form of psychopathology; and, in instances of underachievement, psychotherapy with young people and their parents aimed at expressing underlying resentments, relieving parental pressure, and resolving concerns about rivalry.

When passive-aggressive underachievement is of recent onset and based on concerns that are readily accessible in psychotherapy, treatment for only a few months is often sufficient to resolve the problem. The longer the underachievement has lasted, on the other hand, and the less openly it can be discussed, the more extended the treatment may have to be. Behaviorally oriented school-based programs with underachieving students and their parents and teachers are also proving helpful in avoiding or reversing school failure.

REFERENCES

ALTMANN, H. A., CONKLIN, R. C., & HUGHES, D. C. Group counselling of underachievers. *Canadian Counsellor*, 1972, 6, 112–115.

BACHMAN, J. G., O'MALLEY, P. M., & JOHNSTON, J. *Adolescence to adulthood: Change and stability in the lives of young men.* Ann Arbor, Mich.: Institute for Social Research, 1979.

BAKER, H. S. The conquering hero quits: Narcissistic factors in underachievement and failure. *American Journal of Psychotherapy,* 1979, *33,* 418–427.

BERGER, E. M. Willingness to accept limitations and college achievement. *Journal of Counseling Psychology,* 1961, *8,* 140–144.

BERMAN, G., & EISENBERG, M. Psycho-social aspects of academic underachievement. *American Journal of Orthopsychiatry,* 1971, *41,* 406–415.

BLAINE, G. B., & MCARTHUR, C. C. Problems connected with studying. In G. B. Blaine & C. C. McArthur (Eds.), *Emotional problems of the student* (2nd ed.). New York: Appleton-Century-Crofts, 1971.

BOIKE, M., GESTEN, E. L., COWEN, E. L., FELNER, R. D., & FRANCIS, R. Relationships between family background problems and school problems and competencies of young normal children. *Psychology in the Schools,* 1977, *14,* 283–290.

BROEDEL, J. W., OHLSEN. M. M., PROFF, F. C., & SOUTHARD, C. The effects of group counseling on gifted underachieving adolescents. *Journal of Counseling Psychology,* 1960, *7,* 163–170.

BROOKOVER, W. B. Elementary school social climate and school achievement. *American Educational Research Journal,* 1978, *15,* 301–318.

BROWN, C. *Manchild in the promised land.* New York: Macmillan, 1965.

BROWN, M., JENNINGS, J., & VANIK, V. The motive to avoid success: A further examination. *Journal of Research in Personality,* 1974, *8,* 172–176.

BRY, B. H., & GEORGE, F. E. The preventive effects of early intervention on the attendance and grades of urban adolescents. *Professional Psychology,* 1980, *11,* 252–260.

BUCK, M. R., & AUSTRIN, H. R. Factors related to school achievement in an economically disadvantaged group. *Child Development,* 1971, *42,* 1813–1826.

BUYS, C. J., FIELD, T. K., & SCHMIDT, M. M. A comparison of low socio-economic Mexican American students' and parents' attitudes toward college education. *Personality and Social Psychology Bulletin,* 1976, *2,* 294–298.

CANAVAN-GUMPERT, D., GARNER, K., & GUMPERT, P. *The success-fearing personality.* Lexington, Mass.: Heath, 1978.

CASS, L. K., & THOMAS, C. B. *Childhood pathology and later adjustment.* New York: Wiley, 1979.

CERVANTES, L. F. *The drop out: Causes and cures.* Ann Arbor: University of Michigan Press, 1965.

CHRISTOPHER, S. Parental relationships and value orientation as factors in academic achievement. *Personnel and Guidance Journal,* 1967, *45,* 921–925.

COLEMAN, J. S. *The adolescent society.* New York: Free Press of Glencoe, 1961.

COLEMAN, J. S. The adolescent subculture and academic achievement. *American Journal of Sociology,* 1970, *65,* 337–347.

CONDRY, J., & DYER, S. Fear of success: Attribution of cause to the victim. *Journal of Social Issues,* 1976, *32,* 63–83.

COVINGTON, M. V., & OMELICH, C. L. Effort: The double-edged sword in school achievement. *Journal of Educational Psychology,* 1979, *71,* 169–182.

CRANDALL, V. C. The Fels study: Some contributions to personality development and achievement in childhood and adulthood. *Seminars in Psychiatry,* 1972, *4,* 383–397.

DALSIMER, K. Fear of academic success in adolescent girls. *Journal of the American Academy of Child Psychiatry,* 1975, *18,* 719–730.

DAVIDS, A., & HAINSWORTH, P. K. Maternal attitudes about family life and child rearing as avowed by mothers and perceived by their underachieving and high-achieving sons. *Journal of Consulting Psychology,* 1967, *31,* 29–37.

DUDEK, S. Z., & LESTER, E. P. The good child facade in chronic underachievers. *American Journal of Orthopsychiatry,* 1968, *38,* 153–160.

DULIT, E. Adolescent thinking à la Piaget: The formal stage. *Journal of Youth and Adolescence,* 1972, *1,* 281–301.

ELKIND, D. From ghetto school to college campus: Some continuities and discontinuities. *Journal of School Psychology,* 1971, *9,* 241–245.

ELKIND, D. *Children and adolescents: Interpretive essays on Jean Piaget.* (2nd ed.) New York: Oxford University Press, 1974.

ELTON, C. F., & ROSE, H. A. Longitudinal study of the vocationally undecided male student. *Journal of Vocational Behavior,* 1971, *1,* 85–92.

FITZSIMMONS, S. J. CHEEVER, J., LEONARD, E., & MACUNOVICH, D. School failures: Now and tomorrow. *Developmental Psychology,* 1969, *1,* 134–146.

FREUD, S. (1901) The psychopathology of everyday life. *Standard Edition,* Vol. VI. London: Hogarth, 1960.

FREUD, S. (1916) Some character-types met with in psychoanalytic work. *Standard Edition.* Vol. VI. London: Hogarth, 1957.

GALLAGHER, J. M., & NOPPE, I. C. Cognitive learning and development. In J. F. Adams (Ed.), *Understanding adolescence.* (3d ed.) Boston: Allyn & Bacon, 1976.

GARDNER, G. E., & SPERRY, B. M. School problems: Learning disabilities and school phobia. In S. Arieti (Ed.), *American handbook of psychiatry.* Vol. II. New York: Basic Books, 1974.

GESTEN, E. L., SCHER, K., & COWEN, E. L. Judged school problems and competencies of referred children with varying family background characteristics. *Journal of Abnormal Child Psychology,* 1978, *6,* 247–253.

GILBREATH, S. H. Appropriate and inappropriate group counseling with academic underachievers. *Journal of Counseling Psychology,* 1968, *15,* 506–511.

GOLDBURGH, S. J., & PENNEY, J. F. A note on counseling underachieving college students. *Journal of Counseling Psychology,* 1962, *9,* 133–138.

GREENBERG, J. W., & DAVIDSON, H. H. Home background and school achievement of black urban ghetto children. *American Journal of Orthopsychiatry,* 1972, *42,* 803–810.

GRUNEBAUM, M. G., HURWITZ, I., PRENTICE, N. M., & SPERRY, B. M. Fathers of sons with primary neurotic learning inhibitions. *American Journal of Orthopsychiatry,* 1962, *32,* 462–472.

GUTTENTAG, M., & KLEIN, I. The relationship between inner versus outer locus of control and achievement in black middle school children. *Educational and Psychological Measurements,* 1976, *36,* 1101–1109.

HARRIS, I. D. *Emotional blocks to learning.* New York: Free Press, 1965.

HARVEY, M. G., & KERIN, R. A. The influence of social stratification and age on occupational aspirations of adolescents. *Journal of Educational Research,* 1978, *71,* 262–266.

HATHAWAY, S. R., & MONACHESI, E. D. *Adolescent personality and behavior.* Minneapolis: University of Minnesota Press, 1963.

HATHAWAY, S. R., REYNOLDS, P. C., & MONACHESI, E. D. Follow-up of the later carrers and lives of 1,000 boys who dropped out of high school. *Journal of Consulting and Clinical Psychology,* 1969a, *33,* 370–380.

HATHAWAY, S. R., REYNOLDS, P. C., & MONACHESI, E. D. Follow-up of 812 girls 10 years after high school dropout. *Journal of Consulting and Clinical Psychology,* 1969b, *33,* 383–390.

HELLMAN, I. Some observations on mothers of children with intellectual inhibitions. *Psychoanalytic Study of the Child,* 1954, *9,* 259–273.

HESS, R., & SHIPMAN, V. Cognitive elements in maternal behavior. In J. Hill (Ed.), *Minnesota symposium on child psychology.* Minneapolis: University of Minnesota Press, 1967.

HEWITT, L. S. Age and sex differences in the vocational aspirations of elementary school children. *Journal of Social Psychology,* 1975, *96,* 173–177.

HOGENSON, D. L. Senior neurosis: Cause-effect or derivative. *School Psychologist,* 1974, *28,* 12–13.

HOLLAND, J. L., & HOLLAND, J. E. Vocational indecision: More evidence and speculation. *Journal of Counseling Psychology,* 1977, *24,* 404–414.

HORNER, M. S. Sex differences in achievement motivation and performance in competitive and non-competitive situations. Unpublished doctoral dissertation, University of Michigan, 1968.

HOWARD, M. A., & ANDERSON, R. J. Early identification of potential school dropouts: A literature review. *Child Welfare,* 1978, *57,* 221–231.

HUMMEL, R., & SPRINTHALL, N. Underachievement related to interests, attitudes, and values. *Personnel and Guidance Journal,* 1965, *44,* 388–395.

JARVIS, V. The visual problem in reading disability. *Psychoanalytic Study of the Child,* 1958, *13,* 451–470.

JOHNSTON, L. D., & BACHMAN, J. G. Educational institutions. In J. F. Adams (Ed.), *Understanding adolescence.* (3d ed.) Boston: Allyn & Bacon, 1976.

JOINT COMMISSION ON MENTAL HEALTH OF CHILDREN. Crisis in child mental health. New York: Harper & Row, 1970.

JONES, M. C., & MUSSEN, P. H. Self-conceptions, motivations, and interpersonal attitudes of early- and late-maturing girls. *Child Development,* 1958, *29,* 491–501.

JONES, R. T., & KAZDIN, A. E. Childhood behavior problems in the school. In S. M. Turner, K. S. Calhoun, & H. E. Adams (Eds.), *Handbook of clinical behavior therapy.* New York: Wiley, 1981.

KATKOVSKY, W., PRESTON, A & CRANDALL, V. J. Parents' attitudes toward their personal achievements and toward the achievement behaviors of their children. *Journal of Genetic Psychology,* 1964a, *104,* 67–82.

KATKOVSKY, W., PRESTON, A., & CRANDALL, V. J. Parents' achievement attitudes and their behavior with their children in achievement situations. *Journal of Genetic Psychology,* 1964b, *104,* 105–121.

KATZ, I. The socialization of academic motivation in minority group children. *Nebraska Symposium on Motivation,* 1967, *15,* 133–191.

KEATING, D. P. Thinking processes in adolescence. In J. Adelson (Ed.), *Handbook of adolescent psychology.* New York: Wiley, 1980.

KEATING, D. P., & SCHAEFER, R. A. Ability and sex differences in the acquisition of formal operations. *Developmental Psychology,* 1975, *11,* 531–532.

KELLEGHAN, T. Relationship between home environment and scholastic behavior in a disadvantaged population. *Journal of Educational Psychology,* 1977, *69,* 754–760.

KELSO, G. I. The influences of stage of leaving school on vocational maturity and realism of vocational choice. *Journal of Vocational Behavior,* 1975, *7,* 29–39.

KOHN, M. *Social competence, symptoms and underachievement in childhood: A longitudinal perspective.* New York: Winston, 1977.

LACHER, M. The life styles of underachieving college students. *Journal of Counseling Psychology,* 1973, *20,* 220–226.

LICHTER, S. O., RAPIEN, E. B., SIEBERT, F. M., & SKLANSKY, M. *The dropouts: A treatment study of intellectually capable students who drop out of high school.* New York: Free Press, 1962.

LISS, E. Motivations in learning. *Psychoanalytic Study of the Child,* 1955, *10,* 100–116.

LIVSON, N. & PESKIN, H. Perspectives on adolescence from longitudinal research. In J. Adelson (Ed.), *Handbook of adolescent psychology.* New York: Wiley, 1980.

LOOFT, W. R. Sex differences in the expression of vocational aspirations by elementary school children. *Developmental Psychology,* 1971, *5,* 366.

LORAND, R. L. Therapy of learning problems. In S. Lorand & H. I. Schneer (Eds.), *Adolescents: Psychoanalytic approach to problems and therapy.* New York: Hoeber, 1961.

LUNNEBORG, P. W. Interest differentiation in high school and vocational indecision in college. *Journal of Vocational Behavior,* 1975, *7,* 297–303.

MCARTHUR, C. C. Distinguishing patterns of student neuroses. In G. R. Blaine & C. C. McArthur (Eds.), *Emotional problems of the student.* (2nd ed.) New York: Appleton-Century-Crofts, 1971.

MCINTYRE, P. M. Dynamics and treatment of the passive-aggressive underachiever. *American Journal of Psychotherapy,* 1964, *18,* 95–108.

MANDEL, H. P., ROTH, R. M., & BERENBAUM, H. L. Relationship between personality change and achievement change as a function of psychodiagnosis. *Journal of Counseling Psychology*, 1968, *15*, 500–505.

MARCUS, I. M. Family interaction in adolescents with learning difficulties. *Adolescence*, 1966, 1, 261–271.

MONDANI, M. S., & TUTKO, T. A. Relationship of academic underachievement to incidental learning. *Journal of Consulting and Clinical Psychology*, 1969, *33*, 558–560.

MORROW, W. R. Academic underachievement. In C. G. Costello (Ed.), *Symptoms of psychopathology*. New York: Wiley, 1970.

MORROW, W. R., & WILSON, R. C. Family relations of bright high-achieving and under-achieving high school boys. *Child Development*, 1961, *32*, 501–510.

MUSSEN, P. H., & JONES, M. C. Self-conceptions, motivations, and interpersonal attitudes of late- and early-maturing boys. *Child Development*, 1957, *28*, 243–256.

MUSSEN, P. H., & JONES, M. C. The behavior-inferred motivations of late- and early-maturing boys. *Child Development*, 1958, *29*, 61–67.

MUUSS, R. E. Jean Piaget's cognitive theory of adolescent development. *Adolescence*, 1967, *2*, 285–310.

NADER, P. R. The frequency and nature of school problems. In R. J. Haggerty, K. J. Roghmann, & I. B. Pless (Eds.), *Child health and the community*. New York: Wiley, 1975.

NEIMARK, E. D. Intellectual development during adolescnce. In F. D. Horowitz (Ed.), *Review of child development research*. Vol. 4. Chicago: University of Chicago Press, 1975.

NEWMAN, C. J., DEMBER, C. F., & KRUG, O. K. "He can but he won't": A psychodynamic study of so-called "gifted underachievers." *Psychoanalytic Study of the Child*, 1973, *28*, 83–129.

NIELSEN, A., & GERBER, D. Psychosocial aspects of truancy in early adolescence. *Adolescence*, 1979, *14*, 313–326.

NUTTALL, E. V., & NUTTALL, R. L. Parent-child relationships and effective achievement motivation. *Journal of Psychology*, 1976, *94*, 127–133.

OVESEY, L. Fear of vocational success. *Archives of General Psychiatry*, 1962, *7*, 82–92.

PAPNEK, E. Re-education and treatment of juvenile delinquents. *American Journal of Psychotherapy*, 1958, *12*, 269–296.

PARENS, H., & WEECH, A. A. Accelerated learning responses in young patients with school problems. *Journal of the American Academy of Child Psychiatry*, 1966, *5*, 75–92.

PEARSON, G. H. J. A survey of learning difficulties in children. *Psychoanalytic Study of the Child*, 1952, *7*, 322–386.

PESKIN, H. Influence of the developmental schedule of puberty on learning and ego functioning. *Journal of Youth and Adolescnce*, 1973, *2*, 273–290.

PETERSEN, A. C., & TAYLOR, B. The biological approach to adolescence: Biological change and psychological adaptation. In J. Adelson (Ed.), *Handbook of adolescent psychology*. New York: Wiley, 1980.

PIERCE, J. V., & BOWMAN, P. H. *Motivation patterns of superior high school students. The gifted student.* Washington, D.C.: Cooperative Research Monograph No. 2, U.S. Department of Health, Education and Welfare, 1960.

RICHER, S. Middle-class bias of schools: Fact or fancy. *Sociology of Education*, 1974, *47*, 523–534.

ROMER, N. The motive to avoid success and its effects on performance in school-age males and females. *Developmental Psychology*, 1975, *11*, 689–699.

ROTH, R. M., & PURI, P. The direction of aggression and the Non-Achievement Syndrome. *Journal of Counseling Psychology*, 1967, *14*, 277–281.

SATTLER, H. E., & VAN WAGENER, K. Motivation as an outcome of schooling. *Perceptual and Motor Skills*, 1975, *41*, 993–994.

SCHAEFER, C. Motivation: A major cause of underachievement. *Devereux Forum*, 1977, *12*, 16–29.

SCHECHTER, M. D. Psychiatric aspects of learning disabilities. *Child Psychiatry and Human Development*, 1974, *5*, 67–77.

SCHERESKY, R. The gender factor in six- to ten-year-old children's views of occupational roles. *Psychological Reports,* 1976, *38,* 1207–1210.

SCHULTZ, C. B., & AURBACH, H. A. The usefulness of cumulative deprivation as an explanation of educational deficiencies. *Merrill-Palmer Quarterly,* 1971, *17,* 27–39.

SCHUSTER, D. B. On the fear of success. *Psychiatric Quarterly,* 1955, *29,* 412–420.

SHAW, M. C., & GRUBB, J. Hostility and able high school under-achievers. *Journal of Counseling Psychology,* 1958, *5,* 263–266.

SHAW, M. C., & MCCUEN, J. T. The onset of academic underachievement in bright children. *Journal of Educational Psychology,* 1960, *51,* 103–108.

SHECHTMAN, A. Age patterns in children's psychiatric symptoms. *Child Development,* 1970, *41,* 683–693.

SHERMAN, J. A. Social values, femininity, and the development of female competence. *Journal of Social Issues,* 1976, *32,* 181–195.

SILBERMAN, C. E. *Crisis in the classroom.* New York: Random House, 1970.

SLAUGHTER, D. T. Parental potency and the achievements of inner-city black children. *American Journal of Orthopsychiatry,* 1970, *40,* 433–440.

SPERRY, B. M., STAVER, N., & MANN, H. E. Destructive fantasies in certain learning difficulties. *American Journal of Orthopsychiatry,* 1952, *22,* 356–365.

SPERRY, B. M., STAVER, N., REINER, B. S., & ULRICH, D. Renunciation and denial in learning difficulties. *American Journal of Orthopsychiatry,* 1958, *28,* 98–111.

TEAHAN, J. E. Parental attitudes and college success. *Journal of Educational Psychology,* 1963, *54,* 104–109.

WATTS, B. H. Discontinuity between home and school as a hazard in child development. In E. J. Anthony, C. Koupernik, & C. Chiland (Eds.), *The child in his family.* Vol. 4. Vulnerable children. New York: Wiley, 1978.

WEINER, I. B. Psychodynamic aspects of learning disability: The passive-aggressive underachiever. *Journal of School Psychology,* 1971, *9,* 246–251.

WEINSTEIN, R. S., & MIDDLESTADT, S. E. Student perceptions of teacher interactions with male high and low achievers. *Journal of Educational Psychology,* 1979, *71,* 421–431.

WEISBERG, P. S. Demographic, attitudinal, and practice patterns of adolescent psychiatrists in the United States. In S. C. Feinstein & P. L. Giovacchini (Eds.), *Adolescent psychiatry.* Vol. VI. Chicago: University of Chicago Press, 1978.

WEITZ, S. *Sex roles.* New York: Oxford University Press, 1977.

WESLEY, F., & WESLEY, C. *Sex-role psychology.* New York: Human Sciences Press, 1977.

WILLIAMS, J. E., BENNETT, S. M., & BEST, D. L. Awareness and expression of sex stereotypes in young children. *Developmental Psychology,* 1975, *11,* 635–642.

ZUCKERMAN, M., & ALLISON, S. N. An objective measure of fear of success: Construction and validation. *Journal of Personality Assessment,* 1976, *40,* 422–430.

ZUCKERMAN, M., & WHEELER, L. To dispel fantasies about the fantasy-based measure of fear of success. *Psychological Bulletin,* 1975, *82,* 932–946.

DELINQUENT BEHAVIOR

11

Delinquent behavior consists of acts that violate the law. Despite the apparent clarity of this statement, delinquency is difficult to define and measure. In the first place, delinquent behavior may involve a single delinquent act, a single episode of multiple delinquent acts, occasional but repetitive delinquent acts, or a continually delinquent way of life. Second, delinquent acts may range in severity from major crimes against people or property (assault, theft) to relatively minor offenses (disorderly conduct, vandalism), and they also include **status offenses,** which are illegal only by virtue of the youthfulness of the person committing them (curfew violations, running away). Third, only some of the young people who commit delinquent acts are caught; of those who are caught, only some are arrested; of those arrested, only some come to trial in a juvenile court; and of those tried, only some are adjudicated as delinquent (Eldefonso, 1973, Chapter 3; Erickson & Empey, 1969; Gold, 1970, Chapter 6).

For these reasons, there is no simple way to determine how much delinquency there is, who should be called a delinquent, or which kinds of young people should be studied to learn more about the nature and origins of delinquent behavior. Any general statement about the frequency of delinquent behavior that fails to consider these complexities should therefore be taken with a grain of salt. Similarly, global references to "juvenile delinquents," as if these youngsters constitute some homogeneous group, should be viewed with skepticism. *Delinquency* can be uniformly defined according to what acts it consists of, regardless of who does them or why; *delinquents,* on the other hand, are a markedly heterogeneous group from a psychological point of view.

In terms of their psychological makeup, some youngsters who commit delinquent acts are *sociological* delinquents, in that they have few psychological problems and are well-integrated members of a delinquent subculture. Other delinquent youngsters, whose deviant behavior results from psychological problems, show one of three patterns of disturbance. In one pattern delinquent acts reflect a *characterological* style marked by chronically irresponsible, aggressive, and inconsiderate behavior; in a second pattern delinquent behavior is primarily a *neurotic* symptom that expresses some underlying concerns; and in the third pattern antisocial conduct derives from *psychotic* or *organic* impairments of judgment, impulse control, and other integrative functions of the personality (Hetherington, Stouwie, & Ridberg, 1971; Quay, 1965; Smiley, 1977; Weiner, 1975).

This chapter will first review available data on the prevalence of delinquent behavior and some of the issues involved in interpreting these data. Separate sections will then elaborate the nature and origins of sociological, characterological, neurotic, psychotic, and organic delinquency. A final section will discuss methods of intervention in various kinds of delinquent behavior.

PREVALENCE OF DELINQUENT BEHAVIOR

For an adequate perspective on what is known about the frequency of delinquency, it is necessary to distinguish between two sources of data: *official delinquency statistics* and *actual delinquency estimates.* Official statistics consist of government reports on arrests and dispositions of lawbreakers under age 18. Although limited to young people who have been arrested and adjudicated, these reports have the advantage of providing systematic annual information of the age, sex, race, place of residence, and offenses of the total national population of juveniles who enter the criminal justice system.

Actual estimates come from studies of randomly chosen, presumably representative samples of young people who are asked about their involvement in illegal activity. Such research has the advantage of measuring delinquent behavior independently of whether it has come to legal attention, and it can also cover many more features of delinquents' lives than are usually included in official statistical reports. Unlike official statistics, however, these estimates may or may not approximate true population figures, depending on how good the sampling is, and they are rarely repeated on a systematic annual basis that helps to identify trends and changes. Both kinds of data, though imperfect, combine to provide what current knowledge there is about the prevalence of delinquent behavior.

Official Delinquency Statistics

Statistical reports from the U.S. Department of Justice indicate that official delinquency is a major and steadily increasing problem. Each year approximately 4 percent of American children between the age of 10 and 17 appear in juvenile court for offenses other than traffic violations, and the rate of juvenile court cases has increased more rapidly than the population of young people almost every year since 1961 (see Figure 11.1). A White House Conference in 1970 estimated that one out of every nine young people in the United States will make a court appearance before his or her 18th birth-

Figure 11.1
Rates of juvenile court cases per 1000 population of 10- to 17-year-olds. (From U.S. Department of Justice data reported by Flanagan et al. (1980).)

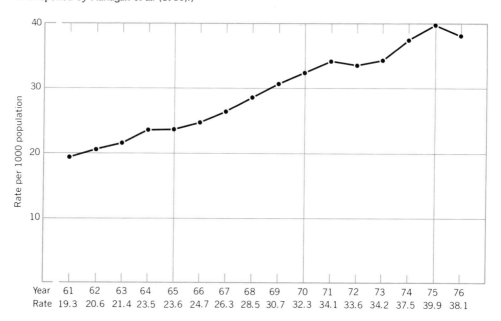

Year	61	62	63	64	65	66	67	68	69	70	71	72	73	74	75	76
Rate	19.3	20.6	21.4	23.5	23.6	24.7	26.3	28.5	30.7	32.3	34.1	33.6	34.2	37.5	39.9	38.1

day, and there is no reason to believe that this rate has become anything but larger since that date (Hess, 1970).

Among juveniles arrested, boys outnumber girls by a ratio of 3.7 to 1. Although some writers suggest that delinquent behavior is increasing dramatically among girls, this sex ratio has changed only slightly over the past 25 years and hardly at all since 1970. Females accounted for 19 percent of juvenile court cases in 1958 and 24 percent in both 1970 and 1976. There is, furthermore, no evidence that violent crimes have been increasing significantly among young females, as is sometimes asserted (Flanagan, Hindelang, & Gottfredson, 1980; Sarri, 1979; Simon, 1975).

There are some clear sex differences in the crimes for which young males and females are most likely to be arrested, however. Compared to the 3.7:1 male:female ratio for all juvenile arrests, males are arrested 12 times more often than females for vandalism; 11 times more often for buying, receiving, or possessing stolen property; 10 times more often for arson and drunk driving; and 9 times more often for violent crimes (murder, manslaughter, rape, robbery, and assault). Females, on the other hand, are arrested 2 times more often than males for prostitution and commercialized vice and 1.5 times more often for running away (Flanagan et al., 1980).

With respect to race, white youngsters outnumber nonwhites by a ratio of 3.1 to one among arrested offenders under age 18. This figure is somewhat smaller than the general population ratio of whites to nonwhites, which indicates an overrepresentation of nonwhites among arrested juveniles. As in the case of sex differences, certain offenses are especially likely to account for arrests of both racial groups. Whites account for 75.7 percent of all juvenile arrests, but for 85 percent or more of arrests for drug abuse, drunkenness, drunk driving, liquor-law violations, running away, and embezzlement. Nonwhite youngsters account for 24.3 percent of the total arrests, but for 45 percent or more of arrests for violent crimes, prostitution, gambling, and fraud (Flanagan et al., 1980).

The distribution of juvenile court cases according to place of residence is shown in Table 11.1. The vast majority of delinquent young people live in cities and suburbs; the population rates indicate that rural youngsters are less likely than city dwellers to appear in a juvenile court. This residential difference must be considered in light of the fact that having a juvenile court in a community appears to increase the likelihood of

TABLE 11.1 Juvenile Court Cases and Degree of Urbanization

Place of Residence	Court Cases (%)	Rate (per 1000 population under 18)
Urban	57	41.8
Semiurban	35	50.4
Rural	8	33.4
Total	100	39.9

Source. Based on data reported by U.S. Department of Justice (1979).

Figure 11.2
Disposition of juveniles taken into police custody. (From U.S. Department of Justice data reported by Flanagan et al. (1980).)

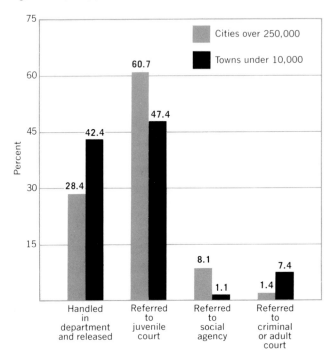

an adolescent's being arrested, perhaps because police are more willing to arrest juveniles when there are special facilities for dealing with them. The establishment of juvenile courts in cities and towns may well have contributed to a greater frequency of arrests in urban than rural areas. Likewise, at least some of the increase in juvenile court cases noted in Figure 11.1 may be attributable to expanding juvenile court facilities rather than to more frequent delinquent behavior.

Figure 11.2 provides some support for questioning official delinquency statistics in this way. Young people who are taken into custody in large cities, where more juvenile facilities can be presumed to exist, are relatively likely to appear in a juvenile court or be referred to a social agency; those picked up by the police in small towns, where special facilities are fewer in number, are relatively likely either to be released or sent to an adult court. It is not unreasonable to hypothesize, then, that additional juvenile court facilities in these less populated areas would result in fewer detected delinquents being released and a corresponding increase in the frequencies of juvenile arrests and juvenile court cases.

The meaning of official statistics is complicated further by the sex and social class of juveniles who break the law. There is some evidence to suggest that boys and lower-class youngsters are more likely to be arrested than girls and middle-class adolescents

Figure 11.3

Adult and Juvenile arrests for major crimes. (From U.S. Department of Justice data reported by Flanagan et al. (1980).)

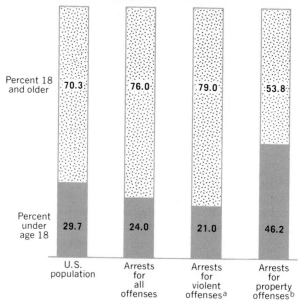

Percent 18 and older

| 70.3 | 76.0 | 79.0 | 53.8 |

Percent under age 18

| 29.7 | 24.0 | 21.0 | 46.2 |

| U.S. population | Arrests for all offenses | Arrests for violent offenses[a] | Arrests for property offenses[b] |

[a] Murder, manslaughter, rape, robbery, assault.
[b] Burglary, larceny, auto theft.

who have committed the same offense (Gold, 1970, Chapter 6; Wirt & Briggs, 1965). To the extent that this is the case, the official data on young people who appear in court may say more about who gets arrested for crimes than who commits them.

Finally, the significance of juvenile crime must be assessed in relation to the adult crime rate and the nature of the offenses committed. As shown in Figure 11.3, young people below the age of 18 constitute 29.7 percent of the population and account for 24.0 percent of the total arrests in the United States (excluding traffic violations). Of this under-18 groups, however, those under 13 constitute about 20 percent of the population but account for only 2 percent of the arrests. This leaves the 13- to 17-year-olds involved in a disproportionately high share of arrests—about 22 percent even though they constitute only about 10 percent of the population. The figure shows further that young people under 18 are less likely than adults to be arrested for violent crimes but account for about half (46.2 percent) of all arrests for major crimes against property.

On the other hand, 60.7 percent of the total arrests of juveniles are for various kinds of misdemeanors rather than more serious crimes against people or property. Three status offenses—curfew violations, running away, and liquor-law violations—account alone for almost 20 percent of juvenile arrests; vandalism, disorderly conduct, drunkenness, and minor violations of drug laws account for another 20 percent of the total arrests of youngsters under 18. Although any and all violations of the law are regrettable, these minor infractions, especially when they occur for the first time or only once, are much less predictive of future criminality or psychopathology than major or repetitive delinquency (Robins, 1966), (see Chapter 1).

Actual Delinquency Estimates

In a landmark study done many years ago, Porterfield (1943) asked 337 male and female college students whether they had ever committed any delinquent acts. Almost all of these young adults admitted previous delinquencies, and the acts they reported were similar in kind and seriousness to those of a comparison group of juvenile court youngsters. The college students appeared to have committed delinquent acts less frequently than the court group, however, and they had rarely ended up in court for them.

Subsequently early work confirmed that a previously unsuspected number of young people commit delinquent acts that go undetected, and most authorities have come to recognize that there is a substantial amount of **hidden delinquency**—delinquent behavior that never appears in official statistics—committed by young people who never become subjects in studies of identified delinquent populations (Murphey, Shirley, & Witmer, 1946; Offer, Sabshin, & Marcus, 1965). Fortunately for research purposes, all available evidence suggests that hidden delinquents commit similar offenses, and for the same reasons, as official delinquents. Except for problems in estimating the true

Most adolescents commit one or more minor delinquent acts that go undetected.

prevalence of delinquent behavior, then, most of what is learned from studies of identified delinquents seems to apply to undetected delinquents as well. The fact remains, however, that delinquency research has been done largely with adjudicated delinquents, and there is consequently only a sparse literature on actual delinquent behavior, independent of involvement with the criminal justice system (Gold & Petronio, 1980).

Two relatively recent large-scale studies that do provide some information about actual delinquency are the National Survey of Youth (Gold & Reimer, 1975), which surveyed self-reported delinquent behavior in a representative sample of 1395 11- to 18-year-olds; and the previously mentioned Youth in Transition Study (O'Malley, Bachman, & Johnston, 1977), which followed the self-reported delinquency of a representative sample of tenth-grade boys until age 23. The results of these studies of actual delinquency confirm the earlier indications of its considerable frequency: over 80 percent of American adolescents admit to having committed one or more delinquent acts. Consistent with official statistics, however, most of these are minor offenses, and a relatively small percent of adolescents are responsible for most of the delinquent behavior among their age group.

As shown in Figure 11.4, the frequency of actual delinquent behavior increases sharply during adolescence, with 18-year-olds of both sexes admitting to almost five times as many nontrivial delinquent acts during the previous 3 years as 11-year-old boys and girls. The sharpest increase occurs between 11 and 15, but the total number of delinquent acts continues to rise until early adulthood before it begins to decrease.

The available information on actual delinquency also confirms official statistics with respect to sex differences: three to four times as many males as females commit delinquent acts. Additionally, heavily delinquent youngsters do not appear to come dispro-

Figure 11.4
Mean frequency of nontrivial incidents committed by boys and girls (11 to 18 years old). (From Gold and Petronio (1980). Reprinted with permission of John Wiley & Sons.)

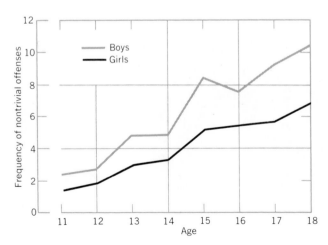

portionately from lower-class or nonwhite groups. Among girls there is no relationship between social class and actual delinquent behavior; among boys there is only a slight relationship, with lower-class youngsters admitting to somewhat more frequent delinquent behavior than middle-class youngsters. Aside from this social class difference, finally, nonwhite adolescents of both sexes are no more delinquent than whites (Gold, 1970; Shanley, Lefever, & Rice, 1966). These findings provide all the more reason to believe that any apparent overrepresentation of lower-class or minority youth in official delinquency statistics may be more a function of who gets arrested than of who breaks the law.

SOCIOLOGICAL DELINQUENCY

Sociological delinquency involves illegal behavior associated with membership in a subculture that endorses *antisocial* standards of conduct. The members of such deviant subcultures join together in committing crimes that reflect their customary way of life and seen entirely appropriate to them. Accordingly, this pattern of delinquency is also referred to as "antisocial," "normal," "socialized," or "subculturally deviant" delinquency (American Psychiatric Association, 1980; Smiley, 1977).

Membership in a delinquent gang can give adolescents feelings of belongingness that are difficult for them to give up.

As this definition indicates, sociological delinquency is characterized by adaptive rather than maladaptive behavior and by social rather than solitary acts. The *adaptive* nature of sociological delinquency was first described by Jenkins (1955, 1957), who did some of the early research on differentiating delinquents according to their personality style. As Jenkins and other writers have elaborated, sociological delinquents engage in planned, easily understandable behavior that breaks the law as an expression of their group's needs and attitudes.

Subcultures that foster group delinquency grant prestige to successful lawbreakers and reject those who refuse to participate in antisocial activities. In this kind of setting delinquent youths experience a sense of self-esteem and belonging, while nondelinquents feel outcast and unworthy. Instead of displaying feelings of personal alienation and social inadequacy, then, sociological delinquents appear psychologically well adjusted. They show a good capacity for interpersonal relatedness, and they are satisfied, secure, and accepted members of the social group that is important to them—namely, their delinquent subculture (Empey, 1969; Friedman, Mann, & Friedman, 1975; Glaser, 1965; Quay, 1979; Short, 1974).

The *social* nature of this form of delinquency refers to the fact that it typically involves group rather than individual behavior and is often appropriately labeled "gang" delinquency. Sociological delinquents rarely commit crimes by themselves and are especially unlikely to keep any solitary criminal acts a secret from their peers. By contrast, a preference for solitary delinquent behavior usually indicates a psychological problem related to individual disturbance rather than group influence. This does not rule out the possibility that some members of a delinquent gang will be psychologically disturbed; often in such cases the group itself has a clear sense of which of its members are relatively unstable and unreliable.

Origins of Sociological Delinquency

Consistent with their being psychologically well-adjusted members of their group, sociological delinquents have usually enjoyed good family relationships during their early life. Attentive parents and siblings have helped them develop basic capacities for judgment, self-control, and interpersonal relatedness as infants and preschoolers. Later, however, as elementary school children and adolescents, they have typically lacked adequate parental supervision and been influenced less by their family than by antisocial models in their neighborhood. Sociological delinquency thus tends to be associated with unsupervised development in a disorganized home that is located in a deteriorated, high-delinquency neighborhood (Brigham, Ricketts, & Johnson, 1967; Duncan, 1971; Jenkins & Boyer, 1968; Jenkins, NurEddin, & Shapiro, 1966).

Yet sociological delinquency is by no means a unique product of lower-class neighborhoods and values. In the first place, neither lack of community cohesion nor inadequate parental supervision is limited to poor neighborhoods. Affluent suburbs, with their sometimes transient population of families on the move and parents preoccupied with their own goals and interests, can also fail to provide young people with a sense of direction and belonging. In a survey of 830 randomly chosen fifth- through twelfth-grade students in an upper-middle-class suburb, Levine and Kozak (1979) found that many had parents who paid very little attention to how or with whom they spent their time.

Second, even though delinquent groups are found more often in lower-class neighborhoods, neither delinquency nor the formation of trouble-making gangs is lacking in middle-class life. In Robins's (1966) previously mentioned study of over 500 child-guidance clinic patients, participation in group delinquent acts was found in 53 percent of the boys from slum areas but also in 26 percent of the boys from better neighborhoods. As for delinquent behavior in general, the indications that official statistics overrepresent lower-class lawbreakers are supported by an extensive literature on the existence and nature of middle-class delinquency (Elkind, 1967; Hennesy, 1978; Miller, 1970; Tobian, 1970; Vaz, 1969).

Third, middle-class adolescents commit just about the same kinds of delinquent acts as lower-class youths. Only two exceptions to this general statement have been noted in studies of actual delinquent behavior: burglary is committed more often by lower-class than by middle-class delinquents, and auto theft is slightly more common among middle-class offenders (Frease, 1973; Herskovitz, Levine, & Spivack, 1959; Nye, Short, & Olson, 1958). Also of interest is more recent evidence (a) that rural adolescents are as likely as urban youths to become involved in group delinquency and (b) that girls as well as boys can become involved in delinquent gangs (Erickson & Jensen, 1977; Thompson & Lozes, 1976). As Levine and Kozak (1979, p. 100) conclude from their survey, then, problems of delinquency "know no class differentiation."

Sociological Theories of Delinquency

According to some influential sociological theories, group delinquency is a fairly common lower-class behavior that represents a consistent, adaptive adherence to norms and values at variance with middle-class standards (Kvaraceus & Miller, 1959; Miller, 1958). However, most people recognize that the actions of delinquent gangs are just as disturbing and unacceptable to law-abiding adults and young people in lower-class neighborhoods as they are to residents of middle-class neighborhoods. Delinquent subcultures are in fact considered deviant by the majority of people within all social classes and do not really serve any adaptive function beyond providing group membership. The wages of crime, including as they do disapproval from most members of society and the constant risk of arrest and imprisonment, call into question how adaptive such acts are, even when they are committed by psychologically stable group delinquents.

Data from Robins's (1966, p. 199) long-term follow-up of her subjects cast further doubt on the adaptive value of antisocial behavior among lower-class youngsters. The relationships she found between youthful antisocial conduct and adult behavior problems were as strong among lower-class as middle-class youngsters. This equal predictability of adult disturbance from childhood antisocial tendencies in lower and middle classes seriously questions the notion that such tendencies serve adaptive functions in the lower class. Hence the "adaptive" nature of sociological delinquency must be understood in a relative sense. Sociological delinquents are less likely to be disturbed than psychological delinquents and are more likely to be misbehaving in response to social influences rather than personal problems. Nevertheless, their behavior should probably not be considered to represent a normal way of life, especially with respect to its future implications.

The issue of adaptation aside, sociological approaches have suffered from an unfortunate tendency to study and interpret delinquent behavior primarily as a lower-class phenomenon. The pioneering and perhaps still best known research on delinquency was done by Sheldon Glueck and Eleanor Glueck (1950, 1952), who studied 500 reform school boys, almost all of whom came from disadvantaged neighborhoods, and a comparison group of nondelinquent boys from similar neighborhoods. As would be expected, their findings—and those of other studies based on such restricted sampling—say more about lower-class life than about the origins of delinquency. For example, Glueck and Glueck (1950, p. 109) report that delinquency is significantly associated with "lack of cultural refinement in the home"; cultural refinement was indeed found lacking in the homes of 92 percent of their lower-class delinquents, but it was also lacking for 82 percent of their lower-class nondelinquent subjects.

When sociological theorists have considered middle- as well as lower-class delinquency, they have traditionally tended to regard adaptive-social delinquency largely as a lower-class phenomenon and maladaptive-individual delinquency as the characteristic form of delinquent behavior among middle-class youngsters. Prominent examples are two widely cited "reaction formation" theories of subcultural delinquency: Cohen (1955) suggests that subcultural delinquency occurs when frustrated efforts to attain middle-class status and prerogatives result in a reactive endorsement of antisocial values; Cloward and Ohlin (1960, p. 78) argue that "pressures toward the formation of delinquent subcultures originate in marked discrepancies between culturally induced aspirations among lower-class youth and the possibilities of achieving them by legitimate means."

Although these theories help to explain why some disadvantaged young people commit crimes, they do not provide an adequate basis for distinguishing between lower- and middle-class delinquency or accounting for delinquent behavior in general. There is no reason to discount the possibility that lower-class youngsters will commit antisocial acts because of psychological disturbance as well as subcultural influence, and we have already seen that middle-class youngsters do become involved in subculturally delinquent groups and commit just about the same kinds of offenses as lower-class youth. In fact, the more closely the distinction between middle-class and lower-class delinquency is examined, the more it is found to consist of little more than differences in socioeconomic status among offenders.

CHARACTEROLOGICAL DELINQUENCY

Characterological delinquency comprises illegal acts that reflect a primarily *asocial* personality orientation. Unlike sociological delinquents, characterological delinquents are usually loners who have no group membership or loyalties. They commit their crimes either by themselves or in temporary alliance with one or two other delinquents, whom they seldom regard as friends. In further contrast to sociological delinquents, they do not maintain two sides to their personality, one a side of trust and loyalty that they reserve for members of their subculture and another a side of disdain and disaffection that they show toward people outside of their group. Instead, characterological delinquents trust no one and are loyal only to themselves—although they may pretend trust and loyalty when it serves their purpose to do so.

The offenses of characterological delinquents occur as a consequence of their disregard for the rights and feelings of others and their inability or unwillingness to control their behavior. These young people typically translate aggressive, acquisitive, and pleasure-seeking impulses into immediate action, with little concern for how anyone else might suffer in the process. Thus they break the law in the course of expressing anger, satisfying a whim, or obtaining something they want, and not in response to group influence or needs for peer acceptance (Weiner, 1975).

For these reasons, characterological delinquency is also classified by various writers as "asocial," "unsocialized," or "undersocialized" delinquency (American Psychiatric Association, 1980; Smiley, 1977). In addition, the interpersonal orientation and behavior patterns of characterological delinquents constitute in budding form a condition typically diagnosed in clinical settings as *psychopathic* or *antisocial personality disorder*. Characterological delinquency can best be understood in relation to the nature, origins, and course of this particular disorder.

Characterological Delinquency and Psychopathic Personality Disorder

Disorders of personality, although sometimes predictable from childhood behaviors, do not begin to take shape until late adolescence or early adulthood, at the time when personality style becomes fairly crystallized. The unique feature of a **personality disorder,** as opposed to a neurotic disturbance, is that its symptoms are not "alien" or distressing to the person who has them; they are simply part of his or her nature and a comfortable way of being. In this respect there is no clear boundary between *personality style* and *personality disorder,* and typically the difference between them is defined by subjective external criteria: an individual's personality style becomes labeled a "personality disorder" when other people regard his or her behavior as incompetent, offensive, self-defeating, or antisocial.

Psychopathic or **antisocial personality** is the most common personality disorder that emerges during adolescence, and it usually comes to light in connection with characterological delinquency. The two basic elements of psychopathic personality are an underdeveloped conscience and an inability to identify with other people. Because they lack conscience, psychopaths feel little guilt about trampling on the rights and feelings of others. Because they lack identifications, they are essentially loveless individuals whose emotional relationships are fleeting and shallow. They do not hate other people, as sociological delinquents may hate "outsiders"; instead, they simply do not care enough about others, one way or another, to have any strong feelings toward them. In addition to their basic guiltlessness and lovelessness, many psychopathic individuals are found to be impulsive, thrill-seeking people with limited capacities for long-term planning or goal-directed behavior (Jenkins, 1960; McCord & McCord, 1964; Schalling, 1978).

These features of their personality make psychopathic youngsters highly likely to engage in characterologically delinquent behavior. Yet there is no necessary relationship between psychopathy and criminality, as is sometimes believed. Law breaking may occur for sociological or psychological reasons that have nothing to do with characterological defects, as noted at the beginning of the chapter. Even among the most frequently and seriously delinquent group of youngsters in Robins's (1966, p. 159) large sample, for example, only half could be diagnosed as psychopathic. Conversely, not all psychopaths become lawbreakers; even though this condition disposes people to engage in antisocial behavior, criminality is by no means an inevitable outcome (Spielberger, Kling, & O'Hagen, 1978; Wagner, 1974).

Problems in Labeling Although there is general agreement concerning the nature of psychopathy, there are differing views on how to label it. *Psychopathic personality* was originally named and distinguished from neurotic and psychotic disorders by Hervey Cleckley (1976) in a book called *The Mask of Sanity,* which first appeared in 1941. Some later writers recommended calling the disorder *sociopathic personality,* to draw attention to its implications for inadequate socialization. Still later the American Psychiatric Association, in both the second and third editions of its *Diagnostic and Statistical Manual* (DSM), elected to call it *antisocial personality* (American Psychiatric Association, 1980; Lewis & Balla, 1975).

This last choice seems unfortunate because the basic nature of the disorder is *asocial,* not antisocial as it is in the case of sociological delinquents. Even more worrisome is the fact that the original term *psychopath* has retained considerable popularity over the years, among both clinicians and researchers. Three widely cited contemporary books use it in their title: *Psychopathic Behaviour* (Hare & Schalling, 1978), *The Psychopath* (Reid, 1978), and *The Psychopath in Society* (Smith, 1978). Hence for the same condition one label is commonly used in the literature (*psychopathic personality*) and a different label is required for official diagnostic purposes in mental health settings (*antisocial personality*).

DSM-III also makes some age distinctions that complicate the labeling process. *Antisocial personality disorder* is acknowledged in the manual to involve numerous characteristics that are present prior to age 15, but it cannot officially be diagnosed in anyone younger than 18. For juveniles showing the features of this disorder, the DSM-III category is **undersocialized conduct disorder.** Although there is some merit in recognizing that personality disorders rarely become crystallized before late adolescence, it may be somewhat arbitrary to label the very same condition one way at age 17 years and 364 days and another way the following day, on the person's 18th birthday—especially when this particular condition is known to show considerable continuity from early adolescence into adulthood (Cass & Thomas, 1979, p. 135). Accordingly, most clinicians and researchers will probably continue to think of juveniles with this disorder as budding psychopaths or antisocial personalities, even though in mental health settings they will have to record a formal diagnosis of undersocialized conduct disorder.

Personality-Oriented and Behaviorally Oriented Descriptions Instead of regarding psychopathy as consisting of certain personality characteristics, some writers prefer to define it strictly in behavioral terms. From this point of view psychopaths are people who rarely form close personal relationships, do poorly in school and on the job, have difficulty supporting themselves and their dependents, and engage regularly in illegal activity. No inferences are made about underlying personality processes that led to this behavior pattern, since such inferences are considered unreliable (Cloninger, Reich, & Guze, 1978; Hare & Cox, 1978; Robins, 1978).

As an illustration of this approach, Robins (1978) notes that some people whom most observers would agree are psychopathic may nevertheless report feeling sorry for things they have done. In these cases, Robins says, believing that inability to feel guilt is a defining characteristic of psychopathy "requires believing that these psychopaths do not really feel the way they claim to feel" (p. 256). Robins argues that personality characteristics must be inferred from what people do, not from what they say, which means that psychopathologists might just as well stick to the behaviors and forget the inferences entirely.

Writers on the other side of this debate argue that precise identification of psychopathy can be achieved only by going beyond overt behavior to a description of underlying personality processes. Many of the behavior patterns associated with psychopathy can also occur as a reflection of schizophrenia, brain damage, mental retardation, or certain other conditions. This means that a diagnostic process based only on the kinds of behaviors listed above, such as a poor work record, must include ruling out a long list of possibly causative disorders. Then, unfortunately, the process will incur the disadvantages of *diagnosis by exclusion* discussed in Chapter 8 (see p. 217). With this in mind, a strong case can be made that psychopathy should be identified not by ruling *out* other possible explanations of illegal or inadequate behavior, but by ruling *in* such distinctive personality attributes as guiltlessness and lovelessness (Lewis & Balla, 1976, Chapter 3; Schalling, 1978).

Psychopathic personality disorder leads to becoming a convicted criminal, but at other times to achieving considerable success as a manipulator of other people.

As for dealing with contrary-to-fact statements by psychopaths, many clinicians do not share Robins's concern about believing that these people may not feel the way they claim to feel. To the contrary, some writers emphasize that psychopathic behavior is determined largely by needs to deceive or outwit other people as a way of gaining their own selfish ends. For this reason, psychopaths are sometimes described as "manipulative personalities" or "charmers" whose words and deeds, especially when they suggest any altruism, cannot be taken at face value (Bursten, 1972; Smith, 1978, Chapter 2; Wagner, 1974).

Asocial Attitudes and Personality Integration   On close inspection, traditional lists of presumably psychopathic characteristics fall into two distinct categories. One category consists of inconsiderate, uncaring actions toward others that reflect the guiltlessness and lovelessness central to this disorder. The other category refers to inadequacies in the integrative functions of the personality that result in poor school and work records, low tolerance for frustration, lack of self-control, limited capacity for long-term planning and goal-directed behavior, and inability to learn from experience.

Over the years a substantial body of research has apparently confirmed that both categories of behavior differentiate psychopathic delinquents from subcultural and neurotic delinquents. For example, studies have suggested that psychopathic youngsters are relatively high in boredom and stimulation-seeking, at the expense of working effectively on laboratory tasks, and relatively low in response to social reinforcement (DeMyer-Gapin & Scott, 1977; Orris, 1969; Skrzypek, 1969; Stewart, 1972).

More recently, however, the adequacy of much of this research has come into question. Because most of these studies have been based on institutionalized delinquents, they include only those psychopaths who have broken the law and been caught and imprisoned. Hence they may sample only *unsuccessful* psychopaths, those who have failed or been deficient in ways that led to their ending up in an institution. Interestingly, some preliminary research data from noninstitutionalized psychopaths suggest that many of them may be quite capable of tolerating boredom, learning from experience, and responding sensitively to social cues (Spielberger, Kling, & O'Hagen, 1978; Smith, 1978, Chapter 4; Widom, 1976, 1978).

It begins to appear, then, that psychopaths may all share in the moral and interpersonal defects that characterize this condition but differ widely in the extent to which the integrative functions of their personality are impaired. Some are well-functioning psychopaths who plan carefully, manipulate others effectively, find ways of attaining academic and vocational success, and rarely show up in mental hospitals or prisons. Others function less well and, as a result of impulsiveness, limited skills, and poor judgment, rarely succeed in life and frequently become detected criminals or mental patients.

Heilbrun (1979) stresses in this regard that cognitive variables always mediate between the core personality characteristics of psychopaths and how they actually behave, and he provides some interesting supportive data. Working in a prison setting, he divided 76 inmates into psychopathic and nonpsychopathic offenders and into high and low scorers on an intelligence test. Having an unsocialized personality was associated with violent and impulsive crime in his sample, but only for the less intelligent psychopaths (average IQ 93.7). The more intelligent psychopaths (average IQ 114.9) were no more likely to have been violent or impulsive than the nonpsychopathic offenders. Additionally, many of these bright psychopaths, despite their criminal history, had achieved noteworthy educational goals.

Origins of Psychopathic Personality Disorder

Much of what has been said in previous chapters about the origins of specific patterns of psychopathology applies to psychopathic personality disorder: the causes of this condition are not fully understood, but they seem to involve some combination or interaction of unfavorable environmental experiences and predisposing genetic factors. As elaborated in this section, psychopathic individuals have usually suffered parental rejection from early in life and been exposed to antisocial family models. In addition, psychopathy shows patterns of familial incidence beyond what can be accounted for in terms of child-rearing or social learning experiences.

Environmental Influences   Psychopathic personality disorder is typically associated with a childhood history of early and severe parental rejection. Youngsters who are deprived from infancy of their parents' affection and interest develop little capacity for interpersonal warmth and compassion. They seldom expect consideration or nurturance from others, and they feel little hesitation in attempting to impose their will on a world they see as hostile and uncaring. There is accordingly good reason to believe that characterologically aggressive, antisocial behavior originates at least partly in the disruption of normal dependency relationships of children to their parents (Bandura & Walters, 1959; Jenkins, 1966; Jenkins, NurEddin, & Shapiro, 1966).

Parental rejection of future psychopaths usually involves not only emotional deprivation in early childhood but also inadequate discipline and supervision during middle childhood and adolescence. In Robins's (1966, pp. 167–168) large sample, for example, only 9 percent of the child-guidance patients who were disciplined adequately or strictly by both parents were diagnosed as psychopathic as adults. Where one or both parents were described as too lenient, however, 29 percent of the youngsters were diagnosed psychopathic as adults, and where one or both exerted no discipline at all 32 percent became psychopathic.

Discipline can be inadequate not only when it is nonexistent, but also when it is inconsistent or punitive. Parents help their children learn good judgment and self-control when they agree on standards of conduct that they regularly enforce. When parents disagree about how their children should behave, or when they punish certain acts sometimes but not always, their youngsters tend to persist in such unsocialized behavior as aggressive, inconsiderate, and irresponsible actions toward others.

Similarly, parents foster internalized moral standards by disciplining their children calmly and appropriately. If instead they angrily scold, spank, or take away privileges in ways that are unrelated or out of proportion to any specific misdeed, they are being more punitive than instructive. Punitive discipline often contributes to children becoming aggressive, short-tempered adolescents and adults whose behavior is governed by an externalized morality—according to which any behavior is acceptable so long as one can get away with it without being caught or punished (Elkind & Weiner, 1978, pp. 274–276; Hoffman, 1977, 1980; Jurkovic & Prentice, 1977).

As testimony to parental influences on emerging psychopathy, the most reliable known predictor of this personality disorder is growing up in a home in which the parents, particularly the father, are prominently antisocial. The long-term follow-up data in Robins's (1966, pp. 160–161; 1978) study revealed that child patients whose parents had no history of psychological disorder or antisocial behavior had a 16 to 18 percent likelihood of developing subsequent psychopathy. In comparison, 32 to 36 percent of those whose father or mother had a history of arrest or desertion or whose father was chronically unemployed were later diagnosed as having a psychopathic personality. A significantly increased risk of psychopathy was also present when the father drank excessively or had failed to support his family.

For both boys and girls in Robins's sample, interestingly, paternal antisocial behavior was the more significant predictor of subsequent psychopathy. Although having a behaviorally disturbed mother in addition to an antisocial father slightly increased the likelihood of psychopathy in the child, the risk of subsequent psychopathy was no greater when only the mother displayed behavior problems than when she did not. Other studies appear to confirm the special importance of the father in influencing his children toward aggressive, delinquent behavior (Anderson, 1968; Becker, Peterson, Hellner, Shoemaker, & Quay, 1959).

Despite superficial appearances to the contrary, identification with parents rarely contributes to this familial incidence of psychopathy. The basic incapacity of psychopaths to identify with anyone has already been noted. Additionally, the dominant importance of the father's pathology in contributing to psychopathy in girls as well as boys cuts across the sex-role influences usually associated with identification. The striking relationship between paternal psychopathy and antisocial personality formation appears to derive not from identification, then, but from the pathogenic child-rearing practices of the antisocial father. That is, a psychopathic father is a particularly likely candidate to ignore his children and to abdicate or abuse his responsibilities for disciplining them.

Genetic Influences. The findings of Robins (1966) and numerous other researchers leave little doubt that psychopathic behavior runs in families. As noted in previous chapters, however, data from twin and adoption studies are necessary to determine whether familial incidence results from genetic transmission or from shared environmental experiences. Twin studies indicate how much concordance there is for a condition in identical (monozygotic) pairs—who share equally common genes and life experiences—and nonidentical (dizygotic) pairs—whose life experiences are generally expected to be more similar than their heredity. Adoption or cross-fostering studies assess the impact on children of being born to and reared by different sets of parents who do or do not show evidence of a particular condition.

As shown in Table 11.2, a much higher average concordance for criminality has been found among identical (54.3%) than nonidentical (21.3%) twin pairs in several studies. The implication of these findings for psychopathic personality disorder is somewhat uncertain, since they come from studies of criminals rather than identified psychopaths. On the other hand, the subjects in these studies were imprisoned adult offenders, about 80 percent of whom are likely to have an antisocial personality (Guze, Goodwin, & Crane, 1969).

TABLE 11.2 Concordance Rates for Criminality in Same-Sexed Identical and Nonidentical Twins

	Identical Twins	Nonidentical Twins
Number of Pairs Studied	219	282
Percent Concordant	54.3	21.3

Source. Based on nine twin studies reviewed by Rosenthal (1975).

TABLE 11.3 Rate of Criminality in Adopted Sons of Criminal and Noncriminal Fathers

	Biological Fathers			
	Criminal		Noncriminal	
Adoptive Fathers	n	Criminal (%)	n	Criminal (%)
Criminal	58	36.2	52	11.5
Noncriminal	214	21.4	333	10.5

Source. Based on data reported by Mednick and Hutchings (1978).

Like these twin studies, adoption data also suggest genetic influences in the origin of psychopathy. Children who are born to antisocial parents and placed for adoption early in life are significantly more likely to be diagnosed psychopathic as adults than adopted-away offspring of parents who have other kinds of diagnosable conditions or no history of psychological disorder. Similarly, tracing back the biological families of adoptees who have become psychopathic reveals a much higher frequency of psychopathy among their first-degree relatives than is found in the biological relatives of nonpsychopathic adoptees (Cadoret, 1978; Cadoret & Cain, 1980; Crowe, 1974; Schulsinger, 1972).

Cross-fostering data indicate further that genetic influences combine with child-rearing factors in an additive way to contribute to psychopathic personality development. Table 11.3 shows that being born to a criminal father increases the likelihood that adopted-away offspring will become criminal, regardless of who rears them (36.2% versus 11.5% for those reared by criminal fathers and 21.4% versus 10.5% for those reared by noncriminal fathers). Simply being reared by a criminal father does not make all that much difference if the biological father is noncriminal (11.5% versus 10.5%). For biological sons of criminal fathers, however, being reared by a criminal adoptive father has an additive effect that increases the likelihood of criminality (36.2% versus 21.4%).

Table 11.4 confirms that the family histories of adopted children who develop criminal records as adults show a higher frequency of criminality among their biological than among their adoptive fathers (49% versus 22%). At the same time, the adoptive fathers of criminal adoptees have more than twice the rate of criminality themselves

TABLE 11.4   Rate of Criminality Among Adoptive and Biological Fathers of Criminal and Noncriminal Adoptees (in percent)

| Adoptees | Fathers | |
	Adoptive	Biological
Criminal	22	49
Noncriminal	10	31

Source.   Based on data reported by Hutchings and Mednick (1974) on 1145 male adoptees.

than the adoptive fathers of children who do not become criminals (22% versus 10%), which bears further testimony to the additive role of the home-rearing climate in contributing to criminality in youngsters who may be genetically disposed in this direction.

The Course of Psychopathic Personality Disorder

Psychopathy is a chronic condition that begins early in life, crystallizes in late adolescence or early adulthood, and typically persists throughout the adult years. Although the current state of knowledge in abnormal psychology justifies very few unqualified statements, such a statement can be made about psychopathic personality disorder: it always starts with certain characteristic childhood behavior problems, and the absence of such developmental problems contraindicates its ever being diagnosed in adulthood (American Psychiatric Association, 1980; Robins, 1978; Robins, Gentry, Munoz, & Marten, 1977; Robins, Murphy, Woodruff, & King, 1971; Rockwell, 1978).

Future psychopaths begin as early as age 5 or 6 to show such antisocial behavior as fighting, lying, stealing, truancy from school, and cruelty to people and animals. By age 10 half or more are misbehaving in these ways and displaying an aggressive, demanding, and self-centered style of life.

In adolescence these childhood characteristics of psychopaths-to-be bring them increasingly into conflict with their peers, family, school, and community. They are more likely than other youngsters to lack friendships, to be argumentative and disobedient at home, and to run away overnight. They are at high risk for skipping school, being expelled or suspended for fighting or other disruptive conduct, and, unless they happen to be bright enough to succeed academically without conscientious effort, being held back one grade or more. They frequently get into trouble with the police and end up being arrested. In addition to engaging in behavior that would be considered socially unacceptable at any age, budding psychopaths also tend to become involved earlier than their peers in activities by which young people seek to feel "grown up," including smoking, drinking, being sexually adventurous, and going off on their own (Hudgens, 1974, Chapter 7; Welner, Welner, & Fishman, 1979).

The life course of psychopaths as adults depends on the extent to which their character defects in morality and interpersonal relatedness are balanced by other personality resources. As noted earlier, those with good attitudes and integrative abilities may fashion successful lives for themselves as charmers and manipulators—although they are likely to be popular only among people who fail to see through them. Those with fewer skills and less well-integrated personalities will be at high risk for criminal records, job failure, alcoholism, and other chronic social problems. People who enter adulthood headed toward a psychopathic life-style seldom change their orientation later. There is some evidence, however, that about one-third "burn out" after age 35 and become less actively aggressive and asocial than before (Rockwell, 1978).

Case 16. *Psychopathic Personality Development in Emerging Characterological Delinquency*

Martin was 13 when his school principal recommended professional help for him. The referral was precipitated by the latest episode in a long history of aggressive behavior, which included numerous unprovoked beatings of younger children. Martin had also been disruptive in class and had recently begun to yell out, "I hate everyone." According to the principal, Martin was "the worst boy we've ever seen at his age."

Martin's father, Andrew, did most of the talking during an initial interview with the parents, both of whom were high school teachers. Andrew said he was very upset by his son's aggressive and unruly behavior in school, and he described Martin further as a lazy, easily frustrated boy who wanted to achieve without working, who could not tolerate losing in anything, and who lied constantly. Andrew could offer no explanation for Martin's misconduct, except to say, "Maybe he was just born bad." On the other hand, he reported that he was a stern disciplinarian and had no trouble with Martin at home. He went on to suggest that perhaps Martin's teachers, by not being sufficiently firm and by picking on him whenever there was a class disturbance, were at least partly responsible for his record of poor conduct.

In a private meeting, Martin's mother, Betty, painted a quite different picture, which she said she had kept to herself during the previous joint interview because she was afraid of arousing her husband's anger. As far as she was concerned, Betty volunteered, Andrew's description of their son was as true of him as of Martin. Although he was highly successful in impressing other people with his maturity, competence, and sincerity, Betty said, Andrew was an irresponsible, lazy, dishonest man who paid little attention to family affairs and frequently absented himself from the home for days at a time without explanation. Much of his self-description, she added, especially about his stern disciplining, was a bald-faced lie: "He likes to think of himself as a big man, but he's never done anything constructive to discipline Martin; when he is home, which isn't often, he can't be bothered."

This new information, supplemented by later evaluation of Martin himself, clarified the likely relation of his behavior problems to a characterologically asocial orientation stimulated by a father who failed to discipline him and set a psychopathic example in his own behavior. In retrospect, the father's blaming the school for his son's problems could be seen as his way of evading any personal responsibility. At the same time, Andrew's attitudes probably suggested to Martin the appropriateness of denying guilt and externalizing blame for difficult situations.

NEUROTIC DELINQUENCY

In **neurotic delinquency** young people commit illegal acts not as well-integrated members of a deviant subculture or in connection with long-standing characterological pathology, but rather as an individualized and very personal attempt to communicate needs that they cannot find other ways of impressing on their environment. In common with many other neurotic behaviors, neurotic delinquency is thus symptomatic of underlying concerns that it serves indirectly to express.

Whereas sociological and characterological delinquency typically involve chronic, recurrent antisocial conduct that becomes a way of life, neurotic delinquency consists of acute, situationally determined lawbreaking. Its onset can usually be traced to the onset or intensification of some personal concerns that are generating feelings of tension, remorse, or discouragement, and it tends to disappear soon after these concerns have been resolved in some way. Accordingly, other labels that have been used for this pattern of antisocial behavior include "acute," "anxious," "accidental," and "situationally provoked" delinquency (Genshaft, 1980; Hare & Cox, 1978; Smiley, 1977; Weiner, 1975).

Consistent with this way of categorizing neurotic delinquents, their previous life patterns contrast sharply with their present pattern of illegal activity. Instead of demonstrating the long-standing antisocial attitudes seen in sociological delinquents or the childhood aggressiveness and selfishness associated with characterological delinquency, neurotic delinquents have typically been conforming, well-controlled youngsters. Those close to them are genuinely surprised that they, of all people, have suddenly lost respect for law and order. As a general principle, the less continuity there appears to be in a delinquent youngster's behavior and the more his or her current delinquency diverges from a past history of model conduct, the more reason there is to consider him or her a neurotic delinquent.

Similarly, the likelihood that delinquent behavior is neurotically determined increases the more there is some evidence of clearly precipitating events occurring at or shortly before the time when a youngster began to misbehave. Neurotic delinquency follows closely on the heels of some "last straw" in a series of rebuffs, rejections, losses, or disappointments that have sharply increased a youngster's unmet needs. When such precipitating events cannot be easily identified, delinquent behavior is more likely to be rooted in subcultural deviance or characterological defects than in neurotic concerns.

Communication of Needs in Neurotic Delinquency

Children and adolescents who commit delinquent acts are often attempting to get other people to respond to needs that they feel are being overlooked or ignored. The specific needs that most commonly underlie such indirect, neurotic efforts to communicate are needs to be recognized and admired and needs to receive help.

Needs for Recognition and Admiration   Youngsters who feel unnoticed and unappreciated in their family and peer groups sometimes resort to delinquent acts in an effort to satisfy their needs to be recognized and admired. These boys and girls may correctly anticipate that a detected delinquent act will serve several purposes: it will command the attention of teachers, police, and other important adults; it will require their parents to become engaged in court, school, or clinical deliberations about them; and it will increase their visibility among their peers.

Acts of daring and bravado, such as attempting to shoplift right under a store clerk's nose or trying to outrace a police car, are well suited for these purposes, as are behaviors that are embarrassing or disruptive to the "establishment," such as calling in a bomb threat that results in a school or movie theater being emptied and searched for naught. The case of Wilma in Chapter 7 (pp. 275–276) provides a good example of attention-seeking delinquency; the use of public antisocial behavior to gain recognition and peer status, especially in youngsters whose self-esteem is being threatened, has been confirmed in numerous other clinical and research studies (Cary, 1979; Gold, 1978; Gold & Mann, 1972; Rosenberg & Rosenberg, 1978).

Because their actions can serve communicative purposes only if they are detected, neurotic delinquents manage almost without exception to get themselves caught. For example, a boy stealing something in school will either do so at a time when he is likely to be seen or will leave the stolen items on his desk or in his locker, where they are certain to be found and traced to him. If despite himself he appears to have gotten away with the theft, he will find some way of letting word of his guilt get out—such as confiding to a friend, as Wilma did. Despite the penalties that may follow, neurotic delinquents are gratified for the moment by the notoriety they achieve in being detected. Indeed, a lack of "carelessness" leading to being caught would suggest that delinquency has other than neurotic origins.

Another identifying feature of neurotically determined delinquent acts is that they usually serve no apparent purpose other than meeting needs for attention and recognition. Items that are stolen are not needed and are not used while they are in the youngster's possession. Demonstrations of bravado provide no personal pleasure beyond what comes from any notoriety that follows. When delinquent acts seem to have been satisfying or enjoyable in their own right, or when they provide young people with things they need and use, sociological or characterological factors are more likely to be involved than neurotic determinants.

Among girls who become neurotically delinquent, needs for recognition are often expressed through sexual behavior. Studies of unwed pregnant adolescents indicate that for many of them engaging in intercourse was a way of feeling attractive and feminine, and having a lover and becoming pregnant by him was a way of gaining peer-group attention and respect (Gottschalk, Titchener, Piker, & Stewart, 1964; Visotsky, 1966). For others, rebelliousness and a wish to punish their mothers for not communicating adequately with them provided part of the motivation to become pregnant (Barglow, Bornstein, Exum, Wright, & Visotsky, 1967; Meyerowitz & Malev, 1973; Roberts, Abrams, & Finch, 1973). In one especially interesting study, low self-esteem and feelings of peer rejection were found to predict more than a year in advance the likelihood of adolescent girls becoming unwed mothers (Kaplan, Smith, & Pokorny, 1979).

Needs for Help. Young people who are experiencing specific problems that they are afraid or embarrassed to tell anyone about, or whose efforts to communicate have fallen on deaf or disinterested ears, may resort to public and sometimes dramatic acts of delinquency as an indirect way of conveying their need for help. The delinquent behavior then forces the environment to recognize the existence of a problem and do something about it. As already noted, for example, inattentive parents who are called before a school principal or a juvenile court judge to discuss their child's misbehavior can no longer deny or overlook problems he or she has been having. In addition, such confrontations commonly result in a referral for needed professional help that the young person might otherwise not have received.

Not uncommonly, the use of delinquent acts to communicate needs for help is associated with an underlying depression. Uncharacteristic aggressive behavior and the sudden onset of stealing can often be traced to events in a young person's life that have left him or her feeling lonely, isolated, discouraged, or helpless (see Chapter 7). As an important example, such behavior frequently appears soon after the loss of some important person in a youngster's life, such as loss of a parent through death or divorce (Burks & Harrison, 1962; Chiles, Miller, & Cox, 1980; Schoor & Speed, 1963).

Sexual promiscuity, especially among young women, may also arise as an expression of ungratified needs for affection and thus reflect underlying depression. As noted in Chapter 7, depressed females may seek sexual intercourse not for erotic reasons, but as a means of establishing intimate contact with another human being, and persistent depression can motivate such youngsters to repetitive, indiscriminate sexual activity. A 17-year-old brought to a psychologist by her parents because of declining school performance, for example, complained that she felt dumb and unattractive, that her friends were snubbing her, and that life did not seem much worth living. She then described her wish to find "some boy who would stick by me," and she confessed to "one-night-stands" with a large number of young men to whom she offered herself sexually in her search for someone "who would accept me and give me a reason for living."

Questions may be raised whether such sexual activity, although clearly maladaptive, should be considered delinquent behavior. However, intercourse among juveniles is in fact a status offense, and the crime of "fornication" is among the minor sexual offenses for which numerous adolescents are arrested each year.

Case 17. *Needs for Attention and Help in Neurotic Delinquency*

Jack was 15 and a high school sophomore when his mother died. She had been the major source of affection and support in his life. His older brother, with whom he had a good relationship, was away at college, and his father, although caring about him, was a busy professional man who had depended on his wife to look after the children. Jack missed his mother very much, and in the absence of any replacement for the nurturance she had provided him, he slipped into a mild but persistent depression. He lost interest in school and other activities, grew listless and lethargic, and became preoccupied with the bleakness of his future.

For a few months Jack suffered mostly inwardly, however, and no one sensed his need for help. He had always been on the quiet side in school, and he was bright enough to continue earning good grades even though he was no longer working very hard. At home he was reluctant to tell his father that he was troubled, primarily because he felt his father had all he could do to handle his own grief.

Then Jack's outward behavior changed as well. He began writing hammer-and-sickle emblems on his papers and textbooks, carrying around the *Communist Manifesto,* and monopolizing class discussions with long-winded comments on the merits of socialism. Before long he was being labeled and teased by his classmates as "the Commie," which apparently met some of his needs to get attention but still brought him little in the way of support or nurturance.

Jack next got hold of a master key to his school and began using it to "borrow" tape recorders and other equipment. He promptly returned these items, but always in such a way that he managed to get caught. This stealing, like his becoming "the Commie," seemed clearly to reflect his underlying depression and his wish to get help in overcoming it. The school recommended professional help, and Jack's attention-seeking and delinquent behavior stopped abruptly after his first interview with a psychologist, during which arrangements were made for ongoing psychotherapy. In succeeding months, as Jack was helped to work through the loss of his mother and develop new relationships, especially among his peers, he gradually regained his previous good spirits and levels of interest and energy.

Family Interaction in Neurotic Delinquency

Unlike the family circumstances surrounding characterological delinquency, the families of neurotic delinquents typically have a history of reasonable stability, mutual affection, and generally law-abiding and socially adaptive behavior. This is not to say that family problems do not exist in association with neurotic delinquency. Neurotic delinquents may use their deviant behavior in part as hostile acts toward their parents, at whom they are angry for not recognizing their needs, and the parents of these youngsters are in turn usually angry or disgusted with them for their misbehavior. If delinquent patterns are truly reflecting neurotic rather than characterological difficulties, however, this current falling out between parents and children will be accompanied by underlying feelings of love and affection and a genuine wish to draw closer together. At the same time, delinquent behavior instead of other types of neurotic problems are especially likely to occur when parents inadvertently foster and reinforce antisocial behavior in their children.

Parental Fostering Parents who are neither psychologically disturbed nor asocial may nevertheless model disrespect for the law in certain ways that foster illegal behavior in their children. For example, generally law-abiding parents who regularly cheat on their income tax or drive over the speed limit communicate to their children that such illegal acts are acceptable. If they take obvious pleasure in their lawbreaking ("I've figured out a neat way to charge off our vacation as a business expense"), they teach their children that flouting the law may be desirable as well as acceptable.

Such teaching makes an especially strong impression when parents are heard to lie about a problem ("Honest, officer, I had no idea I was going over 35"), or deny any plan to change their behavior ("It was worth a try; I'll be more careful next time"), or propose a deception ("Scrunch down so you won't look so tall, and maybe we can get

Children may conclude from their parents' example that it is alright to break the law if you can talk your way out of it.

you in at half-fare''). The more young people are exposed to parental modeling of this kind, the more they are likely to conclude that lying and cheating are appropriate ways to act.

Sometimes parents whose own behavior is above reproach foster delinquency in their children by excessive and unnecessary prohibitions that communicate an anticipation of misbehavior. Parents who constantly caution their youngsters about driving recklessly, drinking, fighting, stealing, getting involved sexually, or hanging around with "bad types" cannot help but convey an expectation that they will act in these ways.

Such delinquency-fostering parents are also usually quick to infer bad behavior from minimal evidence. Noting a new possession, they assume that their son has stolen it, without first asking him where he got it; if their daughter returns home late or disheveled, they suspect her of promiscuity before asking for an explanation. These parental behaviors have an especially telling impact on youngsters who have previously given their parents no cause for such concern. Being constantly accused of shoplifting, drinking, sexual misconduct, or other problem behaviors, previously innocent youngsters may get to the point of feeling that they should do what their parents seem to expect them to do—or, in one boy's words, "I'm getting blamed for it all the time, I might as well be doing it."

Parental Reinforcement Once a delinquent act has been committed, parents sometimes respond in ways that reinforce the antisocial behavior and encourage its repetition. Especially common are situations in which the parents see nothing particularly wrong with what their children have done and hence discipline them in an ambivalent, inconsistent manner that tacitly communicates approval of the delinquent behavior.

For example, delinquency-reinforcing parents typically alternate between complete acceptance of antisocial acts and excessive punishments for them. They deplore the delinquent behavior but collaborate with their youngster to prevent its being detected.

NEUROTIC DELINQUENCY   **415**

Should he or she be caught, they minimize the significance of the offense to the authorities. They accept flimsy excuses for misdeeds and describe them to others in a tone of bemused tolerance. They criticize the outcome of an offense but pay scant attention to the offense itself: "If you had to speed, why did you have to do it right in the center of town where you were sure to be caught," or "If you want to fight, you could at least pick a kid you can handle."

The evidence for such parental fostering and reinforcement in neurotic delinquency comes largely from clinical reports. Nevertheless, the validity of this maladaptive family influence in leading to delinquent acts is supported by observations going back many years and at least some empirical research data (Carek, Hendrickson, & Holmes, 1961; Gallenkamp & Rychlak, 1968; Johnson & Szurek, 1952; Singer, 1974). It has proved especially helpful in understanding initially puzzling instances of delinquency in young people who do not belong to any deviant subculture, who show neither psychopathic nor other serious psychopathological tendencies, who are deriving no obvious gratification from their misbehavior, and whose parents are apparently stable, conforming adults who cannot understand their youngster's conduct. In these situations subtle defects in the parents' code of values and behavior and equally subtle ways in which they are fostering or reinforcing their youngster's illegal actions are often identified in the course of careful clinical investigations.

PSYCHOTIC AND ORGANIC DELINQUENCY

Antisocial character disorders and neurotic symptom formation account for most instances of delinquent behavior that result from psychological causes. However, psychotic and organic brain disorders may also lead to antisocial behavior, perhaps more frequently than is usually recognized. In one study of all children referred to a juvenile court clinic over a 2-year period, one-third were found to show sings of central nervous system impairment or psychosis or both (Lewis, 1976a; Lewis & Balla, 1976, Chapter 7). Although this study was restricted to a special sample of youthful lawbreakers—namely, delinquents who had been caught and adjudicated and who seemed sufficiently disturbed to require referral to a mental health clinic—such a high frequency of psychotic and organic problems within such a group demonstrates that their possible contribution to delinquent behavior cannot be overlooked.

Psychotic delinquency emerges primarily in schizophrenic youngsters whose unrealistic perception of their environment, impaired judgment concerning the consequences of their actions, and limited ability to control themselves may lead to antisocial behavior (see Chapter 6). Organic delinquency occurs most often in connection with one of two patterns of disturbed functioning. In some cases minimal brain dysfunction/attention deficit disorder, with its attendant problems of poor impulse control and low self-esteem, contributes to antisocial conduct in middle childhood and adolescence (see Chapter 4). Brain dysfunction is especially likely to be associated with adolescent delinquency that involves explosive outbursts of rage or violence (Elliot, 1978; Krynicki, 1978; Spellacy, 1977).

In other cases organic delinquency involves a form of epileptic disorder characterized by **psychomotor seizures.** This condition is frequently referred to as **temporal lobe**

elipesy, because brain-wave abnormalities associated with it are typically focused in the temporal lobe, and it may result in episodes of angry, assaultive, antisocial behavior (DeJong, 1957; Ervin, 1975; Stevens, 1966).

Psychomotor seizures consist of a sudden onset of strange body movements that serve no apparent purpose. These actions persist in an automatic, stereotyped fashion for anywhere from a minute to several hours, and efforts to stop the person or change his or her behavior during the attack often provoke combative rage. Afterward the person usually has little or no memory for what he or she has done and sincerely regrets any damage or offense to others that may have occurred. People with temporal lobe epilepsy are also likely to have certain paranoid ideas that, even when they are not having an attack, cause them to get involved in fights in response to imagined threats (Garvin, 1953; Gibbs, 1951; Glaser & Dixon, 1967; Gold, 1974; Lewis, 1976a; Ounsted, 1969).

The prevalence of all forms of epilepsy is estimated at 0.3 to 0.4 percent of the population, and about 20 percent of epileptics are estimated to have psychomotor or temporal lobe seizures (Ervin, 1975). By contrast with these small population frequencies, temporal lobe epilepsy was diagnosed in 6 percent of the young people in the court clinic study mentioned earlier. Of further significance, almost 90 percent of these psychomotor epileptics described paranoid concerns, and 50 percent of the crimes they had committed were offenses against people—compared to just a 2 to 3 percent incidence of violent offenses in the total juvenile court sample studied (Lewis, 1976b; Lewis & Balla, 1976, Chapter 6). These findings confirm that temporal lobe epilepsy plays a not infrequent role in delinquent behavior, especially in cases of sudden, violent, and seemingly unprovoked attacks on other people.

INTERVENTION IN DELINQUENCY

The appropriate treatment for delinquent youngsters varies with the extent to which their antisocial tendencies constitute sociological, characterological, neurotic, psychotic, or organic delinquency. When schizophrenia or brain dysfunctions appear primarily responsible for the misconduct, therapy focuses on treating these disorders in the ways discussed in Chapters 4, 5, and 6. As would be expected, successful treatment of these conditions reduces or eliminates any delinquent behaviors associated with them. Approaches to the other forms of delinquent behavior involve a broad range of interventions, from social-action programs, to outpatient psychotherapy, to residential care. The success of these interventions differs widely, primarily in relation to the kind of delinquency that is present.

Sociological Delinquency

Because sociological delinquency represents group endorsement of antisocial behavior in the relative absence of individual disturbance, efforts to combat it have focused more on prevention through social change than on treatment. These efforts have included such social-action programs as the organization of neighborhood citizen's committees, job-upgrading projects, home-study programs, youth conservation corps, and the Police Athletic League. The goal of such neighborhood-based programs is to convince delinquent youths that there are ways of having fun and making money that can be rewarding as criminal behavior without carrying the risk of going to jail (Amos, Manella, & Southwell, 1965; Eldefonso, 1973, Chapter 6; Rhodes, 1965; Witmer & Tufts, 1954).

The fact that sociological delinquents are already well-integrated members of a group they value has tended to limit the effectiveness of these programs, except in cases where extremely positive interactions with law-abiding adults and peers influence such youngsters to shift their loyalties to a new, nondelinquent group. Likewise, although socialized and psychologically stable delinquents are rarely motivated to become involved in psychological treatment, counseling and psychotherapy can be helpful to them especially when it has an educational focus. Educational efforts with sociological delinquents seek to help them recognize ways in which their current behavior is wasting their talents and energies and could be replaced by rewarding nondelinquent means of getting ahead in school and work situations. To succeed, however, academic and vocationally oriented treatment programs must be tied realistically to the opportunities and constraints existing in the environment from which these delinquents come.

This treatment requirement has been translated into some promising psychosocial approaches to the sociological delinquent. Miller (1965), for example, experimented with a halfway house in which institutionalized delinquent boys from lower-class neighborhoods spent several months gradually getting accustomed to life and work outside the institution. Youngsters with this halfway house experience were less likely to get into further trouble with the law than other groups of delinquents he studied who were discharged directly to the community. Persons (1967) similarly found that psychotherapy yielded better subsequent community adjustment and lower recidivism among institutionalized delinquent boys than a no-treatment condition, but that best results occurred when a successful treatment experience within the institution was combined with adequate community placement and employment after discharge.

This psychosocial approach has also been used successfully in the form of a vocationally oriented psychotherapy program for delinquent boys who had dropped out of school or been expelled. In this program the boys were first contacted in terms of helping them get a job and were then provided preemployment counseling, guidance in such tasks as opening a bank account and getting a driver's license, and psychological support in dealing with various adjustment problems they chose to discuss. A 10-year follow-up indicated that this combined psychotherapy, remedial education, and job-placement approach had helped these boys achieve academic and occupational goals that would probably otherwise have been beyond their grasp (Massimo & Shore, 1963; Shore & Massimo, 1969, 1973).

Although not directed specifically at sociological delinquency, numerous other programs have sought to prevent delinquency through psychosocial intervention with children identified as "predelinquent." The most famous of these programs is the Cambridge-Sommerville Youth Study, which began in 1939. Several hundred 5- to 13-year-old boys, some considered "difficult" and some "average," were referred to the program from schools, churches, welfare agencies, and the police in working-class urban areas of Massachusetts. Half of the boys were assigned to a control group that participated in the study only by providing information about themselves. The other half constituted a treatment group who for an average period of 5 years received twice-monthly family visits from a counselor and some combination of academic tutoring, individual psychotherapy, summer camp placement, and involvement with the Boy Scouts, the YMCA, and other community programs (Powers & Witmer, 1951).

Thirty years later official records and personal contacts were used to assess the effects of this program on 253 men who had been in the treatment group and an equal number of the control group (McCord, 1978). The results were very disappointing, in that the treatment and control subjects were almost equally likely to have committed crimes as juveniles and were equally likely to have been convicted for some crime as adults. Several similar research projects conducted in the 1960s also reported little success in preventing delinquency through multifaceted intervention programs (Craig & Furst, 1965; Empey & Erickson, 1972; Hackler, 1966; Miller, 1962).

Many of these preventive programs were tried prior to recent advances in family and behaviorally oriented treatment and in the use of community-based facilities that take young people out of their home environment without shutting them up in hospitals or reformatories. In the Achievement Place model, for example, a small number of youngsters identified as predelinquent on the basis of aggressive or disruptive behavior are placed in a home-style residence in their community with a pair of professionally trained house parents. The children continue to attend their regular school, but their home life is now managed to provide regular routine, rewards for socially desirable behavior, and individual tutoring or counseling as needed (Hoefler & Bornstein, 1975; Phillips, Wolf, Fixsen, & Bailey, 1976).

Newer strategies are also being applied in drop-in centers and in family programs conducted in the homes of youngsters at risk for delinquency. These include (a) combining material rewards with the reinforcement of peer group participation in efforts to foster nondelinquent values and behavior; (b) preparing formal written contracts between young people and significant people in their environment in which the parties commit themselves to mutually agreeable ways of behaving toward each other; and (c) home-based programs of parent training that result in changes in the patterns of reinforcement young people receive in their family setting (Alexander & Parsons, 1973; Burchard, Harig, Miller, & Amour, 1976; Davidson & Seidman, 1974; Reid & Patterson, 1976). Preliminary findings suggest that these community-based behavioral approaches can help to avoid or reduce certain kinds of delinquent behavior. Further research will be necessary to determine more precisely the contribution they can make to delinquency prevention.

Characterological Delinquency

The relationship of characterological delinquency to psychopathic personality disorder makes it extremely difficult to treat. Delinquents with this kind of psychological disorder rarely trust or identify with other people, they do not reflect critically on their attitudes and behavior, and they feel any need to change. Hence they provide few footholds for even the most skilled therapists to find ways of modifying their delinquency. Psychopathic delinquents are thus notably resistant to treatment efforts and highly likely to persist in inconsiderate, irresponsible, and antisocial behavior. As adults, they are significantly more likely than sociological delinquents to be convicted and imprisoned for criminal behavior (Berman, 1964; Carney, 1978; Henn, Bardwell, & Jenkins, 1980; Hudgens, 1974, Chapter 7; Robins, 1979).

Despite these long odds against success, considerable effort has been devoted to finding treatment approaches that can break into the chronically asocial orientation of characterological delinquents and foster some sense of personal loyalty and concern for others. Work in this area was pioneered by August Aichhorn, who established a residential treatment center for delinquent boys and girls in post-World War I Austria. In a landmark book titled *Wayward Youth,* Aichhorn (1925) provided the first description of how psychological principles could be applied in the treatment of delinquent adolescents. For aggressive delinquents with a history of early emotional deprivation— i.e., psychopaths—he recommended a thoroughly permissive approach. To compensate for these youngsters' lifelong experiences of rejection, no pressures were to be brought to bear on them, no institutional restrictions were to be imposed except as absolutely necessary to prevent physical injury, and the focus was to be on "a consistently friendly attitude, wholesome occupation, plenty of play to prevent aggression, and repeated talks with the individual members" (p. 172).

Although Aichhorn's formulation continues to be influential in some quarters, subsequent clinical experience indicated that such permissive warmth seldom produces any genuine change in the attitudes and behavior of characterological delinquents. Developing psychopaths shun personal intimacy and distrust demonstrations of warmth and affection. Intimacy threatens them with the bitter pill of rejection, which they have been swallowing most of their lives. They regard adults who are consistently tolerant as either stupid or insincere, and they respond to efforts at interpersonal closeness with increasingly aggressive behavior intended to keep others at a distance.

Likewise, despite the apparent logic of treating emotionally deprived youngsters with unbounded love and affection, permissiveness has been found to make matters worse in the treatment of antisocial youth. Lack of restrictions is interpreted as the same kind of weakness or disinterest their parents have shown; firm but fair external controls, on the other hand, convey a caring attitude and also relieve these youngsters of concerns they may have about their own lack of self-control. Contrary to Aichhorn's prescriptions, therefore, controlling rather than permissive treatment approaches are more likely to realize what few opportunities there are for reducing the delinquent behavior of psychopathic youngsters (Bromberg & Rodgers, 1946; Craft, Stephenson, & Granger, 1964; Hacker & Geleerd, 1945; Meeks, 1979).

In addition to cautioning against a permissive approach, clinicians experienced in working with psychopathic delinquents generally recommend a treatment program that is (a) residential, (b) unconventional, and (c) variegated. The defective interpersonal capacities of these young people make it very hard for therapists to form a good working relationship with them on the basis of office visits alone, even if these are scheduled several times weekly. Furthermore, as a reflection of their typical deceitfulness and need to manipulate others, the information and behavior presented by psychopathic individuals during outpatient therapy sessions may bear little relationship to what their lives are really like when they are not being observed or treated. Hence long-term residential care is frequently the only effective way of getting to know and influence these youngsters through a treatment program (Lion, 1978; Marshall, 1979; Meeks, 1979).

Unconventional approaches are necessary in working with psychopathic youngsters because of the extent to which their personality style blunts the caring and warmth that traditionally characterize a therapist's approach to disturbed children and adolescents. Instead, therapists must find ways of being critical, controlling, and apparently not very personally involved while at the same time becoming someone the psychopathic youngster comes to regard as a reliable source of good sense (Eissler, 1950; Noshpitz, 1957; Schwartz, 1967; Unwin, 1968). Variegated treatment is necessary to keep one step ahead of the psychopath's need for stimulation and novelty and to include as many treatment modalities in the program as may be helpful. Accordingly, skillful therapists conduct individual treatment sessions with them with a constant element of change and surprise and involve these youngsters concurrently in group sessions, learning programs, and planned recreational activities in which they have every possible opportunity to learn from or pattern themselves after socialized models (Fleischer, 1975; Gladstone, 1962; Redfering, 1973; Sutker, Archer, & Kilpatrick, 1981).

Although not aimed specifically at any category of delinquent behavior, a modeling approach developed by Sarason (1968, 1976) has shwon promise in this last regard. Delinquent boys admitted to a reception-diagnostic center were engaged in a series of modeling sessions over a 3- to 6-week period. Reading from a prepared script, they role-played such activities as applying for a job, resisting temptation to engage in antisocial acts, and passing up immediate gratification for better opportunities later. Each modeling session was followed by a discussion of the particular coping techniques that had been used in the role-playing situation. At the end of their stay in the reception center, boys who had been in these modeling groups were three times more likely to receive favorable placements (e.g., parole as opposed to reformatory) than boys who had been in discussion groups without a modeling format or who had received no special attention. At follow-ups 1 and 3 years later, the modeling-group boys had a significantly lower rate of subsequent law-breaking than these comparison groups.

Neurotic Delinquency

As an acute symptomatic reaction to current precipitating circumstances, neurotic delinquency typically has a good prognosis and lends itself well to psychological intervention. Of all youthful disorders, symptomatic neuroses are the ones that improve most frequently and rapidly with treatment (see Chapter 8). Neurotic delinquency is accordingly much more likely to have a favorable outcome than delinquency associated with basic characterological defects. This difference illustrates why mental health professionals need to look beyond observable behavior to some understanding of why this behavior is occurring. Delinquent acts occurring as a reflection of psychopathic personality disorder tend to persist, and only long-term residential care holds what little promise there is for achieving behavior change; the very same delinquent acts occurring as a symptomatic expression of neurotic concerns are relatively easy to eliminate through numerous kinds of intervention, often on a short-term basis.

Interventions with neurotic delinquents focus on the needs that they are attempting to communicate through their problem behavior. Unmet needs for recognition and admiration are satisfied in part by having a treatment relationship, since good therapists provide a measure of interest and respect that troubled youngsters may not have been getting elsewhere. Unlike psychopathic youngsters, neurotic delinquents have not only the capacity but also a yearning to receive and respond to such interests. Therapists can then work within the context of a positive treatment relationship to help these young people (a) recognize the attention- and status-seeking motives of their misbehavior and its inevitable self-defeating consequences and (b) identify and carry out more constructive means of gaining the notice and respect of their parents, teachers, and peers.

For delinquent youngsters with previously unnoticed needs for help, having been brought or sent for professional attention can by itself be sufficient to eliminate the motivation to misbehave. Although therapists must work to resolve whatever problems the young person needs help with, the specific delinquent acts that have led to the referral in such cases often stop occurring once a treatment relationship has begun. Especially in cases where underlying depression has contributed to delinquent behavior, adequate therapy aimed at depressive concerns can be expected to stop the delinquency in fairly short order (Toolan, 1974).

Because of the role that parents may play in fostering or reinforcing neurotic delinquency, it is usually beneficial to involve them in the treatment. Unlike the relatives of characterological delinquents, who tend to have little family interest and serious adjustment problems of their own, the parents of neurotic delinquents are usually able and willing to participate actively in their youngster's therapy. These parents can then be helped to understand their child's problem behavior and to identify and modify ways in which they are inadvertently contributing to it.

SUMMARY

Delinquent behavior consists of acts that violate the law. Because the number, nature, and outcome of such acts committed by a young person can vary widely, the prevalence of delinquent behavior is difficult to determine. Likewise, although *delinquency* can be uniformly defined according to the acts it consists of, *delinquents* are a heterogeneous group of children and adolescents about whom few if any psychological generalizations can be made.

Official delinquency statistics, based on government reports on arrested juveniles, indicate that approximately 4 percent of 10- to 17-year-olds appear in juvenile court each year for offenses other than traffic violations. The rate of juvenile court cases has increased more rapidly than the population of young people almost every year since 1961, and youngsters under 18 currently account for 24 percent of all arrests in the United States.

Estimates of actual delinquency, which come from self-reports of representative adolescents independently of whether they have ever become involved with the criminal justice system, indicate that 80 percent of American adolescents commit one or more delinquent acts during their teenage years. However, about 60 percent of the arrests of juveniles are for misdemeanors rather than more serious crimes, and a relatively small percent of repetitively delinquent youngsters are responsible for most of the delinquent behavior among their age group.

In terms of their psychological makeup, some youngsters who commit delinquent acts are *sociological* delinquents, in that they have few psychological problems and are well-integrated members of a delinquent subculture. Some are *characterological* delinquents, in whom delinquent acts reflect a personality disorder marked by chronically irresponsible, aggressive, and inconsiderate behavior. Some are *neurotic* delinquents, whose misconduct is a symptomatic expression of some underlying concerns or conflicts. A final group are *psychotic* or *organic* delinquents, whose inappropriate behavior derives from functioning impairments associated with one or the other of these conditions.

Sociological delinquency is characterized by adaptive rather than maladaptive behavior and by social rather than solitary acts. It is adaptive in that it provides the basis of acceptance and belongingness within a peer group that is socialized and supportive, even though it endorses antisocial standards of conduct. This pattern of delinquency is social in that it typically involves collaborative group or gang lawbreaking.

Sociological delinquents have usually enjoyed good family relationships during their early life, but lacked adequate parental supervision as elementary school children and adolescents. Sociological delinquency is particularly likely to be associated with unsupervised development in a deteriorated, high-delinquency neighborhood in which young people come easily under the influence of antisocial models. However, this form of delinquency cannot be conceived as a unique product of lower-class neighborhoods. Inadequate parental supervision and the formation of trouble-making gangs occur in middle-class life as well, and middle-class adolescents commit just about the same kinds of delinquent acts as lower-class youth. Numerous sociological theories have erred in trying to explain delinquency as a lower-class phenomenon; although these theories help to explain why some disadvantaged young people commit crimes, they do not provide an adequate basis for distinguishing between lower- and middle-class delinquency or accounting for delinquent behavior in general.

Characterological delinquents are usually loners who commit crimes by themselves as a consequence of their disregard for the rights and feelings of others and an inability or unwillingness to control their behavior. These young people translate aggressive, acquisitive, and pleasure-seeking impulses into immediate action, with little concern for how others might suffer in the process. The interpersonal orientation and behavior patterns of characterological delinquents constitute in budding form a *psychopathic* or *antisocial personality disorder,* the two major features of which are an underdeveloped conscience (guiltlessness) and an inability to identify with other people (lovelessness).

Some psychopaths display low frustration tolerance, lack of self-control, limited capacity for planning and goal-directed behavior, and an inability to learn from experience. These people tend to be unsuccessful psychopaths who do poorly in school and on the job and frequently end up as detected criminals, mental patients, or social misfits. Other psychopaths may be well-functioning individuals who mask their underlying asocial orientation by planning carefully, manipulating others effectively, finding ways of attaining academic and vocational success, and avoiding mental hospitals and prisons.

Although the causes of psychopathic personality disorder are not fully understood, they seem to involve some combination of unfavorable environmental experiences and predisposing genetic factors. Psychopathy is typically associated with a childhood history of early and severe parental rejection followed by inadequate discipline and supervision during middle childhood and adolescence. Young people reared in this way develop little capacity for interpersonal warmth and compassion and learn only externalized standards of morality—according to which any behavior is acceptable if one can get away with it.

Psychopathic tendencies run in families, partly because antisocial parents are likely to rear their children in ways that promote psychopathy. As firm evidence for an additional genetic component in the origins of this disorder, however, children who are born to antisocial parents and placed for adoption early in life are significantly more likely to become psychopathic adults than adopted-away offspring of parents who are not antisocial. Similarly, being born to a criminal father increases the likelihood of becoming criminal regardless of who does the rearing.

Psychopathy is a chronic condition that begins early in life. Future psychopaths start as early as age 5 or 6 to show such antisocial behavior as fighting, lying, stealing, truancy, and cruelty to people and animals. By age 10, half or more are also displaying a generally aggressive, demanding, and self-centered style of life, and by adolescence all psychopaths-to-be are coming increasingly into conflict with their peers, family, school, and community. Psychopathy never begins in adulthood in the absence of such a developmental history of esculating antisocial behavior.

In neurotic delinquency young people commit illegal acts not as well-integrated members of a deviant subculture or in connection with long-standing characterological pathology, but as an individualized and very personal attempt to communicate needs that they cannot find other ways of impressing on their environment. Whereas sociological or characterological delinquency typically involves chronic, recurrent antisocial conduct that becomes a way of life, neurotic delinquency consists of acute, situationally determined lawbreaking that is precipitated by current psychological distress and stops when this distress is relieved.

Some neurotic delinquents feel unnoticed and unappreciated in their family and peer groups and misbehave publicly in an effort to satisfy needs for recognition and admiration. Their antisocial behavior attracts attention, makes them more visible among their peers, and punishes their parents for their earlier disregard. Other neurotic delinquents are experiencing specific problems that they cannot easily tell anyone about and resort to sometimes dramatic misbehavior as an indirect way of conveying their need for help. The delinquency then forces the environment to recognize that there is a problem and do something about it. Underlying depressive concerns are especially likely to contribute to symptomatic expression through delinquent behavior of needs for recognition and help.

In contrast to the family circumstances surrounding characterological delinquency, the families of neurotic delinquents typically have a history of reasonable stability, mutual affection, and generally law-abiding and socially adaptive behavior. Nevertheless, delinquent behavior rather than other types of neurotic problems is especially likely to occur when parents inadvertently foster or reinforce antisocial behavior. Sometimes parents who are neither psychologically disturbed nor asocial nevertheless promote illegal behavior in their children by modeling minor disrespect for the law or imposing excessive and unnecessary prohibitions that communicate an anticipation of misbehavior. At other times they encourage the repetition of delinquent behaviors by disciplining their children in an ambivalent, inconsistent manner that tacitly communicates approval.

Psychotic delinquency emerges primarily in schizophrenic youngsters whose unrealistic perception of their environment, impaired judgment concerning the consequences of their actions, and limited ability to control themselves may lead to antisocial behavior. Organic delinquency occurs most often in connection with one of two patterns of disturbed functioning: minimal brain dysfunction/attention deficit disorder, in which problems of poor impulse control and low self-esteem often contribute to antisocial conduct in middle childhood and adolescence; and a form of epileptic disorder characterized by psychomotor seizures, which may lead to episodes of angry, assaultive, antisocial behavior.

The appropriate treatment for delinquent youngsters varies with the origins of their antisocial tendencies. When schizophrenia or brain dysfunction appears primarily responsible for the misconduct, therapy focuses on ways of treating these particulrar disorders. Because sociological delinquency represents group endorsement of antisocial behavior in the relative absence of individual disturbance, efforts to combat it have focused more on prevention through social change than on treatment. The success of these efforts has been limited by the fact that sociological delinquents are well-integrated members of a group they value. However, some educational and psychosocial approaches have shown promise in influencing sociological delinquents to shift their loyalties to nondelinquent adults and peer groups and to replace their lawbreaking with rewarding, nondelinquent use of their talents and energies. These have included combined use of remedial education, job placement, individual counseling, and community-based family-style residential placements.

The origin of characterological delinquency in psychopathic personality disorder makes it extremely difficult to treat. The chronically asocial orientation of psychopathic delinquents resists change in the face of most traditional therapies, and these young people are highly likely to persist in inconsiderate, irresponsible, and antisocial behavior. What little success can be achieved in reducing their delinquency usually requires long-term, highly structured, residential care in which unconventional methods are employed to convince psychopathic youngsters that there is something useful to be gained from learning new ways of relating to people and governing their own behavior.

As an acute symptomatic reaction to current precipitating circumstances, neurotic delinquency typically has a good prognosis and lends itself well to psychological intervention. This intervention focuses on the needs that neurotic delinquents are attempting to communicate through their problem behavior. Coming to understand the motives for their misconduct and benefiting from the increased recognition and help they are receiving through the treatment process, these young people usually give up their delinquent behavior in fairly short order. Because of the role that parents may play in fostering or reinforcing neurotic delinquency, however, effective treatment frequently requires their involvement as well.

REFERENCES

AICHHORN, A. (1925) *Wayward youth.* New York: Viking, 1935.

ALEXANDER, J. F., & PARSONS, B. V. Short-term behavioral intervention with delinquent families. *Journal of Abnormal Psychology,* 1973, *81,* 219–225.

AMERICAN PSYCHIATRIC ASSOCIATION. *Diagnostic and statistical manual of mental disorders* (3d ed.) Washington, D.C.: American Psychiatric Association, 1980.

AMOS, W. E., MANELLA, R. L., & SOUTHWELL, M. A. *Action programs for delinquency prevention.* Springfield, Ill.: Thomas, 1965.

ANDERSON, R. E. Where's Dad? Paternal deprivation and delinquency. *Archives of General Psychiatry,* 1968, *18,* 641–649.

BANDURA, A., & WALTERS, R. H. *Adolescent aggression: A study of the influence of child-training practices and family interrelationships.* New York: Ronald, 1959.

BARGLOS, P., BORNSTEIN, M. B., EXUM, D. B., WRIGHT, M. K., & VISOTSKY, H. M. Some psychiatric aspects of illegitimate pregnancy during early adolescence. *American Journal of Orthopsychiatry,* 1967, *37,* 266–267.

BECKER, W. C., PETERSON, D. R., HELLNER, L. A., SHOEMAKER, D. J., & QUAY, H. C. Factors in parental behavior and personality as related to problem behavior in children. *Journal of Consulting Psychology,* 1959, *23,* 107–118.

BERMAN, S. Techniques of treatment of a form of juvenile delinquency, the antisocial character disorder. *Journal of the American Academy of Child Psychiatry,* 1964, *3,* 24–52.

BRIGHAM, J. C., RICKETTS, J. L., & JOHNSON, R. C. Reported maternal and paternal behaviors of solitary and social delinquents. *Journal of Consulting Psychology,* 1967, *31,* 420–424.

BROMBERG, W., & RODGERS, T. C. Authority in the treatment of delinquents. *American Journal of Orthopsychiatry,* 1946, *16,* 672–685.

BURCHARD, J. D., HARIG, P. T., MILLER, R. B., & AMOUR, J. New strategies in community-based intervention. In E. Ribes-Inesta & A. Bandura (Eds.), *Analaysis of delinquency and aggression.* New York: Erlbaum, 1976.

BURKS, H. L., & HARRISON, S. I. Aggressive behavior as a means of avoiding depression. *American Journal of Orthopsychiatry,* 1962, *32,* 416–422.

BURSTEN, B. The manipulative personality. *Archives of General Psychiatry,* 1972, *26,* 318–321.

CADORET, R. Psychopathology in adopted-away offspring of biologic parents with antisocial behavior. *Archives of General Psychiatry,* 1978, *35,* 176–184.

CADORET, R., & CAIN, C. Sex differences in predictors of antisocial behavior in adoptees. *Archives of General Psychiatry,* 1980, *37,* 1171–1175.

CAREK, D. J., HENDRICKSON, W., & HOLMES, D. J. Delinquency addiction in parents. *Archives of General Psychiatry,* 1961, *4,* 357–362.

CARNEY, F. L. Inpatient treatment programs. In W. H. Reid (Ed.), *The psychopath.* New York: Brunner/Mazel, 1978.

CARY, G. L. Acting out in adolescence. *American Journal of Psychotherapy,* 1979, *33,* 378–390.

CASS, L. K., & THOMAS, C. B. *Childhood pathology and later adjustment.* New York: Wiley, 1979.

CHILES, J. A., MILLER, M. L., & COX, G. B. Depression in an adolescent delinquent population. *Archives of General Psychiatry,* 1980, *37,* 1179–1184.

CLECKLEY, H. M. *The mask of sanity.* (5th ed.) St. Louis: Mosby, 1976.

CLONINGER, C. R., REICH, T., & GUZE, S. B. Genetic-environment interactions and antisocial behavior. In R. D. Hare & D. Schalling (Eds.), *Psychopathic behavior.* New York: Wiley, 1978.

CLOWARD, R., & OHLIN, L. E. *Delinquency and opportunity: A theory of delinquent gangs.* New York: Free Press of Glencoe, 1960.

COHEN, A. K. *Delinquent boys: The culture of the gang.* Glencoe, Ill.: Free Press, 1955.

CRAFT, M., STEPHENSON, G., & GRANGER, C. A controlled trial of authoritarian and self-governing regimes with adolescent psychopaths. *American Journal of Orthopsychiatry,* 1964, *34,* 543–554.

CRAIG, M. M., & FURST, P. W. What happens after treatment? A study of potentially delinquent boys. *Social Service Review,* 1965, *39,* 165–171.

CROWE, R. R. An adoption study of antisocial personality. *Archives of General Psychiatry,* 1974, *31,* 785–791.

DAVIDSON, W. S., & SEIDMAN, E. Studies of behavior modification and juvenile delinquency: A review, methodological critique, and social perspective. *Psychological Bulletin,* 1974, *81,* 998–1011.

DEJONG, R. N. "Psychomotor" and "temporal lobe" epilepsy: A review of the development of our present concepts. *Neurology,* 1957, *7,* 1–4.

DEMYER-GAPIN, S., & SCOTT, T. J. Effect of stimulus novelty on stimulation seeking in antisocial and neurotic children. *Journal of Abnormal Psychology,* 1977, *86,* 96–98.

DUNCAN, P. Parental attitudes and interactions in delinquency. *Child Development,* 1971, *42,* 1751–1765.

EISSLER, K. R. Ego-psychological implications of the psychoanalytic treatment of delinquents. *Psychoanalytic Study of the Child,* 1950, *5,* 97–121.

ELDEFONSO, E. *Law enforcement and the youthful offender.* (2nd ed.) New York: Wiley, 1973.

ELKIND, D. Middle-class delinquency. *Mental Hygiene,* 1967, *51,* 80–84.

ELKIND, D., & WEINER, I. B. *Development of the child.* New York: Wiley, 1978.

ELLIOT, F. A. Neurological aspects of antisocial behavior. In W. H. Reid (Ed.), *The psychopath.* New York: Brunner/Mazel, 1978.

EMPEY, L. T. Delinquent subcultures: Theory and recent research. In C. R. Cressey & D. A. Ward (Eds.), *Delinquency, crime, and social process.* New York: Harper & Row, 1969.

EMPEY, L. T., & ERICKSON, M. L. *The provo experiment: Evaluating community control of delinquency.* Lexington, Mass.: Lexington Books, 1972.

ERICKSON, M. L., & EMPEY, L. T. Court records, undetected delinquency and decision-making. In D. R. Cressey & D. A. Ward (Eds.), *Delinquency, crime, and social process.* New York: Harper & Row, 1969.

ERICKSON, M. L., & JENSEN, G. F. Delinquency is still group behavior: Toward revitalizing the group premise in the sociology of deviance. *Journal of Criminal Law and Crimonology,* 1977, *68,* 262–273.

ERVIN, F. R. Organic brain syndromes associated with elipepsy. In A. M. Freedman, H. I. Kaplan, & B. J. Sadock (Eds.), *Comprehensive textbook of psychiatry* (2nd ed.) Baltimore: Williams & Wilkins, 1975.

FLANAGAN, T. J., HINDELANG, M. J., & GOTTFREDSON, M. R. (Eds.) *Sourcebook of criminal justice statistics—1979.* Washington, D.C.: U.S. Government Printing Office, 1980.

FLEISCHER, G. Identification and imitation in the treatment of juvenile offenders. *Journal of Contemporary Psychotherapy,* 1975, *7,* 41–49.

FREASE, D. E. Delinquency, social class, and the schools. *Sociology and Social Research,* 1973, *57,* 443–459.

FRIEDMAN, C. J., MANN, F., & FRIEDMAN, A. S. A profile of juvenile street gang members. *Adolescence,* 1975, *10,* 563–607.

GALLENKAMP, C. R., & RYCHLAK, J. F. Parental attitudes of sanction in middle-class adolescent male delinquents. *Journal of Social Psychology,* 1968, *75,* 255–260.

GARVIN, J. S. Psychomotor epilepsy: A clinicoencephalographic syndrome. *Journal of Nervous and Mental Disease,* 1953, *117,* 1–8.

GENSHAFT, J. L. Personality correlates of delinquent subtypes. *Journal of Abnormal Child Psychology,* 1980, *8,* 279–283.

GIBBS, F. A. Ictal and non-ictal psychiatric disorders in temporal lobe epilepsy. *Journal of Nervous and Mental Disease,* 1951, *113,* 522–528.

GLADSTONE, H. P. A study of techniques of psychotherapy with youthful offenders. *Psychiatry,* 1962, *25,* 147–159.

GLASER, D. Social disorganization and delinquent subcultures. In H. C. Quay (Ed.), *Juvenile delinquency: Research and theory.* Princeton, N.J.: Van Nostrand, 1965.

GLASER, G. H., & DIXON, M. S. Psychomotor seizures in childhood. *Journal of Nervous and Mental Disease,* 1967, *144,* 391–397.

GLUECK, S., & GLUECK, E. T. *Unraveling juvenile delinquency.* New York: Commonwealth Fund, 1950.

GLUECK, S., & GLUECK, E. T. *Family environment and delinquency.* Boston: Houghton-Mifflin, 1962.

GOLD, A. P. Psychomotor epilepsy in childhood. *Pediatrics,* 1974, *53,* 540–542.

GOLD, M. *Delinquent behavior in an American city.* Belmont, Cal.: Brooks/Cole, 1970.

GOLD, M. Scholastic experiences, self-esteem, and delinquent behavior: A theory for alternate schools. *Crime and Delinquency,* 1978, *24,* 290–308.

GOLD, M., & MANN, D. W. Delinquency as defense. *American Journal of Orthopsychiatry,* 1972, *42,* 463–479.

GOLD, M., & PETRONIO, R. J. Delinquent behavior in adolescence. In J. Adleson (Ed.), *Handbook of adolescent psychology.* New York: Wiley, 1980.

GOLD, M., & REIMER, D. J. Changing patterns of delinquent behavior among Americans 13 through 16 years old: 1967–72. *Crime and Delinquency Literature,* 1975, *7,* 483–517.

GOTTSCHALK, L. A., TITCHENER, J. L., PIKER, H. N., & STEWART, S. S. Psychosocial factors associated with pregnancy in adolescent girls: A preliminary report. *Journal of Nervous and Mental Disease,* 1964, *138,* 524–534.

GUZE, E. B., GOODWIN, D. W., & CRANE, J. B. Criminality and psychiatric disorders. Criminality and psychiatric disorders. *Archives of General Psychiatry,* 1969, *20,* 583–591.

HACKER, F. J., & GELEERD, E. R. Freedom and authority in adolescence. *American Journal of Orthopsychiatry,* 1945, *15,* 621–630.

HACKLER, J. C. Boys, blisters, and behavior: The impact of a work program in an urban central area. *Journal of Research in Crime and Delinquency,* 1966, *12,* 155–164.

HARE, R. D., & COX, D. N. Clinical and empirical conceptions of psychopathy, and the selection of subjects for research. In R. D. Hare & D. Schalling (Eds.), *Psychopathic behaviour.* New York: Wiley, 1978.

HARE, R. D., & SCHALLING, D. (Eds.) *Psychopathic behaviour.* New York: Wiley, 1978.

HEILBRUN, A. B. Psychopathy and violent crime. *Journal of Consulting and Clinical Psychology,* 1979, *47,* 509–516.

HENN, F. A., BARDWELL, R., & JENKINS, R. L. Juvenile delinquents revisited: Adult criminal activity. *Archives of General Psychiatry,* 1980, *37,* 1160–1163.

HENNESSY, M. Broken homes and middle-class delinquency. *Criminology,* 1978, *15,* 505–528.

HERSKOVITZ, H. H., LEVINE, M., & SPIVACK, G. Anti-social behavior of adolescents from higher socio-economic groups. *Journal of Nervous and Mental Disease,* 1959, *125,* 1–9.

HESS, S. *Profiles of children: 1970 White House conference on children.* Washington, D.C.: U.S. Government Printing Office, 1970.

HETHERINGTON, E. M., STOUWIE, R. J., & RIDBERG, E. H. Patterns of family interaction and child-rearing attitudes related to three dimensions of juvenile delinquency. *Journal of Abnormal Psychology,* 1971, *78,* 160–176.

HOEFLER, S. A., & BORNSTEIN, P. H. Achievement Place: An evaluative review. *Criminal Justice and Behavior,* 1975, *2,* 146–148.

HOFFMAN, M. L. Moral internalization: Current theory and research. In L. Berkowitz (Ed.), *Advances in experimental social psychology.* Vol. 10. New York: Academic, 1977.

HOFFMAN, M. L. Moral development in adolescence. In J. Adelson (Ed.), *Handbook of adolescent psychology.* New York: Wiley, 1980.

HUDGENS, R. W. *Psychiatric disorders in adolescence.* Baltimore: Williams & Wilkins, 1974.

HUTCHINGS, B., & MEDNICK, S. A. Registered criminality in the adoptive and biological parents of registered male criminal adoptees. In R. R. Fieve, D. Rosenthal, & H. Brill (Eds.), *Genetic research in psychiatry*. Baltimore: Johns Hopkins University Press, 1974.

JENKINS, R. L. Adaptive and maladaptive delinquency. *Nervous Child*, 1955, *11*, 9–11.

JENKINS, R. L. Motivation and frustration in delinquency. *American Journal of Orthopsychiatry*, 1957, *27*, 528–537.

JENKINS, R. L. The psychopathic or antisocial personality. *Journal of Nervous and Mental Disease*, 1960, *131*, 318–334.

JENKINS, R. L. Psychiatric syndromes in children and their relation to family background. *American Journal of Orthopsychiatry*, 1966, *36*, 450–457.

JENKINS, R. L., & BOYER, A. Types of delinquent behavior and background factors. *International Journal of Social Psychiatry*, 1968, *14*, 65–76.

JENKINS, R. L., NUREDDIN, E., & SHAPRIO, I. Children's behavior syndromes and parental responses. *Genetic Psychology Monographs*, 1966, *74*, 261–329.

JOHNSON, A. M., & SZUREK, S. A. The genesis of antisocial acting out in children and adults. *Psychoanalytic Quarterly*, 1952, *21*, 323–343.

JURKOVIC, G. J., & PRENTICE, N. M. The relationship of moral and cognitive development to dimensions of juvenile delinquency. *Journal of Abnormal Psychology*, 1977, *86*, 414–420.

KAPLAN, H. B., SMITH, P. G., & POKORNY, A. D. Psychosocial antecedents of unwed motherhood among indigent adolescents. *Journal of Youth and Adolescence*, 1979, *8*, 181–207.

KRYNICKI, V. E. Cerebral dysfunction in repetitively assaultive adolescents. *Journal of Nervous and Mental Disease*, 1978, *166*, 59–67.

KVARACEUS, W. C., & MILLER, W. B. *Delinquent behavior, culture, and the individual*. Washington, D.C.: National Educational Association, 1959.

LEVINE, E. M., & KOZAK, C. Drug and alcohol use, delinquency, and vandalism among upper middle class pre- and post-adolescents. *Journal of Youth and Adolescence*, 1979, *8*, 92–101.

LEWIS, D. O. Diagnostic evaluation of the juvenile offender: Toward the clarification of often overlooked psychopathology. *Child Psychiatry and Human Development*, 1976a, *6*, 198–213.

LEWIS, D. O. Delinquency, psychomotor epileptic symptoms, and paranoid ideation: A triad. *American Journal of Psychiatry*, 1976b, *133*, 1395–1398.

LEWIS, D. O., & BALLA, D. "Sociopathy" and its synonyms: Inappropriate diagnoses in child psychiatry. *American Journal of Psychiatry*, 1975, *132*, 720–722.

LEWIS, D. O., & BALLA, D. A. *Delinquency and psychopathology*. New York: Grune & Stratton, 1976.

LION, J. B. Outpatient treatment of psychopaths. In W. H. Reid (Ed.), *The psychopath*. New York: Brunner/Mazel, 1978.

MCCORD, J. A thirty-year follow-up of treatment effects. *American Psychologist*, 1978, *33*, 284–289.

MCCORD, W., & MCCORD, J. *The psychopath: An essay on the criminal mind*. Princeton, N.J.: Van Nostrand, 1964.

MARSHALL, R. J. Antisocial youth. In J. D. Noshpitz (Ed.), *Basic handbook of child psychiatry*. Vol. III. New York: Basic Books, 1979.

MASSIMO, J. L., & SHORE, M. F. The effectiveness of a comprehensive, vocationally-oriented psychotherapeutic program for adolescent delinquent boys. *American Journal of Orthopsychiatry*, 1963, *33*, 634–642.

MEDNICK, S. A., & HUTCHINGS, B. Genetic and psychophysiological factors in a social behavior. In R. D. Hare & D. Schalling (Eds.), *Psychopathic behaviour*. New York: Wiley, 1978.

MEEKS, J. E. Behavioral and antisocial disorders. In J. D. Noshpitz (Ed.), *Basic handbook of child psychiatry*. Vol. II. New York: Basic Books, 1979.

MEYEROWITZ, J. H., & MALEV, J. S. Pubescent attitudinal correlates antecedent to adolescent illegitimate pregnancy. *Journal of Youth and Adolescence*, 1973, *2*, 251–258.

MILLER, D. *Growth to freedom: The psychosocial treatment of delinquent youth.* Bloomington: Indiana University Press, 1965.

MILLER, J. G. Research and theory in middle-class delinquency. *British Journal of Criminology,* 1970, *10,* 33–51.

MILLER, W. B. Lower-class culture as a generating milieu of gang delinquency. *Journal of Social Issues,* 1958, *14,* 5–19.

MILLER, W. B. The impact of a "total community" delinquency control project. *Social Problems,* 1962, *10,* 168–191.

MURPHY, F. J., SHIRLEY, M. M., & WITMER, H. L. The incidence of hidden delinquency. *American Journal of Orthopsychiatry,* 1946, *16,* 686–696.

NOSHPITZ, J. D. Opening phase in the psychotherapy of adolescents with character disorders. *Bulletin of the Menninger Clinic,* 1957, *21,* 153–164.

NYE, F. I., SHORT, J. F., & OLSON, V. J. Socio-economic status and delinquent behavior. In F. I. Nye (Ed.), *Family relationships and delinquent behavior.* New York: Wiley, 1958.

OFFER, D., SABSHIN, M., & MARCUS, D. Clinical evaluation of normal adolescents. *American Journal of Psychiatry,* 1965, *121,* 864–872.

O'MALLEY, P. M., BACHMAN, J. G., & JOHNSTON, J. *Youth in transition: Final report.* Ann Arbor, Mich.: Institute for Social Research, 1977.

ORRIS, J. B. Visual monitoring performance in three subgroups of male delinquents. *Journal of Abnormal Psychology,* 1969, *74,* 227–229.

OUNSTED, C. Aggression and epilepsy—rage in children with temporal lobe epilepsy. *Journal of Psychosomatic Research,* 1969, *13,* 237–242.

PERSONS, R. W. Relationship between psychotherapy with institutionalized boys and subsequent community adjustment. *Journal of Consulting Psychology,* 1967, *31,* 137–141.

PHILLIPS, E. L., WOLF, M. M., FIXSEN, D. L., & BAILEY, J. S. The Achievement Place model: A community-based, family-style, behavior modification program for predelinquents. In E. Ribes-Inesta & A. Bandura (Eds.), *Analysis of delinquency and aggression.* New York: Erlbaum, 1976.

PORTERFIELD, A. L. Delinquency and its outcome in court and college. *American Journal of Sociology,* 1943, *49,* 199–208.

POWERS, E., & WITMER, H. An experiment in the prevention of delinquency: The Cambridge-Sommerville Youth Study. New York: Columbia University Press, 1951.

QUAY, H. C. Personality and delinquency. In H. C. Quay (Ed.), *Juvenile delinquency: Research and theory.* Princeton, N.J.: Van Nostrand, 1965.

QUAY, H. C. Classification. In H. C. Quay & J. S. Werry (Eds.), *Psychopathological disorders of childhood.* (2nd ed.) New York: Wiley, 1979.

REDFERING, D. L. Durability of effects of group counseling with institutionalized delinquent females. *Journal of Abnormal Psychology,* 1973, *82,* 85–86.

REID, J. B., & PATTERSON, G. R. The modification of aggression and stealing behavior of boys in the home setting. In E. Ribes-Inesta & A. Bandura (Eds.), *Analysis of delinquency and aggression.* New York: Erlbaum, 1976.

REID, W. H. (Ed.) *The psychopath.* New York: Brunner/Mazel, 1978.

RHODES, W. C. Delinquency and community action. In H. C. Quay (Ed.), *Juvenile delinquency: Research and theory.* Princeton, N.J.: Van Nostrand, 1965.

ROBERTS, R. E., ABRAMS, L., & FINCH, J. R. "Delinquent" sexual behavior among adolescents. *Medical Aspects of Human Sexuality,* 1973, *7,* 162–183.

ROBINS, E., GENTRY, K. A., MUNOZ, R. A., & MARTEN, S. A contrast of the three more common illnesses with the ten less common in a study and 18-month follow-up of 314 psychiatric emergency room patients. *Archives of General Psychiatry,* 1977, *34,* 269–291.

ROBINS, L. N. *Deviant children grown up: A sociological and psychiatric study of sociopathic personality.* Baltimore: Williams & Wilkins, 1966.

ROBINS, L. N. Aetiological implications in studies of childhood histories relating to antisocial personality. In R. D. Hare & D. Schalling (Eds.), *Psychopathic behaviour.* New York: Wiley, 1978.

ROBINS, L. N. Follow-up studies. In H. C. Quay & J. S. Werry (Eds.), *Psychopathological disorders of childhood.* (2nd ed.) New York: Wiley, 1979.

ROBINS, L. N., MURPHY, G. E., WOODRUFF, R. A., & KING, L. J. Adult psychiatric status of black school boys. *Archives of General Psychiatry,* 1971, *24,* 338–345.

ROCKWELL, D. A. Social and familial correlates of antisocial disorders. In W. H. Reid (Ed.). *The psychopath.* New York: Brunner/Mazel, 1978.

ROSENBERG, F. R., & ROSENBERG, M. Self-esteem and delinquency. *Journal of Youth and Adolescence,* 1978, *7,* 279–291.

ROSENTHAL, D. Heredity in criminality. *Criminal Justice and Behavior,* 1975, 2, 3–21.

SARASON, I. G. Verbal learning, modeling, and juvenile delinquency. *American Psychologist,* 1968, *23,* 254–266.

SARASON, I. G. A modeling and informational approach to delinquency. In E. Ribes-Inesta & A. Bandura (Eds.), *Analysis of delinquency and aggression.* New York: Erlbaum, 1976.

SARRI, R. C. Crime and the female offender. In E. S. Gomberg & V. Franks (Eds.), *Gender and disordered behavior.* New York: Brunner/Mazel, 1979.

SCHALLING, D. Psychopathy-related personality variables and the psychophysiology of socialization. In R. D. Hare & D. Schalling (Eds.), *Psychopathic behaviour.* New York: Wiley, 1978.

SCHULSINGER, F. Psychopathy: Heredity and environment. *International Journal of Mental Health,* 1972, *1,* 190–206.

SCHWARTZ, L. J. Treatment of the adolescent psychopath. *Psychotherapy: Theory, Research and Practice,* 1967, *4,* 133–137.

SHANLEY, F. J., LEFEVER, D. W., & RICE, R. E. The aggressive middle-class delinquent. *Journal of Criminal Law, Criminology, and Police Science,* 1966, *57,* 145–152.

SHOOR, M., & SPEED, M. H. Delinquency as a manifestation of the mourning process. *Psychiatric Quarterly,* 1963, *37,* 540–558.

SHORE, M. F., & MASSIMO, J. L. Five years later: A follow-up study of comprehensive vocationally-oriented psychotherapy. *American Journal of Orthopsychiatry,* 1969, *39,* 769–773.

SHORE, M. F., & MASSIMO, J. L. After ten years: A follow-up study of comprehensive vocationally-oriented psychotherapy. *American Journal of Orthopsychiatry,* 1973, *43,* 128–132.

SHORT, J. F. Youth, gangs and society: Micro- and macrosociological processes. *Sociological Quarterly,* 1974, *15,* 3–19.

SIMON, R. J. *Women and crime.* Lexington, Mass.: Lexington Books, 1975.

SINGER, M. Delinquency and family disciplinary configuration. *Archives of General Psychiatry,* 1974, *31,* 795–798.

SKRZYPEK, G. J. Effect of perceptual isolation and arousal on anxiety, complexity preference, and novelty preference in psychopathic and neurotic delinquents. *Journal of Abnormal Psychology,* 1969, *74,* 321–329.

SMILEY, W. C. Classification and delinquency: A review. *Behavioral Disorders,* 1977, *2,* 184–200.

SMITH, R. J. *The psychopath in society.* New York: Academic, 1978.

SPELLACY, F. Neuropsychological differences between violent and nonviolent adolescents. *Journal of Clinical Psychology,* 1977, *33,* 966–969.

SPIELBERGER, C. D., KLING, J. L., & O'HAGAN, S. E. J. Dimensions of psychopathic personality: Antisocial behavior and anxiety. In R. D. Hare & D. Schalling (Eds.), *Psychopathic behaviour.* New York: Wiley, 1978.

STEVENS, J. R. Psychiatric implications of temporal lobe epilepsy. *Archives of General Psychiatry,* 1966, *14,* 461–471.

STEWART, D. J. Effects of social reinforcement on dependency and aggressive responses of psychopathic, neurotic, and subcultural delinquents. *Journal of Abnormal Psychology,* 1972, *79,* 76–83.

SUTKER, P. B., ARCHER, R. P., & KILPATRICK, D. G. Sociopathy and antisocial behavior: Theory and treatment. In S. M. Turner, K. S. Calhoun, & H. E. Adams (Eds.), *Handbook of clinical behavior therapy.* New York: Wiley, 1981.

THOMPSON, R. J., & LOZES, J. Female gang delinquency. *Corrective and Social Psychiatry,* 1976, *22,* 1–5.

TOBIAN, J. J. The affluent suburban male delinquent. *Crime and delinquency,* 1970, *16,* 273–279.

TOOLAN, J. M. Masked depression in children and adolescents. In S. Lesse (Ed.), *Masked depression.* New York: Aronson, 1974.

U.S. DEPARTMENT OF JUSTICE. *Sourcebook of criminal justice statistics—1978.* Washington, D.C.: Criminal Justice Research Center, 1979.

UNWIN, J. R. Stages in the therapy of hospitalized acting-out adolescents. *American Journal of Orthopsychiatry,* 1968, *13,* 115–119.

VAZ, E. W. Juvenile delinquency in the middle-class youth culture. In D. R. Cressey & D. A. Ward (Eds.), *Delinquency, crime, and social process.* New York: Harper & Row, 1969.

VISOTSKY, H. M. A project for unwed pregnant adolescents in Chicago. *Clinical Pediatrics,* 1966, *5,* 322–324.

WAGNER, E. E. The nature of the psychopath: Interpretation of projective findings based on structural analysis. *Perceptual and Motor Skills,* 1974, *39,* 563–574.

WEINER, I. B. Juvenile delinquency. *Pediatric Clinics of North America,* 1975, *22,* 673–684.

WELNER, A., WELNER, Z., & FISHMAN, R. Psychiatric adolescent inpatients. *Archives of General Psychiatry,* 1979, *36,* 698–700.

WIDOM, C. S. Interpersonal conflict and cooperation in psychopaths. *Journal of Abnormal Psychology,* 1976, *85,* 330–334.

WIDOM, C. S. A methodology for studying non-institutionalized psychopaths. In R. D. Hare & D. Schalling (Eds.), *Psychopathic behaviour.* New York: Wiley, 1978.

WIRT, R. D., & BRIGGS, P. F. The meaning of delinquency. In H. C. Quay (Ed.), *Juvenile delinquency: Research and theory.* Princeton, N.J.: Van Nostrand, 1965.

WITMER, H. L., & TUFTS, E. *The effectiveness of delinquency prevention programs.* Washington, D.C.: U.S. Children's Bureau Publication No. 350, 1954.

12

SUICIDAL BEHAVIOR

As part of the normal developmental process, young people struggling with difficult psychological problems may have fleeting thoughts of harming themselves. Overt suicidal acts, however, in which children or adolescents actually take their own lives or attempt to do so, are never a normal variation; instead, they reflect pathological concerns that require careful professional evaluation. The present chapter will review some basic facts about youthful suicidal behavior and discuss its origins, assessment, and treatment.

BASIC FACTS ABOUT YOUTHFUL SUICIDAL BEHAVIOR

Actual suicide is fortunately rare among children and adolescents. Of 26,832 known deaths by suicide in the United States in 1976, only 5 involved children less than 10 years old, 158 were 10- to 14-year-olds, and 1556 were youngsters aged 15 to 19. As shown in Figure 12.1, these young people committed just 6.9 percent of the suicides reported for the entire population that year, whereas young adults (age 20 to 29) and persons over 60 each accounted for more than 20 percent.

As these data suggest, the suicide rate increases sharply during the adolescent years— from 0.8 per 100,000 among 10- to 14-year-olds to 7.6 per 100,000 at 15 to 19. Among adults the suicide rate continues to climb steadily from 16.4 per 100,000 at age 25 to 34 to 20.1 per 100,000 at age 45 to 54, and it remains at about this level until age 85 (see Figure 12.2).

Although these frequency rates might suggest that suicide is a problem of aging rather than youth, three additional facts make suicidal behavior an important topic in developmental psychopathology.

Figure 12.1
Distribution of suicides in the United States by age groups. (Based on data provided in *Vital Statistics of the United States* (1979b).)

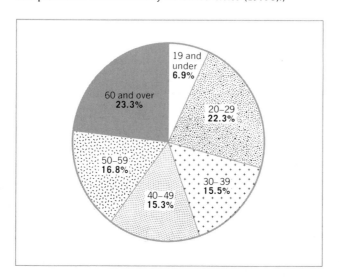

Figure 12.2

Suicide rates by age groups in the United States. (Based on data from *Vital Statistics of the United States* (1979a).)

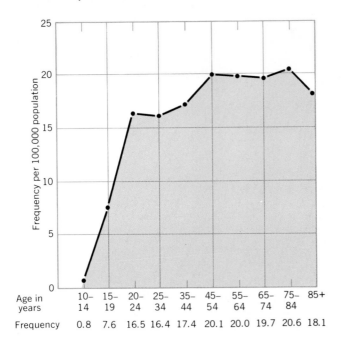

Age in years	10–14	15–19	20–24	25–34	35–44	45–54	55–64	65–74	75–84	85+
Frequency	0.8	7.6	16.5	16.4	17.4	20.1	20.0	19.7	20.6	18.1

1. Youthful suicide appears to be increasing at an alarming rate. During the 10 years from 1962 to 1972, the suicide rate per 100,000 people grew by about 10 percent for the population in general but by almost 80 percent among 15- to 24-year-olds (*Vital Statistics*, 1963–1976). As a result, young people accounted for twice as large a percent of the suicides in the United States in 1972 than a decade earlier (see Figure 12.3).

2. Suicide is more frequently a cause of death during the late teen years than at any other time of life. This is due in part to the fact that adolescents as a group enjoy relatively good physical health. They no longer contract various childhood diseases, and they are not yet susceptible to many of the chronic illnesses that plague older people. As shown in Table 12.1, suicide was the ninth leading cause of death in the general population in 1976, but the third leading cause among 15- to 19-year-olds, after accidents and homicide.

3. Attempted suicide becomes a noteworthy risk during adolescence. One adolescent in every thousand attempts suicide each year in the United States. Whereas adolescents account for fewer than 6 percent of the annual suicides in the United States, they make 12 percent of the known suicide attempts. Compared to approximately 6 to 10 suicide attempts for each actual suicide in the general population, for adolescents the ratio of attempted to completed suicides is estimated

Figure 12.3
Percent of total suicides in the United States committed by young people in 1962 and 1972. (Based on data reported by Petzel and Cline (1979).)

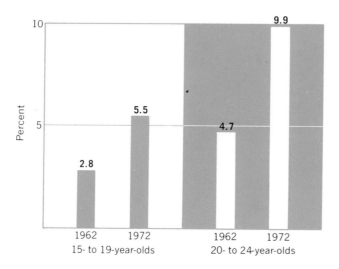

to run as high as 50:1 or even 100:1 (Jacobinzer, 1965; McAnarney, 1975; Seiden, 1969; Stengel, 1964). In child psychiatric clinics 7 to 10 percent of the youngsters seen have been referred for threatened or attempted suicide (Shaffer, 1974). Among persons admitted to psychiatric units in general hospitals, a history of suicide attempts is found in 10 to 15 percent of adult patients but in 25 to 40 percent of adolescents (Garber & Polsky, 1970; Hudgens, 1974; Schneer, Perlstein, & Brozovsky, 1975).

TABLE 12.1   Leading Causes of Death Among Adolescents in the United States

Cause	Age 15–19		General Population	
	Rate per 100,000	Rank	Rate per 100,000	Rank
Accidents	57.4	1	48.4	4
Homicides	9.6	2	10.0	12
Suicide	7.6	3	12.7	9
Cancer	6.0	4	171.1	2
Heart disease	2.0	5	336.2	1
Congenital anomalies	1.6	6	6.2	13
Influenza and pneumonia	1.5	7	26.1	5
Cerebrovascular disease	1.1	8	91.1	3
Anemia	0.4	9	1.5	15
Diabetes mellitus	0.2	10	16.5	6

Source.   From *Vital Statistics of the United States* (1979a, 1979b).

Fatal one-car, one-driver accidents sometimes reflect suicidal intent.

These prevalence data very probably underestimate the true frequency of suicidal behavior, especially among young people. There is reason to believe that up to 50 percent of suicides are mistakenly regarded or recorded as accidents (Toolan, 1975). Suicidal intent is thus particularly likely to go undetected in 15- to 19-year-olds, among whom accidents are so frequently a cause of death. In this vein, almost three-fourths (71.5 percent) of the fatal accidents among adolescents involve automobiles, compared to less than half (46.7 percent) for the population in general (Vital Statistics, 1979). Although intentionality is difficult to determine in automobile and other kinds of fatal accidents, at least some of them—especially one-car accidents in which a teenager was driving alone—are very likely to have been suicides. Similar underreporting no doubt characterizes suicide attempts, which well-meaning professionals may be inclined to record as accidents and which parents understandably tend to deny or conceal (Holinger, 1979; Mishara, 1975; Toolan, 1975; Weissman, 1974).

Sex Differences

Among adolescents who consider suicide, boys are far more likely than girls actually to kill themselves, by a ratio of more than three to one; on the other hand, girls account for 80 to 90 percent of adolescent suicide attempts (Haider, 1968; Seiden, 1969; Vital Statistics, 1975). The same sex difference holds for adults, with men being three times more likely to commit suicide and women three times more likely to attempt it. The reasons for this sex difference are not clearly understood, although they may relate to different sex-role attitudes and preferences. Completed suicide tends to be seen as more "masculine" than attempted suicide, which suggests that males may be more likely than females to consider suicide only when they intend to complete the act (Lester, 1979).

In this regard, there has been a slight decrease in sex differences in suicidal attempts since 1970. To the extent that this change reflects the general trend in our society toward less distinct sex roles, their importance in leading to this difference in the first place is being confirmed (Kraft & Babigian, 1976; Shneidman, 1975; Weissman, 1974). On the other hand, the most recent data available on actual suicide indicates that males

Figure 12.4
Methods used by 15- to 19-year-olds to commit suicide. (Based on data from *Vital Statistics of the United States* (1963–1976).)

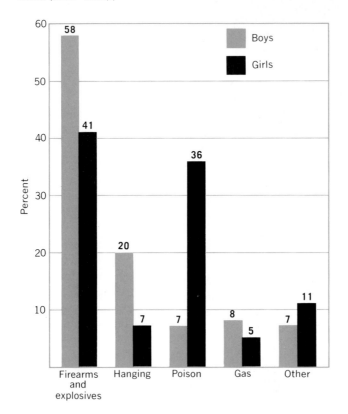

in the United States continue to take their own lives 2.9 times more frequently than females (*Vital Statistics Report,* 1979).

Methods Used

As shown in Figure 12.4, firearms and explosives are the methods most frequently used by both boys (58 percent) and girls (41 percent) to kill themselves. Girls who commit suicide are almost as likely to poison (36 percent) as to shoot themselves, whereas boys rarely take their own lives in this way (7 percent). When young people make suicide *attempts,* however, poison is by far the most commonly chosen method, in about 80 percent of the boys and 90 percent of the girls (Bergstrand & Otto, 1962; Tuckman & Connon, 1962.

This difference between actual and attempted suicide probably reflects the relative lethality of these methods. Taking poison allows more chance for survival, given the wide range of possible nonlethal doses, than shooting oneself, and people who wish to make a suicide attempt but not to die tend to choose methods that do not endanger their lives (Beck, Beck, & Kovacs, 1975). It is of course possible for adolescents to misjudge the effects of what they decide to do to themselves in a suicide attempt. Then, to take a tragic example, the belief that "a few of these can't hurt me" can result in a fatal overdose of some highly toxic substance, and what began as a suicide attempt ends in a death.

ORIGINS OF YOUTHFUL SUICIDAL BEHAVIOR

Suicidal behavior in young people has at times been regarded as a sudden, impulsive response to some disappointment or frustration, such as failing a test, being jilted by a boyfriend or girlfriend, or losing an argument with one's parents. In point of fact, however, youthful suicidal behavior has much more complex origins than these. Typically it occurs as the end result of an unfolding process with the following four characteristics:

1. *Long-standing Family Instability and Discord*   Suicidal adolescents are much more likely than their peers to have grown up in disrupted, disorganized homes. Sometimes through death or desertion of a parent, sometimes through chronic mental or physical illness in the family, sometimes as a result of parental criminality or alcoholism, sometimes in response to marital disharmony, and sometimes because of frequent moves, these youngsters have frequently passed through their childhood with little reason to feel that they could rely on their parents for support or on their home as a place of sanctuary (Cantor, 1972; Stanley & Barter, 1970; Toolan, 1962). Hendin (1975, p. 327) comments vividly in this regard that "what was revealed in the lives of young people who had made suicide attempts were the ways in which death, depression, and misery had been part of their lives since childhood, and had been built into their relationship to their parents."

   As in the case of unraveling the disposition to depression, however, growing up in a broken home cannot be assumed by itself to increase the risk of suicidal behavior. A broken home becomes causally significant for suicide only when frequent moves, marital disharmony, and other patterns of social disorganization are also present. Moreover, apparent disorganization affects young people only to the extent that they *experience* it as stressful. The breakup of an unhappy, strife-filled marriage may produce a calmer and more stable home that, although now "broken," improves an adolescent's sense of psychological well-being. By contrast, suicidal adolescents have almost always regarded such events as divorces, separations, and moves as unwelcome (Bruhn, 1962; Jacobs & Teicher, 1967).

2. *Escalating Family Problems*   Suicidal adolescents have typically experienced an escalation in their family problems for at least a few months prior to their attempting or committing suicide. Frequent parental separations have become permanent divorce, for example, or especially serious illness has prevented the parents from earning the family's living, or a particularly wrenching move to a new school or community has occurred.

   In addition, the months preceding youthful suicidal behavior have usually seen a sharp increase in parent-child conflict. Often the parents have become highly critical of their youngster during this period and have imposed rigid, restrictive limits on his or her behavior. The adolescent has in turn usually complained bitterly about the parents' attitudes and impositions, and angry confrontation has become the order of the day. Almost always the adolescent has come away the loser in these confrontations and has grown to feel powerless to influence his or her destiny (Corder, Page, & Corder, 1974; Schneer, Kay, & Brozovsky, 1961).

3. *Dissolving Social Relationships*   Feeling alienated from uncaring and overcontrolling parents, suicidal adolescents have typically sought a close relationship with some other relative, a teacher, or a boyfriend or girlfriend. Because of their desperate need for such a relationship, however, presuicidal adolescents have had little tolerance for its being disrupted for any reason. What is often found in the recent history of suicidal adolescents, then, is either failure to establish compensatory contacts with other people or the dissolving of such desperately needed relationships, as by a relative dying, a teacher moving away, or a boyfriend or girlfriend no longer wanting a "steady" relationship.

Cantor (1976) found this feature of presuicidal behavior useful in separating young people who frequently think about suicide from those who actually attempt it. Among female college students she studied, both those who had thought about suicide often and those who had made one or more attempts showed strong needs to be close to people and to be nurtured by them, combined with little ability to tolerate frustration of these needs. However, those who had just thought about suicide had been successful in satisfying these needs in their interpersonal relationships, whereas those who had attempted suicide had been unable to reach out and establish supportive relationships with others.

4. *Unsuccessful Problem-Solving Efforts.*   In addition to failing to find or hold onto supportive relationships, suicidal adolescents have usually progressed without success through a series of increasingly desperate efforts to resolve their escalating problems. Often they have begun with reasonable attempts to iron out their differences with their parents or to find support and stability elsewhere. These efforts have then given way to more provocative attempts to convey their distress and influence a change in their circumstances, such as rebelling, running away, or ignoring their school work. With neither reason nor provocation solving their problems, these young people have often developed numerous symptoms of anxiety and depression and finally decided that suicide was the only means left for them to escape their distress or to make some impact on the important people in their lives (Levenson & Neuringer, 1971; Otto, 1964; Teicher, 1973, 1979; Yusin, 1973).

Lonely, alienated young people from disrupted or disorganized homes who have already failed in numerous efforts to resolve mounting problems thus constitute a high-risk group for suicidal behavior. Some specific event will then usually provide a "last straw" that precipitates a suicidal act, such as losing one more argument at home or one more close friend at school; although they may be mentioned by adolescents as their reason for a suicide attempt, such events almost always turn out to have been just the fuse on a long-developing powder keg.

Especially important in the unfolding process that leads young people to attempt suicide is their need to communicate their concerns, particularly to their parents, and to bring about a change in how they are being treated by others. For this reason, attempted suicide is often called "a cry for help" (Darbonne, 1969; Farberow & Shneidman, 1961). Several research findings reflect the need of suicidal adolescents to make an impact on their parents: they typically feel that their parents are unaware of or indifferent to their problems; their attempts are usually made at home, often while their parents are in the house; and their parents commonly have little understanding of what has been bothering the youngsters and precipitated their suicide attempts (Tuckman & Connon, 1972).

None of these individual or family characteristics occurs in all suicidal young people, nor do all adolescents who share them become suicidal. The factors that turn high risk for suicidal behavior into actual or attempted are not fully understood. One factor that appears clearly to influence suicide-risk youngsters to become suicidal is the presence of a suicidal model. In one group of adolescents who had taken their own lives, for example, 13 percent were found to have experienced suicidal behavior by a parent or sibling (Shaffer, 1974). In a study of adolescent attempters, 44 percent knew of an actual or attempted suicide by one or more close friends or relatives, and 25 percent of their mothers or fathers had previously attempted suicide (Teicher & Jacobs, 1966). The extent to which these frequencies exceed general population figures for actual (0.01 percent per year) and attempted (0.1 percent per year) suicide strongly suggests a relationship between observing suicidal behavior and considering it for oneself.

How parents react to adolescent suicide attempts frequently determines whether they will be repeated. Parents who are startled by suicidal behavior into recognizing their youngster's difficulties and offering to help with or at least talk about these difficulties can usually forestall another attempt. On the other hand, parents who show little reaction to a suicide attempt, who do not see it as any reason for changing their behavior, or—even worse—who respond with anger or ridicule rather than with sympathetic understanding set the stage for further and more serious attempts.

Research reports bear grim testimony to the aftermath of suicide attempts that fail to achieve their purpose. Of adults who kill themselves, 75 percent have previously made suicide attempts or gestures, and more than 20 percent of adults who make a suicide attempt eventually die by their own hand (Dorpat & Ripley, 1967; Shneidman & Farberow, 1957). Among adolescents who attempt suicide, 50 to 65 percent have been found to have previously threatened or attempted suicide, which far exceeds the 0.1 percent yearly rate among adolescents in general (Barter, Swaback, & Todd, 1969; Shaffer, 1974).

ASSESSING THE SERIOUSNESS OF SUICIDE ATTEMPTS

The seriousness of suicide attempts refers to how physically damaging they are and the likelihood of their being repeated, perhaps with even more severe self-destructive consequences. In clinical practice, assessments of such future risk are guided by certain known implications of the onset, method, and intent of suicidal behavior.

With respect to *onset,* the more suddenly suicidal behavior develops, the better the chances of reducing the risk of further attempts through brief psychotherapy or environmental manipulation focused on the immediate situation. Conversely, a long-standing history of self-destructive behavior patterns, especially when they include previous suicide attempts, increases the risk of subsequent attempts and calls for extensive treatment or surveillance, perhaps including hospitalization.

Concerning the *method* by which a young person has attempted suicide, much depends on its lethality and the possibilities that were left open for rescue. Youngsters who have survived hanging or shooting themselves are at much greater risk for further suicidal behavior than those who have swallowed a few aspirin. As mentioned earlier, however, the person's own appraisal of lethality must be taken into account. An adolescent who has taken a dozen aspirin tablets expecting them to cause death is probably a greater suicide risk than a youngster who has become seriously ill after swallowing a highly toxic substance that was thought to be relatively harmless.

Likewise, young people who have thoughtfully selected a particular time, place, and method for attempting suicide that maximized both lethality and isolation from potential rescuers pose a relatively serious continued risk of actual suicide. On the other hand, the more they have acted on the spur of the moment, with whatever means were to hand, or picked a time and place with responsible people nearby or expected to come on to the scene, the better are the prospects that further or more serious suicidal acts can be averted.

As for *intent,* considerable importance attaches to whatever communicative or manipulative purposes were involved in the behavior. The more clearly a suicide attempt has been meant to impress others or to influence their actions or attitudes, the fewer the implications for further, more serious self-destructive acts. By contrast, youngsters who do not talk about a suicide attempt they have made in interpersonal terms, or cannot even recognize possible motives for it in relation to other people, are at considerable risk for eventually taking their own lives. Most serious of all is a young person whose suicide attempt occurred in total isolation from others and was accompanied by a conscious wish to die (Beck, Kovacs, & Weissman, 1979).

The following two cases illustrate suicidal behavior of differing severity. Both involve the kinds of mounting family difficulty that typically lead to youthful suicide attempts. In the first case a sudden onset of mild suicidal behavior was followed by a fortunate outcome and minimal future risk. In the second case a more serious situation with a long history led to a near-tragic outcome and a very uncertain prognosis for the future.

Case 18   *A Mild Suicide Attempt*

Noreen, age 13, had swallowed 8 ounces of straight whiskey and been brought to the hospital unconscious. She had drunk the alcohol in the bathroom at home following an argument with her parents. The sound of her falling to the floor had alerted her parents, who rushed to her assistance. Significantly, they found the bathroom door unlocked and standing ajar.

When Noreen was interviewed the following day, she was willing to talk about what she had done but could offer no explanation. She could only repeat that it was a silly and stupid thing to have done and that she had no wish to kill herself. From her parents it was learned that the argument preceding her suicide attempt concerned her relationship with a girlfriend of whom they disapproved. For some months they had been telling her to spend less time with this girl, whom they considered too nonconforming and nonintellectual for their tastes. In the course of the preattempt argument, they came to the point of forbidding any further association with her. This information revealed Noreen's concern about having to give up a valued friendship and her needs to impress her parents with her distress and influence them to change their mind. When these communicative and manipulative aspects of her suicidal behavior were suggested to her, she quickly recognized and acknowledged them. She added that her parents generally did not understand her and that getting through to them when something was troubling her had often proved difficult.

Fortunately, despite the previous communication gaps within the family, these parents were sympathetically concerned about Noreen's behavior. They requested and effectively utilized counseling on why Noreen had attempted suicide, how they might have contributed to her quandary, and what they might do to minimize the likelihood of any further such behavior. The positive treatment response of all family members gave promise that the communication gap between them could be closed sufficiently to prevent further suicidal behavior, and there were in fact no recurrences during the time of an 18-month follow-up.

Case 19. *A Serious Suicide Attempt*

Sara, age 16, had been in constant conflict with her mother, Kate, since Kate had remarried 6 years earlier. Sara's father had died when she was 4, and she and her mother had been alone together from that time until the arrival on the scene of her stepfather, whom she disliked intensely. Sara and Kate fought about anything and everything—dress, friends, table manners, dating privileges, proper attitude toward stepfather, and so forth. When Sara was 15, Kate had sought professional help to improve their relationship.

In the course of brief psychotherapy, Sara and Kate both came through as strong-willed, argumentative, stubborn individuals who magnified minor disagreements and their differences. During some joint sessions they analyzed the various sources of tension between them and agreed to a truce, with compromises on both sides.

Matters improved steadily for almost a year after these sessions. Rules of conduct were discussed and negotiated, and family bickering waned. Then on New Year's Eve, as Sara was dressing for a date that had been arranged weeks in advance, her mother suddenly decided that she was not old enough for a New Year's Eve date and could not go. Instead, she was to remain at home with the family. Sara stayed at home, crushed by this arbitrary decree, only to have her mother and stepfather subsequently go out and leave her alone in the house. At this point, feeling abandoned and hopeless and convinced that her parents cared little for her needs, she swallowed some barbiturates. She was careful, however, to limit herself to a small dose that only made her groggy. She went to bed and the next morning told her parents what she had done.

Her mother became furious at this news and felt so unable to deal with the situation that she called her sister to come over to the house to advise her. The aunt's approach was to call Sara an actor and a fake and to accuse her of trying to drive her mother crazy. At the height of these accusations Sara went upstairs and slashed deeply into both of her wrists with a razor blade. She then came downstairs, dripping blood, to ask, "Am I faking now?" The failure of her initial, mild suicide attempt to focus constructive attention on family issues had thereby precipitated a second, much more serious self-destructive act. The family was unfortunately lost to follow-up after Sara had received medical treatment for her injuries. However, this history would point to continued risk of life-threatening behavior in the absence of improved family relationships.

TREATMENT OF SUICIDAL BEHAVIOR

There is one overriding consideration in treating young people who have made a suicide attempt: *every such attempt must be taken seriously.* Although suicide attempts vary in lethality and in their implications for subsequent suicidal behavior, even the mildest attempt is intended to communicate problems for which no solution seems available. As illustrated in the case of Sara, suicidal behavior that is treated lightly or unsympathetically by the important people in a youngster's life is often followed by further, increasingly more dangerous self-destructive actions.

Whatever the particular circumstances that bring a suicidal youngster to professional attention, the treatment usually assumes that some unappreciated distress and some breakdown in interpersonal relationships have contributed to his or her actions. Accordingly, clinicians focus first on opening up lines of communication between suicidal youngsters and those around them and then seek to identify the motives underlying their self-destructive behavior (Gleser, 1971; Kovacs, Beck, & Weissman, 1975; Teicher, 1979; Toolan, 1978).

Opening Lines of Communication

Suicidal youngsters have frequently become convinced that they are cut off from the affection, nurturance, and support of others. A psychotherapist, by being at least one interested and concerned person, eager to listen and understand, can begin to alter this conviction. Quite literally, the therapist makes an intense, explicit commitment to becoming, for as long as necessary, the young person's "lifeline." This commitment includes being reachable around the clock to talk about troubling concerns, especially thoughts of another suicide attempt. By restoring hope that drastic action may not be necessary to get someone to pay attention and by creating opportunities to talk about before acting on any further suicidal impulses, such intervention sharply reduces the immediate risk of recurrent attempts.

Once a therapist has established lines of communication with a suicidal youngster, the next and eventually much more important step is to extend them to his or her family and friends. Working with the parents or meeting in family sessions is essential if the therapy is to have any sustained effect. The parents must be helped to recognize that they have not been as aware of or concerned about their youngster's problems as they might be, and the young person must be helped to find more effective ways of communicating with his or her parents through words rather than actions. Family discussions in the therapist's presence often reveal just how and where communication breaks down and provide a setting for encouraging more positive patterns of family interaction.

In individual sessions, therapists work on helping suicidal youngsters expand or enrich their friendships. The breakup of friendships that often precedes suicide attempts has typically contributed to feelings of hopelessness. Encouragement to seek new friends and guidance in more effective ways of handling these relationships can lead to a more optimistic view of the future and a more gratifying sharing of feelings and concerns with others. The more people with whom youngsters can communicate, the less likely they are to contemplate suicide. Hence the need for continuing professional care following a suicide attempt depends heavily on how much progress has been made in opening up lines of communication outside the therapist's office.

Identifying Underlying Motives

Adolescents who have attempted suicide often describe their behavior as a mystery to them or attribute it entirely to the final argument or disappointment that preceded it. Moreover, when they are feeling encouraged by a prompt, supportive response from a therapist and from their parents, they are inclined to brush their attempt off as "just one of those things" and to get on with their lives without talking further about it. Therapists usually resist this wish, because suicidal risk persists so long as the young person fails to understand and acknowledge the motives underlying the attempt.

Once open communication has been established in therapy, then, the treatment reviews the entire sequence of long-standing and mounting family problems, dissolving social relationships, and unsuccessful problem-solving efforts that preceded the suicide attempt. The young person needs to vent the feelings associated with these events and to see how they led to a decision to take such drastic action. The therapist also explores the specific communicative or manipulative purposes the suicide attempt was intended to serve. What was the young person trying to communicate, and to whom? What changes was he or she hoping to bring about in whose behavior? Answers to these questions, openly discussed, provide a basis not only for eliminating suicidal behavior as a problem-solving effort, but also for resolving the problems that brought matters to such a pass in the first place.

Parents, too, must be helped to understand the motives for their youngster's suicide attempt. Once family members begin to communicate more openly, they need to have in mind the specific bones of contention from which the suicidal behavior originated. Only then can they work on the problems that need addressing and make helpful decisions about thinking or acting differently.

In summary, then, the treatment approach with suicidal young people is governed by the expectation that the more they encounter warm concern, attempts to understand their behavior, and desired changes in family patterns, the less likely they are to consider suicide attempts in the future. This formulation may appear contrary to principles of reinforcement, which indicate that a rewarding experience subsequent to an act increases the likelihood of the act's being repeated. However, an adequate treatment approach reinforces the communication, not the suicide attempt, and fosters ways of communicating that are neither as painful nor as dangerous as attempting suicide.

SUMMARY

Youthful suicidal behavior always identifies pathological concerns that require understanding and prompt intervention. Actual suicide is rare among young people, with youngsters under 18 accounting for only about 6 percent of the suicides committed each year in the United States. However, youthful suicide has been increasing at an alarming rate, and suicide is more likely to be a cause of death during the late teen years than at any other time in life. Moreover, adolescents are just as likely as adults to make suicide attempts, at the rate of one of every 1000 persons per year.

Among adolescents who consider suicide, boys are three times more likely than girls to kill themselves, whereas girls are four times more likely to make suicide attempts. The reasons for this sex difference, which also exists among adults, are not clearly understood, although they may well derive from differences in sex-role attitudes and preferences. Firearms and explosives are the methods most frequently used by both boys and girls to take their own lives, whereas poison is the most common method used in suicide attempts. This difference between actual and attempted suicide is probably due to the relative lethality of these methods.

Suicidal behavior in young people typically occurs as the end result of an unfolding process that involves (a) long-standing family instability and discord; (b) escalating family problems; (c) dissolving social relationships; and (d) unsuccessful problem-solving efforts. Lonely, alienated young people from disrupted or disorganized homes who have already failed in numerous efforts to resolve mounting problems thus constitute a high-risk group for suicidal behavior. Running through the unfolding process that leads young people to attempt suicide is a need to communicate their distress, particularly to their parents, and to bring about changes in how they are being treated by others. The degree to which these purposes are achieved has considerable bearing on whether further, more serious suicide attempts will occur.

The more suddenly suicidal behavior develops, the less lethal the method used in an attempt, and the more clearly communicative or manipulative purposes are involved, the less serious are the future implications or a suicidal act. Conversely, a long-standing history of self-destructive behavior, an attempt planned to maximize lethality and isolation from potential rescuers, and a conscious wish to die rather then to communicate increase the risk of subsequent attempts and the need for extended treatment or surveillance.

Although suicidal behavior varies in severity, the overriding consideration in treating suicidal young people is that every such attempt must be taken seriously. When circumstances bring suicidal youngsters to professional attention, the treatment focuses first on opening up lines of communication between them and the important people in their lives and second on identifying the motives underlying their actions. Key features of the therapy include the therapist's becoming actively and directly involved in averting further suicide attempts, working with the family to help them understand and respond more effectively to their child's needs, and helping the young person develop nonsuicidal channels of communicating about and attempting to solve life problems.

REFERENCES

BARTER, J. T., SWABACK, D. O., & TODD, D. Adolescent suicide attempts: A follow-up study of hospitalized patients. *Archives of General Psychiatry*, 1969, *19*, 523–527.

BECK, A. T., BECK, R., & KOVACS, M. Classification of suicidal behaviors: I. Quantifying intent and medical lethality. *American Journal of Psychiatry*, 1975, *132*, 285–287.

BECK, A. T., KOVACS, M., & WEISSMAN, A. Assessment of suicidal intention: The scale for suicide ideation. *Journal of Consulting and Clinical Psychology*, 1979, *47*, 343–352.

BERGSTRAND, C. G., & OTTO, U. Suicidal attempts in adolescence and childhood. *Acta Paediatrica*, 1962, *51*, 17–26.

BRUHN, J. G. Broken homes among attempted suicides and psychiatric outpatients: A comparative study. *Journal of Mental Science*, 1962, *108*, 772–779.

CANTOR, P. The adolescent attempter: Sex, sibling position, and family constellation. *Life-Threatening Behavior*, 1972, *2*, 252–261.

CANTOR, P. C. Personality characteristics found among youthful suicide attempters. *Journal of Abnormal Psychology*, 1976, *85*, 324–329.

CORDER, B. F., PAGE, P. V., & CORDER, R. F. Parental history, family communication, and interaction patterns in adolescent suicide. *Family Therapy*, 1974, *1*, 285–290.

DARBONNE, A. R. Study of psychological content in the communications of suicidal individuals. *Journal of Consulting and Clinical Psychology*, 1969, *33*, 590–596.

DORPAT, T. L., & RIPLEY, H. S. The relationship between attempted suicide and committed suicide. *Comprehensive Psychiatry*, 1967, *8*, 74–79.

FARBEROW, N. L., & SHNEIDMAN, E. S. (Eds.) *The cry for help*. New York: McGraw-Hill, 1961.

GARBER, B., & POLSKY, R. Follow-up of hospitalized adolescents: A preliminary report. *Archives of General Psychiatry*, 1970, *22*, 179–187.

GLESER, K. Suicidal children: Management. *American Journal of Psychotherapy*, 1971, *25*, 27–36.

HAIDER, I. Suicidal attempts in children and adolescents. *British Journal of Psychiatry*, 1968, *114*, 1113–1134.

HENDIN, H. Growing up dead: Student suicide. *American Journal of Psychotherapy*, 1975, *29*, 327–338.

HOLINGER, P. C. Violent deaths among the young: Recent trends in suicide, homicide, and accidents. *American Journal of Psychiatry*, 1979, *136*, 1144–1147.

JACOBINZER, J. Attempted suicides in adolescence. *Journal of the American Medical Association*, 1965, *191*, 7–11.

JACOBS, J., & TEICHER, J. D. Broken homes and social isolation in attempted suicides of adolescents. *International Journal of Social Psychiatry*, 1967, *13*, 139–149.

KOVACS, M., BECK, A. T., & WEISSMAN, A. The use of suicidal motives in the psychotherapy of attempted suicides. *American Journal of Psychotherapy*, 1975, *29*, 363–368.

KRAFT, D. P., & BABIGIAN, H. M. Suicide by persons with and without psychiatric contacts. *Archives of General Psychiatry*, 1976, *33*, 209–215.

LESTER, D. Sex differences in suicidal behavior. In E. S. Gomberg & V. Franks (Eds.), *Gender and Disordered Behavior*. New York: Brunner/Mazel, 1979.

LEVENSON, M., & NEURINGER, C. Problem-solving behavior in suicidal adolescents. *Journal of Consulting and Clinical Psychology*, 1971, *37*, 433–436.

MCANARNEY, E. R. Suicidal behavior of children and youth. *Pediatric Clinics of North America*, 1975, *22*, 595–604.

MISHARA, B. L. The extent of adolescent suicidality. *Psychiatric Opinion,* 1975, *12,* 32–37.

OTTO, U. Changes in the behavior of children and adolescents preceding suicidal attempts. *Acta Psychiatrica Scandinavia,* 1964, *40,* 386–400.

PETZEL, S. B., & CLINE, D. W. Adolescent suicide: Epidemiological and biological aspects. In S. C. Feinstein & P. L. Giovacchini (Eds.), *Adolescent Psychiatry.* Vol. VI. Chicago: University of Chicago Press, 1978.

SCHNEER, H. I., KAY, P., & BROZOVSKY, M. Events and conscious ideation leading to suicidal behavior in adolescents. *Psychiatric Quarterly,* 1961, *35,* 507–515.

SEIDEN, R. H. *Suicide among youth.* Washington D.C.: U.S. Department of Health, Education, and Welfare, Public Health Service Publication No. 1971, 1969.

SHAFFER, D. Suicide in childhood and early adolescence. *Journal of Child Psychology and Psychiatry,* 1974, *15,* 275–291.

SHNEIDMAN, E. S. Suicide. In A. M. Freedman, H. I. Kaplan, & B. J. Sadock (eds.), *Comprehensive Textbook of Psychiatry.* (2nd ed.) Baltimore: Williams & Wilkins, 1975.

SHNEIDMAN, E. S., & FARBEROW, N. L. (Eds.) *Clues to suicide.* New York: McGraw-Hill, 1957.

STANLEY, E. J., & BARTER, J. T. Adolescent suicidal behavior. *American Journal of Orthopsychiatry,* 1970, *40,* 87–96.

STENGEL, E. *Suicide and attempted suicide.* Baltimore: Penguin, 1964.

TEICHER, J. D. A solution to the chronic problem of living: Adolescent attempted suicide. In J. C. Schoolar (Ed.), *Current Issues in Adolescent Psychiatry.* New York: Brunner/Mazel, 1973.

TEICHER, J. D. Suicide and suicide attempts. In J. D. Noshpitz (Ed.), *Basic Handbook of Child Psychiatry.* Vol. 2. New York: Basic Books, 1979.

TEICHER, J. D., & JACOBS, J. Adolescents who attempt suicide: Preliminary findings. *American Journal of Psychiatry,* 1966, *122,* 1248–1257.

TOOLAN, J. M. Suicide in children and adolescents. *American Journal of Psychotherapy,* 1975, *29,* 339–344.

TOOLAN, J. M. Therapy of depressed and suicidal children. *American Journal of Psychotherapy,* 1978, *32,* 243–251.

TUCKMAN, J., & CONNON, H. E. Attempted suicide in adolescents. *American Journal of Psychiatry,* 1962, *119,* 228–232.

VITAL STATISTICS OF THE UNITED STATES, 1960–1973. Rockville, Md.: U.S. Department of Health, Education, and Welfare, 1963–1976.

VITAL STATISTICS OF THE UNITED STATES, 1975. Vol. II. Mortality. (Part A) Hyattsville, Md.: National Center for Health Statistics, 1979a.

VITAL STATISTICS OF THE UNITED STATES, 1976. Vol. II. Mortality. (Part B) Hyattsville, Md.: National Center for Health Statistics, 1979b.

VITAL STATISTICS REPORT. *Final Mortality Statistics,* 1979. Washington, D.C.: U.S. Department of Health, Education, and Welfare, Public Health Service Publication No. 79–1120, 1979.

WEISSMAN, M. M. The epidemiology of suicide attempts, 1960–1971. *Archives of General Psychiatry,* 1974, *30,* 737–746.

YUSIN, A. S. Attempted suicide in an adolescent: The resolution of an anxiety state. *Adolescence,* 1973, *8,* 17–28.

13

ALCOHOL AND DRUG ABUSE

The decade from 1965 to 1975 was a period of markedly increasing drug use by adolescents in the United States. This increase is usually attributed to illegal drugs becoming more available and more widely publicized during the late 1960s than before. The emergence of drug trafficking as a profitable criminal activity played a large part in these developments, as did the "hippie" movement with its theme song of "Turn on, tune in, drop out." Timothy Leary, the self-proclaimed high priest of the hippie drug culture, gained great notoriety with predictions that being high on drugs would soon become an American way of life (Leary, 1968; Roszak, 1968, Chapter 5). Although this prophecy proved false, research findings clearly document increased use of illegal drugs among high school and college students during the 10 years preceding 1975 (Kopplin, Greenfield, & Wong, 1977; McGlothlin, 1975; National Commission on Marijuana and Drug Abuse, 1973).

High school students also showed a steady increase in alcohol use during this period (Harford, 1975; Lee, 1978). Interestingly, however, drinking on college campuses during the mid-1970s remained the same as it had been over the previous 25 years; neither the percent of college students who drink nor the proportion having problems associated with heavy drinking changed appreciably from 1950 to 1975 (Engs, 1977; Hanson, 1977). This suggests that youthful drinkers, while not increasing in number, were beginning their drinking at an earlier age than before.

The fact that drinking has not increased among college students in the last generation is mentioned in introducing this chapter because it differs from a widely held belief that drinking is a more serious campus problem than it used to be. Many such common misconceptions of alcohol and drug use among young people have resulted from two sources: (a) selective attention to data from samples that are not representative of the adolescent population at large, and (b) overly dramatized calls for action to combat drug-related problems. In the early 1970s, for example, the professional literature included statements that "drug use has become an integral part of current youth culture" (Proskauer & Rolland, 1973, p. 32) and that "the overwhelming majority of high school students use marijuana" (Millman & Khuri, 1973, p. 143), and the *New York Times* reported that on the college campus "marijuana is the common denominator among all groups" (Darnton, 1971)—none of which is or ever was true.

These are just a few of a great many assertions that could be quoted to demonstrate that mythology abounds in what has been written about youthful alcohol and drug use. Yet it must also be recognized that this is a difficult topic to study. Patterns of drug use change rapidly and vary considerably with individual circumstances. There is great temptation to gloss over such complexities, in a well-meaning effort to say something definitive and help close the large gaps in knowledge in this area.

As a case in point, statements about youthful alcohol and drug use often refer in broad terms to some "percent of adolescents" who "use drugs." Such statements have limited value and rarely merit serious consideration. Adolescents of different ages differ substantially in their patterns of alcohol and drug use; the frequency of and reasons for drug-taking vary widely among individuals and have different psychological implications; and most features of drug use differ for different kinds of drugs. To be meaningful, then, statements about youthful drug use need to specify the age of the people who are using a particular kind of drug with a certain frequency for a particular purpose at a given point in time. This chapter will elaborate the importance of these distinctions and conclude with a discussion of treatment and prevention of drug abuse.

EPIDEMIOLOGY OF YOUTHFUL ALCOHOL AND DRUG USE

Literally hundreds of surveys on youthful alcohol and drug use have been conducted since 1965. Many of these studies are difficult to compare with each other because they were conducted at different times and asked different questions (for example, "Have you *ever used* marijuana?" versus "Do you *use* marijuana?"). On the other hand, analyses of self-report questionnaires on drug use indicate that they can and do provide valid information, especially in large-scale surveys (Petzel, Johnson, & McKillip, 1973; Single, Kandel, & Johnson, 1975; Smart, 1965). The following discussion draws primarily on surveys of junior and senior high school students that (a) are relatively recent, (b) report answers to similar kinds of questions, and (c) include a sufficiently broad and representative subject sample to paint an accurate picture of adolescent involvement with drugs.

Table 13.1 indicates the percent of 12- to 17-year-olds in the United States who report ever having used alcohol, marijuana, stimulants, sedatives, hallucinogens, cocaine, and heroin. The data on alcohol come from young people sampled in working-class, middle-class, and upper-middle-class communities, and the data on the other drugs represent statewide and national samples. The figures exclude medically prescribed use of these substances.

These data indicate that alcohol is by far the most commonly used drug among young people, followed by marijuana and then, at much smaller frequencies, by stimulants, hallucinogens, cocaine, sedatives, and heroin. They show further that, with the

TABLE 13.1 12- to 17-Year-Olds Reporting Ever Having Used Various Drugs

Drug	Percent
Alcohol	66.8–87.2
Marijuana	28.2–31.8
Stimulants	5.2–8.7
Hallucinogens	4.6–6.0
Cocaine	4.0
Sedatives	3.1–5.6
Heroin	1.1

Source. Based on data reported by Abelson, Fishburne, and Cisin (1978) (nationwide sample of 1272); and by Levine and Kozak (1979) and Wechsler & McFadden (1976) (community samples of 2322).

Figure 13.1
Percent of adolescents and adults never having used various drugs.
(Based on data reported by Adelson et al. (1978).)

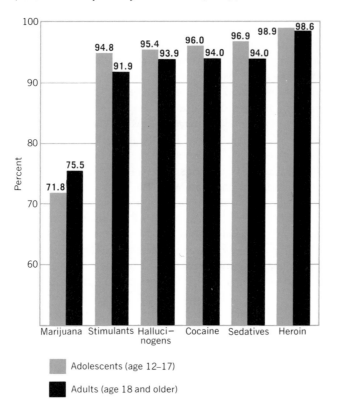

exception of alcohol, the prevailing pattern among adolescents is nonuse of drugs. Figure 13.1 compares the percent of young people who report never having used various drugs with reports from the adult (over 18) population. The two age groups show the same ordering of use among the various drugs; adults are somewhat more likely than adolescents to have had no experience with marijuana, however, and somewhat less likely to have avoided use of the other drugs.

However interesting and reliable these data may be, they represent only the beginning in grasping the complex epidemiology of youthful alcohol and drug use. There are significant age differences within the adolescent population and notable variations in how often drugs are used, as already mentioned, and there are also some apparent sex differences, trends over time, and stages of drug use that need to be identified.

Age Differences

All studies comparing younger and older adolescents have found that the frequency of ever having used drugs increases with age. Figure 13.2 shows such comparisons among

Figure 13.2

Age differences in the percent of adolescents ever having used various drugs. (Based on data reported by Carman (1977); Gould, Berberian, Kasl, Thompson, & Kleber (1977); Johnston, Bachman, & O'Malley (1978); Levine & Kozak (1979); Lipton (1977); and Wechsler & McFadden (1978).)

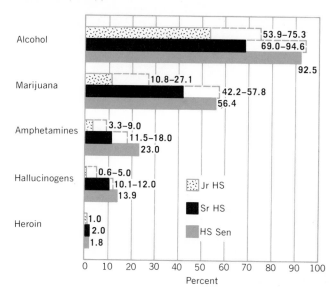

junior high school students (grades 7 to 8), senior high school students (grades 9 to 12), and high school seniors for five drugs. Although the studies on which this figure is based differ in the frequencies they report for some categories, the overall picture of a progression with age emerges clearly.

These marked age differences indicate how misleading it can be to refer to the frequency of "adolescent" drug use without making some distinction between younger and older teenagers. On closer inspection, moreover, even data on how many adolescents of different ages have ever used certain drugs are not particularly meaningful. With increasing age of the sample, the percentage who have "ever used" a drug can only go up, as additional people try it; previous users remain counted, even if they no longer use the drug. Thus the "ever used" statistic says nothing about the prevalence of *current* use. Furthermore, because it assigns the same weight to occasional use as it does to regular use of a drug, the "ever used" statistic gives no information on how often particular drugs are being taken by individual users.

Nevertheless, the number of people who have ever used various drugs does provide a barometer of drug familiarity in a given population at a particular time, and it is the statistic most often cited in the drug literature. Because its cumulative nature makes it the largest statistic on drug use, the "ever used" figure is especially likely to be chosen in efforts to dramatize drug-related problems. Regrettably, the "ever used" figure is sometimes even presented or interpreted as if it were an indication of how many people are currently using drugs. To the contrary, the data presented in the next paragraphs

Figure 13.3

High school students reporting various frequencies of drug use. (Based on data reported by Gelineau, Johnson, and Pearsall (1973); Gould, et al. (1977); and Levine and Kozak (1979).)

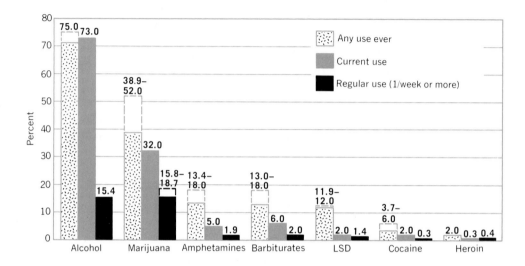

indicate a wide difference between the percent of young people who have ever used a drug and the percent who are currently using it.

Differences in Frequency

The majority of adolescents who report having tried drugs other than alcohol say they did so only a few times and are no longer using them (Forslund, 1977–1978; Konopka, 1976; Myers, 1977). More specifically, Figure 13.3 shows the ranges found in several studies of the frequencies of any use, current occasional use, and current regular use (once weekly or more) for several drugs. As was true for Figure 13.2, the ranges in some categories reflect how difficult it is to be precise about indices of youthful drug use. Despite such variations—which result from differences in when, where, and how the data were collected—Figure 13.3 leaves little doubt that the percentage of young people who have ever used drugs far exceeds the percentage who become regular users. The number of high school students who use these drugs regularly is fewer than 20 percent of those who have tried them for every drug except marijuana, for which it is about 35 percent.

Sex Differences

The important distinction between any use and regular use of a drug has particular significance for what is known about differences between adolescent boys and girls. In the case of alcohol, boys had been found for many years to be much more likely to drink than girls. This margin began decreasing in the 1960s, however, and by the mid-1970s most investigators were finding little or no difference in the percent of both junior and senior high school boys and girls who reported having drunk alcohol. On the other hand, boys remain more likely than girls to be regular drinkers, and they are substantially more inclined to drink heavily and to become intoxicated (Harford, 1975; Harford & Mills, 1978; Lee, 1978; Levine & Kozak, 1979; Wechsler & McFadden, 1977–1978).

Use of other drugs follows this same pattern. The percentage of adolescents who have ever used them is just about the same among boys and girls, except for slight tendencies for boys to be more likely to have used marijuana and for girls to be more likely to have used stimulants and sedatives. For all illegal drugs, however, boys are more likely than girls to become frequent or heavy users (Abelson et al., 1978; Krug & Henry, 1974; Levine & Kozak, 1979; Rosenberg, Kasl, & Berberian, 1974; Wechsler & McFadden, 1976).

Trends over Time

As noted in the introduction to this chapter, young people apparently began drinking at an earlier age during the 1960s and early 1970s. The percent of college students who had ever used alcohol remained the same as in the past during this period, whereas the percent of high school students who have drunk increased steadily. During the late 1970s this trend seemed to be leveling off. In annual nationwide surveys involving many thousands of high school seniors, Johnston, Bachman, and O'Malley (1978) found that the percent who reported any previous use of alcohol was 90.4 in 1975, 91.9 in 1976, and 92.5 in 1977.

Likewise, in contrast to the large increase in adolescent use of illegal drugs from 1965 to 1975, the later 1970s generally showed a leveling off or decline in frequency of any use. Figure 13.4, based on national samples of approximately 1000 12- to 17-year-olds for each year, shows increased experience from 1972 to 1974 for each of the drugs included. Thereafter, in 1976 and 1977, the frequency for any use of hallucinogens, stimulants, sedatives, and heroin decreases or remains essentially the same. There is a slight increase in experience with cocaine from 1976 to 1977, and a marked increase in any use of marijuana during this year.

Stages in Drug Use

Youthful drug use has been found to progress through a sequence of stages. Kandel (1975) identifies four such stages: (a) beer and wine; (b) hard liquor and cigarettes; (c) marijuana, which is often referred to as a "mild" or "soft" drug; and (d) other illegal drugs, frequently referred to a "strong" or "hard" drugs. Her findings and those of numerous other investigators indicate that, with very few exceptions, only young people who have used drugs at one stage become users at the next stage. Thus almost all adolescents who drink hard liquor have previously drunk beer or wine; almost all who smoke marijuana have previously drunk hard liquor; and almost all who become involved with stimulants, hallucinogens, or heroin have had prior experience with marijuana. Previous nonusers of drugs rarely try marijuana without having progressed through the stage of alcohol use, and drinkers rarely experiment with other illegal drugs without first having tried marijuana (Cockerman, 1977; Gould et al., 1977; Kandel & Faust, 1975; Robins & Wish, 1977; Whitehead & Cabral, 1975–76).

Figure 13.4

Trends over time in percent of adolescents ever having used various drugs. (Based on data reported by Abelson et al. (1978) on nationwide sample of 12- to 17-year-olds.)

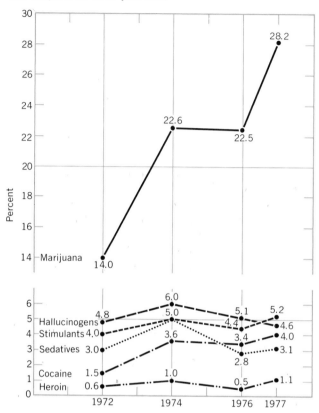

The fact that strong drug use evolves from mild drug use—which is known as the "stepping-stone hypothesis"—does not mean that one drug *necessarily* leads to another. Adolescents who drink are not inevitably on the road to marijuana, and those who use marijuana are not doomed to becoming hard drug users. As the data in Figure 13.2 suggest, most adolescent drinkers do not progress to marijuana and most marijuana users do not progress to hard drugs.

On the other hand, the existence of this progressive sequence does mean that the likelihood of using a substance at a particular stage is higher among young people who have used a substance at a previous stage than among those who have not. In a 5- to 6-month follow-up study of high school students, for example, Kandel and Faust (1975) found that 27 percent of those who smoked or drank subsequently used marijuana, whereas only 2 percent of those who neither smoked nor drank did so. Similarly, 26 percent of the marijuana users had gone on to try LSD, amphetamines, or heroin, but only 1 percent of those who had never used marijuana did so.

The reasons why some youngsters progress from alcohol to marijuana to harder drugs while others do not are complex. In part they involve social and psychological influences on various categories of drug use discussed in the next section. Additionally, research on the stepping-stone phenomenon indicates that whether young people progress from one stage to another is directly related to the intensity of their drug use. In one study, for example, marijuana use was found in 20 percent of light drinkers, 39 percent of moderate drinkers, and 88 percent of heavy drinkers (Kandel & Faust, 1975; Noble & Barnes, 1971; Wechsler, 1976).

CATEGORIES OF DRUG USE

Of many possible ways in which patterns of drug use can be categorized, one useful approach is to distinguish among *experimental, social, medicinal,* and *addictive* users. Young people who *experiment* with drugs try them once or perhaps a few times out of curiosity or to have a new experience and then stop using them. Curiosity is the reason most frequently given by adolescents for why they first become interested in drugs, and for those who never go beyond this experimental use drug involvement cannot be said to constitute any kind of personal or psychological problem (Frenkel, Robinson, & Fiman, 1974; Proskauer & Rolland, 1973).

Social users take drugs as a way of participating in a pleasurable group activity with their peers. Although adolescents may in some cases get together primarily to share a drug experience, social drug use is largely limited to parties, dances, and other special occasions. Like experimental drug use, then, social use tends to involve only occasional or infrequent drug involvement (Forslund, 1978; Levine & Kozak, 1979).

Medicinal drug use is the taking of a drug to relieve anxiety or tension or to enjoy a drug experience for its own sake. Because of the purposes it serves, medicinal drug use is much more likely than social drug use to become a regular or customary way of dealing with or escaping from life problems. In further contrast to social use, medicinal drug use is primarily an individual experience; although two or more people may take drugs together for medicinal purposes, they are likely in doing so to focus more on their own experiences than on any personal interaction. Approximately 15 percent of adolescents who have had any drug experience report that they became interested in drugs as a way to "relieve pressures" and that they typically use drugs alone rather than in the company of other people (Blumenfield, Riester, Serrano, & Adams, 1972; Forslund, 1977–1978; Frenkel et al., 1974).

Addictive drug use, which is also an individual experience, consists of habituation to one or more drugs. Any drug can become habit-forming, if a person comes to depend on its effects to feel good either physically or psychologically. The defining characteristic of addictive drug users is that they suffer real physical or psychological distress (**withdrawal symptoms**) when they are deprived of drugs. As a result, addictive drug users are the most likely of these four types to use drugs regularly and frequently (Millman, 1978; Nystrom, Bal, & Labrecque, 1979).

The differences between these four categories of drug use help to identify an important distinction between drug *use* and drug *abuse*. From a psychological point of view, using a drug is not necessarily an abuse; people can take small amounts of mild drugs

More than 90% of adolescents drink on at least one occasion by the time they finish high school. Personal decisions about how one is to deal with alcohol are thus an important part of growing up.

(alcohol or marijuana) occasionally without doing themselves any harm. Legal and moral issues aside, then, it is the heavy use of drugs and the taking of strong drugs (which almost always implies heavy use of milder drugs) that are most likely to *abuse* a person's physical and psychosocial functioning. Experimental and social drug use seldom results in such abuse, whereas medicinal use may have this result, and addiction to a drug always constitutes drug abuse.

Despite the increase in adolescent alcohol and drug use noted earlier, there appears to be relatively little drug *abuse* among young people. Figure 13.3 indicates clearly that the vast majority of adolescents who have tried drugs are experimental or social users; only a very small minority show the pattern of current, regular drug-taking that characterizes medicinal or addictive use. This distinction has very definite implications for psychopathology. Most investigators have found substantial evidence of psychopathology in drug abusers, whereas drug users—the experimental and social types—are much more like their normal, nondrug-using peers (Amini, Salasnek, & Burke, 1976; Wieder & Kaplan, 1969).

Generally speaking, the heavier the use of alcohol and other drugs by young people the more likely they are to do poorly in school, withdraw from peer-group activities, engage in delinquent behavior, feel personally disaffected, and have a variety of other adjustment difficulties (Albas, Albas, & McCluskey, 1978; Holroyd & Kahn, 1974; Millman & Su, 1973; Stein, Soskin, & Korchin, 1975; Wechsler & Thum, 1973). Whether heavy drug use is a cause or a result of such psychosocial difficulties is difficult to determine from available research. There is little doubt, however, that heavy drug use and problems in living go hand in hand.

FACTORS ASSOCIATED WITH DRUG USE

Independently of whether adolescents are psychologically disturbed, certain personal, social, and familial factors are associated with how frequently they use drugs and with the likelihood of their beginning to use them in the first place. These experiential factors exert different kinds of influences at the different stages of drug use described earlier. For those who become addicted to drugs, genetic factors may also contribute to their drug abuse pattern.

Personal, Social, and Familial Factors

With respect to personal characteristics, the inclination to use drugs is directly related to a high degree of openness to experience, tolerance of deviance, and interest in independence, on the one hand, and a low degree of conformity, social inhibition, interest in achievement, and involvement with religion, on the other hand. Conversely, cautious, dependent, conforming, socially inhibited, achievement-oriented, and religious youngsters are relatively unlikely to try drugs or to use them with any frequency (Brook, Lukoff, & Whiteman, 1977, 1978; Burkett, 1977; Krug & Henry, 1974; Jessor, 1976, Jessor & Jessor, 1977; Victor, Grossman, & Eisenman, 1973).

Socially, the disposition to use drugs is influenced by the nature of adolescents' peer relationships. The more their friends use drugs, the more closely they interact with these friends, and the more they value these friends' affection and approval, the more likely adolescents are to become involved with drugs (Brook et al., 1977; Gorsuch & Butler, 1976; Huba, Wingard, & Bentler, 1979; McKillip, Johnson, & Petzel, 1973; Spevack & Pihl, 1976).

As for familial factors, drug use of all kinds by young people is directly related to how often their parents use—or are perceived to use—alcohol, tobacco, stimulants, and sedatives. Parents who rarely take drugs themselves seldom have children who do so (Brook et al., 1977; Gorsuch & Butler, 1976; Huba et al., 1979; Smart & Fejer, 1972; Spevack & Pihl, 1976; Tolone & Dermott, 1975). Adolescents who use drugs heavily also tend to have permissive or rejecting parents and a generally negative climate at home. Hence drug-using parents may have drug-using offspring because of the example they set and also because they are neglectful parents whose failure to provide adequate control and support fosters many kinds of problem behavior in their children, including drug abuse (Jessor, 1976; Krug & Henry, 1974; Prendergast & Schaefer, 1974; Streit & Oliver, 1972; Tec, 1974).

Brook and her colleagues (Brook et al., 1977, 1978) found further that these personality, peer, and parental influences on adolescent drug use operate independently of each other. As is the case whenever several different factors interact to shape some outcome, this finding has two important implications. First, the maximum likelihood of trying drugs or using them heavily arises when all three kinds of influence—personality, peer, and parental—coexist to a large extent. Second, a particularly strong influence of one kind or another may be sufficient to foster drug use even when the other influences are minimal. Thus, for example, a strong drug "tradition" and a negative climate in the family can lead to drug use in youngsters who are not all that personally oriented toward drugs and are not experiencing much social influence in this direction; similarly, a personal attraction to drugs and strong peer pressure can result in drug use even when parents are neither modeling drug use nor neglecting their parental responsibilities.

Stage-Related Influences on Drug Use

Studies by Kandel and her colleagues have revealed that the relative importance of personality, peer, and parental influences on drug behavior differs for the three stages of hard liquor, marijuana, and hard drug use (Kandel, Kessler, & Margulies, 1978; Kandel, Treiman, Faust & Single, 1976). Starting to use hard liquor is determined primarily by parental and peer influences and not very much by personality characteristics. Parental and peer influences for this stage of drug use carry about equal weight and are exerted in a similar way, through modeling effects. More than anything else, then, adolescents who start to drink hard liquor are imitating the behavior of important people in their lives. Neither the quality of the parent-child relationship nor the parents' attitudes and values seem to have much influence at this stage.

Starting to use marijuana is more likely than the initiation into drinking to involve some of the personality factors associated with drug use. These include relatively liberal, nonconforming attitudes as well as views that marijuana is a nonharmful substance that should be legalized. Young people who begin using marijuana are also likely to have been drinkers and to show some of the problem behaviors associated with drug use, such as minor delinquencies and relatively poor school performance. They are not especially likely to have serious psychological problems, however.

The initiation to marijuana use differs further from beginning to use alcohol in being much more influenced by peers than by parents. Drug use by their friends is in fact a more important influence on using marijuana than it is on using either alcohol or harder drugs. When parental influence does occur, moreover, it is not a modeling effect but a function of the parents' attitudes. The more strongly parents discourage marijuana use, the less likely their children are to try it; the more permissive they are in this regard, the more likely their children are to start using it.

Finally, beginning to use harder drugs is the stage most likely to involve serious personality problems. Hard drug users will have a previous history of heavy or at least regular marijuana use, and they are especially likely to feel depressed and alienated and to be dealing unsuccessfully with a variety of life situations. Very often the best friends of hard drug users will be habitual users. However, because adolescents who start to use hard drugs tend to be withdrawn or cut off from peer group activities and well beyond the use of drugs for social purposes, peer-group influence in the general sense does not play a particularly important role in becoming involved with hard drugs.

Parental influences, on the other hand, assume a major role at this stage. Although the attitudes that parents hold toward hard drugs do not make much difference in whether their offspring use them, both the models they set and the quality of family life they provide do. Parental use of hard liquor, stimulants, and sedatives is an important predictor of adolescent initiation into drugs other than marijuana. In addition, parental neglect and lack of close family relationships exert a strong influence on movement to this stage of drug use.

This analysis confirms the complexities noted earlier of making any broad statements on aspects of youthful alcohol and drug use. It also helps contribute to predicting whether an adolescent who has begun to drink hard liquor will progress to other stages of drug use. In addition to the intensity of drug use at a particular stage determining whether the following stage will ensue, movement from hard liquor to marijuana will depend on the extent of certain kinds of peer influences, and movement from marijuana to harder drugs will depend on the extent of personal psychological problems and disturbed parent-child relationships.

Genetic Factors in Addiction

In addition to the influence of personal, social, and familial experiences on the inclination to alcohol and drug use, there is emerging evidence that genetic factors contribute to the disposition to become an addictive drug user. Alcoholism in particular has been found to run strongly in families, and, as in the case of demonstrable genetic influences on conditions discussed in previous chapters, studies of twins and adoptees identify family patterns that cannot be accounted for in terms of shared experience or parental modeling.

Specifically, among adults who have been placed for adoption very early in life, alcoholism is much more frequent in those whose biological parents abuse alcohol than in those who do not have a history of heavy drinking in their biological relatives (Bohman, 1978; Cadoret & Gath, 1978; Cloninger, Christiansen, Reich & Gottesman, 1978; Goodwin, 1979). Since heavy drinking increases the likelihood that alcohol users will progress to stages of marijuana and hard drug use, any genetic influences on becoming addicted to alcohol could also play a role in how frequently or heavily young people are likely to use these other drugs as well.

TREATMENT AND PREVENTION OF DRUG ABUSE

Treatment is seldom necessary for young people who are experimental or social drug users. They either stop taking drugs of their own accord or use them infrequently in ways that do not interfere with their psychosocial functioning. Medicinal and addictive use of drugs, on the other hand, typically prevents people from realizing their personal capacities and therefore calls for professional intervention. Such intervention includes both treatment programs for young people with established drug habits and programs of drug education intended to prevent drug abuse from occurring.

Treatment

Appropriate treatment of drug-abusing adolescents encompasses the personal, social, and familial factors known to be associated with taking drugs. With respect to personal factors, various forms of individual psychotherapy are employed to help these young people resolve the psychological concerns that are contributing to their needs to use drugs heavily. Medicinal users, who are seeking to escape feelings of anxiety or depression, usually respond well to treatment aimed at easing their tensions and finding more effective means of coping with difficult life situations. As in the case of other behavior problems that are secondary to some psychological disorder, adequate treatment of the underlying concerns eliminates or reduces the problem behavior by modifying its basic cause.

By contrast, addictive drug use, whatever its original sources, has usually become a primary disorder in its own right. Like characterological delinquency, it is less a reaction to current specific circumstances than a chronic way of life. Drug-addicted youngsters therefore present the same kinds of obstacles to effective psychotherapy as characterological delinquents (see Chapter 11). They have difficulty admitting to any psychological problems, they deny needing help, and they resist close or trusting relationships with a therapist. Office visits, no matter how frequent, can rarely influence them to change what has become a deeply ingrained life-style.

For these reasons, most authorities believe that addictive drug use can be successfully treated only in a residential setting that provides a total therapeutic community over an extended period of time. The main strategy in such treatment programs consists of attracting these young people to sources of satisfaction and means of self-control other than drug use, so that they opt for some life-style that is not drug-dependent (Amini & Salasnek, 1975; Hochhauser, 1978a; Proskauer & Rolland, 1973).

In the social sphere, good treatment programs for drug-abusing youth are tailored not only to their individual psychopathology but also the interpersonal context of their lives. To the extent that peer modeling, friendships based on shared drug involvement, or the lack of rewarding relationships with others are contributing to a drug problem, they become a central treatment focus. Well-designed efforts to eliminate or reduce drug problems may accordingly include group therapy or neighborhood counseling programs. The more that socially influenced drug abusers can be helped to form friendships with peers and adults from similar backgrounds who do not abuse drugs, the better their prospects are for identifying and choosing a nondrug alternative life-style (Bratter, 1973; Dembo & Burgos, 1976; Millman, 1978).

As for familial factors, the role that parents can play in the drug use of their children by the example they set cannot be overlooked. It has even been suggested that the best way to get adolescents to stop using drugs is to persuade the adult generation to do so (Smart & Fejer, 1972). In practical terms, however, a more important treatment target derives from the extent to which a negative family climate is contributing to youthful drug abuse. Therapists and drug counselors need to recognize when family problems exist and to focus their treatment efforts in such cases on the family group. Depending on the particular circumstances, the young person's motivation to abuse drugs may be reduced by success in improving the marital relationship between his or her parents, opening channels of parent-child communication, and modifying other aspects of the familial interaction that seem to play a role in the drug-abusing behavior (Millman, 1978; Tec, 1974).

Prevention through Drug Education

Because the chronic, characterological nature of addictive drug use makes it difficult to eliminate—even with a well-conceived and individually tailored combination of long-term personal, social, and family-oriented interventions—many people have concluded that the only really effective way of overcoming it is to prevent it from occurring in the first place. With this in mind, enormous resources have been poured into programs of drug education. The rationale for these programs is that adolescents who are informed about the hazards of using drugs will keep away from them.

Unfortunately, drug education programs, at least through the mid-1970s, have not proved very effective. Experience in a drug education program has not been found to deter adolescents from future drug use and/or to differentiate between users and non-users of drugs. Moreover, drug users consistently display more knowledge about drugs than nonusers, which has suggested to some writers that providing young people factual information not only fails to keep them away from drugs, but may even contribute to their becoming involved with drugs (Fejer & Smart, 1973; Frenkel et al., 1974; Halpin & Whiddon, 1977; Stock & Ruiz, 1977; Tolone & Dermott, 1975). An alternative to concluding that drug education programs do more harm than good is to seek ways of improving these programs. For example, there is reason to believe that drug education has frequently failed because it was begun too late. Basic factual information provided for high school students, at an age when drug use has already begun for most of those who will subsequently have drug-related problems, cannot be expected to pack much preventive wallop. Similarly, moralistic preaching or scare tactics aimed at youngsters of this age, when their value systems have already been largely shaped by family and peer influences, are likely to fall on deaf ears. In recent years schools have accordingly been urged to aim their drug education programs at junior high and even elementary school students, and many have started to do so. Future evaluation studies will indicate whether these programs for younger children will have more of an impact on subsequent drug use than previous efforts with adolescents (Burkett, 1977; Dembo & Burgos, 1976; Krug & Henry, 1974).

Question can also be raised about the qualifications and preparation of the teachers who have been assigned responsibility for drug education programs. Too often this task appears to have fallen to regular classroom or physical education teachers who have not had any special knowledge about drugs or about health education. Hochhauser (1978b, 1978c) has called attention to the need for college-level courses in substance abuse for educators who are to provide drug programs in the schools. Certainly the potential effectiveness of such programs cannot be determined independently of their being provided by adequately trained teachers.

SUMMARY

The use of alcohol and illegal drugs by young people increased markedly during the period from 1965 to 1975, but appeared to level off during the late 1970s. Patterns of alcohol and drug use are difficult to summarize, however, since they change rapidly and vary considerably with individual circumstances. To be fully meaningful, statements on this subject need to specify the age of the adolescents who are believed to be using a particular kind of drug with a certain frequency for a particular purpose at a given point in time.

Recent broad-scale surveys indicate that alcohol is by far the most commonly used drug among young people, followed in decreasing order of frequency by marijuana, stimulants, hallucinogens, cocaine, sedatives, and heroin. With the exception of alcohol, which approximately 90 percent of adolescents have tried by the time they graduate from high school the prevailing pattern among contemporary young people is nonuse of drugs. Over 70 percent of 12- to 17-year-olds have never tried marijuana and 95 percent or more have never used stimulants, hallucinogens, cocaine, sedatives, or heroin.

Use of all the above drugs increases with age, so that older adolescents are more likely than younger adolescents to have had experience with them. Of those adolescencets who report having tried drugs other than alcohol, however, the majority say they did so only a few times and are not currently using them. The number of high school students who use these drugs regularly (once weekly or more) is fewer than 20 percent of those who have tried them for every drug except marijuana, for which it is about 35 percent. Adolescent boys and girls are about equally likely to report alcohol use, but boys are more likely than girls to drink regularly or heavily. For other drugs the percent of adolescents who have ever used them is also just about the same for boys and girls, although boys are again more likely than girls to become frequent users.

Adolescent involvement with drugs progresses through a sequence of stages, from beer and wine to hard liquor to "soft" drugs (marijuana) to harder drugs (other illegal substances). With very few exceptions, only young people who have used drugs at one stage become users at the next stage. Although this "stepping-stone hypothesis" does not mean that drinking alcohol necessarily leads to use of marijuana, which in turn leads to hard drug use, the likelihood of using a substance at a particular stage is much higher among young people who have used a substance at a previous stage—especially when their use has been heavy—than among those who have not.

People who use drugs can be placed in four categories: *experimental* users, who try drugs a few times out of curiosity and then stop using them; *social* users, who take drugs as part of participating in pleasurable peer-group activities; *medicinal* users, who turn to drugs as a way of relieving anxiety or tension; and *addictive* users, who have become habituated to a drug and depend on its effects to feel good either physically or psychologically. The vast majority of adolescents who have had any drug experience are experimental or social users who take drugs infrequently. Legal and moral issues aside, their drug behavior cannot be said to constitute any kind of personal or psychological problem. Approximately 15 percent of adolescents who report drug experience are medicinal or addictive users whose regular or heavy use of drugs constitutes drug *abuse* and interferes with normal physical and psychosocial functioning.

Certain personal, social, and familial factors are associated with how frequently adolescents use drugs and with the likelihood of their beginning to use them in the first place. The inclination to drug use is directly related to a high degree of openness to new experience, tolerance of deviance, and interest in independence, on the one hand,

and a low degree of conformity, social inhibition, interest in achievement, and involvement with religion, on the other hand. The more adolescents' friends are using drugs and the more closely they interact with these friends, the more likely they are to become involved with drugs. The more often their parents use various drugs or provide a generally negative home atmosphere, the more likely young people are to try drugs or to use them heavily.

The maximum disposition to drug involvement occurs when all three of these influences are present. However, each one, if strong enough, can lead to drug use independently of the other two. Furthermore, the relative importance of personality, peer, and parental influences on drug behavior differs for the stages of liquor, marijuana, and hard drug use. Peer and parental modeling contribute equally to decisions to begin drinking; movement from hard liquor to marijuana depends primarily on the strength of certain kinds of peer influences; and progression from marijuana to harder drugs is especially likely to be a function of personal psychological problems and disturbed parent-child relationships.

Treatment is seldom necessary for young people who are experimental or social drug users, since their drug-taking is infrequent and rarely interferes with their psychosocial functioning. Medicinal and addictive use of drugs, on the other hand, because it prevents people from realizing their personal capacities, calls for interventions that address the personal, social, and familial circumstances involved in the disposition to drug use.

For medicinal users, psychotherapy aimed at easing their tensions or dealing effectively with difficult life situations has good prospects for modifying the drug behavior by reducing the primary problems that is causing it. Addictive drug use, by contrast, usually constitutes a primary disorder in its own right that has become a chronic way of life rather than a reaction to specific current circumstances. Hence, even with a well-conceived and individually tailored combination of personal, social, and family-oriented interventions, addictive drug use is difficult to eliminate. The best prospects for improvement involve long-term residential treatment programs in which addicted young people can be helped to find rewarding alternative life-styles that do not include habituation to drugs.

Because drug abuse is so difficult to eliminate once it is established, considerable effort has been devoted to efforts to prevent it from occurring through programs of drug education. So far such programs have not proved very effective; drug information provided to adolescents has had no impact on the extent or nature of their drug involvement. In recent years attention has turned toward directing such education at younger children, before they become exposed to drugs, and to training teachers specifically in how to provide such education. Future evaluation studies will be necessary to determine whether these newer approaches will be more effective than past efforts.

REFERENCES

ABELSON, H. I., FISHBURNE, P. M., & CISIN, I. *National survey on drug abuse, 1977.* Washington, D.C.: U.S. Government Printing Office, 1978.

ALBAS, D., ALBAS, C., & MC CLUSKEY, K. Anomie, social class and drinking behavior of high-school students. *Journal of Studies on Alcohol*, 1978, *39*, 910–913.

AMINI, F., & SALASNEK, S. Adolescent drug abuse: Search for a treatment model. *Comprehensive Psychiatry*, 1975, *16*, 379–389.

AMINI, F., SALASNEK, S., & BURKE, E. L. Adolescent drug abuse: Etiological and treatment considerations. *Adolescence*, 1976, *11*, 281–299.

BLUMENFIELD, M., RIESTER, A. E., SERRANO, A. C., & ADAMS, R. L. Marijuana use in high school students. *Diseases of the Nervous System*, 1972, *33*, 603–610.

BOHMAN, M. Some genetic aspects of alcoholism and criminality. *Archives of General Psychiatry*, 1978, *35*, 269–276.

BRATTER, T. E. Treating alienated, unmotivated, drug abusing adolescents. *American Journal of Psychotherapy*, 1973, *27*, 583–598.

BROOK, J. S., LUKOFF, I. F., & WHITEMAN, M. Peer, family, and personality domains as related to adolescents' drug behavior. *Psychological Reports*, 1977, *41*, 1095–1102.

BROOK, J. S., LUKOFF, I. F., & WHITEMAN, M. Family socialization and adolescent personality and their association with adolescent use of marijuana. *Journal of Genetic Psychology*, 1978, *133*, 261–271.

BURKETT, S. R. Religion, parental influence, and adolescent alcohol and marijuana use. *Journal of Drug Issues*, 1977, *7*, 263–273.

CADORET, R. J., and GATH, A. Inheritance of alcoholism in adoptees. *British Journal of Psychiatry*, 1978, *132*, 252–258.

CARMAN, R. S. Internal-external control and drug use among junior high school students in a rural community. *International Journal of the Addictions*, 1977, *12*, 53–64.

CLONINGER, C. R., CHRISTIANSEN, K. O., REICH, T., & GOTTESMAN, I. I. Implications of sex differences in the prevalences of antisocial personality, alcoholism, and criminality for familial transmission. *Archives of General Psychiatry*, 1978, *35*, 941–951.

COCKERHAM, W. C. Patterns of alcohol and multiple drug use among rural white and American Indian adolescents. *International Journal of the Addictions*, 1977, *12*, 271–285.

DARNTON, J. Many on campus shifting to softer drugs and alcohol. *New York Times*, Jan. 17, 1971.

DEMBO, R., & BURGOS, W. A framework for developing drug abuse prevention strategies for young people in ghetto areas. *Journal of Drug Education*, 1976, *6*, 313–325.

ENGS, R. C. Drinking patterns and drinking problems of college students. *Journal of Studies on Alcohol*, 1977, *38*, 2144–2156.

FEJER, D., & SMART, R. G. The knowledge about drugs, attitudes toward them and drug use rates of high school students. *Journal of Drug Education*, 1973, *3*, 377–388.

FORSLUND, M. A. Drug use and delinquent behavior of small town and rural youth. *Journal of Drug Education*, 1977–1978, *7*, 219–224.

FORSLUND, M. A. Functions of drinking for native American and white youth. *Journal of Youth and Adolescence*, 1978, *7*, 327–332.

FRENKEL, S. I., ROBINSON, J. A., & FIMAN, B. G. Drug use: Demography and attitudes in a junior and senior high school population. *Journal of Drug Education*, 1974, *4*, 179–186.

GELINEAU, V. A., JOHNSON, M., & PEARSALL, D. A survey of adolescent drug use patterns. *Massachusetts Journal of Mental Health*, 1973, *3*, 30–40.

GOODWIN, D. W. Alcoholism and heredity: a review and hypothesis. *Archives of General Psychiatry*, 1979, *36*, 57–61.

GORSUCH, R. L., & BUTLER, M. C. Initial drug abuse: A review of predisposing social psychological factors. *Psychological Bulletin*, 1976, *83*, 120–137.

GOULD, L. C., BERBERIAN, R. M., KASL, S. V., THOMPSON, W. D., & KLEBER, H. D. Sequential patterns of multiple-drug use among high school students. *Archives of General Psychiatry,* 1977, *34,* 216–222.

HALPIN, G., & WHIDDON, T. Drug education: Solutions or problem. *Psychological Reports,* 1977, *40,* 372–374.

HARFORD, T. C. Patterns of alcohol use among adolescents. *Psychiatric Opinion,* 1975, *12,* 17–21.

HARFORD, T. C., & MILLS, G. S. Age-related trends in alcohol consumption. *Journal of Studies on Alcohol,* 1978, *39,* 207–210.

HANSON, D. J. Trends in drinking attitudes and behaviors among college students. *Journal of Alcohol and Drug Education,* 1977, *22,* 17–22.

HOCHHAUSER, M. Drugs as agents of control. *Journal of Psychedelic Drugs,* 1978a, *10,* 65–69.

HOCHHAUSER, M. Educational implication of drug abuse. *Journal of Drug Education,* 1978b, *8,* 69–76.

HOCHHAUSER, M. Drug education: For whom? *Journal of Alcoholism and Drug Education,* 1978c, *23,* 24–33.

HOLROYD, K., & KAHN, M. Personality factors in student drug use. *Journal of Consulting and Clinical Psychology,* 1974, *42,* 236–243.

HUBA, G. J., WINGARD, J. A., & BENTLER, P. M. Beginning adolescent drug use and peer and adult interaction patterns. *Journal of Consulting and Clinical Psychology,* 1979, *47,* 265–276.

JESSOR, R. Predicting time of onset of marijuana use: A developmental study of high school youth. *Journal of Consulting and Clinical Psychology,* 1976, *44,* 125–134.

JESSOR, R., & JESSOR, S. L. *Problem behavior and psychosocial development: A longitudinal study of youth.* New York: Academic, 1977.

JOHNSTON, L. D., BACHMAN, J. G., & O'MALLEY, P. M. *Drug use among American high school students, 1975–1977.* Washington, D.C.: U.S. Government Printing Office, 1978.

KANDEL, D. Stages in adolescent involvement in drug use. *Science,* 1975, *190,* 912–914.

KANDEL, D., & FAUST, R. Sequence and stages in patterns of adolescent drug use. *Archives of General Psychiatry,* 1975, *32,* 923–932.

KANDEL, D. B., KESSLER, R. C., & MARGULIES, R. Z. Antecedents of adolescent initiation into stages of drug use: A developmental analysis. *Journal of Youth and Adolescence,* 1978, *7,* 13–40.

KANDEL, D. B., TREIMAN, D., FAUST, R., & SINGLE, E. Adolescent involvement in legal and illegal drug use: A multiple classification analysis. *Social Forces,* 1976, *55,* 438–458.

KONOPKA, G. *Young girls: A portrait of adolescence.* Englewood Cliffs, N.J.: Prentice-Hall, 1976.

KOPPLIN, D. A., GREENFIELD, T. K., & WONG, H. Z. Changes in patterns of substance use on campus: A four-year follow-up study. *International Journal of the Addictions,* 1977, *12,* 73–94.

KRUG, S. E., & HENRY, T. J. Personality, motivation, and adolescent drug use patterns. *Journal of Counseling Psychology,* 1974, *21,* 440–445.

LEARY, T. *High priest.* New York: World, 1968.

LEE, E. E. Female adolescent drinking behavior: Potential hazards. *Journal of School Health,* 1978, *48,* 151–156.

LEVINE, E. M., & KOZAK, C. Drug and alcohol use, delinquency, and vandalism among upper middle class pre- and post-adolescents. *Journal of Youth and Adolescence,* 1979, *8,* 91–101.

LIPTON, D. S. A survey of substance use among junior and senior high school students in New York State. *American Journal of Drug and Alcohol Abuse,* 1977, *4,* 153–164.

MCGLOTHLIN, W. H. Drug use and abuse. *Annual Review of Psychology,* 1975, *26,* 45–64.

MCKILLIP, J., JOHNSON, J. E., & PETZEL, T. P. Patterns and correlates of drug use among urban high school students. *Journal of Drug Education,* 1973, *3,* 1–12.

MILLMAN, D. H., & SU, W. Patterns of illicit drug and alcohol use among secondary school students. *Journal of Pediatrics,* 1973, *83,* 314–320.

MILLMAN, R. B. DRUG and alcohol abuse. In B. B. Wolman (Ed.), *Handbook of treatment of mental disorders in childhood and adolescence.* Englewood Cliffs, N.J.: Prentice-Hall, 1978.

MILLMAN, R. B., & KHURI, E. T. Drug abuse and the need for alternatives. In J. C. Schoolar (Ed.), *Current issues in adolescent psychiatry.* New York: Brunner/Mazel, 1973.

MYERS, V. Drug use among minority youth. *Addictive Diseases,* 1977, *3,* 187–196.

NATIONAL COMMISSION ON MARIJUANA AND DRUG ABUSE. *Drug use in America: Problems in perspective.* Washington, D.C.: U.S. Government Printing Office, 1973.

NOBLE, P., & BARNES, G. G. Drug taking in adolescent girls: Factors associated with the progression to narcotic use. *British Medical Journal,* 1971, *2,* 620–623.

NYSTROM, K. F., BAL, A. L., & LABRECQUE, V. Substance abuse. In J. D. Noshpitz (Ed.), *Basic handbook of child psychiatry.* Vol. II. New York: Basic Books, 1979.

PETZEL, T. P., JOHNSON, J. E., & MCKILLIP, J. Response bias in drug surveys. *Journal of Consulting and Clinical Psychology,* 1973, *40,* 437–439.

PRENDERGAST, T. J., & SCHAEFER, E. S. Correlates of drinking and drunkenness among high-school students. *Journal of Studies on Alcohol,* 1974, *35,* 232–240.

PROSKAUER, S., & ROLLAND, R. S. Youth who use drugs: Psychodynamic diagnosis and treatment planning. *Journal of the American Academy of Child Psychiatry,* 1973, *12,* 32–47.

ROBINS, L. N., & WISH, E. Childhood deviance as a developmental process: A study of 223 urban Black men from birth to 18. *Social Forces,* 1977, *56,* 448–473.

ROSENBERG, J. S., KASL, S. V., & BERBERIAN, R. M. Sex differences in adolescent drug use: Recent trends. *Additive Diseases,* 1974, *1,* 73–96.

ROSZAK, T. *The making of a counter culture.* New York: Doubleday, 1968.

SINGLE, E., KANDEL, D., & JOHNSON, B. D. The reliability and validity of drug use responses in a large scale longitudinal survey. *Journal of Drug Issues,* 1975, *5,* 426–443.

SMART, R. G. Recent studies of the validity and reliability of self-reported drug use, 1970–1974. *Canadian Journal of Criminology and Corrections,* 1975, *17,* 326–333.

SMART, R. G., & FEJER, D. Drug use among adolescents and their parents: Closing the generation gap in mood modification. *Journal of Abnormal Psychology,* 1972, *79,* 153–160.

SPEVACK, M., & PIHL, R. O. Nonmedical drug use by high school students: A three-year study. *International Journal of the Addictions,* 1976, *11,* 755–792.

STEIN, K. B., SOSKIN, W. F., & KORCHIN, S. J. Drug use among disaffected high school youth. *Journal of Drug Education,* 1975, *5,* 193–203.

STOCK, W. P., & RUIZ, E. M. Drug abuse: Bridging the multidimensional ignorance gap. *Drug Forum,* 1977, *5,* 335–344.

STREIT, F., & OLIVER, H. G. The child's perception of his family and its relationship to drug use. *Drug Forum,* 1972, *1,* 283–289.

TEC, N. Parent-child drug abuse: Generational continuity or adolescent deviancy? *Adolescence,* 1974, *9,* 351–364.

TOLONE, W. L., & DERMOTT, D. Some correlates of drug use among high school youth in a midwestern rural community. *International Journal of the Addictions,* 1975, *10,* 761–777.

VICTOR, H. R., GROSSMAN, J. C., & EISENMAN, R. Openness to experience and marijuana use in high school students. *Journal of Consulting and Clinical Psychology,* 1973, *41,* 78–85.

WECHSLER, H. Alcohol intoxication and drug use among teen-agers. *Journal of Studies on Alcohol,* 1976, *37,* 1672–1677.

WECHSLER, H., & MCFADDEN, M. Sex differences in adolescent alcohol and drug use. *Journal of Studies on Alcohol,* 1976, *37,* 1291–1301.

WECHSLER, H., & THUM, D. Teen-age drinking, drug use, and social correlates. *Journal of Studies on Alcohol,* 1973, *34,* 1220–1227.

WHITEHEAD, P. C., & CABRAL, R. M. Scaling the sequence of drug using behaviors: A test of the stepping-stone hypothesis. *Drug Forum,* 1975–1976, *5,* 45–54.

WIEDER, H., & KAPLAN, E. H. Drug use in adolescents. *Psychoanalytic Study of the Child,* 1969, *24,* 399–431.

14
UNIFYING THEMES

DEFINITION AND PREVALENCE

What to Count

Whom to Ask

When to Measure

Best Estimates

CAUSES

Biogenetic Factors

Psychosocial Factors

Interaction Factors

COURSE AND OUTCOME

Continuity and Change over Time

The Cumulative Nature of Persistent Disorder

Age and Nature of Onset

Likelihood of Improvement

TREATMENT AND PREVENTION

Psychotherapy: Dynamic and Behavioral Approaches

Drug Therapy

Institutional Care

Family Counseling

Educational Planning

Prevention

Textbooks on psychopathology can be organized either around individual patterns of disorder, such as mental retardation and schizophrenia, or around common themes in all disorders, such as their prevalence, cause, course, and treatment. The former approach was chosen for this book, to facilitate a detailed review of available knowledge and provide cohesive descriptions of the various kinds of psychological disturbance. As a consequence, many important issues have been discussed in bits and pieces, as they became relevant in each chapter.

This final chapter pulls together previous observations and conclusions that touch on major unifying themes in child and adolescent psychopathology. The content of this integration has been elaborated in earlier discussions, and the supporting evidence and citations will not be repeated.

DEFINITION AND PREVALENCE

Despite an extensive and rapidly growing body of knowledge on developmental psychopathology, there is no easy answer to the question of how many young people are psychologically disturbed. To begin with, three different ways of defining *normality* lead to considering differing proportions of people as abnormal. If normality is defined as an *ideal* way of coping with life's demands and circumstances, then most people are more or less maladjusted; if it is defined as being *average,* then many but not most people fall into maladjusted categories; if, as seems most sensible, being psychologically abnormal is defined as having mental or emotional difficulties that interfere more than mildly or transiently with the ability to deal adaptively with social and school or work situations, then it can be said that approximately 20 percent of adolescents and adults alike suffer psychological disturbances.

A similar estimate for preadolescent children cannot be made, since there are no adequate survey data on the extent of moderately or severely incapacitating disorder among preschool and elementary school youngsters. However, many of the disorders of early childhood (e.g., childhood psychosis) are rare, and the frequency of some relatively common disorders (e.g., schizophrenia, affective disorder) increases rapidly during the adolescent years. Hence it is reasonable to conclude that a smaller percentage of children than adolescents suffer from major adjustment difficulties.

With respect to the prevalence of particular forms of disorder among young people, several issues influence how available data should be interpreted. These include *what to count, whom to ask,* and *when to measure;* each needs to be considered before turning to prevalence estimates.

What to Count

The frequency with which a condition is counted as being present in a group of people depends on how broadly or narrowly it is defined. In the case of mental retardation, for example, a broad definition based solely on measured intelligence (IQ less than 70) yields a prevalence rate twice as large (3 percent) as a narrower definition involving low intelligence plus adaptive failure (1.5 percent).

Estimates of the prevalence of neurotic disorders are particularly unreliable because of variations in how they are defined. At one extreme, almost every second person in some surveys of adults is considered neurotic; at another extreme, some studies of adolescents report a very high frequency of situational adjustment reactions and almost no neurotic disorders. A balanced view of available information suggests that the first extreme results from using a definition of neurosis that is too broad and inclusive, whereas the second extreme reflects a too narrow, exclusive definition.

Where the truth lies between such alternatives is often difficult to say. Major advances have been made in recent years in formulating precise, behavioral definitions of neurotic and other disorders, especially through DSM-III and multivariate approaches to classification. However, the application of these improved reliable definitions in epidemiological studies is still only in its early stages for many disorders.

A particularly troublesome problem in defining what to count in prevalence studies is the distinction between *symptoms* and *syndromes*. Virtually everyone shows signs of depression from time to time, and many people display obsessive concerns or compulsive mannerisms. But how much depression constitutes a diagnosable depressive disorder, and how many obsessions and compulsions does it take to make an obsessive-compulsive disorder? Usually such judgments must be made on a subjective or arbitrary basis. For some conditions the availability of rating scales with precise cutting scores for identifying how much symptomatology constitutes a syndrome improves the reliability of assigning a diagnostic label to some but not other people. Yet even then the decision as to where this cutting point should be on a particular scale has had to be subjective in the first place. Depending on where the line is drawn between normal variations and a psychopathological extent of symptom formation, then a smaller or larger number of people will be counted as having a particular disorder.

Similar considerations apply to specific behavioral events in determining how many it takes to justify recording a label. For example, how many delinquent acts of what kind does it take to make a "delinquent?" About 4 percent of 10- to 17-year-olds appear in juvenile court each year, but 80 percent of young adults admit to having committed at least one illegal act during their adolescence. Is the prevalence of delinquency 4 percent or 80 percent, then, or something in between? Likewise, about 50 percent of high school students report ever having used marijuana, but fewer than 20 percent report regular (once weekly or more) use of this drug, and fewer than 2 percent report regular use of other illicit drugs. What is the frequency of youthful "drug abuse," then—50 percent, or 20 percent, or 2 percent?

The only defensible answer to such questions is that there are no simple answers. The conclusions drawn will depend on how "delinquency" or "drug abuse" is to be defined. Many additional complicating facts have to be considered as well, such as that both delinquent acts and drug use are more frequent among high school seniors than high school freshmen, and more frequent in some geographic locations than others. This means that broad summary statements about the prevalence of these and other kinds of problem behavior can be very misleading and conceal more information than they provide. Such statements should therefore be viewed with skepticism when they occur and, if possible, avoided in favor of detailed information concerning specific groups of young people who are found to engage in certain kinds of problem behavior with a particular frequency.

Whom to Ask

The challenge that uncertain or inconsistent definitions pose for prevalence estimates is matched by difficulties in choosing among possible data sources. National statistics on people being treated in mental health facilities provide extensive patient-population information on the prevalence of different kinds of diagnosed disorder in relation to age, sex, and geographic location. This information source also has the advantage of regular annual publication, which helps to identify trends over time.

On the other hand, these large-scale statistics are limited to superficial demographic characteristics and seldom include detail on the clinical history or life experience of individual patients. Moreover, this national data-gathering does not monitor how diagnoses are assigned in the reporting agencies. In the absence of any assurance of uniformity there is no way to determine the extent to which agency-reported figures reflect diagnostic errors or biases rather than the true clinical status of patients.

A second important source of prevalence data is studies done over time of people seen in individual clinical settings. This approach allows investigators to establish uniform diagnostic criteria for all patients in the study and to collect detailed information, including follow-up evaluations. The broadly representative sampling of national surveys is lost, however, and the distribution of diagnoses can be affected by the particular kinds of people who are served in the clinical setting where the research is done.

Both national and local data from clinical settings have the additional limitation of providing information only on those young people who are referred for professional help. It is estimated that no more than 50 percent of young people in the United States who need mental health services are receiving them. This means that there is a substantial gap between the *detected* incidence of developmental psychopathology and the *referred* incidence of developmental psychopathology. Hence the patient populations of clinics and hospitals give an incomplete picture of how many disturbed children and adolescents there are in the population and what kinds of disorders they have.

On the other hand, detected disorders of some kinds are much more likely than others to result in a referral. Retarded or psychotic children rarely fail to come to professional attention during their developmental years, whereas mildly depressed or neurotic youngsters are often viewed—perhaps correctly—as not requiring any help beyond what the family, school, family doctor, or clergy member can provide. Referral data from mental health settings are consequently a more reliable index of detected disorder for the more serious forms of disturbance than for the milder ones, and these data are likely to underestimate the percentage of mild disturbance among all disorders.

To sample detected disorder, a third approach in prevalence research is community surveys that identify disturbed people independently of whether they have been referred for professional help. Collecting sufficient information from community samples to chart the epidemiology of psychological disorder is a very large and costly undertaking, however, and data of this kind are still limited. Some researchers doing community studies have focused on general adjustment level rather than the prevalence of specific kinds of disorder. Others have concentrated on the prevalence and course of just a single disorder, such as depression or phobia. Consequently, best estimates of community frequencies still have to be pieced together from various scattered sources, and much basic work remains to be done in this area.

When to Measure

The nature and prevalence of various patterns of psychopathology change dramatically from early childhood to early adulthood. Mild mental retardation and minimal brain dysfunction/attention deficit disorder (MBD/ADD) become most noticeable during the elementary school years and may no longer be apparent in early adulthood. Affective disorder, delinquent behavior, suicidal behavior, and drug abuse are rare in childhood but become increasingly frequent during adolescence, even from one year to the next. Childhood psychosis and school phobia show certain characteristic peaks of onset (the first 30 months or after age 7 in the first case; at entrance to elementary or junior high school in the second case). Whether the question relates to *prevalence* (how many cases there are) or *incidence* (how many new cases develop within a given period of time), the answer will accordingly depend on the age of the young people being sampled.

This means that data on how many people under age 18 have a certain disorder or have engaged in some problem behavior are not very meaningful. Regrettably, many of the most extensive and systematic national surveys are presented in this way. Even reports on the 10 to 17 or the 12 to 18 age groups, which are commonly chosen for epidemiological data analyses, fail to reflect substantial differences between early and late adolescents in their normal and abnormal behavior patterns.

Best Estimates

The issues raised so far may seem to preclude any reasonable summary statement about the prevalence of psychological disorders in young people. However, attention to the limitations of current knowledge should never diminish appreciation for what is known, and uncertainty should not prevent best available estimates from being put to appropriate use. Accordingly, while elaborating the various problems in collecting and interpreting prevalence data, previous chapters have included appropriately qualified estimates based on these data. These estimates are summarized in Table 14.1.

CAUSES

Psychopathology runs in families. For every pattern of psychological disturbance and every kind of problem behavior described in this book, the likelihood of people developing it is increased if it has appeared in one or more of their relatives. Furthermore, the more closely two people are related, the more likely they are to show the same kinds of disturbed or deviant behavior.

These well-documented facts are open to different interpretations, however. They could mean that patterns of psychopathology are transmitted genetically from parents

TABLE 14.1 Prevalence Estimates in Developmental Psychopathology

Mental retardation	3% of population with IQ below 70; 1–1.5% of population labeled retarded at any one time
Minimal brain dysfunction/attention deficit disorder	5–6% of grades K–9 (age 5–14); sex ratio of 3–7:1, male:female
Childhood psychosis	3–5/10,000 (4.5); of these 1–2/10,000 (2.1) with early-onset form (infantile autism); sex ratio for autism 3.4:1, male:female
Adolescent schizophrenia	Gradual increase during adolescence to 1% population prevalence at any one point in time; 2–3% lifetime prevalence; most common diagnosis among adolescents in mental hospitals, accounting for 25–30% of admissions
Affective disorder	Community survey data unavailable for children and adolescents; depression diagnosed in 3.3% of psychiatric patients under age 18, but no similar data for mania; depression rare under age 10, increases dramatically during adolescence toward adult population frequencies of 6% point prevalence, 25% lifetime prevalence; for mania, 3–4/1000 point prevalence and 1% lifetime prevalence for adult population[a]
Phobic disorder	Excessive, incapacitating fears develop in 5% of children, usually between ages 4–7
Obsessive-compulsive disorder	Community data unavailable; diagnosed in 1–2% of children and adolescents and 1.5–3% of adults seen in psychiatric clinics
Conversion disorder	Diagnosed in 4–5% of children and adolescents seen in psychiatric clinics
School phobia	1–2% of school population; 5–8% of students referred for professional care
Academic underachievement	25% of schoolchildren achieve below their intellectual potential; 30–35% of youthful clinic patients referred because of learning problems
Delinquent behavior	4% of 10–17-year-olds appear in juvenile court each year: sex ratio 4:1 male:female; 80% of young adults admit to one or more delinquent acts as adolescents
Suicidal behavior	0.8/100,000 age 10–14 commit suicide each year, 7.6/100,000 age 15–19. 1/1000 adolescents make a suicide attempt each year
Alcohol and drug use	Regular use (once weekly or more) among high school students—alcohol, 75%; marijuana, 15.8–18.7%; other illicit drugs, less than 2%. Any use of drug ever—alcohol, 69–94%; marijuana, 42.4–57.8%; amphetamines, 11.5–18.0%; hallucinogens, 10.1–12.0%; heroin, 1.8%.

[a] Lifetime prevalence refers to percent of population experiencing the disorder sometime during their lives; point prevalence refers to percent of population showing the disorder at any particular point in time.

to their children, or they could mean that parents pass their own adjustment difficulties on to their children by how they rear them and the example they set. These alternatives define the *biogenetic* and *psychosocial* approaches to explaining the origins of psychopathology. In combination they provide a third alternative, known as *gene-environment, interaction,* or *diathesis-stress* theories. All three possibilities must be taken into account in summarizing what is known about the causes of psychological disturbance.

Biogenetic Factors

The most important consideration in evaluating possible biogenetic causes of psychological disorder is the distinction between *suggestive* and *compelling* evidence. Familial incidence suggests genetic causation, but it is equally suggestive of transmission of disorder through shared family experience. For this reason, much attention in exploring the genetics of psychopathology has focused on comparisons between monozygotic (identical) and dizygotic (nonidentical) twins. If twins are assumed to share the same developmental experiences, then differences between monozygotic and dizygotic pairs must be due to the former having exactly the same heredity, whereas dizygotic twins are no more alike genetically than siblings are.

For many disturbances on which data are available, concordance rates run much higher among identical than nonidentical twins, with the latter showing no more similarity than other siblings. Yet such evidence is still only suggestive rather than compelling with regard to genetic causation, since a case can be made that identical twins share a much more common set of life experiences than nonidentical twins.

Compelling evidence for genetic factors in psychological disturbance can come from adoption or cross-fostering studies, in which children born to disturbed or nondisturbed parents are separated from these biological parents at an early age and reared by disturbed or nondisturbed adoptive or foster parents. The more such children share disturbances in common with their biological parents (from whom they have had little or no psychosocial influence) than with their adoptive parents (with whom they have no shared heredity), the more compelling is the evidence that these disturbances are genetically determined.

Based on available adoption data, the developmental disorders in which genetic factors appear to play the largest role are mental retardation, child and adolescent schizophrenia, and affective disorder. Within affective disorder the bipolar form (manic-depressive disorder) shows a stronger genetic influence than the unipolar form (depression). No current findings identify the exact contribution of genetic factors to these conditions, however, as in saying that a particular condition is a certain percent genetically determined. Anyway, as will be mentioned shortly, the nature of gene-environment interaction makes it meaningless to attempt to assign any specific proportion of the causation of psychological disorders to either biogenetic or psychosocial influences.

Two other types of disorder discussed in previous chapters for which some genetic component has been demonstrated in adoption studies are psychopathic personality disorder and drug addiction. These findings mean that delinquent behavior rooted in psychopathy and habituation to drugs results at least in part from hereditary influences.

For neurotic disorders there is some suggestive evidence but as yet no compelling evidence of genetic determinants. These disorders do run in families, and twin studies point toward some genetic transmission. However, the more conclusive types of adoption research have not yet been conducted with respect to phobic, obsessive-compulsive, conversion, and habit disorders.

Biogenetic determinants of psychological disorder consist largely of genetic dispositions transmitted from parents to their children. In three cases, however, there is compelling or at least suggestive evidence that biological abnormalities resulting from harmful prenatal or early life experiences, not from heredity, are responsibile for pathological conditions discussed in this book. First, the intellectual limitations of about 25 percent of mentally retarded children result from demonstrable biological impairments related to injury, infection, deprivation, or arrested growth during pregnancy or early in life.

As the second and third cases, children with MBD/ADD and infantile autism are found to have a high frequency of pregnancy and birth complications, and their cognitive impairments are similar to those seen in people with known brain damage. Although highly suggestive of biological determination, these findings will not be conclusive until further longitudinal studies are done to confirm a cause-and-effect relationship between early physical trauma and subsequent manifestations of MBD/ADD or autism.

Psychosocial Factors

One of the most impressive findings in support of genetic contributions to psychopathology is the fact that approximately 50 percent of identical twins of schizophrenics suffer schizophrenia themselves, compared to an 8 to 9 percent concordance among nonidentical twins and siblings and a 1 percent prevalence in the general population. At the same time, however, this fact bears impressive testimony to the importance of psychosocial factors in the origin of psychological disorder. If only half of the people who share identical heredity with schizophrenic persons become schizophrenic themselves, then environmental experience must have a powerful influence on who does or does not develop this disorder. This conclusion is even more true for other disorders, none of which except for low intelligence has shown as much identical twin concordance as schizophrenia.

Knowing that psychosocial factors contribute to psychological disorder is not the same as being able to demonstrate precisely how and why they do, however. As in the case of biogenetic factors, available research findings comprise mainly suggestive rather than compelling evidence. The chief limitations of research in this area are that it has tended to be *correlative* rather than *causative* and *overgeneralized* rather than *representative*.

Correlative research on the psychosocial origins of psychopathology involves identifying an association between certain life experiences and the presence of some disorder. For example, disturbed patterns of communication are frequently found in the families of schizophrenic adolescents. No matter how strong this association is, however, it does not establish a cause-and-effect relationship. Does poor communication contribute to a child's becoming schizophrenic, or is it one result of a family's having a schizophrenic child in its midst?

Retrospective research is one way of attempting to resolve such cause-and-effect

pathology combine to reach some threshold. These two components of the interactive relationship are thus additive, so that disorder appears when a certain sum total of causative factors has taken effect.

To illustrate this additive interaction, people with a strong biogenetic disposition to becoming disturbed may break down in the face of only minimal life stress, whereas others with only a minimal disposition may be able to withstand enormously stressful life experiences without becoming psychologically disturbed. Similarly, people who appear to be at high biogenetic risk for disturbance may be spared such an outcome by favorable and supportive life circumstances, whereas even people with strong psychological constitutions may break down if subjected to sufficient stress. This interactive relationship explains why two people with the same heredity or seemingly identical life experiences can differ in their vulnerability to developing psychopathology.

Symptom selection has been explained in part by recent advances in identifying the contribution of genetic factors to schizophrenia and bipolar affective disorder. If people have specific genetic dispositions to these disorders, then the combination of a sufficiently strong disposition and sufficiently stressful life experience to cause psychological breakdown will result in these specific disorders. However, for unipolar depression, a broad range of neurotic disorders, and numerous kinds of problem behavior a much more complex and as yet largely unidentified set of interactive factors appears to determine what kind of breakdown will occur once the threshold of additive biogenetic and psychosocial influences is crossed.

The best available hypotheses about symptom selection in these cases revolve around the nature of an individual's personality. People who tend to be timid and fearful, for example, appear relatively likely to develop phobias if they become disturbed, and people with an ideational style of coping with experience are relatively likely to develop obsessive-compulsive symptoms. People who tend to turn anger inward and blame themselves when things go wrong are candidates for depressive disorder, whereas those who externalize blame are more likely to develop paranoid ideas or behave aggressively toward others.

Much more work is necessary to spell out how such dispositions contribute to causing specific psychological disorders. Also of interest is how these personality dispositions originate. To some extent they are determined by how parents rear their children; children who are taught and encouraged to deal with experience ideationally are likely to end up doing so, for example. In addition, many features of personality grow out of an individual's *temperament,* which consists of certain ways of reacting to experience that are inborn and apparently genetically transmitted. The more that has been learned about symptom selection, the more it seems to be influenced by the same kinds of interaction between biogenetic and psychosocial factors that cause psychological disturbance to occur.

As for shaping, neither psychological disturbances nor the factors that cause them are all-or-none phenomena. Individual disturbances, once manifest, vary in how incapacitating they are and in how long they last, and these variations stem from the strength of the biogenetic and psychosocial influences that determine them. In mental retardation, for example, the eventual extent of intellectual handicap people suffer is a complex function of their inborn limitations and how much encouragement to learn they receive early in life. Mirroring such environmental shaping of outcome, genetic influences can limit the extent to which even the most positive environment—including treatment programs—can modify the severity or duration of disorder.

COURSE AND OUTCOME

As in the case of prevalence studies, research on the course and outcome of psychopathology is complicated by questions of what to count, whom to ask, and when to measure. Because investigators have seldom answered these questions in the same way, comparable follow-up data from different studies of the various disorders, or even from studies of the same disorder, are in short supply. Although consequently spotty and sometimes inconsistent, available information on the life course of disturbed people allows some definite conclusions to be drawn concerning (a) continuity and change during the developmental years in the symptoms of disorder; (b) the cumulative nature of persistent disorder; (c) relationships between the age and nature of onset of disorders and their severity and duration; and (d) the general likelihood of improvement or recovery from psychological disorder.

Continuity and Change over Time

Psychological disorders reflect certain basic dimensions of impairment. Minimal brain dysfunction/attention deficit disorder (MBD/ADD) involves particular perceptual-cognitive and behavioral impairments, for example; schizophrenia consists of impairments in the capacities for coherent and logical thinking, accurate perception, interpersonal relatedness, and self-control; and affective disorder consists of disturbances in mood, attitudes, energy level, and bodily functioning. Each of these dimensions of a disturbance remains continuously in place so long as the disturbance lasts, although each may become less apparent as the disturbed person improves. By contrast, the manifest symptoms of many disorders change over time, partly because of normal age differences in behavior and partly because persistent disturbance produces various secondary reactions.

With respect to age differences, the symptoms of all disorders are colored by the maturity level of the person suffering from them and by the life situations he or she must face. In early childhood the most prominent manifestation of MBD/ADD is hyperactivity; in later childhood, when normal maturation has provided all children with increased motor control and when adjustment to school has become a major developmental task, learning disabilities and interpersonal problems become more prominent features of this disorder than hyperactivity. Among adolescents who are depressed, older teenagers are more likely than early adolescents to express negative self-attitudes, because both a self-reflective stance and a willingness to admit personal limitations are normally more characteristic of late than early adolescence.

MBD/ADD and depression also provide good examples of how secondary reactions to a basic disorder can influence its manifest symptoms. In adolescence youngsters with

MBD/ADD often act aggressively toward others, and depressed adolescents sometimes steal or become sexually promiscuous. In both cases the behavior is not primarily "delinquent," but has occurred as a way of expressing or reacting to the basic disorder. Although such distinctions between what is primary and what is secondary are not always immediately apparent, recognizing the basic continuity of dimensions of disturbance and attempting to identify the disorder that is responsible for certain manifest symptoms are important steps in planning effective treatment.

The Cumulative Nature of Persistent Disorder

While they persist, psychological disorders have a cumulative maladaptive impact on personality and social development. Typically a vicious circle is set in motion in which the presence of a disorder increases the stresses that have contributed to it, which in turn makes the disorder worse. A child or adolescent who is underachieving at school becomes depressed by receiving low grades; the depression results in decreased energy and diminished effort in school, which leads to even lower grades and even more depression. A socially anxious youngster draws back from interpersonal contacts, which leaves him or her even less confident socially and increasingly likely to withdraw.

In addition to being cumulative because of the negative effect they generate, psychological disorders also deprive young people of the academic and social experiences they need to learn and grow normally. Because much of school learning is cumulative, underachievers fall further behind their peers each year that their problem persists. Likewise, the longer young people are removed from peer interactions, the more they miss out on and the harder it becomes for them to reenter their peer group.

For this reason, every effort should be made to identify developmental disorders early and modify them promptly. This prescription is easy to overlook in mild disorders that tend to disappear of their own accord, which is true of most neurotic disorders. Even in these cases, however, adequate intervention provides opportunities to shorten the duration of the disorder, to spare young people psychological pain, and to minimize the risk of maladaptive secondary and cumulative effects—which is more than sufficient basis for taking mild disturbances seriously. The fact that completed suicide almost always occurs as the end result of escalating adjustment difficulties that were not adequately recognized and responded to by others bears eloquent testimony to the importance of early intervention.

Age and Nature of Onset

The age at which young people first manifest psychological disorders or problem behaviors and the manner in which the disorders begin have clear implications for how seriously incapacitating they will be and how long they will last. With respect to age of onset, the *earlier* disorders appear, the *worse* their prognosis is, except in the case of neurotic disorders. Specifically, the younger the age at which children first show signs of childhood psychosis, schizophrenia, or affective disorder, the more serious their disturbance is likely to become and the less favorable their prospects will be for improvement or recovery. Early onset of academic underachievement, delinquent behavior, suicidal behavior, or drug abuse similarly has a more serious prognosis than a later onset of these problem behaviors.

This relationship between early onset and poor prognosis is not fully understood. One reasonable hypothesis is that those young people who break down with a particular disturbance earlier are more vulnerable to it—and hence subject to more prolonged and recurrent episodes of it—than those who do not begin to show the disturbance until later.

There is one exception to this general finding: the outcome of neurotic disorders is more favorable if they occur early in life. The younger people are when they develop phobic reactions (including school phobia), obsessive-compulsive disorder, and conversion reactions, the briefer and less incapacitating their disturbance is likely to be. The most likely reason for this difference from the relationship between age of onset and prognosis in other disorders is found in the conceptualization of neurotic disorders as exaggerations of normal childhood fears, rituals, and bodily concerns.

To elaborate this point, personality develops gradually over time, and each year normally brings increasing stability of personality characteristics. This means that what people are like at age 5 will change more than what they are like at age 10, which in turn will change more than what they are like at age 15. Conversely, adults do not have as much personality change ahead of them as they did as adolescents, when they had less personality change ahead of them than they did as children. If neurosis represents an exaggeration of normal developmental concerns, then, early developing neurotic disorders will be more likely than later developing neurotic disorders to be transient phenomena that will disappear with maturation.

The nature of onset of psychological disorders affects their prognosis in relation to whether they begin in a relatively *acute* or a relatively *chronic* fashion. The more suddenly disorders appear, in response to dramatic precipitating events and in the absence of prior signs of breakdown, the more likely they are to be mild and short-lived. By contrast, disorders that mount slowly, from subtle initial indications to gradually more pervasive symptomatology, and that reach a diagnosable degree of severity in the absence of any obvious precipitants, tend to be relatively incapacitating, long-lasting, and unresponsive to treatment efforts. Good examples of this relationship between onset and course are provided by clinical distinctions between acute (good premorbid) and chronic (poor premorbid) schizophrenia; reactive and endogenous depression; acute and chronic school phobia; and situational and characterological delinquency.

Likelihood of Improvement

The data on the long-term outcome of psychological disorders are more abundant than they are systematic. Varying criteria of improvement have been used in different studies, and the populations on which follow-up information is available are sometimes hospital patients, sometimes clinic or office patients, sometimes community samples, and sometimes combinations of all three. Table 14.2 summarizes available outcome information for several disorders; the incompleteness of the table and the lack of comparability across categories reflect the current state of the literature.

TABLE 14.2   Long-Term Expectations in Child and Adolescent Psychopathology

Mental retardation	Intellectual handicap permanent; mildly retarded children may blend with the general population as adults, be identified as "slow" but not "abnormal," once school years are passed; moderately and severely retarded youngsters likely to require institutional care as adults
Minimal brain dysfunction/attention deficit disorder	15% improve significantly; 50% show moderate or marked improvement; 35% fail to improve
Infantile autism	25% make substantial progress, but still achieve only fair adjustment; others 75% do poorly, and 50% become permanently institutionalized by adulthood
Childhood schizophrenia	35 to 50% achieve moderately good social adjustment, including 20% who recover completely; remaining 50% have a marginal or poor adult adjustment, and 35% eventually require residential care
Adolescent schizophrenia	Of those hospitalized, 25% recover, 25% improve but have lingering symptoms or relapses, and 50% make little or no progress; by contrast, schizophrenia beginning in adulthood shows 25% recovering, 50% improving, and 25% making little or no progress
Affective disorder	Of those hospitalized, 35% with unipolar depression recover, remaining 65% subject to recurrences; when hospitalization not required, most cases show spontaneous remission
Phobic disorder	90% of children are likely to get over excessive fears, whereas only 20–30% of adults with phobias overcome them completely and only an additional 30% show some improvement
School phobia	90% of children under age 11 recover; recovery rate for children 11 or older is 50%

TREATMENT AND PREVENTION

Child and adolescent psychopathology is treated by various combinations of psychotherapy, drug therapy, institutional care, family counseling, and educational planning. None of these modalities is best for all kinds of psychological problems, nor is there any problem that can be alleviated only by one particular method. Treatment programs must be carefully tailored to meet the needs of individual youngsters. Moreover, whether disturbed young people benefit from a treatment program depends less on the methods employed than on how skillful, sensitive, dedicated, and well trained their therapists are. In addition to addressing recovery from disorders, therapists must also be concerned with preventing or minimizing disorders before they occur.

Psychotherapy: Dynamic and Behavioral Approaches

There are two major theoretical approaches in psychotherapy. In the *dynamic* approach disturbed or problem behavior is regarded as stemming from underlying concerns of which the person is not fully aware. The treatment focuses on helping people understand why they are thinking, feeling, or acting as they are, in the expectation that increased self-awareness will allow them to find ways of resolving their concerns or dealing with them more effectively. In the *behavioral* approach maladaptive thoughts, feelings, and actions are viewed as being the disturbance or problem, and the treatment focuses directly on modifying these maladaptive patterns or shaping new patterns to replace them.

At times the dynamic focus on understanding and the behavioral focus on symptom removal are debated as if they were mutually exclusive. In these debates dynamically oriented therapists are sometimes criticized for paying insufficient attention to promoting positive behavior change; behaviorally oriented therapists are criticized in turn for failing to promote sufficient self-understanding for people to sustain by themselves any improvements they achieve.

Neither of these criticisms is justified. Adequately trained dynamic therapists view increased self-awareness not as an end in itself, but only as a means toward achieving positive behavior change. Likewise, contemporary behavior therapy stresses that meaningful, lasting behavior change requires people to grasp why they got into difficulty, how the treatment has helped them, and what they can do on their own to avoid or minimize any recurrences.

For these reasons, there is substantial complementarity between these two approaches. Most therapists employ techniques drawn from both orientations, and successful therapy for most conditions involves some combination of efforts to increase self-understanding and remove symptoms.

Turning to individual disorders, psychotherapy is most often the primary treatment of choice in neurotic disorders and for certain problem behaviors. Specific neurotic symptoms, especially phobias, are especially likely to respond favorably to behavioral methods, and imaginative techniques for reducing anxiety and shaping different behaviors can be very helpful to obsessive-compulsive and school-phobic children. In cases where academic underachievement or delinquent behavior reflects underlying neurotic concerns, dynamically oriented psychotherapy has proved highly effective, and suicidal behavior in particular calls for efforts to identify and resolve concerns that are not being adequately recognized or communicated.

In affective disorder psychotherapy of various kinds can help young people work through their sense of loss, reassess and reshape their negative attitudes, and get their lives moving again. In schizophrenia psychotherapy plays an important treatment role as an avenue for promoting interpersonal relatedness and contact with reality. Psychotherapy with autistic children typically combines dynamically and behaviorally oriented techniques aimed at overcoming their interpersonal aversion and training them in basic social skills.

Psychotherapy has little impact on the perceptual-cognitive impairments of children with MBD/ADD but can help them reduce their hyperactivity, distractibility, and impulsivity. Behavioral techniques for promoting self-control are especially useful in this regard. Although dynamically oriented psychotherapy cannot address the primary manifestations of MBD/ADD, it is often helpful in alleviating some of the secondary consequences of this disorder, particularly low self-esteem and negative interpersonal attitudes. Similarly, in working with mentally retarded children, psychotherapy has little impact on low intelligence but can help retarded children avoid secondary psychological reactions to their handicap and promote their social adaptation.

Drug Therapy

Drug therapy makes its major contribution to treating developmental psychopathology in instances of MBD/ADD. Stimulant medication, primarily amphetamines, relieves the primary symptoms of this disorder in 60 to 70 percent of cases. Medication can also play a role in the treatment of autistic and schizophrenic children and adolescents, but not as often or as directly as in MBD/ADD. Antipsychotic drugs, especially the phenothiazines, have a calming, anxiety-reducing effect on autistic and schizophrenic youngsters that curtails their more extreme symptoms and makes them more accessible to psychotherapy.

In younger children, however, a large enough dose of phenothiazines to have this calming effect often has an undesirable sedative effect as well. In adolescents overreliance on drugs in the treatment can have the disadvantage of making youngsters feel manipulated and not in control of themselves. For these reasons, drugs are generally regarded as an adjunct in the treatment of autistic and schizophrenic disorders, to be used to facilitate psychotherapy, rather than as a cure or primary treatment for the condition.

One other specific drug treatment of demonstrable effectiveness is the use of lithium to reduce manic symptoms in affective disorder. Most of what is known about this effect has been observed in adults, however, and the utility of lithium with younger manic persons has only recently begun to be investigated. Similarly, for depression, several kinds of antidepressant medication are known to be helpful in work with adults but are so far of unknown value in the treatment of depressed children and adolescents.

Very little use is made of drugs in treating young people with neurotic disorders, and, with special exceptions, there is no evidence that they are helpful. These exceptions involve beneficial effects of certain drugs in relieving habit disorders, including haloperidol in cases of tics and imipramine in cases of enuresis. Drugs play no role in helping children and adolescents overcome other problem behaviors, except when these behaviors stem from an underlying MBD/ADD or schizophrenic disorder that is the primary focus of the treatment.

Institutional Care

When young people are so severely disturbed that they cannot achieve even a marginal adjustment at home and school, and especially when they are at risk for harming themselves or others, their treatment may have to be conducted in a residential setting. Because hospitalization takes children and adolescents out of the normal developmental stream, great care is necessary in determining whether, when, how, and for how long to place them in an institution. Nevertheless, failure to opt for inpatient treatment when it is necessary can be as psychologically damaging to young people and their parents as hospitalizing them unnecessarily.

One of the major issues in the institutional care of young people is whether adolescents should be treated in an all-adolescent unit or in a mixed adult-adolescent unit. Firm convictions are held in some quarters that one or the other of these approaches is by far the better. However, available evidence indicates that successful treatment depends less on the mix of the patient population than on whether the unit includes staff who are particularly interested in and knowledgeable about adolescent problems.

Family Counseling

With very few exceptions, adequate treatment for disturbed children and adolescents requires involvement of their parents. Parents must be helped to understand the nature of their child's difficulties and the role they play in them. If properly done, such counseling can avoid or at least minimize two kinds of destructive parental reaction: one in which parents blame themselves for the problem and become depressed and oversolicitous toward their child, and one in which they blame the child and become angry and rejecting. Continued contact with parents during their child's treatment contributes to their maintaining a realistic perspective on the problem and can also provide a vehicle for helping them modify their own behavior in ways that promote and sustain their child's recovery.

The degree of parental involvement in treating disturbed children and adolescents varies with the nature and severity of the problem and the parents' capacity to participate and to change. In some cases, when the problem has arisen primarily as a reaction to parental attitudes or behavior, counseling with the parents may constitute the only necessary treatment. One important example of this circumstance is academic underachievement caused specifically by excessive expectations or unwelcome demands that parents are placing on their youngster.

Educational Planning

Mental retardation, MBD/ADD, and academic underachievement revolve around problems in school learning. Although other conditions may affect performance and behavior in school, and thereby require special attention in the classroom, these three call especially for careful educational planning as an integral part of any treatment program. Decisions must be made concerning the skills and subject areas that youngsters with these problems should be expected to master, the particular methods that should be used in instructing them, and the type of classroom setting in which they should be placed.

Two major issues in educational planning for psychologically handicapped youngsters are (a) whether they should be taught in special or regular classes (mainstreamed) and (b) whether the teaching should emphasize tasks or processes. There are no single answers to these questions. Both special and regular class instruction have certain advantages and disadvantages, academically and psychologically, and individual assessment is necessary to determine whether one or the other, or some combination of both in the daily schedule, will help a youngster learn and grow to his or her fullest potential.

Similarly, some children with a learning problem (e.g., reading disability) benefit more from basic skill or process training (e.g., eye-movement exercises), whereas others benefit more from direct task training (e.g., reading exercises). Once again, individual assessment provides the basis for selecting the best treatment approach, as it also does in helping high school students select courses that build on their academic strengths without overtaxing their weaknesses.

Prevention

Approaches to treating psychopathology in people who have already become psychologically disturbed constitute what is known as *tertiary prevention*. Clinicians and researchers must also be concerned with *secondary* prevention, which involves the early identification of children who are at risk for or are just beginning to show certain disorders, followed by efforts to prevent the disorder from occurring or becoming full-blown; and *primary* prevention, which consists of interventions that eliminate or minimize the risk of disorders even beginning to occur.

Work on secondary prevention to date has focused on "tagging" children in whom mild behavioral or learning problems suggest the likelihood of further, more serious problems. Preliminary results indicate that carefully designed counseling and educational programs can effectively reduce the frequency and severity of subsequent adjustment difficulties in high-risk children.

Work in primary prevention is limited by current understanding of basic causes of the various patterns of psychopathology and of realistic opportunities to modify these causes. The most dramatic success to date involves phenylketonuria (PKU), in which otherwise inevitable mental retardation can be averted by dietary controls early in life. Because of what is known about familial retardation, genetic counseling can also play a significant preventive role in mental retardation. The less clearly that psychopathology can be traced to specific biogenetic causes, however, the more difficult it becomes to institute primary prevention successfully. Pathogenic parental modeling and child-rearing practices are difficult to identify and modify in advance of their being psychologically harmful, and sociocultural determinants of disordered behavior call for social change that is usually beyond the capacity of mental health professionals to implement.

GLOSSARY

Abulia. Chronic uncertainty and indecisiveness.

Academic underachievement. A disparity between capacity and performance in which students receive lower grades than they are intellectually capable of earning.

Adjustment. The degree to which people are able to cope effectively with life experience; being well adjusted consists of being able to enjoy rewarding interpersonal relationships and work productively toward self-fulfilling goals.

Affective disorder. A form of psychopathology consisting of maladaptive changes in a person's mood, attitudes, energy level, and physical status.

Affective psychosis. A psychotic degree of disturbance involving extreme states of elevated or depressed mood.

Agoraphobia. A common form of phobic disorder involving excessive, unrealistic fears of leaving one's house or being among crowds of people.

Amniocentesis. A procedure for extracting fluid from the uterus of pregnant women, which can be analyzed to identify certain biological abnormalities in the fetus.

Anhedonia. A pervasive inability to experience pleasure in any setting or activity.

Anorexia. A pathological loss of interest in eating, usually accompanied by physically debilitating weight loss.

Anoxia. An inadequate supply of oxygen to the brain that can occur in newborns who have difficulty starting to breath and can cause mental retardation.

Aphasia. A brain disorder that interferes with the ability to understand or express thoughts in words.

Antisocial personality. A personality disorder characterized by an underdeveloped conscience (guiltlessness) and an inability to identify with other people (lovelessness); used synonymously with *psychopathic personality.*

Attention deficit disorder (ADD). A new term that refers to the condition of *minimal brain dysfunction* but involves no assumption of central nervous system impairment.

Bipolar affective disorder. A form of affective disorder manifest in episodes of mania or alternating episodes of mania and depression.

Borderline disorder. A form of psychopathology that combines certain features of psychotic, neurotic, and characterological disturbance; its chief manifest features are intense affect, poor self-control, illusory social adaptation, strained interpersonal relationships, and vulnerability to psychotic episodes.

Borderline personality. A subcategory of borderline disorder that includes individuals in whom chronic instability in moods and interpersonal relationships is the most prominent feature of the disorder.

Brief reactive psychosis. A schizophrenic-like reaction with rapid onset and a duration of less than 2 weeks.

Bulimia. An excessive, insatiable need to consume food.

Cerebral palsy. A neurological disorder in which damage to the brain produces motor difficulties and, in 45 to 60 percent of cases, mental retardation as well.

Characterological delinquency. Illegal acts that reflect a primary asocial personality orientation.

Childhood schizophrenia. A rare but severely disabling form of schizophrenia that appears in children between 2½ and 12 years of age, mainly after age 7.

Compulsions. Repetitive, nonproductive acts that people feel required to carry out, even against their better judgment.

Contact hypothesis. A view that normally functioning people will have more favorable attitudes toward disturbed or handicapped people if they have opportunities to get to know and interact with them in their customary everyday activities.

Conversion reactions. Sensory or motor impairments for which there is no organic cause, usually in the form of pain, numbness, or loss of muscle control in one or more parts of the body.

Coprolalia. Obscene speech; occurring in uncontrollable outbursts, it is the most distinctive feature of Gilles de la Tourette's syndrome.

Cross-fostering. A research method for distinguishing between hereditary and environmental influences in which the subjects are children born to either normal or disturbed parents but, as a result of adoption or foster-home placement, reared by other either normal or disturbed parents.

Cultural-drift hypothesis. A view that the higher incidence of mental retardation and other serious psychological handicaps in lower than in middle or upper socioeconomic classes results from the tendency of families with a history of such handicaps to drift toward a lower socioeconomic class because of their limited social and vocational capacities.

Custodial retardates. Severely retarded (IQ 25 to 39) and profoundly retarded (IQ below 25) persons who are largely incapable of taking care of themselves and require institutionalization, usually early in life.

Delinquent behavior. Acts that violate the law; how many such acts, of what kind, and with what outcome make a young person a "delinquent" are moot points.

Delusions. Unrealistic but fixed beliefs that derive from faulty reasoning.

Depression. A psychological state involving sadness, negative attitudes, low energy level, and a sense of ill health that are out of proportion to actual circumstances.

Diasthesis-stress model. A view that biogenetic and psychosocial factors interact to cause many psychopathological conditions that neither constitutional dispositions nor environmental influences would be sufficient to cause by themselves.

Dissociation. A disruption in the sequence of thoughts so that one thought does not flow continuously from another.

Displacement. A process by which affects and attitudes are transferred from their real source to a previously neutral object or situation; this process often contributes to the development of phobias.

Down's syndrome. A chromosomal abnormality that almost always produces moderate or severe mental retardation and is the most common biological disorder resulting in intellectual handicap.

Dyslexia. A pattern of reading retardation in which a person's attainment falls significantly below what would be expected from his or her age, intelligence, and opportunities for reading instruction in his or her native language.

Dysgraphia. Problems in writing that derive from basic impairments in the perceptual-motor abilities necessary to master this skill.

Echolalia. A speech abnormality that consists of automatically repeating the words spoken by other people.

Educable mental retardates. Mildly retarded persons who have a Wechsler IQ between 55 and 69, reach between a third and sixth-grade education in school, and as adults can usually do unskilled or semiskilled work and meet the routine demands of social living.

Elation. A normal reaction of joy to happy events.

Electroencephalogram (EEG). A measure of patterns of electrical activity in the brain that is useful in identifying certain kinds of neurological disorder.

Endogenous depression. A form of depressive disorder in which the depress-

ing circumstances are more fantasized than real; tends to be a chronic and lingering condition.

Enuresis. Nocturnal bed-wetting that persists beyond age 3, by which time most children have achieved total bladder control.

Epidemiology. The study of how conditions are distributed in the population, with particular respect to how frequently they occur in relation to the age, sex, race, social class, place of residence, and other objective characteristics of people who develop it.

Ethnocentric judgments. Evaluations of people or events that are based on the conviction that one's own ways of doing things are the best and only right ways.

Familial retardation. Mild to moderate mental retardation (Wechsler IQ 50 to 69) in persons without identifiable biological defects but a family history of retardation.

Fetal alcohol syndrome (FAS). A pattern of facial deformities, growth deficiency, and mental retardation that occurs in one-quarter to one-third of children born to alcoholic mothers.

Flight of ideas. A manifestation of mania in which thoughts flow in such quick succession that the person loses track of them.

Gilles de la Tourette's syndrome. A special form of tic disorder involving twitching movements, involuntary vocal noises, and uncontrollable outbursts of obscene speech.

Grief. A normal, temporary depressive reaction to distressing experiences, especially the loss of a loved person or object.

Habit disturbances. Undesirable traits that represent neurotic ways of behaving but occur as learned habits or as a result of delayed maturation and are not necessarily associated with other indices of maladjustment.

Hallucinations. Sensory impressions for which in reality there are no external stimuli.

Heritability. The proportion of the variability among people in their IQ test scores that can be ascribed to their genetic inheritance.

Hidden delinquency. Delinquent behavior that never appears in official statistics because it is not detected or, if detected, does not result in arrest or adjudication.

High-risk research methods. studies in which children who are considered to have an above-average likelihood of developing psychopathology are followed longitudinally to determine whether and under what circumstances they become psychologically disturbed.

Hyperactive child syndrome (HACS). A behavior disorder characterized primarily by a heightened activity level and distractibility; this term is largely synonymous with *minimal brain dysfunction* but involves no assumption of central nervous system impairment.

Hypochondriasis. An exaggerated concern with health and bodily functions.

Hysterical personality style. A characterological tendency to deal with experience in an emotional labile, superficial, impulsive, and self-centered manner.

Ideas of reference. Mistaken beliefs that general and public events have a specific and unique reference to oneself.

Identity crisis. Incapacitating distress experienced by adolescents who are having an abnormal degree of difficulty in integrating their sense of personal identity.

Identity formation. The process by which late adolescents and young adults arrive at some fairly clear and enduring sense of what kind of person they are, what they believe in, and what they want to do with their lives.

Imipramine. The most commonly used of the tricylic drugs in treating depression.

Infantile autism. A rare but very serious disorder that begins early in life and is characterized by failure to develop normal attachments to people, intolerance for changes in the environment, language peculiarities, and certain kinds of cognitive and intellectual impairments.

Isolation. A process in which affective experience is minimized by separating emotions from thoughts they would ordinarily accompany.

Learning disability. A deficit in essential learning processes that causes children to achieve below expectation in school in the absence of any general intellectual deficit, emotional handicap, or inadequate opportunity to learn.

Life-history research methods. Studies of the possible origins of normal or abnormal behavior patterns that are based on data recorded during the subjects' childhood.

Lithium. A mood-stabilizing drug that is effective in relieving the symptoms of mania.

Mainstreaming. A treatment philosophy that every possible effort should be made to educate children with learning and behavior problems in their regular classes, with their normally developing peers, rather than in special classes.

Mania. A psychological state involving elation, positive attitudes, high energy level, and a sense of well-being that are out of proportion to actual circumstances.

Manic-depressive disorder. A term for bipolar affective disorder that refers to alternating episodes of mania and depression.

Minimal brain dysfunction (MBD). A disorder of behavioral and perceptual-cognitive functioning that is assumed to involve some impairment of the central nervous system.

Neuroleptic drugs. A group of psychoactive chemicals that act on the nervous system to decrease spontaneous motor activity, reduce reactivity to stimulation, and blunt emotional responses.

Neurotic behavior. Repetitively immature, inappropriate, or maladaptive ways of responding to people and situations.

Neurotic delinquency. Illegal acts commited as individual, personal attempts to communicate needs that young people cannot find other ways of impressing on their environment.

Object splitting. An immature orientation toward the world in which other people are seen as either ''all good'' or ''all bad.''

Obsessions. Recurrent ideas, fears, or doubts that people cannot prevent from intruding on their conscious awareness despite finding them unpleasant and wanting to avoid them.

Obsessive-compulsive personality style. A characterological tendency to deal with experience in a rigid, over-controlled, excessively orderly, and perfectionistic manner.

Organic psychosis. A psychotic degree of disturbance resulting from brain-damaging effects of tumors or other disease processes, of deterioration associated with aging, or of alcohol or other toxic substances.

Paranoid disorder. A maladaptive cognitive style and set of attitudes toward the environment that results in people being rigid, inflexible, and narrow-minded and seeing the world as a hostile, dangerous place with which they must deal cautiously.

Paranoid schizophrenia. A form of schizophrenic disorder that involves prominent paranoid styles and attitudes.

Passive-aggressive behavior. Purposeful inactivity intended to vent underlying feelings of anger and resentment that cannot be expressed directly without causing considerable anxiety.

Passive-agressive underachievement. A pattern of psychological disturbance in which learning difficulties are determined by unresolved hostile impulses toward family members, fears of competing with parents and siblings, and a passive-aggressive behavioral style.

Perinatal stress. Complications of pregnancy and the birth process that appear to increase vulnerability to learning and behavioral problems.

Personality disorder. A maladaptive behavioral style in which the symptoms of disorder are not distressing to the person who has them but are simply a

PHOTO CREDITS

CHAPTER 10
Page 361: Laimute Druskis/EPA. *Page 365:* Elizabeth Hamlin/Stock Boston. *Page 370:* Doug Magee/EPA. *Page 375:* Miriam Reinhart/Photo Researchers. *Page 377:* Marcia Weinstein.

CHAPTER 11
Page 396: Tower/EPA. *Page 398:* Michael Abramson/Liaison. *Page 404* (left): Sylvia Johnson/Woodfin Camp. *Page 404* (right): Bettmann Archive. *Page 415:* Marc Riboud/Magnum.

CHAPTER 12
Page 437: Syd Greenberg/Photo Researchers.

CHAPTER 13
Page 458: Charles Gatewood/Stock Boston.

AUTHOR INDEX

Kruger, R., 136
Krugman, S., 98
Krynicki, V. E., 416
Kuna, D. J., 157
Kupfer, D., 153
Kupietz, S., 249
Kushida, E., 98
Kvaraceus, W. C., 400
Kysar, J. E., 27, 31

Labrecque, V., 457
Lacker, M., 378, 381
LaCrosse, J., 9, 323, 348
LaFranchi, S., 180
Lahey, B. B., 130, 139, 153
Laing, R. D., 200
Laird, J. D., 19
Lambert, N. M., 130, 137, 153
Lamprecht, M. J., 48
Lancet, M., 277
Lander, H., 202
Landesman-Dwyer, S., 98
Landis, R., 65
Lang, P., 232
Langer, E. J., 50
Langford, W. S., 153
Langhorne, J. E., 131
Langmeier, J., 101
Langner, T. S., 12, 28
Langsley, D. G., 249, 348, 350
Lansky, S., 345
Laplin, B., 227
Lapouse, R., 9, 11, 303, 318, 322
Largo, R. H., 321
Larsen, S. C., 142
Lasky, E. Z., 137
Lassers, E., 348
Laufer, M., 284
Laufer, M. W., 153
LaVietes, R., 91, 113
Lawler, C., 98
Laybourne, P. C., 319
Layman, D., 154
Leary, T., 450
Leckman, J. F., 280–281
Lee, E. E., 450, 455
Leeman, M. M., 282
Lefever, D. W., 398
Leff, J. P., 200
Leff, R. I., 206
Lefkowitz, M. M., 265, 268, 272
Lefton, L. A., 139
Lehmann, H. E., 230, 248

Lehman, S., 47
Leifer, R., 51
Leigh, G. K., 103
Leighton, A. H., 28
Leighton, D. C., 28
LeMay, M., 184
Lemkau, P. V., 46, 86–87
Lena, B., 288
Lenkowsky, R. S., 140
Lennox, C., 195
Leon, G. R., 274
Leonard, E., 358
Lerer, M. P., 151
Lerer, R. J., 151
Lerner, J. W., 157
Lerner, R. M., 26
Leslie, S. A., 27
Lesse, S., 275
Lesser, G. S., 26
Lesser, I. M., 29
Lessing, E. E., 10, 11
Lester, D., 316, 437
Lester, E. P., 321
Leton, D. A., 341
LeUnes, A., 350
Levenson, E. A., 340, 343
Levenson, M., 440
Levenstein, S., 243
Leventhal, T., 343, 348
Levin, H. S., 147
Levine, E. M., 399–400, 451, 453–455, 457
Levine, J., 234
Levine, P. M., 269
Levinson, D. J., 250
Leviton, H., 157
Levy, N. J., 277
Lewine, R. R., 231, 234, 239
Lewinsohn, P. M., 284, 286
Lewis, J. M., 32, 245, 250
Lewis, D. O., 403–404, 416–417
Lewis, S. B., 250
Lewittes, D. J., 50
Lichter, S. O., 357
Lichty, E. C., 153
Lidz, T., 200, 247
Liebowitz, M. R., 234
Lief, H. I., 24, 31
Liem, J. H., 200
Lindzey, G., 86, 102
Ling, W., 274
Link, B., 12, 28
Linton, R., 2
Lion, J. B., 421

Palkes, H. S., 130, 149, 152
Pambakian, R., 59
Papanek, E., 379
Parens, H., 380
Parke, R. D., 154
Parker, B., 246
Parker, R. M., 142
Parmelee, A. H., 99
Parsons, B. V., 419
Paternite, C. E., 131
Paton, S., 277
Patrick, V., 280
Patterson, F., 52
Patterson, G. R., 419
Patterson, J. H., 328
Paulauskas, S. L., 142
Paykel, E. S., 282
Pearl, R., 142
Pearsall, D., 454
Pearson, G. H. J., 369
Peck, A. L., 340
Pederson, A., 19
Pedulla, B. M., 323–324, 326
Penney, J. F., 380
Penniman, J. H., 243
Perkins, S. A., 98, 101
Perlman, T., 146
Perlstein, A. P., 279, 436
Perry, J. C., 235
Persons, R. W., 418
Peskin, H., 368
Peters, J. E., 135, 137–138, 141, 144–145
Petersen, A. C., 367
Peterson, D. R., 407
Petronio, R. J., 397
Petzel, S. V., 436
Petzel, T. P., 451, 459
Philage, M. L., 157
Philips, I., 86, 91, 268
Phillips, D., 46–47
Phillips, E. L., 419
Phillips, V. A., 32, 245, 250
Piaget, J., 227, 366
Pierce, C. M., 321
Pierce, J. V., 358
Pierce, S., 180
Piggott, L. R., 195
Pihl, R. O., 459
Piker, H. N., 412
Pincus, J., 134
Piotrowski, Z. A., 226
Pirozzolo, F. J., 139
Pitt, R., 239

Pittman, F. S., 348, 350
Pittmen, G. D., 243
Pitts, F. N., 282
Pokorny, A. D., 412
Pollack, J. M., 315
Pollack, M., 240, 243
Pollack, Y., 234, 240
Pollin, W., 197
Pollitt, E., 101
Polsky, R., 436
Pontius, W., 194
Pope, H. G., 269
Popper, K., 315
Porterfield, A. L., 396
Pottenger, M., 265
Powell, G. F., 101
Powers, E., 419
Poznanski, E. O., 275, 306
Prange, A. J., 287
Prawat, R. S., 139
Prazar, G., 317
Prendergast, T. J., 459
Prentice, N. M., 376, 406
Prentky, R. A., 239
Preodor, D., 269
Preston, A., 360
Price, J., 280
Prinz, R. J., 202
Prior, M. R., 180–181, 183
Proctor, J., 318
Proff, F. C., 380
Prosen, M., 187
Proskauer, S., 450, 457, 462
Prout, H. T., 154
Pruitt, A. W., 328
Prusoff, B. A., 287
Pruyser, P. W., 54
Puig-Antich, J., 272
Puri, P., 371
Purohit, A. P., 274
Putterman, A. H., 234
Puzantian, V. R., 264

Quarrington, B., 195
Quast, W., 32, 243
Quay, H. C., 65, 69–71, 129, 391, 399, 407
Quinlan, D., 190, 268, 283
Quinn, P. O., 151

Rachman, S. J., 309
Radin, S., 339
Radloff, L. S., 268
Rae, D. S., 268

Waterhouse, L., 238
Waterman, A. S., 25, 29
Waterman, C. K., 25, 29
Watson, J. B., 307
Watson, L. S., 113
Watt, N. F., 15, 234, 239–241
Watts, B. H., 362
Wayne, H. L., 318
Weber, D., 183
Wechsler, H., 451, 453, 455, 457–458
Weech, A. A., 380
Wein, S. J., 283
Weinberg, R. A., 103
Weinberg, W. A., 144, 266, 272, 274, 285
Weinberger, G., 348
Weiner, A. S., 25
Weiner, B., 49
Weiner, I. B., 26, 28, 31–32, 48, 54, 64, 150, 187,
    224–225, 227–228, 231, 233–235, 268,
    273–275, 277–278, 284–285, 303, 316, 369,
    371, 391, 402, 406, 411
Weinstein, R. S., 363
Weintraub, S., 202
Weisberg, P. S., 247, 357
Weiss, G., 128–129, 136–137, 144–146
Weiss, M., 343, 350
Weissenburger, F. E., 153–154
Weissman, A., 442, 444
Weissman, M. M., 175, 265, 267–269, 285, 287,
    437
Weithorn, C. J., 152
Weitz, S., 365
Welcher, D. W., 98
Wells, K. C., 11, 327
Welner, A., 32, 64, 149, 285, 409
Welner, J., 197
Welner, Z., 32, 149, 285, 409
Wender, P. H., 128, 131, 146, 152, 197–198, 234
Wener, A., 146
Werble, B., 31, 234
Werner, E. E., 17, 100, 147
Werry, J. S., 135, 137, 151, 177, 181, 195, 248,
    287, 318, 322–323
Wesley, C., 364–365
Wesley, F., 364–365
West, J. L., 200
West, K. L., 31
Westman, J. C., 19
Wetherby, B., 113
Wetzel, R. D., 279
Whalen, C. K., 151–152
Wheeler, L., 376
Whiddon, T., 463

White, J., 269
White, L., 199
Whitehead, P. C., 455
Whiteman, M., 459
Whiteside, M. F., 327
Whitmore, K., 12, 18, 130, 140, 302, 341
Widom, C. S., 405
Wieder, H., 277, 458
Will, L., 67
Willerman, L., 148
Williams, D., 265
Williams, J. B. W., 65
Williams, J. E., 364
Williams, N., 86, 91
Williams, S., 203
Williamson, M., 98
Willits, F. C., 26
Willows, D. M., 139
Wilson, P. T., 59
Wilson, R. C., 371
Wilson, R. S., 135, 139, 148
Wilson, W. C., 128
Wilson, W. P., 28
Winer, G., 156
Wing, J. K., 243
Wing, L., 177, 180–181, 185
Wingard, J. A., 459
Winick, M., 101
Winnicott, D. W., 24
Winokur, G., 264–265, 269, 280–282
Winokur, H., 231
Winsberg, B. G., 249
Wirt, R. D., 395
Wish, E., 17, 149, 455
Witmer, H. L., 396, 418–419
Wittes, J. T., 103
Woerner, M. G., 240
Wolf, M. M., 419
Wolfensberger, W., 112
Wolff, P., 135
Wolff, S., 182, 238
Wollersheim, J. P., 47, 110
Wolman, B. B., 287
Wolpert, E. A., 269
Wolraich, M., 151
Wong, H. Z., 450
Wood, D. R., 146
Wood, J. W., 98
Woodrow, K., 318
Woodruff, D. S., 31
Woodruff, R. A., 409
Woolson, R. F., 153, 285
Work, H. H., 87, 113

Worland, J., 202
Wright, M. J., 55
Wright, M. K., 412
Wright, S. W., 86
Wunsch-Hitzig, R., 12, 28
Wyatt, J., 199
Wynne, L. C., 200, 247

Yamamoto, K., 46
Yannet, H., 100
Yarrow, M. R., 14
Yates, A. J., 317–318
Yeates, S. R., 177
Yellin, A. M., 133, 151
Yiu, L., 151
Yoeli, M., 100
Yoshida, R. K., 110
Young, R. D., 128, 277, 341, 348
Youngerman, J., 288
Yule, W., 12, 18, 27, 140, 206, 266, 341
Yusin, A. S., 135, 440

Zagorin, S. W., 10, 11
Zahn, T. P., 152
Zajonc, R. B., 103
Zaks, M. S., 27
Zambelli, A. J., 144
Zax, M., 12, 19, 104
Zeiss, A. M., 285
Zentall, S. S., 156
Zentall, T. R., 156
Zerbin-Rudin, E., 16
Zigler, B., 234
Zigler, E., 84–85, 93, 103, 105, 108–110, 112, 234
Zinn, D., 249
Zinobar, J. W., 84
Zis, A. P., 269
Zubin, J., 60, 202–203, 231, 238, 300
Zuckerman, M., 376
Zuk, G. H., 247
Zukow, A. H., 132
Zukow, P. G., 132
Zwilling, M., 287
Zybert, P., 103

SUBJECT INDEX

Behavior therapy: in academic underachievement, 381
    in characterological delinquency, 421
    in childhood psychosis, 206–207
    in drug abuse, 462
    in habit disturbances, 322–323
    in MBD/ADD, 153–154
    in neurotic disorders, 323–325
    in school phobia, 349–350
    in sociological delinquency, 419
    summary of, 486
Bipolar affective disorder, *see* Depression; Mania
Birth complications, 98–100, 147, 195
Borderline disorder, 234–236
Brief reactive psychosis, 231
British National Child Development Study, 147
Buckinghamshire Child Survey, 11, 18
Bulimia, 271

Cambridge-Sommerville Youth Study, 418–419
Cerebral palsy, 99
Characterological delinquency: case illustration of, 410
    intervention in, 419–421
    nature of, 401–402
    and psychopathic personality, 402–410
    see also Psychopathic personality disorder
Childhood psychosis: age of onset in, 176–177
    case illustrations of, 186–187, 190–191
    characteristics of, 178–193
    drug therapy in, 208
    epidemiology of, 175–178
    origins of, 193–202
    outcome of, 203–205
    prevalence of, 177
    sex differences in, 177–178
    treatment of, 205–208
    see also Childhood schizophrenia; Infantile autism
Childhood schizophrenia: behavior therapy in, 206–207
    biological factors in, 199
    case illustration of, 190–191
    causes of, 195–202
    communication deviance in, 200–201
    course of, 190
    as differentiated from infantile autism, 192
    diasthesis-stress model of, 202
    disordered thinking in, 187–188
    family therapy in, 206–207
    genetic factors in, 195–199
    inaccurate perception in, 188–189
    inadequate controls in, 189–190

    interpersonal ineptness in, 189
    nature of, 187–190
    psychotherapy in, 205–206
    risk research on, 201–202
    social learning factors in, 199–201
    see also Childhood psychosis
Classification: approaches to, 55–62
    benefits of, 52–55
    and communication, 55
    descriptive-behavioral approach to, 56–58
    descriptive-inferential approach to, 58–62
    and DSM-II, 63–64
    and DSM-III, 65–68
    dynamic-etiological approach to, 62–63
    and GAP report, 64–65
    harmful effects of, 44–52
    and interpersonal stigma, 46–50
    and psychological dehumanization, 44–46
    reliability of, 58–61, 66–68
    and research design, 53–54
    schemes for, 63–70
    and social and political deprivation, 50–52
    and treatment planning, 54–55
Collaborative Perinatal Project, 17, 100, 148
Communication deviance, 200–201
Compulsions, 309
Contact hypothesis, 110
Conversion reaction: frequency of, 317–318
    hysterical personality style in, 319–320
    nature of, 317
    origins of, 318–320
Coprolalia, 318
Cross-fostering, 197, 476
Cultural drift hypothesis, 103
Custodial mental retardates, 93

Delinquent behavior: actual estimates of, 396–398
    characterological determinants of, 401–410
    definition, 391
    hidden, 396–397
    intervention in, 417–422
    neurotic determinants of, 411–416
    official statistics on, 392–396
    organic determinants of, 416–417
    prevalence of, 391–398
    psychotic determinants of, 416–417
    sex differences in, 393, 397–398
    social class variables in, 399–401
    sociological determinants of, 398–401
    sociological theories of, 400–401
    see also Characterological delinquency; Neurotic delinquency; Sociological delinquency
Delusions, 188

skill *vs* task training in, 156–157
stimulant medication in, 151–153
treatment of, 151–158
writing problems in, 140
Mental retardation: absolute definitions of, 88
and age, 87
biological causes of, 93–101
birth complications in, 98–101
case illustrations of, 91–92, 94–96
categories of, 88–93
causes of, 93–103
and cerebral palsy, 99
characteristics of, 88–93
definition, 82–83
degrees of, 85
and Down's syndrome, 94–97
environmental view of, 102–103
familial, 84–85, 101–103
and fetal alcohol syndrome, 98
genetic counseling in, 105
genetic factors in, 101–102
institutional programs for, 111–113
interaction view of, 103
maternal ill health in, 98
mild, 89–92
moderate, 92–93
nutritional factors in, 100–101
and phenylketonuria, 97–98
postnatal factors in, 100–101
prevalence of, 83–85
prevention of, 104–114
primary prevention of, 104–105
profound, 93
psychotherapy in, 113–114
relative definitions of, 88
school programs for, 108–110
secondary prevention of, 105–108
severe, 93
and social isolation syndromes, 101
and sociocultural background, 86
tertiary prevention of, 109–114
two-group theory of, 84–85, 86
Middle-class delinquency, 400–401
Milwaukee Project, 106–107
Minimal brain dysfunction, *see* MBD/ADD

National Survey of Youth, 397
Neurosis, *see* Neurotic disorders
Neurotic delinquency: case illustration of, 413–414
communication of needs in, 411–414
family interaction in, 414–416
intervention in, 421–422
nature of, 411

needs: for help in, 412–413
for recognition and admiration in, 411–412
parental fostering of, 414–415
parental reinforcement of, 415–416
sexual behavior in, 412–413
Neurotic disorders: behavior therapy in, 323–325
definition, 300–301
diagnosis of, 300–302
drug theory in, 327–328
experiential factors in, 306–308, 314–316, 319
family involvement in treatment of, 325–327
genetic factors in, 313–314
prevalence of, 300–302
psychotherapy in, 323–325
temperamental factors in, 319
treatment of 323–328
underdiagnosis of, 301–302
unreliability in diagnosis of, 300–301
see also Conversion reaction; Habit disturbances; Obsessive-compulsive disorder; Phobic disorder
New York Longitudinal Study, 319
Normal Adolescent Project, 25
Normality: absolute and relative criteria for, 5–6
as adjustment, 4–6, 471
as average, 2–3, 471
as continuous with abnormal behavior, 6–8
definitions, 2–6, 471
as differentiated from abnormal behavior, 8, 28–29
as ideal, 3–4, 471
Nutritional factors: in MBD/ADD, 150
in mental retardation, 100–101

Object splitting, 234
Obsessions, 309
Obsessive-compulsive disorder: affect in, 311
behavior in, 311–313
case illustration of, 316
definition, 308–309
frequency of, 309–310
ideation in, 310–311
nature of, 310–313
origins of, 313–316
social relationships in, 311
Obsessive-compulsive personality style, 309, 314–315
Organic delinquency, 416–417
Outcome of psychopathology, summary of, 481–484. *See also specific disorders*

Paranoid disorder, 232–234